1977-78 EDITION

DOLLARWISE GUIDE TO

ITALY

By Stanley Haggart and Darwin Porter

Sponsored by

Alitalia

Published by

THE FROMMER/PASMANTIER PUBLISHING CORPORATION

380 Madison Avenue

New York, New York 10017

Distributed by

SIMON AND SCHUSTER

A GULF+WESTERN COMPANY

1230 Avenue of the Americas

New York, New York 10020

671-22725-4

Distributed outside the USA and Canada by

FLEETBOOKS

c/o Feffer and Simons, Inc.

100 Park Avenue

New York, New York 10017

Distributed in Canada by

PJ PAPERBACKS LTD.

330 Steelcase Road East

Markham, Ontario L3R2M1

NOTE: Although every effort was made to insure the accuracy of price information appearing in this book, it should be kept in mind that prices can and do fluctuate in the course of time.

Also, any opinions and judgments appearing in this book are those of the authors alone, and not Alitalia's.

CONTENTS

MAPS

A DOLLAR-WISE GUIDE TO ITALY

THE REASON WHY

THE SUBJECT OF THIS book is Italy. Admittedly, trying to cram that country between the covers of any book—regardless of size—is really an almost impossible task. But, having assumed that our readers will be average visitors with less than a lifetime to spend exploring one nation, we've tried to sample the finest of Italy in a reasonable number of pages.

The "finest" in this sense is interpreted to include not only cities and sightseeing attractions, but hotels, restaurants, and night spots as well. Part of the philosophy of this book is based on the belief that the finest need not be the most expensive. Hence, our ultimate aim—beyond that of familiarizing you with offerings of the boot of Europe—is to stretch your dollar power . . . to reveal to you that you need not always pay scalpers' prices for charm, comfort, and gourmet-level food.

In this guide, we'll devote a great deal of attention to those old tourist meccas, Rome, Florence, and Venice, with both their main and hidden treasures. But those ancient cities are not the full "reason why" of this book. Important as they are, they simply do not fully reflect the widely diverse and complicated country that is Italy.

To seek out the wonders of this often perplexing land, you must also go to Naples, to Sicily, the Dolomites, the Lake District, the Piedmont section, Milan, the Riviera, the Adriatic, and that galaxy of inland art cities—Siena, Pisa, Vicenza, Brescia, Bergamo, to name only a few.

We think we're fairly safe in saying that no country in Europe was designed—per square foot—to captivate pilgrims as much as Italy was. It was in the grand tour business when the "Americans" were still using smoke signals as their only means of cross-country communication.

It's really presumptuous to give you reasons "why" to go to Italy. Every person with a dream of foreign travel has already answered that question for himself or herself. We'll merely add a few that may not have occurred to you:

(1) To savor the history of art

—You're standing in front of a Raphael Madonna, as a guide slyly tells you that the artist's mistress, La Fornarina (the baker's daughter), posed for the painting—the same mistress whose unceasing sexual demands contributed to his demise at the age of 37.

(2) To meet old Stateside acquaintances who went to Italy and never returned

—You're having an apéritif at a Mediterranean villa painted in Easter egg colors. Your hostess with the vampiric eyebrow markings is known along the Amalfi Drive as "The Contessa," though back home as Betty Lou Broyhill.

(3) To pick up the trail of "La Dolce Vita"—this time as uniquely lived in Florence

—You're at Harry's Bar as Princess Galitzine parades in with her black manicured poodle Tshiort ("Black Satan"), dressed in a sea-green flannel coat belted in Roman gold. The mutt gets more attention than the princess.

(4) To see how "The West" was won

—You're in the little town of Tirrenia, with its movie colony, watching the filming of an Italian potboiler western. As the "cowpoke" bites the dust, his girl friend races across the sagebrush-strewn sands, screaming: "Mamma mia."

(5) To do something really majestic

—You're standing under the ruins of the Doric temple of Segesta on a lonely windswept hill in Sicily—with only a lizard on a rock to keep you company. As you look across the field, you suddenly feel, as never before, your link to the heritage of Western man.

(6) To discover the Italian people themselves, who can exasperate you to hysteria one moment then lull you with their charm the next

—You're in maddening traffic, literally taking your life in your hands. A man leans out the window, shouting damnations at you that even Dante didn't will on the lowliest denizens of Hell. In an hour you're cooling off on a terráce beside the pool of your hostess who's saying to her American guest, "I don't think a man's interesting until he's 30"—knowing full well that her visitor has just turned 30.

(7) To meet the "pagan" face to face

—You arrive innocently in a little town in Piedmont, and suddenly you're greeted with an overripe orange, right in the kisser. You wipe off your face to discover young men dressed in raspberry red shirts—with a spade sewn on their backs—throwing citrus missiles. Their actions, your innkeeper explains later, will assure a bountiful harvest.

And finally,

(8) To see what Luigi Barzini has called "The Perennial Baroque"

—You're reading *The Italians* (his fine book on a controversial subject), and you come across these lines: "What happened to Italy is what usually happens to old ladies who were once famous beauties. Just as they relinquish only reluctantly the gestures, curls, witticisms and fashions of their sunset years, Italy still clings to the manners and ideals of the two centuries which followed the coronation of Charles V."

Soon we'll discover for ourselves what he meant, but first, this explanation of our task:

DOLLAR-WISE—WHAT IT MEANS: In brief, this is a guidebook giving specific, practical details (including prices) about Italy's hotels, restaurants, sightseeing attractions, and nightlife. Establishments in *all* price ranges have been documented and described, from the extravagantly revamped chambers of the Grand Hotel Et De Rome ($45.24 double), to a clean but basic pensione in Taormina, Sicily ($10.32 a day per person, full board), which is only spectacular in that it overlooks the active volcano of Mount Etna.

In all cases, establishments have been judged by the strict yardstick of value. If they "measured up," they were included in this book—regardless of price classification. The uniqueness of the book, we think, lies in the fact that it could be used by a society matron ("we always stay at the Hassler"), or a free-wheeling, lire-lean collegian ("there's this great restaurant in Bologna that'll serve you a big spread for a buck fifty").

But the major focus of the book is not centered either on the impecunious whose sole resources jingle in their pockets, or the affluent whose gold rests in numbered accounts in Zurich. Rather, our chief concern is the average, middle-income-bracket voyager who'd like to patronize the almost wholly undocumented establishments of Italy—that is, the second-class hotels and the two-fork restaurants.

The Dollar-Wise Guide attempts to lead the reader through the maze of major sights, such as the Colosseum in Rome; then introduce him or her to a number of more esoteric locales, such as the macabre catacombs at Palermo. Most importantly, the hours of opening and the prices of admission of these attractions have been detailed.

All these specifics are presented against a backdrop of history and culture that has spanned centuries, from the mysterious Etruscans to the baroque "skies of Tiepolo" to the present-day Romans as depicted by novelist Alberto Moravia ("Signora Cecilia was very like some kind of exotic bird with a tiny body and an enormous, fantastic head").

A proper balance has been struck, we think, between serious sightseeing in the Renaissance art cities and fun-time resorts—holiday centers stretching from Rimini on the Adriatic, to Portofino on the Riviera, to the rocky cliffs of Sorrento.

An Antipasto of Bargains

In our journeys through every province of Italy, through its big cities and small villages, we have discovered surprising luxury offered for little cost, or establishments where the homemade or creative touch of their proprietors lifts them far above the ordinary. For a truer understanding of what dollar-wise means, we'll recall only a few as examples, though you'll meet dozens more in the pages ahead—perhaps discover some all on your own when you actually go to Italy.

—A 16th-century monastery high in the clouds with a breathtaking view of the Amalfi coast below. You walk down a long monastic corridor to your antique-filled bedroom. The cost of your accommodation, breakfast, and a bountiful lunch and dinner prepared by an artist chef comes to $16.24 per person daily. Nothing spoiled, nothing crass—a rarity on the choicest sunstrip in Italy.

—A 12th-century villa, surrounded by gardens, flowers, and a swimming pool, lying at the edge of Florence. The home of a charming countess and her family, the lovely hotel is graced with heirloom antiques, wall murals, and a dramatic frescoed loggia, as well as with delightful and discerning clients. The cost of full pension in a palazzo-sized room with private bath: from $27.84 to $32.48 a day per person.

—A time-weathered Tyrolean chalet, at the edge of an alpine village. Under the eaves are large, rambling rooms, each opening onto wide wooden balconies, with abundantly growing flowering vines. In the rustic dining room, the hearty, table-loaded meals combine the culinary artistry of Italy with the mountain cooking of Austria. Full pension comes to $18.56 per person daily.

—A country-style tavern—right in the heart of Rome's famous Parioli district—that offers ambitious portions on an all-you-can-eat basis for a blanket price of $8.12 per person. The atmosphere, the hustle and bustle are straight from a Joseph Levine movie. A basket overflowing with assorted sausages is placed on your table, even an herb-flavored baked ham—and that is just the first course.

THE $10-A-DAY TRAVEL CLUB: In just a few paragraphs, you'll begin your exploration of Italy. But before you do, you may want to learn about a device for saving money on all your trips and travels; we refer to the now widely known **$10-a-Day Travel Club,** which has gone into its 13th successful year of operation.

The Club was formed at the urging of readers of the $10-a-Day Books and the Dollar-Wise Guides, many of whom felt that the organization of a Travel Club could bring financial benefits, continuing travel information, and a sense of community to economy-minded travelers in all parts of the world. We thought—and have since learned—that the idea had merit. For by combining the purchasing power of thousands of our readers, it has proved possible to obtain a wide range of exciting travel benefits—including, on occasion, discounts to members from auto rental agencies, restaurants, sightseeing operators, hotels, and other purveyors of tourist services throughout the United States and abroad.

In keeping with the budget concept, the membership fee is low and is immediately exceeded by the value of your benefits. Upon receipt of $8 to cover one year's membership, we will send all new members by return mail (book rate), the following items:

(1) The latest edition of any *two* of the following books (please designate in your letter which two you wish to receive):

Europe on $10 a Day
England on $15 a Day
Greece on $10 a Day
Hawaii on $15 & $20 a Day
India (plus Sri Lanka and Nepal) on $5 & $10 a Day
Ireland on $10 a Day
Israel on $10 & $15 a Day
Mexico and Guatemala on $10 a Day
New Zealand on $10 a Day
Scandinavia on $15 & $20 a Day
South America on $10 & $15 a Day
Spain and Morocco (plus the Canary Is.) on $10 & $15 a Day
Turkey on $5 & $10 a Day

Washington, D.C. on $10 & $15 a Day

Dollar-Wise Guide to California
Dollar-Wise Guide to England
Dollar-Wise Guide to France
Dollar-Wise Guide to Germany
Dollar-Wise Guide to Italy
Dollar-Wise Guide to Portugal
(Dollar-Wise Guides discuss accommodations and facilities in all price categories, with special emphasis on the medium-priced.)

Where to Stay USA
(By the Council on International Educational Exchange, published in cooperation with the American Revolution Bicentennial Administration, this extraordinary guide is the first to list accommodations in all 50 states that cost anywhere from 50¢ to $10 per night.)

Whole World Handbook
(Prepared by the prestigious Council on International Educational Exchange, this publication deals with more than 1,000 programs of student travel, study, and employment in Europe, the Near East, Africa, Asia, Australia, and Latin America.)

(2) A copy of **Arthur Frommer's Guide to New York,** a newly revised pocket-size guide to hotels, restaurants, night spots, and sightseeing attractions in all price ranges throughout the New York area.

(3) A copy of **Surprising Amsterdam**—a 192-page pocket-size guide to Amsterdam by Arthur Frommer.

(4) A one-year subscription to the quarterly Club newsletter—**The Wonderful World of Budget Travel**—which keeps members up-to-date on fast-breaking developments in low-cost travel to all areas of the world.

(5) A voucher entitling you to a $5 discount on any Arthur Frommer International, Inc. Tour booked by you through travel agents in the United States and Canada.

(6) Your personal membership card, which, once received, entitles you to purchase through the Club all Arthur Frommer Publications for a third to a half off their regular retail prices during the term of your membership.

These are the immediate and definite benefits which we can assure to members of the Club at this time. Even more exciting, however, are the further and more substantial benefits (including, in particular, a comprehensive grant of reductions and discounts on travel accommodations and facilities in numerous areas), which it has been our continuing aim to achieve for members. These are announced to members at frequent intervals throughout the year, and can be obtained by them through presentation of their membership cards. Equally interesting has been the development of the Club's newsletter, *The Wonderful World of Budget Travel,* which has now become an eight-page newspaper, and carries such continuing features as "The Travelers' Directory"—a list of members all over the world who are willing to provide hospitality to other members as they pass through their home cities; "Share-a-Trip"—offers and requests from members for travel companions who can share costs; advance news of individual and group tour programs operated by Arthur Frommer International, Inc.; discussions of freighter travel; tips and articles on other travel clubs (air travel clubs, home and apartment exchanges, pen pals, etc.) and on specific plans and methods for travel savings and travel opportunities.

If you would like to join this hardy band of international budgeteers and participate in its exchange of travel information and hospitality, simply send your name and address together with your membership fee of $8 to: $10-a-Day Travel Club, Inc., 380 Madison Avenue, New York, N.Y. 10017. Remember to specify which *two* of the books in section (1) above you wish to receive in your initial package of members' benefits.

Chapter I

GETTING THERE

1. Traveling to Italy
2. Traveling Within Italy

"ALL ROADS LEAD TO ROME" in ways the emperors never dreamed —by super-fast autostrade, ships, freighters, and last but certainly not least, by jet plane. Indeed, of all the various ways of reaching Italy, the airplane comes off as the best . . . and for the U.S.-to-Italy run, the cheapest.

Getting to Italy is what this chapter is all about. In the first section we'll cover the methods of traveling to Italy. In the second section we'll discuss traveling within Italy—by air, train, rental car, etc.—and find the best ways to save lire.

1. Traveling to Italy

THE CHOICE OF AIRLINE: It certainly seems appropriate if you're flying to Italy to fly **Alitalia,** the national airline of Italy. Alitalia is a fully international airline, and, interestingly enough, the first European airline to go all-jet. Today, Alitalia's full fleet of jets—everything from 747's and 727's to DC-10's to DC-8's—services six continents. In some 30 years it has been in operation, it has created an elaborate, dependable and fully computerized world-wide air network.

Modern comfort and style are what you can expect when you board an Alitalia jet. The interiors are the work of top Italian and international designers, the mood cosmopolitan. In this setting, you'll dine on fine Italian cuisine, listen to stereophonic music, settle back and perhaps watch a movie. The service is warm and gracious—a fitting introduction to the Italian way of life.

Buon viaggio!

AIRFARES: The bold red and green "A" of Alitalia can be seen flying over the Atlantic from New York to Italy 19 times a week. There are 12 direct 747-jet flights to Rome every week in summer, seven to Milan. Airfares vary according to season and there is quite a difference in price. Basic Season is September 15 to May 31 eastbound, October 15 to June 14 westbound. Peak season is June to September 14 eastbound, June 15 to October 14 westbound. (The seasons are slightly different for the APEX excursions—see below.)

All fares set forth in the following pages are valid from April 1, 1977 through March 31, 1978, subject to government approval. In each case, the figure represents the *round-trip* rate from New York, on, of course, a jet aircraft. To determine the approximate fare from your own town, merely add the cost of transportation from where you live to New York.

REGULAR ECONOMY-CLASS FARES: The fares presented here are those you would pay if you could not avail yourself of any of the decidedly cheaper excursion plans—an unlikely possibility. They are calculated from New York to the following cities and represent, as mentioned, the round-trip rates.

	Basic Season	Peak Season		Basic Season	Peak Season
Amsterdam	$ 650	$ 822	London	$626	$764
Athens	978	1132	Madrid	652	824
Barcelona	660	848	Nice	762	916
Berlin	706	894	Oslo	694	878
Brussels	650	822	Paris	650	822
Copenhagen	694	878	Rome	826	966
Frankfurt	694	878	Stockholm	750	934
Hamburg	694	878	Tangier	652	824
Helsinki	782	970	Vienna	762	946
Istanbul	1008	1166	Zurich	694	878

The round-trip fare to these cities from Montreal is, generally, about $17 less than the above; the round-trip fare from Houston is some $180 more. You'll receive a 50% reduction for children between the ages of two and 12, and a 90% reduction for infants under the age of two. If you're not a child or infant, and still want to lower the fare, read on:

14- TO 21-DAY EXCURSIONS: A first way to cut the cost of your air transportation to Europe is by taking a 14- to 21-day "excursion"—which simply means that you plan a trip of from 14 to 21 days' duration. If, under this plan, you go for a minimum of 14 days, but return no later than midnight of the 21st day following your day of departure, you'll realize a substantial saving. Here, then, are the 14- to 21-day round-trip excursion rates between New York and the following cities.

	Basic Season	Peak Season		Basic Season	Peak Season
Amsterdam	$587	$681	London	$541	$631
Athens	769	875	Madrid	587	681
Barcelona	618	711	Nice	666	758
Berlin	643	736	Oslo	634	725
Brussels	587	681	Paris	587	681
Copenhagen	634	725	Rome	717	807
Frankfurt	634	725	Stockholm	704	797
Hamburg	634	725	Tangier	603	696
Helsinki	747	838	Vienna	678	770
Istanbul	783	895	Zurich	634	725

These fares are available for Monday-through-Thursday departures only; if you fly transatlantic on a weekend, you'll pay a $15 supplement for eastbound ocean crossings on Fridays and Saturdays, westbound crossings on Saturdays and Sundays.

22- TO 45-DAY EXCURSIONS: And you can even go cheaper. For 1977, the airlines have again created a 22- to 45-day (minimum 22 days, maximum 45 days) excursion fare that descends to a truly remarkable level—as little as $565 round-trip between New York and Rome in Basic Season, $689 in Peak Season. Once again, these fares represent round trip costs between New York and the following destinations.

	Basic Season	Peak Season		Basic Season	Peak Season
Amsterdam	$487	$601	Madrid	$487	$601
Berlin	526	644	Munich	526	644
Brussels	487	601	Oslo	511	628
Copenhagen	511	628	Paris	487	601
Frankfurt	511	628	Rome	565	689
Hamburg	511	628	Stockholm	548	665
Istanbul	615	754	Vienna	551	665
London	467	587	Zurich	511	628

As with the 14- to 21-day fares, there's a supplement for the weekend use of 22- to 45-day excursion fares: $15 for eastbound trips on Fridays and Saturdays, $15 for westbound crossings on Saturdays and Sundays.

APEX EXCURSIONS: Meaning Advance Purchase, the APEX excursion fares allow you to fly to and from Rome for close to *half* what you would pay on a regular economy ticket. All you have to do to qualify is purchase your ticket *more than* 45 days in advance of your departure. And, if you are traveling before October 1, 1977, you must stay abroad a minimum of 22 days and a maximum of 45 days. As of October 1, 1977, however, the minimum stay will drop to only 14 days; the maximum stay will remain the same.

There is one disadvantage to the APEX fares that you should consider before you purchase such a ticket: cancellation, no matter what the reason, entails a penalty charge of 10% of the fare or $50, whichever is higher.

As mentioned earlier, the duration of the "seasons" differs with the APEX fares. APEX Basic Season is September through May, eastbound or westbound. Peak Season is June, July, and August, either direction. An additional difference: eastbound in July, westbound in August, you will be required to pay a "peak of Peak" surcharge: $20 one way, $40 round trip. And, as with all excursion fares, there is a $15 supplement for eastbound travel on Fridays and Saturdays, the same for westbound crossings on Saturdays and Sundays.

Here we go, then, with the APEX excursion fares, round trip from New York to the cities listed. Remember that they are based on 22 to 45 days until October 1, 1977, and 14 to 45 days thereafter. These fares do not reflect the "peak of Peak" surcharge or the weekend supplement.

	Basic Season	Peak Season		Basic Season	Peak Season
Amsterdam	$376	$477	Madrid	$355	$445
Berlin	407	518	Munich	407	518
Brussels	376	477	Oslo	392	498
Copenhagen	392	498	Paris	376	477
Frankfurt	392	498	Rome	459	571
Hamburg	392	498	Stockholm	419	525
Istanbul	532	647	Vienna	435	554
London	350	440	Zurich	392	498

ADDITIONAL CITIES FOR NO EXTRA FARE: One drawback to the 22- to 45-day and APEX excursion fares: they permit no air stopovers on the way to your destination. What's the impact of that "stopover" rule? Look again at our chart of basic airfares to Europe. Those prices will appear somewhat lower to you when you realize that they can be made to cover not only the expense of traveling to Europe, but also of traveling *within* Europe.

The key to this feat is the so-called "extra-city" system, which, on a non-excursion ticket, permits you to stop free at any of the European cities on the way to, and on the way back from, your ultimate destination. Conceivably, you could incur no extra transportation costs whatever! The same extra-city privileges are provided on a 14- to 21-day excursion flight, but only for five cities (two on the inbound flight, two on the outbound flight, plus the point of turnaround).

Does this save money? Emphatically, yes. Your round-trip fare, you see, is calculated according to the mileage along the straight-line route from New York to your destination. But the cities in which you can stop along the way are not always on the straight-line route; many involve considerable detours. This added mileage comes to you free under the extra-city plan. In fact, your transportation costs within Europe are thus reduced to not much more than they would be by train. And, since most major European cities are separated by only an hour or two of flying time, the extra-city system conserves large portions of your vacation time that would otherwise be spent in weary train trips.

GO NOW, PAY LATER: Thus far we have been investigating the "cheap" ways to fly to Europe—but of course the cost of the ticket is in any case a substantial one. To ease the burden of the initial outlay, all the airlines permit the purchasing of tickets on an installment-payment basis. This plan permits you to avoid the necessity of paying your entire fare all at once, and instead to pay simply $50-or-so down, and the remainder in installments over 3 to 24 months.

You should apply for a pay-later plan at least ten days before you expect to pick up your plane tickets. No collateral is required. You merely fill out a form, furnish a couple of references, and sign your name. If you have any sort of earning power, your application will be approved. We know a young woman who was able to obtain a ticket, installment-style, at a time when she was working as a researcher for $130 a week.

The initial down payment is about 10% of the price of your ticket. Depending then on your own desires or the strength of your credit rating, you'll have from three to 24 months to pay off the rest.

Naturally, any installment purchase device adds a slight amount in interest charges to the ultimate cost of your ticket; it's a money-delayer, not a cash-saver. Still, it's a useful arrangement that avoids an immediate, substantial depletion of your travel funds.

THE LATEST CHARTERS: Besides the three excursion plans explained above, there are lots of other ways to hie yourself to Rome. For example, there's a whole alphabet worth of charter plans now available to the general public from travel agents: ABCs, GITs, ITCs, OTCs, TGCs, etc. The most up-to-date are the ABC (Advance Booking Charter) and the OTC (One Stop Tour Charter). On an ABC you must book and pay at least 45 days in advance. Minimum stay seven days; no maximum; and *no* compulsory land arrangements. An

OTC is similar to an ABC, but the fare quoted includes a mandatory land package of at least $15 a day. You must reserve and pay 30 days in advance.

These charter packages offer fantastic savings on transportation. Check them carefully though. Cancellation fees range from 5% to the full amount depending on days before departure and if the seat is reassigned. Do find a reliable travel agent—preferably via personal recommendation.

2. Traveling Within Italy

ALITALIA AND ATI DOMESTIC SERVICE: Italy's domestic air network is one of the largest and most complete in Europe. There are some 40 airports serviced regularly from Rome, and most flights are under an hour. Fares vary, but all can be lowered if you are able to take advantage of these discounts: passengers 12 to 22 years old receive 30% off; a family group taking a night flight receives 30% off for the head of the family, 50% off for the wife and free fares for all children under 12 (one free fare for every 30% and 50% fare paid).

For schedules and cities serviced by air, get in touch with any Alitalia office (see end of chapter for listing of Alitalia addresses in key çities).

EURAILPASS: Many travelers to Europe have for years been taking advantage of one of its greatest travel bargains, the Eurailpass, which permits unlimited first-class rail travel in any country in Western Europe, except the British Isles and Finland. Passes are purchased for periods as short as 15 days or as long as three months.

Here's how it works: The pass is sold only in North America. Vacationers in Europe for 15 days can purchase a Eurailpass for only $170; 21 days cost $210; a one-month pass costs $260; two months, $350; and three months, $420. Children under four travel free providing they don't occupy a seat (otherwise, they must pay half fare). Children under 12 pay half fare. Students between the ages of 14 and 26 get the best break—they can purchase a **Student-Eurailpass,** entitling them to unlimited second-class transportation for two months for only $230.

The advantages are tempting. No tickets, no supplements—simply show the pass to the ticket collector, then settle back to enjoy the scenery. Obviously, the two or three-month traveler gets the greatest economical advantages; the Eurailpass is ideal for such extensive trips. A passholder can visit all of Italy's major sights, from the Alps to Sicily, then end his vacation in Norway.

Fourteen-day or one-month voyagers have to estimate rail distance before determining if such a pass is to their benefit. To obtain full advantage of the ticket for 15 days or one month, you'd have to spend a great deal of time on the train.

Eurailpass holders are entitled to considerable reductions on certain station buses and ferry boats. For example, you'll get a 10 or 15% reduction for bus trips from Venice to Florence or Rome to Naples. You'll get a 20% reduction on second-class accommodations from certain companies operating ferries between Naples and Palermo, or for crossings to Sardinia and Malta.

Travel agents in all towns, and railway agents in such major cities as New York, Montreal, Los Angeles, or Chicago, sell all these tickets. Readers who live elsewhere can write to: Eurailpass, Box 191, Madison Square Station, New York, N.Y. 10010, or Italian State Railways, 500 Fifth Avenue, New York, N.Y. 10036.

SPECIAL ITALIAN TOURIST SEASON TICKETS: These are recommendable if you wish to travel a great deal via train only within Italy. These special tickets, purchasable in the United States and Canada as well as Italy, allow unlimited travel while the ticket is valid. They include trips made by fast trains *(Rapido)* without payment of extra charges, except on the Settebello and on the Trans-European trains. On these, the full supplement must be paid. The period of validity begins within 10 days of entry into Italy, but the ticket must be stamped at the station on commencement of the journey to establish the validity period. Adult second-class fares for eight days are $43.20; 15 days, $52.20; 21 days, $61.20; and 30 days, $75.60. For comparison, in first class, an eight-day ticket goes for $68.40. Children four to 14 pay half fare, but go free if under four. A family of four traveling together is entitled to a reduction of 40% for adults (passport required). Family tickets must be purchased in Italy.

TRAINS IN ITALY: This can be an inexpensive means of transportation, even if you don't buy the Eurailpass or Special Italian Railway Tickets. A typical adult fare, *Diretto* between Rome and Florence, would be $14.90 first class, dropping to $8.30 in second class. Between Florence and Venice, the charge is $12.10 in first class and $6.80 in second. The fare from Rome to Naples is $10.20 in first, $5.80 in second.

In a land where mamma and bambini are highly valued, families (minimum of four passengers) are granted reductions: adults up to 40%, children 4-14, half fare. If you've ignored birth-control (a family of five or more), you'll get 50% off for adults, 75% off for each bambino.

Classification of trains: *Rapido* are fast trains running between main cities. In some Rapido trains, seats must be reserved in advance, and only first class is offered. *Direttissimo,* long-distance express trains, feature both classes. *Diretto-Express* trains also offer both classes. *Accelerato* are local trains stopping at all stations, and containing both classes. The *Settebello* is a deluxe train running between Milan-Bologna-Florence-Rome. A special surcharge, which includes seat reservations, must be paid in advance. In addition, there are the **Trans-European Express** trains operating in Italy, with only first-class seats.

Get in touch with **Italian State Railways,** 500 Fifth Avenue, New York, N.Y. 10036 (tel. 212-354-9830). There are also offices in Chicago, Los Angeles, San Francisco, Montreal, and Toronto.

CAR RENTALS: Hertz and Avis, of course, are well represented in Italy, with rental counters at the Roma and Milano airports. But, for our purposes, we'd recommend a more European-based company, **Europcar,** which has about 60 offices and offers reliable service stations throughout Italy and its major islands.

Because gasoline is super expensive in Italy, we'd recommend renting the smallest car comfortably possible. Italy, naturally, is a feast of sights, and many visitors find a car imperative, as they want to explore places where trains or buses do not reach.

Europcar has an extra benefit for those requiring a car a minimum of two weeks. You can leave the car, without charge, in Austria, Belgium, Denmark, Germany, Holland, Spain, Sweden, and Switzerland.

Drivers must be 21 years old and possess licenses at least one year old. Five categories of cars are available, the cheapest in Group A. For example, a Fiat 127 rents for 7,200 lire ($8.35) a day. However, the best rate is to take the unlimited kilometers for a minimum of one week at a cost of 129,000 lire ($149.64). A tax of 12% is added to all tariffs. Be forewarned that rates do increase in these days of inflation, so check in advance.

The charges quoted are for on-the-spot rentals in Italy. If you plan ahead, you can realize a savings by reserving in advance in the United States. Call this toll-free number: 800/328-4567.

Gasoline Coupons

The Italian Government has reinstated gasoline coupons for foreign tourists and Italians residing abroad, using vehicles of non-Italian registration. A first allotment of a maximum of 400 liters (equivalent of 104.6 gallons) of gasoline for automobiles; 200 liters (equivalent of 50.3 gallons) for motorcycles of the 125 cc class and above, and 100 liters (equivalent of 26.4 gallons) for smaller engined vehicles will be sold at a time, with the possibility of a second allotment of equal measure allowed during the same calendar year. Regular gasoline, which costs (as of this writing) $2.10 per gallon, is available at $1.65 per gallon, and super, which is sold at $2.65 per gallon, can be obtained at $2.15 per gallon through use of the gasoline discount coupons.

A gasoline and tourist card (Carta Carburante e Turistica-CCT) is issued free to tourists. You can purchase the coupons before departure at the Banca Nazionale del Lavoro, 25 West 51st Street, New York, N.Y. 10019. The bank charges a small fee for handling and postage. The coupons can also be bought at ACI (Automobile Club of Italy) offices at the Italian border. Unused coupons may be submitted for refund (less six percent) to the Italian Government Travel Office (ENIT), 630 Fifth Avenue, New York, N.Y. 10020.

ITALIAN TOURING CLUB: The Italian Touring Club (ITC) is affiliated with touring clubs throughout the world and will be able to offer the traveler in Italy advice, assistance of any kind, itineraries and maps. To become a member write for an application form to the head office in Milan, at Corso Italia 10, or contact **CIT Travel Service** at 500 Fifth Avenue, New York, N.Y. 10036. Membership fee is $11. At CIT, incidentally, you can inquire about the **Tourist Motor Fuel Card,** entitling travelers bringing a car into Italy to receive gasoline discounts.

ALITALIA—SOME KEY ADDRESSES: Alitalia offices in Italy are mentioned throughout this book, under particular cities. For your convenience, here is a list of some international Alitalia offices, in addition to those of the major Italian cities.

		Phone
Amsterdam	15, Leidsestraat	269937
Atlanta	235 Peachtree St., N.E.	577-1320
	Peachtree Center Office Tower	
Bombay	Industrial Assurance Bldg.	316444
	Churchgate Bombay 20	
Boston	The Case Building	567-7740
	535 Boylston St.	
Brussels	23 Avenue Louise	5388970
Buenos Aires	887, Avenida Santa Fé	313194 or
		310730
Catania	Corso Sicilia, 113	224860
Chicago	138 South Michigan Ave.	427-4720
Cleveland	Hanna Bldg.	771-0520
	1422 Euclid Ave.	861-3615

Dallas	8350 Central Expressway	800-241-2550
		or 748-9891
Detroit	620 Book Building	800-223-9770
	1249 Washington Blvd.	
Florence	Lungarno Acciaiuoli, 10/12	2788
Frankfurt	Rubenstrasse, 2	639111
Hamburg	21/23 Gansemarkt	342756/8
Hong Kong	Hong Kong Hilton Hotel	5-237041/9
Johannesburg	Colonial Mutual Building	8343121
	Corner Fox and Loveday Street	
	P.O.B. 1369	
Lagos	Bristol Hotel,	26606/7
	2 Martin St.	20308
Lisbon	Avenida de Liberdade, 225	536141
	Edificio La Equitativa	
London	251/259 Regent St.	01-7344040
Los Angeles	5670 Wilshire Blvd.	800-223-5730
Madrid	Torre de Madrid	2418900/7/8/9
Melbourne	Pearl Assurance Bldg.	601171
	143 Queen St.	
Miami	The Northeast Airline Bldg.	800-223-5730
	150 S.E. 2nd Ave.	
Milan	Via Albricci, 5	6281
	Viale Luigi Sturzo 37	6281
Montreal	2055 Peel St.	842-5201
Munich	2 Pacellistrasse	260-4485
Naples	Via Miguel Cervantes, 78	312200
New York	666 Fifth Ave.	262-4480
Palermo	Via Libertá, 29	583733
Paris	138, Champs Elysées	2566633
	73, Champs Elysées	2466500
Philadelphia	1704 J. F. Kennedy Blvd.	569-1122
Rio de Janeiro	Avenida Atlantica	
	19-36 Copacabana	2573701
Rome	Via L. Bissolati, 13	4688
San Francisco	421 Powell St.	800-223-5730
Singapore	Holiday Inn, Scots Road	373166
Sydney	124 Phillip Str.	922-1444
Tokyo	Tokyo Club Building	
	2-6 Kasumigaseki	580-2171/181
	3-chome, Chiyoda Ku	
Toronto	85 Richmond St. West	416-363-2001
Venice	Campo San Moise, 1463	704666
Washington D.C.	1001 Connecticut Ave. N.W.	393-6841 or
		393-2829
Zurich	Talstrasse, 62	273891

Chapter II

HOTELS AND RESTAURANTS OF ROME

1. Deluxe and First-Class
2. The Medium-Priced Range
3. The Budget Range
4. The Pick of the Pensions
5. The Restaurants of Rome

ROME IS "THE DIVINE COMEDY." If you don't believe that, take a seat at a cafe on the Via Veneto any night in season and watch the passing parade. In a nationwide television show, Sammy Davis, Jr. related his experiences on this fashionable street, characterizing them as "instant image." By that, he meant it's difficult to be yourself while sitting in the midst of the milling throngs. At the tables, conversation attempts not to be so mundane—but rather more daring. The game of seduction with the eyes is played with consummate skill.

Along the Via Veneto, all the way to its end at the Aurelian Wall, you'll see the human drama in action. It's a wide-ranging spectrum: a singer with his guitar and suit of chartreuse sequins; an American woman—an insurance widow—who likes to show off her mauve hair, green-patterned hosiery, mink coat, and 20-year-old Italian lover.

On one side of the street, you'll find chicly dressed young women (Irma la Douce types have long faded from the scene in style-conscious Rome). They patrol the streets in search of expense-account junketeers, while their more prosperous sisters cruise by in convertibles.

In the old days, during the heyday of the Via Veneto, you might even have seen ex-King Farouk battling the naughty *paparazzi* (Rome's aggressive band of freelance photographers who shoot for the tabloids and delight in recording the foibles and invading the privacy of the city's foreign visitors—as, for example, Ms. Bardot sunbathing in the nude on her terrace).

If this seems a backhanded way to introduce Rome, it's based on the theory that what makes The Eternal City eternal is its life. The life of Rome is composed of two elements: the Romans and the visitors. Both are virtually inseparable. Paris remains indubitably French, even with its hordes of aliens.

But in Rome the visitor and the local are entwined. The city almost seems to exist as a host to its never-ending stream of sightseers. It wines them, dines them, and entertains them.

In the following chapter, we'll take you on seemingly endless treks through ancient monuments and basilicas. But monuments are not the total picture. In Rome, you'll find yourself embracing life with an intensity. In other words, "when in Rome. . . ."

To help you navigate better, we'll provide a brief preview of transportation before moving on to our hotel recommendations.

GETTING AROUND ROME: Walking, of course, is the only way you'll see Rome. In days of yore, Rome was practically consumed by its automobile jams. Now pedestrians are reasserting their ancient privileges, along narrow streets dating from the days of the Caesars.

Oases of tranquil peace have replaced bumper-to-bumper traffic. In 1975 some 124 additional acres in the downtown historic center were closed to vehicles. The restriction of traffic began with the closing of the Villa Borghese in 1972 to vehicular traffic. Plans call for the eventual transformation of 500 acres in downtown Rome into pedestrian malls.

Trams and Buses

For only 100 lire (12¢) you can ride around to most parts of the city (though not to the outlying districts) on the quite good tram (streetcar) and bus hookups. Never, but never, ride the trams when the Romans are going to or returning from work, or you'll be flattened flatter than fettuccine. Buses and trams stop at areas marked *Fermata,* where you'll also find a map summarizing the particular routes stopping here. You can get a detailed map of the surface transportation system at the A.T.A.C. office *(Azienda Tramvie ed Autobus del Comune di Roma)* at 65 Via Volturnó.

Subways

Every time the Roman starts to dig for the Metro, he discovers an old temple. Consequently, for that and other reasons, the underground remains embryonic. However, you can ride on a short stretch of subway from the Terminal (railway station) to the Colosseum to "Modern Rome" (E.U.R.) to the Lido di Roma (the beach). The fare, even to the end of the line, is never higher than 800 lire (93¢).

Rush Hours

Rome has four rush hours. The first is in the morning, of course, as Romans head for work. The second rush hour is for the time-honored siesta, followed by traffic jams after the rest period. The final rush hour is around 8 in the evening when the local populace heads for home, or wherever they are going. Try to avoid traveling on public transportation, including taxis, at these times.

Taxis

Walter Galling, in the *Daily American,* wrote: "Italy's best salesmen are its cab drivers. They even open the door!" Conversely, prices are quite dear. The meter drops at 340 lire (40¢). Watch that you don't pay the previous occupant's fare. In other words, if you are accustomed to hopping a cab in New

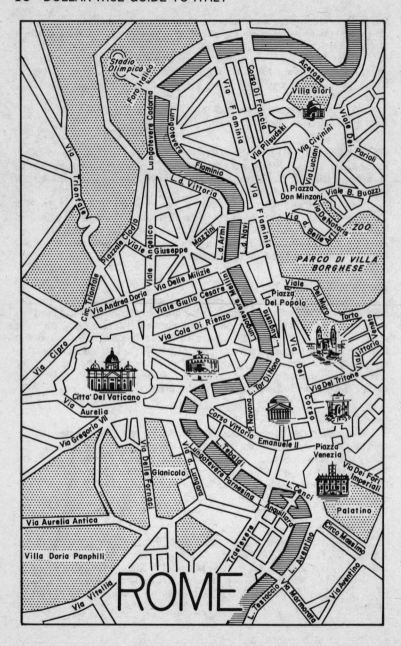

York, then do so in Rome. If not, take another less expensive means of transport. After 10 p.m. and until 7 a.m., there is an additional charge of 250 lire (29¢). You must also pay 100 lire (12¢) per suitcase, and on Sundays, a

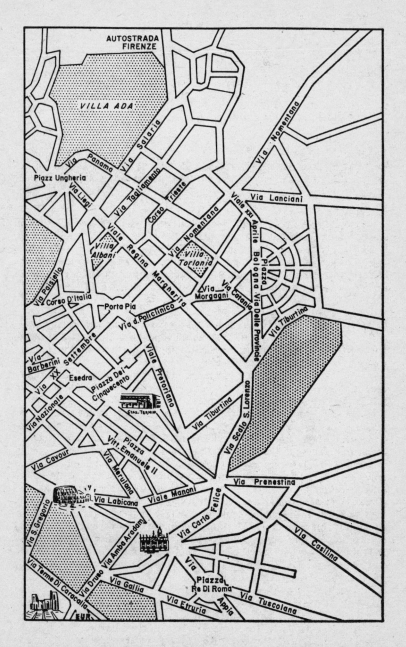

100-lire penalty is charged. Avoid paying with large bills. Invariably, taxi drivers have no change. But you'd better.

Tip: Don't count on hailing a taxi on the street or even getting one at a stand. Have your hotel clerk call one. At a restaurant, ask the waiter or cashier to dial for you. Otherwise, you may be stranded in some remote section of Rome.

Mail

The post office is often chaotic. Mail may take a month or sometimes not be delivered at all. However, many measures are currently being taken to improve services. Meanwhile your best bet is to use the Vatican Post Office which manages to see that the mails go through. It closes at noon.

Alitalia Office

In Rome, the representative office for *Alitalia* is at 13 Via L. Bissolati (tel. 489-171), and the ticket office is at 20 Via L. Bissolati (tel. 4688).

Organized Tours

One of the best and most comprehensive ways to get acquainted with Rome is on a conducted tour operated by one of the leading travel agencies. Recommendable is **Appian Line,** 171 Via Veneto (tel. 06/475-5184), which operates a fleet of comfortable and air-conditioned coaches under the guidance of experienced multilingual guides. A sightseeing tour of Rome lasts about three hours, and is a real bargain for your money. The cost is 4,500 lire ($5.22).

THE HOTEL SITUATION: The Italians are never simple. If you aren't aware of that, you soon will be as you find yourself coping with the myriad of Italian hotel prices and classifications. A handy computer or a brain-trust accountant would be ideal to carry along with you.

Cardinal rule: if you want to enjoy average, "middle-class" comfort, but keep your wallet fairly intact, patronize the top-rated second-class hotels and their equivalents, the first-class pensions. Patronage of a second or even a third-class hotel does not reflect on your social standing. In fact, many of the more cultivated of the world's social, literary, and artistic colony have habitually frequented little unheralded establishments in Rome, not because of financial need—but because of the charm and atmosphere they found there.

Italy controls the prices of its hotels, designating a minimum and a maximum rate. The difference between the two may depend either on the season or the location of the room, even its size. Hotels are divided into deluxe, first class, second class, third class, and fourth class. Many second-class hotels stun the visitor with their seeming grandeur. "Why second class?" is an often asked question. "This is luxury." Government ratings do not depend on sensitivity of decoration or on frescoed ceilings—but rather on facilities such as elevators and the like. Many of the finest hostelries in Italy are rated second-class because they do not serve meals, other than breakfast (a blessing really for those seeking to escape the pension requirements).

1. Deluxe and First-Class Hotels

Le Grand Hotel Et De Rome, 3 Via Vittorio Emanuele Orlando (tel. 489-011), is the grand dowager of Rome hotels—comparable to the Plaza in New York. Its roster included some of the greatest names in European history (royalty among them), and such New-World visitors as Henry Ford and J. P. Morgan. And, thanks to upholsterers and painters and considerable spending by the CIGA chain, the Grand is still the most elegant hotel in Rome. The main hall is palacelike, with an arched, ornate ceiling, frosted Venetian chandeliers, gilt furnishings. Other lounges are almost as voluptuous. The main dining room, Le Maschere, is also ornately decorated with bright murals and crystal, and is the setting for culinary festivals where international chefs vie with each other for prestigious meals. While most selections are à la carte, there are set meals in the 9,000 lire ($10.44) to 12,000-lire ($13.92) range. The small cafe bar is an old-world hangout, where you can have drinks and light snacks in an atmosphere of potted palms and soft music. Also for drinks and light meals, there is the Scottish room, Le Rallye, replete with Tartan carpeting and hunting horns utilized as wall sconces.

Bedrooms are mostly one of a kind, with old-world opulence such as baroque headboards and fragile Venetian chandeliers. All rooms are sound-proofed with attractively coordinated furnishings, televisions, small bar refrigerators, telephones, dressing rooms, and tiled baths. It's not cheap to stay here, but considering its prestigious position, quite reasonable. For normal singles, you'll pay 28,000 lire ($32.48), and 39,000 lire ($45.24) for doubles. For super-deluxe singles and doubles, you'll pay an additional 5,000 lire ($5.80) to 11,000 lire ($12.76) per room. The 12% I.V.A. tax is extra, but service and air conditioning are included in the tariffs.

Hassler Villa Medici, 6 Piazza Trinità de' Monti (tel. 679-2651), the sole deluxe hotel in this old part of Rome, uses the Spanish Steps as its grand entrance. This lush hotel, with its ornate decor, has long been favored by such Americans as the Kennedys, Eisenhowers, and Nixons—and by titled Europeans and movie stars. The brightly colored rooms, the lounges with a mixture of modern and traditional furnishings, the bedrooms with their "Italian Park Avenue" trappings, strike a 1930s note.

The bedrooms have a personalized look—Oriental rugs, tasteful draperies at the French windows, brocaded furnishings, super-soft beds, and (the nicest touch of all) bowls of fresh flowers. The suites, of course, are super expensive. But you can rent a single room with bath and shower for 30,500 lire ($35.38); a double with bath for 45,000 lire ($52.20). Taxes are included. The hotel's 100 rooms, all with private bath, are equally divided between singles and doubles. Dining at the Hassler is an event: either in the sub-tropical patio, or on the roof garden with its panoramic view of the city and its soft music at dinner.

FIRST-CLASS HOTELS: Here's a rundown of first-class establishments, presented in geographical order:

Near the Piazza Navona

Hotel Raphaël, 2 Largo Febo (tel. 65-69-051), is known to the discerning who prefer a palace buried in the heart of Old Rome. A tasteful place, furnished with fine old Italian pieces, it lures with its sophisticated and restful atmosphere. International celebrities check in and out unobtrusively. All of its air-conditioned bedrooms have a private bath or shower, and a few have their own terraces. A single rents for 12,700 lire ($14.73), a double for 20,150 lire ($23.37). Rates include breakfast, which is obligatory. The bedrooms are individually decorated, simply done, with wood-grained built-ins. The hotel is air-conditioned. In the lounges are fine antiques, excellent art objects, ornate gilt mirrors, and high-backed chairs. The dining room has a big fireplace, and the bar carries its liquor inside a gilded baroque cabinet. But the special delight is the rooftop terrace, with its many levels. You can have drinks here, enjoying the vista of tiled rooftops of nearby buildings.

In the Quartiere Prati

Giulio Cesare, 287 Via degli Scipioni (tel. 31-02-44), is an elegant villa, the former home of the Countess Paterno Solari, now converted into a tasteful hotel. In a sedate part of Rome, across the Tiber from the landmark Piazza del Popolo, the baroque-styled villa is entered up a flight of red-carpeted, white marble steps flanked with large potted plants. In the guest salon, where the Countess once entertained diplomats from all over the globe, the furnishings are antique reproductions for the most part, in rose velvet and dusty blue, resting on Oriental carpets. In the public rooms, you'll find tapestries, Persian rugs, mirrors, ornate gilt pieces, and crystal chandeliers. In yet a smaller salon, guests gather for drinks in an atmosphere of fruitwood paneling and 18th-century-styled furnishings. The carpeted bedrooms are furnished as in a tasteful private home, with a single color theme (of many shades) predominating. Needlepoint chairs are placed discreetly in the rooms. The cost of a single is 13,500 lire ($15.66); 25,800 lire ($29.93) in a double. Service is included, but the I.V.A. tax must be added. On the roof garden is a restaurant-bar (you take your continental breakfast at 1,800 lire or $2.09 here as well).

In the Parioli District

The **Ritz,** 43 Piazza Euclide (tel. 803-751), is a jewel box inside, though it lies in Parioli, far from the center of town. The reception lounge introduces you to what's in store—wood paneling, needlepoint provincial chairs, old statues banked with ferns, and other antiques, all sedately glamorous. Its lounge is a rotunda with an intricate sunflower marble floor design, the encircling wall is of deep red, set off by white-fluted pilasters, crystal sconces, a circular balcony, and a huge theatrical chandelier. The formal dining room has velvet provincial chairs, gold draperies, and elaborate paneling. The Empire Bar is all white, gold, and glitter. Each of the bedrooms has an individual touch, furnished mostly with reproductions of good French, English, and Italian designs (many colorful touches). All the 130 rooms have private baths. Singles rent for 21,200 lire ($24.59), doubles for 35,00 lire ($40.60), including service and air conditioning (add I.V.A. tax). On the premises are a beauty parlor, cocktail lounge, and the Regency Restaurant.

Near the Spanish Steps

Grand Hotel de la Ville, 67-71 Via Sistina (tel. 688-941), stands at the top of the Spanish Steps, next door to the deluxe Hassler, on a street lined with boutiques. The severe facade doesn't begin to reveal the beauty of the interior. Most of the bedrooms harbor furnishings of the past, with fine antiques. Singles with bath are 19,800 lire ($21.97); doubles with bath are 30,500 lire ($35.38). You may want to take the demi-pension rates, which range from 27,000 lire ($31.32) in a single to 45,000 lire ($52.20) for two persons. To all bills, add 9% I.V.A. tax; service and air conditioning, however, are included.

At the Grand Hotel de la Ville, a multitude of formal lounges and loggias are decked out in a harmonious white, with fruitwoods, reddish browns and golds. A new wing has been added with a Scandinavian modern decor, though you may prefer to stay in one of the rooms truer to the baroque. The villa opens onto a rear garden, nestled against the hillside. A large-scaled patio is created, where guests dine under the moonlight—surrounded by balconies with flowering plants and vines. Candles glow softly, and the cuisine is first rate. At night, the panoramic view from the roof terrace is inspiring.

Valadier, 15 via della Fontanella (tel. 679-225), could at one time have been the setting of "A House Is Not a Home." But it's been totally transformed into one of the most tasteful and elegant of the little hotels of Rome. Now even the most fastidious will find a home away from home. For a first-class hotel, the tariffs are surprisingly low: 10,000 lire ($11.60) in a single, rising to 17,000 lire ($19.72) in a double—these rates including taxes, air conditioning, and service as well. The rooms have flair, with good reproductions of fine furniture styles, plus an occasional ornate gilt overlay. Each accommodation contains a private bath as well. Not to be ignored is the hotel's restaurant, Le Renoir, where you can enjoy good-tasting Roman viands for around 5,600 lire ($6.50) per dinner.

Near the Colosseum

Hotel Forum, 25-30 Via Tor de' Conti (tel. 679-2446), off the Fori Imperiali, offers an elegance that savors the drama of Old Rome, as well as tasteful, sometimes opulent, accommodations. It's a medium-sized nugget (90 rooms—all with bath or shower), whose accommodations and dining roof terrace look out upon the sights of the ancient city—the Colosseum or Forum. The hotel itself is built around a medieval bell tower, incorporating it happily. The bedrooms are exquisitely appointed with fine antiques, mirrors, marquetry, Oriental rugs. In high season, the Forum charges an inclusive 35,000 lire ($40.60) for a double, 21,000 lire ($24.36) for a single. Reserve in advance. The Forum's lounges are as conservatively conceived as a country estate, with paneled walls, and furnishings that skillfully combine Italian and French provincial. Dining is an event—either sitting on tapestry-covered chairs in front of picture windows, or on the spacious terrace. You can enjoy an *aperitivo* at the hotel's bar on the roof, surveying the timeless Roman Forum.

Off the Via Veneto

Victoria Roma, 41 Via Campania (tel. 480-052), will foot you. As you sit on wrought-iron chairs on its roof garden, drinking your apéritif in a forest of palms and potted plants—all overlooking the Borghese Gardens—you'll think you're at a country villa. But the Via Veneto's just across the way. Even the lounges and living rooms retain that country house decor, with simple, soft touches, including high-backed wing chairs, large oil paintings, bowls of freshly cut flowers, provincial tables, and Oriental rugs. The Swiss owner, H. A. Wirth, has set unusual requirements of innkeeping (no radio, no television, no groups), and has attracted a fine clientele over the years—diplomats, executives, artists. The bedrooms are well furnished and maintained. All the rooms have private baths. Rates go from 21,000 lire ($24.36) in a single; from 34,000 lire ($39.44) in a double. Meals can be taken à la carte in the elegant grill room, which serves the best of Italian and French cuisine. Air conditioning is optional at 1,500 lire ($1.74) per person.

La Residenza, 22 Via Emilia (tel. 460-789), successfully combines the intimacy of a good-sized town house with the facilities of a small hotel. For many, the location is supreme—in the neighborhood of the Via Veneto, the American Embassy, and the Villa Borghese. A converted villa, the aptly named La Residenza is furnished with traditional furniture. A favorite spot for conversation and drinks is the Louis XVI salon, complete with a fireplace and a baroque mirror. In contrast, the skylit main living room evokes a country home, with parquet floors and cretonne upholstery. Each of the bedrooms—28 in all, 25 with baths and showers—is individually decorated in conservative taste. Some open onto the hotel's private garden. A single with bath and breakfast costs 16,000 lire ($18.56); a double with bath and breakfast is 26,000 lire ($30.16), including service and tax. Breakfast is the only meal served, freeing you to swim in the sea of Roman restaurants.

2. The Medium-Priced Range

NEAR THE COLOSSEUM: Colosseum Hotel, 10 Via Sforza (tel. 475-1228), offers baronial living on a miniature scale. Someone with insight and lire notes designed this 50-room hotel (with private baths) in excellent taste—a reflection of the best in Italy's design heritage. The bedrooms are furnished with well-conceived antique reproductions (beds of heavy carved wood, dark paneled wardrobes, leatherwood chairs)—and all with monk-like white walls. Opened in the summer of 1965, the Colosseum charges an inclusive 21,000 lire ($24.36) for a double in season. Singles pay 13,000 lire ($15.08) in season. The half pension rate ranges from 15,000 lire ($17.40) to 17,000 lire ($19.72) per person. The drawing room, with its long refectory table, white walls, red tiles, and provincial armchairs, invites lingering. The reception room, with its parquet floors, arched ceilings, and Savonarola chair, makes a good impression. Highly recommended for the discerning.

IN THE PARIOLI DISTRICT: Hotel Degli Aranci, 11 Via Barnaba Oriani (tel. 870-202), is a former private villa on a tree-lined residential street, surrounded by similar villas now used as consulates and ambassadorial town houses. Most of the rooms have tall windows opening onto pleasant views, and are filled with provincial furnishings or English-styled reproductions. Doubles with bath rent for 12,800 lire ($14.85), but only 9,500 lire ($11.02) without. Singles pay 7,400 lire ($8.58) with bath, 6,500 lire ($7.54) without. Rates are inclusive. The breakfast room, built at the rear, has walls of glass, opening onto the tops of flowering orange trees. The cane and velvet chairs, the bronze chandeliers, add a warm touch. To reach the hotel, take bus No. 3.

NEAR THE SPANISH STEPS: Carriage, 36 Via delle Carrozze (tel. 679-4106), is aptly named, for it caters to the "carriage trade," including many members from the British and French embassies, plus an increasing number of stars (such as Terence Stamp and Ms. Mangano) and film directors. Right near the Spanish Steps, the 18th-century facade covers some charming, though small, accommodations (if you reserve, ask for one of the two rooftop bedrooms). Antiques have been used tastefully, creating a personal aura, even in the bedrooms, with their matching bedcovers and draperies. All 25 of the accommodations have bath, telephone, and radio. For one of the stylish bedrooms, you pay 15,300 lire ($17.75) in a single; 22,850 lire ($26.51) in a double, these rates including I.V.A. tax and a continental breakfast. To meet your fellow guests, head for the Renaissance-styled salon that is called an American Bar.

　　Hotel d'Inghilterra, 14 Via Bocca di Leone (tel. 689-010), nostalgically holds onto its traditions and heritage. Rightly so, for it's been the favorite of many a discriminating "personage"—Anatole France, Ernest Hemingway, Alec Guinness. (In the 19th century, the King of Portugal met here with the

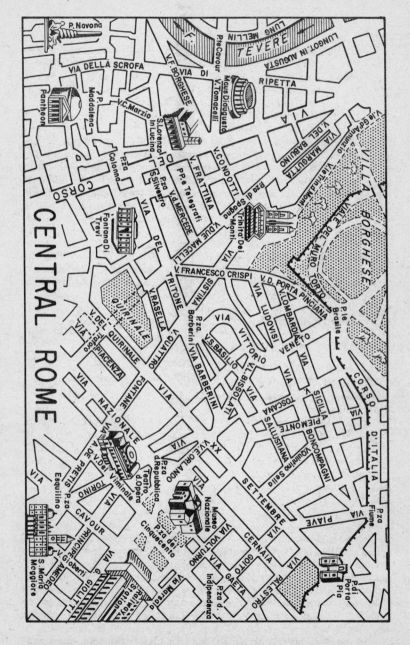

Pope.) The bedrooms have mostly old pieces—gilt and much marble, along with mahogany chests and glittery mirrors. Rates quoted include a continental breakfast, as well as taxes and service charges, except for the I.V.A. tax which will be added. A bathless single goes for 9,300 lire ($10.79); 15,000 lire ($17.40) with bath. Doubles pay 14,700 lire ($17.05) in a bathless room, 22,600 lire ($26.22) with bath. Of the 100 rooms, 70% have baths. The main salon of the hotel is dominated by an impressive gilt mirror and console, surrounded by furniture fit for a small palace. The preferred bedrooms are higher up, opening onto a tiled terrace, with a balustrade and a railing covered with flowering vines and plants. The bar is a favorite gathering spot in the evening, with its paneled walls, tip-top tables, and old lamps casting soft light.

Internazionale, 39 Via Sistina (tel. 679-30-47), is part of the past—built in the 1890s and reflecting the traditional ease of life in those days. But some of its rooms go as far back as the 16th century! It's only a short walk from the Spanish Steps, perhaps one of the choicest locations in Rome. No sophistication here—just a happy accumulation of old pieces, and many bedrooms with ornate furnishings (carved and gilded). The hotel has been a popular tourist nesting place since the '20s. The double rooms—some with private balconies—go for 24,000 lire ($27.84) with bath, 18,000 lire ($20.88) without bath. Singles range from 10,000 lire ($11.60) to 16,000 lire ($18.56), depending on the plumbing. Rates include service, taxes, and air conditioning, as well as continental breakfast with fruit juice.

The **Madrid Hotel,** 93 Via Mario de' Fiori (tel. 679-1243), is a winner for its convenient location near the Spanish Steps in "boutique land." It's a mellowed squash-colored fin de siècle building, completely neat and clean. Its furnishings are up-to-date, but totally utilitarian, with beds set against wood-grained headboards, bedside lights, and telephone. The rates are the same year-round and include service and taxes. In a double room, prices are 26,000 lire ($30.16). A few suites, suitable for three persons, go for 36,000 lire ($41.76). These tariffs include breakfast, I.V.A., TV, and service.

NEAR ST. PETER'S: **Hotel Alicorni,** 11 Via Scossacavalli (tel. 565-786), beds you down on the virtual doorstep of St. Peter's Square. The 16th-century palace, built around a colonnaded courtyard, has been mercifully preserved. Now it's a quiet, well-kept little hotel, with some 50 bedrooms (20 of which have their own private baths). Architecturally, it retains its old features, reflecting the mood of another era. But its furnishings and modern equipment provide the amenities very much of today. Family operated (you'll see a large portrait of mamma and papa in wedding dress at the top of the winding staircase), it makes for a well-oiled stay in the Italian capital. Singles without bath rent for 4,450 lire ($5.22); with bath for 6,000 lire ($6.96). Doubles cost 8,600 lire ($9.98) without bath, 10,300 lire ($11.95) with bath. A continental breakfast is included.

Columbus Hotel, 33 Via della Conciliazione (tel. 564-874), is a rarity—an impressive 15th-century palace within a few minutes' walk of St. Peter's. Once it was the private home of a wealthy cardinal under Julius II, the curse of Michelangelo's life. Its trim, even austere, Renaissance facade belies its rather handsome interior, much overhauled. Some of its dramatic rooms are still intact, with ornate painted ceilings, overscaled antique furnishings, and a courtyard with colonnaded arches. Many of the 120 bedrooms have private baths and showers, big enough to have housed Pinturicchio and his fellow fresco artists. Some of the bedrooms have a view of the basilica. Singles without bath rent for 8,500 lire ($9.86); singles with bath, 12,000 lire ($13.92). Doubles go for 14,000 lire ($16.24) without bath; 20,000 lire ($23.20) with bath. If you want full pension, the charge is a peak 17,000 lire ($19.72) per person, if you're staying in one of the rooms with bath. These rates remain the same year round and are inclusive.

NEAR THE PIAZZA VENEZIA: Tiziano, 110 Corso Vittorio Emanuele (tel. 656-5019), is an antique patrician palace, entirely renovated. The hotel unfortunately has taken the modern route instead of the traditional path in its lobby and bedroom furnishings. If you can forgive the incongruity of functional modern with palace-like architecture, then you may find a stay here rewarding. A bathless single is 9,000 lire ($10.44), 12,000 lire ($13.92) with bath. A bathless double is 18,000 lire ($20.88), 21,000 lire ($24.36) with bath. Service is included in the tariffs, as is a continental breakfast. The half-pension rate ranges in price from 13,000 lire ($15.08) to 15,000 lire ($17.40) per person. The cooking combines Roman dishes with an international cuisine. The Tavernette bar offers a relaxing atmosphere.

NEAR THE PANTHEON: Hotel Sole al Pantheon, 63 Piazza del Pantheon (tel. 679-33-29), may be the oldest hotel in Rome, built in 1496. It has sheltered such creative people as Pietro Mascagni, the Italian opera composer. Its position is romantic, on a tiny plaza with a tall central fountain overlooking the Pantheon. Although the facade has been preserved, the interior has been totally remodeled, offering modern comforts and furnishings. Front doubles with shower rent for 22,650 lire ($26.27); doubles in the rear, 20,050 lire ($23.26). Singles cost 11,050 lire ($12.82). For a continental breakfast, there's an additional charge of 1,300 lire ($1.51).

NEAR THE PIAZZA COLONNA: Hotel Cesàri, 89 Via di Pietra (tel. 679-23-86), since 1787 has been a favored choice of the "literati" and political personalities, attracting such names as Stendhal, Garibaldi, Mazzini. Its interior has been thoroughly overhauled, with many baths installed and a bar drawing a lively social crowd. Today's visitor can be assured of a good accommodation in a history-rich district of Rome. No lunches or dinners are offered—just rooms and breakfast. Bathless singles go for 9,000 lire ($10.44); 13,500 lire ($15.66) with bath. Doubles rent for 13,300 lire ($15.40) without bath; 18,000 lire ($20.88) with bath, Breakfast costs 1,700 lire ($1.97) per person. The charges are reduced considerably from December through February. While rooms generally are furnished in a rather impersonal modern, a few have nice old brass beds. The Cesàri is handy to the Temple of Neptune and many little antique shops.

NEAR TERMINAL STATION: Fiamma, 61 Via Gaeta (tel. 478-912), is exquisite—underrated as second class. It opens directly onto the historic Baths of Diocletian, just a minute from the railway station plaza. Like an exclusive boutique, the atmosphere reflects the sophistication of its owner, Marchese Della Casapicolla. All of the well-appointed rooms have private baths and showers and some even contain ample sitting room areas (gilt cherubs and photomurals) tasteful enough for entertaining guests. Doubles go for 25,000 lire ($29). Singles are 18,000 lire ($20.88). You pay 1,000 lire ($1.16) extra for air conditioning. The I.V.A. tax and service are included. There are meals served, other than breakfast. The long drawing room is divided into several conversational group areas, with down-cushioned sofas covered in gold silk. Appropriately, there are many old pieces—inlaid desks, chests, urns of fresh flowers,

Oriental rugs, and gilt-framed paintings. An alternate group of rooms has a garden atmosphere—little salons suitable for tête-à-tête apéritifs.

Rex, 149 Via Torino (tel. 462-743), near the Opera, still retains much of the architectural dignity it had when it was the private palazzo of a Spanish duke. You'll still find the marble stairway, the original high coffered ceilings, crystal chandeliers, and a baronial carved stone fireplace in the living room. However, the former gardens have long ago given way to a modern bedroom annex with up-to-date amenities. The antique accommodations have far greater flair. Rooms are available with and without private baths. Singles range from 6,870 lire ($7.97) to 10,040 lire ($11.65); doubles, from 11,620 lire ($13.48) to 15,850 lire ($18.29). Breakfast is extra. There is an American bar where you can order drinks throughout the evening.

Lux Messe Hotel, 32 Via Volturno (tel. 464-620), nestles on a convenient spot, opposite the railway station and facing the Baths of Diocletian. It has a classic brown marble facade, tastefully severe, and many creature comforts inside. The furnishings are in high-flying modern (bedroom headboards obviously designed by an airplane propeller expert!). But, brushing past the jazz, you'll find the rooms compact, practical, and most comfortable. Everything is immaculate. Double rooms go for an inclusive 14,200 lire ($16.47) without bath, for 18,200 lire ($21.11) with bath or shower. Singles range from 8,700 lire ($10.09) to 11,200 lire ($12.99). No pension terms are offered. On the premises are an elevator and a bar.

NEAR THE BARBERINI PALACE: 4 Fontane, 149a Via 4 Fontane (tel. 475-49-36), enjoys a handsome situation between the Barberini Palace and the Quirinal. The little second-class hotel contains only 50 rooms, but it is most inviting. The lobby, for example, is decked out with crystal chandeliers, glowing wall sconces, a palace-like ceiling, well-upholstered traditional pieces, and thick carpeting. There is a bar for apéritifs. Though small, the rooms are homelike and comfortable, with color-coordinated fabrics. The bed-and-breakfast rate in a bathless single is 5,100 lire ($5.92); 8,800 lire ($10.21) with bath. Doubles without bath cost 10,500 lire ($12.18); 12,600 lire ($14.62) with bath and shower. Service and tax are included.

Anglo-Americano, 12 Via 4 Fontane (tel. 462-572), is especially favored by Americans. Its location near the Piazza Barberini is unbeatable. The hotel has been given a new lease on life, as befits its position next to the Barberini Palace. The interior of both the public and private rooms are carpeted, and come complete with air conditioning, an automatic switchboard, baths in all the rooms, TV and radio, even a "barfridge." Lavish use is made of leather and wood, even fabric on the walls. The rate in a single is 11,000 lire ($12.76); 16,000 lire ($18.56) in a double. Another 1,000 lire ($1.16) are charged for air conditioning. Breakfast at 1,200 lire ($1.39) is taken on the roof garden.

3. The Budget Range

NEAR THE PANTHEON: Albergo Minerva, 69 Piazza della Minerva (tel. 686-551), is a villa-styled hotel, standing on one of the most interesting squares of Old Rome, (the square boasts a stone elephant supporting an obelisk). The hotel reflects a fascinating past—the great South American soldier and statesman, San Martín, was a guest in 1846. Once the Minerva was one of Rome's great hotels, and it still contains many interesting architectural details; it is currently being renovated and refurnished, though the pace seems to be gradual. It still has its glass-domed rotunda, complete with a statue of the goddess Minerva. The formal dining room with its gilt mirrors and antiques aims for style. If you get a renovated room, you'll be assured of plenty of space and comfort. A bathless single rents for 6,800 lire ($7.89) to 7,500 lire ($8.70); 9,600 lire ($11.14) to 10,800 lire ($12.53) with bath. Bathless doubles tally up at 12,900 lire ($14.96) to 14,200 lire ($16.47), and at 17,600 lire ($20.42) to 19,500 lire ($22.62) with bath. Breakfast is an additional 1,600 lire ($1.86).

NEAR THE PIAZZA NAVONA: Hotel Portoghesi, 1 Via dei Portoghesi (tel. 564-231), stands in a tangle of narrow streets opposite an ancient tower. The albergo seems to have been an old town mansion, but it's now been adapted to the needs of international travelers, attracting, in particular, a host of young clients. Each floor has its own guest lounge, made cheery with chintz-covered chairs and fresh flowers. There are some 20 bedrooms, each with a private bath or shower. Doubles rent for 8,500 lire ($9.86); singles, 5,500 lire ($6.38). A grandfather clock and 18th-century prints add a personal touch to the narrow reception lounge. The hotel is on a street that intersects Via Scrofa between the Mausoleum of Augustus and the Piazza Navona.

NEAR THE PIAZZA BARBERINI: The **Memphis**, 36a Via degli Avignonesi (tel. 475-1955), is recommendable on many counts. Its location, only a couple of blocks from the Piazza Barberini and four blocks from the Trevi Fountain, is terrific. It's tiny and immaculate, an elevator hotel that has a decided character without being glamorous. The entrance is modest, with a mini-bar and lounge. The emphasis is on the comfortable bedrooms. Although the building is an old-timer, the accommodations have modern facilities, each containing a private bath with either a tub or shower. A single costs 5,500 lire ($6.38); a double, 9,000 lire ($10.44). The Memphis is a good, safe bet.

NEAR THE BATHS OF CARACALLA: Hotel Santa Prisca, 25 Largo Manlio Gelsomini (tel. 571-917), is an unheralded hotel away from the center of the city in the Aventino residential district. It is set aside from the hysterical traffic by a private garden. A newish building erected for Argentine nuns, it puts aside half of its space for visitors to Rome. You won't, we assure you, find a cloistered life here, though one of peace and quiet. The public rooms, as well as the private bedrooms, are furnished in simple modern. All of the rooms have a private bath and shower, as well as a telephone. The furnishings are grained wood pieces, and there's even an American Bar. Singles rent for an inclusive 6,100 lire ($7.08), while couples pay 8,500 lire ($9.86). You can stay and have all your meals for 13,900 lire ($16.12) per person.

The **Hotel-Pensione S. Anselmo,** 2 Piazza S. Anselmo (tel. 573-547), is really three hotels in one. Highly recommended by many of its illustrious clients, it offers a slightly out-of-the-way location on a tranquil hill in the Aventino section. As such, it's better for longer stays. The hotel lies on the far side of the Palatine Hill, beyond the Circus Maximus. The other villas are **Aventino,** 10 Via S. Domenico (tel. 572-831), and **Villa S. Pio,** 19 Via S. Anselmo (tel. 57-41-325). The hotels are owned by Enzo Piroli, who is genial and skilled in his trade. Each location has a pleasant garden and featured in the main dining room are good Roman meals. In a double with bath, the charge is 12,500 lire ($14.50); 8,600 lire ($9.98) in a single with bath.

NEAR THE SPANISH STEPS: Hotel Homs, 71-72 Via della Vite (tel. 678-0482), is a fairly good choice for those who want to be near the Piazza di Spagna and the American Express lifeline. The rooms are quite basic, but they are as clean as Dutch Cleanser. No meals, other than breakfast, are served. The single rooms—all without private baths—cost only 5,000 lire ($5.80). A few doubles, however, have baths, and rent for an inclusive 12,000 lire ($13.92). The bathless doubles, by far the majority, cost only 9,000 lire ($10.44). Extra beds can be added at an additional charge. Breakfast can be served on a little terrace. It's convenient and quite good, considering the price.

Pensione Suisse, 56 Via Gregoriana (tel. 678-3649), can fulfill one's desire to live inexpensively near the Spanish Steps. This 35-room hotel is owned by Signore Jole Ciucci and stands on the fourth and fifth floors of an ancient elevator building. The decor, if you can call it that, is rather old-fashioned and casual, with parquet or tiled floors, occasional throw rugs, and overstuffed armchairs in the lounge. On the roof you can order breakfast. Bedrooms are overscaled—unadorned, but comfortable—equipped with "blond" furniture, and occasionally blended with so-so antiques. More than a dozen have private bath, and the rest offer running water. Bathless singles cost 5,600 lire ($6.50), rising to 7,000 lire ($8.12) with bath. A bathless double goes for 4,600 lire ($5.34) per person, increasing to 6,000 lire ($6.96) per person with bath. Add I.V.A. to all tariffs, though a continental breakfast and service are included in the above-quoted prices.

NEAR THE TERMINAL: Sitea, 90 Via Vittorio Emanuele Orlando (tel. 481-047), is directly across from the elegant Grand Hotel, only three minutes from the railway station plaza. It's family run, and bears the stamp of excellent personal taste and a sense of how to run a good hotel. Perhaps that explains the coterie of painters, writers, and embassy personnel who have been attracted here over the years. Most of the rooms have private baths and air conditioning, and the bedrooms have individual styles—Venetian, provincial, old pieces, or reproductions. In all, a happy use of color. Single rooms with bath cost 18,000 lire ($20.88). Two persons pay around 26,000 lire ($30.16) for a room with private bath. The I.V.A. tax is additional. There is a large, air-conditioned roof bar. In one corner of the dining room is a circular fireplace with a raised brick hearth.

Pavia, 83 Via Gaeta (tel. 479-090), is in the third-class category and a little seedy—not for the fastidious. However, it has elements to recommend it. Entered through a wisteria-covered, narrow passageway, just off the busy railroad station plaza, it was once a private villa. Despite the hustle and bustle outside, it manages to be quiet and private. The key feature of the Pavia is its old-fashioned, country-style, home cooking, featuring such specialties as risotto alla pescatora. Meals cost 3,500 lire ($4.06). Non-hotel guests are welcomed to the table. In summer, meals are served in an adjoining garden. A bathless single with breakfast costs 4,500 lire ($5.22). Couples pay 8,000 lire ($9.28) in rooms with baths, also including breakfast. While strong on convenience, the Pavia's furnishings are time worn.

Albergo Venezia, 18 Via Varese (tel. 49-50-036), has three points in its favor: (1) it's convenient to the railway station; (2) it is economical; (3) it is clean and efficiently run. The owner Mrs. Rosemarie Diletti is Swiss, and her sophisticated taste is reflected in the decorations. Two sitting rooms, with their blue and white theme, are eye-catching. The twin dining room is also intimate, again in a blue and white color theme. You can stay here on the breakfast-only plan, though most guests prefer to take the delicious dinner. The rooms are prettily decorated, simple but comfortable. The rate, in a double with bath, is 6,500 lire ($7.54) per person. Some rooms accommodate three persons at 5,500 lire ($6.38) per person, with bath. A single costs 7,500 lire ($8.70). For accommodations with private showers, figure on a supplement of 1,500 lire ($1.74) per person.

Igea, 97 Via Principe Amedeo (tel. 73-11-212), is one of the older hotels in the vicinity of the railway station. But it's been renovated and offers fresh and up-to-date accommodations—at reasonable prices. A single room with shower costs 7,000 lire ($8.12), 5,000 lire ($5.80) without. Doubles pay 9,000 lire ($10.44) for a room without bath, 12,000 lire ($13.92) with shower. Winter heating, service, and taxes are included in the rates quoted. The bedrooms are quite nice, in spite of their severity, softened by white walls and modern walnut beds and night tables.

4. The Pick of the Pensions

To judge from the facades, you might think all Roman pensions can be checked off in Alfred Korzybski fashion (father of general semantics): house$_1$, house$_2$, house$_3$, etc. Not so! Once you enter them, you'll find considerable differences. Most of these "boarding houses" occupy one or two floors of a large apartment building; others, particularly on the outskirts, are housed in once-private villas.

The "pensione" is generally more intimate and personal than a hotel—in one, the nature and quality of the welcome depend largely on the host or hostess, who might also be the cook and chief maid. As a general rule, a first-class pension in Rome is the equivalent of a second-class hotel. A third-class hotel and a second-class pension are "spiritual sisters." In most of these pensions, you'll be asked to take demi-pension arrangements, though not always. We'll first survey our favored recommendations, then follow with even cheaper choices.

NEAR THE TERMINAL: Pensione Texas, 47 Via Firenze (tel. 485-627), is a surprise. Bank clerks cashing checks of Texas guests do a double take at the name: "No, Signor . . . not where you're from. The name of your hotel in Roma." The pension is a unique combination of elements, the creation of two men—one, Marvin Hare, a superb painter, gourmet, and former head of Elizabeth Arden in South America; the other, Guido Agnolucci, who comes from a fine Florentine family. Both men have utilized their individual talents in making this establishment a select place to stay for many discerning visitors, including several Broadway stars. The Texas is but a five-minute walk from the railway station, three from the Opera. Clients generate a lively atmosphere in the salons furnished partially with antiques from Mr. Agnolucci's home in Florence. At the end of the day, everybody gathers to drink martinis and to meet fellow guests (everyone is introduced). Many of the bedrooms are handsomely furnished with antiques and contain private baths. For these, you pay from 10,200 lire ($11.83) up per person in a double room. Less expensive doubles, without private facilities, go for only 7,800 lire ($9.05). These rates include a continental breakfast and choice of lunch or dinner. The Texas has a charming breakfast room. For the main meals, you will be furnished with a voucher which can be used at a good restaurant nearby. And the owners will deduct 2,000 lire ($2.32) for each lunch or dinner you might miss. The palazzo itself was the home of Count Sacconi, who designed the monument to Victor Emmanuel. Obviously the count had better taste in his selection of a home than he had in monuments. Mr. Hare and Mr. Agnolucci also manage the **Pensione 7 Hills** underneath the Texas. It has the same rates.

NEAR THE VATICAN: Orsini, 4 Via Orsini (tel. 312-829 or 315-656), is a private villa, in an area of Gothic villas popular with Vatican nobility. The Orsini is a fine old building, about a block from the river, with a small garden for before-dinner drinks. The ingratiating owner, Leda Mainoldi, and her mother, Bianca, converted this former private home, installing more bathrooms while creating a tasteful place for receiving guests. Their living room-gallery has a high wood-carved and beamed ceiling, and is furnished with the family antiques. All the 11 bedrooms are decked out simply, but are most comfortable and spotless. Rates, including a continental breakfast, are 11,000 lire ($12.76) double; 7,500 lire ($8.70) single, with either a bath or shower. Without a bath, doubles cost 9,300 lire ($10.79); singles, 6,200 lire ($7.19).

NEAR VILLA BORGHESE: The Villa Borghese, 4 Via Giovanni Sgambati (tel. 861-035), is ideal for couples who want a shuttered old villa, with only a busy street separating it from the Borghese Gardens. It has mellowed furnishings, and its rear rooms escape the noise of traffic. To stay here, it's necessary to take all your meals—but the viands are most savory. The rate per person ranges from 8,000 lire ($9.28) to 9,000 lire ($10.44) depending on whether you have a private bath. If there is no room at the inn, you may be in luck at the villa's villetta across the street (even quieter). The English love it here.

NEAR THE SPANISH STEPS: Scalinata di Spagna, 17 Piazza Trinità dei Monti (tel. 679-3006), sits snugly at the little plaza at the top of the Spanish Steps, keeping incongruous company with the deluxe Hassler across the way. The pension's facade, with fluted pilasters and bas relief ceramics, sets the style level. Inside, the rooms have intimacy and individuality, making for a delightful stay. The neat rooms have many antiques, but best of all is the roof garden, where you can have your morning coffee in spring or summer with a view of St. Peter's across the Tiber.

A single with hot and cold running water rents for 7,000 lire ($8.12), increasing to 10,000 lire ($11.60) with bath. Doubles with showers (no toilets) range from 11,000 lire ($12.76) to 14,000 lire ($16.24), peaking at 16,000 lire ($18.56) with complete bath. The rates include breakfast, but a 12% service goes on the final total. Poets and artists seem to like it here.

Elite, 49 Via Francesco Crispi (tel. 678-30-83), really means business. Everything has been done to make it up-to-date, immaculate, and most comfortable. For example, all the bedrooms have been equipped with private baths, along with a tasteful selection of furnishings. Even the lobby has been refurbished in a restrained way, though it maintains a certain homey quality. Singles pay an inclusive 17,000 lire ($19.72) for full board; doubles, 15,500 lire ($17.98) per person for a room and meals. The singles with bath and continental breakfast rent for 9,000 lire ($10.44); doubles for 15,000 lire ($17.40).

ON THE OUTSKIRTS: Villa del Parco, 110 Via Nomentana (tel. 864-115), is an old Roman villa, set up from the boulevard in the midst of trees and shrubbery. The atmosphere is decidedly non-commercial. It has a small, tree-shaded front terrace, where guests gather in the late afternoon to chat and sip Campari. The interior suggests a country house on the Mediterranean, with a few antiques intermingled with tasteful upholstered lounge chairs. The living room has a cozy bar and television area, mellowed photographs, and prints of Old Rome. All the rooms have private baths. The bed-and-breakfast charge for a single is 12,500 lire ($14.50). Doubles pay 17,000 lire ($19.72). High season, full-pension rates range from 16,700 lire ($19.37) to 18,500 lire ($21.46), and in summer, 2,500 lire ($2.90) extra are charged for air conditioning. The bedrooms are well appointed and well kept. To reach the villa, take bus 36, 60, or 62.

EVEN CHEAPER PENSIONS: Daria, 24 Via Sicilia (tel. 460-797), is rated by the government as a second-class pension, but it is only a moment away from the Via Veneto, near the American Embassy and across the street from the deluxe Excelsior Hotel. The pension attracts a lively crowd—embassy personnel, opera singers, writers, and painters. The living room is filled with homelike antiques, overflowing into the corridors and the casually furnished bedrooms. All rooms have private bath or shower. For a room and breakfast, two persons pay 11,000 lire ($12.76); one guest, about 7,000 lire ($8.12). Reserve well in advance.

Forti's Guest House, 2 Via Cosseria (tel. 382-431), provides a "safe" accommodation for those seeking a shelter that is not only inexpensive, but where American whims are appreciated. It's owned by an American ex-G.I. and English teacher, Charles Cabell, and his Verona-born wife, Renata. Their guest house venture is the familiar story of a Yank who fell in love with an Italian girl ("I'm her Romeo, she's my Juliet"). Once he was sports editor of the *Rome Daily American,* but now he takes in paying guests "to make ends meet." Their simple pension is a block from the river (on the Vatican side), set in a residential district occupying the lower floors of a plain apartment house. A family-style living room is available, complete with TV and a collection of prints and engravings. Guests exchange touring tips in the cozy dining room, with its African wood collection and red-checkered tablecloths. The accommodations are utterly simple, though six contain private baths. Singles range from 5,000 lire ($5.80) with breakfast; doubles, from 7,000 lire ($8.12) to 8,500 lire ($9.86), also with breakfast. Ask for the budget special—that is, 7,500 lire ($8.70) per person for bed, breakfast, a boxed lunch, and a four-course dinner. Take bus 78 or 99 from the Terminal Station to a nearby corner (the first stop after crossing the Tiber).

LIVING CHEAPLY IN A NUNNERY: Rome, the spiritual center of the Catholic church, maintains dozens of nunneries, a few of which accept paying guests at especially economical rates. These are more ideal for families and single girls than roving bachelors. There is always a curfew imposed. Many are worth considering if you are watching your lire and don't mind the simple life. Perhaps the most offbeat is the **Centro Diffusione Spiritualita,** Casa d'Ospitalità 44 Via dei Riari (tel. 65-61-296), which is maintained by the Sisters of Pro Sanctitate. It's the only accommodation we know of in the colorful and characteristic Trastevere section. The sisters welcome visitors who do not require private baths and are satisfied with basically furnished rooms and three square meals a day. The cost of full pension is 8,000 lire ($9.28) per person daily. No English is spoken, and there's an 11 p.m. curfew.

5. The Restaurants of Rome

The largest task confronting guidebook writers is to compile a list of best restaurants in such cities as Rome and Paris. For everybody—locals, expatriates, even those who have chalked up only one visit—has favorites ("what . . . you don't know about that little trattoria three doors down from the Piazza Navona?").

What follows is not a list of all the best restaurants of Rome, but simply a running commentary on a number of personal favorites. For the most part, we've preferred not to document every deluxe citadel—known to all big spenders. Rather, we've tried to seek out equally fine (or better!) establishments, such as the Taverna Flavia, often patronized by some of the finest palates in Rome (but not necessarily by the fattest wallets).

Rome's cooking is not subtle, but its kitchen is among the finest in Italy, rivaling anything the chefs of Florence or Venice can turn out. Another feature of Roman restaurants is their skill at borrowing—and sometimes improving upon—the cuisine of other Italian regions. Throughout the capital, you'll come across Neapolitan, Bolognese, Florentine, even Sicilian specialties. If you don't like the food, you may enjoy the view—either of the Piazza Navona, the Spanish Steps, or the Via Veneto.

Some restaurants offer a **tourist menu** at an inclusive price. The tourist menu includes soup (nearly always minestrone) or pasta, followed by a meat dish with vegetables, topped off by dessert (fresh fruit or cheese), as well as a quarter liter of wine or mineral water, along with the bread, cover charge, and service (you'll still be expected to tip something extra).

If you order from the tourist menu, you'll avoid the array of added charges the restaurateur likes to tack on. You'll not get the choicest cuts of meat, nor will you always be able to order the specialties of the house, but you'll probably get a filling and quite good repast if you pick and choose your restaurants carefully.

What about the *prezzo fisso*? A confused picture. A fixed-price meal might even undercut the tourist menu, offering a cheaper meal of the "casa." On the other hand, it might not include wine, service, bread, or cover charge—for which you'll be billed extra. If you're on the most limited of budgets, make sure you understand what the prezzo fisso entails—so as to avoid misunderstandings when you settle the tab.

THE TOP RESTAURANTS: Sans Souci, 20 Via Sicilia (tel. 460-491), is the most elegant and sophisticated dining choice in Rome, and it also serves some of the finest food. With this unbeatable combination, it is no wonder that it has a chic—and frequently famous—clientele. An additional plus is its location—right off the Via Veneto. To begin your evening, you'll enter the dimly lit small lounge/bar to the right at the bottom of the steps. Here, amidst tapestries and glittering mirrors, the maître d' will present you with the menu, and you can leisurely make selections while sipping a drink. We've found, in general, it's best to skip the chef's suggestions of the day and, instead, order from the highly imaginative à la carte menu. Recommended is the espadon (swordfish) at 5,200 lire ($6.03) or the duck in orange sauce, also 5,200 lire. The house specialty is mazzancolle flambée Danilo, 6,500 lire ($7.54)—a double treat as the waiters achieve "fireworks" spectaculars with their flambé dishes. We also heartily endorse the cheese soufflé, 6,500 lire ($7.54) for two persons. It's expensive, but worth it. Go for dinner only, and reserve in advance. Closed Mondays. You'll be treated to the finest service in the capital. It may spoil you for other places.

"La Tavernetta" Villa Miani, 151 Via Trionfale (tel. 349-87-07), is an outstanding private villa at Monte Mario, on the outskirts of Rome. A long and winding private driveway leads to this formal palace, with its stunning view of the capital. The splendid building, complete with its elaborately baroque interior, handles mostly catered affairs, though you can dine year round in the lower-level tavern, with its cove ceilings and humorous murals. In a cozy around-the-fireplace chair, you can order pre-dinner drinks. Put yourself in the hands of the skilled maître d' who will suggest an Italian dinner, complete with two wines and dessert. Expect to pay at least 15,000 lire ($17.40) per person. The antipasto is delicious, as are the pasta dishes. We've also liked the risotto with champagne, plus the melt-in-your-mouth entrecôte. Bring a healthy appetite for good food and you'll fare well. Go for dinner only, except on Mondays. A taxi is mandatory. For your return, the staff will radio one to pick you up.

Hostaria dell'Orso (The Inn of the Bear), 93 Via di Monte Brianzo (tel. 561-835), is the most elegant restaurant in Rome. Jane and Ira Avery compared it to New York's 21 or Paris' Tour d'Argent, but it's different, of course. You may want to stop first for a drink at the Blue Bar, with its flickering candles in the chandeliers and seductive background music from a pianist. Then you can ascend into the upper 14th-century salon dining rooms, with their luxurious, high-fashion furnishings. The Hostaria was once a simple inn, constructed in 1300. Reportedly, St. Francis of Assisi once stayed here, as did Dante during the Jubilee Year. Later, as a hotel, it was to attract such guests as Rabelais, Montaigne, and Goethe. Falling into disrepute at the turn of the century (skeletons discovered in the walls), it was taken over in 1940 and launched on its present fame as a gathering spot of international society.

You can go here for dinner only (dress in your finest). For a three-course minimum dinner, expect to pay 10,000 lire ($11.60), excluding wine. The varied menu includes such good dishes as cannelloni Hostaria (stuffed with meat and cheese), antipasti, chicken stewed in French champagne, sirloin steak in red wine, and veal scaloppine. The dessert wagon will force you to abandon your "chastity" vows.

L'Eau Vive, 85 Via Monterone (tel. 654-1095), qualifies as an off-beat adventure. One of the most exciting additions to the Roman dining scene in many a year, it is run by lay missionaries who wear the dress or costumes of their native countries. In other words, if the lay woman waiting on you is from Thailand, you might know what to expect. However, if she's from Los Angeles, you take your chances. The menu is international, although French specialties —such classic ones as pâté, coq au vin, omelette aux champignons—seem to predominate. Delectable appetizers include six escargots at 2,200 lire ($2.55); quiche Lorraine at 800 lire (93¢); or perhaps a Vietnamese soup at 1,700 lire ($1.97). Main dishes range anywhere from guinea hen with onions and grapes in a wine sauce at 2,500 lire ($2.90) to couscous at 3,500 lire ($4.06). A smooth finish is the chocolate mousse at 1,300 lire ($1.51). Under vaulted ceilings, the atmosphere is deliberately kept subdued, though the place settings—with fresh flowers and good glassware—are most tasteful. However, some of the most flamboyant members of international society have adopted L'Eau Vive as their favorite spot. A cosmopolitan list of habitués includes artists, priests, ambassadors, journalists, bankers, even families who live in nearby villas. The somewhat restrained ambience is quickly forgotten when you see the smile of the hostess waiting to seat you, and when the food is put before you. An excellent choice for "la bonne cuisine." On a narrow street in Old Rome, it is hard to find. Closed Sundays.

Near the Piazza Colonna

31 Al "Vicario," 31 Via Uffici del Vicario (tel. 672-251), is an undisputed choice for super-good Roman food, with a menu selection expansive enough to appeal to most tastes. Known to European gourmets as that special place in Rome, it's a sedate restaurant in the "classico" style—its tone set by a tall, elegant entranceway, flanked by bronze lanterns. The several dining rooms are in beige and white, enlivened by occasional gilt torchiers and contemporary watercolors. For starters, the classic dish is risotto verde at 1,600 lire ($1.86), though we're invariably attracted to the vermicelli alle vongole (baby clams) at 2,400 lire ($2.78). In fish, a good main dish is the shrimp Newburg at 4,500 lire ($5.22). The châteaubriand for two is also recommendable at 9,500 lire ($11.02). To finish, why not go all the way and request crêpes suzette at 3,500 lire ($4.06)? Closed Sundays.

Near the Spanish Steps

Ristorante G. Ranieri, 26 Via Mario de' Fiori, (tel. 679-15-92), off the Via Condotti at the foot of the Spanish Steps, is well launched into its second century (it was founded in 1843) as an intimate dining spot for the cognoscenti. Here is an atmosphere evocative of Anaïs Nin's *Under a Glass Bell*—rose petals, gold brocade, crystal chandeliers. But Victorian trappings aren't all Ranieri offers. The food titillates your taste buds. Over the years, the lasagne verdi (green noodles), topped with cheese, has earned the greatest salvos; it costs 1,000 lire ($1.16) a dish. Dozens of meat and fish entrees are featured, averaging from 2,000 lire ($2.32) to 3,000 lire ($3.48). The most loyal habitués always finish with zabaglione, a foamy delicate treat, made here with bits of pineapple —one of Italy's greatest desserts, costing 700 lire (81¢).

George's, 7 Via Marche (tel. 484-575), is one of the most expensive restaurants in Rome. Also, one of the best. It's been a favorite of ours ever since Romulus and Remus were being tended by the She-Wolf. First of all, the proprietor, a distinguished gastronome, isn't named George and is tired of being called that. He is C. Vernon Jarratt, and he's English. You're ushered into a bar with a seasoned ambience. Here, in this clubby atmosphere, you can sip your apéritif, enjoying piano music in the evening and a decor of New Yorker cartoons, photographs, and prints. English is spoken. While your own table lamp softly lights your menu, you can select such delicious cold soups as gazpacho or vichyssoise, both 1,800 lire ($2.09). Another delightful opener is the smoked trout at 2,900 lire ($3.36), accompanied by a creamy, freshly made horseradish with a kick. A host of main dishes is offered, including roast duck Tour d'Argent style, 9,000 lire ($10.44) for two persons, or planked steak for two, 13,750 lire ($15.95). An unusual dessert is the syllabub at 1,550 lire ($1.80). George's is behind the deluxe Excelsior Hotel, right off the Via Veneto. The restaurant is closed in August.

Near the Villa Bonaparte

Taverna Flavia, 9 Via Flavia (tel. 489-214), is a favorite of the visiting movie star, as its famous line-up of celeb photographers will testify—everybody from Frank Sinatra to "Ben Hur" himself. Crowded and bustling, the taverna is a romanticized version of the Roman trattoria. Vogue hairdos intermix casually with the most arrived of the artist colony. Thankfully, the kitchen isn't overlooked in this array of glamor. The meals are prepared with consummate artistry, with even the simple dishes managing a creative flair. A good beginning is the vine-ripened melon with figs and prosciutto at 2,800 lire ($3.25).

Main dishes include a risotto with scampi at 2,200 lire ($2.55), and fish dishes from 3,400 lire ($3.94) to 5,000 lire ($5.80). Try spaghetti al whiskey at 1,300 lire ($1.51). A different regional dish is featured daily. Desserts begin at 600 lire (70¢). In the words of one visitor, Gloria Swanson—"It's divine, dear heart."

Will the Real Alfredo's Please Stand Up?

In the old days, the tourist to Rome penciled at the top of his itinerary: "See the Colosseum and lunch at Alfredo's." Today, the notation is likely to be the same. The question is, which Alfredo's? There are three major ones, but the big two are **Alfredo alla Scrofa,** 104 Via Della Scrofa (tel. 654-0163), where it all began, and **Alfredo l'Originale** 30 Piazza Augusto Imperatore (tel. 681-672), with the most exciting situation.

With so many claims, it's difficult to figure out which is the original. It doesn't matter anyway, as the real Alfredo is dead. (He was presented with a golden spoon and fork with which to mix the fettuccine by Mary Pickford and Douglas Fairbanks.) Both houses still serve the greatest fettuccine (noodles made of eggs) in town, and we can't find any appreciable difference between the food at either of them—hence, we gravitate to the least expensive.

At Alfredo alla Scrofa, you'll find the walls decked out with photos of such celebs as Charlie Chaplin, Clark Gable, or Gregory Peck and Audrey Hepburn (stars of "Roman Holiday"). The dish to order here is maestose fettuccine al triplo burro, costing only 1,200 lire ($1.39). It's well worth it—enhanced as it is by loads of butter and cheese. For fettuccine aficionados, the waiters are real choreographers when they're mixing the dish. The next recommended main-course specialty: filetto di tacchino dorato for 2,500 lire ($2.90)—a delicious sautéed breast of turkey covered with thin slices of white truffles from Piedmont. An Irish coffee at 1,600 lire ($1.86) makes a good finish. Sad-faced strolling musicians add a dour note, but the diners supply their own entertainment. Closed Tuesdays. (Alfredo l'Originale is closed Sundays.)

THE SPECIALTY RESTAURANTS—ALL PRICE RANGES: Césarina, 109 Via Piemonte (tel. 460-828), off the Via Veneto, is the finest citadel of the Bolognese cuisine in the Eternal City. As you may know, Bologna is considered the gastronomic capital of Italy. The hearty empress here is Césarina Masi, who looks like everybody's mamma mia (she even lectures you if you don't finish your tagliatelle). As big and bustling as a New York kosher delicatessen restaurant, the semi-rustic Césarina features at least two specialties that tower over the rest: one is the misto Césarina, offering three kinds of pasta made by hand and costing 1,800 lire ($2.09); the other, served as a main course, is the cotoletta alla bolognese, a veal cutlet with ham, baked with cheese—a savory delight when prepared well (and mamma sees that it's always prepared well). The cost of this dish is 3,000 lire ($3.48). The dessert specialty, wheeled to your table and dished out from the cart, is semifreddo Césarina at 1,200 lire ($1.39). Césarina is closed Fridays.

Massimo d'Azeglio, 18 Via Cavour (tel. 46-06-46), is in a hotel, but don't be put off by that. This restaurant is celebrated throughout Europe, having dispensed the haute cuisine, Roman style, since 1875. Angelo Bettoja runs it today, and it was his great-great grandfather who founded it. It was built near the terminal station, which was considered a fashionable address in the 19th century. The cognoscenti frequent it. Mr. Bettoja was once inspired to create pheasant porthos—that is, a boned pheasant stuffed with partridge breast which had been lined with breast of thrush which contained a ball of foie gras! The game birds came from Mr. Bettoja's estate near Orvieto. Specialties include tagliolini d'Azeglio, a masterful pasta dish at 2,500 lire ($2.90). We'd recommend spaghetti alla carbonara at 1,800 lire ($2.09). Also good is filetto di manzo (beef) flambé, at 4,900 lire ($5.68).

Girrarrosta Toscano, 29 Via Campania (tel. 464-292), faces the walls of the Borghese Gardens. It draws a coterie of sophisticated guests from Via Veneto haunts. Under vaulted ceilings in a cellar setting, some of the finest Tuscan specialties in Rome are served. You often have to wait, being tantalized by the aroma of meats on the open charcoal grill. In the meantime, you can enjoy an enormous selection of antipasti which the waiters bring around to you: succulent little meatballs, vine-ripened melon with prosciutto, an omelette, mozzarella, and especially delicious Tuscan salami. You're then given a choice of pasta, such as fettuccine in a cream sauce. Priced according to weight, the bistecca alla Fiorentina is the best item to order, though it's likely to be expensive. This is a grilled steak seasoned with oil, salt, and pepper. For dessert, we'd recommend what everybody has—an assortment of different flavors of ice cream, called a "gelati misti." A complete meal will cost about 12,000 lire ($13.92) per person with wine, possibly more if you order a big beefsteak.

Ambasciata d'Abruzzo, 26 Via Pietro Tacchini (tel. 878-256). If you like ambitious portions on an all-you-can-eat basis, a place where the food is well-cooked and tasty, and also inexpensive for the value received, then strike out for this little, hard-to-find restaurant in the Parioli district. It's not only superb value, but great fun, providing you are ravenously hungry and enjoy bountiful dining. It accomplishes the seemingly impossible, not skimping on quality for quantity. First, the price is a blanket 7,000 lire ($8.12) per person. The atmosphere is exceedingly informal, and you may have to stand in line if you didn't reserve a table. It's in the true tavern style, with strings of sausages, peppers, and garlic. As soon as you're seated, the culinary parade commences, with a basket over-flowing with assorted sausages placed on your table, even an herb-flavored baked ham is presented, resting on a cutting board with a knife. Help yourself—but go easy, as there's more to come. Another wicker basket holds moist crunchy peasant-styled bread, from which you tear off huge hunks. Next a hearty mass of spaghetti vongole (with baby clams) is placed before you. Then you proceed to an overloaded antipasto table, with its awesome selections, including marinated artichokes, salads, whatever. Later those still remaining at the table are served a main dish such as grilled fish. Then comes the large salad bowl, mixed to your liking, followed by an assortment of country cheese, plus a basket brimming with fresh fruit. You're even given your choice of a dessert. On our latest rounds, the waiters pronounced it "Boston cream pie." A pitcher of the house wine is at your disposal, and the price not only includes coffee, but an entire bottle of Sambuca is placed on your table. Again, it's help yourself. Closed Sundays.

Dal Bolognese, 1-2 Piazza del Popolo (tel. 380-248). If "La Dolce Vita" were being filmed in the 70s, the director would probably use this restaurant as a backdrop. It is one of those rare dining spots that is not only chic, but noted for its food as well. Young actors, shapely models, artists from the nearby Via Margutta, even industrialists on an off-the-record evening on the town, show up here, quickly booking the limited sidewalk tables. Because of the mounting popularity of this restaurant, you must reserve a table in advance. The canopy and awning partially conceal the clientele, although the sidewalk tables do open onto a view of the twin baroque churches. To launch you into your repast, we'd suggest the savory Parma ham at 2,200 lire ($2.55), or perhaps the melon and prosciutto at 2,800 lire ($3.25) if you're feeling extravagant. Incidentally, try a little freshly ground pepper on the latter—you'll be surprised (happily) at the results. For your main course, the chef does a truly superb osso bucco with peas at 3,000 lire ($3.48) and an entrecôte Bordelaise at 3,200 lire ($3.71). Dal Bolognese is closed on Mondays. Instead of lingering in the restaurant, you may want to cap your evening by calling on the Rosati next door (or its competitor, the Canova, across the street), and enjoying one of the tempting pastries. The most beautiful girls in Rome show up here after midnight! You'll find them available providing you look like Alain Delon or Robert Redford.

Ristorante Nino, 11 Via Borgognona (tel. 679-56-76), off the Via Condotti, a short walk from the Spanish Steps, is a simple tavern mecca for writers, artists, and an occasional model from one of the nearby high-fashion houses. Nino's enjoys deserved acclaim for its Tuscan dishes—everything from "Devilish done chicken" to "entrails and paw after the Florentine cuisine!" The cooking is hearty and completely unpretentious. The restaurant is particularly known for its steaks shipped in from Florence and charcoal broiled—around 7,500 lire ($8.70) for a big one. A maddeningly filling bowl of zuppa di fagioli (bean soup) costs 850 lire (99¢). Other good dishes include the fried scampi at 3,200 lire ($3.71) and the cannelloni at 950 lire ($1.10). Typical desserts average around 950 lire also. "Sundays closed for weekly rest." Don't miss it! The annual closing is from July 20 to September 1.

Lon Fon, 44 Firenze (tel. 475-52-61), is the splashiest and most acclaimed Chinese restaurant in Rome, though connoisseurs will claim concessions have been made to the Italian palate. It lies on a fashionable street, near the Opera House, and is an attractive, almost festive place in which to dine. Bamboo trees, lots of lanterns, and much brilliant red make the two large dining rooms joyous. For openers, we'd recommend the hot and sour soup at 800 lire (93¢), followed by Pekinese duck at 12,000 lire ($13.92). Three other heartily recommendable specialties include "Beggar's Chicken" at 10,000 lire ($11.60); squirrel shredded chicken at 3,000 lire ($3.48), and big meatballs with Chinese sauce at 3,600 lire ($4.18).

Scoglio di Frisio, 256 Via Merulana (tel. 734-619), is the choice suprême to introduce yourself to the Neapolitan kitchen. While at it, you might as well get reacquainted with pizza (pizza pie is redundant!), abandoning your Yankee concepts and appreciating the genuine article. At night, you can begin with a plate-sized Neapolitan pizza (crunchy, oozy, and excellent) with clams and mussels, 1,150 lire ($1.34). After devouring the house specialty, you may then settle for chicken cacciatore, hunter's style, 1,950 lire ($2.26), or veal scaloppine, 2,150 lire ($2.50). For the "nostalgic American," spaghetti and meatballs —not an Italian dish—is offered for 1,350 lire ($1.57). Scoglio di Frisio also has entertainment—so it makes for an inexpensive "night on the town." All the fun, cornball "O Sole Mio" elements spring forth in the evening—a weeping violin, a passionate accordion, a strolling tenor who acts like Mario Lanza reincarnate. The decor's nautical in honor of the top-notch fish dishes—complete with a high-ceilinged grotto with craggy walls, fishermen's nets, crustaceans, and a miniature three-masted schooner hanging overhead. It's closed Mondays. The restaurant is on a broad street, south of the railway station. Bus No. 93.

Dining in Trastevere

"Da Meo Patacca," 30 Piazza de' Mercanti (tel. 581-6198), would certainly have pleased Barnum and Bailey. On a gaslit plaza from the Middle Ages in Trastevere, it serves bountiful self-styled "Roman country" meals to flocks of tourists. The atmosphere is one of extravaganza—primitive, colorful, theatrical in a carnival sense, but good fun if you're in the mood. From the huge open spit and the charcoal grill, many tempting platters are cooked. Downstairs is a vast cellar, studded with waves of strolling musicians and singers—a smash hit. Utilizing a taverna theme, the restaurant is decked out with wagon wheels, along with garlands of pepper and garlic. And the offerings are as adventurous as the decor: wild boar, wild hare, quail, corn on the cob, even pork and beans. A recent complete dinner for two, including coffee, bread, wine, and three courses, plus service, came to 15,000 lire ($17.40). The antipasti are huge and filling—many succulent tidbits—with an order costing 3,000 lire ($3.48). In summer, you can dine at outdoor tables.

This extravaganza was born in 1959, the creation of Remington Olmsted, who had visited Rome as Jud in "Oklahoma." Its success was so phenomenal that he took over other properties on the same piazza. Featured at **Da Ciceruacchio** are charcoal-broiled steaks and chops, along with lots of local wine on tap. Located at 1 Via del Porto (tel. 580-60-46), it was once a sunken jail—the ancient walls dating from the days of the Roman Empire. Mr. Olmsted's third venture on the same square is **Ar Fieramosca,** 3 Piazza Mercanti (tel. 589-0289), named after a medieval knight hero. This latest venture is super rustic, with large fireplaces, waiters dressed as fishermen, and musicians. House specialties are seafood and pizzas, the latter beginning at 800 lire (93¢). You can pay as much as 7,000 lire ($8.12) for a complete meal here, depending on what you order. Closed Tuesdays.

Sabatini, 18 Vicolo di S. Maria in Trastevere (tel. 58-83-07), attracts food-wise habitués in the increasingly fashionable district of Trastevere. It's just right for that special dining occasion, easily absorbing its widely varied international clientele. First of all, it's romantically situated right off a hideaway square, deep in the heart of the sector. At night, the Piazza S. Maria—a setting for Fellini's "Roma"—itself is the center of lively movement, with its cafes and ecclesiastical illuminations. Incidentally, our recommendation is not to be confused with another Sabatini opening directly onto the piazza. In fair weather, you can sit at one of the outside tables across the way. Inside the side-street restaurant, the atmosphere is rich in the old tavern style, with deep arches, a beamed ceiling, even frescoed decorative effects. Unquestionably, the pacesetter is the large open charcoal fire you see at the entrance. Delicate white fish is grilled there daily. For beginners, try the antipasto mistomare, with its delicious "fruits of the sea" at 2,200 lire ($2.55). An excellent alternative is the zuppa di cozze (mussels), at 2,600 lire ($3.02). Most meat dishes cost 2,500 lire ($2.90). For a main course, we'd recommend the gamberi alla marinara at 2,500 lire ($2.90), though the sole is also good, priced according to weight. Desserts are in the 700 lire (81¢) to 900 lire ($1.04) bracket in this medium-priced establishment.

Romolo, 7 Via Porta Settimiana (tel. 588-284), is a Trastevere gem. You can sit in a Renaissance garden that once belonged to Raphael's mistress, della Fornarina (the baker's daughter), who posed for some of his madonnas. Now it's known and has been patronized by everybody from celluloid heroes (Kirk Douglas) to political personalities (Clare Boothe Luce or Margaret Truman) to collegians. Favorite dishes offered? To begin your meal, try the fettuccine with meat sauce for 900 lire ($1.04), followed by scaloppine al marsala for 1,800 lire ($2.09), or deviled chicken at 2,400 lire ($2.78). A fresh garden salad costs 500 lire (58¢) extra. For dessert, try a "charlotte" for 650 lire (75¢)—a sponge cake lathered with whipped cream and topped by a decorative motif. Even if the garden isn't in use, you'll like the cozy interior, with its bric-a-brac of copper, wood, and silver.

La Cisterna, 13 Via della Cisterna, lies deep in the heart of Trastevere—and has for some time. For the last 50 years or so, it's been run by the Simmi family, who are genuinely interested in serving only the best as well as providing a good time for all the guests. The Cistern in the name comes from an ancient well discovered in the cellar, dating from the heyday of Imperial Rome. When the weather's good, you dine outside at sidewalk tables, serviced by waiters in short pants with red sashes. If it's rainy or cold, you can select from one of a series of inside rooms decorated with murals—many of which are amusing, particularly the Rape of the Sabine Women. Roman specialties are featured. In summer you can inspect the antipasto—a mixed selection of hors d'oeuvres—right out on the street before going in. The cost is 2,400 lire ($2.78), and you may not want another bite. Recommendable are roasted meat dishes, such as veal, at 2,500 lire ($2.90), and fresh fish, rarely averaging more than 3,700 lire ($4.29) per serving. The best desserts will run you 850 lire (99¢).

Near St. Peter's

Il Matriciano, 55 via dei Gracchi (tel. 359-52-47), is a family-style restaurant that enjoys patronage by a devoted set of habitués. Its location in the gastronomic wasteland in and around St. Peter's makes it all the more distinguished. The food is good, but it's only country fare—nothing fancy. The decor, likewise, is kept to a minimum. In summer, try to get one of the sidewalk tables behind a green hedge and under a shady canopy. The luncheon clientele seems to linger a long time, perhaps out of reluctance to get back to their offices. For openers, you might prefer a simple zuppa di verdura at 600 lire (70¢), or ravioli di ricotta, 950 lire ($1.10). The preferred choice, however, is tagliolini con tartufi, 2,200 lire ($2.55). For main dishes, we'd recommend scaloppa alla Valdostana, 2,200 lire ($2.55); abbacchio (baby lamb) al forno, 2,800 lire ($3.25), and trippa alla Romano, 2,000 lire ($2.32). Desserts begin at 700 lire (81¢). Closed Wednesdays.

Trattoria Vincenzo, 173 Via della Lungaretta (tel. 585-302), is surrounded by far more expensive restaurants in the Trastevere district. It has never wasted the cost of an anchovy on fancy trappings; instead, it hauls out some of the best prepared dishes—particularly seafoods—in this colorful section of the city. And the prices are kind to those on the budget safari. Small, popular (always crowded with Flea Marketeers at Sunday lunch), the Vincenzo serves a zuppa di pesce (really a stew that doesn't need to play second bass to the most savory bouillabaisse), costing 2,700 lire ($3.13). The delicately spiced and grilled scampi, another specialty of the house, goes for 3,000 lire ($3.48). Want a little bit of everything? Try the fritti misti di mare (mixed seafood platter), including red mullet and crisp bits of squid, for 2,700 lire ($3.13). The trattoria doesn't overlook the pasta dishes either—sample the cannelloni for 900 lire ($1.04). It's closed Sunday nights and Mondays.

In the Roman Ghetto

Piperno Monte Cenci, 9 via Monte de Cenci (tel. 65-40-629), is the leading choice in the Eternal City's old Jewish ghetto. However, it's not a kosher restaurant. Come here to sample a vegetable for which Rome is known in gastronomic circles—carciofi alla guidia, artichokes sliced crosswise and deep-fried to a golden-brown crispness. These artichokes are unique in the world, having little in common with the tough-leaved variety grown in the United States. The cost is 1,800 lire ($2.09) for two persons. Almost equally good is fiori di zucca ripieni e fritti (fresh squash blossoms, deep-fried to a golden brown), 2,200 lire ($2.55). As you enter the simple restaurant, a delectable array of antipasto misto at 1,800 lire ($2) awaits your selection. For a main course, we'd recommend filetti di baccalà, strips of codfish fillets batter fried, 2,000 lire ($2.32). A tourist menu costs 3,000 lire ($3.48). Closed Mondays.

da Giggetto, Via del Portico d'Ottavia (tel. 6561-105), nestles in the old ghetto of Rome, a short walk from the Theater of Marcellus. Not only does this budget choice stand side-by-side with colorful ruins, but old Roman columns extend practically to its doorway. Once you walk into its maze of dining rooms, you'll be entering a bustling, exciting trattoria. The Romans flock here for their special traditional dishes. None is more typical than carciofi alla giudia, the baby-tender fried artichokes—thistles to make you whistle with delight. The cost is just 600 lire (70¢). This is a true delicacy. Another well-recommended dish is filetti di baccalà, slender strips of codfish fillets batter-fried in oil, only 500 lire (58¢). The cheese concoction, mozzarella in carozza, is another delight at 1,500 lire ($1.74). Shrimp grilled or with wine sauce goes for 2,500 lire (58¢). In spring you might sample the fresh strawberries from Nemi, 1,300 lire ($1.51). Closed Mondays.

Angelino a Tormargana, Piazza Margana, about three blocks from the Piazza Venezia, is housed in Goethe's historic inn. In this setting of old palazzi and charmingly ancient cobblestoned squares, you can dine al fresco at tables hedged with greenery. At night the colored lanterns are turned on, and you're often treated to the sound of strolling musicians. A somewhat elegant clientele is attracted to the inn, and the atmosphere is surprisingly sophisticated. Also in the square are three pieces of steel and plexiglass modern sculpture. The food is very much in the typical Roman trattoria style—not exceptionally imaginative, but good for what it is. Expect a tab of 4,500 lire ($5.22) to 6,000 lire ($6.96) for a complete meal, including a carafe of the house wine. We'd recommend the eggplant parmigiana, followed by chicken with peppers. Add 15% for service. Closed Sundays.

Vecchia Roma, 18 Piazza Campitelli (tel. 656-4604), is a charming trattoria, budget priced, in the heart of the ghetto (a short walk from Michelangelo's Campidoglio). Head in the direction of the Theater of Marcellus, but turn right at the Synagogue. Everybody from Bardot to Niven frequents the place, sitting at one of the crowded tables. The room in the back, with its bas relief, is more popular—but not because of the bas relief! On the way in, you'll pass a table laden with tempting hors d'oeuvres. Try artichokes alla giudia at 650 lire (75¢). Another good beginning is a pasta dish called agnolotti at 600 lire (70¢). It's stuffed with minced meat, a smaller version of ravioli. Among the main dishes, the cotoletta alla Bolognese at 2,000 lire ($2.32) is recommended. To accompany your meal, why not a rice-stuffed tomato at 600 lire (70¢), for garlic devotees only? Expect a 350 lire (41¢) cover charge.

Near the Piazza Navona

Passetto, 14 Via Giuseppe Zanardelli (tel. 654-0569), a minute's stroll from the Piazza Navona, draws a faithful coterie of epicures who know of its delights and consider it one of the finest deluxe restaurants in the Roman capital. For example, it takes one of the mainstays of the Italian kitchen—cannelloni, the stuffed pasta dish—and turns it into a platter worthy of Caesar. For a main course, we recommend the scaloppine alla pizzaiola, which is done very well. But the real scene stealer, when featured is abbacchio, baby lamb, as well as mint and garlic-flavored carciofi (artichokes). You might begin your meal with cannelloni at 1,300 lire ($1.51) or a delicious soup at 1,000 lire ($1.16). For a change of pace, however, we'd recommend speck, a Tyrolean meat, sliced razor thin, the color of dried beef, costing 1,900 lire ($2.20). Good main dishes include roast quail (two of them), also 1,900 lire, and a fonduta alla Piemontesa with truffles at 4,300 lire ($4.99). For dessert, the chef's specialty is crêpes suzette at 2,300 lire ($2.67). Passetto is closed Sundays.

Papa Giovanni, 4 via dei Sediari (tel. 656-53-08), is our secret restaurant address in Rome. It's expensive but worth it for that very special treat. For many years, Signor Renato, alias Papa Giovanni, has been at the stove. However, he now greets guests courteously, showing them to a table in his tiny restaurant of narrow rooms, his walls cluttered with rows of wine bottles and picture postcards. In this informal tavern atmosphere, some of the upper-crust of Rome society shows up, along with an occasional movie star. Your smiling waiter is likely to recommend your course for the day, so you can dispense with menus. One of Papa Giovanni's secrets is "truffles with everything." However, these tiny shavings of that delicious morsel will cost you an additional 1,400 lire ($1.62) every time you order them. The mushroom salad with dandelions is among the best we've ever sampled, the cost, 2,000 lire ($2.32). For a main course, we'd recommend involtini (rolled meat) di manzo, 3,000 lire ($3.48), or perhaps fonduta alla Valdostana, also 3,000 lire. Everything tastes better with vino di Papa Giovanni, 2,000 lire ($2.32). Closed Sundays. Reservations are imperative, and the restaurant serves dinner after 8:30. This place is for the discriminating visitor to the Eternal City who is appreciative of good food and wants to linger long over his or her meal.

Da Pietro, 19 Via dei Pianellari, is the name of a simple-looking trattoria, but the food is superb and the clientele may range from an internationally known film star to a painter taking a break from an exhibition at the nearby Piazza Navona. There's plenty of Roman atmosphere to make you enjoy such delicious dishes as gnocchetti di spinaci e ricotta, cannelloni, crêpes aux fromages, or the exceptional manzo al Barolo (a tender meat with Barolo wine sauce). A complete, though necessarily basic meal, will cost about 5,000 lire ($5.80) including your wine and cover charge. The wine list reflects a large variety of good selections, and the bottles aren't too expensive. The Hostaria da Pietro suddenly became famous among foreign journalists living in Rome after an American newsman mislaid some notes and a gold pen. Pietro himself took the trouble to call all the possible addresses where U.S. journalists normally can be found. He found his man. Closed on Sundays.

The **Trattoria Mastrostefano,** 93-95 Piazza Navona (tel. 651-669), is our preferred medium-priced choice on this magnetic piazza, with its Bernini Fountain of the Four Rivers. With its sidewalk tables, the trattoria offers a ringside view, a mecca for the in-the-know-crowd who wisely avoid the overstuffed Tre Scalini across the way. The prices at the Mastrostefano are lower, and we've found that the food is equally good—though served in less pretentious surroundings. Why not introduce yourself to a yummy spaghetti carbonara at 1,000 lire ($1.16)? The veal dishes are the specialties—none finer than the scaloppini served with a Marsala wine sauce for 2,800 lire ($3.25). Osso bucco is also good at 2,800 lire. Closed Mondays. Since you're so near the **Tre Scalini,** you might well stroll across the piazza to its "Gelateria" and try its famous tartufo (bittersweet chocolate-coated ice cream with cherries and whipped cream). If you order two to take out, it'll cost you 950 lire ($1.10) each. Your sweetheart will be much sweeter after downing this concoction. Tre Scalini is closed on Wednesdays.

Trattoria Febo, 12 Largo Febo, is a good bet if the high-priced restaurants of the nearby Piazza Navona are too much for you. Although it is just across the street from one of Rome's most deluxe hotels, the Raphael, the Febo is modest in both price and decor. It's frequented primarily by Romans who know they can get good food in a jovial ambience. The dining area is really a garden where tables are set out under trees. The whole is bordered by beds of bright flowers. For starters, you might try the spaghetti with clams at 800 lire (93¢), although the risotto with saffron, at 800 lire also is good. Chicken grilled over an open fire, at 2,000 lire ($2.32), is highly recommended, as is the sirloin at 2,700 lire ($3.13). The tipsy cake at 600 lire (70¢) is guaranteed to make you the same. For service 12½% is automatically added to your bill.

Near the Trevi Fountain

Quirino, 84 Via delle Murate, is a good place to dine right after you've tossed your coin into the Trevi Fountain. The atmosphere inside is typically Italian, with hanging Chianti bottles, a beamed ceiling, and muraled walls. Table service is thoughtful, but you won't be overly solicited. The food is strictly in the "home-cooking" style of the Roman trattorie. At times you can enjoy fresh chicory that is perfumed and bitter at the same time. All the ritual dishes of the Roman kitchen are here, including tripe at 2,500 lire ($2.90) a serving. We're also fond of a mixed fry of the tiny shrimps and squid rings which resemble onion rings, 2,500 lire also. For an opening course, we'd recommend the cannelloni at 700 lire (81¢). For dessert, a basket of fresh fruit will be placed on your table for 600 lire (70¢). Expect to pay a 300 lire cover charge.

Near Trajan's Forum

Ristorante "Ulpia," 2 Foro Traiano (tel. 689-980), is for atmospheric dining. It's been a restaurant for 175 years, and is now under the direction of Paolo Giardini, who maintains that it's "the most aristocratic and distinguished place in the heart of Imperial Rome." High praise, but Ulpia merits it. It grew out of a tavern constructed in the old Ulpian Trajan Road, across from Trajan's Forum. Inside are old Roman museum pieces. Featured in the restaurant is the house specialty, fettuccine Ulpia at 1,200 lire ($1.39), as well as chicken fiamma sacra, at 3,000 lire ($3.48). You might begin with antipasti vari at 2,700 lire ($3.13), finishing with crêpes suzette at 3,000 lire ($3.48). Expect to pay a cover charge of 600 lire (70¢), plus 15% for service. Bottles of red wine, such as Bardolino or Chianti, go for 2,800 lire ($3.25). In the evening, Ulpia becomes a nightclub, with music and dancing. Closed Sundays.

Near Piazza Ungheria in Parioli

Al Ceppo, 2 Via Panama (tel. 861-379), greets you with a glittering antipasto tray, including such delectable suggestions as stuffed yellow and red peppers, finely minced cold spinach blended with ricotta, unpeeled eggplant with a topping of tomato, mozzarella, and anchovy, and at least two dozen other dishes, many of which taste good either hot or cold. Because of its somewhat hidden location (though it's only two blocks from the Villa Borghese), the clientele is likely to be Roman rather than foreign. "The Log," as the name is in English, features an open fireplace which is fed with wood. On it, the chef does lamb chops, even quail, liver and bacon, to charcoal perfection. The beefsteak, which hails from Tuscany, is also delicious. If you can order both a pasta and the hors d'oeuvres, we'd suggest linguine con peperoni. These are thin noodles blended with green peppers cut thin like matchstick. Expect to pay 6,000 lire ($6.96) for a really filling repast, including a carafe of the house wine. Closed Mondays and in August.

Near the Pantheon

Ristorante Le Cave di St. Ignazio, 169 Piazza S. Ignazio (tel. 67-97-821), lies in the heart of Old Rome on a miniature plaza, but it lures with a dash of sophistication and glamor. The atmosphere is a combination of luxury set against a semi-crude backdrop. The old walls of the primitive architecture contrast well with the smartness of the decoration. Of the à la carte selections, the following are singled out: zuppa alla pavese (broth with a poached egg) for 650 lire (75¢), or risotto alla milanese (broth-cooked rice with giblets, mushrooms, and cheese) for 800 lire (93¢) . . . just for starters. For a mouthwatering specialita dello chef, order the cheese soufflé for only 1,700 lire ($1.97)—but allow at least 40 minutes, as it's prepared to order. Cooked equally well is the more filling chicken with rice smothered in sauce suprême, also for 1,700 lire. If you skipped the cheese soufflé for a main course, you may want to try the chocolate soufflé with vanilla sauce for dessert—another 1,700 lire.

Hostaria Angoletto, 51 Piazza Rondanini, is on the ground floor of an old palazzo. Under umbrellas or awnings, you dine on wooden floorboards. At night it attracts a lively and chic crowd of Romans, drawn to this romantic spot deep in Rome, near the Pantheon. The food is good, though not exceptionally inventive. The chef usually features Roman specialties. That means the egg drop soup, stracciatella at 800 lire (93¢), or saltimbocca (veal with ham and cheese) at 3,000 lire ($3.48). Tripe for aficionados is offered on Saturdays, costing 2,000 lire ($2.32). We also like the ravioli con ricotta, 900 lire ($1.04). The special dessert is ice cream with whiskey, 1,000 lire ($1.16). In addition, you'll pay a cover charge of 500 lire (58¢).

Near the Piazza di Campo dei Fiori

Ristorante da Pancrazio, 92 Piazza del Biscione (tel. 561-246), is a dining oddity. It serenely occupies the ruins of Pompey's ancient theater. The lower section of the theater and the rugged stone vaulted cellar have been converted into a restaurant that is a national monument, its walls witnessing 2,000 years of history. A simple tavern decoration sets the informal mood in several of the dining halls. However, the main room is more dignified, with tall marble columns and a coffered ceiling. An especially good opener for your meal is risotto alla pescatora (with an assortment of fruits of the sea), 1,000 lire ($1.16). Main courses include two roasted quail at 1,800 lire ($2.09) and eggplant parmigiana at 1,500 lire ($1.74). The fish dishes are also good, especially the mixed fish fry at 2,600 lire ($3.02) and the scampi at 3,700 lire ($4.29). For a dessert, try the fruit salad at 750 lire (87¢). Closed Wednesdays and in August.

Valle-la-Biblioteca, 9 Largo del Teatro Valle (tel. 651-292). Don't be misled by the name. It's not the kind of library where you check out books—rather one of the most unusual restaurants in Old Rome. It was created out of a wine cellar, and its walls are still lined with bottles, as well as pictures of celebrities. Big and popular, La Biblioteca is one of Rome's special restaurants. Many traditional Italian dishes are prepared here with flair, including a varied assortment of delicious pastas, such as lasagne di casa al forno at 900 lire ($1.04). Other typical dishes are carciofi (artichokes) alla Romana at 750 lire (87¢) and mozzarella in carrozza at 1,300 lire ($1.51). Main dishes include capriccio di pesce at 2,500 lire ($2.90) and chicken suprême with risotto at 2,200 lire ($2.55). The hard-to-find restaurant is on a satellite square of the Piazza di S. Andrea della Valle, off the Corso Vittorio Emanuele II. Closed Sundays and in August.

Near the Piazza Venezia

Abruzzi, 1 Via de Vaccaro (tel. 679-3897), takes its name from a little explored region known for its haunting beauty and curious superstitions. Its Roman namesake is at one side of the Piazza SS. Apostoli, just a short walk from the Piazza Venezia, with its memories of Mussolini. For some reason, a long list of sophisticated young people have selected this restaurant as their enduring favorite—probably because they get good food here at moderate prices. The chef is justly praised for his satisfying assortment of cold antipasto (hors d'oeuvres). You can make your own selection from the trolley cart for 1,250 lire ($1.45). With your beginning, we'd suggest a liter of garnet-red wine at 1,100 lire ($1.28). Once we had one whose bouquet was suggestive of the wild flowers of Abruzzi. If you'd like a soup as well, you'll find a good stracciatella (made with a thin batter of eggs and grated Parmesan cheese poured into a boiling chicken broth), 550 lire (64¢). A typical main dish is saltimbocca, the amusing "jump-in-the-mouth" name for tender slices of veal which have been skewered with slices of ham, sautéed in butter, and seasoned with Marsala, 1,900 lire ($2.20). The decor is not pretentious, and the atmosphere is friendly. It's closed Saturdays and for part of August.

Near the Spanish Steps

Otello alla Concordia, 81 Via della Croce, about two blocks from the Spanish Steps, is most central. The food is genuinely Roman and Tuscan, owing to the origin of the charming couple who own the restaurant. Very often they prepare either the excellent cannelloni alla Concordia or the spaghetti alla carbonara, either one costing 800 lire (93¢). If featured, the sizzling abbacchio (a very tender suckling lamb), at 2,000 lire ($2.32) is preferred, although you can order a scaloppine al Marsala at 1,800 lire ($2.09) if you're keeping costs low. A full three-course dinner, including a pasta opener, a main meat course, and dessert, will run at least 3,500 lire ($4.06). One of the main attractions, besides the good and inexpensive food, is the beautiful courtyard in the garden, a real oasis of peace in the center of Rome. Closed on Sundays.

"La Cantinella" da Emilio il Sardo, 19 Via Francesco Crispi (tel. 67-50-69), specializes in the cuisine of that ancient land of myth and legend, Sardinia. The Mediterranean island has a deserving place among Italy's gastronomic centers. The best introduction is porceddu (suckling pig seasoned with herbs, especially myrtle), costing 1,400 lire ($1.62). You might also want to try prosciutto di cinghiale all Nurghe, 1,200 lire ($1.39). This is black wild boar and ham, served thinly sliced. Pasta specialties include culuxionis (a ravioli stuffed with cheese) and malloreddus (little dumplings of corn flour and saffron, served with a spicy sauce and sprinkled with grated goat cheese), from 650 lire (75¢) to 800 lire (93¢). Everything tastes better with pane frattau—a Sardinian bread with eggs and tomato sauce. Desserts average around 600 lire (70¢). A simple tourist menu goes for 2,500 lire ($2.90). The family-run restaurant occupies two tiny rooms (the kitchen is between them). The location's just off the Via del Tritone, which runs into Piazza Barberini and its famous fountain.

Osteria Margutta, 82 Via Margutta, is on a street that traditionally has housed the nucleus of Rome's art colony. On Sundays, art shows are staged along the street, and it is the most fun then, although you can visit the galleries any day of the week. Should you get hungry during your stroll, drop in at this rustic tavern, given added style by the use of art posters, even paintings by children. You'll pass by tables of tempting antipasto, which are priced at 1,500 lire ($1.74). Excellent entrees include Hungarian goulash at 1,800 lire ($2.09) and tripe in the Roman style at 1,450 lire ($1.68). Handkerchiefs placed over lamps with soft bulbs make everyone look attractive. This restaurant is inexpensive and good.

Ristorante Mario, 55-56 Via della Vite (tel. 678-3818), is noted for its game specialties, all inexpensively priced. Mario also does excellent Florentine dishes, although the typical beefsteak is too costly these days for most budgets. You can dine in air-conditioned comfort on the street level or descend into the cellars. A good beginning is a wide noodle dish, pappardelle, best when served with a game sauce (caccia), costing 600 lire (70¢). Capretto (kid) is served in the Florentine fashion for 1,900 lire ($2.20), though you may prefer two roasted quail with polenta at 1,600 lire ($1.86). We heartily recommend the gelato misto, a selection of mixed ice cream, at 500 lire (58¢). You can order a fiasco (1.75 liters) of red Tuscan wine at 2,000 lire ($2.32).

Near the Colosseum

Trattoria l'Albanese, 148 Via dei Serpenti. For years visitors always found it difficult to locate a good and inexpensive restaurant while exploring the core of Imperial Rome. However, there is one that is quite fine, although it's small. As compensation for its size, it has a garden in the rear where you can order lunch. A set dinner goes for 2,500 lire ($2.90), and it's not bad, or you can order from an à la carte menu. Soups begin at 400 lire (46¢), and most meat and fish dishes are priced at 1,500 lire ($1.74). The trattoria is closed Tuesdays.

On the Island of Tibertina

Sora Lella, 16 Via dei Ponte Quattro Capi, is recommended primarily for its medieval location, on the boat-shaped island of Tibertina, right in the middle of the river. It's housed in a tower at the foot of a bridge, with busy traffic hurrying by. Somewhat of a dining curiosity, it is regionally decorated with hanging lanterns, tavern tables, and a cozy fireplace. Pasta dishes go for 900 lire ($1.04), and most meat courses cost 2,700 lire ($3.13). A basket of fresh fruit rounds out the repast at 650 lire (75¢). Closed Sundays.

Near the Circus Maximus

Circo Massimo, 53 Via dei Cerchi, is as close as Rome comes to having a genuine provincial inn. It's at the edge of the world-famed Circus Maximus, with its memories of Ben Hur. Here is all the cornpone decor associated with Italian taverns, including pigtails of garlic, corn on the cob hanging from the ceiling, and rolls of fat sausages. You can begin with the antipasto at 1,100 lire ($1.28) or one of the fine pasta dishes, such as fettuccine, at 900 lire ($1.04). Meat courses average around 3,000 lire ($3.48). A basket of fresh fruit at 600 lire (70¢) rounds out the repast, along with the "last of the wine." Try to linger longer making an evening of it—the atmosphere is mellow. Closed Mondays and in August.

On the Via Nazionale

Ristorante e Pizzeria Ricci, 29a Via Genova, are the "Gemini" pizza parlor and trattoria of The Eternal City. Linked by the same ownership, they stare across the street at each other at the end of a cul-de-sac street, with sidewalk tables, all of this a block from the Via Nazionale, within walking distance of the railway station. The pizza parlor is unmarred by the modern invasion, with a respectable patina on its wood paneling. Best of all are the sizzling hot pizzas, in many varieties, that adorn the plates. A far cry from the

American offerings, the pizzas here represent imagination running riot. But when in Rome, you should do as the Romans do and order their own particular variation—capricciosa—for 1,400 lire ($1.62). It's served with ham, mushrooms, stuffed mussels, cheese, and a bull's eye of a cooked egg! Across the way at the opposite side of the constellation is a restaurant-pizzeria that serves a 3,900-lire ($4.52) tourist dinner. Both establishments shut down on Mondays.

Birreria Bavaria, 251a Via Nazionale (tel. 462-077), is for the devotee of the specialties of Bavaria. Across the street from the Quirinale, near the Opera House, the restaurant is a reproduction of a German beer tavern, that attempts a *gemütlichkeit* atmosphere. The keller with thick arches splits into many wood-paneled rooms, where you can dine inexpensively at crude tables. Your meal can be either German or Italian. For a typical, albeit heavy, beginning, try the goulash soup at 1,500 lire ($1.74). For a meat dish, we'd suggest the wurstel, with sauerkraut and potato salad, at 1,500 lire also. You'll enjoy the low-bowing and smiling waiters, the dessert cart laden with goodies, the rugged plank floors, even the patrons whose waistlines attest to many a stein of Löwenbräu. Closed Mondays. There's a 400-lire (46¢) cover charge, plus 12% for service.

Down on the Farm (the Appian Way)

Hostaria l'Archeologia, 139 Appia Antica (tel. 788-04-94), on the historic Appian Way, is only a short walk from the catacombs of St. Sebastian. The restaurant's like a 1700s village tavern—crude, with lots of atmosphere, strings of garlic and corn, oddments of copper hanging from the ceiling, earth-brown beams, and sienna-washed walls. In summer, guests dine in the garden out back sitting under the spreading wisteria, with Chinese pheasants and wandering ducks for company—plus an occasional peacock for a touch of elegance. The kitchen is Roman, and the victuals are first rate. The Gianpaolo family produces an appetizing specialty as a beginning: fettuccine al vaccara at 1,000 lire ($1.16), cream and pâté de foie gras are combined to make the sauce. There's even a touch of nutmeg to lend further spice. To follow in a spectacular manner, request the pollo al fuoco di Roma at 4,500 lire ($5.22), which is flamed on a bed of bay leaves. Also recommendable is the scaloppine Cecilia Metella (veal scallops laced with cognac and flavored with sage and anchovy) 2,500 lire ($2.90). Desserts begin at 600 lire (70¢).

SELF-SERVICE CAFETERIAS: Piccadilly, 12 Via Barberini (near Bernini's famous Triton fountain), is a large, bustling, modern, self-service cafeteria, the finest in Rome. It's really a complex of restaurants and bars, including a coffee shop. Cockney pub, sidewalk cafe, and a restaurant on the roof. The management advertises a $1.50 (U.S.) ham & eggs breakfast served till noon. The staff also knows what cheeseburgers, 600 lire (70¢) and milkshakes, 400 lire (46¢) are. Pizzas range from 650 lire (75¢) to 850 lire (99¢). Often noisy, always crowded, the Piccadilly is open daily, except Sundays, from noon to 3 p.m. and from 7 to 10:30 p.m.

Self-Service Falcioni, 47 Piazza dei Cinquecento, is a cafeteria diagonally across from the super modern Termini. Don't be put off by the stand-up *tavola calda* on the street level (strictly for the eat-on-the-run working person). Proceed downstairs to the brightly lit "catacombs" where some fine food values are found. The cuisine is not exceptional, but it occasionally offers some subtle touches for such a low-budget establishment. For example, our most recent entree of sliced pork had been studded with carrots before roasting. Incidentally, the house specializes in roasts. Main dishes begin at 700 lire (81¢), rarely going beyond 1,500 lire ($1.74). You might start with a hearty bowl of mine-strone at 450 lire (52¢), or pasta e fagioli (beans), also 450 lire. A busboy carries your tray to your table and should be rewarded with a small tip.

STATESIDE SNACKS: The Cowboy, 68 Via Francesco Crispi, is for the wandering *griglia*. The best corral in Rome for those with a hankering for the vittles of Texas, it offers chili at 1,200 lire ($1.39); southern-fried chicken with french fries at 1,300 lire ($1.51); and a Texasburger with cheese at 900 lire ($1.04). For dessert you can order a homemade apple pie with ice cream at 700 lire (81¢), followed by American-styled coffee at 300 lire (35¢).

Time Out for Tea

Babington's Tea Rooms, 23 Piazza di Spagna (tel. 67-86-027). Back when Victoria was on the throne in England, an English spinster lady arrived in Rome and couldn't find a place for "a good cuppa." With stubborn determina-tion, she opened her own tea rooms right near the foot of the Spanish Steps. Surprisingly, the rooms are still going strong, decorated with Tudor-styled glass windows, beamed ceilings, and mahogany chairs. You can order every-thing from a banana split at 1,800 lire ($2.09) to a club sandwich at 1,800 lire ($2.09) to Ceylon tea at 1,000 ($1.16). It's closed Thursdays, but open otherwise for breakfast (waffles and omelettes are featured), luncheons, and teas.

READERS' RESTAURANT SUGGESTIONS: "We found a jewel in the St. Peter's area. It is **La Caravella** (proprietor F. Magistri), 32b Via Degli Scipioni (three blocks north of Piazza Risorgimento, up Via Ottaviano and one block east on the northwest corner, lighted by a huge sign depicting a boat). The genial owner with his excellent chef, Genio, will, for 1,700 lire ($1.97), provide vegetable soup (the best we had in Italy) or pasta, fish or meat, with a little salad or french fries, bread and all service and taxes included. Drinks are extra. All courses were liberal. Inciden-tally, the price-fixed menu is not displayed. It is necessary to ask for it" (Robert J. Sandy, Woodland Hills, Calif.). . . . "You've got to send people to a great little *cheap* restaurant, **Vertec-chi,** on Via Frattina, near the Spanish Steps. The food was terrific, it was crowded with Italians, and amazingly reasonable, around 2,400 lire ($2.78). We had a super eggplant parmigiana" (Pam King, New Haven, Conn.). . . . "After six visits to Rome, we have found the tourist's dream budget restaurant. We highly recommend the **Tavola Calda 'Magenta'** just two short blocks to the right as you leave the terminal. It's at 20 Via Magenta, on the corner of Via Marghera. It is owned by the four Donati brothers who speak English. The atmosphere is very warm and friendly. They have a large variety of pizzas, lasagne, ravioli, gnocchi, spaghetti, and steaks. For less than $2 you can have a delicious full-course meal. We usually paid $1.50" (Mr. and Mrs. Joseph Rinkus, Bedford, Ohio).

READER'S TIPS TO THE STARVATION BUDGETEER: "There's the danger of skimping on food to save money. A wiser course, and one that increases the fun of traveling, is to buy most of your food in the local markets. For example: in Italy, go to a cafe in the morning for a glass of hot milk (add sugar, as Italians do, and it's like cocoa) and a doughnut. For a mid-afternoon lunch, buy a couple of large soft rolls in a paneficio. Get some luncheon meat or cheese from another store. What Italians call Parisian salami, and what we call, ironically, bologna, can be had. Buy some fresh fruit, large, juicy pears, for instance. Or buy a small head of lettuce. You'll be full enough so that all you'll need in the evening is a bowl of pasta at a tavola calda. Food cost for the day, about $2—and you'll have eaten more than you would get in any restaurant serving. Some will say, 'But if you don't eat in the restaurants, you miss out on Europe.' On the contrary. By all means, eat out often enough to sample the local food. But you'll meet many more people on a much more natural basis by buying your own food" (John Goldrosen, Chapel Hill, N.C.).

Despite its epicurean delights, you surely didn't come to Rome just to dine (although that wouldn't be a bad idea). The time has come to wander back through the city's history—a period covering 2,700 years.

Chapter III

ROME: DAY AND NIGHT

**1. The Top Sights
2. The Secondary Sights
3. Rome After Dark
4. Ring Around Rome**

AS ONE OF THE GREATEST centers of Western civilization, Rome is thickly studded with ancient monuments that silently evoke its pageantry. In the millennium of The Eternal City's influence, all roads led to Rome with good reason. It became the first truly cosmopolitan city on earth, importing slaves, gladiators, great art—even citizens—from the far corners of the Empire.

With all its carnage, with all its mismanagement, it left a legacy of law and an uncanny lesson in how to conquer an enemy by absorbing his culture. Rome's Pantheon of Gods became a galaxy.

But Ancient Rome is only part of the spectacle. Having the papal household in Rome has had an unfathomed effect on making the city a center of world tourism. Though Vatican architects stripped down much of the glory of the past, they created great treasures of the Renaissance, occasionally incorporating the old—as Michelangelo did in turning the Baths of Diocletian into a church.

In the years to come, Bernini was to adorn the city with the wonders of the baroque—especially fountains. The modern sightseer even owes a debt (as reluctant as we are to pay it) to Mussolini, who did much to dig out the past, as at the Imperial Forum. Il Duce was a better archaeologist, however, than an architect (see "Modern Rome"). Of course, dictators are dangerous business —regardless of their accomplishments—and Mussolini almost got Rome wiped off the map. We can be grateful today that it was spared the wrath of Allied bombers.

Besides being the capital of the Italians, Rome, in a larger sense, belongs to the world. And here are some of its sights.

1. The Top Sights

The sights of Rome are multifarious. To see even the most important ones may make you feel like an elephant of Hannibal's crossing the Alps. For that reason, we've selected a representative sampling of "The Top 12," which will take several days to cover. We hope though, you'll be in Rome long enough to view at least a dozen more secondary sights, descriptions of which immediately follow the Top 12.

We don't want to bewilder you, but it would be a shame and a loss to strike out for Naples or Florence, without having at least visited Hadrian's Villa and the Villa d'Este in the environs—and we haven't even told you of Palestrina and Ostia Antica yet. We'll begin our formidable task with:

(1) ST. PETER'S: As you stand in Bernini's Piazza San Pietro (St. Peter's Square), you'll be in the arms of an ellipse. Like a loving mother, the Doric-pillared colonnade reaches out to embrace the faithful. Hugging 300,000 is no problem in this square.

In the center of the square is an Egyptian obelisk, brought from the ancient city of Heliopolis on the Nile Delta—and used to adorn Nero's Circus, which was nearby. Flanking the obelisk are two 17th-century fountains—the one on the left (facing the basilica) by Bernini himself; the other by Carlo Maderno, who designed the facade of St. Peter's.

Inside (open from 7 a.m. to 7 p.m. in summer; 7 a.m. to 5:30 p.m. in winter), the size of the world's largest church is awe-inspiring—though its dimensions are not apparent at first. Guides like to point out to American parties that the basilica is like two football fields joined together. St. Peter's is said to have been built over the tomb of the crucified saint himself. Originally, it was erected on the orders of Constantine, but the present structure is essentially Renaissance and baroque, having employed the talents of some of Italy's greatest artists, Bramante, Raphael, and Michelangelo.

In a church of such grandeur—overwhelming in its detail of gilt, marble, and mosaic—you don't expect subtlety. But the basilica is rich in art. The truly devout are prone to kiss the feet of the 13th-century bronze of St. Peter, attributed to Arnolfo di Cambio (at the far reaches of the nave, against a corner pillar on the right). Under Michelangelo's dome is the celebrated "baldachin" by Bernini, resting over the papal altar. The canopy was created in the 17th century—in part from bronze stripped from the Pantheon.

In the nave on the right (the first chapel) is the best-known piece of sculpture, the Pietà that Michelangelo sculptured while still in his early 20s. In one of the most vicious acts of vandalism on record, a geologist screaming "I am Jesus Christ" attacked the Pietà, battering the Madonna's stone arm, the folded veil, her left eyelid, and nose. Now restored, the Pietà is protected by a wall of reinforced glass *Time* magazine has labeled "prophylactic."

Much farther on, in the right wing of the transept near the Chapel of St. Michael, rests Canova's neo-classic sculptural tribute to Pope Clement XIII.

In addition, you can visit the Sacristy and Treasury, filled with jewel-studded chalices, reliquaries, and copes. One robe worn by Pius XII casts a simple note in these halls of elegance. It costs 200 lire (31¢) to visit the Historical-Artistic Museum, which is open from 9 a.m. to 1 p.m. and from 2 to 4:30 p.m. Later, you can pay an underground visit to the Vatican Grottoes, with their tombs—ancient and modern (Pope John XXIII gets the most adulation). They are open from 7 a.m. to 12:45 p.m. and from 2:30 to 6:30 p.m. in summer; from 7 a.m. to 12:45 p.m. and from 2:30 to 5 p.m. in winter.

The grandest sight is yet to come: the climb to Michelangelo's dome, towering about 375 feet high. Though you can scale the steps (200 lire), we recommend the elevator for as far as it'll carry you (300 lire round-trip). The dome is open from 8 a.m. to 7 p.m. You can walk along the roof, for which you'll be rewarded with a magnificent view of Rome and the Vatican.

Note: to be admitted to St. Peter's, women are advised to wear longer skirts or pants—anything that covers the knees. Also, sleeveless tops are a no-no.

(2) THE VATICAN AND SISTINE CHAPEL: In 1929, the Lateran Treaty between Pope Pius XI and "Il Duce" created the world's smallest independent state, lying on a man-made island in Rome. Traditions long abandoned in the courts of Europe live on here.

This state may be small, but it contains a gigantic repository of treasures from antiquity and the Renaissance—labyrinthine gallery after gallery, an art that reaches its apex in the Sistine Chapel (save this for last, as everything else will be anticlimactic after seeing Michelangelo's panels).

The Vatican Museum (really a house of museums) in itself is a series of lavishly adorned palaces on Viale Vaticano, a long walk around from St. Peter's Square. Take bus 30 or 64, or else streetcar 30. The museum is open daily, except Sunday and religious holidays, from 9 to 2. It charges the steepest admission price of any museum in Italy—1,000 lire ($1.16)—but that's cheap when you see what's inside. In July, August, and September, hours are from 9 to 5.

A dozen museums and galleries should be inspected. Obviously, one, two, or even 20 trips will not be enough to see the wealth of the Vatican, much less digest it. With that in mind, we've previewed only a representative sampling of masterpieces.

After climbing the spiral stairway, keep to the right which will take you to the:

Pinacoteca (Picture Gallery)

Some of the most enduring works of art from the Byzantine (Room I) to the baroque are displayed here. But for a break with the Byzantine, see one of the Vatican's finest art works—the "Stefaneschi Polyptych" (six panels), by Giotto and his assistants in Room II. In Room III we are introduced to the works of Fra Angelico, the 15th-century Dominican monk who distinguished himself as a miniaturist (his Virgin enthroned with child is justly praised—look for the microscopic eyes of the Madonna).

In the Raphael salon (Room VIII), you'll find three paintings by a giant of the Renaissance—including the "Virgin of Foligno" and "The Transfiguration" (completed by assistants following his death). There are also 10 tapestries made by Flemish weavers from cartoons by Raphael. In Room IX is Leonardo da Vinci's masterful—though uncompleted—St. Jerome with the lion, as well as Giovanni Bellini's entombment of Christ. One of Titian's greatest works, the "Virgin of Frari," hangs in Room X. Finally, for a view of one of the masterpieces of the baroque period, head for Room XII and Caravaggio's "Deposition from the Cross."

Egyptian-Gregorian Museum

The sarcophagi, the mummies, statues of goddesses, vases, jewelry, red-granite queens as well as hieroglyphics, review the grandeur of the Pharaohs. But even more interesting is the:

Etruscan-Gregorian Museum

With its sarcophagi, a chariot, bronzes, urns, jewelry and terracotta vases, this gallery affords a remarkable insight into a mysterious people. One of the most acclaimed exhibits is the Regolini-Galassi tomb, unearthed at Cerveteri (see "Ring Around Rome") in the 19th century. It shares top honors with the "Mars of Todi," a bronze sculpture that probably dates from the fifth century B.C.

Pius Clementinus Museum

These rooms are filled with Greek and Roman sculptures, many of them masterpieces that will bring immediate recognition because of the widespread reproductions. In the Rotunda is a large gilded bronze of Hercules that dates from somewhere around the time of Christ. Other major works of sculpture are to be seen under porticoes in rooms opening onto the Belvedere courtyard. Laocoön and his two sons (first century B.C.) are locked in their eternal struggle with the serpents (the original statue is broken in parts; the completed version nearby is a copy). The incomparable Apollo of Belvedere (Roman reproduction of an authentic Greek work from the fourth century B.C.) has become, of course, the symbol of classic male beauty. The "Torso of Belvedere" is the partially preserved Greek statue from the first century B.C. (the rippling muscles and the intricate knowledge of the human body, as revealed in this work, pre-dated Michelangelo by centuries, but equaled his achievements).

Chiaramonti Museum

In these galleries, the array of Roman statuary, plus copies of Greek originals, continue to dazzle us. One of the most remarkable pieces of sculpture from antiquity is displayed—"The Nile," a magnificent reproduction of a long-lost Hellenistic original. The imposing statue of Augustus presents him as a regal commander.

Vatican Library

So richly decorated and frescoed, the Library detracts from its own treasures—manuscripts under glass. In the Sistine Salon are sketches by Michelangelo, drawings by Botticelli to illustrate the *Divine Comedy,* plus a Greek Bible from the 4th century A.D.

The Stanze of Raphael

While still a young man, Raphael was given one of the greatest assignments of his short life: the decoration of a series of rooms for Julius II, who saw to it that Michelangelo was busy in the Sistine Chapel. In these works, Raphael achieves the Renaissance concept of the blending of classic beauty with realism. In the first chamber, the Stanza dell' Incendio, you'll see much of Raphael's pupils, but little of the master himself—except the fresco across from the window. Look for the figure of the partially draped man rescuing an older comrade (to the left of the fresco).

Raphael reigns supreme in the next and most important salon, the Stanza della Segnatura. In this chamber, the majestic "School of Athens," depicting such figures as Aristotle and Plato (even Raphael himself), is one of the artist's best-known works. Across from it is another well-known masterpiece, the "Disputà" (Disputation). The Stanza d'Eliodoro, also by the master, manages to flatter Raphael's papal patrons (Julius II and Leo X), without compromise to his art. However, one rather fanciful fresco depicts the Pope driving Attila from Rome. Finally, the Sala di Costantino was completed by his students after Raphael's death.

The Loggia of Raphael: This loggia is frescoed with more than 50 scenes from the Bible, designed by Raphael, though the actual work was done by his loyal students who always flocked around him.

The Borgia Apartment

Before entering the Sistine Chapel, you may want to visit this apartment frescoed with Biblical scenes by Pinturicchio of Umbria, along with his assistants. The apartment was designed for Pope Alexander VI (the famous Borgia Pope). The rooms, though generally badly lit, have great splendor and style. At the end of them is the Chapel of Nicholas V, an intimate interlude in an otherwise field of museums. The chapel was frescoed by the Dominican monk Fra Angelico, probably the most saintly of all Italian painters.

The Museum of Modern Art

In the Borgia Apartments in the Vatican Complex, this gallery represents the first invasion of American artists into the Vatican. Until this museum opened in 1973, the church limited its purchases to European art, and usually did not exhibit any works created after the 18th century. But Pope Paul's hobby has changed all that. Of the 65 galleries in the new museum complex, at least 12 are devoted solely to American artists. All the works chosen for the museum were judged on the basis of their "spiritual and religious values," but other religious groups outside the church are represented as well. Among the American works is Leonard Baskin's five-foot bronze sculpture of "Isaac." Modern Italian artists such as di Chirico and Manzù are also displayed, and there's a special room for the paintings of the French artist Georges Rouault.

The Sistine Chapel

The struggle of Michelangelo in the painting of the ceiling of the Sistine Chapel was dramatized by Irving Stone in *The Agony and the Ecstasy,* with Charlton Heston doing the neck-craning in the film version—thus earning a world-wide audience for one of the classic stories of art history. Michelangelo, of course, considered himself a sculptor, not a painter. While in his 30s, he was virtually commanded by Julius II to stop work on the Pope's own tomb and to devote his considerable talents to painting frescoes on the ceiling—an art form of which the Florentine master was contemptuous.

Michelangelo, taxing himself physically (he permanently damaged his eyesight), labored for four years over this epic project, and had to contend with the Pope's incessant urgings that he hurry up. At one point, Julius threatened to topple Michelangelo from the scaffolding—or so Vasari relates.

It is ironic that a project undertaken against the artist's wishes would form his most enduring legend. Glorifying the human body as only a sculptor could, Michelangelo painted nine panels from the pages of Genesis, surrounded by prophets and sibyls. The most notable are the expulsion of Adam and Eve from the Garden of Eden, and the creation of man—with God's outstretched hand imbuing Adam with spirit.

The great Florentine master was in his 60s when he began to paint the masterly Last Judgment on the Altar Wall. Again working against his wishes, Michelangelo presents a more jaundiced view of mankind and his fate, with God sitting in judgment and sinners being plunged into the mouth of Hell.

A master of ceremonies under Paul III, Monsignor Biagio, protested to the Pope against the "shameless nudes" painted by Michelangelo. Michelangelo showed he wasn't above petty revenge by painting the prude with the ears of a jackass in Hell! When Biagio complained to the Pope, Paul III maintained he had no jurisdiction in Hell. However, Daniele de Volterra was summoned to drape clothing over some of the bare figures—thus earning for himself a dubious distinction as a haberdasher.

On the side walls are frescoes by other Renaissance masters—artists such as Botticelli, Luca Signorelli, Pinturicchio, Cosimo Rosselli, and Ghirlandaio. We hazard a guess that if these paintings had been displayed by themselves in other chapels, they would be the object of special pilgrimages. But having to compete unfairly against the artistry of Michelangelo, they're virtually ignored by the average visitor.

The History Museum

This museum, founded by Pope Paul VI, is a recent addition to the Vatican's collection of museums. Exhibiting arms, armor, and uniforms, it was specifically established to tell the history of the Vatican. Some pieces of armor date back to the early days of the Middle Ages. The carriages on display are those used by popes and cardinals in religious processions. Among the show-cases of dress uniforms are the colorful outfits worn by the Pontifical Army Corps, which was discontinued by Pope Paul several years ago.

The Ethnological Museum

The Ethnological Museum, another recent addition, is an assemblage of works of art and objects of cultural significance from all over the world. The principal route is a one-half mile walk through 25 geographical sections which display thousands of objects covering 3,000 years of world history. Especially interesting is the section devoted to China. Although the History and Ethnological Museums are related, you must pay a separate admission fee of 300 lire for each.

The Vatican Gardens

Separating the Vatican on the north and west from the secular world are 58 acres of lush, carefully tended gardens, filled with winding paths, brilliantly colored flowers, groves of massive oaks, ancient fountains and pools. In the midst of this pastoral setting is a small summer house, the Villa Pia, built for Pope Pius IV in 1560 by Piero Ligorio.

Visitors may view the gardens by obtaining a permit at the Permit Office near the Arca della Campane. (It's wise to request it at least two days in advance.) The permit is free, but must be used on the day issued, between 8 a.m. and 2 p.m.

(3) THE ROMAN FORUM: When it came to cremating Caesar, raping Sabine women, purchasing a harlot for the night, or sacrificing a naked victim, the Roman Forum was a swinging place. Traversed by the Via Sacra, it was built in the marshy land between the Palatine and the Capitoline Hills. It flourished as the center of Roman life in the days of the Republic, gradually losing in prestige to the Imperial Forum (see "Ancient Rome").

Be duly warned: expect only fragmented monuments, an arch or two, and lots of overturned boulders. That any semblance of the Forum remains today is in itself miraculous, as it was used, like the Colosseum, as a quarry for years—eventually reverting to what the Italians call a campo vaccino (cow pasture). But excavations in the 19th century began to bring to light one of the most historic spots of Western civilization.

By day, the columns of the now-vanished temples, the stones from which long-forgotten orators spoke, are mere shells. Bits of grass and weed grow where a triumphant Caesar was once lionized. But at night, when the Forum is silent in the moonlight, it isn't difficult to imagine that the Vestal Virgins are still guarding the sacred fire in the temple. (Historical footnote: the function of the maidens was to keep the sacred fire burning—but their own flame under control. Failure to do the latter sent them to an early grave . . . alive!)

You can spend at least a morning wandering through the ruins of the Forum alone. If you're content with just looking at the ruins, you can do so at your leisure. But if you want to give meaning to the stone, you'll have to purchase a detailed plan, as the temples are hard to locate otherwise.

Some of the ruins are more important than others, of course. The best of the lot is the handsomely adorned Temple of Castor and Pollux, erected in the fifth century B.C. in honor of a battle triumph. The Temple of Faustina and Antonius, with its lovely columns and frieze (griffins and candelabra), was converted into the San Lorenzo in Miranda Church. The facade is in the baroque style.

The senators used to meet in the Curia, walking on marble floors from Egypt. Diocletian reconstructed the Senate, and it was later transformed into a medieval church. Across from the Curia is the "Lapis Niger," a black marble slab said to be the tomb of Romulus, legendary founder of the city (you can go downstairs).

The Temple of the Vestal Virgins and its nearby "casa" always draw an audience. Some of the statuary, mostly headless, remains. The Temple of Saturn was founded in the days of the Republic in the first century B.C., but what you see today is largely from the fourth century A.D.

The Temple of Julius Caesar was ordered constructed by Octavian, in honor of the place where Caesar's body was cremated following his assassination. Rather oddly placed is the Church of Santa Maria Antiqua, with Christian frescoes that go back to the seventh century A.D. It was built on the site of a far more ancient structure of uncertain origin.

Finally, the two arches are memorable. One is the Arch of Septimius Severus, erected in 203 A.D. with bas reliefs, and the Arch of Titus, with much better carving—commemorating a victory in Jerusalem.

The Roman Forum, on Via dei Fori Imperiali, can be reached by taking trams "ED" or "ES," buses 85, 62, or 64, or the subway to "Colosseo." It is open daily, except Monday, from 9 a.m. to 1 p.m. and 3 to 6 p.m., in winter 10 a.m. to 5 p.m. Admission is 200 lire (23¢); 100 lire (12¢) on Sunday, when its hours are from 9 a.m. to 1 p.m. The same hours are in effect and the same ticket will admit you to our next major attraction.

(4) PALATINE HILL: A long walk up from the Roman Forum leads to one of the seven hills of Rome. The Palatine, tradition tells us, was the spot on which the first settlers built their huts, under the direction of Romulus. In years to come, the hill was turned into an elegant patrician residential district—attracting such citizens as Cicero. In time, though, it was gobbled up by imperial palaces—drawing such a famous and infamous roster of tenants as Caligula (he was murdered here), Nero, Tiberius, and Domitian.

Only the ruins of its former grandeur remain today, and you really need to be an archaeologist to make sense of them, as they are more difficult to understand than those in the Forum. But even if you're not interested in the past, it's worth the climb for the magnificent sweep of both the Roman and Imperial Forums, as well as the Capitoline Hill and the Colosseum.

Of all the ruins to inspect, none is finer than the so-called House of Livia (the "abominable grandmother" of Robert Graves' *I, Claudius*). Actually, recent archaeological research indicates that the house was, in fact, the "casa" of her husband, Augustus. Livia used to slip him maidens noted for their discretion. A guard who controls the gate will show you the mythological frescoes reminiscent of those discovered at Herculaneum and Pompeii.

The Imperial Palace—the "Domus Augustana"—is an easy walk away, lying in the virtual heart of the Palatine. Domitian called the palace home. In the middle of the once-lavish estate—now stripped to the brick—is a large peristyle, with a fountain. The same emperor also ordered the building of the Palatine Stadium or "Hippodrome" below. In addition, Domitian was responsible for a once-remarkable structure, the Palace of Flavii, with its triclinium or great hall. When not overseeing real-estate construction, Domitian was seeing to it that his name would become one of the immortals in the history of vice.

When the glory that was Rome has completely overwhelmed you, you can enjoy a respite in the cooling **Farnese Gardens,** laid out in the 16th century, even incorporating some of the designs of Michelangelo.

The Palatine Hill looks down on the Circus Maximus, now a large dusty field on which Roman boys play ball on Sundays. Once it evoked memories of Ben Hur, when chariots raced across its bowl, while as many as a quarter of a million spectators cheered from their hard position on marble seats. Along with the Colosseum, the Circus was the most important structure in Ancient Rome, but every last bit of it has long ago been carted off. The building was completed as early as the second century B.C., although touches of adornment were also added by Caesar Augustus, Trajan, and Caracalla, even Constantine. The last performance—when the population of Rome was reduced to just a few beaten souls—was in 548. The "emperor," his head spinning with dreams of imperial glory, was Totila the Goth.

(5) THE COLOSSEUM: In spite of the fact that it's a mere shell of itself, the Colosseum remains the greatest architectural inheritance from Ancient Rome. Called the Amphitheatrum Flavium, the elliptically shaped bowl was ordered built by Vespasian in 72 A.D. and was launched by Titus in 80 A.D. with a many-weeks-long bloody combat between gladiators and wild beasts.

At its peak, under the cruel Domitian, the Colosseum could seat 50,000 spectators. The Vestal Virgins from the temple screamed for blood, as more and more exotic animals were shipped in from the far corners of the Empire to satisfy jaundiced tastes (ever seen two naked women battle a hippopotamus?). Not-so-mock naval battles were staged (the canopied Colosseum could be flooded), in which the victorious combatants might have their lives spared if they put up a good fight.

One of the most enduring legends linked to the Colosseum—that is, that Christians were fed to the lions here—is considered to be without foundation by many historians. Long after it ceased to be an arena to amuse sadistic Romans, the Colosseum was struck by an earthquake. Centuries later, it was used as a quarry, its rich marble facing stripped away to build palaces and churches.

On one side, part of the original four tiers remain—the first three levels being constructed in Doric, Ionic, and Corinthian to lend it variety. The Colosseum is at the Piazzale Colosseo (streetcars 5 or 11, or subway to "Colosseo"). As of this writing, the Colosseum is open on a limited basis in summer from 9 a.m. to 3 p.m. (winter from 9 a.m. to 2 p.m.), and charges an admission fee of 150 lire (17¢).

Also at the Piazzale Colosseo is the **Arch of Constantine,** one of Rome's most enduring landmarks, having been built in 315 A.D. to celebrate a military victory of Constantine—and it's still in good shape. Under this arch marched the victor and the vanquished.

After visiting the Colosseum, it is also convenient to explore the **Domus Aurea,** or the Golden House of Nero on the Via Labicana, facing the Colosseum. Adjacent to the Forum, Nero built one of the most sumptuous palaces of all time. Floors were made of mother of pearl, furniture of gold. The area that is the Colosseum today was an ornamental lake, reflecting the grandeur and glitter of the Golden House. Nero constructed the estate after that disastrous fire that swept over Rome in 64 A.D. The hollow ruins—long stripped of their lavish decorations—lie near the entrance of the Oppius Park, extending on one of the two Esquiline heights.

During the Renaissance, painters such as Raphael chopped holes in the long-buried ceilings of the Domus Aurea to gain admittance. Once there, they were inspired by the frescoes and the small "grotesques" of cornucopia and cherubs. The word grotto came from this palace, as it was believed to have been built underground. Remmants of these original 2,000-year-old frescoes remain, along with fragments of mosaics. The Domus Aurea is open from 9 to 2 p.m., charging an admission fee of 100 lire (12¢).

(6) CAPITOLINE HILL (CAMPIDOGLIO): Of the Seven Hills of Rome, Campidoglio is considered the most sacred—its origins stretching way back into antiquity (an Etruscan temple to Jupiter stood on this spot). The most dramatic approach to Capitoline Hill is to walk up the Via di Teatro Marcello from the Piazza Venezia, the center of Rome.

On your left, you can climb the steps designed by the master himself, Michelangelo. At the top of the approach is the perfectly proportioned square of the Piazza di Campidoglio, also laid out by the Florentine genius.

Michelangelo even positioned the bronze equestrian statue of Marcus Aurelius in the center. A most remarkable treasure, the statue was made in the second century A.D. All other imperial bronze equestrian statues have been lost to history, but this one was discovered in the mud of the Tiber. The bronze emperor on his horse, it is believed, once rode atop a column—hence, the seeming distortion of the present work when viewed up close.

One side of the piazza is open; the others are bounded by the Senatorium (Town Council), the statuary-filled Palazzo dei Conservatori, and the Capitoline Museums (see "Museums and Galleries"). The Campidoglio is especially dramatic at night (walk around to the back for a regal view of the floodlit Roman Forum). On your return, head down the small steps on your right. You'll pass two caged wolves, a commemorative gesture to the "Capitoline Wolf," who is said to have suckled Romulus and Remus, legendary founders of Rome. If you care to climb the other steps adjoining Michelangelo's approach, they'll take you to Santa Maria d'Aracoeli (see "Churches of Rome").

(7) CASTEL SANT' ANGELO: From its vantage landmark position on the Tiber (at Largo Castello), this overpowering structure was originally built in the second century A.D. as a tomb for the Emperor Hadrian, and it continued as an imperial mausoleum until the time of Caracalla. Cylindrically shaped, it is an imposing and grim castle with thick walls. If it looks like a fortress, it should, as that was its function in the Middle Ages (linked by an underground passageway to the Vatican, much used by the fleeing papacy trying to escape unwanted visitors, such as the sacker of the city, Charles V).

In the 14th century, it became a papal residence, enjoying various connections with Boniface IX, Nicholas V, even Julius II, patron of Michelangelo and Raphael. But its legend rests largely on its link with Pope Alexander VI, whose mistress bore him two famous children—Cesare and Lucrezia Borgia.

Of all the ladies of the Renaissance in Italy, Lucrezia is the only one who could command universal recognition in the Western world, her name a virtual synonym for black deeds, such as poisoning. Again, popular legend is highly unreliable: many of the charges against her that her biographers have suggested (such as incestuous involvements with her brother and father), may have been successful attempts to blacken her name. In addition to being a link with an infamous family, she was a patroness of the arts and a devoted charity worker, especially after she moved to Ferrara. Of course, her brother Cesare is without defense—a Machiavellian hero who is remembered accurately as a symbol of villainy and cruel spite.

Today, the highlight of the castle is a trip through the Renaissance Apartments, with their coffered ceilings and lush decoration. Their walls have witnessed some of the arch treachery of the High Renaissance—plots and intrigues. Later, you can go through the dank cells that once rang with the screams of Cesare's victims of torture, such as Astorre Manfredi of Faenza, who was finally relieved of his pain by murder.

Perhaps the most famous figure imprisoned here was Benvenuto Cellini, the eminent sculptor and goldsmith, remembered chiefly for his classic, candid autobiography. Cellini kept getting into trouble—murdering people etc.—but was jailed here on a charge of "peculation" (embezzlement of public funds). He escaped, was hauled back to jail, but finally freed.

Now a military and an art museum, the castle shelters halls displaying the history of the Roman mausoleum, along with a wide-ranging selection of arms and armaments. Don't fail to climb to the top terrace for another one of those dazzling views of The Eternal City. The museum, which can be visited on your way to St. Peter's, is open daily—except Monday—from 8:30 a.m. to 1 p.m. (Sundays 8:30 a.m. to noon). Admission is 200 lire (23¢), 100 lire (12¢) on holidays. Take tram 29, or buses 88, 66, 39, 20, or 21.

(8) BATHS OF CARACALLA: When Romans took baths, they liked an audience. And, at the once-spectacular Baths of Caracalla, they were assured of hundreds of fellow bathers. The baths, completed in the early part of the third century, were named after the Emperor Caracalla (their construction probably the cleanest thing he ever did). Actually, they were started during the reign of his father, Septimius Severus.

Of course, the richness of decoration has been carted off, and we can only judge its lushness from the shell of brick ruins that remains today. But it's a most scenic ruin (Shelley found the setting so inspiring he wrote *Prometheus Unbound* here). Well worth inspecting during the day, it is open from 9 a.m. till one hour before sunset. But the ideal time to come to call is during one of the summer operatic presentations (see "Rome After Dark"). To reach the baths, take tram "ED" or "ES" to the Parco di Porta Capena, outside the city.

(9) APPIAN WAY AND THE CATACOMBS: Of all the roads that led to Rome, the Appia Antica—built in 312 B.C.—was the queen. It eventually stretched all the way from Rome to the seaport of Brindisi, through which trade with the colonies in Greece and the East was funneled. If you've never been to Rome, you may recall the Appian Way from the MGM spectacular of the early 50s, "Quo Vadis," with Robert Taylor and Deborah Kerr. According to the Christian tradition, it was on the Appian Way that an escaping Peter encountered the vision of Christ, which caused him to go back into the city to face subsequent martyrdom.

Along the Appian Way, the patrician Romans built great monuments above the ground, while the Christians met in the catacombs beneath the earth. The remains of both can be visited today. In some dank, dark grottoes (never stray too far from either your party or one of the exposed lightbulbs), you can still discover the remains of early Christian art. At the height of the persecution, the Christians fled deep into the catacombs to avoid arrest, torture, and death.

Only someone wanting to write a sequel to "Quo Vadis" would want to visit all the catacombs. Of those open to the public the Catacombs of St. Callistus and those of St. Sebastian are the most important. Both can be reached by taking bus 118. Each one charges 300 lire (35¢) admission.

The **Catacombs of St. Sebastian,** 136 Via Appia Antica, lie under the fourth-century Church of St. Sebastian. These four-tiered catacombs house the tomb of the martyred St. Sebastian. St. Peter and St. Paul were buried nearby, before their tombs were subsequently removed. It is estimated that the grottoes, if stretched out, would reach a distance of seven miles. In the dark tunnels, you'll find frescoes, mosaics, and graffiti. These catacombs are open from 8:30 a.m. to noon and from 2:30 to 5:30 p.m.; on Sundays, hours are from 9 a.m. to 1 p.m.

The **Catacombs of St. Callistus,** 126 Via Appia Antica, are visited chiefly because they were the tombs of the Popes in the third century. One of the earliest catacombs, and the last to be rediscovered (1852), St. Callistus is also the largest, extending for more than 10 miles of burial galleries. Guided tours take visitors to the Crypt of the Popes (nine Popes were buried there) and to the Crypt of St. Cecilia. An early Christian martyr, she received three strokes on her head (maximum allowed by Roman law), but they failed to kill her— that is, not until after three days of agonizing pain. Also to be seen are a variety of early Christian symbols (most notable being that of the fish) and many frescoes. Visiting hours are from 8:30 a.m. till noon and from 3 to 6:30 p.m. in summer (from 8:30 a.m. till noon and from 2:30 to 5 p.m. in winter). As mentioned above, admission is 300 lire (35¢).

Of the Roman monuments, the most impressive one is that of the **Tomb of Cecilia Metella,** within walking distance of the catacombs. Cylindrically shaped, the tomb honors the wife of one of the military commanders of Caesar. Why such an elaborate tomb for such an unimportant person in history? Cecilia Metella happened to be singled out for enduring fame, simply because her tomb remained and the others decayed. The tomb may be visited daily, except Wednesday, from 9 a.m. to noon and from 3 to 6 p.m. (in winter, 9 a.m. to noon and 2:30 to 5 p.m.). Take bus 118.

(10) THE PANTHEON: Of all the great buildings of Ancient Rome, only one remains intact: the Pantheon ("all the Gods"). Built in 27 B.C. by Marcus Agrippa, it was later reconstructed by the Emperor Hadrian in the first part of the second century A.D. This remarkable building is listed among the architectural wonders of the world, because of its concept of space and its dome. Byron described the temple as "simple, erect, austere, severe, sublime."

Once it was ringed with white marble statues of pagan gods, such as Jupiter and Minerva, in its niches. Animals were sacrificed and burned in the center, the smoke escaping through the only means of light, an opening at the top—27 feet in diameter. The Pantheon is 142 feet wide, 142 feet high. Michelangelo came here to study the dome before designing the cupola of St. Peter's (the dome of the Pantheon is two feet larger than that of St. Peter's).

Other statistics are equally impressive. The walls are 25 feet thick, and the bronze doors leading into the building weigh 20 tons each. The temple was converted into a church in the early seventh century (is there no one with a healthy respect for the pagan?).

About 125 years ago, the tomb of Raphael was discovered in the Pantheon (fans still bring him flowers). Victor Emmanuel II, king of Italy, was also interred here.

The admission-free Pantheon lies at the Piazza della Rotonda (take bus 87 or 94). It's open from 9 a.m. till sunset.

(11) THE PIAZZA DI SPAGNA (SPANISH STEPS): The Spanish Steps were the last view of the outside world that Keats saw before he died in a house at the foot of the stairs (see "Poets' Corner"). The steps—filled, in season, with flower vendors, young jewelry salesmen, and photographers snapping pictures of tourists—and the square take their names from the former Spanish Embassy that used to have its headquarters here.

At the foot of the steps is a nautically shaped fountain that was designed by Pietro Bernini (Papa is not to be confused with his son, Giovanni Lorenzo Bernini, who proved to be a far greater sculptor of fountains). About two centuries ago, when the foreign art colony was in its ascendancy, the 136 steps were flanked with young men and women wanting to hire out to pose for the painters—the men with their shirts unbuttoned to show off what they hoped was a Davidesque physique, the women consistently draped like Madonnas.

At the top of the steps is not only a good view, but the 16th-century church of Trinitá dei Monti, built by the French, with twin towers.

(12) THE FOUNTAINS OF ROME: Rome is a city of fountains—a number of such exceptional beauty that they're worth a special pilgrimage. Some of the more famous ones are the Four Seasons and Bernini's Triton Fountain at the Piazza Barberini, but the two that hold the most enduring interest are the **Fountains of Trevi** and the waterworks at the **Piazza Navona.**

The Piazza Navona is one of the great squares of Rome, built in the shape of an ellipse. In Domitian's day, chariot races—reminiscent of Ben Hur—were staged here. Of the three fountains in the piazza, the center one dates from the 17th century and is by Bernini. Called the Fountain of the Four Rivers, it is surmounted by an obelisk that came from Egypt, believed to have been erected in the days of Rameses II.

Finally, for a fit farewell to Rome, the Fountains of Trevi, at the Piazza di Trevi represent the last big "splash" of the baroque in Rome. They were designed by Nicholas Salvi in 1762, though with their rippling cascades, they evoke Bernini. Neptune towers over all . . . the most theatrical fountains in Rome. After you've seen them (illuminated till midnight), you will have had the best of the fountains. On your last night in the city, tradition compels you to visit Trevi and toss a coin over your shoulder into the fountains to insure your return to Rome. Remember "Three Coins in the Fountain"?

2. The Secondary Sights

MUSEUMS AND GALLERIES: For those not tossing their lire into the Trevi Fountain—and who can stick around for a more extended stay—we'll now discuss some other important sights, museums, and galleries:

National Roman Museum

Near the Piazza dei Cinquecento, which fronts the Railway Station, this museum (also called the Museum of the Thermae) occupies part of the third-century (A.D.) Baths of Diocletian and a section of a convent that may have been designed by Michelangelo. Today it houses one of the finest collections of Greek and Roman sculpture, and early Christian sarcophagi in Europe.

The Ludovisi Collection is the apex of the museum, particularly the statuary of the Gaul slaying himself after he's done in his wife (a brilliant copy of a Greek original from the third century B.C.). However, this section is closed as of this writing, but it may be temporary.

Across the hallway in Gallery II is another prize, a one-armed Greek Apollo. Adjoining in Gallery III is a galaxy of sculptured treasures: "The Discus Thrower of Castel Porziano" (an exquisite copy); Aphrodite of Cirene (a Greek original); and, finally, "Personaggio Virile," a Greek original of an athlete with a lance. In Room 4, the "Sleeping Hermaphrodite" (Ermafrodito Dormente), an original Hellenistic statue, sprawls out. Don't fail to stroll through the cloisters, filled as they are with statuary and fragments of antiquity, including a fantastic mosaic.

The museum is open daily, except Mondays, from 9 a.m. to 2 p.m. (holidays and Sundays, 9 a.m. to 1 p.m.); 200 lire (23¢) for admission. It's free on Sundays.

National Museum of Villa Giulia (Etruscan)

A 16th-century papal palace in the Villa Borghese gardens shelters a priceless collection of the art and artifacts of the mysterious Etruscans, who pre-dated the Romans. Known for their sophisticated art and design, the Etruscans left as their legacy sarcophagi, bronze sculptures, terracotta vases, and jewelry, among other items.

If you have time only for the masterpieces, head for "Sala 7," with its remarkable Apollo from Veio from the end of the sixth century B.C.—clothed for a change! The other two widely acclaimed pieces of statuary in this gallery include "Dea con Bambino" (a goddess with a baby) and a greatly mutilated, but still powerful, Hercules with a stag. In the adjoining room, Sala 8, you'll see the lions' sarcophagus from the mid-sixth century B.C., excavated at Cerveteri, north of Rome.

Finally, one of the world's most important Etruscan art treasures is the bride and bridegroom coffin from the sixth century B.C., also dug out of the tombs of Cerveteri (in Sala 9). Near the end of your tour, another masterpiece of Etruscan art awaits you in Sala 33: the "Cista Ficoroni," a bronze urn with paw feet, mounted by three figures—dating from the fourth century B.C.

The address of the museum is 9 Piazza di Villa Giulia (tram 30 or bus 19). It is open daily, except Mondays, from 9 a.m. to 1 p.m. (Sundays, 9 a.m. to noon), and charges 100 lire (12¢) for admission (free on Sundays).

The Borghese Gallery and Museum

Housed in a handsome villa in the Villa Borghese gardens, the gallery contains some of the finest paintings in Rome, with a representative collection of Renaissance and baroque masters, along with important Bernini sculpture. On the main floor is the sculpture collection, the most celebrated piece being in the first room—the so-called "Conquering Venus" by Antonio Canova, Italy's greatest neo-classic sculptor. Actually, the early 19th-century work created a sensation in its day, as it was posed by Pauline Bonaparte Borghese, sister of Napoleon (if the French dictator didn't like to see his half sister naked, he was even more horrified at the Canova version of himself totally nude!). In the rooms that follow are three of Bernini's most widely acclaimed works: "David," "Apollo and Daphne" (his finest piece), and, finally, "The Rape of Persephone."

Upstairs hang the paintings, a display of canvases almost too rich for one visit. If pressed for time, concentrate on three works by Raphael in Room 9 (especially the young woman holding a unicorn in her lap and his recently restored "Deposition from the Cross").

But the finest salon at the Borghese is Room 14, devoted to the works of Caravaggio (1569-1609), the master of chiaroscuro and leader of the "Realists." His paintings include such works as the "Madonna of the Palafrenieri." In Room 18 is one of Rubens' favorite themes: the elders lusting after poor Susanna. Titian's "Sacred and Profane Love" is exhibited in Room 20, along with three other works by the same master.

The gallery is open daily except Mondays from 9 a.m. to 2 p.m. (holidays, 9 a.m. to 1 p.m.); entrance fee is 200 lire (24¢); holidays, 100 lire (12¢).

After visiting the gallery, you may want to join the Italians in their strolls through the Villa Borghese, replete with zoological gardens and small bodies of water. Horse shows are staged at the Piazza di Siena.

Capitoline Museum & Palace of the Conservatory

At the Piazza del Campidoglio are two museums—housing some of the greatest pieces of classical sculpture in the world. **The Capitoline Museum** itself was built in the 17th century, based on an architectural sketch by Michelangelo. The exhibit was originally a papal collection, having been founded by Sixtus IV in the 15th century.

In the first room is a statue that brings instant recognition the world over, "The Dying Gaul," a work of majestic skill, a copy of a Greek original that dates somewhere from the second or third century B.C. But in a special gallery all her own is "The Capitoline Venus," demurely covering herself—the symbol of feminine beauty and charm down through the centuries (Roman copy of the Greek original from the third century B.C.). Finally, "Amore" (Cupid) and Psyche are up to their old tricks!

The **Palace of the Conservatori** across the way was also based on an architectural plan by Michelangelo. It is rich not only in classical sculpture, but paintings as well. One of the most notable bronzes—a work of incomparable beauty—is the "Spinario" (the little boy picking a thorn from his foot). The Greek classicistic bronze dates from the first century B.C. In addition, you'll find "Lupa Capitolina" (the Capitoline Wolf), a rare Etruscan bronze that may possibly stretch back to the sixth century B.C. (Romulus and Remus, the legendary twins that the wolf suckled, were added at a later date).

The palace also contains a "Pinacoteca"—mostly paintings from the 16th and 17th centuries. Notable canvases include Caravaggio's fortune-teller and his curious John the Baptist; the holy family by Dosso Dossi; Romulus and

Remus by Rubens; and Titian's "Baptism of Christ." Both museums are open daily, except Monday, from 9 to 2 (also open Tuesday and Thursday evenings from 5 to 8, Saturday until 11:30 p.m.) and charge a 400-lire (46¢) admission during the day and 500 lire (58¢) at night (free on Sundays). The same ticket admits you to both museums.

National Gallery of Modern Art

On the Viale delle Belle Arti (reached by trams 19 and 30), the museum is in the Villa Borghese gardens, a short walk from the Etruscan Museum. With its neo-classic and romantic paintings and sculpture, it's a dramatic change from the glories of the Renaissance and the Romans. Its 75 rooms house the largest collection in Italy of 19th- and 20th-century artists, including a comprehensive collection of modern Italian paintings. The highlight of this group is a small, but impressive selection of Modiglianis, the greatest Italian painter of the 20th century. Look for his "La Signora dal Collaretto," and the large "Nudo." Several important sculptures, including one by Canova, are on display in the museum's gardens. The gallery also houses a large collection of foreign artists, including French impressionists Degas, Cézanne, and Monet, and the post-Impressionist, Van Gogh. Surrealism and Expressionism are well represented in works by Klee, Ernst, Braque, Miró, Kandinsky, Mondrian, and Pollock. In addition to the paintings, you'll find sculpture by Rodin, and etchings by Beardsley. The gallery frequently changes its exhibitions. Open daily, except Monday, from 9 to 2 (Sundays until 1 p.m.), the museum charges 150 lire (17¢) admission (free on Sundays).

Palazzo Doria Pamphili

Off Via del Corso, the museum offers visitors a look at what it's really like to live in an 18th-century palace. The mansion, like many Roman palaces of the period, is partly leased to tenants (on the upper levels), and there are even shops on the street level, but all this is easily overlooked after you enter the grand apartments of the historical Doria Pamphili family. Currently inhabited by the Princess Orietta Doria Pamphili who traces her line back to before the great 15th-century Genoese admiral Andrea Doria, the regal apartments surround the central court and gallery of the palace. The colorful 18th-century decor pervades the magnificent ballroom, the studies, dining rooms, and even the family chapel. Gilded furniture, crystal chandeliers, Renaissance tapestries, and portraits of family members are everywhere. The Green Room is especially rich in treasures, with a 15th-century Tournay tapestry, paintings by Memling and Filippo Lippi, and a semi-nude portrait of Andrea Doria by Sebastiano del Piombo. The Andrea Doria Room is dedicated to the admiral and to a ship of the same name. It contains a glass case with mementos of the great maritime disaster.

Skirting the central court is a picture gallery containing a memorable collection of frescoes, paintings, and sculpture. Most important among a number of great works are the portrait of Innocent X by Velázquez, Salome by Titian, and works by Rubens and Caravaggio. Most of the sculpture came from the Doria country estates. They include marble busts of Roman emperors, bucolic nymphs, and satyrs. Even without the paintings and sculpture, the gallery would be worth a visit—just for its fresco-covered walls and ceilings. Both the apartments and gallery are open to the public only on Tuesday, Friday, Saturday, and Sunday, from 10 to 1. Admission is 500 lire (58¢) for each of the two attractions. The entrance is at la Piazza del Collegio Romano.

The Museum of Palazzo Venezia

At the Piazza Venezia, in the geographic heart of Rome, is the building that served as headquarters for Mussolini during his Fascist regime. The balcony, from which he used to harangue the populace of Rome in the grand manner of Braggadocio, is rarely missed by the first-timer to Rome.

Surmounting the hill at the piazza is the 19th-century monument to **Victor Emmanuel II,** king of Italy—a lush work that has often been compared to a birthday cake. Here you'll find the tomb of the Unknown Soldier, created in World War I.

Less known is the museum in the Palazzo Venezia, a former papal residence that dates back to the 15th century. You can now walk through the rooms, including Il Duce's study (Romans used to stroll by at night to see if the lights were burning).

The rooms and halls contain oil paintings, antiques, porcelain, tapestries, ivories, ceramics, and arms. No one particular exhibit stands out; it's the sum total that adds up to a major attraction. Hopefully, you'll be able to see a changing exhibit which is often displayed in the palace (on one recent occasion, a rare collection of Russian icons were shown). The palace is open daily, except Monday, from 9 to 2 (Sundays until 1 p.m.), for a 200-lire admission. It is free on Sundays.

ANCIENT ROME: Even in the days of the Republic, the population explosion was a problem. Julius Caesar saw the overcrowding and began to expand, beginning what were known as the Imperial Forums in the days of the Empire. After the collapse of Rome and the oncoming Dark Ages, the forums were lost to history—that is, until Mussolini set out to restore the grandeur of Rome. He knew that one way to do that was to remind his countrymen of their glorious past. He cut through the years of debris and junky buildings to carve out the **Via dei Fori Imperiali,** linking the Piazza Venezia to the Colosseum. Excavations began at once, and much was revealed. Today, the boulevard makes for one of the most fascinating walks in Rome.

Beginning at the Piazza Venezia, we come first to the **Forum of Trajan** at the Piazza del Foro Romano. Built to the specifications of Apollodorus of Damascus in the early second century A.D., this is the most grandiose of all the Imperial Forums—though its two libraries have long ago been sacked and the Basilica of Ulpia leveled. But the vaguest outline remains of what it was like, for those who don't mind pumping their imagination a bit.

Its crowning achievement is **Trajan's Column,** soaring about 100 feet high, whose sculptures, glorifying the victories of the Emperor Trajan in Dacia, were carved with surprising attention to historical accuracy. A statue of St. Peter now mounts the column. Trajan's Forum is open to visitors who want to go below, or else you can confine your search to walking around the railing. It is open daily, except Monday, from 9 to 2 and from 3 to 6 in summer (10-5 in winter) for a 100-lire admission charge.

A more substantial ruin lies a short walk away—**Trajan's Markets,** at 94 Via IV Novembre. The crescent-shaped structure is now filled with tiers of empty stalls, but once the Roman peddlers sold everything from the blonde tresses of barbarian slave girls from Northern Europe to sow's udders! The market, charging 100 lire (12¢) for admission, is open daily, except Mondays, from 9 a.m. to 1 p.m. and from 3 to 6 p.m. Sundays, mornings only, it's free. In winter it's open regularly from 10 to 5.

Back on the Via dei Fori Imperiali, you'll pass by the **Forum of Caesar** on your right. This area was the site of the first expansion away from the old

Roman Forum, dating back to around 55 B.C. Today you can still see the pillars of a temple honoring Venus.

Across the way (on your left walking toward the Colosseum) is the **Forum of Augustus,** on the Via Campo Carleo. Originally, this was the site of a temple dedicated to Mars, the ruins of which you can explore today. The remains of a wall designed to shelter the temple were also excavated during the big dig of the late 20s.

Back on the Via dei Fori Imperiali are the remains of the **Forum of Nerva** (sometimes known as the "Transitorium"). Just the chopped-off blocks of the Temple of Minerva remain, as well as a couple of Corinthian pillars.

All of the imperial forums may be visited daily, except Monday, from 9 to 1 and from 3 to 6 (Sundays, 9 to 1, for a free admission charge). In winter the hours are from 10 to 5. The admission to each forum costs 100 lire, but most sightseers settle for a look from the street.

Tracing our steps back to the Piazza Venezia, we head up the Via de Teatro Marcello, past Capitoline Hill on our left, for the best-preserved Roman ruins yet. Near the entrance to the old Roman Ghetto lies:

The Theatre of Marcellus: Originally conceived by Julius Caesar, but completed in the reign of Augustus, this was the scene of many public spectacles. Now consisting of two levels of arches, it holds a former palace resting on its decay. You're free to wander around the base of the ruins at your leisure. Romans who escaped Mussolini's urban renewal still live on top of it.

Further up the street on the Via del Mare (at the Piazza St. Maria in Cosmedin), we come to the Ionic temple of **Fortuna Virile.** Now showing its age and propped up, it is, nevertheless, a handsome heritage. At last a ruin that provides a clear conception of what a Roman temple looked like, this one dating from the Republican period.

The ring-shaped **Temple of Vesta,** on the other hand, employs Corinthian columns and was built in the days of the Empire, probably in the time of Augustus. Why were these pagan temples preserved and the others destroyed? They were converted into churches in the Middle Ages. To reach the temples, take tram "ED" or bus 30 or 90.

Finally, for still another look at Imperial Rome, head for the **Column of Marcus Aurelius,** at the Piazza Colonna (near La Rinascente department store). Standing about 90 feet high, it was built to commemorate the military triumphs of the philosophizing emperor. Like Trajan, Marcus Aurelius was de-throned from his position atop the column, only to be replaced by St. Paul. The column may be climbed for a superb view.

MODERN ROME: At the height of Mussolini's power, he launched a complex of modern buildings—many of them in cold marble—to dazzle Europe with a scheduled world's fair. But Il Duce got strung up, and E.U.R.—the area in question—got hamstrung. The new Italian government that followed inherited the uncompleted problem, and decided to turn it into a center of government and administration. It has also developed into a residential section of fairly deluxe apartment houses. Most of the cold granite edifices fail to escape the curse of "Il Duce moderno," but the small "city of tomorrow" is softened considerably by a man-made lagoon, which you can row across in small rented boats.

Italy's greatest architect, Milan-born Pier Luigi Nervi, designed the "Palazzo della Sport" on the hill. One of the country's most impressive modern buildings, it was the chief site of the 1960 Olympics. Another important structure is the Palazzo dei Congressi in the center, an exhibition hall with changing displays of industrial shows. It's well worth a stroll. You'll also spot versions of architecture reminiscent of Frank Lloyd Wright, "Aztec modern," and a building that evokes the design of the United Nations in New York.

If you want to turn your jaunt into a major outing, you can visit the **Museum of Roman Civilization,** on the Piazza Giovanni Agnelli, housing Fiat-sponsored reproductions that recapture life in Ancient Rome. Its major exhibition is a plastic representation in miniature of what Rome looked like at the apex of its power. You'll see the impressive Circus Maximus, the Colosseum as it looked when intact, the Baths of Diocletian—and lots more. The museum is open daily, except Monday, from 9 to 2 (in addition from 5 to 8 on Tuesday and Thursday nights). It charges 200 lire (23¢) for admission except on Sundays when it's free and it's open from 10 a.m. to 1 p.m. To reach E.U.R., take the "Metro" to "Expositione." (E.U.R. can be visited en route to Ostia Antica and the Lido of Rome.) For still another look at Mussolini's architectural achievements, head across the river from E.U.R. to the:

Foro Italico: Shades of 1932! This complex of sports stadiums blatantly honors Il Duce. At the entrance to the forum, an obelisk bears the name—MVSSOLINI—so firmly engraved that to destroy the lettering would be to do away with the monument. It stands defiantly. Visitors on a sunny day walk across a mosaic courtyard with DVCE in the pavement more times than La Rosa has noodles. The big attraction of this freakish site is the "Stadium of Marbles," encircled with 50 marble nude athletes—draped discreetly so as not to offend the eyes of the Golden Madonna on the hill beyond. Take bus 32 or 48 or streetcar 1 to the Piazza Lauro De Bosis when you tire of looking at the forums of ancient dictators and want to see that of a more contemporary one. Incidentally, the mosaics at the Foro Italico—even the marble statuary—reaffirm the observation that fascism and notable art are about as ill matched as a rhinoceros and a bird of paradise.

THE CHURCHES OF ROME: St. Peter's is not the only church you should see in Rome. The city's hundreds of churches—some built with marble stripped from ancient monuments—form a major sightseeing treasure. We've highlighted the best of the lot, including four patriarchal churches of Rome that are extraterritorial, belonging to the Vatican. Others are equally worth viewing, especially one designed by Michelangelo. Our selections follow:

Basilica of San Giovanni in Laterano

At the Piazza di San Giovanni in Laterano is the seat of the Archbishop of Rome. St. John's—not St. Peter's—is the Cathedral of Rome. Originally built in the fourth century by Constantine, the cathedral has suffered the vicissitudes of Rome itself, being badly sacked and forced to rebuild many times. Only fragmented parts of the Baptistry remain from the original structure.

The present building is characterized by its 18th-century facade by Alessandro Galilei (statues of Christ and the apostles ring the top). Borromini gets the credit (some say blame) for the interior, built for Innocent X. It is said that in the misguided attempt to redecorate, frescoes by Giotto were destroyed (remains believed to have been painted by Giotto were discovered in 1952 and are displayed). In addition, look for the unusual ceiling, the sumptuous transept, and explore the 13th-century cloisters.

The Popes used to live next door at Lateran Palace before the move to Avignon in the 14th century. But the most unusual sight is across the street at the "Palace of the Holy Steps," called the **Scala Santa.** It is alleged that these were the actual wooden steps that Christ climbed when he was brought before Pilate. These steps are supposed to be climbed only on your knees, as you're likely to see the faithful doing throughout the day. One vigorous German boy we recently saw scaled them on his knees in 30 seconds, but we suspect that this set his karma back years.

Basilica of St. Mary Major (Maria Maggiore)

At the Piazza di Santa Maria Maggiore, you'll find the third great church of Rome, founded in the fifth century, then later rebuilt. Its campanile, erected in the 14th century, is the loftiest one in the city. Much doctored in the 18th century, the church's facade is not an accurate reflection of the treasures inside. The basilica is especially noted for the fifth-century Roman mosaics in its nave, as well as for its coffered ceiling, said to have been gilded with gold brought from the New World. In the 16th century, Domenico Fontana built a now-restored "Sistine Chapel." In the following century, Flaminio Ponzo designed the Pauline (Borghese) Chapel in the baroque style. The church contains the tomb of Bernini, Italy's most important architect during the flowering of the baroque in the 17th century. Ironically, the man who changed the face of Rome with his elaborate fountains was buried in a tomb so simple it takes a sleuth to track it down (to the right near the altar).

The Basilica of St. Paul's

On Via Ostiense lies the fourth great patriarchal church of Rome. Tracing its origins back to Constantine, it burned in the 19th century and was subsequently rebuilt. This basilica is believed to have been erected over the tomb of St. Paul, much as St. Peter's was built over the tomb of that saint. Inside, its windows appear at first to be stained glass, but they are alabaster—the effect of glass created by the brilliant light shining through. With its forest of single-file columns and its mosaic medallions (portraits of the various popes), it is one of the most streamlined and elegantly decorated churches in Rome. Its single most important treasure is a 12th-century candelabrum, designed by Vassalletto, who is also responsible for the remarkable cloisters—in themselves worth the trip "outside the walls." On Wednesday afternoons, the Benedictine monks and students sell a fine collection of souvenirs, rosaries, and bottles of Benedictine. The visit to the Basilica and cloister is free. The gift shop is open every day except Sunday and feasts of precept.

St. Peter in Vincoli

From the Colosseum, head up a "spoke" street, the Via degli Annibaldi, to a church founded in the fifth century A.D. to house the chains that bound St. Peter in Palestine. The chains are preserved under glass. But the drawing card is the tomb of Julius II, with one of the world's most famous pieces of sculpture, "Moses" by Michelangelo. As readers of Irving Stone's *The Agony and the Ecstasy* know, Michelangelo was to have carved 44 magnificent figures for Julius' tomb. That didn't come about, of course, but the Pope was given one of the greatest consolation prizes—a figure intended to be "minor" that is now numbered among Michelangelo's masterpieces. Of the stern, ever foreboding, father symbol of Michelangelo's Moses, Vasari, in his *Lives of the Artists,* wrote: "No modern work will ever equal it in beauty, no, nor ancient either."

Church of Santa Maria Degli Angeli

At 12 Piazza della Repubblica, adjoining the National Roman Museum near the railway station, stood the "tepidarium" of the third-century Baths of Diocletian. But in the 16th century, Michelangelo—nearing the end of his life—converted the grand hall into one of the most splendid churches in Rome. Surely the artist wasn't responsible for "gilding the lily"—that is, putting trompe l'oeil columns in the midst of the genuine pillars. The church is filled with tombs and paintings, but its crowning treasure is the statue of St. Bruno by the great French sculptor Jean Antoine Houdon. His sculpture, to your right as you enter, is larger than life and about as real. No admission is charged, and you can visit throughout the day.

Church of St. Clement

From the Colosseum, head up Via di San Giovanni in Laterano, which leads to the Basilica of Saint Clement. This isn't just another Roman church. Far from it. In this church-upon-a-church, centuries of history peel away like stalks of fennel which the Romans eat for dessert. In the fourth century, a church was built over a second-century pagan temple dedicated to Mithras (god of the sun), which in itself was erected over a secular house of the first century A.D. Down in the eerie grottoes (which you can explore on your own—unlike the catacombs on the Appian Way), you'll discover well-preserved frescoes from the first through the third centuries A.D. You can visit the grottoes from 9 to 2 (until 1 p.m. on Sundays) for a well-spent 150 lire. After the Normans destroyed the lower church, a new one was built in the 12th century. Its chief attraction is its bronze-orange mosaic (from that period) which adorns the apse, as well as a chapel honoring St. Catherine of Alexandria (murals by Masolino de Panicale who decorated the Brancacci Chapel in the Church of Carmine in Florence in the 15th century).

Church of Santa Maria in Cosmedin

At the Piazza della Verità, near the Museum of Rome, is a charming little church that was founded in the sixth century, but subsequently rebuilt—a campanile being added in the 12th century in the Romanesque style. The church is ever popular with pilgrims to Rome, drawn here not by its great art treasures—but by its "Mouth of Truth," a large disk under the portico. According to tradition, it is supposed to chomp down on the hand of any liar who inserts his or her paw (although Audrey Hepburn escaped with her pretty mitt untouched in "Roman Holiday"). On our last visit to the church, a little woman, draped in black, sat begging a few feet from the medallion. A scene typical enough—except this woman's right hand was covered with bandages.

The Church of Santa Maria D'Aracoeli

Sharing a spot on Capitoline Hill (but unfortunately, reached by a long flight of steps different from those leading to the Piazza di Campidoglio), this landmark church was built for the Franciscans in the 13th century. According to legend, Augustus once ordered a temple erected on this spot, where a sibyl, with her gift of prophecy, forecast the coming of Christ. On the interior of the present building, you'll find a nave and two aisles, two rows with 11 pillars each, a Renaissance ceiling, and a mosaic of the Virgin over the altar in the Byzantine style. If you're sleuth enough, you'll also find a tombstone carved by the great Renaissance sculptor, Donatello.

THE POETS' CORNER OF ROME:

The **Keats-Shelley Memorial,** at 26 Piazza di Spagna, is the 18th-century house where Keats died of consumption on February 23, 1821—carefully tended to by his close friend, Joseph Severn. "It is like living in a violin," wrote the Italian author, Alberto Savinio. The apartment where Keats spent his last months shelters a museum, with a strange death mask of Keats as well as the "deadly sweat" drawing by Severn. For those really interested in the full story of the involvement of Keats and Shelley in Italy, a good little book compiled by Neville Rogers is sold on the premises. The memorial house is open from 9 a.m. to noon and from 4 to 6, daily except Saturday afternoons and Sundays; it charges 500 lire (58¢) for admission.

Near St. Paul's Station, in the midst of a setting of cypress trees, lies the old **Protestant Cemetery** where John Keats was buried. In a grave nearby, Joseph Severn, his "death-bed" companion, was interred beside him, six decades later. Dejected and feeling his reputation as a poet diminished by the rising vehemence of his critics, Keats asked that the following epitaph be written on his tombstone: "Here lies one whose name was writ in water." A great romantic poet Keats certainly was. But a prophet, never.

Shelley, author of *Prometheus Unbound,* was drowned off the Italian Riviera in 1822—before his 30th birthday. His ashes now rest alongside those of Edward John Trelawny, fellow romantic and man of the sea. Trelawny maintained that Shelley may have been murdered, his boat being overrun by petty pirates bent on robbery.

Although it's not part of "English Rome," it's good to tie in a visit to the Protestant Cemetery with the neighboring **Pyramid of Caius Cestius,** which adjoins it on the Piazzale Ostiense (streetcar "ED" or bus 30). Dating from the first century B.C., it is about 90 feet high, and looks as if it belongs to the Egyptian landscape. The pyramid can't be entered, but it's fun to circle and photograph. Who was Caius Cestius? A judge of sorts, a man less impressive than his tomb.

THE FLEA MARKET:

This sprawling open-air market is held in Rome every Sunday morning—at which time every peddler from Trastevere and the surrounding "Castelli Romani" sets up his temporary shop. The vendors are likely to sell merchandise ranging from second-hand paintings of Madonnas (the Italian market's glutted with these), to termite-eaten Il Duce wooden medallions (many of the homes of the lower-income groups still display likenesses of the murdered dictator), to pseudo-Etruscan hairpins to bushels of rosaries, to 1947 television sets, to books printed in 1635. Serious shoppers can often ferret out a good buy. Go to the Flea Market (bus 75 to Porta di Portese, then a short walk away to the Via Portuense) to catch the workaday Roman in an unguarded moment. If you've ever been impressed with the bargaining power of the Spaniard, you haven't seen anything till you've viewed an Italian housewife.

ROME'S MOST MACABRE SIGHT:

It's the **Cemetery of the Capuchin Fathers,** in the Church of the Immaculate Conception, 27 Via Veneto, a short walk from the Piazza Barberini. You enter the cemetery from the first staircase on the right of the church, at the entrance to the Friary. Guidebooks of old used to rank this sight along with the Forum and the Colosseum as the top attractions in the city. Qualifying as one of the most horrifying sights in all Christendom, it is a cemetery of skulls and crossbones woven into "works of art." To make this allegorical dance of death, the bones of more than 4,000 Capuchin brothers were used. Some of the skeletons are intact, draped with Franciscan habits. The creator of this chamber of horrors? The tradition of the friars is that it was the work of a French Capuchin. Their literature suggests that the cemetery should be visited keeping in mind the historical moment of its origins, when Christians had a rich and creative cult for their dead, when great spiritual masters meditated and preached with a skull in hand. Those who have lived through the days of crematoriums and other such massacres may view the graveyard differently, but to many who pause to think, this macabre sight of death has a message. Not for the squeamish! Charging no admission, the cemetery is open in summer from 9 to noon and from 1 to 7 p.m. (winter hours, from 9:30 to noon and from 3 to 6 p.m.).

ROME'S NEWEST PARK: The press had a field day. One editorial writer said that Roman "bambini" would be bitten by poisonous vipers. The pro-Communist press cried that the land should have been used for schools and hospitals. The center of the furor is Rome's newest parkland, the **Villa Doria Pamphili,** opened to the public in 1971 and acquired from Princess Orietta Doria Pamphili at a reported cost of $3.2 million. (The Princess is descended from the world-famous naval commander, Andrea Doria.) Behind the Vatican, the park is about half as large as Central Park in New York, but is more than double the dimensions of the previously described Villa Borghese. Regardless of press criticism, the Villa Pamphili fulfills a sad lack in the Roman capital, providing some much-needed green space. At one time, the park belonged to Pope Innocent X, who planted it with exotic shrubbery, trees, and flowers.

ON TOP OF OLD JANICULUM: From many vantage points in The Eternal City, the views are magnificent. Scenic gulpers, however, have traditionally preferred the outlook from Janiculum Hill (across the Tiber), not one of the "Seven Hills," but certainly one of the most visited (a must on many coach tours). The view is seen at its best at sundown, or at dawn when the skies are often fringed with mauve. Janiculum was the site of battle between Giuseppe Garibaldi and the forces of Pope Pius IX in 1870—an event commemorated today with statuary. To reach "Gianicolo" without a private car, take bus 41 from Ponte Sant' Angelo.

THE BARGAIN PASS: The best all-around museum pass—available to all regardless of profession or academic connection—can be purchased in North America, before your trip to Italy. It costs only $1, but can save you a considerable sum of money (your meager initial fee will be recouped after a visit to only two or three museums). If you plan to do considerable touring throughout Italy, you'll save many $$$.

The pass entitles visitors to be admitted free to *all* of Italy's national museums and galleries. But note the word *national.* In other words, don't present the card at Vatican City, as we recently noted a number of indignant Americans were doing.

To obtain the pass, apply at any office in North America of **Alitalia.** Principal Alitalia offices are at 666 Fifth Avenue and Kennedy International Airport in New York; at 2 East Monroe Street in Chicago; 1001 Connecticut

Avenue (N.W.) in Washington, D.C.; 5670 Wilshire Boulevard in Los Angeles; 2055 Peel Street or at the International Airport in Montreal.

CITY PASS: The City of Rome operates two tourist bus lines from the central railway station to major sightseeing targets of Rome. Drivers (in English) give running commentaries on the sights. The fare is the equivalent of $2.40, and stops include the Colosseum, the Forum, Castel Sant'Angelo, the Piazza di Soagna, the Piazza Venezia, the Pantheon, and St. Peter's Basilica.

PAPAL AUDIENCES: Private audiences are virtually impossible to obtain, unless your name happens to be Mrs. Rose Kennedy. Public audiences with the Pope are held regularly—usually on Wednesday mornings inside Vatican City (in summer, often at the papal villa at Castelgandolfo, 16 miles from Rome). A huge new audience hall designed by Pier Luigi Nervi and accommodating up to 14,000 people has been constructed near the south wall of Vatican City at a cost of $6 million. General audiences, of course, are open to the public at large. Tickets or invitations may be obtained by writing to the Prefect of the Apostolic Palace, Vatican City. Another way for U.S. citizens to apply is at the North American College, 30 Via dell' Umiltà. Canadians should seek invitations at the Collegio Pontifico Canadese.

Before leaving for Rome (assuming you're a Catholic), you should ask the priest of your parish for a letter of introduction. The Vatican prefers women to wear long-sleeved and skirted dresses and to have their heads covered. Men should wear that old reliable, the dark suit and tie.

3. Rome After Dark

In summer, the nightclub pickings in Rome are sometimes as slim as the grain left for Ruth and Naomi—that is, a few bundles, and not the rich fields you'd associate with the city of La Dolce Vita. The legitimate nightclubs tend to be dull and expensive—highlighted only by call girls plying their trade. Younger people fare better, as the discotheques open and close with free-wheeling abandon.

To a Roman, a night on the town means dining late at a trattoria. The local denizens like to drink wine and talk after their meal, even when the waiters are putting chairs on top of empty tables.

Unless you're dead set on making the Roman nightclub circuit, you may experience a far livelier scene simply by sitting late at night on the Via Veneto or the Piazza del Popolo (see below)—all for the cost of a cup of espresso. However, in the earlier part of the evening, you may want to witness:

THE SPECTACLE: For our tastes, the city's best nighttime diversion is to go wandering around ancient monuments, which are illuminated then. For an organized spectacle, drive to Tivoli, then walk through the floodlit splendor of the fountains of **Villa d'Este**. From May 1 till the end of September, the Villa is illuminated every night from 9 to midnight, except Monday and Friday, and can be visited for an admission charge of 900 lire ($1.04).

But for the greatest nighttime event on the entire Roman calendar, try to attend:

AN OPERA AT THE BATHS OF CARACALLA: When the Romans stage something, they like it to be of epic quality. At the Imperial Baths of Caracalla, at Parco di Porta Capena (bus 93 from the Terminal, tram 5, or the subway), you can attend performances of Grand Opera at 9 p.m., usually from the first of July till the middle of August (dates tend to vary from year to year). Sponsored by the Rome Opera House, the season is likely to include Verdi's "Aïda," the best selection for employing the grandeur of the setting.

"Aïda" ends with a smash—the celebrated "double scene," the floodlit upper part representing the Temple of Vulcan, the part underneath, the tomb. And for sheer unrivaled Cecil B. de Mille, it's worth going just to see the phalanx of trumpeters enter in the second act, playing the "Grand March." They are followed by Egyptian troops, with banners, chariots, Ethiopian slaves, dancing girls—a spectacular crescendo.

To purchase tickets go to the **Rome Opera House,** the box office location at 1 Piazza Beniamino Gigli (tel. 461-755). The most expensive seats cost 10,000 lire ($11.60), though you can get excellent ones for anywhere from 3,500 lire ($4.06) to 7,000 lire ($8.12). The Opera House box office is open from 9:30 a.m. to 1 p.m. and from 4 to 6 p.m. daily. You can also purchase tickets at the Baths of Caracalla, on the day of the performance only—the box office opening at 8 p.m. After the opera lets out, you'll find buses waiting to take you to all parts of Rome.

Incidentally, the Rome Opera House itself, one of the most renowned in Europe, has its regular season from the end of November till May, with tickets for the best seats usually peaking at 13,000 lire ($15.08), though good ones are available in the 3,500-lire ($4.06) to 10,000-lire ($11.60) bracket.

THEATERS: Teatro Goldoni, Vicoloto de' Soldati, just north of the Piazza Navona, offers theatricals in English. To see what's playing, call 56-11-56. For the average performance, tickets range from 3,000 lire ($3.48) to 4,500 lire ($5.22). In the 18th-century foyer, incidentally, is a fine bar, offering not only snacks but afternoon teas.

ON THE VIA VENETO: Back in the 1950s—a decade that *Time* magazine gave to Rome, in the way it conceded the 60s to London—the Via Veneto rose in fame and influence as the choicest street in Rome, crowded with movie stars, aspirant and actual, their directors, and a fast-rising group who were card-carrying members of the so-called jet set. Fashions, of course, are one of the most fickle elements in man's culture. Today, movie stars and directors wouldn't be caught on the Via Veneto—even with night-owl sunglasses! In the course of a decade, the Via Veneto has moved into the mainstream of world tourism, and lays its own claim to having interest (no first-timer should miss it). It's about as in and undiscovered today as pretzels. But you may want to spend some time there. A "coffee house" that enjoys continued popularity is **Café de Paris.** People like to come here to see and be seen. In winter, enclosed see-through booths keep out the chill, but not the view of the passing parade. A cup of the de Paris' cappucino costs 700 lire (81¢), a whiskey, 1,500 lire ($1.74). A club sandwich costs 2,400 lire ($2.78); a beer, 900 lire ($1.04); and most ice creams, 1,100 lire ($1.28).

The other most frequented cafe is the **Doney,** 139-143 Via Veneto. This is one of Rome's more enduring cafes. Legend has it that only foreigners go there, but they must like it, as they return year after year. Of course, new recruits are added all the time. While you're eating lunch, pedestrians walk right through the maze, inspecting your chicken salad sandwich. A hamburger costs 1,300 lire ($1.51) at any time of the day; an omelette, 1,500 lire ($1.74); a Campari, 1,000 lire ($1.16). If you've got it, you can flaunt it at the Doney! Nowadays the stars at night are big and bright—deep in:

THE HEART OF THE PIAZZA DEL POPOLO: The **Café Rosati,** Piazza del Popolo, attracts the Fellini, Zeffirelli entourage, plus an assortment of guys and dolls of all types and persuasions who drive up in Maseratis and Porsches. The Rosati, which has been around since 1923, is really a sidewalk cafe, ice-cream parlor, candy store, confectionery that has been swept up in the fickle world of fashions. The later you go, the more interesting is the action. At one of the sidewalk tables, a Campari goes for 900 lire ($1.04); an espresso for 450 lire (52¢); a gin and tonic, 1,800 lire ($2.09); a whiskey for 1,900 lire ($2.20). The also-popular **Canova** across the street isn't overlooked either. The lucky few quickly grab the sidewalk tables, ordering a Campari at 1,200 lire ($1.39) or an espresso at 600 lire (70¢). In cool weather, the crowd retreats to the maze of rooms in the rear. The standard tourist menu, either at lunch or dinner, costs about 5,500 lire ($6.38). At night you can order a delicious pizza for 1,500 lire ($1.74). Incidentally, it doesn't matter whether you're an important director or a film star. The fun of the game is to act the part.

The piazza itself is haunted with memories. According to legend, the ashes of Nero were enshrined there, until 11th-century residents began complaining to the Pope about his imperial ghost. The Egyptian obelisk seen there today dates from the 13th century B.C., removed from Heliopolis to Rome during the reign of Augustus. Originally, it stood at the Circus Maximus. The present piazza was designed by Valadier, the architect of Napoleon, in the early 19th century. The twin baroque churches also stand on the square, overseeing the never-ending traffic.

THE CAFES OF TRASTEVERE: Just as the Piazza del Popolo lured the chic and sophisticated from the Via Veneto, several other cafes in the colorful district of Trastevere, across the Tiber, are threatening to do the same for Popolo. Fans who saw Fellini's "Roma" know what the Piazza Santa Maria, deep in the heart of Trastevere, looks like. The square—filled with milling throngs in summer—is graced with an octagonal fountain and a church dating from the 12th century. On the traffic-free piazza, children run and play, and occasional spontaneous guitar fests are heard when the weather's good. For drinks, try either the **Galeassi** or **Di Marzio.** Several of our well-recommended restaurants also lie off this square.

BAR HOPPING: Le Pavillon Bar, Grand Hotel, 8 Via Vittorio Emanuele Orlando (tel. 489-011), attracts (quietly) Roman society to its precincts, everybody from Moravia to Mastroianni. The atmosphere is vaguely chinoiserie, with white and pink garden lattice work, a ceramic bird collection, semitropical greenery, and simulated bamboo chairs and tables. A pianist entertains after 7 p.m. The reigning king of the bar is Ricardo Vettor, famous for his Venetian cocktails. Most drinks average between 1,000 lire ($1.16) and 2,500 lire ($2.90). Light meals are also served.

Pino's, 80 Via Marche (tel. 462-474), off the Via Veneto, might become your own personal living room in Rome. The setting is intimate, the drinks good. If you're dropping in before dinner, an apéritif of Campari costs 850 lire (99¢). Whiskies begin at 2,000 lire ($2.32). Soft rose-colored sofas and ottomans are grouped for conversational gatherings, and the walls are hung with old

English prints and cartoons. Overscaled brass lamps and parquet floors add to the atmosphere. Open till 2 a.m. Closed Sundays.

Harry's Bar, 148 Via Veneto. Every major Italian city, such as Florence and Venice, has to have a Harry's Bar. Rome is no exception. After all, a watering spot is needed for the IBF—International Bar Flies. The one at the top of the Via Veneto is elegant, chic, and sophisticated. In summer, sidewalk tables are placed outside, but off season the ambience is more intimate, with walls of tapestry, ornate wood paneling, carved pilastering, and Florentine sconces. Some of the attractive girls in Rome show up here to drink or whatever. In back is a small dining room, serving such dishes as risotto with mushrooms at 1,400 lire ($1.62) or beef stroganoff at 4,300 lire ($4.99). You're welcomed to the bar if you order an espresso at 800 lire (93¢) or a whiskey at 2,000 lire ($2.32). Closed Sundays.

THE MOST FASHIONABLE COFFEE HOUSE: Antico Caffè Greco, 86 Via Condotti, is the poshest and most fashionable coffee bar in Rome, and has been on and off since 1760. Attired in the trappings of the turn of the century, it has for years enjoyed a reputation as the gathering place of the literati. Previous sippers included Stendhal, Goethe, even D'Annunzio. Keats would also sit here and write. Today, however, you're more likely to see dowagers and American tourists. In the front is a wooden bar, but beyond this is a series of small salons, decorated in the 19th-century style with oil paintings in gilded frames. You sit at marble-topped tables of Napoleonic design, against a backdrop of gold or red damask, romantic paintings, and antique mirrors. Waiters are attired in black tailcoats. A cup of cappucino costs 750 lire (87¢); sandwiches go for 500 lire (58¢); a scotch and soda, 1,300 lire ($1.51). However, the house specialty is a paradiso, made with lemon, orange, cherries, and grapefruit, costing 1,500 lire ($1.74). There's plenty of atmosphere here.

SOOTHING THE SWEET TOOTH: Giolitti, 40 Via Uffici del Vicario, is one of the most popular gathering spots in nighttime Rome for devotees of gelato (ice cream). In the evening, this colorful section of Rome throngs with strollers with a sweet tooth. Satisfying that craving admirably is the whipped-cream-topped coppa-Giolitti, costing 950 lire ($1.10), or such tempting flavors as pistachio, banana, coconut. During the day, you can get wonderful snacks here, too. The elegant ice-cream parlor is behind the Piazza Colonna. When Ingrid Bergman lived in Rome, this section was a favorite spot for her.

THE NIGHTCLUBS: La Cabala, above the deluxe restaurant, the Hostaria dell' Orso, 93 Via Monte Brianzo (tel. 564-221), is the most elegant nighttime rendezvous in all of Europe. Tradition has it that Dante, even Montaigne and Rabelais, at various times occupied this 14th-century Renaissance palazzo. The clientele usually wears stunning clothes (but not formal). You'll pay 6,000 lire ($6.96) for the first drink, and 4,000 lire ($4.64) for each additional drink—and there's no cover charge. Discotheque music is played for dancing, and it's fun to sip and admire the scenery. Truly magnificent Roman splendor, but it may be shut down in summer—so telephone in advance.

Scarabocchio, 8 Piazza dei Ponziani (tel. 580-04-95), in Trastevere, is a combination discotheque and nightclub, which operates in the English fashion—as a private club. To this day we can't figure out how the doorman evaluates who is acceptable and who is not. One thing we do know: elegant dress is *de* *rigueur.* Drinks are 5,000 lire ($5.80). We don't know which is the more impressive show, the performer or the guests.

L'Arciliuto, 5 Piazza Monte Vecchio (tel. 659-419), is one of the most romantic candlelit spots in Rome. Its associations are unusual—owned by the famous musician, Enzo Samaritani, it was the former studio of Raphael. You probably have heard recordings of Samaritani, and will enjoy him on his home ground. His Neapolitan songs are most winning—a night here is like a concert, especially when he plays some of his more elaborate guitar arrangements. The setting and atmosphere are intimate. A first drink will cost 5,000 lire ($5.80). Highly recommended, but hard to find. Within walking distance of Piazza Navona.

Capriccio, 38 Via Liguria (tel. 489-961), off the Via Veneto, books a combo for dancing between 10:30 p.m. and 4 a.m. nightly. The atmosphere is somewhat elegant, with torchiers and baroque mirrors—plus plenty of gilt and red silk. The well-dressed clientele likes the music subdued. For your first drink, you pay 5,000 lire ($5.80), 3,500 lire ($4.06) for your second *consumazione.* Closed in July and August.

Club 84, 84 Via Emilia, is stuffed as tight as a jar of Italian olives till around 4 a.m., when most of Rome is sleeping. Noisy, with a smoke-gets-in-your-eyes atmosphere, Club 84 usually has hip combos, which play dance tunes to souped-up modern overtones. Two live groups alternate every two hours, playing from 10:30 to 4 a.m. The dance floor is mini-sized—so you do the elbow trot. To keep the 3,000 lire ($3.48) price tag on their drinks, men and their dates hover close to the bar. Otherwise the charge is 5,000 lire ($5.80) at a table. At the club, catering mainly to couples, a cinerama projection encircles the room with slides of abstract patterns and scenic views.

Club Gattopardo, 97 via Mario de' Fiori (tel. 67-84-838), means "Leopard," the name of a famous novel about Sicily. It's one gigantic living room decorated with contemporary paintings. Attracting a sophisticated crowd, it provides dancing to a live combo. You pay 3,500 lire ($4.06). A dinner will run 8,000 lire ($9.28). The location is a block above Via Capo le Case, a short walk from the Spanish Steps.

Piper Theatre Restaurant, 9 Via Tagliamento, is fantastico—the best of its type in Rome. Take bus 35 from the terminal station to Piazza Buenos Aires. Look for a neon sign of a green serpent eating a red apple. You can dine here for 15,000 lire ($17.40), with wine, one drink, and service included; or just drink, costing 6,000 lire ($6.96) for the first one, 3,500 lire ($4.06) for each one thereafter. You are then thrown into a snake pit of exhibitionist dancers and rock groups, interspersed with name acts such as Diana Ross and splashy Paris-type cabaret. The trick here is to dress to attract as much attention as possible—perhaps a suit so flaming yellow that it ignites the breath of imbibers who've downed more than one litre! Whether you're with it, against it, or simply couldn't care less, the Piper is a whirlpool in the Dead Sea of Roman nightlife. The demimonde arrives after midnight. Two male readers have written to complain of some "very thirsty" English girls who hang out at the Piper, waiting for free-spending Yankees. One of the men signed his name, "Fleeced."

FOLKLORE EVENINGS: Fantasie di Trastevere, 6 Via di Santa Dorotea (tel. 589-29-86), combines Roman rusticity with theatrical flair. It's housed in the former "people's theater" (Teatro di Tiberino) where the famous actor, Petrolini, made his debut. After the theater declined, it housed a printing press until purchased by Constanti Brugnoli, who pumped a wheelbarrow of lire into transforming it into one of the most robust spots on the Roman nighttime circuit.

Dressed in regional garb of Italian provinces, the waiters serve with drama. The cuisine isn't subtle—still good and bountiful. Such dishes as the classic saltimbocca (ham with veal) are prepared, preceded by tasty pasta (including one with a sauce made with red peppers)—everything aided by the wines from the "Castelli Romani." Accompanying the main dishes is a big basket of warm, country-coarse herb bread (you'll tear off hunks). Expect to pay 15,000 lire ($17.40), excluding wine and beverages. Some two dozen folk singers and musicians in regional costumes perform, making it a friendly, festive affair. Lasting two hours, the folklore show features both Roman and Neapolitan favorites. Try to arrive before 9:30 p.m. It's closed Mondays.

HONKY-TONK: **Red Banjo,** 76 Via San Nicola da Tolentino (tel. 489-348), is speakeasy Numero Uno in Rome. Rinky-tink and Roaring 20s, ragtime and honky-tonk, folk and gay (90s, that is), New Orleans and Western—you name it. On our latest rounds, the piano-player even sang "Amazing Grace!" Neapolitan folk songs are occasionally thrown in to please the young Italians who frequent the establishment, along with the many Americans (some in Stars and Stripes shirts) and Canadians. You're invited to sing along to your favorite tunes. A frosty mug of beer goes for 2,200 lire ($2.55), a pitcher for 3,800 lire ($4.41). Booze is from 1,900 lire ($2.20).

Never a cover or a service charge. American bar and American management. In the Pan Am Building, just off the Piazza Barberini.

FILMS: In Trastevere, not too far from the Piazza Santa Maria, the little **Pasquino** draws a faithful coterie of English-speaking fans, not only Italians, but expatriates. To find out what is playing, call 580-36-22. The location is at Vicolo del Piede, a small street, deep in the district, across the Tiber. The average films—and usually they are of recent vintage—cost 1,000 lire ($1.16).

READER'S AFTER-DARK TIP: "A new little spot, the **Cuscio Club,** 5 via Capo d'Africa (tel. 73-79-53), is delightful and inexpensive. The evening includes typical Italian songs and folk music, dancing, and entertainment by the two owners who have a flair for show biz themselves" (Laurabelle Yoder, Waterloo, Belgium).

4. Ring Around Rome

Most capitals of Europe are ringed with a number of scenic attractions. For sheer variety, Rome tops all of them. Just short miles away, you can walk in silence across the cemetery of U.S. servicemen killed on the beaches of Anzio in World War II, or go back to the dawn of Italian history and explore the dank tombs the Etruscans left as their legacy.

You can wander around the ruins of the "queen of villas of the ancient world" (Hadrian's), or be lulled by the music of baroque fountains in the Villa d'Este. You can drink the golden wine of the Alban hill towns ("Castelli Romani"), or turn yourself bronze on the beaches of Ostia di Lido—or even explore the ruins of Ostia Antica, the ancient seaport of Rome.

Unless you're rushed beyond reason, allow at least three days for taking a look at the attractions in the environs. We'll highlight the best of the lot, beginning with:

TIVOLI: Known as Tibur to the ancient Romans, Tivoli was the playground of emperors. Today, its reputation continues unabated: it is the most popular half-day jaunt visitors take from Rome. The ruins of Hadrian's Villa as well as the Villa d'Este, with their fabulous fountains and gardens, remain the two chief attractions of Tivoli—and both should be seen, even by those who must curtail their sightseeing in Rome itself. The town of Tivoli lies 20 miles from the capital, out the Via Tiburtina. Even if you don't have a car, you won't have to take a guided tour, as a motorcoach leaves from the corner of the Via Gaeta in Rome (Piazza dei Cinquecento) nearly every 20 minutes.

Right inside the town itself, we can look at two villas before heading to the environs of Tivoli and the ruins of Hadrian's Villa.

The Villa D'Este

Like Hadrian centuries before, Cardinal Ippolito d'Este of Ferrara believed in heaven on earth. In the mid-16th century, he ordered a villa built on a hillside (entered from the Piazza Trento). The dank Renaissance structure, with its second-rate paintings, is hardly worth the trek from Rome, but the gardens below—designed by Pirro Ligorio—dim the luster of Versailles.

Visitors descend the cypress-studded slope to the bottom, and on their way are rewarded with everything from lilies to gargoyles spouting water, torrential streams, and waterfalls. The loveliest fountain—on this there is some agreement—is the "Fontana dell'Ovato," designed by Ligorio himself. But nearby is the most spectacular achievement—the hydraulic organ fountain, dazzling visitors with its water jets in front of a baroque chapel, with four maidens who look tipsy. The work represents the French genius of Claude Vénard.

Don't miss the moss-covered, slime-green Fountain of Dragons, also by Ligorio, and the so-called "Fountain of Glass" by Bernini. The best walk is along the promenade with 100 spraying fountains. The garden itself, filled with rhododendron, is worth hours of exploration, but you'll need frequent rest periods after those steep climbs. If possible, visit the Villa d'Este on a summer night (see "Rome After Dark"). The splashing fountains are illuminated then, and rank among the wonders of Italy! But they're mighty impressive in the noon-day sun, too (open from 9 a.m. to 7:30 p.m.; till 4 p.m. off season). The admission is 300 lire (35¢).

While at Tivoli, you may want to visit another attraction—

The Villa Gregoriana

Whereas the Villa d'Este dazzles with manmade glamor, the Villa Gregoriana relies more on nature. At one point on the circuitous walk carved along a slope, visitors stand and look out onto the most spectacular waterfall (Aniene) at Tivoli. The trek to the bottom on the banks of the Anio is studded with grottoes, plus balconies opening onto the chasm. The only problem is, if you do make the full journey, you may need to have a helicopter lowered to pull you up again (the climb back is fierce.). From one of the belvederes is an exciting view of the Temple of Vesta on the hill. The gardens were built by Pope Gregory XVI in the 19th century. The villa is open from 9:30 a.m. to 12:30 p.m. and from 1 to 6, and costs 250 lire (29¢) to enter.

Hadrian's Villa on the Outskirts of Tivoli

Of all the Roman emperors dedicated to La Dolce Vita, the globe-trotting Hadrian spent the last three years of his life in the grandest style. Less than four miles from Tivoli, he built one of the greatest estates ever erected in the world, filling acre after acre with some of the architectural wonders he'd seen on his many trips.

Perhaps as a preview of what he envisioned in store for himself, the emperor even created a representation of Hell centuries before Dante got around to recording its horrors in a poem. A patron of the arts, a lover of beauty, and himself something of an architect, Hadrian directed the staggering construction task that created not a villa, but a self-contained world for a vast royal entourage and the hundreds of servants and guards they required to protect them, feed them, bathe them, and satisfy their libidos.

On the estate were erected theaters. baths, temples, fountains, gardens, and canals bordered with statuary. The palaces and temples Hadrian filled with sculpture, some of which now rests in the museums of Rome. In the centuries to follow, barbarians, popes, and cardinals, as well as anyone who needed a slab of marble, carted off much that made the villa so spectacular. But enough of the fragmented ruins remain for us to piece together the story.

For a glimpse of what the villa used to be, see the plastic reconstruction at the entrance. Then, following the arrows around, look in particular for the Marine Theatre (the ruins of a round structure with Ionic pillars); the Great Baths, with some of the mosaics intact, and the Canopus, with its group of Caryatids—their images reflected in the pond, as well as a statue of Mars. For a closer look at some of the items excavated, you can visit the museum on the premises. Hadrian's Villa is open from 9 a.m. to 7:30 p.m. (till 5 p.m. in winter), and charges 200 lire (23¢) for admission (free on Sundays). From Tivoli, take a "B" bus to the gateway of the villa.

Where To Eat in Tivoli

Dining is an event at Tivoli. The best of the restaurants is **Villa Gregoriana,** 33 Ponte Gregoriano (tel. 200-26), at the bridge. Its main attraction is its cantilevered terrace extending out over a gorge with a good view of the Vesta Temple. Behind its sienna-colored walls, delicious Roman specialties are served, including cannelloni, fresh fish, and veal. You'll pay a minimum of 3,800 lire ($4.41) for your repast, though your bill could easily run up to 6,000 lire ($6.96). Add 15% for service.

Sibilla, 50 Via della Sibilla, earns its laurels not only for atmosphere and regional cooking—but for its view. In fair weather, you can choose a table on the graveled terrace shaded by creeping wisteria. The Sibilla hangs out on a precipice and in its garden is the Temple of Vesta, with its Corinthian columns dating from the 2nd century B.C. Add a glimpse of the cliffside houses, the sound of a cascading waterfall, and the soft guitar-playing and singing of a village balladeer—and you have the general idea. Throw in a good kitchen, and you've got an unbeatable blending of elements. Specialties: cannelloni, 1,000 lire ($1.16); trout freshly caught in the Anio, 2,800 lire ($3.25); a mouth-watering soufflé for 1,200 lire ($1.39). Another well-prepared dish—and an entree you should try at least once while in Italy—is pollo alla diavolo (deviled chicken) for 2,700 lire ($3.13). It's delicious.

An alternative choice nearby is the **Eden Sirene,** 4 Piazza Massimo (tel. 21-352), with its equally spectacular view, both of the Temple of Vesta and the Villa Gregoriana. Its dining terrace is cantilevered into space—far above the valley and the waterfall. Opening onto a central plaza, it is reached by descending several flights of steps. Ask first to see the famous trout grotto, where you may prefer to select your dinner at 3,000 lire ($3.48) a plate. A good beginning would be the cannelloni at 1,000 lire ($1.16). Another recommendable specialty is chicken from Valdarno at 1,500 lire ($1.74). It's closed Mondays. If you're planning to stay overnight, you can get fair double rooms with baths—all with excellent views—for 5,500 lire ($6.38) a night.

It's also possible to dine right at the entrance to Hadrian's Villa. The **Adriano** (tel. 329174) is all "rustico" and bustle, but you may enjoy it if you're in the mood. Though slightly rundown, it is strong on character. If you're able to attract the eye of a waiter, you'll be served pasta dishes, ranging in price from 750 lire (87¢) to 1,000 lire ($1.16). Meat dishes go from 2,000 lire ($2.32) to 2,500 lire ($2.90). Everything tastes better accompanied by the mixed salad at 700 lire (81¢).

READER'S EATING SUGGESTION: "At **Ricky's Hamburgers,** in the righthand corner of the main square, 1 Largo Garibaldi, a real, good, old-fashioned American hamburger can be had for the most reasonable price in all Europe. About 75¢ buys you a hearty burger complete with the best conversationalist in all Italy, Emily Newton, who runs the place. For all those who are tired of pasta, this is the place to eat" (Vivian Thompson, Saskatoon, Saskatchewan, Canada).

Staying Overnight

Residence Torre S. Angelo, Via Quintilio Varo (tel. 23292), has been adapted from a 15th-century castle. Built of natural stone, it stands on the ledge of a hill that is dominated by a five-story square tower. The bedrooms are in the provincial style, with terracotta floors and furnishings of the 17th-century idiom. All of the accommodations offer magnificent views. Singles with bath rent for 8,000 lire ($9.28); doubles, 11,900 lire ($13.80). Dining is baronial in a lofty room with beams, towering windows, and tiled floors. Well-chosen colors and more provincial furnishings characterize the guest lounges. The swimming pool invites relaxation at Tivoli.

OSTIA: If you want to see all of Rome—both ancient and modern—take the Metropolitana (subway) at Termini Station. With your bathing suit in hand, ride it until you reach the stop at "Ostia Antica," about 16 miles from Rome. However, remember to change at the stop called Piramide. There you can catch another train which stops right at Ostia Antica. You can then walk to the ruins (see below). Later, you can board the underground again for the Lido di Ostia, the beach.

Ostia Antica

At the mouth of the Tiber, Ostia Antica was the port of Ancient Rome. Through it were funneled the riches from the far corners of the Empire. Actually it was founded in the fourth century B.C., but the engineering work of dredging it into a major port and naval base was carried out primarily under three later emperors: Claudius, Nero, and Trajan.

A thriving prosperous city developed, full of temples, baths, theaters, and patrician homes. Ostia Antica flourished for about eight centuries from the date of its founding, eventually withering, as the wholesale business of carting off its art treasures began. Gradually, it became little more than a malaria bed, a buried ghost city that faded into history.

But in the 19th century, a papal-sponsored commission launched a series of diggings, though the major work of unearthing was carried out under Mussolini's orders from 1938 to 1942, having finally to stop because of the war. The city is only partially dug out today, but it is believed that all the chief monuments have been uncovered.

Ostia Antica is one of the major attractions in the environs of Rome, particularly interesting to those who can't make it to Pompeii. All the principal monuments are clearly labeled. The most important spot in all the ruins is the Piazzale delle Corporazioni, an early version of Wall Street. Near the theater, this square contained nearly 75 corporations, the nature of their businesses identified by the pattern of mosaics preserved.

Greek dramas were performed at the ancient theater, built sometime in the early days of the Empire. The classics are still aired here in summer (check with the Tourist Office for specific listings), but the theater as it looks today is the result of much rebuilding. Every town the size of Ostia had a forum. Uncovered during the excavations were a number of pillars of the ancient Ostia Forum. At one end is a second-century B.C. temple honoring a trio of gods, Minerva, Jupiter, and Juno (little more than the basic foundation remains). In addition, there is a well-lit museum within the enclave, displaying Roman statuary, along with some Pompeii-like frescoes. The ruins, which take at least a couple of hours to explore, are open from 9 a.m. to sunset, and cost 150 lire (17¢) admission.

Lido di Ostia

It may be a strongly Catholic country, but the Romans, unlike their fellow Latins, the Spanish, don't allow religious conservatism to affect their bathing attire. Shapely Italian girls know how to wear a wild bikini. This is the beach where the denizens of the capital frolic on the seashore, at times creating a merry carnival atmosphere, with dance halls, cinemas, and pizzerie. The Lido is set off best at Castelfusano, against a backdrop of pinewoods. This stretch of shoreline is often referred to as The Roman Riviera.

Where to Eat in Ostia

The **Vecchia Pineta,** Piazzale dell' Aquilone (tel. 602-9277), at the end of the walk from the Ostia di Lido subway stop, borders the ocean. In a holiday-making atmosphere, it serves seafood specialties. The zuppa di cozze is a favorite of Latium province—really a tangy soup of mussels found in the Gaeta Bay and dished up in a marinade. We've often made a luncheon out of this gourmet dish alone, which costs 1,400 lire ($1.62). Another specialty worth citing is the frito misto mare, a mixed fish fry—squid, red mullet, sole, shrimps —going for 2,200 lire ($2.55). But the pièce de résistance is risotto with scampi, the rice being cooked in a rich broth and served with succulent tidbits of the fish—for 3,000 lire ($3.48). There's dancing evenings, and the weekends tend to be crowded.

CASTELLI ROMANI: For both the Roman emperor and the wealthy cardinal in the heyday of the Renaissance, the Castelli Romani (Roman Castles) exerted a powerful lure. They still do. Of course, the Castelli are not castles, but hill towns—many of them with a history that is ancient. The wines from the Alban hills will add a little *feu de joie* to your life. They're that delicious. The ideal way to explore the hill towns is by car. But you can get a limited preview by taking one of the motorcoaches that leaves every 20 minutes from Rome on the Viale Carlo Felice. Our selection of a string of the most interesting towns follows, beginning with—

Marino

About 14 miles from Rome, out the Via Appia, this hillside town is the most easily reached of Rome's satellites. It was the birthplace of the poetess

Victoria Colonna, whose platonic relationship with Michelangelo greatly influenced his life. In spite of its charming fountains and interesting churches, it is being encroached upon by "moderno," which is draining much of its charm.

Other towns in the Castelli Romani are more intriguing—except at grape harvesting time in October. Then Marino is the liveliest spot in all of Italy. The fountains start spouting wine (you can drink all you want—free), as Bacchus-like revelry reigns supreme. The only trick is to avoid the snake-like line of homeward-bound Romans afterward. When stone sober, the Roman drives as if the Madonna were his or her own special protector. When filled with the golden wine of the Alban hills, he or she descends like the Normans did in their sack of the city.

Castelgandolfo

Since the early 17th century, this resort on Lake Albano, 16 miles from Rome, has been the summer retreat of the Popes. As such, it attracts thousands of pilgrims yearly, though the papal residence, Villa Barberini, and its surrounding gardens, are private—open only on special occasions. As a sardonic side note, the Pope's summer place incorporates part of Domitian's imperial palace (but the pastimes have changed).

On days that the Pope grants a mass audience, thousands of visitors—many of whom arrive by foot—stream into the audience hall about 100 yards long. Built by Pius XII, the air-conditioned structure protects the faithful from the elements. The former Pope once expressed alarm at the thousands of persons waiting out in the rain to see him. On summer Sundays, the Pope usually appears on a small balcony in the palace courtyard, reciting with the crowd the noon Angelus prayers.

The seat of the papacy opens onto a little square in the center of the town, where holiday-makers sip their wine—nothing pontifical here. A chair lift transports visitors from the hillside town to the lake, where some of the aquatic competitions were held in the 1960 Olympics. The church of St. Thomas of Villanova, on the principal square, as well as the fountain, reveal Bernini's hand. If you need more selling, remember Castelgandolfo was praised by such an eminent guidebook writer as Goethe.

Rocca di Papa

Easily approached from Frascati is the star sapphire in the Castelli Romani crown. Towering over all, the medieval village lies near what was supposedly the camping grounds of Hannibal's legions. The most colorful time to visit is on market day, but any time can be good for the athletic. The narrow lanes are filled with kinks, swirls, ups and downs—more suitable for the donkeys of Rocca di Papa than those who grew up in the elevator era. The snug little houses hug the slopes like cliff dwellings. A greater peak still—3,130 feet high—is Monte Cavo, to be driven . . . not walked from Rocca di Papa. It's the most scenic spot in the hill towns.

Nemi

The Romans flock here in droves, particularly from April through June, for the succulent strawberry of the district—acclaimed by some gourmets as the finest in Europe. (In May, there's a strawberry festival.) Nemi was also known to the ancients. To the huntress Diana, a temple was erected on Lake Nemi—said to be her "looking glass."

In 37 A.D., Caligula built luxurious barges to float on the lake. Mussolini had Nemi drained in another era. The Caligula barges, as predicted, were discovered. Regrettably, it was a dangerous time to excavate them from the lake's bottom, as they were senselessly destroyed by the Nazis during their infamous retreat.

What remained after the destruction—principally the hulls—along with latter-day small-scale reconstructions, can be seen at the Museum of the Ships of Nemi (signs in the town point the way), which is open daily, except Monday, in summer from 10 to 1 and from 3:30 to 7 (in winter, from 10 to 4:30).

The 15th-century Palazzo Ruspoli, a baronial estate, is the focal point of Nemi, but the hill town itself invites exploration—particularly the alleyways the local denizens call streets and the houses with balconies jutting out over the slopes. While darting like Diana through the Castelli Romani, try to time your schedule for lunch in Nemi.

Where to dine in Nemi: Offering a large array of the dishes of the region, as well as a "rustico" atmosphere, **La Taverna di Panetta Alberto,** 13 Via Nemorense (tel. 93-61-35), is worth the trouble of trying to reach. In April the fragole (wild strawberries) signs go out. These berries cost 1,000 lire ($1.16) per serving. Spring is also the time to order pappardella al sugo di lepre (large noodles with wild game sauce)—costing 850 lire (99¢), and worthy of the goddess of the hunt herself. Lake trout—grilled with bay leaves—is the choicest main dish, at 2,700 lire ($3.13). If you really want to have a Roman feast, accompany it with large roasted mushrooms, priced according to size, and a small fennel salad at 500 lire (58¢). To top off the galaxy of goodies, it's traditional to order sambuca, a clear white drink, like anisette, "with a fly in it." The "fly," of course, is a coffee bean, which you suck on for added flavor.

Frascati

About 13 miles from Rome out the Via Tuscolana, Frascati is one of the most beautiful of the hill towns—known for the wine to which it lends its name and its villas. Romans drive up on a Sunday just to drink vino. Although bottles of Frascati are exported—and served in many of the restaurants and trattorie of Rome—tradition holds that the wine is best near the golden vineyards from which it came. Some 1,073 feet above sea level, the town bounced back from the severe destruction caused by bombers in World War II.

If you stand in the heart of Frascati, the Piazza Marconi, you'll see the most important of the estates: **Villa Aldobrandini.** The finishing touches to this 16th-century villa were applied by Maderno, who designed the facade of St. Peter's. Only its gardens (free) may be visited—daily from 9 a.m. to noon and from 3 to 6 p.m. With its grottoes, yew hedges, statuary, and splashing fountains, it makes for an exciting outing.

If you have a car, you can continue on past the Villa Aldobrandini to **Tuscolo,** about three miles beyond the villa. An ancient spot with the ruins of an amphitheater dating from the first century B.C., Tuscolo offers what may be one of Italy's greatest views—with the campagna laid out before you.

If you're in Frascati on a summer evening, you may also want to go to the bombed-out **Villa Torlonia.** Its grounds have been converted into a public park, whose chief treasure is the "Theater of the Fountains," also designed by Maderno. A "Sound, Light, and Water" spectacle is staged.

Dining in Frascati: Cacciani Restaurant, 4 Via Armando Diaz (tel. 940-378), is the choicest restaurant in a town where the competition's always been tough (Frascati foodstuff once attracted Lucullus, the epicurean). A large, modern restaurant, with a terrace commanding a view of the valley, Cacciani in the past drew such celebs as Clark Gable. Nowadays it's more likely to attract Anthony Quinn or Gina Lollobrigida. The kitchen is exposed to the public, and it's fun just to watch the women clean the sand off the spinach. The tourist menu at 4,500 lire ($5.22) includes one half of a good-sized roast chicken. But many Romans prefer to order à la carte, particularly the pasta specialties—such as fettuccine (thin noodles) or agnolotti (stuffed pasta "envelopes"), each costing only 900 lire ($1.04). For a main course, the scaloppine al Marsala at 2,700 lire ($3.13) is always reliable. The restaurant is closed Tuesdays.

Cantina Comandini, Via E. Filiberto, at the steps of the station, right off the central Piazza Roma, is a wine cellar that's reason enough for going over the hill to Frascati. On a hot summer day, to sneak away to this cool wine cellar and sample the golden dry vino is reason enough to live. It's cheap: only 700 lire (81¢) per liter. The proprietor, Mr. Comandini, sells wine in this rustico tavern from his own vineyards. He'll even show visitors the grottoes where his choicest wine is stored. In the evenings there is singing. The cantina is closed Sundays. To sum up, here you'll find good revelry, Bacchus style.

PALESTRINA: If you go out the Via Prenestina for about 24 miles, you'll eventually come to Palestrina, a medieval hillside town overlooking a wide valley. When U.S. airmen flew over in World War II, bombing part of the town, they scarcely realized they were launching Palestrina as an important tourist attraction. The debris cleared, a pagan temple—once one of the greatest in the world—emerged: the **Fortuna Primigenia,** rebuilt in the days of the Empire, though dating from centuries before.

The **Barberini Palace,** high on a hill overlooking the valley, today houses Roman statuary found in the ruins, plus Etruscan artifacts, such as urns the equal of those in the Villa Giulia museum in Rome. But the most famous work—worth the trip itself!—is the "Nile Mosaic," an ancient Roman work, amazingly well preserved, the most remarkable one ever uncovered. The mosaic details the flooding of the Nile, depicting a shepherd's hut, mummies, ibises, Roman warriors—and lots more. The palace is open Sundays and Thursdays from 9:30 a.m. to 1:30 p.m., and charges 100 lire (12¢) admission. Closed Mondays. In winter, the hours are from 10 a.m. to 4:30. To reach Palestrina, you can take a bus leaving from the Viale del Castro Pretorio, near the Central Station.

ANZIO AND NETTUNO: These two towns are peaceful seaside resorts today, but to many an American and Englishman they conjure up bitter memories. On January 22, 1944, an Allied amphibious task force landed the U.S. VI Corps at Anzio and Nettuno, as a prelude to the liberation of Rome. Fighting against terrific odds, the Allies lost many lives.

In Nettuno, the Italian government presented 77 acres to the United States for a cemetery. The graves are visited today by parents, wives, brothers, sisters, and other relatives who lost men in the campaign. The cemetery contains graves not only of those who died on the beaches of Anzio and Nettuno (where holiday-makers now revel), but also of those who were killed in the Sicilian campaign.

The fields of Nettuno contain 7,862 U.S. dead—39 percent of those originally buried (the others have been returned home by their relatives). In Nettuno, a Graves Register office helps visitors locate the markers of particular servicemen. The neatly manicured fields are peppered with crosses and stars of David, plus the saddest sight of all: 488 headstones that mark the graves of the unknowns. The cemetery is open from 8 a.m. till 6 p.m. daily.

In Anzio, you can visit the British cemetery filled with war dead. One memorial to B. J. Pownell, a gunner in the Royal Artillery, seems to symbolize the plight of all the young men who died on either side: "He Gave the Greatest Gift of All: His Unfinished Life." Gunner Pownell was struck down on January 29, 1944. He was 20 years old.

Anzio was the birthplace of both Nero and Caligula. Many wealthy Romans once erected villas there at the port said to have been founded by Antias, the son of Circe and Odysseus. In the ruins of Nero's fabulous villa, the world-famous statue of Apollo Belvedere was discovered.

Motorists can visit Ostia Antica in the morning, Anzio and Nettuno in the afternoon. Tourists dependent on public transportation can either take a train from Terminal Station in Rome, or else a bus from the Via Carlo Felice in the capital.

FREGENE: The fame of this coast city north of the Tiber dates back to the 1600s when the land belonged to the Rospigliosi, a powerful Roman family. Pope Clement IX, a member of the wealthy family, planted a forest of pine extending along the shoreline for 2½ miles and half a mile deep to protect the land from the strong winds of the Mediterranean. Today, the wall of pines makes a dramatic backdrop for the golden sands and luxurious villas of the resort town.

For food or accommodations, there is the following recommendation.

"La Conchiglia," 4 Piazzale a Mare (tel. 64-60-229), means The Shellfish in Italian—an appropriate name for this hotel and restaurant right on the beach, offering views of the water and of the pine trees. Its circular lounge is painted white, with curving wall banquettes built in and facing a cylindrical fireplace with a raised hearth. It seems a setting for one of those modern Italian films, with its cubical upholstered chairs. However, the resort aura is created by the large green plants. Facing the terrace, the bar in the cocktail lounge is also circular, with foot-wide plastic rolls for seats! The rooms are comfortable and well furnished, costing 18,000 lire ($20.88) to 21,000 lire ($24.36) per person for full pension in high season. You have to stay a minimum of three days to get these rates. An arrangement is made with a nearby lido club for free entrance and 50% reduction on cabins. It's also possible to stop by for a meal. The food is good. Try, for example, gnocchi at 1,000 lire ($1.16), then perhaps follow with scampi al curry at 3,000 lire ($3.48). Many excellent meat dishes begin at 2,000 lire ($2.32). The restaurant's in the garden, shaded by bamboo. Oleander flutters in the sea breezes.

THE ETRUSCAN ZONE: As you walk through the Etruscan Museum in Rome (Villa Giulia), you'll often see the word **Caere** written under a figure vase or a sarcophagus. This is a reference to the nearby town known today as Cerveteri. Caere was one of the great Etruscan cities of Italy, its origins dipping back into antiquity—maybe to the 9th century B.C. Of course, the Etruscan town has long faded, but not the **Necropolis of Cerveteri.** The effect is eerie, often called a "city of the dead."

When you go beneath some of the mounds, you'll discover the most striking feature of the necropolis—the tombs are like rooms in Etruscan homes. The main burial ground is called the Necropolis of Banditaccia. Of the graves thus far uncovered, none is finer than the **Tomba Bella** (sometimes called the

Reliefs' Tomb), the burial ground of an Etruscan family by the name of Matuna. Articles such as utensils, even house pets, were painted in stucco relief. Presumably these paintings were representations of items the dead family would need in the world beyond.

Experts believe that the Euphronios vase sold in 1972 to the Metropolitan Museum of New York for $1 million may have come from one of the tombs near Cerveteri. Sold by art dealer Robert Hecht, the vase dates from about 500 B.C. Recent finds include a carved stone head of the demon Tuculka, an Etruscan deity.

The necropolis is open from 9 to 1 and 4 to 7 except Mondays, and charges 200 lire (23¢) for admission. Cerveteri can be reached by motorcoach from Rome, leaving from the Viale Castro Pretorio. If you're driving, head out the Via Aurelia, northwest of Rome, for a distance of 28 miles.

If you wish to see even more striking and more recently excavated tombs, go to **Tarquinia,** about 13 miles above the port of Civitavecchia.

The medieval turrets and fortifications atop the rocky cliffs overlooking the sea seem to contradict the Etruscan name of Tarquinia. Actually, Tarquinia is the adopted name of the old medieval community of Corneto, in honor of the major Etruscan city which once stood nearby. The main attraction within the town is the **Tarquinia National Museum,** Piazza Cavour, which is devoted to Etruscan exhibits and sarcophagi excavated from the necropolis a few miles away. The museum is housed in the Palazzo Vitelleschi, a Gothic palace dating from the mid-15th century. Among the exhibits are gold jewelry, bronze busts of elegant Etruscan women, black vases with carved and painted bucolic scenes, and sarcophagi decorated with carvings of animals and relief figures of priests and military leaders. But the biggest attraction of all, is in itself worth a drive all the way from Rome. This is the almost life-sized pair of winged horses taken from the pediment of a Tarquinian temple. The gilded finish is worn here and there, and the terra-cotta color shows through, but the relief stands as one of the greatest Etruscan masterpieces ever discovered. The museum is open daily, except Monday, from 9 to 1 and from 4 to 7, and charges 200 lire (23¢) admission (free on Sundays).

Just four miles southeast of the town is the **Etruscan necropolis,** covering more than 2½ miles of rough terrain near where the ancient Etruscan city once stood. Thousands of tombs have been discovered here, some of which have not been explored even today. Others, of course, were discovered by looters, but many treasures remain even after countless pieces have been removed to museums and private collections. The paintings on the walls of the tombs have helped historians reconstruct the life of the Etruscans—a heretofore impossible feat without a written history. A guide will lead you to and open up the most important tombs, including the Tomba dei Leopardi and the Triclinium. The paintings depict feasting couples in vivid colors mixed from iron oxide, lapis-lazuli dust, and charcoal. One of the oldest tombs (from the 6th century B.C.) depicts young men fishing while dolphins play and colorful birds fly high above. Many of the paintings convey an earthy, vigorous, sex-oriented life among the wealthy Etruscans. The tombs are generally open from about 9 to 1 and 4 to 7 except Mondays, and the guide naturally expects a tip.

VITERBO: The 2,000 years that have gone into the creation of the city of Viterbo make it one of the most interesting day trips from Rome. Just a two-hour drive on the Autostrada North (to the Orte exit), Viterbo traces its history back to the Etruscans. The bulk of its historical architecture, however, dates from the Middle Ages and the Renaissance, when the city was a residence

—and hideout—for the popes. The old section of the city is still surrounded by thick stone walls which once protected the inhabitants from papal (or anti-papal, depending on the situation at the time) attacks.

The only way to see Viterbo properly is on a walking tour of the medieval town, wandering through the narrow cobbled streets and pausing in front of its remarkable structures. Beginning at the Piazza del Plebiscito, which is dominated by the 15th-century Town Hall, one is impressed with the fine state of preservation of Viterbo's old buildings. The courtyard and attractive fountain in front of the Town Hall and the 13th-century Governor's Palace are a favorite meeting place for townfolk and visitors alike.

Just down the Via San Lorenzo is the Palazzo San Lorenzo, the site of Viterbo's Cathedral, which sits atop the former Etruscan acropolis. The Duomo, dating from 1192, is a composite of architectures, from its pagan foundations to its Renaissance facade, to its Gothic bell tower. Next door is the 13th-century Palazzo Papale, built as a residence for the pope, but also serving as a hideout when the pope was in exile. It was also the site of three papal elections. The outside staircase and the colonnaded loggia all go to make up one of the finest examples of civil Roman architecture from the Gothic period.

The finest example of medieval architecture in Viterbo is the **San Pellegrino Quarter,** reached from the Piazza San Lorenzo by a short walk past the Piazza della Morte. This quarter, inhabited by working class Viterbans, is a maze of narrow streets, arched walkways, towers, steep stairways, and ornamental fountains.

Worth a special visit is the **Convent of Santa Maria della Verita,** dating from 1100. The church itself is interesting enough, with 15th-century frescoes by Lorenzo da Viterbo, student of Piero della Francesca. But the real reason for visiting the convent is to see the Etruscan collection in the Municipal Museum, housed in the cloisters. Among the contents of the museum are several Etruscan sarcophagi, including a red-haired lady and a red-faced fat man with a broken nose. The collection also includes sculpture (an excellent Etruscan lion) and pottery. Adjoining the museum is a picture gallery containing a painting of the dead Christ, the finest work by Sebastiano del Piombo, a student of Michelangelo. The museum and gallery are open daily from 9 to 4 (Monday 9 to 1).

READER'S SIGHTSEEING TIP: "The visitor to Viterbo is in for several wonderful surprises at a short distance from the city. One of them is the **Villa Lante,** at Bagnaia, which Sacheverell Sitwell hailed as the most beautiful garden in Italy. When I first read Sitwell's rapturous account of the Villa Lante, I felt that he was probably exaggerating. After all, Italy abounds in superb landscape gardens—one has only to mention the Villa d'Este north of Rome. But when my wife and I saw the Villa Lante with our own eyes, we had to confess that Sitwell told the truth. Words cannot do justice to this manmade Renaissance paradise, where water, stone, and vegetation are combined harmoniously to produce a vision of earthly perfection.

"The other splendid surprise in the Viterbo area is **Bomarzo,** with its park of grotesque figures carved from natural rock. No one knows precisely why these figures were created, but the available evidence suggests that they were commissioned by Vicino Orsini, an eccentric member of an aristocratic family that played a dramatic role in Italian history. The figures probably date from about 1560, as Annibale Caro, a Renaissance poet, refers to them in a letter he wrote in 1564. They rise mysteriously from the wild Tuscan landscape, covered with strangling weeds and moss. Nature and art have joined hands to create a surrealistic fantasy unlike anything in the world. Salvador Dali visited Bomarzo and was astonished by what he saw. Manuel Mujica-Lainez, a modern Argentine author, has written a novel entitled *Bomarzo,* and also furnished the libretto for Ginastera's opera of the same name. Bomarzo is mentioned in several books on Mannerist art. Despite signs of interest in the place, Bomarzo has not received the attention it deserves" (Dr. Alfred Dorn, Long Island City, N.Y.).

Dining Near Viterbo

Instead of dining at Viterbo, we suggest a detour to La Quercia, less than two miles from the medieval center. There you'll find **Aquilanti** (tel. 31-911). La Quercia is the seat of the Basilica of the Madonna of Quercia, with its cloister by Bernini, its bell tower of Sangallo, and its ceramic portal by Della Robbia. Commanding a view of an Etruscan burial ground, the dining room does not disappoint those seeking good quality Italian fare. Specialties include fettuccine allo stennarello, ravioli di ricotta e spinaci all'etrusca, plus vitella (veal) alla montanara, as well as a fabulous array of fruit and vegetables. The wine is from Orvieto. Expect to pay 8,500 lire ($9.86) for a complete meal. Closed Tuesdays.

MANZÙ: The **Collection of the Friends of Manzù** is housed in a simple but effective museum in the village of **Ardea.** A short drive through the pine and eucalyptus-studded countryside outside Rome, it is a unique tribute to a living artist by his friends. Giacomo Manzù, who lives in a nearby villa, is a remarkable sculptor, strongly influenced by the 15th-century works of Donatello and Rosso. His combination of classicism and individuality are especially apparent in his ecclesiastical figures. His portraits of his friend Pope John XXIII (they both came from Bergamo), and especially the huge bronze sculpture of "Il Grande Cardinale," demonstrate this. Several sculptures are portraits of Manzù's wife, Inge, and his children. Look for the oversized pram with the likenesses of the children atop it. Also on display are articles of jewelry created by Manzù during the past 30 years.

FIUGGI FONTE: Beautiful landscapes and healthy mountain air have combined with "the waters" to make this resort renowned for its curative powers since the 13th century. Michelangelo, his neck strained from painting the Sistine Chapel, went here for the cure, a fact commemorated by a hotel named after him. The resort lies 38 miles south of Rome and can easily be tied in with a sightseeing visit to the previously described Palestrina. The spa is so little known by North Americans that visitors can add it to their list of offbeat European sights.

Accommodations in Fiuggi Fonte

Grand Hotel Vallombrosa & Majestic, 120 Via Vecchia Fiuggi (tel. 55-531), is unknown to many seasoned Italian travelers. It's a hotel spa that is both spacious, airy, and contemporary. Life here moves at a slow pace, the tranquil quality enhanced by trees and gardens. The establishment is just 300 feet from the Spa Baths. Within the hotel itself are generous lounges, a guest tavern, plus a cozy bar and restaurant. In the garden, the heated swimming pool is a further draw. All the well-furnished and comfortable bedrooms contain private baths and air conditioning. For full pension, you pay 20,000 lire ($23.20) per person in May, June, and September, that tariff increasing to 24,000 lire ($29) per person in July and August, service and taxes included.

A Dining Detour

If you're touring through this part of Italy, we'd suggest a detour to **Ferentino** for a meal at **Bassetto,** via Casilina Sud (tel. 394-931). This is the domain of Signor Enrico Concutelli, more popularly known as "Shorty." He became the local celebrity after being featured in an Italian film. He does two fabulous pasta dishes, including maccheroncini Bassetto and fettuccine ciociara. His main-dish delight, however, is pollo (chicken) Sofia. Everything tastes better with his local wine, Colli di Cotannazzo. Expect to pay 6,000 lire ($6.96) for a truly fine repast. The restaurant is open daily. Incidentally, Signor Concutelli will also accommodate you in one of his fine rooms, charging 5,000 lire ($5.80) in a single, 10,000 lire ($11.60) in a double. One reason for staying over is to do some exploring in this Latium town, overlooking the Sacco Valley. You can see the imposing Acropolis there, attributed to Alexandrine workers; visit an ancient Roman theater and view the church of Santa Maria Maggiore—a Cistercian structure with Gothic features from the 13th century. Ferentino is 15 miles from Fiuggi.

Chapter IV

HOTELS AND RESTAURANTS OF FLORENCE

WHEN THE LAST RENAISSANCE artist capitulated to the baroque, and pundits began to evaluate the era, the question was asked, "Why was Florence the city chosen for the 'rebirth'?" Some long-forgotten individual emerged with the opinion that the Renaissance didn't choose Florence, but Florence chose the Renaissance as its own bambino.

The Florentines are a unique lot. A Genoese sailor could persuade Isabella to finance his expedition to the Americas, but it took a Florentine by the name of Amerigo Vespucci to get the country named after himself. The Florentines are the champions of the vigorous life. To adapt another saying, they believe in taking the dilemma by the horns. Thus, the Florentine, Dante, wrote the *Divine Comedy* in the vernacular—and not only persuaded his readers to accept such a "vulgar" work, but helped make the Tuscan dialect and language *the* tongue of Italy.

To appreciate Florence, to understand its treasures, we need to know something, however meager, of the boldness and tenacity of its people. So we'll check into our hotel first, look over the city's restaurants, and then, in the following chapter, set out on our task.

Note: In Florence, Alitalia has offices at 10/12 Lungarno Acciaioli and 1 Piazzetta dell'Oro (tel. 263-051).

THE HOTEL SITUATION: Florence was always a leader in architecture. Consequently, with the decline and fall of the great aristocratic families of Tuscany, many of the city's grand old villas and palaces have been converted into hotels. For sheer charm and surprising luxury, the hotels of Florence are among the finest in Europe. There are not too many tourist cities where you can find a 15th- or 16th-century palace—tastefully decorated and most comfortable—rated as a second-class pension. Florence is well equipped with hotels —in virtually all price ranges and of widely varying standards, comfort, service, and efficiency. Our recommendation in every major government classification follows, beginning with:

1. Deluxe Hotels

The **Hotel Excelsior Italie,** 3 Piazza Ognissanti (tel. 294-301), is the glamour queen on the Arno, a center of total luxury. It offers a broad assortment of facilities and a time-tested and sharpened service, which has won world-wide acclaim for it.

Totally revamped, the hotel offers the well-known Donatello Bar, patronized by the high-fashion people of Florence, and a terrace from which you'll have a view of the Arno. Its public rooms have grandeur, but in a quiet, low key. All of the sumptuous double rooms contain private baths, as do most of the singles, but each bedroom varies in style and ornamentation.

Singles range from 27,000 lire ($31.32) to 36,000 lire ($41.76); doubles, 42,000 lire ($54.52) to 54,000 lire ($62.64). In high season, lunch and dinner are served on the roof, which offers a view of the Arno and most of Florence.

Villa La Massa, 8 Via La Massa (tel. 630-051), lies on the outskirts of Florence at Candeli, about a 10-minute drive from the city, a distance of four miles from the railway station. In its special classification, the villa—the 15th-century home of the Count Giraldi family—is a preferred choice for those who don't mind the trek (its location is far favored in summer).

One of the loveliest spots in all the hill country, the villa is on a projection of parkland that has the Arno snaking around on three sides. All the spacious drawing rooms, private library, and dining salons open onto a central covered courtyard-lounge, with a surrounding arched passageway. The bedrooms on the floor above open onto this courtyard, or onto the river and gardens. Top-level taste has been summoned up in converting the villa into a hotel, now containing 44 rooms—all with private bath, some with air conditioning. A single with bath rents for 18,000 lire ($20.88), a double for 32,000 lire ($37.12). Rates are inclusive, except for the I.V.A. tax. For demi-pension, the charge is 26,000 lire ($30.16) per person. Off season, November 1 to March 14, rates are reduced.

The rooms, both public and private, are lavishly furnished with excellent antiques or fine reproductions. The furnishings couldn't be more appropriate: gilt and red velvet armchairs, old-gold velvet sofas, Oriental carpets, tiled floors, gilt chairs. The glittery bar was once an altar, and the Corinthian-columned dining room is formal, with a vaulted ceiling and a stone fireplace— ideal for baronial meals at 8,500 lire ($9.86).

In addition, you'll find a sun terrace and a small swimming pool, along with flowers and shade trees. But that isn't all: there's another building, near the riverside, where dining is accompanied by excellent dance music. A Cellar (Club La Cave) offers an American-style bar and occasional entertainment. A hotel bus transports visitors into the city.

Villa Park San Domenico, 55 Via della Piazzola (tel. 576-697), provides a fortunate opportunity to live in the grand style, in one of the finest old villas in Florence. It lies in the hills, yet within the city limits, a taxi ride from the center. Surrounded by elaborately formal terraced gardens, the villa is set in a 10-acre park, the largest privately owned one in Florence. Many people come here for dining (see our restaurant recommendations).

The villa is steeped in history, dating from 1350. The family who created it founded La Scala Opera in Milan. Once it was used exclusively by titled families, but now public guests can enjoy one of the few bedrooms, each impressive (and containing private baths and telephones). The bed-and-breakfast rate in a single is 16,000 lire ($18.56), 27,800 lire ($32.35) for a double. A single party pays 21,800 lire ($25.29) for demi-pension; two persons, 39,400 lire ($45.70). Rates include taxes and service. You may fall heir for the night to a room of lush antiques, including a princely fourposter. Rare carpets, aged furniture, and unmarred architectural beauty predominate. Guests have the use of the drawing room, with its coved ceiling, baronial furnishings, and concert grand piano. There's even a fascinating "winter bar," with antiques and more contemporary frescoes. Note the confessional booth in the reception lounge, which has been converted into a telephone booth.

2. First-Class Hotels

NEAR PIAZZALE MICHELANGELO: Grand Hotel Villa Cora, 18-20 Viale Machiavelli (tel. 228-451), is a grandiose, Renaissance, neo-classic palace on the hill near Michelangelo Square above the city. Built by the Napoleons and once lived in by the Italian ambassador to the U.S., the luxury hotel stands in its own formal gardens, with a special recreation area, including an open-air swimming pool. The public rooms have architectural splendor, with the drawing rooms opening off the domed circular rotunda. Marble, ornate bronze, white and gilt doors, frescoed ceilings, parquet floors, and silk damask walls characterize the decor. Some of the bedrooms—the more expensive ones—are one of a kind, although the others are well furnished with tasteful reproductions of the 19th-century pieces. All are air-conditioned with "frigo-bars." Singles rent for 15,000 lire ($17.40); doubles, 27,000 lire ($31.32). In the lower-level restaurant, Taverna Machiavelli, you can enjoy truly fine food. From the rooftop solarium, a panoramic view of the rooftops of Florence unfolds.

NEAR THE RAILWAY STATION: Hotel Kraft, 2 Via Solferino (tel. 284-273), was created by the son of one of Italy's greatest hotel men (the father, Herman Kraft, of Berne, Switzerland, sparked the fabulous Excelsior in the 19th century). The present-day Kraft is far removed from the baroque—rather, it meets the requirements of today quite beautifully. It's at the side of a quiet square, close by the railroad station and almost next to the Arno and the American Consulate. Fine antiques or reproductions are used in the lovely and comfortable bedrooms. Many have little terraces, perfect for morning coffee, and all have streamlined bathrooms. A single with bath costs an inclusive 16,500 lire ($19.14); two persons pay 27,000 lire ($31.32), including taxes, air conditioning, and service. The full-pension rate is 23,000 lire ($26.68) per person. The Kraft is crowned on top with a dining room—worthy of gourmets—opening onto a covered terrace. Several terraces higher is an open-air swimming pool. Imagine swimming with a view of the Duomo, the Piazzale Michelangelo, and Fiesole. Being so near the Opera House, the Kraft is popular with maestros and singing stars.

Aerhotel Baglioni, 6 Piazza Unità Italiana (tel. 218-441), formerly known as the Baglioni Palace, for years was a landmark hotel near the railway station. It is now owned by Aerhotel, a new chain jointly created by Alitalia and S.M.E., one of the major Italian financial holdings, partly owned by the government. Completely renovated, the first-class hotel offers a total of 220 accommodations, all with private bath and air conditioning, plus radio and television. In high season, a single rents for 20,000 lire ($23.20); a double for 32,000 lire ($37.12). However, in the off season, the tariff drops to only 15,000 lire ($17.40) in a single; 23,500 lire ($27.26) in a double. Candlelight meals, and good ones at that, are served on the panoramic roof garden of the hotel. A set luncheon or dinner costs about 6,000 lire ($6.96). The period furnishings and the excellent standard of service make this hotel one of the leaders in Florence. The new Melarancio Restaurant is ideal for quick breakfasts, business lunches, even late-night snacks.

Grand Hotel Minerva, 16 Piazza S. Maria Novella (tel. 284-555), is one of the most streamlined choices near the railway station. Its 108 rooms all have private bath or shower, and the hotel is air-conditioned. The bedrooms themselves are pleasantly furnished with modern pieces. A single room with bath or shower rents for 18,000 lire ($20.88) to 22,000 lire ($25.52); a double for 27,000 lire ($31.32) to 39,700 lire ($46.05). Half pension is 10,000 lire ($11.60) per person in addition to the room rate. The most popular feature of the Minerva is its rooftop swimming pool, a choice spot considering the view of the city. The hotel is well protected against noise, billing itself as "the really quietest hotel of the town."

Hotel Astoria, 9 Via del Giglio (tel. 298-095), is blessed with a magnificent structure. Its interior evokes days of grand living—high baroque ceilings, ornate doorways, and overscaled paintings. But the furnishings themselves are fairly modern. The bedrooms are spacious enough, nicely decked out with matching pieces in the traditional Italian manner. All of the 90 rooms have private baths and air conditioning. For room and breakfast, singles pay 23,000 lire ($26.68); doubles, 35,000 lire ($40.60). Rates are inclusive. The dining room is informal, with a glassed-in portion, opening onto a garden. There is also a grill-room restaurant, offering à la carte selections, and a snack bar.

NEAR CASCINE PARK: Anglo-American Hotel, 9 Via Garibaldi (tel. 282-114), occupies an old Florentine palace. Its streetside buildings enclose a covered garden room, lounge, and loggia—spring-like the year around. The older parts of the hostelry have exquisite architectural features, as does the dining room, with its ornate plaster designs on the wall—cameolike in pink, red, and white. Crystal chandeliers and towering gilt mirrors grace the public salons. The bedrooms continue the same good taste level, combining fine old pieces with serviceable modern. All rooms have a private bath or shower and air conditioning. A single with bath costs 22,000 lire ($25.52), increasing to 35,000 lire ($40.60) in a double, taxes, service, air conditioning, and continental breakfasts included. The half-pension rate in a single is 27,000 lire ($31.32), rising to 45,000 lire ($52.20) for two in a double. A special winter plan of reduced tariffs is in effect from November 1 to March 15. The hotel is well placed near the Arno, close to the Opera House and the United States Consulate. A garage for your car is available nearby.

OFF THE VIA TORNABUONI: Hotel de la Ville, 1 Piazza Antinori (tel. 261-805), stands about three short blocks from the Arno and American Express. It has a glittering and luxurious appearance as you enter (with flowering plants, Venetian sconces, mirror-bright marble floors). The autumnal-colored chairs make the lounge most appealing. Three elevators whiz visitors to the revamped bedrooms; most accommodations have private entryways with luggage racks; beds have ultra-convenient side tables with gadgets for summoning the maid; the modern baths have new-fangled water faucets, laundry bags for overnight washing service, and plenty of light. Singles pay 17,700 lire ($20.53) for a room with bath; couples are charged 31,300 lire ($46.31) for the standard room with bath. No pension terms are offered, though you pay 1,800 lire ($2.09) for breakfast. On the premises are a grill room and restaurant, an American bar, and a garage.

A FORMER CONVENT AT FIESOLE: Villa S. Michele, 4 Via Doccia (tel. 59-451). The setting is memorable, even breathtaking. On a hill just below Fiesole, the former 15th-century monastery, complete with gardens, was built on a wide ledge. After being damaged in World War II, the villa was carefully restored. It is said that the design of the facade and the loggia was based on sketches by Michelangelo. A curving driveway, lined with blossoming trees and flowers, leads to the entrance.

A 10 arch-covered loggia continues around the view side of the building to the Italian gardens at the rear. On the loggia, elegant chairs are set out for drinks and moonlight dinners. Most of the bedrooms open onto the panoramic view, or the inner courtyard. Each room is unique, some with iron or wooden canopy beds, antique chests, Savonarola chairs, formal draperies, old ecclesiastical paintings, candelabra, and statues. In other words, a stunning tour de force of rich, but restrained design. Poets and artists have stayed at San Michele, singing its praise. Open from March 20 to November 1, the hotel charges 32,800 lire ($38.05) in a single with bath, 51,800 lire ($60.09) for half pension. A double with bath is 48,300 lire ($56.03), based on double occupancy. The half-pension rate is 43,000 lire ($49.88) per person.

ON THE ARNO: Hotel Principe, 34 Lungarno Vespucci (tel. 284-848), is a real "find." Its facade is dignified, like an old embassy town house, and its 22 bedrooms have been well adapted. Each bedroom is treated differently, reflecting the high taste level of owner-director Prof. Bronzi, who blends antique and modern. Every room has a private bath—the original mammoth marble ones retained on the lower two floors. Ask for one of the terrace rooms, where tables and chairs are set out for breakfast fronting the Arno. Double glass doors protect the bedrooms from street noises. There is central air conditioning. Singles with bath rent for an inclusive 15,000 lire ($17.40), and doubles cost 27,000 lire ($31.32). Finally, one of the nicest features of the hotel is its little walled garden in back where drinks are served.

3. The Medium-Priced Range

NEAR THE PONTE VECCHIO: Hotel Continental, 2 Lungarno Acciaiuoli (tel. 282-392), occupies some choice real estate, right at the entrance to the Arno-spanning Ponte Vecchio. Through the lounge windows and from some of the bedrooms, you can see the little jewelry and leather shops flanking the much-painted bridge. Despite its perch in the center of historic Florence, the hotel cut its teeth in the 60s, so its style of accommodation is most utilitarian, with functional modern furniture, softened by the placement of decorative accessories. You reach your bedroom either by the elevator, or by climbing a wooden staircase (note that parts of the old stone structure have been retained). The air-conditioned bedrooms are furnished with Italian provincial pieces, color coordinated. The management likes to put up Americans, knowing they'll be attracted to the dramatic roof terrace, a vantage point for viewing the Piazzale Michelangelo, the Pitti Palace, the Duomo, the Campanile, Fiesole. Artists fight to get the tiny simple room up in the tower ("Torre Guelfa dei Consorti"). All the 62 bedrooms have private baths or showers. The rate is 7,400 lire ($8.58) in a bathless single. In the bedrooms with bath or shower, singles pay 11,650 lire ($13.51); couples, 22,200 lire ($25.75). No pension terms are offered, but a continental breakfast is available for an additional 1,250 lire ($1.45).

Lungarno, 14 Borgo San Jacopo (tel. 260-397). As you stand on the banks of the Arno, looking at the facade of the 10 floors of the hotel, you find it difficult to believe it was built entirely after the flood. It's proof that an exciting modern and comfortable hotel can be created in the old style, without sacrificing conveniences of the 20th century. Imagine sitting in a stone-built tower suite, enjoying a room-long view through a picture window of the rooftops of Florence, including the Duomo and Campanile. Throughout the hotel is a collection of contemporary water colors and oils. Around the fireplace is a "clutter wall" of framed art. On sunny days, guests congregate on the upper terrace, enjoying drinks and a view of the bridges spanning the Arno. The bedrooms are consistently well designed and attractive, each having its own color theme. For the average accommodations, including service, taxes, and air conditioning, the rate in a single with shower is 15,000 lire ($17.40), 26,100 lire ($30.28) in a double with bath.

Augustus e dei Congressi, Piazzetta dell'Oro (tel. 283-054), is for those who require modern comforts in a setting of historical and monumental Florence. The Ponte Vecchio is just a short stroll away, as is the Uffizi Gallery. The exterior is rather pillbox modern, but the interior seems light, bright, and comfortable. The expansive lounge and drinking area is like an illuminated cave, with a curving ceiling and built-in conversational areas interlocked on several levels. Forest green couches, white stucco room dividers, and lemon-yellow decorative accents form an inviting backdrop. Some of the bedrooms have forsythia-yellow color accents, and they open onto little private balconies with white garden furniture. Single rooms with shower rent for 20,000 lire ($23.20); doubles with private bath or 34,400 lire ($39.90), with an extra sitting room going for anywhere from 10,000 lire ($11.60) to 13,000 lire ($15.08). Included are air conditioning, service, and taxes.

OFF THE PIAZZA DELLA SIGNORIA: Grand Hotel Cavour, 3 Via del Proconsolo (tel. 287-102), opposite the Bargello museum, is an elaborate palace, built originally in the 13th century. In a convenient position, the Cavour maintains its architectural splendor—but not in its furnishings. The coved main lounge, with its frescoed ceiling and crystal chandelier, is of special interest, as is the old chapel, which is now used as a dining room. The altar and confessional are still there. The ornate ceiling and stained-glass windows reflect superb craftsmanship. An elevator has been installed, as well as central heating. Many of the simply furnished bedrooms have private baths, and all have hot and cold running water. Singles pay 7,500 lire ($8.70) for a bathless room; couples, 11,000 lire ($12.76). In rooms with bath singles are charged 9,500 lire ($11.02); couples, 16,000 lire ($18.56). The half-pension rate ranges from 12,000 lire ($13.92) to 16,000 lire ($18.56), depending on the kind of room you occupy.

AT THE PIAZZA S. MARIA NOVELLA: Pietrobelli Hotel Roma, 8 Piazza S. Maria Novella (tel. 270-366), is a holdout for the old-fashioned style of living.

A long-popular, family-run hotel, the Roma stands on the famous Florentine square, near the railway station. Known for its kitchen and wine cellar, the hotel receives guests in its 60 bedrooms, half of which have private baths. Public rooms are fitted with pilasters, paneled walls, pillars, and parquet floors. Most of the bedrooms have furnishings evoking the turn of the century in decor; and the rooms are spacious, with high mahogany beds covered by soft downy coverlets. Bathless singles go for 6,800 lire ($7.89); with bath, 10,000 lire ($11.60). Bathless doubles rent for 12,000 lire ($13.92); with bath, 18,000 lire ($20.88). A continental breakfast is extra.

4. The Budget Range

ON THE ARNO: Hotel Columbus, 22a Lungarno Cristoforo Colombo (tel. 677-251), is a modern hotel, built and furnished with good taste, offering 101 rooms with bath or shower, and private balcony. Though it's set quite a way off from the city's major attractions, it is still within walking distance of the Ponte Vecchio. The air-conditioned public rooms, with light-inviting windows, have pleasant, informal furnishings. The dining room has round tables, with ladder-backed chairs, potted greenery, and a sense of space. Each of the bedrooms is compact, in the motel fashion, with everything built in: bedside table, lights, and all. There's no fussy decor—severe but restful. Singles are charged 11,400 lire ($13.22) in rooms with private baths; doubles, 18,800 lire ($21.81) with private bath. The half-pension rate is 15,900 lire ($18.44) per person in high season. Taxes and service are included. You'll be assessed 1,300 lire ($1.51) extra for air conditioning.

ON THE OUTSKIRTS: Villa Belvedere, 3 Via Benedetto Castelli (tel. 222-501). Found on the edge of Florence, about a seven-minute drive from the center, the villa grounds once belonged to the Medici, though the present building is a reconstruction. It's suitable for those wanting the quiet of the country at night, gardens for sunbathing, a swimming pool for quick dips, and a tennis court for exercise. The 27 rooms, with private baths and air conditioning, are efficient—well-planned, though the modern decor is a bit spartan. The villa is closed in December, January, and February. In high season, April to October, it requires demi pension (the food is first rate). Singles pay 16,000 lire ($18.56) for a room and breakfast. Doubles are charged from 27,000 lire ($31.32) to 30,000 lire ($34.80) for a room and breakfast. *Note:* some doubles have a veranda with a panoramic view of Florence. The use of the swimming pool, tennis court, and garage parking is free, and the I.V.A. tax is included in the tariffs. The villa lies on the Siena-Roma road (take bus 11 or 37; the stop is Poggio Imperiale).

OFF THE PIAZZA D'AZEGLIO: Umbria Hotel, 3 Piazza d'Azeglio (tel. 587-655), lies a bit apart from the shopping and sightseeing center of Florence, but has its own garden, across from a park. Lodging here is quiet and restful. A well-built, old-styled villa, the Umbria offers tasteful, pleasant bedrooms. The rooms opening onto the garden have arched windows, coordinated fabrics, and swan-slatted headboards. All of the accommodations have up-to-date bathrooms. For air-conditioned rooms with showers and radios, singles pay 17,000 lire ($19.72); couples, 29,500 lire ($34.20), including breakfast. I.V.A. is extra. There are three dining rooms—the smaller and cozier one paneled in mahogany; and another, a newer addition, has a slanted beamed ceiling, with rush-seated chairs overlooking the garden. At the rear of the hotel is parking space. If you're going to Rome, you'll find the Umbria's well-run sister, the Lord Byron.

AT THE PIAZZA DELLA SS. ANNUNZIATA: Hotel Morandi, 3 Piazza della SS. Annunziata (tel. 212-687), is sheltered in a former Renaissance monastery on one of the most exciting old squares of Florence. Imagine waking up every morning and looking out your window at the Foundling Hospital with Andrea della Robbia's terra-cotta medallions of the swaddling babies in the cortile over Brunelleschi's loggia (the first building of the Florentine Renaissance). Across the way is the Church of the Annunciation, baroqued up to its seven-year-old molars (Florentine brides come here with their bouquets of white roses, which they then place on the chandelier-draped altar to the Madonna). The hotel itself is dated, so don't arrive expecting streamlined modern. An English lady, known to most of her guests as Kathleen Doyle (though she's married to an Italian, Signor Antuono), runs things very well, aided by her children. She studied the classics at a nearby university, and is an expert in Latin. The bedrooms of her rambling, roomy hotel are furnished in a plain way, with blonde woods, severe lines—but plenty of comfort and cleanliness. The bed-and-breakfast rate ranges from 4,000 lire ($4.64) to 6,000 lire ($6.96) per person per day, depending on whether you occupy a single or double room, with or without bath. The I.V.A. tax is additional. The Morandi does not provide meals, but there are many good and inexpensive restaurants in the neighborhood. Even the rear rooms have their own view, overlooking the Art Academy gardens, where students make sculpture molds under the trees.

OFF THE PIAZZA D'AZEGLIO: Hotel Liana, 18 Via Vittorio Alfieri (tel. 587-608), was the English Embassy between 1864 and 1870, a gracious villa opening onto a tree-shaded rear garden, with gravel walks set among flowerbeds. Most of the bedrooms are nicely furnished, with good beds and a few antiques. Half of the 22 rooms have private baths and telephones. Bathless singles go for 5,900 lire ($6.84). Doubles cost anywhere from 10,200 lire ($11.83) for a bathless room to 13,500 lire ($15.66) for a room with bath. Rates are inclusive, except for an 800-lire (93¢) supplement for use of the public baths. The central hallway is impressive, with an arched ceiling and columns, opening onto the garden. Generally, the lounges seem to have comfy pieces left over from the days when Britannia ruled the waves. To reach this third-class-rated hotel, take bus 6.

NEAR THE RAILWAY STATION: Villa Azalee, 44 Viale Fratelli Rosselli (tel. 260-353), is a remake of a gracious 19th-century corner villa, with a big garden. This small hotel is run by Roberto Bellini and his American wife. They have provided a personal touch in both atmosphere and decor. The decorating is good: tall, white-paneled doors with ornate brass fittings, parquet floors, crystal chandeliers, and good antiques intermix with credible reproductions. The lounge is as in a private home, and the bedrooms have distinction (one, in particular, boasts a flouncy canopy bed). With a private bath, plus a continental breakfast, doubles rent for 19,000 lire ($22.04); singles, 7,550 lire ($8.99). Service is included but tax is extra. Air conditioning is also available at a cost of 1,300 lire ($1.51) per person daily.

Aprile, 6 Via della Scala (tel. 216-237), is a 15th-century Medici palace (Palazzo del Borgo), recently renovated for guests. You'll be given an enthusiastic reception by the youthful owner, Riccardo Zucconi, a sort of Italian Alain Delon. He has created a sophisticated setting, using excellent furnishings to complement the lines of the traditional architecture. He's even installed an elevator to take guests to their bedrooms. These private rooms—with stylish old and contemporary pieces—have a personal touch that is reflected everywhere. All rooms have telephones. The charge for room and continental breakfast is 6,250 lire ($7.25) per person in a bathless single; 6,900 lire ($8) per person in a room with bath or shower. The I.V.A. tax is extra.

Martelli, 8 Via Panzani (tel. 217-151), is near the railway station, yet most of its accommodations are quiet, as the majority of them overlook the interior courtyard. Much of the original architectural glory of this converted Medici palace remains, as reflected by the frescoed ceilings and crystal chandeliers. Many of the bedrooms have been glamorously furnished, though others are modest by comparison. Bathrooms have been installed, and, in some cases, air conditioning. The owner-manager, Signor Croce, has promised on a "stack of Da Vinci's" to give a 10% reduction to readers who show a copy of this guide. For half pension in season, the rate is 15,000 lire ($17.40) per person. Bed and breakfast is 10,000 lire ($11.60) per person. Meals are provided in the formal dining room, with its coved ceiling, fireplace, and high-backed chairs.

Locanda Tony's Inn, 77 Via Faenza (tel. 217-975), is a romance story. A young Canadian girl, Rosemarie, not only fell in love with the museums and churches of Florence, but also a handsome Florentine, Antonio Lelli. They were married. Hard work and good fortune combined to allow them to acquire a small, but modern, second-floor *locanda* (in this case an apartment rooming house). The accommodations are large, with hot and cold running water, adequate bathroom facilities, plus tasteful furniture that creates a pleasing and comfortable atmosphere. Prices are reasonable: 8,000 lire ($9.28) for a double, 10,800 lire ($12.53) in a triple. Scott and Demaris Somers, Cleveland Heights, Ohio, have already tried it out. They write, "Our best stay in Europe."

OFF THE PIAZZA DELL'INDIPENDENZA: **Rapallo,** 7 Via Santa Caterina d'Alessandria (tel. 472-412), gets an "A" for effort, as all its rooms have indications of attempts to make them liveable and comfortable. Without succeeding in being typical of Florence, it is, nevertheless, newish (completely revamped), fresh, and inviting. The lounge, ingeniously using small space, is brightened by planters, Oriental rugs, and crude barrel stools set in the corners for drinking and conversation. The bedrooms—31 in all, some with private bath—are furnished mostly with blonde-wood suites, quite pleasant. The twin-bedded rooms have end-to-end beds, as in Scandinavia. A bathless single goes for an inclusive 7,000 lire ($8.12); bathless doubles for 11,000 lire ($12.76). The rooms with bath rent for 8,500 lire ($9.86) for singles; 14,000 lire ($16.24) for couples. The full-pension rate ranges from 14,500 lire ($16.82) to 16,000 lire ($18.56) per person. The I.V.A. tax is added to the bill. The hotel is easy to find, at the far corner of the Piazza del'Indipendenza.

5. The Pick of the Pensions

NEAR THE DUOMO: **Pensione Monna Lisa** (yes, that's the right spelling), 27 Borgo Pinti (tel. 296-213), is a privately owned Renaissance palazzo, astonishingly well preserved. On a narrow street, where carts once were driven, the palace facade is forebodingly severe, in keeping with the style of its day. But when one enters the reception rooms, the atmosphere is most inviting. Most of the great old rooms overlook either an inner patio, or the garden in the rear. Each of the salons is handsomely furnished in a restrained way, utilizing many fine antiques and oil paintings. The gracious owner, Countess N.D. Oslavia Ciardi-Dupré, will welcome you. The bedrooms vary greatly, but all have private baths. Everywhere is a stamp of individuality and good taste. The ideal way to stay here is to take demi-pension arrangement (continental breakfast and one main meal). Depending on the plumbing, the half-board rate in a single is 14,900 lire ($17.28). Singles are available only in the off season. In a double, the half-pension charge is 13,800 lire ($16.01) per person, plus I.V.A. tax. You dine here on high-backed, leather-tooled chairs, in the best Florentine style, and the food is, of course, home prepared. No long menu—just simply delicious fare. The idea that you're entering a Renaissance museum is quickly dispelled when you meet the unsinkable manager, Lallo Batacchi, who is seen after 6 p.m. at the Two Roses Bar, mixing some of the best martinis in Florence. The multi-lingual free-wheeling and witty gentleman was a former cruise director on the Italian liner *Michelangelo.*

AT COLONNATA DI SESTO FIORENTINO: Villa Villoresi, 63 Via delle Torri (tel 448-9032), is five miles from the heart of Florence and about two miles from exit 19 on the Autostrada del Sole. The 12th-century villa, surrounded by flowers and gardens, is managed by a charming young Contessina, Cristina Villoresi de Loche. Across the front of the villa is a long Tuscan loggia, with garden chairs set out for guests, overlooking the swimming pool below. The inner gallery, which must be nearly 125 feet long, is furnished with family antiques and paintings—set against five wall murals. Most of the lovely old rooms, such as the reading salon, have fine furnishings. The high-ceilinged and beamed dining hall is a good background for the appetizing and pleasing meals served. Many of the well-furnished bedrooms—with private bath—open onto an inner courtyard, with fruit trees and flowering plants. On a second—or even a first!—honeymoon, ask for the *camera matrimoniale,* an overscaled bedroom, grandly furnished, opening onto the loggia. A single room with bath goes for 12,500 lire ($14.50); a double with bath costs 22,000 lire ($25.52). Tariffs include service, taxes, and I.V.A. The recommended pension rate ranges from 24,000 lire ($27.84) to 28,000 lire ($32.48).

NEAR AMERICAN EXPRESS: Tornabuoni Beacci, 3 Via Tornabuoni (tel. 272-645), is on the principal shopping street of Florence. Near the Arno and the Piazza S. Trinità, the pension occupies the three top floors of a 14th-century palazzo. All its living rooms have been furnished in a tatty provincial style, with bowls of flowers, parquet floors, a formal fireplace, old paintings, murals, and tasteful rugs. The decades have brought wear and tear, but there is an air of gentility. The roof terrace, surrounded by potted plants and flowers, is for late-afternoon drinks. The view of the nearby churches, towers, and rooftops is worth experiencing. A great deal of the continued popularity of the pension is due to its attractive owner, Signora Lensi-Orlandi-Beacci, who knows how to "mix" her guests. Her guest books are numerous, including in days of yore many famous personalities such as John Steinbeck, the Gish sisters, and Frederic March. The bedrooms themselves are only moderately well furnished. Every room of the first-class pension has hot and cold running water, and a number have private baths, some not in the best of shape. The demi-pension rate ranges from 12,250 lire ($14.21) to 17,250 lire ($20.01) per person—according to plumbing assignment—including I.V.A. tax, service, and heating. Good value—and there's an elevator and air conditioning.

La Residenza, 8 Via Tornabuoni (tel. 284-197), lies right in the hub of Florence, on an elegant shopping street of fashion houses, boutiques, and palaces. It occupies the top floors of a Renaissance building, just a few blocks from American Express and the Arno, right next door to the Palazzo Strozzi. The pension offers freshness, comfort, and style. Antiques are extensively used. The rooms on the top floor are the newest (and the best), with reproductions, color-coordinated pieces, and many private balconies. You can have morning coffee here, enjoying the wisteria, pots of flowering plants, and especially the view. Demi pension is offered for 10,000 lire ($11.60) per person in a bathless room, 12,000 lire ($13.92) per person in a room with bath. The I.V.A. tax is additional.

NEAR THE PONTE VECCHIO: Pension Hermitage, 1 Vicolo Marzio (tel. 287-216), is offbeat and intimate, a charming place to stay right at the Ponte Vecchio, on the Arno, with a sun terrace on the roof, providing a view of much of Florence, including the nearby Uffizi. Here you can take your breakfast under a leafy arbor, surrounded by potted roses and geraniums. The success of the pension spins around its English-speaking owner, Rina Migliorini, one of the loveliest women in Florence. She is assisted by Anna Consigli, a gentle-speaking American from the South. The owner has made the Hermitage an extension of her home, furnishing it with antiques and well-chosen reproductions. Best of all is her warmth with her guests, many of whom keep coming back, enjoying the gatherings in the top-floor living room, where they sit around the woodburning fireplace on nippy nights. The bedrooms are pleasantly furnished, many with Tuscan antiques, rich brocades, and soft beds. The baths are superb; tiled and containing lots of gadgets. Demi-pension rates in a single are 15,500 lire ($17.98) with bath. Depending on the plumbing, demi-pension for two people costs from 24,000 lire ($27.84) to 28,000 lire ($32.48). The food served in a dignified, beam-ceilinged dining room is quite good.

ON THE LEFT BANK: Pensione Annalena, 34 Via Romana (tel. 222-403), in existence since the 15th century, has gone through many owners, including the Medici. Once a convent, it has, in the past three-quarters of a century, been a haven for artists, poets, sculptors, and writers (Mary McCarthy once wrote of its importance as a cultural center). During a great deal of that period, it was the domain of the late sculptor, Olinto Calastri (his works are placed throughout the palazzo). Now his widow, the gracious and unforgettable Signora Calastri, still accepts paying guests who are sympathetic to the special qualities of Annalena. Most of the drawing rooms, bedrooms, and the dining room overlook the rear gardens—possibly the largest of any private palazzo in Florence. Every lovely old room, every piece of furniture is indelibly interlocked with the past. Each antique has its own life, its own story. For rooms with breakfast, singles pay from 5,600 lire ($6.50) to 6,800 lire ($7.89); doubles from 10,600 lire ($12.30) to 12,500 lire ($14.50). The more expensive tariffs include accommodations with private baths. Service and taxes are included. During the war, the Annalena was the center of much underground work, as many Jews and rebel Italians found safety hidden away in an underground room behind a secret door. The pension lies about a three-minute walk from the Pitti Palace, five from the Ponte Vecchio.

Pensione "Adria," 4 Piazza Frescobaldi (tel. 215-029), provides economy living, right on the Arno, close to the Ponte Trinità, where Dante is said to have seen Beatrice. An eccentric elevator will deliver you to the top floor, where respectable bedrooms at moderate tariffs are to be found. Your hosts are an ingratiating couple, Mr. and Mrs. Zucconi. In season, demi pension is required, and that ranges in price from 8,500 lire ($9.86) to 9,800 lire ($11.37) per person. The special feature of the Adria is its dual-purpose lounge and dining room, complete with "wide-screen" picture window. While downing your pasta, you can enjoy one of the most cherished views in all of Florence, from the far side of the Arno.

A FAMILY VILLA AT FIESOLE: Pensione "Bencista," 4 Via B. da Maiano (tel. 59-163), has been the family villa of Paolo Simoni for years. After his father's death, he opened it to paying guests. Its position, high up on the road to Fiesole, is commanding, with an unmarred view of the city and the hillside villas. A 10-minute ride from the heart of Florence, it is reached by bus 7 from the station, the Piazza Duomo, and the Piazza San Marco. The driveway to the formal entrance, with its circular fountain, winds through olive trees. The widely spread out villa has many lofty old rooms—unspoiled and furnished with family antiques. Bedrooms vary in size and interest, some having private bath, but most with hot and cold running water only. Full pension is from 13,000 lire ($15.08) without bath, to 16,000 lire ($18.56) per person with bath. Guests meet each other in the evenings in front of a huge fireplace. The Bencista is suitable for families who might want to leave their children in the country while taking jaunts into the city. The family-style meals emerge from the vast old kitchen.

LESS EXPENSIVE PENSIONS: Near Piazza S. Marco: Pensione Cellai, 14 Via XXVII Aprile (tel. 475-088), is an attractive, fresh, and comfortable place at which to stay. As you walk up its steps, you'll enjoy the pots of greens and flowers on the landing. The furnishings are Nordic styled, all done in warm colors. The surprise is the top floor, air-conditioned dining room, with a glass wall, pots of bright flowers, and a slanted window. It also has a roof terrace, a pleasant place on which to rest and enjoy a view of the rooftops and towers. The bedrooms are quite fine, with desks, twin beds, end tables, and reading lights. The baths (shower) are small, but efficient. Singles (bathless only) go for 6,500 lire ($7.54). Doubles without bath rent for 10,500 lire ($12.18); with bath for 12,500 lire ($14.50), inclusive. Half pension ranges from 8,000 lire ($9.28) to 10,000 lire ($11.60) per person. The Cellai lies about five minutes from the railway station, near the Academy Gallery, with Michelangelo's David.

Near the Duomo: Il Magnifico, 7 Via Ginori (tel. 284-840), is perfect for those who enjoy "atmosphere" in a fine establishment, made all the more so by its interesting hostess-owner, Mrs. Tilly Loner. It's a late 17th-century Florentine building—actually an old palace with much hand-carved wood and a frescoed ceiling. The bedrooms vary considerably in size and furnishings. Pot-luck bookings will give you a rather grand room with noteworthy antiques, or a smaller and much more basic room with more modern furnishings. Mrs. Loner, who was born in Luxembourg and has lived in Trieste and Genoa, spends much time with her guests. The rates are 9,500 lire ($11.02) for a double room with bath; 8,000 lire ($9.28) for a double without bath. A single room (bathless) goes for 5,000 lire ($5.80). Rates are inclusive. The location of Il Magnifico is ideal, about 300 feet from the Duomo.

Pensione Pendini, 2 Via Strozzi (tel. 270-712), off the Piazza della Repubblica, was founded in 1879. It's still family owned and run. Nadia Pasi offers a homey environment, in a colorful and distinguished setting of Florence. Your room may overlook the active piazza or front an inner courtyard (more peaceful). The pensione offers 34 rooms, many with private baths or showers. In summer demi pension for one person ranges from 12,500 lire ($14.50) to 18,000 lire ($20.88). Two persons in a double pay from 24,000 lire ($27.84) to 30,000 lire ($34.80) for half board. From November to March, 20% discounts are granted. Typical Tuscan-style meals are provided. The all-purpose lounge is furnished family style, with a piano and card tables. The dining room is pleasantly and modestly provincial, and the bedrooms have a great deal of character, with reproductions of antiques.

Near the Piazza d'Azeglio: Losanna, 9 Via Alfieri (tel. 587-516), is a tiny—only nine rooms—family-run place, off the Viale Antonio Gransci, between the Piazzale Donatello and the Piazza d'Azeglio. It's utter simplicity and cleanliness—a good inexpensive choice—and is owned by Vincenzo Campagna and his wife, Anna Maria. Bus 6 stops a block and a half away (get off at Mattonaia). The bedrooms are homey and well kept. You can stay here and have all your meals for 6,000 lire ($6.96) in a bathless room—a remarkable bargain. Half pension will cost you 5,000 lire ($5.80). For room and breakfast only, the price is 3,500 lire ($4.06). The I.V.A. tax is added. There's free parking on a quiet street.

Near the Opera: Ariele, 11 Via Magenta (tel. 211-509), calls itself "Your Home in Florence." Just a block from the Arno, it's an old corner villa which has been converted into a roomy pension. The building itself is impressive architecturally, with large salons and lofty ceilings. The furnishings, however, combine the antique with the functional. The bedrooms are a grabbag of comfort. There are only two singles, but 12 doubles. All but two of these rooms contain private baths. Depending on the plumbing, singles range from 5,900 lire ($6.84) to 8,100 lire ($9.40); doubles, 12,450 lire ($14.44) to 15,050 lire ($17.46). Mr. and Mrs. Bartelloni, the owners, are enthusiastic about entertaining Americans in their villa, especially those guests who enjoy an old style of living.

Pensione Bretagna, 6 Lungarno Corsini (tel. 263-618), is an annex of the Ariele. Run by the skilled and friendly owner and manager, Carlo Bartelloni, the Bretagna offers only bed and breakfast. Depending on the plumbing, singles go from 5,700 lire ($6.61) to 7,300 lire ($8.47). Doubles begin at 10,850 lire ($12.59), increasing to 13,050 lire ($15.14), the latter with private baths. All rates include taxes, service, and I.V.A. Accommodations are furnished in a basic manner, although the public rooms have touches of gilt and crystal. Off the drawing room, a balcony overlooks the Arno.

Pensione "Cosy Home," 5 Via Solferino (tel. 296-818), is a small, inexpensive place at which to stay, especially popular with older visitors drawn to the friendly atmosphere created by the Gastaldo family. Its location is choice, right off the Arno, around the corner from the Opera House. In fact, many operatic singers have stayed here. The rooms are large enough, with the proper necessities, and they're clean. Bathless singles rent for 3,700 lire ($4.29), increasing to 4,650 lire ($5.40) in a single with bath. Doubles with shower go for 8,350 lire ($9.69). Breakfast is an extra 900 lire ($1.04).

READERS' PENSION SELECTIONS: "Soggiorno Iris, 22 Piazza Santa Maria Novella, third floor (tel. 296-735), surpassed even our fondest hopes. Signor Antonio Campagna, the owner, and his wife Teresa were considerate hosts, even to the point of offering to wash our clothes! I recommend Soggiorno Iris to anyone who wants a neat, simply furnished room. Singles, with breakfast, rent for 3,800 lire ($4.41), increasing to 6,000 lire ($6.96) in a double. Our room was the largest and neatest we encountered in Europe. The owners lived in Australia and speak English. Showers cost 400 lire (46¢) and baths go for 500 lire (58¢).

The Iris is central, only a five-minute walk from the train station, eight minutes from the Duomo, and 10 minutes from the Uffizi Galleries. Our room overlooked the Piazza S. Maria Novella, affording us a nice view of the square" (Donald and Cheryle Davis, Tyler, Texas). . . . "We discovered a gem of an inn, **Locanda Ester**, 6 Via Nazionale, second floor (there is a lift) (tel. 272-741). It is directly opposite Via Fiume, two minutes walk from the railway station. Doubles are 4,500 lire ($5.22), triples 7,000 lire ($8.12). The triple room we had was large, with a balcony to hang out your wash (which the proprietress takes in and folds should it start to rain). The signora woke us up daily by bringing us a tray of steaming, excellent coffee with as many rolls, butter, and jam as we could eat. I felt our things were safe at the Ester. The door was always locked, and only the guests would be admitted. Showers are 500 lire (58¢), and you get a large bath towel" (Mrs. Helen Chadim, Curtin, A.C.T., Australia). . . . "The **Soggiorno Caterina**, 8 Via di Barbano (tel. 483-705), is near the central railroad station. The proprietor, Mr. Afferni, is fluent in English, among other languages, and extraordinarily helpful in every way possible. The pension is spotlessly clean. In a single without bath, the rate is 5,500 lire ($6.38), increasing to 9,500 lire ($11.02) for a double without bath. These tariffs include breakfast, taxes, and service. A deposit is requested for bookings made in advance. Mr. Afferni provides many pleasant, homey touches. Guests are free to do their laundry in their rooms, and he hangs wash out to dry, returning your clothes the next morning. He provides a refrigerator and, besides a good continental breakfast, he often pops in with a cup of espresso or a plate of fruit as an afternoon pick-me-up. Occasional fresh flowers in the rooms are only one of many small touches that make guests feel well cared for and comfortable" (Judith Green, Toronto, Canada). . . . "**Locanda Panichi**, 89 Via Faenza (tel. 272-039), has been completely redone and refurnished. The decor is a cheery orange and white, and the host and hostess could not be nicer. English is spoken fluently. The continental breakfast was the best we had anywhere. A double room with breakfast costs 7,000 lire ($8.12), a double with bath and breakfast, 9,000 lire ($11.02). Multiple accommodations are available at lower student rates, with breakfast. Moreover it is spotless" (Linda Brughelli Bolton, Davis, Calif.).

"The **Soggiorno Erina**, 17 Via Fiume (tel. 284-343), just around the corner from the side exit of the train station, is strongly recommended. We had a large white-painted airy, double with a balcony, for 6,000 lire ($6.96), with free baths and breakfast served in the room" (R.E. Shelgren, Paris, France). . . . "For women traveling, I suggest the most inexpensive, historical, and beautiful place you will find, **Soggiorno Sereno**, 3 Piazza San Domenico, S. Domenico di Fiesole (tel. 59-225). It is the ex-monastery where Beato Angelico lived, and there is even a fresco done by him four centuries ago. It was occupied by Dominican priests until recent years. It is in the residential suburbs of Florence, just 10 minutes from the center. Bus No. 7 stops in front and takes you downtown to the railway station center. The price is 2,000 lire ($2.32) a day. Look for the fountain just across the street, where men such as Leonardo da Vinci, Fra Angelico, Lorenzo il Magnifico, Alexander Dumas, Thomas Gray, and many others have meditated, contemplating the beauty of the area" (Lucia Lozano Loyala, Mexico City, Mexico). . . . "For readers (like us) on a sub-starvation budget, in Florence, within walking distance of the train station is the **Pensione Vienna**, 14 Via XXVII Aprile (tel. 483-256), where two can rent a clean, cozy, and comfortable double room without bath for 4,500 lire ($5.22), increasing to 5,500 lire ($6.38) for a double with bath, inclusive. The Pensione Vienna came as a godsend" (Magnolia Young, San Francisco, Calif.). . . . "High recommendation is rated by **Locanda Castelli**, 25 Borgo SS. Apostoli (tel. 214-213), housed in a beautiful ancient building, with exquisite furniture. We were charged 4,000 lire ($4.64) for a double room, including service and taxes. On each floor was a free bath. No breakfast is served. The inn is run by very kind people" (Dr. Heinz G. Vogelsang, Germany).

"The **Pensione Pitti Palace** is at 2 Via Barbadori, at the foot of the Ponte Vecchio (tel. 282-257). It was 17,500 lire ($20.30) a night for a double without bath, and it is insane to take a room with bath, as the one in the hall is almost always empty, it seems. Request a room away from the street, though, as it is a bit trafficky. Amadeo Pinto, who speaks fluent English, is assisted by his wife, Mary Ann, an American. They are gracious and helpful, distributing maps like crazy and willing to make telephone calls. A good breakfast is served in a cheerful room, and a lovely sitting room is available for guests. In all, there are about 25 rooms" (Pam King, New Haven, Conn.). . . . "I obtained the cheapest room of my European tour at the **Romagna Hotel**, 4 Via Panzani (tel. 211-005). For 4,000 lire ($4.64) my bathless single room faced the back and was very quiet. I had been warned about the traffic noise of that street. There seemed to be quite a few single rooms there for 6,000 lire ($6.96) with bath. Bathless doubles cost 7,500 lire ($8.70), rising to 9,500 lire ($11.02) with bath" (Lynn Peterson, Hollywood, Calif.). . . . "A delightful pension is **Locanda Nella**, 69 Via Faenza (tel. 284-256). The rooms are spotless and the hospitality cordial. One extra special feature of the Nella is some very quiet rooms at the back, which, for older people, would be an advantage. Prices are from 2,500 lire ($2.90) a night for bed and breakfast" (June

Salmons, Swansea, England). . . . "A lovely tourist house in Florence is called **Pensione Serena,** 20 Via Fiume (tel. 23-643). It's 60 yards from the train station (one block from the side of the station) in a building with an elevator and a most charming proprietor, Enés Carresi, who speaks some English and makes every attempt to be helpful. His wife, mother-in-law, and he operate this impeccably clean pension which has huge rooms with balconies, sink, and in some, a shower. We had a double room which included a continental breakfast served in the room (no shower) for 6,800 lire ($7.89) for the two of us. A tremendous bathroom is down the hall, where you can take a hot shower or bath for 500 lire (58¢). The location is ideal, but the most impressive point of this pension was Mr. Carresi, whose warmth was amazing and most welcome" (Allyson Jill Kleiman, Brooklyn, N.Y.). . . . "I can thoroughly recommend the **Pensione Parodi** (tel. 211-866) to anyone requiring accommodation in Florence. Its location is superb—opposite the Medici Chapels, at 8 Piazza Madonna in the Palazzo Aldobrandini. The Duomo is three blocks away and the station four blocks. This spotless establishment is charmingly furnished and the ablution facilities were the best encountered in Europe during a two months' stay. The bright and cheery rooms and lounge mirror the personality of Signor Parodi, who is a mine of information and ever ready to help his guests with a screwdriver, bottled water, or suggesting inexpensive parking, all in excellent English. The cost of a double room with shower is 6,900 lire ($8) to 7,400 lire ($8.58) per night. Although officially classified as a locanda or inn, this place has an exceptionally high standard among pensions visited in Europe" (J.F. Vinsen, Durban, South Africa).

After checking into your hotel (and assuming you've escaped the pension requirement, at least for one meal), you'll begin an even more interesting search—this time for a restaurant that may represent your introduction to Florentine cuisine.

6. The Restaurants of Florence

The Tuscan cuisine should please most North Americans (except for some of the hair-raising specialties), as it's simply flavored, without rich spices, based on the hearty, bountiful produce brought in from the hills. Florentine restaurants are not generally acclaimed by gourmets as much as those of Rome, but many dishes are prepared so well that the Tuscan kitchen is considered among the finest in Italy. The Florentines themselves often assert that the cooking in the other regions of Italy "offends the palate."

The case was stated most critically by Mary McCarthy, who wrote: "The food in the restaurants is bad, for the most part, monotonous, and rather expensive. Many of the Florentine specialties—tripe, paunch, rabbit, and a mixture of the combs, livers, hearts and testicles of roosters—do not appeal to the foreign palate." The statement is funnier than it is true, though we concede the point about some of the specialties.

But one of the most typical platters is the Florentine beefsteak, savored by foreigners and locals alike. We don't know where Ms. McCarthy dined in Florence, which admittedly has many expensive citadels dispensing viands at "Grand Duke" prices. On the other hand, the city often stuns its many visitors with its sheer preponderance of good budget eating establishments, which pop up in surprising places.

The one Italian wine all foreigners recognize, the ruby-red Chianti, usually in a straw bottle, comes from Tuscany. Though shunned by some wine snobs, it is a fit complement to many a local repast.

Armed with a knife and fork, we'll eat our way down through the pick of the restaurants. We hasten to point out that the reference to "down" is in price only. Many of our most memorable and top-level dinners have been in some of the completely unheralded trattorie and "buca" (cellar) restaurants of the city.

THE TOP RESTAURANTS: Doney, 48r Via Tornabuoni, is on a street of palaces, boutiques, and houses of fashion. In rather opulent trappings, you can dine on faultlessly prepared Italian specialties, or stick closely to viands made to please the international palate. Seldom in Tuscany will you find such appetizing and well-cooked food, even if you stick to the relatively simple dishes. We recommend the green ravioli Doney, a pasta variation that rarely disappoints, 1,000 lire ($1.16). Chef's specialties we've liked: sautéed kidneys for 2,400 lire ($2.78); pizzaiola veal escalopes, the pièce de résistance, also 2,400 lire. For dessert, the chocolate mousse (superb whipped cream) is unimpeachable, for 800 lire (93¢). In the late afternoon, Doney is Florence's supreme spot for afternoon tea. Even the mouth-watering Italian pastries are snobbish. Closed Mondays and for part of August.

Ristorante Villa Park San Domenico, 55 Via della Piazzola (tel. 576-697), is a setting for a cuisine that has been acclaimed by some as one of the ten best in Europe! You could hardly find a more enthralling setting in which to dine: in an ancient villa, dating from 1350, set in a private park of 10 acres, with terraces, flowers, sculpture, and old trees. Best of all is the view of Florence from the panoramic terrace. But whether you dine on this wide panoramic veranda, or inside in the baronial hall, with its tall stone fireplace and high-backed leather chairs, you'll be impressed. The manager, G. Ignesti, is rightly proud of his unusually high gastronomic standing. He honors with a gift of a ceramic plate those who order his specialty, "bigoncia fiorentina trifolata," at 3,000 lire ($3.48). This is a savory concoction, blending veal with truffles, cheese, mushrooms, and ham—simmered in wine and cream. A good beginning might be the smoked salmon at 2,000 lire ($2.32), the tagliatelle or the tortellini, each at 800 lire (93¢). The special Florentine cake, zuccotto, costs 800 lire also. Call for a reservation. It's a taxi ride into the hills from the center of Florence.

Harry's Bar, 22r Lungarno Vespucci, is an enclave of expatriate and well-heeled visiting Yankees. From its prime position on the Arno, it deserves its well-earned reputation. You not only get a friendly welcome from Lio at the bar and Maestrelli in the dining room, but here you'll find the easiest place in Florence to meet your fellow Americans and (at least for a while) escape from some of the glory of the Renaissance. On a recent visit, we heard three words of Italian, from a frustrated woman from Alabama, who was kindly assured by the Tuscan waiter (in English) that she need struggle no more. As if by inner radar, martini drinkers and hungry diners know they'll be able to order from an international menu—small, but select, and beautifully prepared. Several soups are featured daily, including onion for 1,500 lire ($1.74), or cream of chicken for the same price. The gamberetti (crawfish) cocktail is most tempting, at 2,000 lire ($2.32). Harry has created his own tortellini (stuffed pasta) for 1,900 lire ($2.20). But Harry's hamburger at 2,900 lire ($3.36) and his club sandwich at 2,500 lire ($2.90) are the most popular items. The chef also prepares about a dozen specialties every day: breast of chicken "our way" for 3,500 lire ($4.06), grilled giant-sized scampi for 4,900 lire ($5.68), a lean broiled sirloin steak for 4,800 lire ($5.57). You'll have to pay 1,000 lire ($1.16) extra for vegetables and salad. An apple tart with fresh cream costs 1,000 lire also, and you must pay 600 lire (70¢) for a cover charge, plus service and tax. The bar is open from 11:30 a.m. to midnight—daily except Sunday. Closed from December to January 15.

Ristorante Oliviero, 51 Via della Terme, has a long tradition and a top-drawer reputation, and is frequented by some of the most fashionable denizens of Florence. Its cuisine is appropriate for the city of Donatello: original and imaginative dishes rarely equaled in the Tuscan capital. Come here only with a large appetite for rich and, at the same time, subtle food. Under the clever eye of the director, guests are welcomed from all over the world to consummate service and courtesy. To begin your dinner, we recommend the crêpes alla Fiorentina, 1,400 lire ($1.62) or maccheroncetti alla Fiorentina, a delicious pasta, 800 lire (93¢). Among fish dishes, the filetti do sogliola Oliviero at 4,300 lire ($4.99) would please Neptune. Delicie di vitello alla moda du chef, 4,300 lire ($4.99), is another specialty. For dessert, either crêpes suzette at 2,600 lire ($3.02) or a soufflé for two at 2,800 lire ($3.25) is recommended. Open nightly, except Sunday, from 4 p.m. At 8 p.m., there's music in the piano bar. Closed for vacation in August.

Buca Lapi, 1r Via del Trebbio, also off the Piazza S. Maria Novella (tel. 23-768), a cellar restaurant founded in 1880, is big on glamor, good food, and the almost gemütlich enthusiasm of fellow diners. Its decor alone—under the Palazzo Antinori—makes it fun: vaulted ceilings covered with travel posters from all over the world. There's a long table of interesting fruits, desserts, and vegetables. The cooks know how to turn out the most classic dishes of the Tuscan kitchen with superb finesse. Specialties: pâté di fegato della casa, 1,500 lire ($1.74), a liver pâté; cannelloni at 1,000 lire ($1.16); scampi giganti alla griglia, 3,500 lire ($4.06), super-sized shrimp; bistecca alla Fiorentina (local beefsteak), 8,500 lire ($9.86). In season, the gagioli Toscani all'olio at 900 lire ($1.04)—Tuscan beans in the native olive oil—are considered a delicacy by many palates. For dessert, you can order the international favorite crêpes suzette, or the local choice, zuccotto, 700 lire (81¢), a Florentine cake that's "delicato." Evenings can be quite festive, as the singing becomes contagious—a friendly boat. Closed Mondays.

Paoli, 12r Via dei Tavolini, near the Piazza della Signoria (tel. 276-215), between the Duomo and the Piazza della Signoria, is one of the finest restaurants in Florence, turning out a host of specialties. But it could be recommended almost solely for its medieval tavern atmosphere, with arches and ceramics stuck into the walls like medallions. The walls are adorned with frescoes. Its pastas are homemade. The fettuccine alla Paoli at 900 lire ($1.04) is served piping hot. The chef also does a superb rognoncino (kidney) trifolato at 2,000 lire ($2.32) and a sole meunière at 2,500 lire ($2.90). A recommendable side dish is piselli (garden peas alla Fiorentina), 600 lire (70¢). Closed Tuesdays.

Otello, 36r Via Orti Oricellari, near the railway station (tel. 275-819). "Mangi, mangi, mangi!" the waiter urges. That means "Eat, eat, eat!" And the Otello has plenty of victuals to stir the most lethargic of appetites. To begin with, one of the most delicious arrays of Tuscan antipasti is wheeled to your table. Even tender roast pork is part of the offerings, and this opening feast represents merely the hors d'oeuvres. The price of this inaugural plateful is based on what you order. For main courses, the Florentine beefsteak is priced according to weight. But we'd recommend arrosto misto, also priced according to what you have—a cart is wheeled to your table containing "everything that walks or flies," and you're asked by the waiter to make your selection. Two other good main dishes include chicken curry at 2,200 lire ($2.55) and veal scaloppini Otello at 2,600 lire ($3.02). If you can manage pasta as well, we'd suggest taglierini all'Otello at 1,000 lire ($1.16). For desserts, the specialty is zuccotto alla Fiorentina, a rich Florentine cake, 700 lire (81¢). Closed Tuesdays.

THE MEDIUM-PRICED RANGE: For fine meals, at reasonable prices, sample the following establishments:

Near the Duomo

Giannino in S. Lorenzo, 37r Borgo S. Lorenzo, a short walk from the Duomo, prepares some of the finest steaks and roasts in Florence. Serving diners upstairs and down, Giannino crackles with an open-fire grill, usually chock full of golden brown roast chickens turning on the spit. Thus, its reputation as a rosticceria. Its English roast beef costs 2,500 lire ($2.90) per serving; its even better pork roast goes for the same price. For one of the juicy, charcoal-grilled Florentine steaks, your tab will average around 4,200 lire ($4.87) for this platter alone. For starters, tortellini alla panna at 700 lire (81¢) is a house specialty. To finish, the Florentine cake, zuccotto, at 700 lire also, will completely destroy your waistline, but please your taste buds. Giannino is further suited to low budgeteers: it serves a 4,000-lire ($4.64) tourist menu, for which you must specifically ask the waiter. Late at night you may want to drop in for a pizza, as the restaurant's also a pizzeria. The best one we've tried here is the Roman pizza capricciosa, usually made with "the works"—ham, mushrooms, stuffed mussels, cheese, asparagus, even a cooked egg. The cost? 1,600 lire ($1.86).

Buca di S. Giovanni, 8 Piazza S. Giovanni, facing the Baptistery, is an intimate cellar restaurant that serves beautifully prepared dishes. Lasagne at 900 lire ($1.04) or a salad of the sea at 1,400 lire ($1.62) are the traditional openers. Main dishes can be ordinary, but well prepared, including roast chicken at 1,900 lire ($2.20); or they can be more exotic, as represented by tacchino (turkey) alla cacciatora at 1,600 lire ($1.86). Desserts average around 900 lire ($1.04).

Near the Ponte Vecchio

Alfredo sull'Arno, 46 Via de Bardi (tel. 283-808), offers good and unpretentious food in a setting right on the Arno. Call for a reservation, and chances are you'll be given an outdoor table on a veranda overlooking the river. The food is home style—well prepared, with hefty portions. The service from English-speaking (usually) waiters is friendly. This restaurant has been a special favorite of ours since the 50s, and it's always been run by the Giachetti family. Try, for a starter, the risotto Corsara at 1,500 lire ($1.74). Perhaps you'll follow with scaloppine vitella (veal) forestale, 4,200 lire ($4.87), or else prawns roasted on the spit, 3,900 lire ($4.52). Desserts range from 700 lire (81¢) to 950 lire ($1.10), and a cover charge of 550 lire (64¢) is imposed. Closed Wednesdays.

Near Ponte S. Trinità

Ristorante "Natale," 80r Lungarno Acciaioli, between the Ponte Vecchio and the Ponte S. Trinità, is an excellent choice for good food and leisurely dining along the Arno. Though its setting is relatively unpretentious, we've found its kitchen among the best in Florence—and its prices far below more heralded establishments. You might begin with rice the Florentine way at 900 lire ($1.04), then follow with some delicious scallops at 2,300 lire ($2.67). Among the meat and other fish dishes, we'd recommend the breast of chicken at 2,200 lire ($2.55) or grilled trout at 1,900 lire ($2.20). Desserts, including delicious cakes, range in price from 600 lire (70¢) to 800 lire (93¢). Closed Tuesdays.

Near the Piazzale Michelangelo

Ristorante Le Rampe, 1 Viale Poggi (tel. 663-063), is on the *rampa* leading to the Piazzale Michelangelo. Marcello Pieri, who has had success with the Buca dell'Orafo, has selected a site that gives a magnificent view of Florence. The restaurant is like a rustic chalet, with walls of glass, an overhanging roof, natural woods, a rugged stone wall, and a raised fireplace. The furnishings are rustic, including crude ladderback chairs and plaid tablecloths. The chef offers a version of an Italian smorgasbord, really a self-service antipasto counter, including many specialties of the Tuscan kitchen, priced according to consumption, with an average cost of 1,500 lire ($1.74). Except in the peak of the summer season, an open charwood fire is used for the rotisserie, turning out those tempting Florentine steaks, priced according to weight. Fish dishes are also featured. Try especially the fried scampi with zucchini at 3,000 lire ($3.48). Desserts range in cost from 600 lire (70¢) to 750 lire (87¢), the latter price for ice cream with whiskey. It's recommended that you reserve a table, but if you don't, you can wait in the American bar. Closed Wednesdays.

La Loggia, Piazzale Michelangelo (tel. 287-032). You shouldn't have any trouble locating this popular restaurant housed in a 100-year-old former art gallery. It occupies one of the most prominent positions in Florence, a panoramic piazza where all first-time visitors appear to drink in the view of the City of the Renaissance. The food is good, too. If the weather's fair, try for one of the outside dining spots. In winter, you must retreat to one of the glassed-in tables. The menu is variable, but pasta dishes average around 1,200 lire ($1.39). Most main dishes, including breast of chicken and steak Diana, are in the 3,000-lire ($3.48) to 5,000-lire ($5.80) range, with a basket of fresh Tuscan fruit placed on your table for 850 lire (99¢).

Near the Piazza Taddeo Gaddi

Trattoria Vittoria, 52r Via Fonderia (tel. 225-657), is unheralded and untouristy, but it serves some of the finest fish dishes in Florence. A big, bustling trattoria, it offers you a chance to dine in one of several rooms. Service is frenetic. Most of the fresh fish dishes of the day are priced according to weight. Sole is the most expensive, though you can also order equally tempting lower-priced dishes. Two outstanding choices to begin your meal include risotto alla marinara at 650 lire (75¢) and spaghetti alla vongole (clams) at 550 lire (64¢). The mixed fish fry gives you a little bit of everything at 2,200 lire ($2.55). Desserts cost from 550 lire (64¢).

BUDGET RESTAURANTS: In this category, Florence is a city that boasts many a good—and inexpensive—restaurant.

Near the Duomo

Sasso di Dante, 6r Piazza delle Pallottole, is great on a sunny day (its outdoor tables overlook the Duomo). In cooler weather, you can hover closer to the warm victuals in the kitchen. On a shaded terrace outside, the waiter shows you the menu that includes a beginning course, Tuscan salami at 700 lire (81¢) and minestrone at 500 lire (58¢). Roast beef at 1,500 lire ($1.74) with a green salad at 450 lire (52¢) pleases many, followed by the fresh fruit of the season at 250 lire (29¢). The house specialty is fillet Sasso di Dante at 2,600 lire ($3.02). The waiters are most congenial, as is the atmosphere. Closed Fridays.

Near the Piazza della Santa Maria Novella

Sostanza, 25r Via del Porcellana, is "pretend peasant." For years, it's been a tucked-away little trattoria where working people could go to get excellent food inexpensively. But, in more recent times, the invading sophisticates have been pouring in to share tables with them. The management has been watching the transition with amazement. You enter through a hole-in-the-wall into a small dining room, with over-crowded family-style tables. The rear kitchen is open, its secrets exposed to friendly diners. When you taste what comes out of that kitchen, you'll know that fancy decor would be superfluous. Specialties include breaded chicken breast at 2,800 lire ($3.25) and a succulent T-bone steak at 6,000 lire ($6.96). You might also want to try tripe here the Florentine way—that is, cut into strips, then baked in a casserole with tomatoes, onions, and Parmesan cheese, 1,500 lire ($1.74). A fine beginning is the tortellini at 750 lire (87¢), and a fit ending is Florentine cake at 650 lire (75¢). It's closed Sundays.

Near the Piazza S. Trinità

Ristorante Walter e Nandina, 684 Borgo SS. Apostoli, is such a well-established budget restaurant with tourists that it prints its menu in English. Its prezzo fisso is 3,200 lire ($3.71)—and here is one restaurant that doesn't hide its budget menu. For the fixed price, you'll usually be served scallop-shaped ravioli with meat sauce (or spaghetti), followed by chicken on the spit or roast beef, then fresh fruit for dessert. Chef's specialties include scampi curry rice pilaff at 3,900 lire ($4.52) and piccatine di vitella (veal) a piacere at 2,800 lire ($3.25). Tables are set out on the sidewalk near the church. But, on a cool day, why not eat in the kitchen? For your background music, there's a symphony of pots and pans. The family-run Walter e Nandina is just off the Arno, a four-minute walk from the Uffizi. Closed Fridays.

"Al Lume di Candela," 23r Via delle Terme, is uniquely located in a 13th-century tower that was partially leveled when its patrician family fell from grace (the prestige of Tuscan families was once reflected in how high their family towers soared). With its rustic tavern decor, the restaurant offers a typically Florentine cuisine, under the guiding, deft hand of the padrone in the kitchen. In a candlelit atmosphere, it makes for a romantic dining place, having drawn celebrities in the past. Despite its popularity, its prices are low. Main dish specialties include entrecôte alla Diana at 3,500 lire ($4.06) and a small capon Principessa at 2,500 lire ($2.90). The most spectacular dessert is the crêpes suzette, 3,500 lire ($4.06) for two persons. The bistro lies off the major shopping artery, the Via Por Santa Maria, near the Straw Market.

Near Piazza della Signoria

Trattoria Antico Fattore (Da Luigi I'coco), on tiny Via Lamberfesca, a few hundred feet from the Piazza della Signoria, is one of the most unusual restaurants in the city of the Renaissance. The cuisine here is decidedly farmer style. It serves Florentine food based on recipes that surely must date back two or three hundred years. For a beginning, try pappa al pomodoro, a thick tomato and bread soup. Other local fare includes crostini (chicken liver canapés), zuppa alla contadina (with beans), sausages and beans all 'uccelletto (that is, cooked in oil with chopped onions and sage-flavored tomatoes). Incidentally, the bread here is called stinchi and pronounced "stinky." Most main dishes run about 2,600 lire ($3.02). Soup is 400 lire (46¢).

Near the Ponte Vecchio

Buca dell'Orafo, 28r Via dei Girolami (tel. 23-619), is one of the many cellars or buca-type establishments beloved by Florentines. It's a stepdown bistro in an arcade to the left of the Ponte Vecchio on the Right Bank. In summer, the trattoria is stuffed at noontime with its regular habitués, who know they can fill up on charcoal-grilled steaks, good pastas, or a big fish soup that's really a stew. Soups average around 600 lire (70¢). Main dishes are in the 1,800-lire ($2.09) to 3,000-lire ($3.48) range, and desserts cost an extra 600 lire (70¢). Even if you know your Italian, it won't help much, as the menu seems to have been written in hieroglyphics. Our more adventurous readers will find a nice feeling of camaraderie among the local diners.

Near the Railway Station

Ristorante Giannino, 15 Via Panzani, across from the Baglioni Palace Hotel, is far removed in spirit from that deluxe citadel. Rather, it is a simple, but good, trattoria. Usually an ornamental fowl display case can turn on hearty appetites, providing one is not a vegetarian, of course. The soups at 600 (70¢) and the pastas at 600 lire also make the most traditional beginnings. Main meat courses, such as chicken breasts and veal, are in the 1,700 lire ($1.97) to 1,900 lire ($2.20) range. The dessert special, cassata, costs 600 lire (70¢). Closed Thursdays.

On the Left Bank

Trattoria Cammillo, 57 Borgo S. Iacopo, is one of the most popular—and perhaps the finest—of the Left Bank dining spots housed on the ground floor of a former Medici palace. It's good enough to lure the snobbish owners of the boutiques, who cross the Arno regularly to feast here. They know they'll get such specialties as tortellini alla panna for 500 lire (58¢), or zuppa alla certosina at 800 lire (93¢), to begin their feast. The characteristic trattoria also does a delicious scaloppa alla parmigiana for 3,000 lire ($3.48), and that old standby, beloved by the locals, Florentine tripe, for 2,200 lire ($2.55). In modest but attractive surroundings, the trattoria is between the Ponte Vecchio and the Ponte S. Trinità. Because of increased business, one is likely to be rushed through a meal.

Mamma Gina, 37r Borgo S. Iacopo (tel. 296-009), is a rustic Left Bank restaurant that's a winner for fine foods prepared in the traditional manner. This trattoria is exceptional, well worth the trek across the Ponte Vecchio. The trattoria is a center for hearty Tuscan fare. The chef does an excellent tortelloni verdi (a green pasta dish) at 800 lire (93¢). You can follow with any number of fish or meat dishes, ranging in cost from 1,500 lire ($1.74) to 3,000 lire ($3.48). Desserts begin at 800 lire (93¢). Closed Sundays and in August. Mamma Gina is ideal for lunch after visiting the Pitti Palace.

For Lire Watchers

Frizzi, 76r Borgo degli Albizi (tel. 294-163), is a surprising combination of atmosphere and budget meals. It's housed in an old palace, with an elegant entrance, which you enter through high doors. Some of the tables are in the courtyard; others inside the vaulted dining rooms. Part of the past, the restaurant is lit by a massive wrought-iron chandelier. It's not elaborately voguish—in fact, it caters to students and the working people of Florence, who eat here regularly. They never seem to tire of the major offering, a 2,000-lire ($2.32) prezzo fisso meal. Usually one gets both a first and a second course (a choice of a dozen different items), as well as fruit, a quarter liter of wine, bread, and service. On the à la carte, you might begin with a risotto alla Fiorentina e piselli (peas) at 700 lire (81¢), then follow with a quarter of a roast chicken at 900 lire ($1.04) or sole in butter at 2,000 lire ($2.32).

The **Giannino in S. Lorenzo,** 31 Borgo S. Lorenzo (tel. 272-206), is a self-service cafeteria with a rustic decor, only a short walk from the Duomo. The food is several notches above what you might expect in cafeteria fare, and the portions are large and filling. Pastas, such as lasagne, are 500 lire (58¢), and are dished out from huge serving pans fresh from the kitchen. The meat entrees are equally good, with a breaded veal cutlet in the Milanese style going for 1,500 lire ($1.74). Desserts are priced from 300 lire (35¢) to 400 lire (46¢). At night, pizzas are a specialty, ranging in price from 600 lire (70¢) to 1,200 lire ($1.39). Closed Tuesdays. The same owners run a more expensive restaurant next door.

Near the Piazza della Signoria: Casa di Dante, 4 Via D. Alighieri, is a family-style place, operated informally. The waiters speak some English. The food is top-notch, produced with skill by the women in the kitchen. The trattoria offers many Florentine specialties on its à la carte menu. A filling and most delicious dish is spaghetti alla carbonara at 700 lire (81¢). To follow, you can have deviled roast chicken at 1,500 lire ($1.74). A Florentine cake, zuccotto, rounds out the meal at 500 lire (58¢). The Casa di Dante is on a narrow street, near the poet's former house, about a five-minute walk from the Duomo in the direction of the Uffizi.

THE ATTRACTIONS OF FLORENCE

FLORENCE WAS THE FOUNTAINHEAD of the Renaissance, the city of Dante and Boccaccio. Characteristically it was the city of Machiavelli, but uncharacteristically of Savonarola. For three centuries, it was dominated by the Medici family, patrons of the arts, masters of assassination. But it is chiefly through its artists that we know of the apogee of the Renaissance: Ghiberti, Fra Angelico, Donatello, Brunelleschi, Botticelli, and the incomparable Leonardo da Vinci and Michelangelo.

In Florence, we can trace some of the steps by which man freed himself from the shackles of medievalism and entered an age of "re-birth." For example, all modern painters owe a debt to an ugiy, awkward, unkempt man who died at 27. His name was Masaccio (Vasari's "Slipshod Tom"). Modern painting began with his frescoes in the Brancacci Chapel in the Church of S. Maria del Carmine. You can go see them today. Years later Michelangelo was to paint a more celebrated Adam and Eve in the Sistine Chapel, but even so great an artist was never to realize the raw humanity of Masaccio's Adam and Eve fleeing from the Garden of Eden.

Ralph Roeder in a 1930 book, *The Man of the Renaissance,* wrote: "In the broadest sense the Renaissance might be described as one of those recurring crises in the annals of the race when a ferment of a new life, like a rising sap, bursts the accepted codes of morality and men revert to Nature and the free play of instinct and experience in its conduct."

To understand more fully the remarkable achievement of which Roeder wrote, we'll begin with:

1. The Top Sights

In the heart of Florence, at the Piazza del Duomo and the Piazza S. Giovanni (named after John the Baptist), is a complex of ecclesiastical buildings that form a triumvirate of three top sightseeing attractions, beginning with:

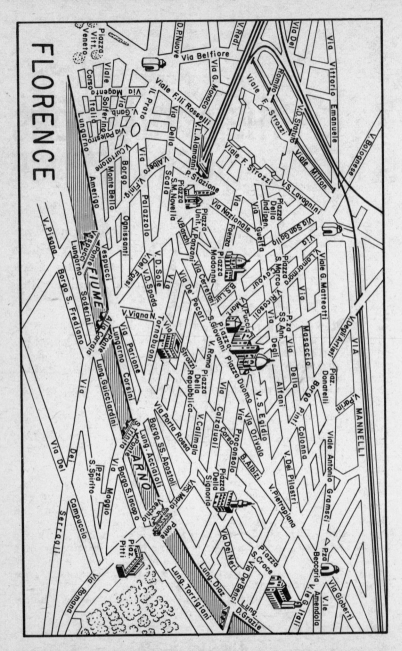

(1) GIOTTO'S BELL TOWER: Giotto, if we can believe the accounts of his contemporaries, was the ugliest man ever to walk the streets of Florence. In an ironic touch, he left to posterity the most beautiful bell tower or campanile in Europe, rhythmic in line and form. That Giotto was given the position of "capomastro" and grand architect (and pensioned for 100 gold florins for his service) is remarkable in itself, as his fame rests on his genius in freeing painting from the confinements of Byzantium. The campanile was designed by Giotto in the remaining two or three years of his life, and he died before its actual completion.

The final work was admirably carried out by Andrea Pisano, who was one of the greatest Gothic sculptors in Italy (see his bronze doors on the nearby Baptistery). The 274-foot tower, a most "Tuscanized" Gothic, with bands of colored marble, can be scaled for a panorama of the sienna-colored city, a view that surely will rank among your most memorable—encompassing the enveloping hills and Medici villas. If a medieval pageant happens to be passing underneath (a likely possibility in spring), so much the better. After Giotto's death, Pisano, as well as Luca della Robbia, did some fine bas relief and sculptural work at the base of the tower. Charging 350 lire (41¢) for admission, the campanile is open in summer from 8:30 a.m. to 12:30 p.m. and from 2:30 to 6 p.m.; in winter from 8:30 a.m. till 12:30 p.m. and from 2:30 to 4:30 p.m.). Closed on Sunday afternoons from November 1 to February 28.

(2) THE BAPTISTERY: Named after patron saint Giovanni (John the Baptist), the present octagonally shaped building dates from the 11th and 12th centuries. The oldest structure in Florence, the Baptistery is a highly original interpretation of the Romanesque style, with its bands of pink, white, and green marble. Visitors from all over the world come to gape at its three sets of bronze doors.

In his work on two sets of doors, Lorenzo Ghiberti reached the pinnacle of his artistry in "quattrocento" Florence. To win his first commission on the North Door, the then 23-year-old sculptor had to compete against such formidable opposition as Donatello, Brunelleschi (architect of the dome crowning the cathedral), and Siena-born Jacopo della Quercia. Upon seeing Ghiberti's work, Donatello and Brunelleschi conceded. By the time he completed the work, Ghiberti was around 44 years old. The gilt-covered panels represent scenes from the New Testament, including the "Annunciation," the "Adoration," and Christ debating the doctors in the temple—a flowing rhythmic narration in bronze.

After his long labor, the Florentines gratefully gave Ghiberti the task of sculpting the East Door (directly opposite the entrance to the Duomo). On seeing the doors, Michelangelo is said to have exclaimed, "The Gateway to Paradise!" Given carte blanche, Ghiberti designed his masterpiece, choosing as his subject familiar scenes from the Old Testament, including Adam and Eve at the creation. This time, Ghiberti labored over the rectangular panels from 1425 to 1452 (he died in 1455). The gilded panels were swept away in the flood waters of 1966, but have been restored.

Shuttled off to adorn the south entrance and to make way for Ghiberti's "gate" to paradise were the oldest doors of the Baptistery by Andrea Pisano, mentioned earlier for his work on Giotto's Bell Tower. For his subject, the Gothic sculptor represented the "Virtues" as well as scenes from the life of John the Baptist, whom the Baptistery honors. The door was completed in 1336. On the interior (just walk through Pisano's doors—no admission), the dome is adorned with 13th-century mosaics, dominated by a figure of Christ.

The third part of the ecclesiastical compound is:

(3) THE CATHEDRAL OF S. MARIA DEL FIORE (THE DUOMO):

Il Duomo, graced by Brunelleschi's dome, is the crowning glory of Florence. But don't rush inside too quickly, as the view of the exterior, with its bands of white, pink, and green marble—geometrically patterned—is the best feature, along with the dome, of course.

One of the world's largest churches, Il Duomo represents the flowering of the "Florentine-Gothic" style. Begun in 1296, it was finally consecrated in 1436, though finishing touches on the facade were applied as late as the 19th century. Actually, the cathedral was designed by Arnolfo di Cambio in the closing years of the 13th century, the funds being raised in part by a poll tax. As was typical of the history of cathedrals, construction stretched over centuries. In tribute to Arnolfo di Cambio's original foundation, it was miraculous that it supported the double-thick dome of Brunelleschi.

The efforts of Brunelleschi to build the dome (1420 to 1436) would in themselves make the subject of a film, as did Michelangelo's vexations over the Sistine Chapel. Before his plans were eventually accepted, the architect was once tossed out on his derrière and denounced as an idiot. He eventually won the commission by a clever "egg trick," as related in Vasari. His dome—a "monument for posterity"—was erected without supports. When the time came for Michelangelo to construct a dome over St. Peter's, he said in tribute to Brunelleschi's earlier cupola in Florence: "I am going to make its sister larger, yes, but not lovelier."

Inside, the overall effect of the cathedral is bleak, except when you stand under the cupola, frescoed in part by Giorgio Vasari, to whom we owe a debt in this book (as do authors of all other books dealing with Italian Renaissance art) for his *Lives of the Painters,* written in the 16th century. Some of the stained-glass windows in the dome were based on designs by Donatello (Brunelleschi's friend) and Ghiberti (Brunelleschi's rival). If you resisted scaling Giotto's Bell Tower, you may want to climb Brunelleschi's ribbed dome. And if so, you can from 8:30 a.m. to 12:30 p.m. and from 2:30 to 6 p.m. for a 350 lire (41¢) admission. The view is well worth the trek.

Also in the cathedral are some terra-cottas by Luca della Robbia. In 1432 Ghiberti, taking time out from his gateway to paradise, designed the tomb of St. Zenobius. Still another chapel is graced with the unfinished "Pietà" of Michelangelo, carved between 1548 and 1555 when the artist was in his 70s. It's interesting to compare it with his youthful Pietà in St. Peter's in Rome. In this vintage work, a figure representing Joseph (but said to be Michelangelo's face) is holding Christ. The great Florentine intended it for his own tomb, but is believed to have grown disenchanted with it and to have attempted to destroy it.

Recent excavations in the depths of the cathedral have brought to light the remains of the ancient Cathedral of S. Reparata (tombs, columns, and floors), probably founded in the fifth century, and transformed in the following centuries until it was demolished to make way for the actual cathedral. Admission is 150 lire (17¢).

Incidentally, during some 1972 excavations the tomb of Brunelleschi was discovered. New discoveries indicate the existence of a second tomb near that of the architect of the dome. Giotto's tomb, which has never been found, may be in a right nave of the cathedral, beneath the campanile which bears his name.

After coming out of the entrance to the cathedral, turn to the right, then head down Via Ricasoli to:

(4) THE ACADEMY GALLERY (MICHELANGELO'S "DAVID"): This museum at 60 Via Ricasoli contains paintings and sculpture, but is completely overshadowed by one work, Michelangelo's colossal "David," unveiled in 1504. One of the most sensitive accounts we've ever read of how Michelangelo turned the 17-foot "Duccio marble" into David is related in *"The Giant"* chapter of Irving Stone's *The Agony and the Ecstasy.* Stone describes a Michelangelo "burning with marble fever" who set out to create a David who "would be Apollo, but considerably more; Hercules, but considerably more; Adam, but considerably more; the most fully realized man the world had yet seen, functioning in a rational and humane world." How well he succeeded is much in evidence today.

"David" once stood in the Piazza della Signoria, but was removed in 1873 to the academy, a copy being substituted. Apart from containing the masterwork, the sculpture gallery also is graced with Michelangelo's unfinished quartet of slaves, carved around 1520 and intended for the ill-fated tomb of Julius II, and his "St. Matthew," which he worked on (shortly after completing "David") for the Duomo. His unfinished "Palestrina Pietà" displayed here is a much later work, dating from 1550.

In the connecting picture gallery is a collection of Tuscan masters, such as Botticelli, and Umbrian works by Perugino (teacher of Raphael). You can visit the Academy daily, except Monday, from 9 a.m. to 2 p.m. for 150 lire (17¢). On Sundays (9-1), admission is free.

While still suffused with the rich legacy of Michelangelo, it's only fitting that we pay a call on:

(5) THE MEDICI CHAPELS: A mecca for all pilgrims, the Medici Tombs are sheltered adjacent to the Basilica of San Lorenzo (see "Churches of Florence"). The tombs, housing the "blue-blooded" Medici, are actually entered in back of the church by going around to the Piazza Madonna degli Aldobrandini. First, you'll pass through the octagonally shaped, baroque "Chapel of the Princes," with its colored marble, but cold decoration. In back of the altar is a collection of Italian reliquaries.

But the real reason the chapels are visited en masse is the "New Sacristy," built to the design of Michelangelo. Working from 1521 to 1534, the Florentine artist created the Medici tomb in a style that foreshadowed the coming of the baroque. One of the greatest names in the history of the Medici family—Lorenzo the Magnificent—a ruler who seemed to embody the qualities of the Renaissance itself, was buried near Michelangelo's uncompleted "Madonna and Child" group, a simple monument that evokes a promise unfulfilled.

Sardonically, the finest groups of sculpture—of world renown—were reserved for two Medici "clan" members, "who" (in the words of Mary McCarthy) "would better have been forgotten." Both are represented in sculptured figures by Michelangelo as armored, regal; idealized princes of the Renaissance. In fact, Lorenzo II, Duke of Urbino, depicted as "the thinker," was a young man (just out of his teens before he died) who was deranged! Clearly, Michelangelo was not working to glorify these two Medici dukes. Rather, he was chiseling for posterity. The other two figures on Lorenzo's tomb are most often called "Dawn" and "Dusk", with the morning represented as woman, the evening, man.

The two best-known figures—Michelangelo at his most powerful—are "Night" and "Day" at the feet of Giuliano, the Duke of Nemours. "Night" is chiseled as a woman in troubled sleep; "Day," a man of strength awakening to a foreboding world. These two figures were not the sculptural works of Michelangelo's innocence.

Discovered in a sepulchral chamber beneath the Medici Chapel was the world's only group of mural sketches by Michelangelo. However, the general public can't be let in, as access is through a trap door and a winding staircase. The walls apparently had been used by the great artist as a giant doodling sheet. Drawings include a sketch of the legs of Duke Giuliano, Christ risen, and a depiction of the Laocoön, the famous Hellenistic figure group. In all, 50 drawings were found, done in charcoal on plaster walls.

The chapel is open from 9 a.m. to 7 p.m. daily (9-1 on Sunday), and charges 200 lire (23¢) for admission. Closed Mondays.

(6) THE UFFIZI GALLERY: When the last grand duchess of the Medici family died, the end of her line, she bequeathed to the people of Tuscany a wealth of Renaissance, even classical, art. The paintings and sculpture had been accumulated by the powerful Grand Dukes in three centuries of rule that witnessed the height of the Renaissance. Vasari himself designed the palace in the 16th century for Cosimo I.

The Uffizi contains the finest collection of art in Italy, and ranks along with the Prado and Louvre as one of the greatest art galleries in the world. To describe its offerings would take a very thick volume all its own, and to see and have time to absorb all the Uffizi paintings would take at least two weeks. We'll present only the sketchy highlights to get the first-timer through a citadel of madonnas and bambini, mythological figures, and Christian martyrs. The Uffizi is nicely arranged—that is, grouped into periods or schools to show the development and progress of Italian art, which later branches out to include European masters in general.

The first room begins with classical sculpture, but in *Room 2* we meet up with those rebels from Byzantium, Cimabue and Giotto, his pupil, with their madonnas and bambini. Since the Virgin and Child seems to be the overriding theme of the earlier of the Uffizi artists, it's enlightening just to follow the different styles over the centuries, from the ugly, almost midget-faced babies of the post-Byzantine works to the chubby, red-cheeked cherubs that glorified the baroque.

In *Room 3* is Simone Martini's "Annunciation," a collaborative venture. The halo around the head of the Virgin doesn't conceal her pouty mouth. In *Room 7* the wall decoration picks up considerably. Here you'll find the canvases of Fra Angelico of Fiesole, a 15th-century painter lost in the world peopled with saints and angels, making his Uffizi debut with a "Madonna and Bambino," naturally. But the special treasures are works by Masaccio, who died at an age when most of us are shedding our diapers, but is credited as the father of modern painting. In his madonnas and bambini, we see the beginnings of perspective in painting. Also in this salon are two important portraits by Piero della Francesca, the 15th-century painter (go to Arezzo to see his frescoes).

Room 8 is super charged. Fra Angelico's "Coronation of the Virgin" is here; but what makes the salon outstanding is the work of another friar—this one Filippo Lippi, a rebel among the brethren, who painted a far superior "Coronation" along with a galaxy of charming madonnas.

Room 10 is the most popular, especially with visitors who come here "to contemplate 'Venus on the Half-Shell.'" The room contains the finest works by Sandro Botticelli. Before being captured by Venus, don't miss "Minerva Subduing the Centaur" a most important painting which brought about a resurgence of interest on the part of painters in mythological subjects. The canvas was one of many Uffizi treasures shipped to Germany in World War II.

Botticelli's "Allegory of Spring" or "Primavera" is a Uffizi gem; it's often called a symphony because you can listen to it. Set in a citrus grove, the painting depicts Venus with Cupid hovering over her head. "The Wind" is trying to capture a nymph; but the three graces, in a lyrical composition, form the painting's chief claim to greatness. Mercury looks out of the canvas to the left.

But it is the "Birth of Venus"—Botticelli's supreme conception of life— that packs them in. Flora is trying to cover the nude goddess, while the gods of the wind are puffing up a storm. Before leaving the room, look for Botticelli's "Adoration of the Magi," in which we find portraits of the Medici (the vain man at the far right is Botticelli himself). *Room 11* is often bypassed, it appears so tiny and unimportant, but it contains Botticelli's small allegorical "Calumny."

On the other hand, in *Room 14* nobody could miss "The Adoration of the Shepherds," a triptych—superb in detail, commissioned for a once-important Tuscan family and painted by Hugo van der Goes, a 15th-century artist. In *Room 15* we come across another of Leonardo da Vinci's unfinished paintings —this one the brilliant "Adoration of the Magi." At the entrance to *Room 16* is Verrocchio's "Baptism of Christ," not a very important painting, but noted because da Vinci painted the angel on the right—when he was 14 years old, already a child prodigy. Also in this salon hangs da Vinci's "Annunciation," a painting of the early years of his genius—with its twilight atmosphere, each leaf painstakingly in place. Proof that Leonardo was an architect? The splendid Renaissance palace he designed is part of the background.

In *Room 18,* the most beautiful in the gallery with its dome of pearl shells, is the Venus of the Medici, occupying center stage, one of the most reproduced of all Greek sculptural works. Also displayed are Apollo, the Wrestler, and the Flaying of Marsyas, from Greek originals of the 3rd and 4th centuries B.C.

In the rooms to follow are works by Perugino, Dürer, Mantegna, Giovanni Bellini, Giorgione, and Correggio. Finally, in *Room 25* is Michelangelo's contribution to the Uffizi, his "Holy Family," as well as Raphael's "Madonna of the Goldfinch," plus his portraits of Julius II and Leo X. *Room 28* might be dubbed the Titian salon, as that painter of the High Renaissance takes over with two of his interpretations of Venus (one depicted with Cupid). When it came to representing voluptuous females on canvas, Titian had no rival. In the rooms to follow, we meet important Mannerists: Parmigianino, Veronese, Tintoretto ("Leda and the Swan"). In the rooms nearing the end are works by Rubens, Caravaggio ("Bacchus"), and Rembrandt.

Recently opened after wartime damage, the famous Vasari Corridor is lined with some of the world's greatest self-portraits. It used to link the Uffizi with the Pitti Palace on the other side of the Arno. The corridor spans the river as the upper part of the Ponte Vecchio. Only 20 visitors are allowed in the corridor in the morning, 20 more at noon. Permission is granted on a first-come, first-served basis. Go when the Uffizi opens and ask for special permission to visit the corridor at a counter next to the regular ticket kiosk. There is no charge, though visitors must hold a regular Uffizi ticket.

The Uffizi at 6 Loggiato degli Uffizi, between the Piazza della Signoria and the Arno, is open daily, except Monday, from 9 a.m. to 2 p.m. and charges no admission. On Sundays, hours are from 9 to 1.

(7) THE PIAZZA DELLA SIGNORIA: This square, though never completed, is one of the most beautiful in Italy—the center of secular life in the days of the Medici. Through it pranced church robbers, connoisseurs of entrails, hired assassins seeking employment, chicken farmers from Valdarno, book burners, and many great men—including Machiavelli on a secret mission to the Palazzo Vecchio, and Leonardo da Vinci, trailed by his inevitable entourage.

On the square is the Fountain of Neptune, the sea god surrounded by creatures from the deep, as well as frisky satyrs and nymphs. It was designed by Ammannati, who later repented for chiseling Neptune in the nude. But Michelangelo, to whom Ammannati owes a great debt, judged the work inferior.

Near the fountain is a medallion marking the spot where Savonarola walked his last mile. The zealous monk, of course, was a fire-and-brimstone reformer who rivaled Dante in conjuring up the punishment Hell would inflict on sinners. Two of his chief targets were Lorenzo the Magnificent and the Borgia pope, Alexander VI, who excommunicated him. Savonarola whipped the Florentine faithful into an orgy of religious fanaticism, but eventually fell from favor. Along with two other friars, he was hanged in the square. Afterward, as the crowds threw stones, the pyre underneath the men consumed their bodies. It is said that the reformer's heart was found whole, grabbed up by souvenir collectors. His ashes were tossed in the Arno. The year: 1498.

For centuries, Michelangelo's "David" stood in the Piazza della Signoria, but it was moved to the Academy Gallery in the 19th century. The work you see on the square today is an inferior copy, commonly assumed by many to be Michelangelo's original.

In the 14th-century Loggia della Signoria (sometimes called Loggia dei Lanzi) is a gallery of sculpture, depicting fierce, often violent, scenes. The most famous and the best piece is a rare work by Benvenuto Cellini, the goldsmith and tell-all autobiographer. Of his exquisite, though ungentlemanly, Perseus holding the severed head of Medusa, critics have said it is the most significant Florentine sculpture since Michelangelo's "Night" and "Day." Two other well-known, though less skilled, pieces are Giambologna's "Rape of the Sabines" and his "Hercules with Nessus the Centaur." For those on the mad rush, we suggest saving the interior of the Palazzo Vecchio (see "Palaces and Museums") for another day.

(8) THE PITTI PALACE: The "Palatine Gallery" on the Left Bank (a five-minute walk from the Ponte Vecchio) at the Piazza Pitti, houses one of Europe's great art collections, with masterpieces hung one on top of the other, as in the days of the Enlightenment. If for no other reason, it should be visited for its Raphaels alone. The Pitti, built in the mid-15th century (Brunelleschi was the original architect) was once the second residence of the powerful Medici family.

After passing through the main door, proceed to the **Sala di Venere** (the Room of Venus), which appropriately belongs to Titian, the favorite admirer of that goddess. In it is his "La Bella," of rich and illuminating color (entrance wall), and his portrait of Pietro Aretino, one of his most distinguished works. On the opposite wall is Titian's "Concert of Music," often attributed to Giorgione, and his portrait of Julius II.

In the **Sala di Apollo** (on the opposite sides of the entrance door) are Titian's "Man with the Gray Eyes"—aristocratic, handsome, a romanticist—as well as his Mary Magdalene with her plunging décolletage. On the opposite wall are Van Dyck portraits of Charles I of England and Henrietta of France.

In the **Sala di Marte** (entrance wall) is an important Madonna and Child by Murillo of Spain, as well as the Pitti's best known work by Rubens, "The

Four Philosophers." On the left wall is one of Rubens' most tragic and moving paintings, depicting the "Consequences of War"—an early "Guernica."

In the **Sala di Giove** (entrance wall) is Andrea del Sarto's idealized John the Baptist in his youth; Fra Bartolomeo's "Descent from the Cross"; and one of Rubens' most exciting paintings (even for those who don't like art): a romp of nymphs and satyrs. On the third wall (opposite the entrance wall) is the Pitti's second famous Raphael, the woman under the veil, known as "La Fornarina," his bakery girl mistress.

In the following gallery, the **Sala di Saturno,** look to the left on the entrance wall to see Raphael's "Madonna of the Canopy," plus other works, such as portraits, by that Renaissance master. On the third wall near the doorway is the greatest Pitti prize, Raphael's "Madonna of the Chair," his best known interpretation of the Virgin—in fact, probably one of the six most celebrated paintings in all of Europe!

In the **Sala dell'Iliade** (to your left on the entrance wall) is a work of delicate beauty, Raphael's rendition of a pregnant woman, painted while he was still searching for a personal style. On the left wall is Titian's "Portrait of a Gentleman," which he was indeed! (Titian is the second big star in the Palatine Gallery). Finally, as you're leaving, look to the right of the doorway to see one of Velázquez' interpretations of the many faces of Philip IV of Spain.

In the rooms that follow, the masterpieces dwindle, but the drama of the salons themselves remains vivid—enhanced by portraits by Justus Sustermans, who could be almost as devastating as Velázquez.

Major works resume again in the **Sala di Prometeo,** notably Filippo Lippi's "Madonna and Child," as well as two Botticelli portraits. In the **Sala dell'Educazione di Giove** hangs Caravaggio's "Sleeping Cupid," and in the **Sala della Giustizia** you'll find Tintoretto's "Virgin and Child," a vintage work by that Venetian master.

After the paintings of the Pitti, the Museum of Silver on the ground floor, with its silver, glass, gold, and ivory objets d'art, seems to dim despite its gleam. The Pitti is open from 10 a.m. to 4 p.m. (till 1 p.m. on Sundays), and charges 200 lire (23¢) for admission. Closed Mondays.

(9) THE NATIONAL MUSEUM (BARGELLO): At 4 Via del Proconsolo

is a fortress palace, dating from the 13th century, that once resounded with the cries of the tortured echoing through its dank underground chambers. Today it's a vast repository of some of the most important sculpture of the Renaissance, housing works by both Michelangelo and Donatello.

As you enter through the turnstile on the ground floor, you'll see another of Michelangelo's "Davids" (referred to in the past as Apollo), chiseled perhaps 25 to 30 years after the statuesque figure in the Academy Gallery. The Bargello David is totally different—even effete when compared to its stronger brother. And in the next gallery to the left you'll find Michelangelo's grape-capped Bacchus (one of his earlier works), tempted by a satyr.

Going up the steps on the right, you enter a foyer of sculpture, the most significant of which is Giambologna's delicately balanced "Mercury." The gallery approached from the loggia contains Michelangelo's truly magnificent bust of Brutus, and a "Madonna and Bambino with John the Baptist" in bas relief. You'll also find a terra-cotta by the master himself, Luca della Robbia. In addition, the salon displays two versions of Donatello's John the Baptist—one emaciated, the other a younger and much kinder edition.

Donatello, of course, was one of the outstanding and original talents of the early Renaissance. In this gallery, you'll learn why. His St. George is a work of heroic magnitude. According to an oft-repeated story, Michelangelo, upon seeing it for the first time, commanded it to "March!" Donatello's bronze "David" in this salon is one of the most remarkable figures of all Renaissance sculpture—the first "free-standing" nude since the Romans stopped chiseling. As depicted, David is narcissistic, a stunning contrast to Michelangelo's latter-day virile interpretation. For the last word, however, we'll have to call back our lady of the barbs, Mary McCarthy, who wrote: "His David . . . wearing nothing but a pair of fancy polished boots and a girlish bonnet, is a transvestite's and fetishist's dream of alluring ambiguity."

On the top floor you can explore a room devoted mainly to the few remaining works of Benvenuto Cellini, the last of the "giants" of the Renaissance sculptors. His more celebrated figures are "Apollo" and "Narcissus," as well as both his bronze and marble version "warm-ups" before he sculptured the Perseus you see in the Piazza della Signoria. Finally, you'll see his regal bust of Cosimo de' Medici, his patron.

In the adjoining room, look for at least one more notable work, another "David"—this one by Andrea del Verrocchio, one of the finest of the 15th-century sculptors. The Bargello contains a large number of terra-cottas by the della Robbia clan.

The museum, a short walk from the Piazza della Signoria, is open daily, except Monday, from 9 a.m. to 2 p.m., and charges 150 lire (17¢) admission. On Sundays, hours are from 9 to 1.

(10) SAN MARCO MUSEUM: At the Piazza San Marco is a handsome Renaissance palace, the walls of its cells decorated with frescoes by the mystical Fra Angelico, one of Europe's greatest 15th-century painters. In the days of Cosimo de' Medici, San Marco was built by Michelozzo as a Dominican convent. It originally contained bleak, bare cells, which Angelico and his students then brightened considerably with some of the most important works of this pious artist of Fiesole, who learned to portray recognizable landscapes in strong, vivid colors. One of his better known paintings found here is "The Last Judgment," peopled with angels on the left dancing in a circle, with lordly saints towering overhead.

But Hell, as depicted on the right, is naïve—Dantesque—infested with demons, reptiles, and sinners, boiling in a stew. If not that, then the denizens of the deep are devouring each other's flesh . . . or worms! Much of Hell was created by his students, as Angelico's brush was inspired only by the crucifixion, madonnas and bambini—or landscapes, of course. Here also are his "Descent from the Cross" and an especially refined interpretation panel of scenes from the life of Mary, including the "Flight into Egypt."

In the following room, the Lavabo, are frescoes by another friar—this one, Bartolomeo, who lived from 1475 to 1517 and worked with Raphael. Note his "Ecce Homo" and his "Madonna and Child." In the Capitolo is a fading, but powerful, Crucifixion, by Angelico.

Turn right at the next door, and you'll enter a refectory devoted to the artistic triumph of Domenico Ghirlandaio, the man who taught Michelangelo how to fresco. In Ghirlandaio's own work in this room, a "Last Supper," he was rather realistic, giving his saints tragic faces, while silently evoking a feeling of impending doom.

Upstairs on the second floor—at the top of the hallway—is Angelico's masterpiece, "The Annunciation." A perfect gem of a painting. From here, you can walk down the left corridor, exploring the cells of the Dominicans, enhanced by frescoes by Angelico and his pupils. Most of the badly lit frescoes depict scenes from the Crucifixion.

After turning to the right, you may want to skip the remaining frescoes, as they appear to be uninspired student exercises. But at the end of the corridor is the cell of Savonarola, the scene of his arrest. The cell contains portraits of the reformer by Bartolomeo, who was plunged into acute melancholy by the jailing and torturing of his beloved teacher. You'll also find pictures of the reformer on the pyre at the Piazza della Signoria.

If you retrace your steps to the entrance, then head down still another corridor, you'll see more frescoes, past a library with Ionic columns designed by Michelozzo. Finally, you'll come to the cell of Cosimo de' Medici, with a fresco by Gozzoli, who worked with Angelico.

A state museum, San Marco is open daily, except Monday, from 8:30 a.m. to 4 p.m. and charges 200 lire (23¢) for admission. On Sundays, it's open till 1 p.m. and is free.

2. The Secondary Sights

THE CHURCHES OF FLORENCE: The wealth of architecture, art and treasures of Florence's churches is hardly secondary, but if you want to see even a sampling of the best, you'll have to schedule an extra day or more in the City of the Renaissance.

Church of Santa Croce

At the Piazza Santa Croce is the Pantheon of Florence, sheltering the tombs of everyone from Michelangelo to Machiavelli, from Dante (he was actually buried at Ravenna) to an astronomer (Galileo) who—at the hands of the Inquisition—"recanted" his concept that the earth revolves around the sun! Just as the Santa Maria Novella was the church of the Dominicans, Santa Croce was the church of the Franciscans, said to have been designed by Arnolfo di Cambio.

In the right nave (first tomb) is the Vasari-executed monument to Michelangelo, whose body was smuggled back to his native Florence from its original burial place in Rome. Along with a bust of the artist, are three allegorical figures representing the arts. In the next memorial a prune-faced Dante looks down, a poet honored belatedly in the city that exiled him. Further on, still on the right, is the tomb of Machiavelli, whose *Prince* became a virtual textbook in the art of wielding power. Nearby is a lyrical bas relief, "The Annunciation" by Donatello.

The "Trecento" frescoes are reason enough for visiting Santa Croce—especially those by Giotto to the right of the main chapel. Once whitewashed, the Bardi and Peruzzi Chapels were "uncovered" in the mid-19th century in such a clumsy fashion that they have had to be drastically restored. Though badly preserved, the frescoes in the Bardi Chapel are most memorable—especially the deathbed scene of St. Francis. The cycles in the Peruzzi Chapel are of John the Baptist and St. John. In the left transept is Donatello's once-controversial wooden "Crucifix"—too gruesome for some Renaissance tastes, including that of Brunelleschi, who is claimed to have said: "You (Donatello) have put a rustic upon the cross." (For Brunelleschi's "answer," go to Santa Maria Novella.) Incidentally, the Pazzi Chapel, entered through the flood-damaged cloisters, was designed by Brunelleschi, with terracottas by Luca della Robbia.

Church of Santa Maria Novella

At the Piazza S. Maria Novella, near the railway station, is one of the most distinguished churches of Florence, begun in 1278 for the Dominicans. Its geometric facade, with bands of white and green marble, was designed in the late 15th century by Leon Battista Alberti, an aristocrat who was the true Renaissance man (that is, philosopher, painter, architect, poet). The church in good harmony borrows from the Romanesque, Gothic, and Renaissance styles.

In the left nave as you enter (third large painting) is the great Masaccio's "Trinity," a curious work that has the architectural form of a Renaissance stage setting, but whose figures—in perfect perspective—are like actors in a Greek tragedy. If you view the church at dusk, you'll see the stained-glass windows in the fading light casting kaleidoscopic fantasies on the opposite wall.

Head straight up the left nave for the Gondi Chapel for a look at Brunelleschi's wooden "Christ on the Cross," said to have been carved to compete with Donatello's same subject in Santa Croce (see above). According to Vasari, when Donatello saw Brunelleschi's completed Crucifix, he dropped his apron full of eggs intended for their lunch. "You have symbolized the Christ," Donatello is alleged to have said. "Mine is an ordinary man." (Some art historians reject this story.)

In the late 15th century, Ghirlandaio contracted with a Medici banker to adorn the choir with frescoes, illustrating scenes from the lives of Mary and John the Baptist. Michelangelo, only a teenager at the time, is known to have studied under Ghirlandaio (perhaps he even worked on this cycle).

If time remains, you may want to visit the cloisters, coming first to the "Green Cloisters," then the splendid Spanish Chapel frescoed by Andrea di Bonaiuto in the 14th century (one panel depicts the Dominicans in triumph over heretical wolves). The cloisters may be inspected from 9 to dusk weekdays for a 150-lire entrance fee (otherwise 9 to noon on admission-free Sundays). Closed Fridays.

Church of S. Lorenzo

At the Piazza San Lorenzo is Brunelleschi's 15th-century Renaissance church, where the Medici used to attend services from their nearby palace on Via Camillo Cavour. Most visitors flock to see Michelangelo's "New Sacristy" with that artist's "Night" and "Day" (see the Medici Chapels under "Ten Top Sights"), but Brunelleschi's handiwork deserves some time, too.

Built in the style of a Latin cross, the church is distinguished by harmonious grays and rows of Corinthian columns. The Old Sacristy (walk up the nave, then turn left) was designed by Brunelleschi and decorated, in part, by Donatello (see his terra-cotta bust of St. Lawrence).

After exploring the Old Sacristy, go through the first door (unmarked) on your right, then turn right again and climb the steps to:

The **Laurenziana Library** (also entered separately from 9 Piazza San Lorenzo) was designed by Michelangelo to shelter the expanding library of the Medici. Beautiful in design and concept, approached by exquisite stairs, the library is filled with some of Italy's greatest manuscripts—many of them handsomely illustrated. One dainty and coy illustrator in either the 10th or 11th century saw fit to depict male figures in the nude, but castrated them so as not to offend public taste. The library is open from 10 to 1 weekdays (free); closed Sunday. After a visit here, you may want to wander through the cloisters of S. Lorenzo, with their Ionic columns.

Santa Maria Del Carmine

At the Piazza Santa Maria del Carmine, a long walk from the Pitti Palace on the Left Bank, is an unprepossessing baroque church, a result of rebuilding after a fire in the 18th century. Miraculously, the renowned Brancacci Chapel was spared—miraculous in that it contains frescoes by Masaccio, who ushered in the great century of "Quattrocento" Renaissance painting. Forsaking the ideal, Masaccio depicted man and woman in their weakness and their glory.

His technique is seen at its most powerful in the expulsion of Adam and Eve from the Garden of Eden. A masterpiece of early perspective, the artist peopled his chapel with scenes from the life of St. Peter, the work originally begun by his master, Masolino. Note especially the fresco, "tribute money," and the baptism scene with the nude youth freezing in the cold waters.

No less an authority than Leonardo da Vinci commented on the decline by imitation in painting following Giotto's breakthrough. But, upon seeing Masaccio's work, he wrote: "Masaccio showed by his perfect works how those who take for their ideal anything but nature—mistress of all masters—tire themselves in vain." Masaccio did the upper frescoes, but because of his early death, the lower ones were completed by Filippino Lippi (not to be confused with his father, Filippo Lippi, a greater artist).

It is open in summer from 6 a.m. to noon and from 3 to 7 p.m. In winter, it keeps the same hours, except it closes at 6 p.m.

PALACES AND MORE MUSEUMS: The most famous and most imposing palace in Florence is, without a doubt, the . . .

Palazzo Vecchio

At the Piazza della Signoria is the secular "Old Palace," dating from the closing years of the 13th century. Its truly remarkable architectural feature is its 308-foot tower, an engineering feat that required supreme skill on the part of the builder. Before entering the palace, you'll see Donatello's bronze, "Judith and Holofernes." Once home to the Medici, the Palazzo Vecchio (also called Palazzo della Signoria) is occupied today by city employees, though much of it is open to the public.

Pause in Michelozzo's Renaissance courtyard long enough to see Verrocchio's much-photographed "Boy with a Dolphin" fountain. On the ground floor is the 15th-century "Hall of the 500" ("Dei Cinquecento"), the most outstanding part of the palace, filled with Vasari & Co. frescoes as well as sculpture. As you enter the hall, look to the right for Michelangelo's "Victory." It depicts an insipid-looking young man treading on a bearded older man (it's been suggested that Michelangelo put his own face on that of the trampled man).

Later you can stroll through the rest of the palace, through its apartments and main halls, without fear of running into any more masterpieces. However, the salons themselves, such as a fleur-de-lis apartment, have their own richness and beauty. Following his arrest, Savonarola was taken to the Palazzo Vecchio for more than a dozen torture sessions, including "twists" on the rack. The torturer pronounced him his "best" customer! Afterward, you can walk along the ramparts for an excellent view of Florence. Charging 250 lire (39¢) for admission, the palace is open weekdays except Saturdays from 9 to 7 (Sundays till noon).

Palazzo Medici-Riccardi

At 1 Via Camillo Cavour, a short walk from Il Duomo, was the home of Cosimo de' Medici before he took his household to the Palazzo della Signoria. Built by palace architect Michelozzo in the mid-15th century, the brownstone was also the scene, at times, of the court of Lorenzo the Magnificent. Art lovers visit today chiefly to see the mid-15th-century frescoes by Benozzo Gozzoli in the Medici Chapel.

Gozzoli's frescoes, depicting the "Journey of the Magi," form his master-piece—in fact are considered a hallmark in Renaissance painting in that they abandoned ecclesiastical themes to celebrate emerging man (he peopled his work with the Medici, the artist's master, Fra Angelico, even himself). Goz-zoli's ability as a landscape artist and a distinguished portraitist (each man in the procession is a distinctly identifiable individual—often elaborately coifed and clothed) is seen at its finest here. The chapel is open from 9 to 1 and from 3 to 6, charging 200 lire (31¢) for admission; free on Sundays when it's open until noon. Closed Wednesdays.

The gallery of Luca Giordano, which has to be entered by another stair-way, was frescoed by that artist in the 18th century, but his work seems merely decorative. The apartments themselves, heavily baroqued, provide their own amusement. The gallery, incidentally, is free.

Archaeological Museum

At 38 Via della Colonna, a short walk from the Piazza della SS. Annun-ziata, this museum houses one of the most outstanding Egyptian and Etruscan collections in Europe. Its Egyptian mummies and sarcophagi are on the first floor, along with some of the more celebrated Etruscan works. In Room X on the first floor, pause to look at the lid to the coffin of a fat Etruscan (unlike the blank faces staring back from many of these tombs, this overeater's counte-nance is quite expressive).

Room XIV is graced with three bronze Etruscan masterpieces, among the rarest objets d'art of these relatively unknown people. They include the "Chi-mera," a lion with a goat sticking out of its back. The lion's tail—in the form of a venomous reptile—lunges at the trapped beast. The others are a statue of Minerva and one of an Orator. These pieces of sculpture range from the fifth to the first centuries B.C. In Room XII is another rare find: an original Greek bronze of a young god.

On the second floor are enough terra-cotta vases to hold half the wine in the vineyards between the Tiber and the Arno. The François vase on the ground floor, from the year 570 B.C., is celebrated. The museum is open from 9 a.m. to 2 p.m. daily, except Monday, charging 150 lire (17¢) for admission. It closes at 1 p.m. on admission-free Sundays.

Duomo Museum

At 9 Piazza del Duomo (across the street but facing the apse of Santa Maria del Fiore) is an unheralded museum beloved by connoisseurs of Renais-sance sculptural works. It shelters the sculpture removed from the Campanile and Il Duomo themselves—not only to protect the pieces from the weather, but from visitors who wanted samples. As you purchase your admission ticket in the reception hall, you'll find a Brunelleschi bust, as well as della Robbia terra-cottas.

Continue left to the second chamber to see bits and pieces from what was the old Gothic-Romanesque fronting of the cathedral, with ornamental statues, as conceived by the original architect, Arnolfo di Cambio. One of Donatello's early works, St. John the Evangelist, is here—not his finest hour certainly, but anything by Donatello is worth looking at.

The major reason for visiting the museum is to see the marble choirs— "cantorie"—of Donatello and Luca della Robbia (both works face each other, and are housed in the first room you enter after climbing the stairs). The Luca della Robbia choir is more restrained, but still "Praise the Lord" choreography in marble—with "clashing cymbals, sounding brass" . . . reaffirmation of life. In contrast, all restraint breaks loose in the "cantoria" of dancing cherubs in Donatello's choir. It's a romp of chubby bambini. Of all of Donatello's works, perhaps this one is the most light-hearted. But, in total contrast, don't miss Donatello's "Zuccone," which some consider to be one of his greatest masterpieces; it was done for Giotto's Bell Tower. The museum is open weekdays from 9:30 a.m. to 1 p.m. and from 3 to 6 p.m. (Sundays till 1 p.m.), charging an admission fee of 300 lire (35¢) (except Sundays). Winter hours are from 9:30 a.m. to 4 p.m.

EVEN MORE SIGHTS: As you're swiftly learning, the sights of Florence are endless . . .

Boboli Gardens

Behind the Pitti Palace are the gardens through which the Medici romped. Originally laid out by that great landscape artist, Tribolo, in the 16th century, the Renaissance gardens are the scene of the annual open-air "Maggio Musicale." The Boboli is ever popular for a promenade or an idyllic interlude in a pleasant setting. It's filled with fountains and statuary, such as a Venus by Giambologna in the "Grotto" of Buontalenti. You can climb to the top of the Fortalezza di Belvedere for a dazzling view of the city. The garden is open in summer until 6:30 p.m. Closes in winter at 4:30.

Piazzale Michelangelo

For a view of the wonders of Florence below and Fiesole above, hop aboard a No. 13 bus from the Central Station and head for the Piazzale Michelangelo, a 19th-century balcony overlooking a view seen in many a Renaissance painting. It's best at dusk, when the purple-fringed Tuscan hills form a frame for Giotto's Bell Tower, Brunelleschi's dome, and the towering hunk of stones sticking up from the Palazzo Vecchio. Dominating the square is another copy of Michelangelo's "David." A note from the Devil's Advocate: at certain times during the day the square is so overcrowded with tour buses and hawking trinket peddlers with claptrap souvenirs that the balcony is drained of its chief drama. If you go at midday in summer, you'll find that the view of Florence is still intact—only you may be run down by a Vespa if you try to enjoy it.

Ponte Vecchio

Spared by the Nazis in their bitter retreat from the Allied advance in 1944, "The Old Bridge" is the last remaining medieval *ponte* that once spanned the Arno (the Germans blew up the rest). The existence of the Ponte Vecchio was again threatened in the flood of 1966—in fact, the waters of the Arno swept over it, washing away a fortune in jewelry from the goldsmiths' shops that flank the bridge.

Today the Ponte Vecchio is back in business, closed to traffic except the *pedoni* type. The little shops continue to sell everything from the most expensive of Florentine gold to something simple—say, a Lucrezia Borgia poison ring. Once the hog butchers of Florence peddled their wares on this bridge.

Foundling Hospital

At the Piazza SS. Annunziata is the hospital of the innocents, the oldest of its kind in Europe. The building, and especially the loggia, with its Corinthian columns, was conceived by Brunelleschi, marking the first architectural bloom of the Renaissance in Florence. In the cortile are terra-cotta medallions, in blues and opaque whites, of babes in swaddling clothes, the work of Andrea della Robbia.

Still used as a hospital, the building also contains an art gallery. Notable among its treasures is a terra-cotta "Madonna and Bambino" by Luca della Robbia, plus works by Andrea del Sarto and Filippo Lippi. One of the gallery's most important paintings is an "Adoration of the Magi," by Domenico Ghirlandaio (the chubby bambino looks a bit pompously at the Wise Man kissing his foot). The gallery is open weekdays, except Mondays, from 9:30 a.m. to 1 p.m. and from 2 to 4:30 p.m. (holidays from 9 to 1); it charges 250 lire admission.

HOUSES OF ARTISTS AND WRITERS: What better place to start than at the house once owned by Michelangelo . . .

Casa Buonarroti

On 70 Via Ghibellina, a short walk from Santa Croce, stands the house that Michelangelo managed to buy for his nephew. Turned into a museum by his descendants, the house was restored in 1964. It contains some fledgling work by the great artist, as well as some models attributed to him. Here you can see his "Madonna of the Stairs," which he did when he was about 17 years old, as well as a bas relief he did later, depicting "The Battle of the Centaurs." The casa is enriched by many of the drawings of Michelangelo—that is, those not owned by the Uffizi. The house is open daily, except Tuesday, from 9 a.m. to 2 p.m., charging 500 lire (58¢) for admission.

Casa Guidi

At 8 Piazza S. Felice, a short walk from the Pitti Palace away from the Arno, was the residence of Elizabeth Barrett and Robert Browning during their self-imposed exile in Florence. For a hundred years, the house was closed to the public, after its sale by the poets' son's estate. Its latter-day occupants were besieged by curiosity seekers—fans of the two poets—who tried to gain admittance to see such sights as the "white doves in the ceiling," of which Elizabeth wrote. In the 1970s, the Browning Institute took over the house, opening it to the general public from 4 to 7 p.m., closed weekends and holidays. Admission is free. In a more cynical age, there is a tendency to reject the Brownings' life and view of Florence as "sentimental." Regardless, it's admirable what the institute has done to pay altogether fitting homage to the two 19th-century poets who were the central figures in "English Florence," just as Keats and Shelley were the stars in "English Rome." Elizabeth died in the house in 1861 and was buried in the English Cemetery in Florence (her tomb may be visited). A heart-broken Browning, who later died in Venice, was buried in Westminster

Abbey in London. The institute plans to include in the apartment a 19th-century literature study center.

Dante's House

For those of us who were spoon-fed Hell, but spared Purgatory, a pilgrimage to this rebuilt medieval house may be of passing interest, though it contains few specific exhibits of interest. Dante was exiled from his native Florence in 1302 for his political involvements. He never returned, and thus wrote his *Divine Comedy* in exile, conjuring up fit punishment in the *Inferno* for his Florentine enemies. Dante certainly had the last word. The house is reached by walking down Via Dante Alighieri, though the entrance to the museum is at 1 Via S. Margherita. The admission-free casa is open daily, except Wednesdays, from 10 a.m. to 1 p.m. and from 4 to 7 p.m. in the summer (from 3 to 6 p.m. in the winter). Between July 1 and August 31, the house is closed for approximately three weeks.

READERS' SIGHTSEEING TIPS: "Any readers traveling to Florence on limited time (two or three days) should try to be there toward the end of the week if possible. We arrived on Sunday afternoon with plans to leave on Wednesday, early in the afternoon. Most museums close at 12:30 or 1 p.m. on Sunday and are closed all day Monday" (Mark and Donna Rand, San Francisco, Calif.). . . . "On the right side (approaching from the city) of the Ponte San Niccoló, there is a bar by the side of the river where one can rent a rowboat for 1,000 lire ($1.16) per hour" (David K. Kirby, Tallahassee, Fla.).

Note: In Florence, **Alitalia** offices are at 10/12 Lungarno Acciaiuoli, 1 Piazza dell'Oro, and 9 Piazzetta dell'Oro (telephone all three at 2788).

3. Florence After Dark

Not an exciting prospect, unless you like simply to walk through the narrow streets or head up toward Fiesole for a view of the city at night (truly spectacular). However, for those seeking more organized action, these recommendations follow:

Perhaps nothing could be more unexpected in this city of Donatello and Michelangelo than a club called the **Red Garter,** 33 Via dei Benci (tel. 263-004), right off the Piazza Santa Croce. You'll think you're right back on an American college campus, circa 1955, when you hear the banjo band. Tap beer is on hand at 900 lire ($1.04), and you can purchase an entire pitcher at 3,000 lire ($3.48). Booze, as it's called here, sells for from 700 lire (81¢) to 1,000 lire ($1.16) a drink. The American Prohibition era not only lives on, it's been exported.

Space Electronic, 37 Via Palazzuolo (tel. 29-30-82), is a multi-media light and sound spectacular on two large floors. International bands play American and English sounds. It's open nightly at 8:30, charging 2,500 lire ($2.90) for the entrance fee, this tab including the price of one alcoholic drink. Additional drinks cost 400 lire (46¢) for a glass of wine, 1,000 lire ($1.16) for a whiskey. Snacks such as hamburgers at 700 lire (81¢) are also served. The most cooperative manager, Ennio, said the club is no longer just for the very young, but also attracts an over-30-ish crowd.

Full Up, 25 Via Della Vigna Vecchia (tel. 293-006), is a discotheque and piano bar that's really quite elegant, with carpeting and mirrors. Patrons of all ages select their own room, after paying an entrance fee of 5,000 lire ($5.80) which includes one drink. Additional drinks cost 3,000 lire ($3.48) at the bar, 3,500 lire ($4.06) at a table.

Finally, to cap your evening, you may want to do what the Florentines do. Head for **Vivoli,** 7 Via dell'Isola. This little establishment serves the finest ice cream we've tasted in Italy. Buy your ticket first and select your flavor, including such delights as blueberry, chocolate mousse, fig, melon, even coffee ice cream flavored with espresso. The gelati ranges in price from 250 lire (29¢) to 900 lire ($1.04). Closed Mondays.

4. Fiesole and the Medici Villas

For more extensive day-trips, refer to the following chapter. But for a virtual suburb of Florence, we'll now explore:

FIESOLE: When the sun shines too hot on the Piazza della Signoria, and tourists try to prance bare-backed into the Uffizi, the Florentine is likely to head for the hills—usually to Fiesole. But he or she will probably encounter more tourists, as this town—once an Etruscan settlement—is the most popular outing from the city. Bus No. 7, leaving from the Piazza San Marco, a breathtaking 25-minute ride, will take you there and give you a fine view along the way. You'll pass fountains, statuary, and gardens strung out over the hill like a scrambled jigsaw puzzle.

When you finally arrive at Fiesole, by all means don't sit with the throngs all afternoon in the central square sipping Campari (though that isn't a bad pastime). Explore some of Fiesole's attractions. You won't find anything as dazzling as the Renaissance treasures of Florence, however, as the charms of Fiesole are subtle. Fortunately, all major sights branch out within walking distance of the main piazza, beginning with:

The Duomo

At first, this cathedral may seem austere, with its cement-gray Corinthian columns and Romanesque arches. But it has its own beauty. Dating from the year 1,000 A.D., it was much altered during the Renaissance. In the Salutati Chapel are important sculptural works by Mino da Fiesole. Around to the side of the cathedral is the:

Bandini Museum

On the ground floor are terra-cottas from the della Robbia school, as well as original work by Nicola Pisano, the biggest name in sculpture in pre-Renaissance Italy. Upstairs is a collection of paintings reflecting ecclesiastical themes, most of them the work of Tuscan artists in the 14th century, with an original by Fra Angelico and Fra Filippo Lippi. The museum is open from 9 a.m. to noon and from 2 to 6 p.m. (in winter from 9 a.m. to noon and from 2 to 5 p.m.), charging 100 lire (12¢) for admission. Across the street is:

The Roman Theater and Archaeological Museum

On this site is the major surviving evidence that Fiesole was an Etruscan city six centuries before Christ, and later a Roman town. In the first century B.C., a theater was built, the restored remains of which we can see today. Near the theater are the skeleton-like ruins of the baths, which may have been built at the same time. Finally, try to visit the Etruscan-Roman museum, with its many interesting finds dating from the days when Fiesole—not Florence—was supreme (a guide is on hand to show you through). The museum and theater are open from 10 a.m. to 12:30 p.m. and from 2 to 7:15 p.m. in summer. Winter hours are more restricted. Admission is 200 lire (23¢). The hardest task you'll have in Fiesole is to take the goat climb up to the:

Convent of San Francesco

You can visit the Franciscan church, in the Gothic style, but it's of routine interest, with mediocre frescoes (some in contemporary dress). In the basement, however, is a museum devoted to objets d'art from China (collected by a father who was sent there as a missionary), along with Etruscan and Roman artifacts, even an Egyptian sarcophagus. The real reason to make the climb is for the unforgettable view.

Where to Dine in Fiesole

11 Tinello, 22 Piazza Mino, is a little dream trattoria at the top of the main plaza. There are three rooms, separated by an old archway screen. The first room has dining tables; the middle room a serving counter, buffet tables with baskets of fresh fruit, and an old raised hearth for grilling. The back salon has a skylight and a raised corner fireplace, with wrought-iron chandeliers. On the à la carte menu, the favorite item is beefsteak Florentine, priced according to weight, though you may prefer the baked lasagne at 500 lire (58¢) or the veal cutlet Milanese at 1,800 lire ($2.09). One must order a full meal—that is, a first and second course. The restaurant is open daily, except Wednesdays.

Trattoria Le Cave di Maiano, 16 Via delle Cave (tel. 591-33), is a mere 15-minute drive from the heart of Florence. It's a very old family-run establishment, which for many years has been an esoteric address to discerning Florentines. It's imperative, incidentally, that you reserve a table before heading here. The trattoria is actually a garden restaurant, with stone tables and large sheltering trees which create a colorful setting for the excellent cooking. Inside, the restaurant is in the true tavern style, with a crude beamed ceiling. Le Cave is open for lunch and dinner every day except Thursday. We'd recommend highly the antipasto at 1,000 lire ($1.16) and the homemade green tortelloni at 800 lire (93¢). For a main course, there is a golden delicious grilled chicken at 2,000 lire ($2.32) or perhaps a savory, herb-flavored roast lamb, 3,000 lire ($3.48). For side dishes, we'd suggest fried polenta, Tuscan beans, and fried potatoes at 600 lire (70¢). As a final treat, the waiter will bring you homemade ice cream with fresh raspberries at 1,000 lire ($1.16) a serving.

THE MEDICI VILLAS: In the hills around Florence are the villas once owned by the Medici. Either on your own or on an organized tour, you can visit some of the more interesting ones, which form a major attraction of the half-day and one-day trips from Florence through the Tuscan hills.

The state-owned **Villa of Poggio a Caiano** is the best of the lot. The architect was Giuliano da Sangallo, who erected the villa for Lorenzo the Magnificent in the 15th century in the village of Poggio, which is about 20 miles northwest of Florence. The villa is noted for its frescoes by Andrea del Sarto. The gardens have been greatly altered over the centuries, and we can only imagine what they looked like during the flowering of the Renaissance. Francis I and his wife died here in 1587 on the same night. The admission-free villa is open in summer from 9:30 a.m. to 1 p.m. and from 3:30 to 7 p.m. Winter hours are from 9 a.m. to 4:30 p.m. A S.A.C.A. bus (terminal at Piazza S. Maria Novella in Florence) goes to Poggio a Caiano if you're visiting on your own.

SIENA, PISA, THE HILL TOWNS

THE HILL TOWNS of Tuscany and Umbria are prized not only for their essential beauty (for example, the unspoiled medieval severity of Siena and San Gimignano)—but for their spectacular art treasures, created by such "hometown boys" as Leonardo da Vinci. From Florence, you can explore numerous nearby art cities, including Pisa, Lucca, and Siena, as well as San Gimignano with its medieval towers.

And if you're traveling between Rome and Florence, why not veer off the autostrada and visit a string of still other hill towns that are, in essence, sanctuaries of the past? These include Spoleto, Assisi (birthplace of St. Francis), Perugia, and Arezzo. You'll be traversing the heart of Italy. And don't assume that these hill towns are obscure or of esoteric interest. Far from it. Siena, Pisa, and Assisi are prime targets of all pilgrims to Italy bent on doing merely the highlights. We'll begin with the best of the lot . . .

1. Siena

After Florence, it's altogether fitting, certainly bi-partisan, to call on what has been labeled in the past her natural enemy. In Rome, we saw classicism and the baroque; in Florence, the Renaissance; but in the walled city of Siena we stand solidly planted back in the Middle Ages. On three sienna-colored hills in the center of Tuscany, "Sena Vetus" lies in Chianti country. Perhaps preserving its original character more markedly than any other city in Italy, it is a showplace of the Italian Gothic (of a different character from Gothic in the French or Flemish sense).

William Dean Howells, the late American novelist (*The Rise of Silas Lapham*), called Siena "not a monument but a flight." About 31 miles south of Florence and regrettably too often visited on a quick day's excursion, it is a city for contemplation and profound exploration. It is characterized by Gothic palaces, almond-eyed madonnas, mansions of long-faced aristocrats, letter-writing St. Catherine (patron saint of Italy), narrow streets, and medieval gates, walls, and towers.

Although such a point of view may be heretical, one can almost be grateful that Siena lost its battle with Florence. Had it continued to expand and change after reaching the zenith of its power in the 14th century, chances are it would be remarkably different today, influenced by the rising tides of the Renaissance and the baroque (represented today only in a small degree.). But Siena retained its uniqueness (we've read that certain Sienese painters were still showing the influence of Byzantium in the late 15th century). Its spiritual sister in Europe—that is, among cities that are holdovers from the Middle Ages—is Toledo, south of Madrid.

A visit to Siena at any time can be of enduring interest, though the best time to visit if you're seeking a spectacle is on July 2 or August 16, the occasion of the **"Palio delle Contrade."** This is an historical pageant and tournament known throughout Europe, drawing thousands annually. In the horse race, each bareback-riding jockey represents a *contrade* (the wards into which the city is divided). The race, requiring tremendous skill, takes place on the shell-shaped Piazza del Campo, the historic heart of Siena. Before the race, much pageantry evoking the 15th century parades by, with colorfully costumed men and banners. The flag-throwing ceremony, depicted in so many travelogue films, takes place at this time. And just as enticing is the victory celebration.

Reader Pam King writes: "Don't buy tickets for the day of the Palio. It's free to stand in the middle—and a lot more fun. Besides, the tickets go for $20. Just get there real early, bring a book, and a thermos. For a great dinner and loads of fun, join one of the 17 contrades, attending a *cena* (supper) that is held outdoors the night before the race. There's good food, plus singing, and friendly folk. Few tourists know they are welcome. We also loved having a *contrade* to root for and really call our own."

THE SIGHTS: Much to see here. Let's start with the **Palazzo Comunale (Pubblico).** Standing in the heart of Siena, the "Town Hall" opens onto the shell-shaped **Piazza del Campo,** described by Montaigne as "the finest of any city in the world." Pause before entering the palazzo to enjoy the "Fonte Gaia," the fountain of joy, with embellishments by Jacopo della Quercia (the present sculptured works are reproductions; the badly beaten original ones are found in the Town Hall itself).

The skyline of Siena is characterized by its lithe **Torre (tower) del Mangia,** dating from the 14th century and soaring to a height of 335 feet. In season (March to October), you can climb the tower daily from 10 to noon and from 2 to 5 p.m., for a 50-lire admission charge (9-2 off season).

The brick Palazzo Pubblico (1288-1309) is filled with important art works by some of the leaders in the Sienese school of painting and sculpture. Upstairs in a museum is the "Sala della Pace," frescoed from 1337-39 by Amborgio Lorenzetti, and showing allegorically the idealized effects of good government and bad government. In this depiction, the most notable figure of the Virtues surrounding the King is "La Pace" (Peace). To the right of the King and the Virtues is a representation of Siena in peaceful times.

On the left, Lorenzetti showed his opinion of "ward-heelers," but some of the sting has been taken out of the frescoes, as the evil government scene is badly damaged. Actually, these were propaganda frescoes in their day, commissioned by the party in power, but they are now viewed as among the most important of all secular frescoes to come down from the Middle Ages.

In the "Sala del Mappamondo" is Simone Martini's "Majesty," a madonna enthroned with her child, surrounded by angels and saints. It is his earliest known documented work (c. 1315). The other remarkable Martini fresco (on the opposite wall) is the equestrian portrait of Guidoriccio da Foligno, general of the Sienese Republic in ceremonial dress.

The palazzo is open from 9:30 a.m. to 12:30 p.m. and from 2 to 5 p.m. from March to October, and charges 150 lire (17¢) for admission. Winter hours are from 9 a.m. to 2 p.m. Closed Mondays.

Il Duomo

At the Piazza del Duomo stands an architectural fantasy. With its colored hands of marble, the Sienese cathedral is an original and exciting building, erected in the Romanesque and Italian Gothic styles and dating from the 12th century. The dramatic facade—designed in part by Giovanni Pisano (but not the modern mosaics, of course)—dates from the 14th century, as does the Romanesque bell tower.

The zebra-like interior, with its black and white stripes, is equally stunning. The floor in itself consists of various embedded works of art, many of which are roped off to preserve the richness in design, which depicts both biblical and mythological subjects. Numerous artists worked on the floor, notably Domenico Beccafumi. For most of the year, wood covers a large part of the cathedral floor, again to protect it.

On the main altar is a glass-enclosed box with an arm that tradition maintains is that of John the Baptist, used to baptize Christ. The octagonally shaped, 13th-century pulpit is by Niccolò Pisano (Giovanni's father), who was one of the most significant Italian sculptors before the dawn of the Renaissance (see his pulpit in the Baptistery at Pisa). The Siena pulpit is considered his masterpiece, revealing in relief such scenes as the slaughter of the innocents and the Crucifixion. The elder Pisano finished the pulpit in 1268, aided by his son and other artists. Its pillars are supported by four marble lions, again reminiscent of the Pisano pulpits at Pisa.

In the chapel of the left transept (near the Library) is Donatello's bronze of John the Baptist. To see another Donatello work in bronze—a bishop's gravemarker—look at the floor in the chapel to the left of the pulpit's stairway. And don't miss the inlaid wooden stalls in the apse, some based on designs by Riccio. A representational blue starry sky twinkles overhead.

Perhaps the artistic highlight of the cathedral is the:

Piccolomini Library

Founded by Cardinal Francesco Piccolomini (later Pius III) to honor his uncle (Pius II), the church is renowned for its cycle of frescoes by the Umbrian master, Pinturicchio. His panels are remarkably well preserved, though they were frescoed in the early 16th century. In Vasari's words, the panels illustrate "the legend of Pope Pius II from birth to the minute of his death." Raphael's connection with the frescoes, if any, is undocumented. The library, charging 200 lire (23¢) for admission, is open from 9 to 1 and from 2:30 to 6:30 p.m. (till 5:30 p.m. on Sunday).

To the right (facing) of the Cathedral is the:

Opera Metropolitana

Housing paintings and sculptures originally created for the cathedral, this museum deserves some attention. On the ground floor, you'll find much interesting sculpture, including works by Giovanni Pisano and his assistants, as well as an exquisite "Three Graces," a Roman copy of a 3rd-century B.C. Greek work from the school of Praxiteles.

But the real reason the museum is visited hangs on the next floor in the "Sala di Duccio": his fragmented "La Maestà," a madonna enthroned, painted from 1308-11. The panel was originally an altarpiece by Duccio di Buoninsegna for the cathedral, filled with dramatic moments illustrating the story of Christ and the Madonna. A student of Cimabue, Duccio was the first great name in the school of Sienese painting.

In the rooms upstairs are the collections of the Treasury, and on the very top floor is a display of paintings from the early Sienese school. The museum, charging 300 lire (35¢) for admission, is open from April to September from 9 to 1 and from 2:30 to 6:30 (Sunday, 9 a.m. to 1 p.m.). In winter the hours are from 9 a.m. to 1 p.m. and from 2:30 to 5 p.m.

From the museum, a walk down some nearby steps in back of the cathedral takes us to:

The Baptistery

On the Piazza S. Giovanni, the facade of the Baptistery dates from the 14th century, but remained uncompleted over the passing centuries. In the center of the interior is the baptismal font by Jacopo della Quercia, containing some bas reliefs by Donatello and Ghiberti. It is a 15th-century Renaissance work of superb design and craftsmanship.

The Pinacoteca (Picture Gallery)

Housed in the 14th-century Palazzo Buonsignori at 29 Via S. Pietro is the national gallery's collection of the Sienese school of painting, which once rivaled that of Florence. Displayed here are some of the giants of the pre-Renaissance. Most of the paintings cover the period from the late 12th century to the mid-16th century.

The principal treasures are found on the second floor, where you'll contemplate the artistry of Duccio in the early salons. The gallery is rich in the art of the two Lorenzetti brothers, Ambrogio and Pietro, who painted in the 14th century. Ambrogio is represented by an "Annunciation" and a "Crucifix," but one of his most celebrated works, carried out with consummate skill, is an almond-eyed Madonna and her Bambino surrounded by saints and angels. Pietro's most important entry here is an altarpiece—"The Madonna of the Carmine"—made for a church in Siena in the 1320s. Simone Martini's "Madonna and Bambino" is damaged, but one of the most famous paintings in the entire collection.

In the salons to follow are works by Giovanni di Paolo ("Presentation at the Temple"—the bambino is terrified); and Sano di Pietro with his eternal fixation on the Madonna and Child. In Room 31 (on the first floor) is a masterpiece of Giovanni Antonio Bazzi (called "Il Sodoma," allegedly because of his sexual interests). It is a picture of Christ at a column, a work of such plastic quality it almost qualifies for publication in a body beautiful magazine.

From May to September, the gallery is open daily from 9 a.m. to 2 p.m. (Sundays, 9-1). In winter it is open daily, except Monday, from 9 a.m. to 2 p.m. The admission is 150 lire (17¢).

St. Catherine's Sanctuary

Of all the personalities associated with Siena, the most enduring legend surrounds that of St. Catherine, acknowledged by Pius XII in 1939 as the patron saint of Italy. The mystic, the daughter of a dyer, was born in 1347 in Siena. She was instrumental in persuading the papacy to return to Rome from Avignon. The house where she lived has now been turned into a sanctuary— really a church and oratory, with many works of art, on the spot where her father had his dyeworks. The sanctuary is open daily from 7 a.m. to noon and from 3 to 8 p.m., and charges no admission—though an offering is expected. Nearby at the 13th-century Basilica of Domenico is a chapel dedicated to St. Catherine. It was frescoed by Il Sodoma, and includes his celebrated "swoon" scene.

HOTELS IN SIENA: You'll *definitely* need hotel reservations for the Palio. Make them way in advance, and secure your room with a deposit. Here are our recommendations in all price ranges:

The First-Class Choices

Villa Scacciapensieri, 24 Via di Scacciapensieri (tel. 41-441), is one of the lovely old villas of Tuscany, where you can stay in a personal and tasteful atmosphere. For example: every morning, as your breakfast tray is placed on your bedside table, a rose is laid on the linen cloth, and there are four kinds of bread (made on the farm) and two kinds of butter from the Dolomites. Says owner-hostess, Signora Emma Nardi, "I like butter from cows who are free in the Alps." Life at this splendid villa is not overpowering or pretentious largely because of the owner's insistence on running it in a homelike way.

Standing on the crest of a hill, with a panoramic view of the Tuscan hills and Siena about two miles away, the villa is approached by a private driveway of sweet-scented shade trees. The bedrooms are individually designed and exquisitely appointed—each having coordinated colors and a theme according to the crest on the door. Only delicate, pure Belgian linen is used on the soft beds ("I like people to feel they're really welcome," says Signora Nardi). Open from the middle of March until the beginning of November, the first-class hotel charges quite moderate half-pension rates considering what it offers: $30 for a single with bath; $26 per person in a double with bath. House guests vary widely: from students of archaeology to Belgian diplomats to painters who visit in the colorful autumn. A look at one season's guest book tells the story: European princesses, Renata Tebaldi, Andre Kostelanetz, and Vittorio Gassman. Evenings in the informal drawing room are worth the trip; guests chat easily as they gather around the log fire burning on a raised hearth. The gardens open onto many vistas. There is bus service into Siena (an eight-minute ride) every half hour. Additions include a handsomely landscaped swimming pool and tennis court, plus a little Swiss villa ideal as a honeymoon cottage.

Park Hotel 16 Via di Marciano (tel. 44-803), is a 15th-century villa, built on its own parklike grounds. It stands proudly on a hilltop, surrounded by olive groves and formal gardens. Long the home of the Zondadari family (many of their portraits still adorn the walls), the villa was eventually sold to Mr. Marzocchi, who transformed it into a hotel (operating since 1958). All of the immense bedrooms have their own private baths and are well furnished and maintained. Singles pay an inclusive 21,000 lire ($24.36) for a room; doubles, 35,000 lire ($40.60). Full-pension terms in high season average around 38,000 lire ($44.08) per person in a double, but you must stay three days to get this rate. The drawing room has a single vaulted ceiling, with Victorian furnishings; one public room is baronial sized, with oak chairs. The little chapel, in red and white, is still intact. Guests enjoy cooling drinks on the graveled terrace, or in the loggia, with a view of the old well. The hotel has been completely renovated to offer a heated swimming pool, a new banquet hall and bar, plus air conditioning in every room.

The Medium-Priced

Garden Hotel, 2 Via Custoza (tel. 47-056), is a well-styled country house, built by a Sienese aristocrat in the 16th century. On the edge of the city, high up on the ledge of a hill, it commands a view of Siena and the surrounding countryside, the subject of many a painting. The hotel stands quite formal and serene, with an entrance on the garden side and a long avenue of clipped hedges. There's a luxurious sense of space (big enough for tennis, it seems) and an aura of newness and freshness. The furnishings (much plastic) emphasize the utilitarian instead of stylistic adornment. The rate for a bathless single room is 7,000 lire ($8.12); with shower, 9,600 lire ($11.14). A bathless double goes for 13,200 lire ($15.31); with bath, for 16,000 lire ($18.56). Full pension ranges from 18,500 lire ($21.46) per person. These rates include taxes and service. An enjoyable spot for morning coffee is the breakfast room, with its flagstone floor, decorated ceiling, and view of the hills. You can take your other meals in an open-air restaurant on the premises. There is a pleasant swimming pool, also.

A Student Favorite

Albergo Centrale, 24 Via Calzoleria (tel. 280-379), a minute's walk from the Piazza del Campo, is rated fourth class by the government, and, as such, it's recommended as a rendezvous for young people, who pass along the word that it's inexpensive and clean. Many students have stayed here who come to Siena to attend the School of Language and Culture, mainly to learn Italian (the Sienese "tongue" is said to be pure—that is, free of dialect). The Centrale is housed in an old building, typical of its surrounding structures, and is reached by a stairway (no elevator, of course). A single room without bath goes for 3,150 lire ($3.66). Doubles without bath are 5,600 lire ($6.50); with bath, 7,500 lire ($8.70). I.V.A. and other taxes are additional. The rooms are quite basic.

The Best Pension within the Walls

Palazzo Ravizza, 34 Pian dei Mantellini (tel. 280-462), has that intangible quality: soul. A first-class pension in Siena, it's really an old palace, within walking distance of the major attractions. In the front is a formal facade, in the rear a terraced garden with shade trees and benches for viewing the sweeping countryside. For years the home of great Tuscan families, it is owned and managed by a lovely lady who has not allowed drastic modernization, except for the installation of water basins and a few private baths. There are 28 well-furnished bedrooms (14 bathrooms), each with a distinct personality, utilizing fine old furniture. Singles rent for 7,000 lire ($8.12) for a bathless room. Bathless doubles go for an inclusive 13,000 lire ($15.08); with bath, 15,000 lire ($17.40). Full pension ranges from 13,000 lire ($15.08) to 14,000 lire ($16.24) per person. The living room and drawing rooms of the second floor possess excellent antiques, including a grand piano. All the rooms are interesting architecturally, with many coved ceilings. The owner has several family retainers who offer old-world service. It's probably one of the finest pension choices in Tuscany.

A Villa in the Country

Villa Terraia, 13 Via dell'Ascarello (tel. 280-361), is a charming country villa, on the rise of a hill, just two miles from Siena. It's not only inexpensive, but an especially ingratiating and restful place at which to stay. Open April through October 15, the third-class hotel has been a haven for artists and intellectuals. Its gracious hostess is Nelly Barzetti, who involves guests in her way of life. In her parlor are reminders of her life and interests, such as a grand piano belonging to her daughter, a concert pianist in London (an Epstein sculpture of her daughter stands on an antique chest). On the piano is an autographed photograph of Paderewski. There are oddly shaped and agreeable bedrooms available. The singles without bath are 4,360 lire ($5.06). Doubles are 6,875 lire ($7.98) without bath, 12,140 lire ($14.09) with bath. To reach the villa, head out Simone Martini, cross Viale Lippo Memmi, turning right on Viale Sardegna, until you come to Via dell'Ascarello, about a 10-minute drive through undulating hills.

DINING IN SIENA: Even half-day trippers sometimes find themselves in Siena for lunch, and that's a happy prospect, as the Sienese are good cooks, in the best of the Tuscan tradition. For one of the best restaurants in the city—with assuredly the most exciting view—find a perch on the central square (our chief recommendations follow).

Al Mangia, 44 Piazza del Campo (tel. 281-121), is one of the finest restaurants in the heart of the inner city, with outside tables overlooking the Town Hall. The food is not only well cooked, but appetizingly presented. To begin with, the house specialty is cannoli alla Mangia at 900 lire ($1.04). If then you crave some savory Tuscan main dish, try a bollito di manzo con salsa verde (boiled beef with green sauce), 2,100 lire ($2.44). Another excellent course is the osso bucco with artichokes at 2,100 also. For dessert, there's one specialty that transcends identification with its home town and is known all over Europe: panforte, made of spicy delights, including almonds and candied fruits, and costing 500 lire (58¢). Closed Mondays.

Guido, 7 Vicolo Pier Pettinaio (tel. 280-042), is a medieval Tuscan restaurant, about 100 feet off the promenade street near the Piazza del Campo. It's decked out with crusty old beams, time-aged brick walls, arched ceilings, and great iron chandeliers. Our approval is backed up by the public testimony of more than 300 famous people, who have left autographed photographs to adorn the walls of three dining rooms—film stars, diplomats, opera singers, and car-racing champions. There's an open grill for steaks, chickens, and roasts. A simple tourist menu goes for 4,000 lire ($4.64), but you may want to order some of the specialties on the à la carte list. Thus, you can have assorted antipasto for 900 lire ($1.04)—most rewarding. Also, try the cannoli alla Guido, the recommended house choice for starters, a cheese-stuffed pancake, costing 750 lire (87¢). For a main dish, you may want to stick to the roasts, especially the piccione (pigeon) with potatoes, 2,500 lire ($2.90). Desserts are in the 600-lire (70¢) range. A complete meal is likely to run 6,000 lire ($6.96). Guido is closed Mondays.

Severino, 6-8 Via del Capitano, probably won't appear in any travel guides—except this one, of course. But to us it represents a continuing manifestation of the "Dollar-Wise" philosophy that you often get your best meals in Italy at little unheralded, inexpensive trattorie. For 3,100 lire ($3.60)—on the "tourist menu"—we had a piping hot and unusually delicious baked lasagne, followed by scaloppe al marsala, accompanied by a mixed salad, then a basket of fresh Tuscan fruit for dessert. We liked the meal so much that we returned for other repasts on our most recent Siena sojourn, sampling some of the à la carte selections. Highly impressive was the Florentine risotto for 700 lire (81¢), really considered an appetizer, though dainty diners fill up on it. The simple roast chicken for 1,400 lire ($1.62) and the scaloppe alla pizzaiola at 1,600 lire ($1.86) are other fine entrees. The Severino is only a short walk down from the Duomo.

READERS' RESTAURANT SUGGESTION: "The **Trattoria Quatro Venti,** 68 Via S. Pietro, has a prezzo fisso meal at 1,800 lire ($2.09). Continue along the Via da Capitano away from the Duomo, past the Severino Restaurant, and veer to the right to get on the Quatro Venti" (Tom and Gale Lederer, Richmond, Calif.).

SIENA IN THE EVENING: In lieu of nightlife, you'll have a most intriguing experience if you go to the 16th-century **Fortezza Medicea** to sample wines. The Italian Wine center there, launched in 1960, is open till midnight. It's in the elegant cellars of the Medici fortress, and you'll find in it bottles of wine from all parts of Italy.

2. San Gimignano

A golden lily of the Middle Ages! Called the Manhattan of Tuscany, the town preserves 13 of its noble brick towers, which give it a skyscraper skyline. The approach to the walled town is dramatic, but once it must have been fantastic, as San Gimignano in the heyday of the Guelph and Ghibelline conflict had as many as 75 towers. Today, its fortress-like severity is softened by the subtlety of its quiet, harmonious squares, and many of its palaces and churches are enhanced by Renaissance frescoes, as San Gimignano, like Florence and Siena, could afford to patronize major painters.

THE SIGHTS: In the center of town is the palazzo-flanked **Piazza della Cisterna** (see our hotel recommendations)—so named because of the 13th-century cistern in its heart. Connecting with the irregularly shaped square is its satellite, the **Piazza del Duomo.** The square's medieval architecture—towers and palaces—is almost unchanged, the most beautiful spot in San Gimignano.

The present **Duomo** dates essentially from the 13th century. Inside, the cathedral is richly frescoed. In the right aisle, panels trace scenes from the life of Christ—the kiss of Judas, the Last Supper, the flagellation, and the crucifixion—painted by an artist most often known as Barna da Siena. In the left aisle are frescoes by Bartolo di Fredi, a mid-14th century cycle representing scenes from the Old Testament, such as the massacre of Job's servants.

On the reverse of the front wall are statues symbolizing the Annunciation by that Sienese master, Jacopo della Quercia. In 1464, Benozzo Gozzoli painted a St. Sebastian replete with arrows (note the attention paid to the landscape). It appears on the back of the Duomo's facade. In the nave on the left is the "Last Judgment," peopled with devils attacking fair damsels, the Inferno-inspired fantasy of Taddeo di Bartolo.

The chief attraction is the **Chapel of Santa Fina,** designed by Giuliano da Maiano. It was frescoed in about 1475 by Domenico Ghirlandaio, who depicted scenes from the life of Saint Fina, as in the memorable death-bed panel. Ghirlandaio, you may recall, was Michelangelo's fresco teacher. The chapel is open the same hours as the Civic Museum (see below), and you can use your ticket from the museum to enter.

Around to the left of the cathedral on a little square (the Piazza Luigi Pecori) is **The Museum of Sacred Art,** an unheralded museum of at least passing interest for its medieval tombstones and wooden sculpture. It also has an illustrated manuscript section and an Etruscan section. Admission is with your ticket from the Civic Museum.

Also opening onto the Cathedral Square is the:

Palazzo del Popolo, a palace designed by Arnolfo di Cambio in the 13th century, with a tower built a few years later—that is believed to have been the tallest "skyscraper" (about 178 feet high), a symbol of the podestà or mayor. For 100 lire (12¢), you can scale the tower and be rewarded with a bird's eye view of this most remarkable town.

Upstairs you can visit the **Civic Museum,** especially the Sala di Dante, where the Guelph-supporting poet spoke out for his cause in 1300. Look for one of the masterpieces of San Gimignano—the "Maestà," or madonna enthroned, by Lippo Memmi (and later "touched up" by Gozzoli).

The first large room you enter upstairs contains the other masterpieces of the museum—a "Madonna in Glory," with Saints Gregory and Benedict, painted by Pinturicchio when perspective was flowering. Flanking it are two different portraits of the "Annunciation" by Filippino Lippi. On the opposite wall, note the magnificent primitive "Crucifix" by Coppo di Marcovaldo.

The museum is open from April 1 to October 31 from 9 to 1 and from 3 to 7 and charges 150 lire (17¢) for admission. Off season its morning hours remain the same, but it closes at 5 p.m. Closed Mondays.

One final attraction lies a pleasant stroll from the center of town—

The **Church of Sant'Agostino.** At the Piazza S. Agostino, this handsome Gothic church was built in the 13th century. It is visited chiefly today by those wanting to see the mid-15th-century cycle of 17 frescoes in the choir by Benozzo Gozzoli. The panels, depicting scenes from the life of St. Augustine, are noted for their backgrounds and for the attention the artist paid to architectural detail and costumes. You can also explore the cloisters, with their simple, but beautiful, architectural lines.

THE HOTELS: La Cisterna, Piazza della Cisterna (tel. 940-328), is a second-class hotel of unusual merit. Thoroughly modernized, it still retains its medieval lines, having been built at the base of some 14th-century patrician towers. In its heyday, La Cisterna was the palazzo of a Tuscan family of nobility. Many tourists visit it just for the day, patronizing "Le Terrazze" restaurant (see our dining recommendations). But lucky is the pilgrim who gets to spend the night, safely ensconced in the spirit of 600 years ago. The bedrooms themselves are generally large and spacious, with some of the more superior lodgings opening onto terraces with stunning views of the Val d'Elsa (the hotel surmounts a hilltop). The Cisterna has 47 bedrooms, some equipped with private baths or showers. Bathless singles go for 4,700 lire ($5.45); bathless doubles for 8,300 lire ($9.63). The more limited (in number) singles with bath rent for 6,600 lire ($7.66); doubles with bath, 10,000 lire ($11.60). The fortunate few who are in San Gimignano long enough to take the pension rate will find that it ranges from 12,500 lire ($14.50) to 13,300 lire ($15.43) per person daily. Within two minutes after leaving the front door, you'll be at all the major sightseeing attractions.

Bel Soggiorno, 41 Via San Giovanni (tel. 940-375), lies on a narrow street running through the town, its rear bedrooms and dining room opening on the lower pastureland and the bottom of the village, a splendid view of the Val d'Elsa. The front is in the unspoiled Tuscan style, with a simple entryway and arched windows. Though rated only third class by the government, the lodgings offered are far superior to what you might expect. The rooms are small, pleasantly revamped, and they offer excellent views (some have antiques and terraces). All of them were designed in the high Tuscan style by an architect from Milan. In all, the Bel Soggiorno contains about 30 rooms, some of which have private baths. Bathless doubles go for 6,000 lire ($6.96). Doubles with bath cost 8,200 lire ($9.51). In high season, you'll be asked to have your meals here—which is no great hardship, as the cuisine is excellent. The full-pension rate peaks at 11,000 lire ($12.76) per person. The I.V.A. tax will be added. Part of the dining room juts out into space, with three sides of glass. Done in the medieval style, it contains murals depicting the hunting of wild boar. There's a country fireplace with crude chairs. Outsiders can drop in for meals.

WHERE TO DINE: The **Ristorante Le Terrazze** in La Cisterna Hotel on the Piazza della Cisterna is the preferred choice, not only for its cuisine, but for its panoramic view through glassed-in windows opening onto the Val d'Elsa. The setting is one of a country inn. The food itself is quite exceptional, a rich and varied assortment of produce from the surrounding Tuscan farm country. Many wonderful-tasting soups and pastas make for good beginnings, though the risotto alla Cisterna at 750 lire (87¢) is a specialty of the house. In meats, the house specialties are vitello alla Cisterna, with beans in butter, for 3,000 lire ($3.48); breaded lamb cutlet with fried artichokes, also 3,000 lire (a most worthy repast); and one-fourth faraona arrosto (roast guinea fowl) with fried potatoes for 3,000 lire.

Traveling by rail or car for about 50 miles west of Florence will take us to our next goal:

3. Pisa

One of the best short stories Katherine Anne Porter ever wrote was called *The Leaning Tower.* A memorable scene in that story dealt with a German landlady's sentimental attachment to a five-inch plaster replica of the Leaning Tower of Pisa, a souvenir whose ribs caved in at the touch of the fingers of one of her prospective clients. " 'It cannot be replaced' said the landlady, with a severe, stricken dignity. 'It was a souvenir of the Italian journey.' " Ironically, the year (1944) Miss Porter published her *Leaning Tower,* a bomb fell near the real campanile, but, fortunately, it wasn't damaged.

Few buildings in Europe have captured imaginations as much as the Leaning Tower of Pisa. It is probably the single most instantly recognizable building in all the Western world. Perhaps people are drawn to it as a symbol of man's fragility, or at least the fragility of his works.

The Leaning Tower may be a landmark powerful enough to entice visitors to come to call, but once there, they usually find other sights to explore. We'll survey the top attractions first, as most visitors pass through just for the day. For those who can settle in, we'll then follow with hotel and restaurant recommendations.

THE SIGHTS: In the middle ages, Pisa reached the apex of its power as a maritime republic, before it eventually fell to its rivals, Florence and Genoa. As is true of most cities at the zenith, Pisa turned to the arts, making contributions in sculpture and architecture. Its greatest legacy remains in the Piazza del

Duomo, which D'Annunzio labeled the "Piazza dei Miracoli" (miracles). Here you'll find an ensemble of the top three attractions—original "Pisan-Romanesque" buildings, including the Duomo, the Baptistery, and the Leaning Tower itself. Nikolaus Pevsner, in his classic *An Outline of European Architecture,* wrote: "Pisa strikes one altogether as of rather an alien character—Oriental more than Tuscan." We'll begin with:

Il Duomo

Dating back to the 1060s, the cathedral was designed by Buscetto, although Rainaldo in the 13th century erected the unusual facade, with its four layers of open-air arches, which diminish in size as they ascend. Reminiscent of the Baptistery in Florence, the Pisa Cathedral is marked by three bronze doors—rhythmic in line—which were damaged in a disastrous fire in 1596, but have been restored. The South Door is considered the most notable, and was designed by Bonanno in 1180.

In the restored interior, the chief art treasure is the pulpit by Giovanni Pisano. Actually the pulpit, damaged in the cathedral fire, was finally rebuilt only in 1926, employing bits and pieces of the original, which was finished by Pisano in 1310. The pulpit is polygonally shaped, held up by porphyry pillars and column statues symbolizing the Virtues (two posts are supported on the backs of lions). The relief panels depict scenes from the Bible. The pulpit is similar to an earlier one by Giovanni's father, Niccolò Pisano, in the Baptistery across the way.

There are other treasures, too—Galileo's Lamp (according to unreliable tradition, the Pisa-born astronomer used the chandelier to formulate his laws of the pendulum); mosaics in the apse said to have been designed by Cimabue; the tomb of Henry VII of Luxembourg; a St. Agnes by Andrea del Sarto; a "Descent from the Cross" by Il Sodoma; and a "Crucifix" by Giambologna.

The Baptistery

Begun in 1153, the Baptistery is like a Romanesque crown capped by Gothic. Although it is at its most beautiful on its exterior, with its arches and columns, it should be visited inside to see the hexagonally shaped pulpit made by Niccolò Pisano in 1260. Supported by pillars resting on the backs of a trio of marble lions, the pulpit contains bas reliefs of the Crucifixion, the Adoration of the Magi, the presentation of the Christ child at the temple, and the Last Judgment (many angels have lost their heads over the years). Column statues represent the Virtues. At the baptismal font is a contemporary John the Baptist by a local sculptor. The echo inside the Baptistery shell has enthralled visitors for years.

The Leaning Tower

Construction began on the eight-story campanile in 1174 by Bonanno, and there has been a persistent legend that the architect deliberately intended that the bell tower lean (but that claim is undocumented). If it stood up straight, the tower would measure about 180 feet.

It is said that Galileo let objects fall from the tower, then timed their descent. From 8 a.m. to 7:30 p.m. in summer, you can scale the tower for a 500-lire (58¢) admission. The sensation of climbing the tilting steps, 294 in all, and going out on the loggia may upset your sense of balance, at least. From the top of the tower, a wonderful view is spread before you. How long you'll be able to climb the tower is a matter of conjecture. The tower is no longer ailing, but is in serious danger of collapse. The government has announced an international competition to solicit plans to save the monument. The tower is said to be floating on a sandy base of water-soaked clay, leaning at least 14 feet from the perpendicular.

The fourth attraction in this meadow of marble is:

Camposanto

This cemetery was originally designed by Giovanni di Simone in 1278, but a bomb hit it in 1944. In more recent times, it has been partially restored. It is said that earth from Calvary was shipped here by the Crusaders on Pisan ships (the city was a great port before its water receded). The cemetery is of interest because of its sarcophagi, statuary, and frescoes. Notable frescoes, badly damaged, were by Benozzo Gozzoli, who illustrated scenes from the Old Testament, paying special attention to the architectural details of his cycle. One room contains three of the most famous frescoes, from the 14th century: the "Triumph of Death," the "Last Judgment," and the "Inferno," with the usual assortment of monsters, reptiles, and boiling caldrons. The Triumph of Death is the most interesting, with its flying angels and devils—superb in composition. In addition, you'll find lots of white marble bas reliefs—including Roman funerary sculpture. The cemetery may be visited from 9 a.m. to 7 p.m. (it closes at 4 p.m. in winter) for a 500-lire (58¢) admission.

The National Museum of St. Matthew

In this handsome, well-planned museum on Lungarno Mediceo, you'll find a good assortment of paintings and sculpture, many of which date from the 13th and 14th centuries. In the museum are statues by Giovanni Pisano; Simone Martini's "Madonna and Bambino with Saints," a polyptych in Room 21, as well as Nino Pisano's "Madonna del Latte" (milk), a marble sculpture; Masaccio's "St. Paul," painted in 1426; Dominico Ghirlandaio's two "Madonna and Saints" depictions; works by Strozzi and Alessandro Magnasco in Room 35; and very old copies of works by Jan and Peter Brueghel. The national museum is open year round from 9 a.m. to 2 p.m. (9 to 1 on Sundays and holidays) for 100-lire (12¢) admission. Closed Mondays.

HOTELS IN PISA: Pisa doesn't lack good accommodations in all price ranges, as you'll see by the following recommendations:

First-Class Hotels

Dei Cavalieri, Piazza della Stazione (tel. 43-290), is an excellently designed hotel, opposite the station square. Although its exterior reflects the regional architecture, with an upper-floor loggia, its interior is modern. The architect was consciously trying to warm the austerity of certain contemporary design. The end result is a mélange of ceramic bas reliefs, strong colors, spiral stairs, and built-in wooden furniture. The bedrooms are inviting, with original room dividers, dressing table and desk combinations, post lamps, good beds, and a liberal splash of color. Most up-to-date, every bedroom has a private bath and telephone. For rooms in this citadel of moderno razz-matazz, singles pay 16,000 lire ($18.56); couples, 28,000 lire ($32.48); add 1,800 lire ($2.09) for air conditioning, plus tax and 2,000 lire ($2.32) for breakfast.

Grand Hotel Duomo, 94 Via Santa Maria (tel. 27-141), is a blending of the talents of an architect and decorator who set out to create a streamlined modern hotel in the heart of Pisa, a short walk from the Leaning Tower. The air-conditioned hotel offers 90 bedrooms; all its chambers have handsome private baths. Contemporary it is, in a severe blue-gray stucco, with a covered roof garden for those uninterrupted views. Inside, there's a liberal use of marble, crystal chandeliers, even tall murals in the dining room. The bedrooms are well furnished, with parquet floors, white curtains on the side window expanse, built-in headrests, individual lights, and telephones. The Duomo charges 12,-000 lire ($13.92) for a single, 21,000 lire ($24.36) for a double, plus 1,500 lire ($1.74) extra for air conditioning.

Second-Class Hotels

California Park Hotel, Via Aurelia at Km. 338 (tel. 83-726), only lacks palm trees to make it true to its name. Just outside the city, the hotel is a tidy, white boxed modern group of bungalows, gathered around an open-air swimming pool, with fir trees that show promise of providing shade. Without doubt, it's the best place for motorists, especially in summer. With its freshness, trimness, it is cool, crisp, and stripped down for action. The rooms are equipped with folding-mirror dressing tables, wall-to-wall draperies, built-in headboards, and strong colors on the comfortable beds. To sum up, a cheerful holiday stopover. The pool has nightly lighting and plenty of space for long-distance swimmers. All rooms have private baths, with singles renting for 9,000 lire ($10.44), doubles for 15,000 lire ($17.40). Tax is included.

D'Azeglio, 26 Via D'Azeglio (tel. 25-045), is a modern structure, right off Piazza Vittorio, near the railway station. With its extending cement balconies, it reaches out to the sun and to a view of the square. It's most contemporary and streamlined throughout, especially in the light and airy bedrooms. The slatted wood headboards, end tables, overhead bedside lamps, built-in closets and desks, make it seem motel inspired. Single rooms with bath go for 7,700 lire ($8.93). Couples pay an inclusive 11,600 lire ($13.46) with bath. No pension terms are offered.

Royal Victoria, 12 Lungarno Pacinotti (tel. 23-381), is impressively and conveniently on the Arno, within walking distance of most of the jewels in Pisa's crown. Its lounge sets the hospitable scene, tastefully decorated, and utilizing good antiques. But the bedrooms are not as devoted to the past, as they have more contemporary furnishings, with an accent on body comfort. The single rooms without bath cost 6,000 lire ($6.96), increasing to 8,500 lire ($9.86) with bath. Bathless doubles rent for 10,000 lire ($11.60), peaking at 13,000 lire ($15.08) with bath.

Hotel Arno, Piazza della Repubblica (tel. 22-243), is one of the best of the second-class hotels, conveniently situated in a quiet position in front of the Tribunal. This modern hotel has 34 rooms, all with private showers. It is furnished throughout with pieces of a functional design. Singles rent for 8,400 lire ($9.74); doubles for 14,560 lire ($16.89), including service and taxes. For full pension, add 7,840 lire ($9.10) per person to the room rate. A lunch or dinner is an extra 3,000 lire ($3.48).

Hotel La Pace, 14 Viale Gramsci (tel. 50-22-66), is a quiet, immaculate, seven-story hotel across the Arno from the Leaning Tower and within walking distance of the railway station. Although classified as "second class" by the government, its service and decor seem to merit a higher rating. The corridors are lined authoritatively with paintings. The bar and dining room are attractive in a modern idiom. Two elevators lead to the rooms which rent for from 5,000 lire ($5.80) to 8,000 lire ($9.28) in a single, from 9,200 lire ($10.67) to 12,000 lire ($13.92) in a double. The more expensive accommodations are for private baths, of course. The hotel advertises air conditioning, charging 1,500 lire ($1.74) for it, though we found it feeble.

A Third-Class Choice

Hotel Cecile, 17 Via A. Volta (tel. 29-328), is the twin of the second-class D'Azeglio, born of the same parent. Both are modern, but each has its own personality. The simpler—and less expensive—life holds forth at the Cecile. It adjoins a broad avenue, about two blocks from the Arno and within walking distance of the Leaning Tower and the Duomo. The bedrooms are streamlined and functional, light and airy, and the 20-room hotel charges 7,250 lire ($8.41) for a bathless double; with bath, 9,250 lire ($10.73), inclusive. No pension terms are offered.

DINING IN PISA: Pisan fare is not the reason you go to Pisa. Nevertheless, our recommendations follow, beginning with the top restaurant.

The **Buzzino**, 42 Via Cammeo (tel. 27-013), is conveniently reached from the Piazza dei Miracoli (the square of miracles with the Leaning Tower). It slightly resembles a Santa Barbara hacienda, with a clerestory window, which filters light down upon the interior brick wall and ladderback dining chairs. The waiter will point out specialties on the à la carte menu, or you can order from the 5,000 lire ($5.80) tourist menu. Though the restaurant resembles "the businessman's choice," the food is really quite good. The chef does a nice scaloppine. If you order at random, you're likely to spend around 5,000 to 8,000 lire ($9.28) for a really fine repast, with wine. Closed Tuesdays and from July 20 to August 20.

Il Montino, 1 Vicolo del Monte, is a pizzeria that serves good food, attracting a faithful list of local habitués, who know of its location off the Piazza S. Felice on a quiet pedestrian walk. Outside is a handful of tables, with a view of the little chapel nearby. Inside, the dining hall is usually crowded, opening onto the service bar where Pisans come in to order slices of superb pies from the ever-hot pizza oven. Most pizzas range in price from 700 lire (81¢) to 1,000 lire ($1.16). You may prefer the delicious ham fritters at 450 lire (52¢). You can also order meals here, including spaghetti alle vongole (baby clams) at 500 lire (58¢); roast veal at 1,200 lire ($1.39); lasagne verdi at 600 lire (70¢). Closed from Saturday at 3:30 p.m. to Monday during July and for the whole month of August.

Emilio, 26-28 Via Roma (tel. 26-028), stands midway between the Arno and the tower. It's convenient, especially for lunch, though dinner is equally as appetizing. The antipasti buffet is tempting, especially the seafood dishes. The menu features the usual Italian fare, though the food is well prepared and particularly good. For a full meal, expect to pay anywhere from 4,000 lire ($4.64) to 6,000 lire ($6.96). With your repast, we'd suggest a local red wine, Bellavista. The dining room is decorated with a painting collection, and overhead are a pair of glittering globular chandeliers. Fresh flowers are placed on every table. Closed Mondays and between July 15 and August 1.

READER'S RESTAURANT SUGGESTION: "We found a fantastic self-service ristorante called **Santa Maria**, just down the street from the tower. It offered a choice of salad or pasta, entree, fruit, and beverage for 2,500 lire ($2.90). A choice from about 12 entrees was possible, plus 15 types of salads and vegetables (everything was fresh and beautifully displayed in a long case), and 10 types of beverages. The cafeteria was on an upper story and was large, with two different rooms for seating" (Judy Feldman, Chicago, Ill.).

Note: In Pisa, the **Alitalia** office is at 21 Via Puccini (tel. 48-025).

4. Lucca

At the time of the collapse of the Roman Empire, Lucca was virtually the capital of Tuscany. Periodically in its valiant, ever-bloody history, it functioned as an independent principality, similar to Genoa. This autonomy attests to the fame and prestige that Lucca enjoyed. Now, however, it is largely bypassed by time and travelers, rewarding the discriminating few who trouble to make the trek.

Linda Arking summarized its special appeal this way: "Thriving, cosmopolitan, and perfectly preserved, Lucca is a sort of Switzerland of the south. Banks have latticed Gothic windows; shops look like well-stocked linen cupboards. Plump children play in landscaped gardens, and geraniums bloom from the roofs of medieval tower houses."

Its city walls, built largely in the days of the Renaissance, enclose the old town, the zone of most interest to visitors, of course. For orientation, you may want to walk (even drive your car) along the tree-shaded ramparts, a distance of 2½ miles.

Afterward, we suggest that you head to the Piazza S. Martino to visit **Il Duomo,** dating back to 1060, though the present structure was mainly rebuilt. The facade is exceptional, evoking the so-called "Pisan-Romanesque" style, but with enough originality to distinguish it from the Duomo at Pisa. Designed mostly by Guidetto da Como in the early years of the 13th century, the west front contains three wide ground-level arches, surmounted by a trio of scalloped galleries with taffylike twisting columns (each one a different design), tapering in size. Towering to the side is a quadrangular campanile or bell tower.

The relic of St. Martin (the name of the cathedral) is the so-called Volto Santo, a crucifix carved by Nicodemus (so tradition has it), from a Cedar of Lebanon. The face of Christ was supposedly chiseled onto the statuary. The main art treasure in the Duomo is Jacopo della Quercia's tomb of Ilaria del Carretto, who died in 1405 (while still young), the wife of Paolo Guinigi. The marble effigy of the young lady, in regal robes, rests atop the sarcophagus—the cathedral's diffused mauve light in the afternoon casting a ghostly glow on her countenance. The tomb in the transept is fringed with chubby bambini.

At the Piazza S. Michele, a short walk away, the **Church of S. Michele** often surprises first-timers to Lucca, who mistake it for the Duomo itself. A 12th-century church, it is the most memorable example of the style and flair the denizens of Lucca brought to the Pisan-Romanesque school of architecture. Its west front, again employing the scalloped effect, is spanned by seven arches on the ground level, then surmounted by four tiers of galleries, utilizing imaginatively designed columns. Dragon-slaying St. Michael, wings outstretched, rests on the frieze-like peak of the final tier. Inside, seek out a Filippo Lippi painting of four saints.

HOTELS IN LUCCA: If you're planning to spend the night, you'll find Lucca adequately supplied with good lodgings.

The Second-Class Choice

Napoleon, Viale Europa (tel. 53-141), is a fairly recently built, second-class hotel of 72 rooms, the finest and most expensive choice for accommodations in Lucca. Lying outside the city walls, near the Autostrada, the Napoleon stands alone off the highway, like a miniature citadel of comfort. There's a circular glass-enclosed stairway attached to the front. Effort has been expended in coordinating the colors, the furnishings, and designs—much of which was successful, creating an island of plushness. Throughout the lounges is exhibited a permanent art collection, and there are areas with modern tables and chairs for relaxing. All the air-conditioned bedrooms have private baths or showers and telephones. The rooms are handsome, in the contemporary style, but softened with decorator touches. Singles with bath go for 12,050 lire ($13.98); doubles with bath for 17,150 lire ($19.89). The pension rate, based on double occupancy, is 26,000 lire ($30.16). There's plenty of parking space.

The Budget Choice

Hotel Ilaria, 20 Via del Fosso (tel. 47-558), is a pleasant little (16 rooms) hotel on a tiny canal. Reminiscent of the houses in a Dutch town, the Ilaria mixes rustico with moderno in its interior—and keeps both clean and well groomed. The building is a fairly new construction, though surrounded by older structures. Many of the pleasingly furnished, but simple, rooms overlook a view of irregular roofs and balconies with flowers and vines. No meals are offered, other than a continental breakfast included in the tariffs. You pay 3,700 lire ($4.29) in a bathless single; 4,300 lire ($4.99) in a single with bath. Couples are charged 6,200 lire ($7.19) in a room without bath, 8,500 lire ($9.86) in an accommodation with bath.

DINING IN LUCCA: **Buca di Sant'Antonio,** 1 Via della Cervia (tel. 55-881), is one of the finest regional restaurants in Tuscany, specializing in game dishes. Right off the Piazza S. Michele, it is tucked away on a hard-to-find mews, but the quality of its produce keeps the visitors and habitués returning. The interior is intimate in the rustic idiom, with a fireplace and such "quaint bits" as copper pots. To begin your meal (if you're there in the right season, autumn), you can order pappardelle alla lepre, a delicious noodle concoction with a spiced hare sauce, 900 lire ($1.04). To be regional, you can partake of codfish with polenta at 1,800 lire ($2.09), though you may prefer one of the game dishes. Featured in season are faraona (guinea fowl) and capretto (kid), both costing 2,000 lire ($2.32) each. Desserts range in price from 350 lire (41¢) to 850 lire (99¢).

5. Arezzo

The most landlocked of all towns or cities of Tuscany, Arezzo lies about 50 miles southeast of Florence, a one-hour train ride from that city. Originally an Etruscan settlement, later a Roman center, Arezzo flourished in the Middle Ages before its capitulation to Florence.

The walled town grew up on a hill, but large parts of the ancient city, including native son Petrarch's house, were bombed out during World War II before the area fell to the Allied advance in the summer of 1944. Apart from Petrarch, famous sons of Arezzo have included Vasari, the painter-architect remembered chiefly for his history of the Renaissance artists, and Guido of Arezzo (sometimes known as Guido Monaco), who gave the world the modern musical scale, before his death in the mid-11th century.

The biggest event on the Arezzo calendar is the **"Giostra (joust) del Saracino,"** staged the first Sunday of September at the Piazza Grande. Horsemen in colorful medieval costumes re-enact the lance-charging ritual—with balled whips cracking the air—as they have since the 13th century. But at any time of the year, the **Piazza Grande** should be visited, for the medieval and

Renaissance palaces and towers that flank it, including the 16th-century Loggia Palace by Vasari.

If you have only an hour for Arezzo, run—don't walk—to the:

Church of St. Francis. At the Piazza di S. Francesco is a Gothic church finished in the 14th century for the Franciscans. In the church is a fresco cycle—"Legend (or Story) of the True Cross"—that Piero della Francesca painted, his masterpiece. Working in the 1450s, the artist of the "Quattrocento" Renaissance was largely ignored by the world for centuries (except by art historians), but now enjoys his rightful position in the foreground of popular taste.

His frescoes are remarkable for their grace, clearness, dramatic light effects, well-chosen colors, and ascetic severity. If the cycle appears composed with consummate precision, it may be recalled that Vasari credited della Francesca as a master of the laws of geometry and perspective. The frescoes depict the burial of Adam, Solomon receiving the Queen of Sheba at the court (the most memorable scene in the cycle), the dream of Constantine with the descent of an angel, as well as Heraclius in triumph, among other subjects.

If time remains, you may want to explore the following sights:

The **Church of Santa Maria della Pieve,** on the Via de' Pileati (a short walk from the Piazza Grande), is a Romanesque structure, with a front of three open-air loggias (each pillar designed differently). Standing near it is a 14th-century bell tower, known as "the hundred holes," as it's riddled with windows. Inside, the church is bleak and austere, though there's a notable polyptych of the Virgin with Saints by one of the Sienese Lorenzetti brothers (Pietro), painted in 1320.

A short walk away, on Via dell'Orto, is **Petrarch's House,** rebuilt after war damage. Born at Arezzo in 1304, Petrarch was, of course, the great Italian lyrical poet and humanist, who immortalized his love, Laura, in his sonnets. His house may be visited from 3 to 4 p.m.

Il Duomo: Built in the so-called pure Gothic style—rare in itself for Tuscany—the cathedral was begun in the 13th century, but the final touches (the facade) weren't applied until the outbreak of World War I. Its art treasures include a Mary Magdalen by della Francesca; stained-glass windows by Marcillat, and a main altar in the Gothic style.

HOTELS IN AREZZO: Most visitors seem to whiz through Arezzo just for the day. But if you're seeking lodgings, you'll find two good second-class hotels.

The **Continentale,** 7 Piazza G. Monaco (tel. 20-251), is a honeycomb-modern invasion on an old tree-filled piazza. Every room has its own small balcony. The Continentale is at its best on its roof terrace with its potted trees, tables for drinks, and panoramic view of the city. Inside, the lounges and private rooms are spick and span modern, most streamlined. The bedroom furnishings are also utilitarian, with color added to make them breezy and cheerful. The year-round hotel has 80 rooms, with 67 bathrooms. Bathless singles go for 3,800 lire ($4.41); bathless doubles for an inclusive 6,500 lire ($7.54). Single overnighters in rooms with bath are charged 5,800 lire ($6.75); couples pay 8,700 lire ($10.09) for rooms with bath.

Albergo Chiavi d'Oro, 4 Piazza San Francesco (tel. 23-601), is at the opposite extreme from the Continentale, reflecting the architectural past of Tuscany. It's like a fine old villa, not quite a small palace. Its living rooms are Victorian oriented, especially a little salon. The bedrooms are well proportioned, not extravagantly furnished, but good for a restful night's sleep. No air conditioning, but on sunny days, the heavy window shutters are closed to keep out the noon-day sun. Singles pay 4,850 lire ($5.63) in a bathless room. A bathless double costs 8,500 lire ($9.86). Singles with bath go for 7,300 lire ($8.47); doubles with bath, 12,400 lire ($14.38). No pension terms are offered. The Albergo is adjacent to the Church of S. Francesco.

READER'S HOTEL SELECTION: "**Hotel Etruria**, 33-35 Via Spinello (tel. 27-611), is opposite the station but on a very quiet piazza. The cost is 2,500 lire ($2.90) per person" (Madeleine Dutour-Gauzé, St. Germain-en-Laye, France).

DINING IN AREZZO: The **Buca di S. Francesco**, 1 Via S. Francesco (tel. 23-271), is the best restaurant in Arezzo—in fact, it holds its own admirably in all of Tuscany. Not only is the food delicious—prepared and served with style—but the atmosphere's appropriate: the buca is decorated in the 14th-century fashion, with a frieze of Tuscan colors, blues and sienna. The one dish worth veering off the autostrada for is the anise-flavored pollo del Valdarno arrosto (roast chicken of the province) for 2,100 lire ($2.44). When the diners pick the bones, the pleased waiter throws up his hands with a "thank you, thank you." For 6,000 lire ($6.96) per person, we recently had a meal that included not only a minestrone *and* a pasta, but the roast chicken as well, along with a fresh garden salad, Chianti, and dessert. Of course, you can dine here less expensively, for about 4,900 lire ($5.68) by ordering from the tourist menu. But you may be tempted to go the whole hog when the victuals are so tasty. For starters, try the superb green noodles with a rich meat sauce, oozing with creamy cheese and topped off with a big hunk of fresh butter. The cellar lies just across the way from della Francesca's eternal frescoes. Closed Tuesdays.

From Arezzo, a 50-mile drive takes us to:

6. Perugia

For one of their greatest cities, the Etruscans chose a setting of remarkable beauty—much like Rome itself, with a group of hills overlooking the Tiber River Valley. In Perugia, we can peel away the epochs. For example, one of the town gates is called the **Arco di Augusto,** or Arch of Augustus. The loggia spanning the arch dates from the Renaissance, but the central part is Roman. Actually, builders from both periods used the reliable Etruscan foundation, the work of architects who laid stones to last. Perugia was one of a dozen major cities in the galaxy of the mysterious Etruscans.

Today, the city is the uncrowned capital of Umbria, retaining much of its Gothic and Renaissance charm, though it's been plagued with wars and swept up in disastrous events. To capture the essence of the Umbrian city, you must head for the **Piazza IV Novembre** in the heart of Perugia. During the day, the square is overrun. Try, then, to go to the piazza late at night when the old town is sleeping. That's when the ghosts come out to play.

THE SIGHTS: As the villages of England compete for the title of most picturesque, so the cities of Italy vie for the honor of having the most beautiful square. As you stand on the Piazza IV Novembre, you'll know that Perugia is among the top contenders for that honor.

In the heart of the piazza is the **Fontana Maggiore** (Grand Fountain), built sometime in the late 1270s by a local architect, a monk named Bevignate. But its artistic triumph stems from the sculptural work by Niccolò Pisano and his son, Giovanni. Along the lower basin of the fountain—the last major work of the elder Pisano—is statuary symbolizing the arts and sciences, Aesop fables, the months of the year and signs of the zodiac, scenes from the Old Testament and Roman history. On the upper basin (mostly the work of Giovanni) is allegorical sculpture, such as one figure representing Perugia itself, as well as saints, biblical characters, even local officials of the city in the 13th century.

After viewing the marvels of the fountain, you'll find that most of the other major attractions either open onto the Piazza IV Novembre, or lie only a short distance away.

The Cathedral of S. Lorenzo: The exterior is rather raw looking, as if the builders were suddenly called away to pour boiling oil on the heads of invaders, and never returned. The basilica is built in the Gothic style, dating from the 14th and 15th centuries. Inside, you'll find "the Deposition" of Federico Barocci. In the museum housing the cathedral works is displayed Luca Signorelli's "Virgin Enthroned," with saints. Signorelli was once a pupil of Piero della Francesca.

On the opposite side of the Piazza IV Novembre is the:

Palazzo dei Priori (The Palace of the Priors), the Town Hall, considered one of the finest secular buildings in Italy, dating from the 13th century. Its facade is characterized by a striking row of mullioned windows. Over the main door is a Guelph (member of the papal party) lion and a griffin of Perugia, holding chains once looted from a defeated Siena. You can walk up the stairway —the Vaccara—to the pulpit. By all means, explore the interior, especially the vaulted Hall of the Notaries, frescoed with stories of the Old Testament and from Aesop. Upstairs in the Palace of the Priors is:

The National Gallery of Umbria. This houses the most comprehensive collection of Umbrian art from the 13th up to the 18th century. Among the earliest paintings of interest is a Virgin and her bambino by Duccio di Buoninsegna, the first important master of the Sienese school. In the second salon you'll find statuary by the Pisano family, who designed the Grand Fountain out front, and by Arnolfo di Cambio, the architect of the Palazzo Vecchio in Florence.

Tuscan artists are represented in Room 7—the pious Fra Angelico's Virgin and bambino with saints and angels, as well as the same subject treated differently by Piero della Francesca and Benozzo Gozzoli. The salon might be labeled Tuscan variations on a theme.

In Room 13 we begin to encounter the works of native-son Perugino, among them his "Adoration of the Magi." Perugino, of course was the master of Raphael. Often accused of sentimentality, Perugino does not enjoy the popularity today that he did at the peak of his career, though he remains a key painter of the Renaissance, noted especially for his landscapes.

Room 15 is the most important in the gallery, devoted to art not only by Perugino, but by Pinturicchio, whose most notable work was the library of the Duomo at Siena. Pinturicchio studied under Perugino. Vasari had few kind words for Pinturicchio: "It seems that fortune's favorites are those who must depend on her alone, unaided by any ability, and of this we have an instance in Pinturicchio of Perugia, whose reputation was far greater than he deserves." In this salon, you can decide for yourself.

The national gallery, charging 150 lire (17¢) for admission, is open from 2 to 4 p.m. On Sundays, it's open from 9 to 1 year-round, and is always closed on Mondays.

Our final attraction in this heartland of monuments is the:

Collegio del Cambio. Right off the Piazza IV Novembre, at 25 Corso Vannucci, the medieval Exchange building opens onto the main street of Perugia, Corso Vannucci (Vannucci was the real name of Perugino). The collegio is visited chiefly by those seeking to view the Hall of the Audience, frescoed by Perugino and his assistants, including a teenaged Raphael. On the ceiling Perugino represented the planets allegorically. On the walls, his warriors look too timid to fight an ant colony. The Renaissance master peopled his frescoes with the virtues, sybils, and such Biblical figures as Solomon. But his masterpiece is his own countenance. It seems rather ironic that—at least for once—Perugino could be realistic. Perugino's self-portrait makes him look like a peddler of pig sausage. The Exchange is open from 9 to 12:30 p.m. year round, and from 2:30 to 5 p.m. May 1 to October 30, and 2:30 to 6 p.m. November 1 to April 30. Admission is 200 lire (23¢).

HOTELS IN PERUGIA: Good accommodations in all price ranges and classes can be found in Perugia.

Brufani Palace, 12 Piazza Italia (tel. 20-741), at the top of the city, was built by Giacomo Brufani in 1884 on the ruins of the ancient Pauline Fortress. It is placed on a cliff edge of town, opening onto a tree-studded square in front. The side and rear bedrooms offer a dramatic view of the Umbrian landscape, so beloved by painters. The hotel is first class—not deluxe—and you can live well here. The bedrooms are consistently comfortable, but most of them don't reach the style set by the public rooms. The entrance is designed around a glassed-in courtyard, with well-portioned encircling arches leading to the lounges. Bathless singles go for 6,800 lire ($7.89); 14,200 lire ($16.47) with bath. Bathless doubles cost 10,500 lire ($12.18), peaking at 21,000 lire ($24.36) with bath. The Panoramic Restaurant, with an American bar and a terraced garden, serves a good Umbrian cuisine, offering a set meal for 5,800 lire ($6.73). Underneath is a garage, offering overnight parking at 1,900 lire ($2.20).

La Rosetta, 19 Piazza Italia (tel. 20-841), is entered through an open old-world courtyard, where tables are set out for dining. Against this background of trailing vines and palm trees is a quite modern 109-bedroom, second-class hotel, offering good service. Arched windows open onto balconies. The furnishings are most contemporary, at their best in the new-wing bedrooms, equipped with gadgets, bedside lamps, radios, and maid bells. But the rooms in the older part are also fine, with all the necessary comforts. Most of the doubles have either a bath or shower, and rent for 15,500 lire ($17.98); three doubles without bath go for 10,600 lire ($12.30). Single rooms range in price from 7,300 lire ($8.47) to 9,900 lire ($11.48), inclusive. The Umbrian cuisine at La Rosetta is widely praised, and you might want to sharpen your knife here even if you aren't staying over (see our restaurant recommendations).

The **Minerva Hotel,** 9 Via Caporali (tel. 61-128), is our lowest-priced entry, popular with students at the University for Foreigners. Though rated third class, it is completely immaculate and fresh appearing. The lounge is minuscule, with the severity and simplicity of vaulted ceilings, natural brick walls, and an uncluttered arrangement of streamlined modern furnishings. The Minerva is within walking distance of the major sights of the Old Town. The rooms are trim and under-decorated, with the emphasis placed solely on functional furnishings and cleanliness. A few of the rooms have showers. The bathless singles go for 3,900 lire ($4.52). Bathless doubles cost 6,400 lire ($7.42); with shower, 8,300 lire ($9.63).

DINING IN PERUGIA: La Rosetta, 19 Piazza Italia (tel. 20-841), has gained

more fame than the hotel in which it's lodged. Food-smart Italian travelers manage to arrive here at mealtime: it's that good and reasonable. You'll find three areas in which to dine: an intimate wood-paneled salon, a main dining area divided by Roman arches and lit by glittering brass chandeliers, a courtyard enclosed by the walls of the villa-styled hotel. Under shady palm trees you can have a leisurely meal. The menu choice is vast, but a few specialties stand out over the rest. To begin, the finest dishes are either spaghetti alla Norcina (with a truffle sauce) for 2,500 lire ($2.90), or vol-au-vent di tortellini Rosetta for 1,200 lire ($1.39). Among the main dishes, the outstanding entries are scaloppine alla Perugina for 2,400 lire ($2.78). Most of the vegetable choices cost 650 lire (75¢), and several desserts, such as fresh fruit and ice cream, are the pick of the after-dinner choices, costing 800 lire (93¢). There's a 550-lire (64¢) cover charge.

Altro Mondo, 11 Via Caporali, in the Minerva Hotel, is home base for those who enjoy inexpensive food, a clean kitchen, and a dining room that is attractive. All seems light and airy, in spite of the stone vaulting. You can look through into the kitchen, a most reassuring sight. Specialties include paglia and fieno all'Altro Mondo (a fine spaghetti in a cream sauce), 900 lire ($1.04), and grigliata all'Altro Mondo (stuffed veal), 2,000 lire ($2.32). You're given a choice of at least a dozen other main dishes.

From Perugia, it's a 15-mile drive to:

7. Assisi

Ideally placed on the rise to Mount Subasio, watched over by the medieval fortress of Rocco, this purple-fringed Umbrian hill town retains a mystical air. The site of many a pilgrimage, Assisi is forever linked in legend with its native son, St. Francis. The gentle saint founded the Franciscan order and shares honors with St. Catherine of Siena as the patron saint of Italy. But he is remembered by many, even non-Christians, as a lover of nature (his preaching to an audience of birds is one of the most famous legends of his life).

THE TOP SIGHT: The **Basilica of St. Francis:** Consisting of both an Upper and Lower Church, at the Piazza di San Francesco, it houses some of the most important cycles of frescoes in Italy, works by such pre-Renaissance giants as Cimabue and Giotto. Both churches were built in the first part of the 13th century. The basilica and its paintings form the most significant monument to St. Francis.

Upon entering the Upper Church through the principal doorway, look to your immediate left to see one of Giotto's most celebrated frescoes, that of St. Francis preaching to the birds. In the nave of the Upper Church you'll find the rest of the cycle of 27 additional frescoes, some of which have been attributed to Giotto, though the authorship of the entire cycle is a subject of controversy. Many of the frescoes are almost surrealist—in architectural frameworks—like a stage setting that strips away the walls and allows us to see the actors inside. In the cycle we see pictorial evidence of the rise of humanism that was to lead not only to Giotto's but Italy's split from the rigidity of Byzantium.

Proceed up the nave to the transept, turning left. Here is a masterpiece of Cimabue, the "Crucifixion." Time has robbed the fresco of its former radiance, but has not diminished its power and ghostlike drama. The cycle of badly ruined frescoes in the transept and apse are other works by Cimabue and his paint-smeared helpers.

From the transept we proceed down the stairs through the two-tiered cloisters to the Lower Church, which will put us in the south transept. Look for Cimabue's faded but masterly "Virgin and Bambino" with four angels and St. Francis looking on from the far right. The fresco is badly lit, but is often reproduced in detail as one of Cimabue's greatest works. On the other side of the transept is the "Deposition (descent) from the Cross," a masterpiece of that Sienese artist, Pietro Lorenzetti, plus a Madonna and Bambino with St. John and St. Francis (stigmata showing). In a chapel honoring St. Martin of Tours, Simone Martini of Siena painted a cycle of frescoes, done with great skill and imagination, depicting the life and times of that saint.

Finally, under the Lower Church is the crypt of St. Francis, validated by the papacy after being closed off for centuries.

Other Sights

The **Church of S. Rufino:** Built in the mid-12th century at the Piazza S. Rufino, the Duomo of Assisi is graced with a Romanesque facade, greatly enhanced by rose windows, all making it one of the finest churches in the hill towns, as important as the one at Spoleto. Adjoining the cathedral is a bell tower or campanile. Inside, the church has been baroqued, an unfortunate decision and a loss of the purity that the front suggests. St. Francis and St. Clare were both baptized here.

The **Basilica of St. Chiara** (Clare), at the Piazza S. Chiara, honors the second important saint of Assisi. A woman of noble ancestry, St. Clare was born in the closing years of the 12th century, but—inspired by St. Francis—she was to forsake her position and create the Order of the Poor Clares. The Roman Catholic Church canonized her in 1255. As a curious side note, Pius XII declared her the patron saint of TV in 1958. Vision-conjuring St. Clare was her own transmitter. After the glory of the Basilica of St. Francis, St. Chiara is bare and bleak in its interior, quite a comedown. But under the church is the tomb of the saint. We recently visited it, along with 25 whispering nuns. Another nun, her hood concealing all but her mouth, spoke to us. At first, it was as if St. Clare herself had risen from the grave. The church, built in the 13th century, is characterized by its beige and salmon facade.

If time remains, you can visit:

The **Temple of Minerva,** which opens onto the **Piazza del Comune,** the heart of Assisi. The square itself is a dream for a lover of architecture from the 12th through the 14th centuries. A pagan structure, with six Corinthian columns, the Temple of Minerva dates from the 1st century B.C. With Minerva-like wisdom, the people of Assisi let it stand, turning it into a baroque church inside so as not to offend the devout. Adjoining the temple is the 13th-century Tower of the People, built by Ghibelline supporters.

The **Rocca Maggiore** (Great Fortress) strides a hill overlooking Assisi. It should be visited if for no other reason than the view of the Umbrian countryside possible from its ramparts. Though the present building—now in ruins—dates from the 14th century, the origins of the structure go back beyond that. There's no admission charged to enter the fort, but the non-salaried guard expects a tip.

The **Prisons' Hermitage:** In a setting 2½ miles east of Assisi (out the Via Eremo delle Carceri), the hermitage dates from the 15th century. The "prison" is not a penal institution—rather a spiritual retreat. It is believed that St. Francis retired to this spot for meditation and prayer. Visitors can go down into the grotto to see the stone bed on which (legend tells us) St. Francis slept. Out back is a gnarled, moss-covered, oak where the saint is believed to have preached to the birds. The monastery contains some faded frescoes. One of the handful of monks who still inhabit the retreat will show you through. The hermitage is open daily from 8 a.m. to sunset. No admission is charged, but an offering would be in order.

HOTELS IN ASSISI: Space in Assisi tends to be tight—so reservations are important. Still, for such a small town, Assisi has a surprising number of accommodations.

The Second-Class Hotels

Hotel Subasio, 2 Via Frate Ella (tel. 812-206), is a second-class hotel with a decidedly old-fashioned East European aura. One of the owners, Mrs. Violante Rossi, likes to keep it this way, surprising her guests with the level of accommodation offered. Virtually an institution, Mrs. Rossi—all motherly, warm, and smiling—is proud that the Subasio has been the unquestioned choice of many a celebrated visitor—the King and Queen of Belgium, the Queen of the Netherlands, Charlie Chaplin, Merle Oberon, Marlene Dietrich, James Stewart. The hotel is linked to the Church of St. Francis by a covered stone arched colonnade, and its dining terrace (extremely good food) is perhaps the most dramatic in Assisi. Your table will be shaded by a sprawling vine. Dining is also an event on the vaulted medieval loggia. The bedrooms at the front open onto balconies with a good view. The rooms are adequately furnished. Singles without bath rent for 5,300 lire ($6.15); with bath, 7,000 lire ($8.12). Bathless doubles go for 8,600 lire ($9.98); with bath, 13,500 lire ($15.66). Footnote: Mrs. Rossi rarely turns anyone away, even during high season when rooms are scarce. She's purchased a first-class pension, the Hermitage, for overflow guests.

Hotel Giotto, 41 Via Fontebella (tel. 812-209), is a most up-to-date and well-run hotel, built at the edge of town on several levels. Near the Basilica of St. Francis, and opening onto panoramic views, the Giotto offers little formal gardens and terraces for meals or sunbathing. It has spacious modern public rooms and an elevator. Most of its well-furnished bedrooms—72 in all—have private baths. Bright colors predominate, and there's a Parmeggiani mural (modern artist from Bologna) over the drinking bar. The following rates are charged: $7.50 for a single without bath; $10 with bath. Bathless doubles go for $10.60; $17.50 with bath. The full-pension rate ranges from $22.95 to a peak $26.48 per person.

Umbra, Piazza del Comune (tel. 812-563), is the most centrally located accommodation in Assisi, in a position right off the main square with its Temple of Minerva. The outdoor terraced dining room forms an important part of the hotel's entryway. You enter through old stone walls covered with vines, and walk under a leafy pergola. The lobby is compact and functional. The bedrooms themselves are most efficient, with comfortable beds; some have a tiny balcony overlooking the crusty old rooftops and the Umbrian countryside. Many of the 28 rooms have private baths or showers. Bathless singles go for 4,600 lire ($5.34); with bath, 6,700 lire ($7.77). Bathless doubles rent for 6,900 lire ($8); with bath, 10,400 lire ($12.06), inclusive. Full pension ranges from 11,300 lire ($13.11) to 12,400 lire ($14.38), inclusive.

The Budget Class

Albergo Minerva, 7 Piazzetta Ruggero Bonghi (tel. 812-416), is on the lower edge of Assisi, a short walk from the Basilica of St. Francis, and many of its rooms open onto excellent views. With the owner, Andrea Lipparelli, directing the show, guests who know a real bargain are welcomed to a friendly atmosphere. The Minerva is sheltered in a remodeled oldish building, with a well-maintained interior. But there are no luxuries or frills, unless you count the vaulted ceilings of the lounge and dining room and the collection of modern paintings. The hotel is well kept and clean, but you must bring your own magic. Bathless singles rent for an inclusive 3,100 lire ($3.60); with bath, 4,300 lire ($4.99). Bathless doubles go for 5,300 lire ($6.15); with bath, 7,200 lire ($8.35). In the same building, the hotel runs a budget restaurant, popular with tourists and locals, as it has not only good cooking, but fine wines from the hill country.

Excelsior, 2/A Via Tiberio d'Assisi (tel. 812-328), is a small third-class hotel, remodeled to accommodate its share of the multitude of visitors who pass through Assisi. About 50 feet off the main Piazza del Comune, the hotel was recently renovated. It is a suitable candidate for those seeking a clean room, a good bed, and inexpensive but filling Umbrian fare. The bathless singles go for 4,200 lire ($4.87); with bath, 5,400 lire ($6.26). Bathless doubles rent for 7,400 lire ($8.58); with bath, 9,300 lire ($10.79). The full-pension rate ranges from 11,500 lire ($13.34) to 12,500 lire ($14.50) per person.

Living in a Medieval Villa

S. Anthony's Guest House, 10 Via Galeazzo Alessi (tel. 812-542), is special, reflecting the spirit of the old Sidney Poitier film, "The Lilies of the Field." It's for those desiring an economical and comfortable accommodation in a medieval villa turned pension. On the upper ledges of Assisi, S. Anthony's contains its own terraced gardens and views. Run by members of the Franciscan Sisters of the Atonement (an order originating in New York), the guest house offers good rooms and complete tranquility. Visitors who pass through the large wooden entrance door are greeted with a smile. In all, 45 guests are accommodated here, and are charged 6,800 lire ($7.89) per person, based on double occupancy and without private bath. This tariff includes three meals as well. The sisters are dedicated to social work and to St. Francis, and finding this former villa was the answer to a prayer. They joyfully go about, polishing and scrubbing, making beds, and serving bountiful platters of good basic hearty food in a restored 12th-century dining room.

READER'S PENSION SELECTION: "**Pensione Nord,** 23E Via Becchetti (tel. 81-91-16), is owned by Ettore Mancini. It's at Santa Maria Degli Angeli, five kilometers from Assisi. I paid 4,000 lire ($4.64) a night. There was a sink in the room, a little balcony with potted flowers, a spotless (even by American standards) bathroom with a huge bathtub, real (i.e. immersed in water) hot baths for 500 lire (58¢). The pièce de résistance is a light right by the bed, so you don't have to get up to turn it out. Coffee is served in the morning in a lovely little china cup" (Joanne Landesman, Santa Cruz, Calif.).

DINING IN ASSISI: **La Taverna dell l'Arco da Bino,** 8 Vicolo S. Gregorio, offers the best cuisine to be found outside the second-class hotels. Perched down a walk of old steps, the tavern captures the atmosphere of the 14th century, with original vaulted ceilings and stone walls. La Taverna offers a limited, but well chosen, à la carte menu. The first plate might be melon and figs at 1,100 lire ($1.28). Main dishes include piccione (pigeon) for 2,700 lire ($3.13), or veal scaloppine in Marsala wine, 1,800 lire ($2.09). Desserts are in the 500-lire (58¢) to 900-lire ($1.04) range.

Ascesi, 7 Via Frate Elia (tel. 812-420), is an inviting little restaurant near the Basilica of St. Francis, where you can get a complete meal for 3,300 lire ($3.83). A typical repast starts with a homemade soup or pasta (the simpler varieties), plus a choice of four main dishes, with vegetables, as well as fresh fruit for dessert. The Ascesi is on the lower floor of a stone structure which houses a hotel with 11 comfortable rooms, each containing bath and shower, its antique vaulted ceiling intact. Good simple meals for low budgets are served here.

Our final stopover in the Umbrian hills brings us about 78 miles north of Rome.

8. Spoleto

Hannibal couldn't conquer it, but Gian-Carlo Menotti did—and how. Before Maestro Menotti put Spoleto on the tourist map, it was known mostly to art lovers, teachers, and students. Today the chic and fashionable, the artistic and arty, the bohemian and the middlebrow flood the Umbrian hill town to attend performances of the world-famed **"Festival dei Due Mondi"** (Festival of the Two Worlds), most often held in June and July. Menotti searched and traveled through many hill towns of Tuscany and Umbria before making a final choice. When he saw Spoleto, he fell in love with it. And quite understandably.

Before Tennessee Williams arrived to premiere a new play, Tom Schippers to direct a musical "Macbeth," Shelley Winters to do three one-act plays by Saul Bellow, Spoleto was known both to St. Francis and to Lucrezia Borgia, the latter having occupied the 14th-century castle that towers over the town, the Rocca dell'Albornoz. The town is filled with palaces of Spoletan aristocracy, medieval streets, and towers for protection from a time when visitors weren't as friendly as those of today. There are churches, churches, and more churches—some of which, such as **S. Gregorio Maggiore,** were built in the Romanesque style in the 11th century.

But the tourist center is the **Piazza del Duomo,** with its cathedral and **Teatro Caio Melisso** (Chamber Theater). Though few visitors may know it, Mr. Menotti has a small house with a terrace opening onto the square. The cathedral itself is a hodgepodge of Romanesque and medieval architecture, with a 12th-century campanile. Its facade is of exceptional beauty, renowned especially for its mosaic by Salsterno. The interior should be visited if for no other reason than to see the cycle of frescoes in the chancel by Filippo Lippi. His son, Filippino, also an artist, designed the tomb for his father. The keeper of the apse will be only too happy to unlock it for you. These frescoes, believed to have been carried out largely by students, were the elder Lippi's last work; he died in Spoleto in 1469. Vasari writes, "Some said he was poisoned by certain persons related to the object of his love." As friars went in those days, Lippi was a bit of a swinger, having run off with a nun, Lucrezia Buti, who later posed as the Madonna in several of his paintings.

Spoleto should be visited even when the festival isn't taking place, as it's a most interesting town. It has a number of sights worth seeking out, including the remains of a **Roman Theater** lying off the Piazza della Libertà. Motorists wanting a view can continue up the hill from Spoleto around a winding road (about five miles) to **Monteluco,** 2,500 feet above sea level. An ancient spot, Montelucco is peppered with summer villas.

A note on the festival: dates, programs, prices of tickets, change yearly. In Spoleto, the general offices of the festival are 10 Via Giustolo. In New York City, an office is at 119 West 57th Street (tel. 582-2746).

HOTELS IN SPOLETO: Spoleto offers an attractive range of hotels, but when the "two worlds" crowd in at festival time, the going's rough (last season a group of students bedded down on the Piazza del Duomo). In an emergency, the Tourist Office at the Piazza della Libertà (tel. 23-190) can probably arrange for you to stay in a private home—at exceptionally low prices: a clean, comfortable double room for around 3,600 lire ($4.18) per night, not including break-fast. The office is open only during regular business hours, but it's imperative to telephone in advance for a reservation. Many of the private rooms are often rented way in advance to artists appearing at the festival. Our specific hotel recommendations follow.

A First-Class Choice

Gattapone, Via del Ponte (tel. 23-125), is more a spectacle than a hotel. Probably the only eight-room hotel in Italy to be rated first class, it's among the clouds, high on a twisting road leading to the ancient castle and the 13th-century Ponte delle Torri, a bridge 250 feet high. The hotel and restaurant occupy two separate stone cottages, side by side—one devoted to guest rooms, the other to serving meals. The buildings cling closely to the road, and each descends down the precipice overlooking the gorge. The hotel has had its viewside equipped with a two-story picture window and an open spiral stairway leading from the intimate lounge to the bedrooms. Each of the rooms—doubles only, all with private bath—is individually furnished, with comfortable beds, antiques, and plenty of space. A double room in high season costs an inclusive 18.500 lire ($21.46). A meal, with that view, averages around 6,800 lire ($7.89). The restaurant is open March to October only.

A Second-Class Entry

Dei Duchi, Piazza della Libertà (tel. 23-105), is a well-designed, modern hotel, within walking distance of the major sights: yet it perches on a hillside with views and terraces. Near the Roman Theater, Dei Duchi is graced with walls of natural brick, open-to-the-view glass, tropical plants, and lounges with Danish furnishings and original paintings. Every bedroom has its own balcony, bedside lights, and telephones, plus brightly colored bed coverings, wood-grained furniture, built-in cupboards—quite a good layout. Singles with private bath or shower rent for 9,000 lire ($10.44); doubles with bath or shower, 14,000 lire ($16.24) per person. You have a choice of two dining rooms—each airy, light, and roomy. Meals are skillfully prepared by high-hatted chefs. Demi- or full pension is required at festival time.

A Budget Choice

Clarici, Piazza della Vittoria (tel. 24-206), is rated only third class, but it's new, airy, and modern—all its rooms featuring a private bath or shower. Each accommodation has a private balcony, opening onto a view. The hotel doesn't emphasize style, but the creature comforts: soft low beds, built-in wardrobes, telephones, steam heat, an elevator. There's a large hanging terrace for sun bathing or sipping drinks. Open year round, the hotel charges 4,300 lire ($4.99) for a single with shower; 6,700 lire ($7.77) for a double with shower, inclusive. Breakfast is an additional 900 lire ($1.04).

DINING IN SPOLETO: **Il Tartufo,** 24 Piazza Garibaldi (tel. 251-36), outside the heart of town near the amphitheater, may serve as your introduction to the Umbrian tartufo (truffle). This immaculately kept, excellent taverna serves at least nine regional specialties using the black tartufo of Spoleto. An ever-popular dish—and a good introduction for neophyte palates who may never have tried truffles—is fettuccine al tartufo at 2,500 lire ($2.90). Alternatively, you may want to start your meal with an omelette—for instance, frittata al tartufo at 3,300 lire ($3.83). Main dishes of veal and beef cost 2,500 lire ($2.90), and you're assessed a 300-lire (35¢) cover charge. Closed Wednesdays and from July 15 to July 31.

Tric-Trac da Giustino, Piazza del Duomo (tel. 352-92), is frequented by an international clientele, the majority of which are Americans at the Festival of the Two Worlds. The setting on this landmark square is in an atmosphere evoking the 16th century. The restaurant as well as Giustino's American bar is beneath Signor Menotti's house. The food is well prepared, the service excellent. For a full-course meal, expect to pay from 6,000 lire ($6.96) to 9,500 lire ($11.02). The restaurant is open only from April to October.

Chapter VII

BOLOGNA AND FOUR EMILIAN CENTERS

1. **Bologna**
2. **Ferrara**
3. **Faenza**
4. **Modena**
5. **Parma**

LYING IN THE NORTHERN REACHES of Central Italy, the district of Emilia-Romagna is known for gastronomy and for its art cities, such as Modena and Parma. Once-great families, including the Renaissance Dukes of Ferrara, rose in power and influence, creating courts that attracted painters and poets, notably Tasso and Ariosto. (For other centers in this region, refer to the Byzantine city of Ravenna and the Adriatic resort of Rimini in the following chapter.)

Bologna, the capital of Emilia, stands at the crossroads between Venice and Florence, and is linked by express highways to both Milan and Tuscany. By centering in the ancient university city of Bologna, you can branch out in all directions: north for 32 miles to Ferrara; southeast for 31 miles to the ceramics-making town of Faenza; northwest for 25 miles to Modena with its Romanesque cathedral, or 34 miles farther to Parma, the legendary capital of the Duchy of the Farnese family in the 16th century.

With the exception of Ferrara, which makes a good stopover for motorists heading south from Venice, all of our sightseeing destinations lie on the ancient Roman road, Via Emilia, that began in Rimini and stretched all the way to the Roman colony of Piacenza, a temptress that often attracted invading barbarians.

This ancient land (known to the Romans as "Aemilia," and to the Etruscans before them) is rich in man-made attractions—the Cathedral and Baptistery of Parma, for instance—and in scenic beauty (the green plains and the slopes of the Apennines). Emilia is one of the most bountiful farming districts in Italy, and sets a table highly praised in Europe—both for its wines and for its imaginative pasta dishes.

First, we'll drop anchor in:

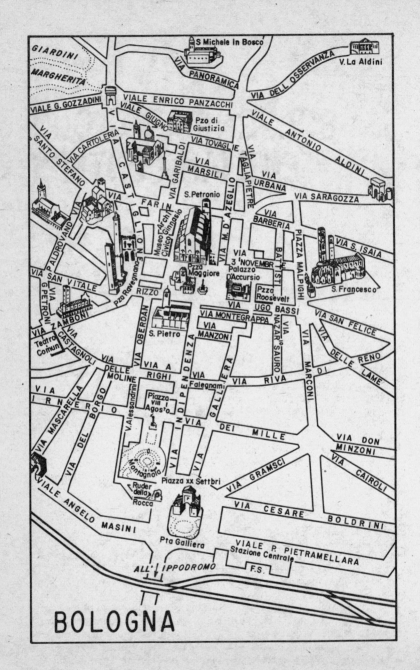

BOLOGNA

1. Bologna

The manager of a hotel in Bologna laments: "You Americans! You spend a week in Florence, a week in Venice. Why not six days in Florence, six days in Venice . . . and two days in Bologna?"

A good question. Bologna is one of the most sadly overlooked (by tourists) cities of Italy, enough so that we've found cavernous accommodation space here in July and August, when the hotels of Venice and Florence were packed as tightly as a can of Progresso clam sauce.

"But what is there to see in Bologna?" is a question also asked. True, it boasts no Uffizi, or Doge's Palace. What it does offer is a beautiful city considered by some to be the most architecturally unified in Europe—a panorama of marbled sidewalks and porticos that, if spread out, would surely stretch all the way to the border.

A city of sienna-colored buildings, perhaps a suitable shade for its left-wing politics, Bologna is the leading city of Emilia. Its rise as a commercial power was almost assured by its strategic location as the geographic center between Florence and Venice. Its university, among the oldest in Europe, has for years generated a lively interest in art and culture.

Bologna is also considered to be the gastronomic capital of Italy. Gourmets flock here just to sample the food—the delicious pasta dishes (tortellini, tagliatelle, lasagne verde), the meat and poultry specialties (zampone, veal cutlet Bolognese, tender breasts of turkey in sauce supreme), and, finally mortadella, the incomparable sausage of Bologna, as distant a cousin to baloney as porterhouse is to the hotdog.

Note: In Bologna, the **Alitalia** office is at 6 Via dei Mille (tel. 226-475 and 226-476).

HOTELS IN BOLOGNA: Before we sample the culinary and sightseeing wares, we'll survey the hotels, beginning with the most expensive, then descending in price.

Deluxe Hotels

Royal Hotel Carlton, 8 Via Montebello (tel. 55-41-41), is new and deluxe, built L-shaped and rising six stories high, with a triangular garden. It is in the extreme modern style, with a balcony and picture window for each bedroom. It is only a few minutes' walk from the railway station and many of the national monuments. Inside, the decorator infused the establishment with warmth. The entrance foyer has a cantilevered staircase, and many of the public rooms wisely employ autumnal colors. Two dining rooms, one with an adjoining American bar, the other a grill, emphasize not only good food, but style and comfort. Bedrooms are cheerful, with such niceties as a radio, television, air conditioning, and a "frigo bar." Doubles are charged 36,000 lire ($41.76); singles, 25,000 lire ($29), these rates including service, taxes, and a continental breakfast.

Grand Hotel Majestic Baglioni (tel. 274-771), is an air-conditioned hotel, a remake of a 16th-century palace, in the heart of Bologna. Many of the public rooms are unspoiled, their original grandeur intact: marble columns, ornately carved and painted ceilings (the one in the dining room, for example, is a Renaissance creation of the Caracci clan), gilt-framed pictures, marble fireplaces, and antique furniture. In the dining room, with its Venetian chandeliers, guests feast handsomely while seated on high-backed, green-velvet chairs, placed on a brilliant red carpet. More than 20 of the bedrooms have antique furniture (at least 10 have private sitting areas); the other rooms are modified, yet still eye-catchingly attractive. Room rates are 16,300 lire ($18.91) for a single; 24,000 lire ($27.84) for a double. A handful of bedrooms, with water basins only, are offered at substantial reductions. The management asks that one main meal be taken at the hotel, for which guests are charged 5,000 lire ($5.80). For 2,000 lire ($2.32), you can shelter your car at the hotel garage.

First-Class Hotels

Grand Hotel Elite, 36 Via A. Saffi (tel. 437-417), on the outskirts of Bologna, close to Autostrada A-1, is highly recommendable. It makes a bold architectural and decorative statement, with tastefully applied primary colors contrasting with bone white. Wood paneling creates a warm ambience. The bedrooms are skillfully designed and decorated, possessing flair. They contain radios, direct-dial telephones, individually controlled air conditioning and heating, and many offer bar and refrigerator areas. Singles rent for 18,000 lire ($20.88); doubles, 29,000 lire ($33.64). Even if you're not staying at the hotel, you may want to patronize the dining room, Cordon Bleu, featuring an array of international specialties, plus classic dishes from Emilia. Also popular is a multi-purpose American bar, with comfortable tufted banquettes, an open fireplace, plus entertainment for music and dancing.

Internazionale, 60 Via dell'Indipendenza (tel. 26-26-85), is in a typical classic palace-style building, over an arched sidewalk colonnade, with a completely contemporary extension. However, its interior has been given the lush Italian "moderno" look. Lounges are dominated by overscaled white plastic armchairs, autumnal colors, and contemporary paintings. The bedrooms have style, each containing a tiled bath. All have been given that decorator touch. Rates, including a continental breakfast, are 18,200 lire ($21.11) in a single, increasing to 29,500 lire ($34.22) in a double.

Jolly, 2 Piazza XX Settembre (tel. 26-44-05), is one of the golden nuggets in this ubiquitous hotel chain. Nicely placed right off the Piazza Medaglie d'Oro, it avoids much of the deafening noise of the heavy traffic. The first-class, fully air-conditioned, 304-bed hotel offers private baths and telephones in all its rooms. The bedrooms themselves escape the usual Jolly simplicity; many have mahogany period furniture and Oriental rugs, combined with soft plain draperies and pastel colors. A double room rents for 29,200 lire ($33.87); a single, 18,050 lire ($20.94). These rates include an American breakfast, service, and taxes. The drinking lounge, all in wood paneling, is a good spot for a before-dinner apéritif or an after-dinner coffee.

Hotel Milano Excelsior, 51 Via Pietramellara (tel. 23-94-42), is a relatively new, first-class hotel near the Piazza Medaglie d'Oro. It has all the trappings and fringe benefits associated with hostelries in its classification: air conditioning, private baths with every room, an American bar, and two restaurants (the more formal one decorated with cane chairs and crystal chandeliers). Frequented largely by a commercial clientele, the Milano Excelsior has a completely modern decor, except that a number of its bedrooms have been filled with the romantic designs of the past—achieving that almost impossible goal: a homey look, with provincial pieces, curved upholstered headboards, and chintz draperies. A couple is charged from 13.500 lire ($15.66) to 19,000 lire ($22.04) for a double room; singles pay from 7,400 lire ($8.58) to 12,000 lire ($13.92). The higher tariffs are for rooms with private baths. No winter reductions are granted.

Second-Class Hotels

Alexander, 47 Via Pietramellara (tel. 27-09-24), is perhaps the best of the hotel buys near the main hub of automotive and rail traffic, the Piazza Medaglie d'Oro, for the wayfarer who wants maximum comfort at minimum price. Perched near the more expensive Hotel Milano Excelsior, the Alexander tempts with its quite good bedrooms, which contain brightly painted foyers, compact furnishings, and neat, tidy baths. The thickness of the double glass in the windows helps to blot out street noises. The main lounge is crisply and warmly paneled in wood, with red leather lounge chairs placed on Turkish rugs. All of the 108 bedrooms have private baths and phones, and they are air-conditioned as well as heated properly in winter. A double costs 16,650 lire ($19.26); a single, 10,500 lire ($12.18).

Roma Hotel, 9 Via D'Azeglio (tel. 23-13-30), right off the Piazza Maggiore, again in the heart of the city, is a small, friendly hotel that has been extensively modernized. It offers superb value, either in its renovated newer section, or in its more time-mellowed older wing, with its sometimes cavernous rooms. The Roma has a small lobby, a combined tearoom and bar, two entrances, and space out back for your car. The two connecting dining rooms (excellent Bolognese cooking) are pleasantly decorated. Cocktails and refreshments are available at the Roof Garden bar and lounge, from which guests can admire the ancient palaces of Bologna. More than half of the Roma's bedrooms have either private baths or showers, for which couples pay 12,700 lire ($14.73); it's 10,000 lire ($11.60) for rooms with water basins. Singles ante up 5,500 lire ($6.38) for the bathless rooms, increasing to 8,200 lire ($9.51) for rooms with bath. I.V.A. tax will be added. Since the food is so good, you may want to take at least demi-pension here.

Third-Class Hotels

Tre Vecchi, 47 Via dell'Indipendenza (tel. 231-991), offers the best food of any hotel in Bologna, and that is a most compelling reason to stay there. However, the accommodations are good as well. Rooms are traditionally and functionally furnished. In spite of the location on a much traveled street, most of the accommodations are noiseless because of the hotel's isolation. The charge is quite reasonable. A bathless double goes for 9,000 lire ($10.44), increasing to 12,000 lire ($13.92) with bath. Bathless singles ring up at 5,500 lire ($6.38), going up to 7,000 lire ($8.12) with bath. Breakfast is extra. On the floors are several lounges where you can relax and watch television. The corridors are brightly lit and warm, with carpeting on the floor.

Albergo Eliseo, 3 Via Testoni (tel. 27-77-38), is a small (only 19 rooms), family owned and run hotel, placed most practically near the heartbeat Piazza Maggiore and the principal shopping district. It is a Bolognese architectural treasure—one of those burnt-orange-colored palaces, with a long row of arches along its facade. Inside, the building forms a quadrangle, with encircling porticoes and potted plants in the center. All of the rooms of this second-floor hostelry open onto this quiet courtyard. While the rooms themselves are not sumptuous, they are practical and immaculate. A double with bath or shower (seven in this category) rents for 9,500 lire ($11.02); for 8,500 lire ($9.86) without bath. None of the singles has a private bath, but they come equipped with water basins, and rent to lone travelers for 5,500 lire ($6.38) a night. I.V.A. tax is additional.

Regina Hotel, 49-51 Via dell'Indipendenza (tel. 23-68-17), is an old-fashioned building recently renewed, with very simple rooms, appealing to budget travelers. Furnished in box-car modern, the rooms themselves are functional, comfortable—good, basic living. The Regina offers about 60 bedrooms, the doubles with private bath renting for 9,500 lire ($11.02). Singles are bathless, going for 5,500 lire ($6.38).

DINING IN BOLOGNA: Even though Bologna is the reigning queen of the Italian cuisine, she does not charge regal prices in her restaurants. One of the city's finest gourmet citadels, Al Pappagallo, is not at all super priced by North American standards. And, happily, Bologna—being a university town—has a number of imaginative dining spots catering to a student clientele. We'll begin with the top restaurants, then descend in price.

The Top Restaurants

Ristorante Al Pappagallo, 3 Piazza Mercanzia (tel. 23-28-07), draws a faithful coterie of gastronomes, some of whom consider it one of the finest restaurants in Italy. "The Parrot" is housed on the ground floor of a Gothic mansion, across the street from the landmark 14th-century Merchants' Loggia (a short walk from the leaning towers). Under a beamed ceiling and crystal chandeliers, diners from many foreign lands are introduced to the Bolognese cuisine. For the best possible introduction, begin your meal with lasagne verde al forno (baked lasagne which gets its green color from minced spinach), 1,500 lire ($1.74). And then, for the main course, the specialty of the house: filetti di tacchino, superb turkey breasts, baked with white wine, parmigiano cheese, and truffles, 4,000 lire ($4.64). Two other well-recommended specialties include tortellini alla Pappagallo at 2,000 lire ($2.32), and cotoletta di vitello alla Pappagallo at 5,000 lire ($5.80). With your meal, the restaurant serves the amber-colored Albana wine and the sparkling red Lambrusco, two of the best known wines from the vineyards of Emilia. Closed Mondays, and from July 1 to 18.

Ristorante Sampieri, (tel. 22-26-50), is another celebrated establishment. Housed in a sienna-colored, 15th-century palace, the Sampieri turns out noble meals in a modernized interior. A well-known Bolognese pasta dish, tortellini, is served with flair here. Tortellini consists of little rings of dough filled with meat, usually veal or pork (as you pass the food stores of Bologna, you'll see women painstakingly stuffing them). Legend has it that tortellini was inspired when a chef gazed upon the navel of Venus. They are served at Sampieri either in a chicken broth or in a ragoût sauce. Either way, the dish is delicious as a starter, costing 1,100 lire ($1.28). For a main course, you may want to sample the cutlet alla Bolognese (a tender slice of veal coated with ham and cheese), 3,100 lire ($3.60). Another excellent regional dish is zampone (stuffed pig's trotters), served with mashed potatoes, 1,900 lire ($2.20). Closed Mondays. At night the restaurant is mainly a nightclub, so it's best to drop in for lunch. The management also runs the excellent pizzeria which adjoins the restaurant. Called **Sampierino,** it offers piping hot pies in the evening at prices that range from 800 lire (93¢) to 1,300 lire ($1.51).

Rostaria Antico Brunetti, 5 via Caduti di Cefalonia (tel. 234-441), is sheltered in a 12th-century tower just off the Piazza Maggiore in the heart of Bologna. The restaurant reportedly is the oldest in town, dating back to 1873. Sometimes the owner Cavaliere Gino Mazzacurati does the cooking, and count yourself lucky if you arrive on one of those nights. His mother is considered one of the most expert pasta-makers in the city where the competition is rough. Antico Brunetti has distinguished itself for its gramigna verde alla moda dello chef, green spaghetti with a sauce made with sausage. The cost: only 1,300 lire

($1.51). On another occasion and for the same price we enjoyed mama's delicious tortellini, those little stuffed squares of dough in a ragoût. With the tortellini, we'd suggest ordering a bottle of Lambrusco di Sorbara, one of the most straightforward, delicious, and best known wines of Italy. It is a brilliant ruby-red and has a natural sparkle. For a main course, we prefer the traditional cotoletta al prosciutto, veal cutlet with a slice of ham and cheese, topped with white truffles, 2,600 lire ($3.02). The dessert specialty is Spuma Chantilly, a foamy whipped cream, 600 lire (70¢). Closed Mondays.

Al Cantunzein, 4 Piazza Verdi (tel. 238-356), occupies a "small corner" on a half-moon-shaped piazza with ocher-tinted Renaissance buildings. It faces the Teatro Communale. The Communist mayor with his family often comes here for a long drawn out feast (but French champagne?). The restaurant has a long tradition. Once it was a stopover for chauffeurs. The chef is especially noted for his many varieties of pasta, including several made with spinach. Our favorites are lasagne farcite alla Cantunzein (stuffed with sausages). The price range for pasta dishes is from 1,300 lire ($1.51) to 1,600 lire ($1.86). For a main course, we'd recommend the bolliti misti (boiled meats carved from a cart), 2,500 lire ($2.90). Sometimes a slice of zampone, the delicious specialty of Modena, is included. This is a pig's foot stuffed with minced and spiced pork. For a complete meal, expect to pay from 6,000 lire ($6.96) to 11,000 lire ($12.76). For your wine, we'd suggest Sangiovese, a dark ruby-red "brut" wine whose name translates as "the blood of Jove." It goes for about 1,800 lire ($2.09) a bottle. Closed Tuesdays and in August.

Montegrappa-da Nello, 2 via Montegrappa (tel. 236-331), has a faithful list of habitués who swear by its pasta dishes. Franco Goldoni and Franco Bolini are your hosts. They insist that all their produce be fresh. Their restaurant, just a short walk from the Piazza Maggiore, offers tortellina Montegrappa at 1,100 lire ($1.28). This pasta favorite is served in a cream and meat sauce. The restaurant is also known for its fresh white truffles and mushrooms. You can try these in an unusual salad, including porcini, the large wild mushrooms, at a cost of 4,200 lire ($4.87). Another salad we prefer is made with truffles, mushrooms, Parmesan cheese, and artichokes (again, fresh), at a cost of 2,500 lire ($2.90). For a main course, we'd suggest misto del cuoco—a mixed platter from the chef, featuring a selection of his specialties, including zampone, cotoletta Bolognese, and scaloppina with fresh mushrooms. It goes for 3,200 lire ($3.71). Expect to pay from 6,000 lire ($6.96) to 8,000 lire ($9.28) for a complete meal, plus 12% for service. Walk on through the ground-floor dining area, heading for the large kitchen and dining room below. The restaurant is closed Mondays and from July 20 to August 23.

Rosteria da Luciano, 19 Via Nazario Sauro (tel. 40-121), is seriously challenging the competition for supremacy. It serves some of the best food in Bologna at prices that are reasonable. On a side street, within walking distance of the center, it is styled like a sophisticated tavern. Preferred is the front room, opening onto the kitchen. As a novelty, there's a see-through window on the street, looking directly into the kitchen. The chefs not only can't keep any secrets from you, but you get an appetizing preview of what awaits you before you step inside. To begin your gargantuan repast, request the manicaretto garisenda piatto del Buon Ricordo, at 1,600 lire ($1.86). This green pasta is rolled with the savory Parma ham as well as the cheese of Parma. Two well-recommended main dishes include the fritto misto all'Italiana at 3,100 lire ($3.60) and the scaloppe al cartoccio, 3,900 lire ($4.52). A dramatic dessert is the crêpes flambée at 3,200 lire ($3.71). Closed Wednesdays and in August.

Budget to Moderate

Trattoria Augusto, 2 Via Testoni (tel. 264-584), is a pleasant, modernized little restaurant, with wood paneling and many original paintings. Only a short walk from the basilica, it is frequented largely by athletes—footballers, mountain climbers, and swimmers. Typical main dishes include manzo bollito (boiled beef) at 1,800 lire ($2.09), and braciolo di vitello at 2,100 lire ($2.44). To begin with, try the lasagne verde al forno at 800 lire (93¢). The dessert specialty is semifreddo all'Augusto, 850 lire (99¢). Closed Wednesdays and from July 26 to August 22.

Ristorante Da Giuseppe, 11 Piazza Maggiore, facing the Church of St. Petronio in the very heart of the city, is no banquet of decoration—but the food is, especially the well-prepared regional dishes. You order à la carte. Two suggestions: a plate of tortellini flavored with a ragoût sauce, 800 lire (93¢), followed by the veal cutlet Bolognese, 1,800 lire ($2.09). Service is 12% extra. Closed Wednesdays.

Trattoria Da Pietro, 18a Via De Falegnami, may win you over with its utter simplicity and local color, a fit foil for the typical Bolognese dishes served here. The trattoria has just a few tables on the lower level. An elaborate and skillfully arranged display of uncooked foods—fresh strawberries, oranges, sausages, apples, strings of garlic, peppers, green tomatoes, fresh asparagus, cherries—is a Lorelei lure. The upper level has several family-style tables, at which you're likely to see a gathering of artists. The English-speaking owner is also likely to say: "Forget about the menu. We'll tell you what we have." Anywhere from 3,500 lire ($4.06) to 6,000 lire ($6.96) should be sufficient for a substantial meal here.

The **Taverna,** 19d Strada Maggiore, is an attractive, two-story tavern, frequented mainly by university students drawn here by the good food. The meals are fine, though not fancy, or elaborately served. For 800 lire (93¢), you can order the house specialty, lasagne verde al forno. And for an appetizer, we'd suggest a plate of antipasto misto, 1,800 lire ($2.09). This selection of hors d'oeuvres will give you a taste treat and an experience with the sausages of Bologna—particularly mortadella, prepared according to all those heavily guarded recipes. The most typical main dish to order is the previously described cotolette alla Bolognese, 1,600 lire ($1.86). Desserts average 800 lire (93¢). The restaurant is housed on the ground floor of a Gothic mansion, the Isolani House, built in the 13th century. Closed Mondays.

THE SIGHTS: Of all the cities of Italy, Bologna is perhaps the easiest to cover on foot, as most of the major sights are in or around the **Piazza Maggiore,** the heart of the city. And such a handsome center it is, dominated by:

The Church of Saint Petronius

Sadly, the facade of this enormous Gothic basilica was never completed. It therefore sits like a lady half out of her dress, glared at by thousands of Peeping Toms. The church honors the patron saint of Bologna. The builders went to work in 1390, but after three centuries the church was still not completed, though Charles V was crowned emperor here in 1530. However, Jacopo della Quercia of Siena did grace the central door with Renaissance sculpture, considered a masterpiece, although today many of the details are buried under layers of Bolognese grime. Inside, the church could accommodate the traffic of Grand Central Station. The central nave is separated from the aisles by pilasters, shooting upward to the flying arches of the ceiling. Of the 22 art-filled chapels, the most interesting is the Bolognini Chapel, the fourth chapel on the left as you enter. It is embellished with frescoes representing Heaven and Hell (the cannibalistic scenes from Hell, the sadism and torture, attract the most attention). The purity and simplicity of line represent some of the best of the Gothic in Italy.

As you come out of the basilica, head left to the second attractive square of Bologna, the **Piazza del Nettuno,** adjoining the Piazza Maggiore. In the center of this satellite square is:

The Fountain of Neptune

Characteristic of the pride and independence of Bologna, this fountain has gradually become the symbol of the city itself—though it was, in fact, designed by a Frenchman, named Giambologna by the Italians (his fame rests largely on the work he did in Florence). Considered irreverent by some, vulgar to other tastes, magnificent by more liberal appraisers, the 16th-century fountain depicts Neptune with rippling muscles, with a trident in one arm and a heavy foot on the head of a dolphin. Around his feet are four cherubs, also with dolphins. At the base of the fountain nestle four sirens, each sprouting five different streams of water from her breasts. After checking out the peculiar mammillary activity of the sirens, head across the street for:

The Palazzo Communale

Built in the 14th century, the Town Hall has seen major restorations, but happily retains its splendor. Enter through the courtyard, then proceed up the steps on the right to the **Communal Collection of Fine Arts** (free; open 9 to 2 p.m.; Sundays 9 a.m. to 12:30 p.m. and 4 to 7 p.m.; closed Tuesdays). But don't harbor hopes too high. The interior of the palace is infinitely more enjoyable than the art, mostly the work of Emilian masters—or, in many cases, pupils.

The Basilica of St. Domenico

At the Piazza St. Domenico, the basilica dates from the 13th century, but has seen many alterations and restorations, achieving a lot of its present drama with pale gray and cream walls, aided by maroon hangings draped across the pilasters. The church houses the tomb of St. Domenico, opposite the main altar. The sculptured tomb—known as an arca—is in itself a masterpiece of the Renaissance, a joint enterprise of Niccolò Pisano, Guglielmo (friar), Niccolò dell'Arca, Alfonso Lombardi, and (perhaps) the young Michelangelo. The choir stalls, the second major artistic work in the basilica, were carved by Damiano da Bergamo, another friar, in the 16th century.

The Leaning Towers

At the Piazza di Porta Ravegnana (one of the most interesting of the old squares of Bologna), the towers keep defying gravity year after year. The Due Torri were built by patricians in the 12th century. In the Middle Ages, Bologna had dozens of these skyscraper towers, anticipating Manhattan. They were status symbols: the more powerful the family, the taller the tower. The smaller one, the Garisenda, is only 162 feet high, leaning approximately 10½ feet. The taller one, 334 feet high (a walk up nearly 500 steps.), inclines 7 2/5 feet. Those who scale the Asinelli (100-lire admission) should be awarded a medal, but instead they're presented with a panoramic view of the tiled roofs of Bologna and the hills beyond. Afterward, take a walk up what must be the most elegant (from the architectural point of view) street in Bologna, the **Via Maggiore,** with its colonnades and mansions.

The Church of St. Stephen

From the Leaning Towers, head up Via Santo Stefano to see a virtual community of churches, linked together like Siamese twins. The first church you enter is the Church of the Crucifix, relatively simple with only one nave plus an uninteresting crypt. It was built in the 11th century. To the left is the entrance to the Church of Santo Sepolcro, its present structure dating principally from the 12th century. Under the altar is the tomb of patron saint Petronius. Continuing left, we enter another rebuilt church, this one honoring Saints Vitale and Agricola. The present building, graced with three apses, also dates from the 11th century. In the apse to the far left is a gilded wood carving showing the three Wise Men paying tribute to the Madonna and her child. Re-entering Sepolcro, we take the back entrance this time into the Courtyard of Pilate, onto which several more chapels open. Through the courtyard entrance to the right, proceed into the Romanesque cloisters, dating from the 11th and 12th centuries. The names on the wall of the Lapidary honor Bolognese war dead. The ecclesiastical complex is open from 6:30 a.m. to noon and from 3 to 6 p.m. (admission free).

The Church of S. Giacomo Maggiore

Off the Via Zamboni at the Piazza Rossini, the Church of St. James originally was a Gothic structure in the 13th century; but like so many others, it has been altered and restored at the expense of its original design. Still, it is one of Bologna's most interesting churches, filled with art treasures. The Bentivoglio Chapel is the most sacred haunt, even though time has dimmed the luster of its frescoes. In back of the main altar (to the left) is a Madonna and Bambino enthroned, one of the most outstanding works of the artist Francesco Francia. The holy pair are surrounded by angels and saints, as well as a half-naked Sebastian to the right. Nearby is a sepulchre of Antonio Bentivoglio, designed by the Sienese, Jacopo della Quercia, who labored so long over the doors to the Basilica of S. Petronio.

The Civic Archaeological Museum

At 2 Dell'Archiginnasio (on the street that runs to the left when facing the Basilica of S. Petronio). Housed in this museum is one of the major Egyptian collections in Italy, as well as important Etruscan discoveries found in Emilia. As you enter, look to the right in the atrium to see a decapitated marble torso, said to be that of Nero. In the first room upstairs are cases of the relics, tools, and artifacts of prehistoric man. But in Rooms 3, 4, and 5, interest picks up considerably, as these salons display the Egyptian collection—notably an array of mummies and sarcophagi. The chief attraction (Room 4) is the cycle of bas reliefs from Horemheb's tomb. In Room 6 is the museum's greatest treasure, Phidias' head of "Athena Lemnia," a Roman copy of a Greek work, dating from the 5th century B.C. In Room 9 search out the miniature Byzantine casket, carved from ivory. The rooms that follow, notably No. 10, comprise the best single exhibition in the museum—the relics of the Etruscans. As you enter, look at the glass cabinet against the wall to the right. In it is displayed a highly stylized "Askos Benacci," depicting a man on a horse which is perched on yet another animal. Also in this long hall is an intriguing terra-cotta urn and a vase depicting fighting Greeks and Amazons. A bronze Certosa jar dates from the 5th century B.C. The admission-free museum is open Tuesdays to Saturdays from 9 a.m. to 2 p.m.; Sundays, 9 a.m. to 12:30 p.m. It is closed Mondays.

The National Picture Gallery

At 56 Via Belle Arti. The most significant works of the school of painting that flourished in Bologna from the 14th century to the heyday of the baroque have been assembled under one roof in this second-floor *pinacoteca*. In addition, the gallery houses works by other major Italian artists, such as Raphael's "St. Cecilia in Estasi." Guido Reni (1575-1642) of Bologna steals the scene with his "St. Sebastian" and his "Pietà," along with his equally penetrating "St. Andrea Corsini," "The Slaying of the Innocents," his idealized "Samson the Victorius," "The Flagellation of Christ," the "Crucifixion," and his masterpiece— "Ritratto della Madre"—a revealing portrait of his mother that must surely have inspired Whistler. Then, don't miss Vitale de Bologna's (1330-1361) rendition of St. George slaying the dragon—a theme in European art that parallels Moby Dick in America. Also displayed are works by Francesco Francia, and especially noteworthy is a polyptych attributed to Giotto. The gallery is open in summer from 10 a.m. to 4 p.m. (in winter, from 9:30 a.m. to 3:30 p.m.). Sunday hours are from 9:30 a.m. to 12:30 p.m. Closed Mondays and holidays. The admission is 100 lire (12¢).

2. Ferrara

When Papa Borgia, otherwise known as Pope Alexander VI, was shopping around for a third husband for the apple of his eye, darling Lucrezia, his gaze fell on the influential House of Este. From the 13th century, this great Italian family had dominated Ferrara, building up a powerful Duchy and a reputation as builders of palaces and patrons of the arts. Alfonso d'Este, son of the shrewd, but villainous, Ercole I, who was the ruling Duke of Ferrara, was an attractive, virile candidate for Lucrezia's much-used hand (her second husband had already been murdered, perhaps by her brother, Cesare, who was the apple of nobody's eye—with the possible exception of Machiavelli).

Though the Este family may have had private reservations (after all, it was common gossip that the Pope "knew" his daughter in the biblical sense), they finally consented to the marriage. As the Duchess of Ferrara, a position she held until her death, Lucrezia was to have seven children (all by Alfonso, we trust). But one of her grandchildren, Alfonso II, wasn't as prolific as his forebear, although he had a reputation as a roué. He left the family without a male heir. The greedy eye of Pope Clement VIII took quick notice of this, gobbling up the city as his fief in the waning months of the 16th century. The great house of Este went down in history, and Ferrara sadly declined under the Papacy.

Incidentally, Alfonso II was a dubious patron of Torquato Tasso (1544-1595), author of the epic *Jerusalem Delivered,* a work that was to make him the most celebrated poet of the late Renaissance. The legend of Tasso—who is thought to have been either insane, paranoid, or at least tormented—has steadily grown over the centuries. Not that it needed any more boosting, but Goethe fanned that legend through the Teutonic lands with his late 18th-century drama, *Torquato Tasso.* It is said that Alfonso II at one time made Tasso his prisoner.

About 30 miles from Bologna, Ferrara today is still relatively undiscovered, especially by the globe-trotting Americano. But the city is richly blessed with much of its legacy intact, including a great cathedral and the Este Castle, along with enough ducal palaces to make for an hysterically frantic day of sightseeing. Its palaces, for the most part, have long been robbed of their lavish furnishings, but the faded frescoes, the paintings not carted off, the palatial rooms, are ghostly remainders of the vicissitudes of power.

THE SIGHTS: We'll begin our tour in the center of the city at the landmark:

Este Castle

A moated, four-towered castle (lit at night), this proud fortress began as a bricklayer's dream near the end of the 14th century. Though its face has been lifted and wrenched around for centuries, it was home to the powerful Este family. Here the Dukes went about their daily chores: murdering their wives' lovers, beheading or imprisoning potential enemies. Though today used for municipal offices, many of its once-lavish rooms may be inspected—notably the "Salon of Dawn," the "Salon of Frescoes," and a chapel that once belonged to Renata di Francia, a daughter of Louis XII.

The Cathedral

A short stroll from the castle, the Duomo weds a delicate Gothic with a more virile Romanesque. The offspring: an exciting marble facade. Behind the cathedral is a typically Renaissance campanile (bell tower). Inside, the massive structure is heavily baroqued, as the artisans of still another era festooned it with trompe l'oeil. The entrance to the **Duomo Museum** lies to the left of the atrium as you enter. It's worth a visit just to see works by Ferrara's most outstanding painter, Cosmè Tura, of the 15th century. Aesthetically controversial, the big attraction here is Tura's St. George slaying the dragon to save a red-stockinged damsel in distress. Opposite is a lackluster "Pietà" by Jacopo della Quercia, depicting a Madonna holding a pomegranate in one hand and her bambino in the other. Also extant from the Renaissance heyday of Ferrara are some bas reliefs, notably a two-headed man, along with some 16th-century tapestries of uncertain appeal. The museum is open from 10 to noon and from 3 to 5 p.m.

The Schifanoia Palace

Restored in 1967, this Renaissance palace at 23 Via Scandiana lures art lovers to its "Salon of the Months." The cycle was painted by Francesco del Cossa, another 15th-century artist of the Ferrara school who played second brush stroke to Tura. He was ably assisted by Ercole de' Roberti, who completed the trio of major Ferrara painters. The frescoes are stylized, yet they have a marvelous naturalism. The "Group of Riders" is the best known. Some of them, slightly impish, are reminiscent of settings for great ballets. The palace is open from 9 a.m. to noon and from 2:30 to 5 p.m. (closed Tuesdays) from May through August. Off season, it is open from 9 a.m. to noon and from 2 to 4 p.m. On Sundays, hours are from 9:30 a.m. to 12:30.

The Este Tomb

At the Monastery of Corpus Domini, 4 Via Pergolato, run by veiled sisters, Lucrezia Borgia, the most famous woman of the Renaissance, lies buried, her secrets with her. The much-married Duchess gave up her wicked ways in Rome when she became the wife of Alfonso I (except for, perhaps, a discreet love affair with the handsome, romantic Venetian poet, Bembo). The woman whose very name (perhaps erroneously) has become synonymous with evil lies under a flat slab, a simple tomb. Frankly, it's not much of a sight, but it would be heretical to come all this way and not pay your respects to the seductive enchantress who in crimson velvet died on a warm Emilian morning on June 24, 1519, having only days before given birth to a daughter. The tomb may be visited from 10 to 11:30 a.m. and from 2:30 to 4:30 p.m.

The Palace of Ludovic the Moor

This ducal Renaissance palace at 124 Via XX Settembre makes a handsome background for the priceless collection of Etruscan works discovered in the necropolis at Spina (in the environs of Ferrara). The **National Archaeological Museum,** in the building, houses the booty unearthed from the Etruscan sarcophagi—including urns, pottery, and jewelry. Downstairs is a salon housing admirable frescoes by Garofalo. In another room are two hand-hewn trees (pirogues) that date from late Roman years. Afterward, you may want to stroll through the gardens behind the palace. The museum is open from May to September, except Mondays, from 9:30 to 1 and from 3 to 6 p.m. (off season hours are from 9:30 a.m. till 4 p.m.). It charges 100 lire for admission.

The Diamond Palace

Another sparkler to d'Este splendor, the palace at 21 Via Corso Ercole I d'Este is so named because of the diamond-shaped stones on its facade. Of the handful of museums sheltered here, the **National Picture Gallery** is the most important, ensconcing the works of the Ferraresi artists—notably the trio of old masters, Tura, del Cossa, and de' Roberti. The collection covers the chief period of artistic expression in Ferrara from the 14th to the 18th centuries. The gallery charges no admission and is open from 9 a.m. to 1 p.m. and from 3 to 6 p.m., except Monday, from June through September (off season from 9 to 4 daily).

The House of Ariosto

67 Via Ariosto. Along with the already-mentioned Tasso, the second major writer to come out of Ferrara was Ludovico Ariosto (1474-1533), who labored three decades over his masterpiece, *Orlando Furioso.* In its day, Ariosto's epic created a literary sensation throughout Europe, as both emperors and grand ladies lounging in salons thrilled to Orlando's (Roland's) love for Angelica. It is believed that William Shakespeare was influenced by Ariosto's style. The house where Ariosto lived and ultimately died doesn't rank in splendor with the d'Este palaces, but it's well worth a visit—though its furnishings are long gone. The house is open from June through August from 9 a.m. to noon and from 3 to 6 p.m. (off-season hours are from 10 a.m. till noon and from 2 to 5 p.m.). No admission is charged but it's customary to tip the attendant.

The Romei House

30 Via Savonarola. A 15th-century palace, this was the property of a rich man, John Romei, a friend and confidante of the fleshy Duke Borso d'Este, who made the Este empire a duchy. John or Giovanni was later to marry one of the Este princesses, though we don't know if it was for love or for power or both. In later years, Lucrezia and her gossipy coterie—the ducal carriage drawn by handsome white horses—used to descend upon the Romei house, perhaps to

receive Borgia messengers from Rome. The house is near the Este tomb. Its once-elegant furnishings have been carted off, but the chambers—many with terra-cotta fireplaces—remain, and the "casa" has been filled with frescoes and sculpture. Noted especially for its graceful courtyards, the Romei House may be visited from 9 a.m. to noon and from 2 to 6 p.m., June through September (afternoon hours, off season, are from 2:30 to 5 p.m.). Ring the bell for the custodian (tip expected).

La Palazzina Marfisa d'Este

This palace at 170 Corso Giovecca was built in the 16th century as a country home (though expanding Ferrara has caught up with it). It has been resurrected and filled with provincial antiques (not the originals, however). The home belonged to Marfisa d'Este, who must have been an exceptional beauty if you can believe Tasso. The bizarre art on the ceiling claims the attention of those mesmerized by too many Tiepolo cherubs. Charging no admission, the "small palace" is open from 9 a.m. to noon and from 2 to 6 p.m., April through September. On summer Sundays it is open from 9:30 a.m. to 12:30 p.m. Off-season hours are 10 a.m. to 12:30 p.m. and 2 to 5 p.m. (Sundays, 9:30 to 12:30).

A SECOND-CLASS HOTEL: Grand Hotel Ferrara, 4 Piazza della Repubblica (tel. 33-015), opens onto a tiny square, with shade trees and a spraying fountain . . . right in the shadow of the Este Castle. The exterior of the second-class hotel is plain, belying the old-fashioned decor retained inside, where antiques are intermixed with leather chairs soft enough for total relaxation. The bedrooms themselves are tight on space, with a more modern design (Nordic furnishings, plain wall-to-wall draperies, bedside reading lights). Thirty of the 70 rooms have baths or showers. Bathless singles go for 4,300 lire ($4.99); with bath, 5,300 lire ($6.15). Bathless doubles cost 6,700 lire ($7.77); with bath, 7,900 lire ($9.16).

WHERE TO DINE: Ristorante Italia "da Giovanni," 32 Largo Castello (tel. 35-775), faces the castle moat—a view to enjoy and remember. It isn't the scenic site, however, that makes the Italia the most outstanding eating spot in the city, but its *tipico* Ferrarese cuisine. Inside, the air-conditioned restaurant is handsomely equipped to prepare and serve fine food. A black-jacketed maître d' seats you, and the service is superb. For the best of the specialties, try a wide noodle dish, pappardelle alla Duchessa, 1,100 lire ($1.28), and grilled fish, 2,700 lire ($3.13). Assorted boiled meats will be brought to your table and carved in front of you at 2,300 lire ($2.67) per plate. For dessert, try a large helping of Italia's homemade ice cream, 1,100 lire ($1.28). Closed Tuesdays.

3. Faenza

Positioned halfway between Bologna and Rimini on the Adriatic, Faenza is famous throughout the Western world for lending its name to a form of ceramics (majolica) known as "faïence." The town flourished in ceramics, an art form that reached its height in Faenza in the 16th century, thereafter declining. Preserving that legacy is the:

INTERNATIONAL MUSEUM OF CERAMICS: On Viale Baccarini, this museum is probably the world's greatest china shop. Originally founded in 1908, it rose again following a 1944 bombing. The "international" in its title is deserving and accurate. Housed here are works that range the world over, including pre-Columbian pottery from Peru. Of exceptional interest are the Etruscan and Egyptian ceramics, as well as a wide-ranging collection from the Orient, and even from the days of the Roman Empire.

But deserving most attention is the modern ceramic art. So impressed were they by Faenza's reputation that many of the greatest contemporary artists have contributed their statement in ceramics. You'll find Picasso vases and a platter with his dove of peace; a platter in rich colors by Chagall; a surprise from Matisse, and a framed ceramic plaque of the crucifixion by Georges Rouault. Another excellent work, the inspiration of a lesser known artist, is a ceramic woman by Dante Morozzi. The museum is open from 9:30 a.m. to 1 p.m. and from 3 to 6 p.m. (afternoon hours are from 2:30 to 5:30 off season). On Sundays, it closes at 1 p.m. and shuts down all day Monday. A 200-lire (23¢) admission is charged.

4. Modena

After Ferrara fell to Pope Clement VIII, the Duchy of the Este family was established at Modena (25 miles northwest of Bologna) in the closing years of the 16th century. Lying in the Po Valley, the provincial and commercial city possesses a great many art treasures that evoke that more glorious past. And, too, the chefs of Modena enjoy an outstanding reputation in hard-to-please gastronomic circles. Traversed by the ancient Roman road, the Via Emilia, Modena (pronounced Mó-dena) is frequented by European art connoisseurs, but rarely visited by overseas travelers. Those who can veer from Northern Italy's main-line attractions for two or three hours or so will be richly rewarded.

THE SIGHTS: The action begins at the **Piazza del Duomo,** with its—

Cathedral

One of the glories of the Romanesque in Northern Italy, the Duomo of Modena's style will be familiar to those who've been to Lombardy. It was founded in the summer of the closing year of the 11th century, and designed by an architect named Lanfranco, though Viligelmo was the decorator (given to sometimes bizarre tastes).

The work was carried out by Campionesi masons from Lake Lugano. The cathedral, consecrated in 1184, was dedicated to St. Geminiano, the patron saint of Modena, a 4th-century Christian and fanatical defender of the faith. Towering from the rear is the "Ghirlandina" (so named because of a bronze garland), a 12th-to-14th-century campanile, 285 feet high. Leaning slightly, the bell tower guards the replica of the *Secchia repita* (stolen bucket), garnered as booty from a defeated Bolognese.

The facade of the Duomo itself features a 13th-century rose window by Anselmo da Campione, Viligelmo's main entryway—its pillars supported by lions—as well as Viligelmo bas reliefs, depicting scenes from Genesis. But don't confine your look to the front. The South Door, the so-called "Princes' Door," was designed by Viligelmo in the 12th century, and is framed by bas reliefs that illustrate scenes in the saga of the patron saint. You'll find an outside pulpit, from the 15th century, with emblems of Matthew, Mark, Luke, and John.

Inside, the overall effect is gravely impressive, with a vaulted ceiling—all wisely and prudently restored by the Modenese during the first part of the 20th century, so that its present look resembles the original design. The gallery above the crypt is an outstanding piece of sculpture, supported by four lions. The pulpit itself, also intriguing, is held up by two hunchbacks. The crypt, where the body of the patron saint was finally taken, is a forest of columns. In it, you'll find Guido Mazzoni's Holy Family group in terra-cotta, completed in 1480.

After visiting the crypt, head up the stairs on the left, where the custodian (tip expected) will lead you to the **Museum of the Cathedral.** In many ways the most intriguing of the Duomo's art, the "metopes" displayed here used to adorn the facade. Like gargoyles, these profane bas reliefs are a marvelous change of pace from solemn ecclesiastical art. One, for example, is part bird, part man—though he has one hoof. But that's not all: he's eating a fish whole.

The next two attractions are sheltered in the 18th-century **Palazzo del Musei** at 48 Largo Sant'Agostino.

Estense Gallery and Library

The Estense Gallery is noted for its paintings from the Emilian or Bolognese schools from the 14th to the 18th centuries. The nucleus of it was created by the Este family, in Ferrara's and afterward Modena's heyday as duchies. Some of the finest work is by Spanish artists, including a miniature triptych by El Greco of Toledo, a portrait of Francesco I d'Este by Velásquez. Other works of art include Bernini's bust of Francesco I, plus paintings by Cosmè Tura, Correggio, Veronese, Tintoretto, Carracci, Reni, and Guercino. The picture gallery is open from 9 a.m. to 4 p.m. and charges an admission of 150 lire (17¢). Closed Mondays.

Considered one of the greatest libraries in Southern Europe, the Estense Library contains around 500,000 printed works and 13,000 manuscripts. An assortment of the more interesting volumes are kept under glass for tourists to inspect (ask the attendant to unlock the door). Of these, the most celebrated volume is the 1,200-page Bible of Borgo d'Este, bordered with stunning miniatures. There is no admission fee.

DINING IN MODENA: As a city noted for gastronomy, Modena offers a number of good restaurants at varying price levels. But for a memorable experience, head for:

Fini, Largo Francesco (tel. 22-33-14). This restaurant alone is well worth making the trip to Modena. Proudly maintaining the high reputation of the city's kitchen, Fini (owned by the Hotel Real-Fini, but in a different part of the city), is one of the best restaurants you're likely to encounter in Emilia-Romagna. For starters, try the green lasagne or the tortellini (prepared in six different ways here—for example, with truffles), at prices that range from 900 lire ($1.04) to 2,700 lire ($3.13). For a main dish, the gran bollito misto at 2,300 lire ($2.67) reigns supreme. A king's feast of boiled meats, accompanied by a selection of four different sauces, is wheeled to your table. Included on this board of meats is zampone, the most famous specialty of Modena. Prepared at Fini's, it is stuffed pig's trotters boiled with beef, a calf's head, ox tongue, chicken and ham. After all this rich fare, you may settle for the fruit salad at 800 lire (93¢). For wines, Lambrusco is the local choice, and it's superb. The Fini is splashed with Picasso-esque murals and equipped with banquettes. Closed Thursdays and from August 5 to August 23.

The **Da Enzo,** 17 Via Coltellini (tel. 225-177), off the Piazza Guiseppe Mazzini (car parking), is kinder to wallets, while still alluring to the palate. Two specialties are noteworthy—lasagne verde for 700 lire (81¢) and zampone, described above, for 1,600 lire ($1.86). The menu's in English. The second-floor restaurant is closed Wednesdays.

5. Parma

Straddling the Via Emilia, Parma was the home of Correggio, Il Parmigianino, Bodoni (of type fame), Toscanini, and Parmesan cheese. It rose in influence and power in the 16th century as the seat of the Farnese Duchy, then in the 18th century under Bourbon rule. For years Parma has been a favorite of art lovers, though a provincial city.

THE SIGHTS: Let's begin our tour of Parma at the **Piazza del Duomo** in:

The Cathedral

Built in the Romanesque style in the 11th century, with Lombard lions from the 13th century guarding its main porch, the dusty pink Duomo stands side by side with a campanile (bell tower)—in the Gothic-Romanesque style—completed in 1294. The facade of the cathedral is highlighted by three open-air loggias. Inside, two darkly elegant aisles flank the central nave. The octagonally shaped cupola was frescoed by the "divine" Correggio. Master of light and color, Correggio (1494-1534) was one of Italy's greatest painters of the High Renaissance. His fresco here, Assumption of the Virgin, foreshadows the baroque. The frescoes, painted from 1522 to 1534, will be illuminated for you for 100 lire, or else you can climb to the dome for 150 lire (17¢). In the transept to the right of the main altar is a Romanesque bas relief, the "Deposition from the Cross," by Benedetto Antelami—somber, each face bathed in tragedy. Made in 1178, the bas relief is the best known work of the 12th-century artist, who is considered the most important sculptor of the Romanesque in Northern Italy. The cathedral is open year-round from 6:30 to noon and from 3 to 7:30 p.m. For Antelami's real achievement, however, head across the square to the:

Baptistery

Listed among the greatest Romanesque buildings in Northern Italy, the Baptistery was the work of Antelami, begun in 1196, though the date of its actual completion is in doubt. Made of salmon-colored marble, it is spanned by four open tiers (the fifth one closed off). Inside, the Baptistery is richly frescoed with biblical scenes: a "Madonna Enthroned" and a "Crucifixion." But it is the sculpture by Antelami that forms the most worthy treasure and provides the basis for that artist's claim to enduring fame, especially his portrayal of the "months of the year." The Baptistery is open from 9 to noon and from 2 to 7, April to September (otherwise from 9 to noon and from 2 to 5). If you wish, the interior will be illuminated for you for 100 lire.

Abbey of St. John

In back of the Duomo at the Piazzale S. Giovanni is a church of unusual interest. After admiring the baroque front, pass into the interior to see yet another cupola by Correggio. Working from 1520 to 1524, the High Renaissance master depicted St. John viewing the Ascension of the Virgin. Vasari liked it so much he became completely carried away in his praise, suggesting the "impossibility" of an artist conjuring up such a divine work and marveling that it could actually have been painted "with human hands." You can have the frescoes automatically illuminated by inserting 100 lire in a box. Correggio also painted a St. John with pen in hand in the transept (over the doorway to the left of the main altar). Il Parmigianino, the second Parmesan master, also did some frescoes in the transept. You can visit the abbey from 9 a.m. to noon and from 4 to 7 p.m.

Other Sights

After viewing this complex of ecclesiastical buildings, you'll find the second batch of attractions conveniently sheltered under one roof at the **Palazzo della Pilotta.** At 4 Via della Pilotta, this palazzo once housed the Farnese family in Parma's heyday as a Duchy in the 16th century. Badly damaged by bombs in World War II, it has been restored and turned into a palace of museums, the most important of which is the **National Gallery.** Filled with the works of Parmesan artists from the late 15th century to the 19th century—notably paintings by Correggio and Parmigianino—the national gallery offers a limited, but well-chosen, selection of art. In Room V is an unfinished head of a young woman attributed to da Vinci. Correggio's "Madonna della Scala" (of the stairs), the remains of a fresco, is displayed in Room VII. But his masterpiece—one of the celebrated paintings of Northern Italy—is St. Jerome with the Madonna and Bambino. Imbued with a delicate quality, it represents age, youth, love—a gentle ode to tenderness. In the next room (8) is Correggio's "Madonna della Scodella" (with a bowl), with its agonized faces. Room X contains Correggio's "Coronation," a golden fresco, a work of great beauty, and his less successful "Annunciation." One of Parmigianino's best-known paintings is here, "St. Catherine's Marriage," with its rippling movement and subdued colors.

The gallery may be visited from 9 a.m. to 2 p.m. for an admission fee of 150 lire (17¢). On Sundays, it's open from 9 to 1.

With the same ticket, you're entitled to view **St. Paul's Chamber,** which Correggio frescoed with mythological scenes, including one of Diana. The chamber lies on Via Macedonia Melloni.

On the same floor as the National Gallery is the **Farnese Theater,** evocative of Palladio's theater at Vicenza. Originally built in 1618, the structure was bombed in 1944 and has been restored. Still in the same palazzo, you can explore the **Antiquities Museum.** This most interesting museum houses Egyptian sarcophagi, Etruscan vases, Roman and Greek-inspired torsos, a bronze portrait of a boy from the 1st century A.D., Bronze Age relics, and a most celebrated exhibition, called "Tavola Alimentaria," a bronze-engraved tablet dating from the reign of Trajan and excavated at Velleia in the province of Parma. The museum is open daily except Tuesdays from April to September, 9 a.m. to 2 p.m. (Sundays, 9 to 1); and the admission is 150 lire (17¢) (free on Sundays).

Still in the same palazzo is the **Bodoni Museum,** a collection of the graphic arts and rare manuscripts, including a rare edition of Homer's *Iliad,* and the **Palatine Library,** which exhibits works from the fallen house of Bourbon.

Finally, to round out your day, go to one of the shops and buy a bottle of "Parma Violet" perfume.

HOTELS IN PARMA: Accommodations are generally a poor lot, especially for those on low budgets, as most of the second-class hotels are second rate. However, those who can afford first-class prices will find three good choices:

Palace Hotel Maria Luigia, 140 Viale Mentana (tel. 21-032), is welcome on the Parma hotel scene. Bold colors and molded plastic built-ins set the up-to-date mood, and bedrooms are made particularly comfortable by sound-proofed walls, air conditioning and TV. There's a very Italian-looking American bar on the premises, plus a restaurant, and garage space. All rooms come with bath and go for 13,000 lire ($15.08) single, 20,500 lire ($23.78) double. Add the I.V.A. tax. Lunch or dinner is an additional 5,500 lire ($6.38), continental breakfast, 1,500 lire ($1.74). This hotel is a good choice.

Park Hotel Stendhal, 3 Piazza Bodoni (tel. 36-653), sits on a quiet square, a few minutes' walk from many of the city's important sights. It offers 45 rooms, all with private bath. Singles go for an inclusive 12,500 lire ($14.50); doubles for 20,150 lire ($23.37). The bedrooms of the hotel are well-maintained, furnished with contemporary pieces. There's a traditional American bar and lounge, with comfortable armchairs for before or after-dinner drinks. You'll find parking space for your car near the entrance.

Milano, 9 Viale Bottego (tel. 35-877), is one of the best of the second-class choices. Near the railway station and a busy thoroughfare, it's an oldish hotel without pretenses. But its bedrooms are fairly large, adequately furnished, and quite clean. The front rooms, of course, face the noisy boulevard. The hotel has 47 rooms, but only a few have a private bath or shower. For the bathless singles, you'll pay 5,400 lire ($6.26); 7,700 lire ($8.93) for the bathless doubles. The limited number of singles with private bath or shower go for 9,700 lire ($11.25); 11,400 lire ($13.22) for a double with bath.

READER'S HOTEL SELECTION: "**Principe,** 46 Via Emilia Est (tel. 40-996), deserves mention. It's inexpensive, very clean, and pleasant. Depending on the plumbing, singles range from 5,000 lire ($5.80) to 6,000 lire ($6.96); doubles, from 7,500 lire ($8.70) to 10,000 lire ($11.60). Furthermore, the owner, Sr. Bruni, speaks English, quite unexpected in this small town somewhat off the beaten path. He was formerly a chef for Cunard Lines. He's a nice man, and as you can imagine, his table is splendid. The price of a meal ranges from 4,000 lire ($4.64) to 5,000 lire ($5.80). The Principe is away from the center, but no more than a 10-minute walk. There are frequent buses as well. Our front room was a bit noisy, however" (William Kaplan, Wilmette, Ill.).

DINING IN PARMA: The chefs of Parma are far more skillful than the innkeepers. Of course, Parmesan cheese has added just the right touch to thousands of Italian dinners, and the word Parmigiano is familiar to diners in American-Italian restaurants.

La Filoma, 15 Via 20 Marzo (tel. 34-269). This is the domain of Signor Ravazzoni, who will tempt you with so many opening dishes you may be bewildered. First, there's tortelli, stuffed with spinach and ricotta cheese, or else "the spaghetti with the four cheeses," including mozzarella and homemade Parmesan. The chef's main dish specialty is cartoccio Filoma—that is, scallops served with raw ham and a slice of mozzarella. All of this good food is enhanced by a bottle of the local wine, Lambrusco. A truly memorable meal, one of the best we've eaten in Italy in a decade, will cost anywhere from 5,500 lire ($6.38) to 7,000 lire ($8.12)—money well spent. Closed Tuesdays and from July 5 to July 20.

The **Aurora Restaurant,** 4 Volta S. Alessandro, Piazza Steccata (tel. 33-954), in the center of the city. Somewhat hard to find, on a little alleyway behind a church, it ignores the decorative touches and concentrates instead on appetizing dishes. Of course, one item that's a virtual "must" for those who make it to Parma is tortelli alla parmigiani for 1,200 lire ($1.39)—little wholesome bits of pasta with the justly celebrated Parmigiano cheese. For a main-dish specialty, try the filetto di tacchina Duchesse (fillet of turkey), 3,000 lire ($3.48). A complete meal will cost from 5,000 lire ($5.80) to 8,000 lire ($9.28).

Chapter VIII

RAVENNA, RIMINI, SAN MARINO

1. Ravenna
2. Rimini
3. San Marino

THE BRISK AIR of the Adriatic Sea sweeps across the marshy land, dunes, and pinewoods. The aromas of the Romagna kitchen waft across the lobby of a pension. Clusters of bodies line the sandy beaches for miles. Ravenna evokes the melancholy memories of the Byzantine in the West. But Rimini makes you forget them again, as you're swept up in a carnival-like atmosphere with Northern Europeans in pursuit of fun by the seashore. And—at sunset— you can hike up Mount Titano to the little Republic of San Marino for a view—high, wide, and handsome.

1. Ravenna

Ravenna, where Dante Alighieri came to die, is one of Italy's greatest art cities—but different from all the rest. The sea long receded, Ravenna is another landlocked city in the way that Pisa is. The waters left behind one of the greatest collections of mosaics in the Western World—many created to decorate 5th- and 6th-century basilicas, during the flowering of Ravenna's artistic expression within the confines of Byzantine and early-Christian art.

THE SIGHTS: If Ravenna existed in some remote corner of Italy, the chances are it would be overrun by tourists and sprinkled with first-class hotels. But all too often it's relegated to a quick day's jaunt from either Venice or Rimini. Though steeped in industry and ravaged by World War II bombings, Ravenna still evokes its illustrious past. But you must follow an inviolable rule: never decide whether to enter a church just by looking at its exterior. Like the Alhambra at Granada, many of Ravenna's basilica facades appear unprepossessing, but contain a wealth of Byzantine mosaics inside. (Incidentally, the mosaic business—now reactivated—is going strong once more in Ravenna. To see the modern artists at work, visit the school of mosaics at 2 Via Chartres.)

To Ravenna went the dubious privilege of being the capital of the Roman Empire in the West. Flavius Honorius, emperor of the West, moved his court to Milan after the sack of Rome. But, again threatened by barbarian hordes, he set up his capital in Ravenna, near his Adriatic fleet for those quick getaways should the need arise. The court was graced with the presence of the legendary Galla Placidia, sister of Honorius, who ruled for a time in place of her son, Valentinian III. With the fall of the Roman emperors, Odoacer came to call, then Theodoric. The Ostrogothic king, Theodoric, converted to Christianity and left many great monuments and reminders of his peaceful reign in Ravenna. He governed for more than 30 years at the end of the 5th century and the beginning of the 6th century. Eventually, Justinian recaptured the city (539), returning it to the folds of the Roman Empire in the East. Ravenna became the outpost of Byzantium in the West. For the glory left behind during all these periods, let's explore:

The Neone Baptistery

At the Piazza del Duomo, near the cathedral, the octagonally shaped Baptistery was built in the 5th century. In the center of the cupola is a tablet, showing John the Baptist baptizing Christ. The circle around the tablet depicts in mosaics the 12 crown-carrying Apostles, dramatic in deep violet blues and sparkling golds. From April to September, the Baptistery is open from 9 a.m. to noon and from 2:30 to 6 p.m., till 5 p.m. in winter (for the custodian, a 50-lire tip is customary). Closed Sunday afternoons. The Baptistery originally serviced a cathedral that no longer stands. The present-day Duomo of Ravenna was built around the mid-18th century and is of little interest—though it has some unusual pews. Beside it is a campanile (bell tower) that dates from the 11th century, perhaps earlier. For a sight far more appealing, walk around in back of the Duomo to the:

Archiepiscopal Museum and Church of St. Andrea

Opening onto the Piazza Arcivesçovado, this twofold attraction is housed in the Archbishop's Palace, dating mainly from the 6th century. In the museum itself, the major exhibit is a throne carved out of ivory for Archbishop Maximian (some of the panels missing), dating from around the mid-6th century. In the chapel or oratory dedicated to St. Andrea are brilliant mosaics. Pause long in the antechamber and look over the entrance for a most intriguing mosaic. Here is an unusual representation of Christ as a warrior, stepping on the head of a lion and a snake. Though haloed, he wears partial armor, evoking "Onward Christian Soldiers." The mosaic workers made Christ's knees embarrassingly low. The chapel itself—built in the shape of a cross—contains other mosaics that are "angelic," both figuratively and literally. Busts of saints and apostles stare down at you with the ox-eyed look of Byzantine art. The museum is open from 9 a.m. to noon and from 2:30 to 6 p.m. (till 5 in winter), and charges 100 lire (12¢) for admission. Closed Sundays and Mondays.

The next cluster of sights is centered a short walk from the Piazza Baracca, beginning with:

Church of St. Vitale

On Via S. Vitale sits an octagonally shaped dome-surmounted church that dates from the mid-6th century. Inside, its mosaics—in brilliant greens and golds, lit by poetic light from translucent panels—are among the most celebrated not only in Ravenna, but the Western world! Covering the apse is a mosaic rendition of a clean-shaven Christ, striding the world, flanked by saints and angels. To the right is the mosaic of the Empress Theodora and her court, and to the left the man who married the courtesan-actress, the Emperor Justinian and his entourage. If you can tear yourself away from the mosaics long enough, you might admire the church itself, with its marble decoration. Seven large arches span the temple, but the frescoes of the cupola are so unimaginative it isn't worth straining your neck to look up at them. St. Vitale is open (free) from 8:30 a.m. to 8 p.m. In winter the hours are from 8:30 a.m. to 5:30 p.m.

The Mausoleum of Galla Placidia

Standing beside the Church of St. Vitale, and built in the 5th century, it is a chapel so unpretentious that you'll think you're at the wrong place. But inside it contains mosaics of exceptional merit—dripping with antiquity, but not looking it. Popular tradition has it that the cross-shaped structure houses the tomb of Galla Placidia, sister of Honorius. But there is evidence that this claim may be false. Translucent panels bring the mosaics alive in all their grace and harmony—rich and vivid with peacock blue, moss green, Roman gold, eggplant, and Navajo orange. The mosaics in the cupola literally glitter with stars. (Same hours as St. Vitale.)

In the courtyard of St. Vitale is the entrance to the:

National Museum

Of minor interest, this museum contains archaeological objects from the early Christian and Byzantine periods—icons, fragments of tapestries, medieval armaments and armory, sarcophagi, ivories, ceramics, and bits of broken pieces from the stained-glass windows of St. Vitale. Charging 150 lire (17¢) for admission, it is open from 9 a.m. to noon and from 2 to 5 p.m.; in winter, from 9 to 2. On Sundays and holidays it shuts down at noon, and is closed all day Monday.

The Arian Baptistery

Lying right off the Piazza Ariani, this Baptistery is not as successful as that of Neone—but it still deserves a visit. Dating from the 5th century, the octagonally shaped structure is also noted for its mosaics. In the center of the cupola is a portrait of John the Baptist baptizing Christ, and the figure of an old man who represents the Jordan River. Like spokes in a wheel, the 12 Apostles—all haloed—branch out. The admission-free oratory is open from 8:30 a.m. to 12:30 p.m. and from 2 p.m. to sunset.

Basilica of St. Apollinare Nuovo

On the Via di Roma (at the intersection of Via Alberoni), this church, dating from the 6th century, was founded by Theodoric. In the nave are some of Ravenna's finest mosaics, illustrating the procession of virgins and martyrs, with their classically rounded faces, in brilliant greens, golds, and whites. On the left are 22 haloed virgins, plus the Madonna and her Bambino, as well as the Three Wise Men and four angels. On the right wall, Christ is depicted seated on his throne with four angels and 26 martyrs carrying crowns. Though repetitious, the processionals create a stunning effect. At one end of the panel depicting the martyrs is a representation of the Palace of Theodoric. Supporting the walls are two dozen Corinthian columns. The admission-free basilica is open from 8:30 a.m. to noon and from 2 to 7 p.m. In winter, the hours are from 8:30 to noon and 2 to 5:30. Adjoining the church is an impressive circular campanile.

Dante's Tomb

On the Via Dante, right off the Piazza Garibaldi, the final monument to Dante Alighieri, "the divine poet," isn't much to look at—graced as it is with a bas relief in marble. But it's a far better resting place than he assigned to some of his fellow Florentines! The author of *The Divine Comedy,* in exile from his home town of Florence, died in Ravenna on September 14, 1321. To the right of the small temple is a mound of earth in which Dante's urn went "underground" from March, 1944, to December, 1945. It was feared in Ravenna that his tomb might suffer in the bombings. Around from the tomb is the Church of San Francesco, dating from the 5th century, in which the poet's funeral was held.

Theodoric Mausoleum

Less than a mile from the above-mentioned attractions (out on the Via della Industrie), the mausoleum honors Theodoric, king of the Ostrogoths (454-526). Though stripped of its art, the two-story tomb, made of Istrian stone, is starkly awesome. In the upper chamber is a porphyry sarcophagus, but the remains of Theodoric have long disappeared, of course. The admission-free mausoleum may be visited from 8:30 to noon and from 2 to 6 p.m. (in winter it closes at 5 p.m.).

The Basilica of St. Apollinare in Classe (also Classis)

About 3½ miles south of the city (it can be visited on the way to Ravenna if you're heading north from Rimini), the church dates back to the 6th century, having been consecrated by Archbishop Maximian. Before the waters receded, Classe itself was a seaport of Rome's Adriatic fleet. Dedicated to St. Apollinaire, the bishop of Ravenna, the early basilica stands side-by-side with a campanile—both symbols of faded glory now resting in a lonely low-lying area. Inside is a central nave, flanked by two aisles, the latter containing tombs of ecclesiastical figures in the Ravenna hierarchy. The floor—once carpeted with mosaics—has been rebuilt (look at the fenced-off section to the right of the entrance for a sense of what it once looked like). Along the central nave are frescoed tablets. Two dozen marble columns line the approach to the apse, where we find the major reason for visiting the basilica. The mosaics are exceptional, rich in gold and turquoise, set against a background of top-heavy birds nesting in shrubbery. St. Apollinaire stands in the center, with a row of lambs on either side lined up as in a processional (the 12 lambs symbolizing the Apostles, of course). The basilica may be visited from 9 to noon and from 2 to 6 p.m. (till 5 p.m. in winter). No admission is charged.

HOTELS IN RAVENNA: Generally an uninspired lot—but adequate and perfectly suitable for overnighting. Our recommendations follow, in all price ranges.

Bisanzio, 30 Via Salara (tel. 27-111), is our preferred first-class choice in Ravenna, ranking ahead of the comparably priced Jolly Mameli. The Bisanzio's location is excellent, just a few minutes' walk from many of Ravenna's treasures, such as the Basilica of St. Vitale and the Mausoleum of Galla Placidia. A pleasantly coordinated modern hotel, with no way-out attempts to create novelty, it's a dignified place at which to stay, with modern furnishings spicing up the old. To brighten the wood paneling are wall-to-wall draperies and Oriental carpets. It's ideal for those who want the absolute comfort of a well-organized hotel, with good bedrooms, offering simplicity, compactness, and tiled baths. Its extra amenities are air conditioning, baths and showers in most of the rooms, telephones, a TV lounge, and an American bar, plus an uncluttered dining room with softly draped windows. Singles with bath go for 14,700 lire ($17.05); doubles with bath for 24,900 lire ($28.88). Bathless singles rent for 9,500 lire ($11.02); bathless doubles for 17,000 lire ($19.72).

Nuovo San Marco, 14 Via XIII Giugno (tel. 24-307), is a smallish second-class hotel, right in the center of the city, with a petite reception lounge, but bedrooms that are fairly spacious. The hotel offers 28 pleasingly furnished rooms, but less than half with private bath or shower. It's a walk-up situation, with quiet and clean rooms, most suitable for one-night stopovers. The Nuovo San Marco's next door to the "leaning tower of Ravenna." The dining room manages to serve appetizing meals. The rooms are most reasonable, with bathless singles costing from 3,000 lire ($3.48) to 4,100 lire ($4.76); bathless doubles, 5,400 lire ($6.26) to 6,900 lire ($8). The limited number of singles with bath go for from 4,100 lire ($4.76) to 5,200 lire ($6.03); doubles with bath for from 7,500 lire ($8.70) to 9,000 lire ($10.44). There's a car park around the corner.

Albergo Cappello, 41 Via IV Novembre (tel. 22-306), has a facade that transcends its interior. It's a brick palazzo with arched street-level windows and doors and a little balcony with a bower of vines and flowers held out like a corsage to welcome visitors. The third-class hotel is reasonably priced, most central, and very clean. In the single rooms without bath, the rate is 4,400 lire ($5.10), rising to 6,500 lire ($7.54) with bath. The doubles range in price from 6,200 lire ($7.19) without bath to 9,500 lire ($11.02) with bath, inclusive. The food also wins high praise, consistently drawing a faithful coterie of locals.

DINING IN RAVENNA: Alla Torri, 3 Via Paolo Costa (tel. 22-098), near the leaning tower, has for years (it was established in 1933) been in the vanguard of good eating establishments of Ravenna. Popular with a multitude of faithful customers with a good nose for the cuisine of Romagna, the restaurant features a 3,300-lire ($3.83) tourist menu, served in a friendly, relaxed atmosphere. It doesn't skimp on the portions either. Among its better dishes on the à la carte menu are rice with ragoût sauce for 500 lire (58¢); fried sole, 2,700 lire ($3.13); and calamaretti fritti, tasty bits of squid fried in a batter, also for 2,700 lire. But to go truly native, order the boiled meat with green sauce at 2,700 lire—a ubiquitous dish of the northern provinces. Closed Tuesdays.

Thirty-three miles south of Ravenna, you'll find:

2. Rimini

The leading resort along the Adriatic, Rimini basks in the gemütlich sun from May to October, then settles down for a long winter's nap. First discovered by Fräuleins & Friends, Rimini was splashed with *zimmer frei* signs, as the Emilians moved in from the hinterlands to open one pension after another, based on the soundness of the West German mark. Then the cheap charter flights from Copenhagen and Stockholm brought more hordes—this time the Vikings, not in horn helmets, but the briefest of bikinis.

The English—who know a good bargain—began to fly in, drawn by the low prices of the Adriatic resort, which are considerably cheaper than similar accommodations on the French and Italian Rivieras. New signs—"English tea like mother makes"—started to compete with the beer and wurst billboards. Now the Americans are discovering that Rimini is a great place at which to wind down between vaporetto rides in Venice and too much cold marble in Florence.

Rimini can be a curvaceous mermaid to some, a battle-scarred sea dragon to others. Go there if you adore invasions of holiday-makers—some of whom have had more than the traditional quarter liter of wine for lunch. The beaches are wide and long, the water clean. The sand is a healthy beige—that is, if you can see the beach under the layers of snow-white bodies cooking a lobster red under the hot July sun.

To arrive in peak season without a reservation guarantees that you'll get a quickly assembled "From Here to Eternity" cot in the maid's pantry. In contrast, those efficient itinerary mappers who always know where they'll be at any given hour—four months in advance—are luxuriating in the beachfront rooms with the picture windows . . . and paying approximately the same price as you are for your humble cell.

Rimini has more beds than San Marino has postage stamps. Most of the hostelries line the beach. Some of the dreary third-class pension boarding houses away from the beach are hot, and bonebare of facilities. Rimini also has a water shortage in summer, so don't be surprised if you're greeted with a dying gurgle when you turn on the tap.

If approached in the right spirit, Rimini can spell fun in the sun. But if you're haunted with fears of the population explosion, get thee to a nunnery.

Note: In Rimini, Alitalia doesn't have an office, but its handling agent is **Adriatour,** 115 Corso d'Augusto (tel. 0541/27-200 or 23-941).

THE SIGHTS: With so much interest centered on the beaches and the modern hotels, it's easy to forget that Rimini is also an ancient seaport. In the center of the city stands the **Arch of Augustus** (27 B.C.), commemorating the joining of the two great Roman roads, the Emilia and the Flaminia. But the real interest in Rimini centers on the Malatesta family, who were to the Adriatic city what the Medici were to Florence. The Malatesta grip on Rimini was tightened to a stranglehold in the 14th century.

The most memorable story of that reign starred Paolo and Francesca, the ill-fated Romeo and Juliet of Rimini. According to legend, Francesca thought she was going to marry Paolo, nicknamed the handsome, but was tricked into wedding his deformed brother, Gianciotto. The cripple later killed both his wife and his brother, who were lovers. Dante immortalized them in the lines: ". . . these two who go together and seem to be so light in the wind." The divine poet wasn't carried away with any schoolgirl romance, however. Unable to condone adultery, he sentenced them both to his Inferno.

The drama of Paolo and Francesca took place, it is said (though some historians discount it), at the 13th-century **Gradara Castle,** which is best visited on a S.I.T.A. tour departing daily in summer at 3 p.m. (it's less than an hour's ride, a distance of only 18 miles, to Gradara) from the Piazza Tripoli. Reservations are made at 44 Via Coletti, and cost 2,500 lire ($2.90). Of course, you can visit Gradara on your own. It's most interesting, encircled by fortress-like medieval walls. The Castle La Rocca was built by the Grifi family, belonging later to the Malatesta and the Sforza. In summer it is open from 8 a.m. to 12:30 p.m. and from 3:30 to 6:30 p.m. In winter, hours are from 8 to 1. Closed Mondays. Admission is 200 lire (31¢).

Sigismondo was another famous member of the Malatesta clan, the subject of numerous legends because of his penchant for getting rid of his wives. The true love of the Rimini lord was his beautiful mistress, Isotta. To show his devotion—and being Italian—he erected a church to her (the **Malatesta Temple** on Via Leon Battista Alberti). The military leader and art patron hired Leon Battista Alberti to design it. Throughout the Renaissance temple—today a sort of Malatesta pantheon—are representations of elephants and roses, the Malatesta symbol, and the initials of Isotta and Sigismondo—knotted together into a dollar sign (with only one line). The present-day temple, heavily damaged in the war, has been restored. Though a church, it remains marvelously secular somehow.

HOTELS IN RIMINI: Our hotel recommendations, in two price ranges, follow.

Second-Class Entries

Kursaal, 80-A Viale Regina Elena (tel. 81-007), at first glance appears to be all sun balconies and no bedrooms. Not so, as the inner core of this six-story, oceanside hotel has 60 compact, ultra-modern bedrooms, each with its own private bath or shower. Considering the quality and the high standards employed, the hotel is most reasonable, costing in peak season (July and August) 6,200 lire ($7.19) in a single, 8,900 lire ($10.32) in a double, inclusive. Open from May 15 to mid-October, the Kursaal charges in the less active months 5,100 lire ($5.92) for a single, only 6,900 lire ($8) for a double. The full-pension rate ranges from 6,000 lire ($6.96) to 9,150 lire ($10.62) per person, depending on the season and the number occupying a room. The lounge and dining room open onto an airy, cantilevered stairway and large sea-view windows. A rear terrace overlooks the private changing cabins on the sands.

Alba, 4 Via F. Gioia (tel. 23-739), is a world unto itself. An old villa, handsomely converted for June-through-September guests, it's placed about three blocks from the sea, set back on a tree-lined street. The owner has brought his own discriminating life and personal good taste to the running of this establishment. For example, he has shared his hobby of collecting fine paintings, displaying them throughout the hotel. The rooms themselves—37 in all, with either private bath or shower—have a flair and are most comfortable. Many are good-sized, with French doors opening onto balconies. In July and August the highest rates are charged—that is 5,900 lire ($6.84) for a single room, 9,200 lire ($10.67) for a double. At all other times, the rates are 5,100 lire ($5.92) in a single, 7,100 lire ($8.24) in a double, and full pension (room and all three meals) can be had for from 5,900 lire ($6.84) to 11,100 lire ($12.88) per person, depending on the season and the number occupying the room.

Aristeo, 106 Viale R. Elena (tel. 81-150) is a recently built, ultra-modern structure with private swimming pool, open all year. Its spacious bedrooms, each with a small private balcony overlooking the Adriatic, are equipped with private baths and utilitarian but comfortable furnishings. Even during the peak season (July and August), the rates are quite reasonable, costing 6,500 lire ($7.54) for a single room; 8,500 lire ($9.86) for a double. During the rest of the year, rates drop to 5,000 lire ($5.80) for a single and 7,000 lire ($8.12) for a double. Full pension ranges from 7,000 lire ($8.12) to 11,000 lire ($12.76) per person, depending on the season and the room.

The Budget Class

Astra, 80 Viale Regina Elena (tel. 80-044), was created for sun worshippers and lovers of the sea. Decked out with private balconies and a rooftop solarium, it enjoys an anchor spot right on the beachfront. Every room here is set for vacation action—simple, Italian modern, quite basic in fact, but with the required conveniences. All of the rooms have their own private shower. The hotel, open from April to September, charges its highest prices in July and

August: 4,700 lire ($5.45) for a single, 6,700 lire ($7.77) for a double, inclusive. Off season, that rate is reduced to 4,320 lire ($5.01) single, 7,500 lire ($8.70) double; while full pension ranges from 5,600 lire ($6.50) to 7,500 lire ($8.70) per person, depending on the season and the room.

Spiaggia Marconi, 100 Viale Regina Elena (tel. 80-368), is a good ocean-front choice—a fairly large (35 rooms), family-run, elevator hotel. Facing the main boulevard, it has shady trees and a graveled terrace on one side, with its own bathing cabins on the seafront. Most of the bedrooms—furnished with utilitarian pieces—have a private shower. The peak season (July and August) rate is 5,000 lire ($5.80) for a single, 9,000 lire ($10.44) for a double, inclusive. Of course, if you check in off season, or get one of the bathless rooms, the rate will be 20% cheaper. The family of Antonio Marconi may win your heart, as they're friendly and helpful. Signora Marconi speaks English. She serves memorable meals, with abundant portions, including, on occasion, tender slices of sauteed veal with garden-fresh asparagus and a bowl of delicate salad greens, with two desserts to finish. The full-pension rate ranges from 5,000 lire ($5.80) to 9,000 lire ($10.44) per person, depending on the season and the room occupied. The open-air modern living and dining room is enhanced with plenty of glass letting in the view of the sea. There's free parking. Open May to October.

The Pick of the Pensions

Belvedere, 50 Viale Regina Elena (tel. 81-247), is a lovely old villa, right on the sea—its front covered with wisteria vines, all partially hidden by leafy trees. It's one of the few remaining old houses, evoking Rimini's past. There are rooms with private baths, and rooms with hot and cold running water. The full-pension rate ranges from 7,000 lire ($8.12) to 11,000 lire ($12.76) per person, depending on the season and the room occupied. The Bianchini family opens the Belvedere in May, shutting it down in October.

RESTAURANTS IN RIMINI: If you ever escape from your hotel's pension requirements, you'll find some good fish dishes from the Adriatic served at the city's limited number of fine restaurants. For the best of the lot, try one of the following recommendations, which begin with the most expensive.

Ristorante Nello, 7 Viale F. Gioia (tel. 27-777), is on the ground floor of a modern building. This place will spread before you a delight of sea fruits. A huge repast, complete with antipasti, zuppa di pesce, grilled fish, dessert, fruit, coffee, wine, and mineral water is likely to run 10,000 lire ($11.60). A large bowl of fish soup—a luncheon in itself—will cost 3,500 lire ($4.06). Not cheap, but Father Neptune prizes his children. Closed Mondays.

Vecchia Rimini, 7 Via C. Cattaneo, off the Piazza Ferrari (tel. 26-610), is one of the finest seafood restaurants along the Adriatic. Deep within the old town, it charges modest tabs, considering the high quality of its cuisine. The atmosphere is roomy and comfortable, the decor enlivened with tanks of fish and ships' models. To get you started, we'd recommend mussels "in the sailor fashion" at 1,100 lire ($1.28), or a savory fish soup at 1,900 lire ($2.20). The risotto with fruits of the sea is also excellent, costing 1,100 lire ($1.28). Among the main-course dishes, the tasty grilled scampi at 2,900 lire ($3.36) is preferred, though you may be drawn to the squid, 3,100 lire ($3.60). The ice cream at 600 lire (70¢) makes for a smooth finish. Closed Tuesdays.

Taverna degli Artisti, 1 Viale Vespucci, Parco dell'Indipendenza (tel. 29-519), is the choice of budgeteers—a good center on the beach. Both a restaurant and tavola calda, it offers a number of dishes prepared well and served at sidewalk tables. Again fish is king, ranging in price from 1,100 lire ($1.28) to 2,300 lire ($2.67). But the regular Italian specialties rank equally well with the palate. Thus, for example, you might try bucatini all'arrabbiata, the house specialty (a type of spaghetti served in a sauce of tomatoes and peppers) for 900 lire ($1.04), or faraona in salmi (guinea hen in red wine and tomato sauce) for 1,300 lire ($1.62). In summer pizza is served for from 800 lire (93¢) to 1,500 lire ($1.74).

RIMINI AFTER DARK: As a resort city, Rimini has lots of nightlife, but only in summer. The **Bus Stop,** Lungomare Vittorio Emanuele III, near the Helicopter Airport, is the rocking-est spot on the beach, attracting lots of young stuff. Featuring dancing to records in the discotheque style and an occasional beat combo, the Bus Stop starts playing as early as 3 p.m. You enter free, but there's a 1,000-lire ($1.16) minimum. Then, from 9 to midnight, at 2,000 lire ($2.32) minimum, it gets packed.

Las Vegas, Viale Duca degli Abruzzi (tel. 50-286; at the Marina Centro, bus stop 9), attracts an older, better-dressed international clientele. The club features dancing every night. When it imports a combo and show, you can't escape for less than 4,500 lire ($5.22) per drink.

The **Paradiso Club,** Colle di Covignano, is similar to one of those Beverly Hills hilltop estates, surrounded by gardens and palms. It's the splashiest place at which to dine, drink, and dance in the environs of Rimini. An orchestra plays for dancing (two in July); and there are two nightly floor shows to enliven the atmosphere. The dancing music is a modified new sound—not too extreme, but not square either. The doors open at 9:30 p.m., and meals are served for around 7,500 lire ($8.70) per person. But if you want only music and dancing, a drink will cost you 4,000 lire ($4.64). The main dining room opens onto a panoramic view of the sea. On warm nights, the outside garden area is used. Paradiso lies a 10-minute taxi ride up in the hills.

Finally, **L'Altro Mondo,** 358 Via Flaminia (tel. 33-151), on the road to San Marino, is the biggest and most popular night spot in the Rimini area in summer. Assessing 2,500 lire ($2.90) as a cover charge, it offers live music every night in summer, as well as a light show. Incidentally, the cover includes the price of a first drink. After that, you pay 1,000 lire ($1.16) per drink.

READERS' TOURING SUGGESTIONS (URBINO): "Urbino is a quiet university town not far from Rimini and Assisi with a superb museum, the **Gallery of the Marches,** * housing 'unfamous' but very fine Renaissance works, many of which have been well restored to their original colors and completeness under the auspices of a mammoth restoration project. The second floor (counter-Reformation works) of the museum can, in our opinion, be forgotten, but the hallway circling the main rooms should not be, if only because of some special crucifixes—simple, dignified, and moving—dating from the 12th and 13th centuries. It is in the ducal palace on Piazza Duca Federico, and is open in summer from 2 to 8 p.m. and 9 a.m. to 2 p.m. off season. The **Raffaello House** is also worth seeing, both because it is a delightful house and because it, too, contains a good collection of paintings" (Tom and Gale Lederer, Richmond, Calif.).

*The Gallery of the Marches in the ducal palace, Piazza Duca Federico (open in summer from 9 a.m. to 1 p.m. and 3 to 6 p.m.; 3 to 4 p.m. off season).

READERS' RESTAURANT SUGGESTION (URBINO): "We put together a good meal for 3,500 lire ($4.06) to 5,000 lire ($5.80) per person at the **Ristorante Self-Service Bonaventura,** 1 Via del Poggio, a block from the main entrance to the palace/museum. We also highly recommend the frulattos (milk, fresh fruit, and sugar blended into a thick drink) which are a filling snack at the tiny bar a half-dozen doors down from the Raffaello House on the same side of the Via Raffaello. Macedonia (with or without whipped cream) is available there, too" (Tom and Gale Lederer, Richmond, Calif.).

3. San Marino

The world's oldest and smallest republic, San Marino is 14 miles from Rimini, reached either by autostrada in your own private car or by bus which leaves frequently in front of the railway station in Rimini. Europe's other peapod nations, Vatican City and Monaco, have less land space, but they aren't republics. San Marino may not have enough land for a decent crow's flight (24 square miles), but it isn't exactly bursting at the seams with population either.

San Marino, also the name of the capital, strides the top slopes of Mount Titano. The origins of San Marino go back to the 4th century A.D. Local tradition holds that Marino, a Dalmatian slave later made a saint, founded the republic. Except for Cesare Borgia's invasion in 1503, and periodic attempts to seize it, the state has enjoyed relative freedom. Napoleon passed this way, finding the nation "amusing," even benevolently offering it more territory. But the people wisely turned him down. Though officially neutral in both world wars, San Marino suffered Allied bombs in World War II (for which Great Britain later paid an indemnity).

Of course, the sovereign adjective to San Marino shouldn't be interpreted too literally. Whenever a republic is small and completely surrounded by a larger nation, it can only exist at that nation's good grace. Unlike Gibraltar, San Marino does not have access to the sea (Rimini is its port). In the post-war years, when San Marino, in the grand tradition of Monaco, opened a gambling casino to attract much-needed revenue, the Italian government brought such pressure that the tiny republic was forced to abandon the operation and the badly needed lucre.

San Marino, instead, has been forced to rely almost entirely on tourists and postage stamps. Prized by collectors the world over, the postage stamps are sold in nearly every shop in San Marino.

On December 15, 1972, San Marino issued its first series of coins in 35 years. On orders from Mussolini, it had stopped minting coins in 1938, relying entirely on the use of Italian lire. Minted in Rome and even designed by an Italian sculptor, the new coins depict such scenes as Garibaldi and his wife, Anita, taking refuge in the little country after the collapse of the Roman republic in 1849. The latter scene is on the 20 lire coin.

SIGHTS: The country is blessed with one super-star attraction: a view seen from one of its trio of medieval towers, Guaita, Cesta, and Montale. Among the specific sights to visit are:

Palazzo del Governo

In the center of town is this handsome Gothic-Florentine-styled building, erected toward the end of the 19th century. It's well worth a visit. It's open from 9 a.m. to 12:30 p.m. and from 2:30 to 7 p.m. In winter, it closes at 5:30 p.m. Admission is 500 lire (58¢), and this also entitles you to visit the Fortress, the Arms Museum, the Museum of History, the Picture Gallery, and the Church of San Francesco.

Dominating San Marino is a **Fortress** or castle that looms like a great ship in the sky. From one of its towers, you can see Rimini, the Adriatic, even the Dalmatian Coast (Yugoslavia).

The Arms Museum

At the top of another hill, also offering a splendid view, is this fairly routine museum filled with such medieval armaments as hatchets, used back in the days when man killed his fellow man one at a time instead of en masse.

San Marino Basilica

This Basilica looks at first like the First National Bank, but is graced by a splendid campanile (bell tower) to its side. When the bells sound, it's a wonder that San Marino (buried inside) doesn't wake up and flee. The interior is less austere, with a central nave and two aisles, adorned with Corinthian columns.

DINING IN SAN MARINO: Chances are you'll be more in need of a good restaurant than a good hotel, as most visitors hike through San Marino in a day, then strike out for another frontier by evening.

La Taverna, Piazza della Liberta (tel. 991-196), is anchored on a site that looks onto the valleys and Apennine landscape. Outside are tables arranged on the belvedere, but inside is a cornball atmosphere. Fortunately, the food is good. A complete meal will run from 3,200 lire ($3.71) to 4,900 lire ($5.68). When the late Tyrone Power was starring in "Prince of Foxes" (filmed in San Marino), he made La Taverna his favorite hangout. With your dinner, why not order a bottle of "Moscato," a characteristic wine of San Marino? Ideal for "real English tea brewed in a pot." Closed from December till January 15.

The **Ristorante Diamond,** 72 Via XXV Marzo (tel. 991-003), is a "grotto" dug out of a rock and sheltered by a hotel. For 3,500 lire ($4.06) you can have many of the regular items on the Italian menu, prepared well and served in goodly portions. We recently enjoyed a large plate of spaghetti with a tangy meat sauce, followed by roast chicken, a green salad, then fresh fruit. The noodles are homemade.

HOTELS AND RESTAURANTS OF VENICE

ONE RAINY MORNING as we were leaving our hotel—a converted palazzo—a decorative stone fell from the lunette, narrowly missing us. For a second, it looked as if we were candidates for the gondola funeral cortège to the island of marble tombs, San Michele. In dismay we looked back at the owner, a woman straight from a Modigliani portrait. From the doorway, she leaned like the Tower of Pisa, mocking the buildings of her city. Throwing up her hands, she sighed: "Venezia, Venezia," then turned and went inside.

Stoically she had long ago surrendered to the inevitable decay that embraces Venice like moss at the base of the pilings. Venice is preposterous, a monument both to the folly and obstinacy of man. It shouldn't exist . . . but it does, much to the delight of thousands upon thousands of tourists, gondoliers, lace-makers, hoteliers, restaurateurs, and glass-blowers.

Fleeing the barbarians, Venetians centuries ago left dry-dock and drifted out to a flotilla of "uninhabitable" islands in the lagoon. Survival was difficult enough, but no Venetian has ever settled for mere survival. The remote ancestors of the present inhabitants created the world's most beautiful city.

However, to your children or their children, Venice may be a mirage of the past. It is sinking at a rate of about 2½ inches every decade. It is estimated that one-third of the city's art will have deteriorated hopelessly within the next 10 years if action is not taken to save it. Clearly Venice is in peril. One headline recently read, "The Enemy's At the Gates."

Working on a campaign to save Venice, John R. McDermott put the case this way: "Venice is under assault by uncontrolled tides, pollution, and old age. Atmospheric acid is eating away its art treasures—stone, bronze and pigment

—and the walls of its buildings are being eroded by floods; industrial waste is polluting its water. Unless these conditions are alleviated and repairs made, some of the loveliest art in the world will be lost forever and eventually the city itself could cease to exist as we know it now."

ARRIVAL IN VENICE: All roads lead not necessarily to Rome, but in this case to the docks on the mainland of Venice. The arrival scene at the unattractive Piazzale Roma is filled with nervous expectation, and even the most veteran traveler can become confused. Whether you arrive by train, bus, auto, or airport limousine, there is one common denominator—everyone walks to the nearby docks to select a method of transport to his or her hotel. The cheapest way is by vaporetto, the more expensive by gondola or motor launch. Here are the advantages and costs of each method:

Gondola (motor launch)

If you are hooked on the idea of arriving at your hotel in a gondola, there is a special rate for this transfer. This service includes an interpreter's meeting and send off, conveyance of clients and their luggage, plus the porter's fees (two normal-sized pieces of baggage per person). The charge for two persons is $19, for three $21, and for four $24. It is the same rate for a private motor launch. (Add approximately $4 more to go to the Lido.) After 8 p.m. or before 8 a.m., there is a 20% supplement.

Vaporetti

Much to the chagrin of the once-ubiquitous gondolier, the motorboats of Venice provide inexpensive, frequent, though not always fast, transportation in the canal-riddled city. The average fare on the "accelerato" (which makes every stop) is 75 lire (9¢), which will take you from St. Mark's to the Lido. The average fare on the "diretto" (only express stops) is 100 lire (12¢)—say, from the Railway Station to the Rialto Bridge. In summer, these vaporetti are fiercely crowded, and you can easily be pushed into the Grand Canal in a stampede—particularly when the Venetians themselves are boarding them to and from work. Try to avoid them at peak hours.

Car parks

If you arrive in Venice by auto, there is a car park near the vaporetti, gondola, and motor-launch docks. You'll find it at the end of the road on your right. You park your car yourself, pick up a ticket, and choose your means of transportation to your hotel. You'll be charged around 1,500 lire ($1.74) daily for a small car. There is a dispatcher at the garage entry who will get you a porter.

Porters

Another tricky problem. If you need help with your luggage to reach a remote accommodation tucked away in Venice, chances are you'll be dependent on the Venetian porter. The porter can carry your luggage aboard the vaporetto (you pay his boat fare), then lead you through the winding narrow streets till he reaches your hotel. Between two points in the city, give him 700 lire (81¢) for one piece of luggage, plus 300 lire (35¢) for each extra piece. If you're having your luggage transferred from the station to one of the hotels on the Lista di Spagna, pay only 250 lire (29¢) for each piece (this rate is in effect all the way to the bridge, Ponte delle Guglie). If you're having your luggage transferred from the railway station to the Lido, you'll have to pay 1,000 lire ($1.16) for the first piece, plus 400 lire (46¢) for each additional piece. This is the official rate, but if a porter thinks you're unaware of that, he may try to charge you more. Protests mean little to these battle-toughened veterans who have stood off the most robust of visitors in sirocco winds under the blazing August sun.

This excessive attention has been devoted to gondoliers, vaporetti, and porters because we've seen too many visits to Venice marred by a hassle that dampens the tourist's enthusiasm for the city at the outset. Providing you can overcome the problem of getting yourself and your luggage transported safely —and without fisticuffs—to your hotel, you'll probably be set to embark upon one of the grandest experiences of a lifetime: the exploration of Venice.

Once you are settled into your hotel, you'll need to know how to get around Venice. At one point, you'll be tempted to enjoy the city on a splurge gondola ride.

More about Gondolas

In *Death in Venice,* Thomas Mann wrote: "Is there anyone but must repress a secret thrill, on arriving in Venice for the first time—or returning thither after long absence—and stepping into a Venetian gondola? That singular conveyance, come down unchanged from ballad times, black as nothing else on earth except a coffin—what pictures it calls up of lawless, silent adventures in the plashing night; or even more, what visions of death itself, the bier and solemn rites and last soundless voyage!"

Mann reflected the point of view of German romanticism, but he didn't tell all the story. The voyage on a gondola isn't likely to be so "soundless"—at least not when time comes to pay the bill. When riding in a gondola, two major agreements have to be reached—one, the price of the ride; two, the length of the trip. If you vaguely suggest in any way one of Barnum's suckers, you're likely to be taken on both counts. It's a common sight in Venice to see a gondolier huffing and puffing to take his passengers on a "quickie," often reducing the hour to 15 minutes. The gondolier, with his eye on the watch, is anxious to dump his load and pick up the next batch of passengers. Consequently, his watch almost invariably runs fast.

There is no longer an accepted official rate schedule for gondoliers. The actual fare depends on how effective you are in standing up to the gondolier's attempt to get more money out of you. Many visitors hire a gondolier for anywhere from $12 to $15 an hour. In fairness to the gondoliers, it must be said that they have an awful job, romanticized out of perspective by the world. For they must row boatloads of tourists across hot, smelly canals with such endearments screamed at them, as "No sing! No pay!" And these fellows must make plenty of lire while the sun shines, as their work ends when the first cold winds blow in from the Adriatic.

Note: Alitalia has offices in Venice at 1463 Campo San Moise (tel. 700-355).

1. Deluxe Hotels

Gritti Palace, 2467 Campo Santa Maria del Giglio (tel. 26-044), is a stately, sumptuous setting for a Venetian fantasy fulfillment. On the Grand Canal, it's the huge renovated palazzo of the 15th-century doge, Andrea Gritti. "Our home in Venice" to Ernest Hemingway, it has for years drawn a select

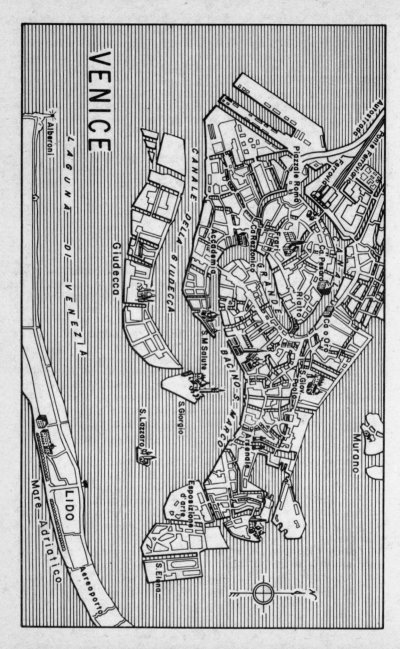

clientele of some of the world's greatest theatrical, literary, political, and royal figures, including Elizabeth and Philip, Greta Garbo, Herbert Von Karajan, the Aga Khan, Gian-Carlo Menotti, Winston Churchill, and W. Somerset Maugham (for his "bottle of Soave in the ice-pail"). The Gritti, a shining star in the CIGA crown, has almost 100 rooms—all air-conditioned and containing private baths. The range and variety seem almost limitless, from elaborate suites to relatively small single rooms. But in every case the stamp of glamor and sophistication is evident. The excellent antiques, in both the bedrooms and public rooms, evoke top-level taste.

For splurge living, ask for Hemingway's old suite, or the Doge Suite once occupied by Maugham. Manager N. Rusconi is used to catering to the whim of the famous, but he doesn't overlook the needs and desires of the first timers from Iowa. The Gritti charges a peak season 35,000 lire ($40.60) for a single; 52,000 lire ($60.32) for a double. These rates, however, are only the price of the room itself, as I.V.A. and city taxes are added on. From November 1 to February 28, prices generally drop by 5,000 lire ($5.80) in a double room. In high season, you are no longer obliged to take half pension. However, the cuisine at the Gritti is among the best—if not the very best—in Venice. The chef, Cesare Gosi, is an artist, the service is flawless, and the setting is romantic. Figure on paying 13,000 lire ($15.08) per person extra for demi-pension rates.

Danieli Royal Excelsior, 4196 Riva degli Schiavoni (tel. 26-480), was built as a grand showcase by the Doge Dandolo in the 14th century. In 1822 it was transformed into a deluxe "hôtel for kings." Placed in a most spectacular position, right on the Grand Canal, it has sheltered not only kings, but princes, cardinals, ambassadors, and such celebrated literary figures as George Sand and her 24-year-old lover, Alfred de Musset. In time, the palace was to play host to such distinguished men as Charles Dickens, D'Annunzio, and Wagner. A star sapphire in the CIGA chain, the palace fronts the canal with the New Danieli Excelsior, a modern wing. Two neighboring palaces as well have been incorporated into this Serenissima ensemble.

"Incredible, breathtaking," said one California visitor. "You enter into a four-story-high stairwell, with Venetian arches and balustrades (one almost expects to see Juliet suddenly appear from behind one of the columns)." Throughout you wander in an atmosphere of silk-flocked walls, gilt mirrors, ornate furnishings, marble walls, decorated ceilings, and Oriental carpeting. Even the balconies opening off the main lounge have been glamorously illuminated by stained-glass skylights. More intimate is the beamed-ceiling drinking lounge, with leather armchairs. The hotel possesses a rooftop dining room, giving you an undisturbed view of the canals and "crowns" of Venice.

The bedrooms, 242 in all, range widely in price, dimension, decor, and vistas, with the ones opening onto the lagoon going for more, of course. The standard accommodations (facing the side) range between 17,000 lire ($19.72) and 27,000 lire ($31.32) in a single; doubles go for 32,000 lire ($37.12) to 46,000 lire ($53.36). For a super accommodation, facing the lagoon, a double is 52,000 lire ($60.32), with sitting rooms costing extra, of course. The service charge is included in the prices, but taxes are additional.

The **Hotel Europa & Britannia,** 2159 San Marco (tel. 700-477), is another Grand Canal citadel of comfort and luxury, but much less expensive. Like the Gritti, it's one of the three deluxe hotels in Venice proper owned by the prestigious CIGA chain. The upgraded Europa & Britannia—recipient of much chain lucre—is a gracious old hotel, handsomely revamped, with a waterfront bar-terrace.

Thoroughly air-conditioned, the hotel offers 146 well-appointed bedrooms, partly furnished with "semi" antiques. The new Tiepolo wing offers 50 completely redecorated rooms with baths. (Warning: canal-view rooms are booked months in advance.) From March 1 to October 31, the hotel charges 29,000 lire ($33.94) for a single with bath; 46,000 lire ($53.36) for a double with bath. To all rates, you must add taxes. Service, air conditioning, and continental breakfast are included in the room rates. For demi-pension arrangements, you'll pay 10,000 lire ($11.60) extra per person. The meals are most elaborate, attractively served on the restaurant terrace.

2. First-Class Hotels

Hotel Regina, 2205 San Marco (tel. 700-544), is a Venetian baroque palazzo, facing the Grand Canal, only a five-minute walk from the Piazza San Marco. Its canal facade is that of a grand old villa, with a waterside al fresco dining area; windows with purple sun shades, and two upper floors with set-back private terraces—all ready for honeymooners. Its lounges incorporate beamed ceilings and marble—all comfortable and inviting. The completely redecorated CIGA hotel has about 65 well-furnished bedrooms with private baths and showers. The single rooms are all modern, with built-in complexes of beds, wardrobes, and desks. Most of the double rooms are more traditional, with a generous use of old Venetian furnishings, and luxury-soft beds. The Regina charges 27,000 lire ($31.32) for a single with bath; 40,000 lire ($46.40) for a double with bath. To this you must add taxes. Service, air conditioning, and continental breakfast are included. Substantial reductions—about 6,000 lire ($6.96)—are granted off season. In high season, preference in room assignment is given to demi-pension arrangements. The half-board rate is 10,000 lire ($11.60) extra per person.

Gabrielli-Sandwirth, 4110 Riva degli Schiavoni (tel. 31-580), is a Venetian-Gothic palace, with blossom-filled balconies, on the fashionable main street bordering the lagoon. The hotel possesses that rarity: a good-sized private garden and courtyard, the center of its life. You'll find a shaded dining terrace, cozy nooks with chairs, swings and hammocks set out. Inside, its lounges have blue-gray marble, beamed ceilings, modern furnishings, and spaciousness. The bedrooms are well furnished and attractively maintained, reflecting the taste level of the owners, the Perkhofer family of Austria. Most of the 110 rooms have private bath or shower, for which singles pay 16,400 lire ($19.02), doubles 27,200 lire ($31.55). The limited number of bathless singles go for 9,800 lire ($11.37), bathless doubles for 12,100 lire ($14.04). These rates are inclusive, except 1,500 lire ($1.74) charged for air conditioning. The food—Austrian-Italian meals—is good. The full-pension rate in high season ranges from 18,000 lire ($20.88) to 26,000 lire ($30.16) per person, inclusive.

Saturnia-Internazionale, 2399 Via XXII Marzo (tel. 708-377), is one of the top choices in Venice, maintaining high standards and top-drawer service. A 14th-century Venetian palazzo near Piazza San Marco, it is part and parcel Old Venice, and as such is recommended mainly to those seeking the romantic past. Wherever you wander throughout this palace, you'll find richly embellished beauty—the grand hallway with its wooden staircase, heavy iron chandeliers, fine paintings, beamed ceiling; the dining salon with its more rustic-style decor, including regal chairs and pillars of bricks, or the more intimate dining gallery in a nautical theme.

The air-conditioned bedrooms are spacious, furnished with chandeliers, Venetian antiques—enriched with tapestry rugs, gilt mirrors, and ornately carved ceilings. Many of these bedrooms overlook the quiet and dignified garden in the back. The cost of staying here varies according to the season. All of the hotel's 96 bedrooms have private baths, for which singles in high season pay 25,000 lire ($29); couples, 39,000 lire ($45.24). The half-pension rate is 34,000 lire ($43.04) in a single; 55,000 lire ($63.80) for two persons. Rates are inclusive. Dining here is an enjoyable event, as the cuisine is excellent.

3. The Medium-Priced Range

The **Hotel Flora,** 2283-A Via XXII Marzo (tel. 25-324), has a jewel setting, right in the full swing of Venetian life, yet set back on a narrow lane in a peaceful garden overlooking the so-called Palazzo of Othello. The little hotel (44 rooms) has its own central patio garden with a graveled terrace, pots of rambling blossoming vines and plants. All the rooms overlook either of these gardens. The hotel is run by an old Venetian family, presided over by Alessandro Romanelli, who is ably assisted by his lovely wife and painter son Ruggero (who looks like a Venetian Bob Dylan). They have given each bedroom—large or small—an individual personality. Some of the rooms have Oriental rugs on terrazzo floors, furniture subtly colored in the Venetian fashion, desks, armchairs, and private baths or showers. Singles with bath go for 14,800 lire ($17.17). Bathless doubles cost 18,500 lire ($21.46); doubles with bath, 23,800 lire ($27.51). Rates quoted are inclusive of continental breakfast. Air conditioning is 1,300 lire ($1.51) per night. In October and March, Mr. Romanelli grants a 20% reduction, and may lower the rates even more in winter. No pension terms are offered, though arrangements can be made for you to take your meals at two nearby restaurants.

Bonvecchiati, 4488 Calle Goldoni (tel. 041-85-017), halfway between the Rialto Bridge and the Piazza San Marco, stands proudly on its little square, looking much like the private villa of a titled Venetian family. The owner, Giovanni Deana (who is also the proprietor of the recommended La Colomba Restaurant), is apparently trying to outdistance Peggy Guggenheim with his collection of modern art. Paintings acquired by him cover most of the lounge halls, corridors, living rooms, even grace some of the bedrooms. Most of the bedrooms are furnished with antiques or good reproductions. A bathless single rents for 10,150 lire ($11.77), increasing to 15,200 lire ($17.63) with bath or shower. A twin-bedded room without bath costs 18,700 lire ($21.69), peaking at 25,450 lire ($29.52) with bath or shower. Rates are lowered from November through March. The cuisine is exceptional. The interior dining room—all in white and ivory, with fluted columns and a central crystal chandelier—has a balcony for overflow dining. But the favored spot for meals is the outside canopied terrace, bordering the canal and decorated with potted plants, lanterns, and garden furniture. The demi-pension rate ranges from 18,850 lire ($21.87) to 24,000 lire ($27.84) per person daily. The drinking bar is purely provincial, warmed by a remarkable collection of copper pots hanging from the beamed ceiling. The lounges are more like personalized living rooms, with paintings and Turkish carpets, and modern plastic furniture.

Boston Hotel, 848 Ponte dei Dai (tel. 87-665), is a very pleasant, 50-room hotel, built in 1962, just a whisper away from St. Mark's. Open from March 18 through October, it's run by an attractive couple, Mario and Adriana Bernardi, who have instilled their good taste and friendliness here. The hotel was named after an uncle who left to seek his fortune in Boston . . . and never returned. The little living rooms skillfully combine the old and new, containing many good antiques and Venetian-type ceilings. For the skinny guest, there's a tiny, self-operating elevator and a postage-stamp street entrance. Most of the bedrooms with parquet floors have built-in features, snugly designed beds, chests, and wardrobes. Fortunately, several have tiny balconies opening onto canals. Many of the rooms are bathless, with hot and cold running water only. For these, singles pay 11,000 lire ($12.76); couples, 19,600 lire ($22.74). For the rooms with a private bath or shower, the single rate is 14,600 lire ($16.94); the double rate is 25,600 lire ($29.70). Rates quoted are inclusive. Air conditioning is 1,500 lire ($1.74) extra per person. The food is good, the portions enormous.

Giorgione, 4587 SS. Apostoli (tel. 25-810), is a recently glamorized little hotel, near the Ca d'Oro vaporetto stop. In spite of its modernization, its decor is lush and traditionally Venetian. The lounges and dining rooms are equipped with fine furnishings and decorative accessories. Likewise, the bedrooms are designed to coddle guests—being very comfortable as well as stylish. Singles with bath peak at 12,300 lire ($14.27), and doubles go for 19,850 lire ($23.03). The owner hawkeyes the running of the dining room, seeing that the cuisine is first rate. Although rated second class by the government, the Giorgione has a higher standard than many of the first-class establishments.

La Fenice Et Des Artistes, 1937-A San Marco (tel. 32-333), is right on the beam for those who yearn for very nice living in a romantic atmosphere fringing on luxury. Your fellow guests are apt to be just as special: a nun working on her book of poetry, a tenor from the visiting opera company, or an escapee from the old jet set. In a select part of Venice (vaporetto stop 15), La Fenice has an architecturally rich staircase leading to its beautifully decorated but petit salons, with red brocaded provincial chairs. The bedrooms are highly individualized—liberally furnished with antiques and excellent reproductions. Your satin-lined room may have an exquisitely inlaid desk and a wardrobe painted in the colorful Venetian manner to match the baroque bed frame. Capping the decor are velvet bed covers, gilt mirrors, and crystal chandeliers. The hotel year-round charges from 16,600 lire ($19.26) to 19,500 lire ($22.62) for a double with bath, from 10,000 lire ($11.60) to 12,000 lire ($13.92) for a single with bath. Singles without bath cost 6,900 lire ($8); doubles without bath, 12,500 lire ($14.50). Air conditioning is 1,500 lire ($1.74) per day extra. Breakfast is the only meal served, for 1,400 lire ($1.62). On sunny days, you can take your morning meal on a terrace under a parasol.

Savoia & Jolanda, 4187 Riva degli Schiavoni (tel. 24-130), is in a prized position on Venice's main street, with a lagoon as its front yard. Most of the bedrooms—71 in all—have a view of the boats and the Lido. While its exterior has much of Old Venice to win you, the interior is somewhat spiritless. But the distinguished gentleman owner, Signore Iganni, makes life here comfortable and relaxed. His hand-picked staff extends the same good manners and thoughtfulness. The bedrooms are neutral modern, with plenty of space for daytime living (desk and armchairs). Most of them have private baths, for which singles pay 10,900 lire ($12.64); doubles, 20,500 lire ($23.78). Rates quoted are inclusive and are charged in peak season. The owner has also transformed his own town house into quarters for paying guests. Just around the corner from his hotel, the private home opens onto a quiet square.

4. The Budget Range

Near the Rialto Bridge: Rialto, 5147 San Marco (tel. 28-299), opens right onto the Grand Canal, at the foot of the Ponte di Rialto, the famous bridge—flanked with budget shops—that spans the main waterway at its center. Admittedly, the albergo is better known for its waterside ristorante, offering delicious "shore dinners," but its bedrooms are quite satisfactory. They combine simple modern with the complexities of ornate Venetian ceilings and wall decorations. The beds are most comfortable. The high-season rate for a bathless single is 7,400 lire ($8.58); 10,100 lire ($11.72) for a single with bath; 12,900 lire ($14.86) for a bathless double; 16,600 lire ($19.26) for a double with bath. Rates quoted are inclusive. Vaporetto stop 7.

Marconi & Milano, 729 San Polo (tel. 22-068), was built in the year 1500, when Venice was at the height of its supremacy on the seas, but now it incorporates a later addition. The older portion, once a wine shop, has been absorbed into the hotel and is bound to titillate lovers of the ornate and dramatic. Drawing room furnishings, for instance, are appropriate for visiting bishops. The hotel lies less than 50 feet from the much-painted Rialto Bridge (vaporetto stop 7). The Savoldi Scherer family operates everything, combining an Italian flair with German efficiency (the German owner married the daughter of the founder). Only four of the lovely old rooms open directly onto the Grand Canal; the others face side and rear streets. The bedrooms are less inspired, with semi-modern furnishings. Singles (bathless—only two in this category) go for 5,750 lire ($6.67). Bathless doubles rent for 10,100 lire ($11.72); with bath, 12,950 lire ($15.02) to 16,500 lire ($19.14) per person. It's fun to have meals in the L-shaped room, sitting rather formally in Gothic chairs. But in summer, you'll want to dine at a sidewalk table on the Grand Canal.

Albergo Da Bruno, 5726-A Salizzada S. Lio (tel. 30-452), combines good rooms and excellent meals. You can't go wrong if you enjoy Italian locanda life. The innkeeper has 24 rooms to rent. Half of these rooms have private showers. The bedrooms are quite satisfactory—nicely furnished, compact, tidy. Ignore the tiny lobby, the lack of a lounge, and concentrate on a good night's sleep. Bathless singles go for 4,600 lire ($5.34); with shower for 6,600 lire ($7.66). Doubles rent for 8,800 lire ($10.21); 11,400 lire ($13.22) with private shower. Da Bruno is halfway between the Rialto Bridge and the Piazza San Marco (vaporetto stop 7 is closer). Open March 15 to October 31.

Mignon, 4535 SS. Apostoli (tel. 37-388), is a small third-class hotel not far from the Rialto Bridge and the Ca' d'Oro vaporetto stop. It has recently been given a face-lift, and now offers some accommodations with private baths. Fortunately, for lone travelers there are many single rooms, a rarity in Venice. Most of the chambers overlook a private garden where breakfast is served, even afternoon tea. Bathless singles cost 4,200 lire ($4.87); bathless doubles, 8,000 lire ($9.28). In the doubles with private bath, the charge is 10,000 lire ($11.60). Service and taxes are included, though a continental breakfast is an extra 750 lire (87¢).

Near Piazza San Marco: San Moisè, 2058 San Marco (tel. 36-720), is off the beaten track for most tourists, providing much-needed peace and privacy, though it's only a short walk from St. Mark's. It's on a cul-de-sac, a little canal (Canale dei Barcaroli) overlooking the private garden of a neighboring palace. The owner, Signora Leah Bardusco Cestari, suggests you arrive by gondola if you can afford it; otherwise, it's a few minutes' walk from vaporetto stop 15. She has renovated the hotel's 18 bedrooms, decorating some with rustic pieces, mixed in with many items hand painted in the Venetian style. Only a continental breakfast is served. A double without bath costs 15,000 lire ($17.40); a double with bath, 18,000 lire ($20.88), inclusive. There are no singles. Open all year.

"Do Pozzi," 2373 Corte do Pozzi (tel. 707-855), is small, new, and centrally located, just a short stroll from the Grand Canal. More of a little country tavern than a hotel, it opens onto a paved front courtyard, with potted greenery. To complete the picture, you can arrive via taxi, boat, gondola, or vaporetto. The sitting and dining rooms are furnished with antiques (and near antiques)—all intermixed with utilitarian modern. Baths have been added, and a major refurbishing has given everything a fresh touch. The price for a single room with shower, including breakfast, is 14,500 lire ($16.82). A twin-bedded room with bath or shower, plus breakfast, is 26,000 lire ($30.16). Air conditioning is included in the rates.

Off the Riva degli Schiavoni: Rio, 4356 Castello (tel. 34-810), is more than just an annex of the nearby Pellegrino. Though assigned an even lesser rating by the government, it's new inside, designed in a compact, totally functional style. Right up front on a pie-shaped campo, it's near three outdoor cafes, convenient for economy meals, as the albergo doesn't offer pension terms. The Rio is fresh and well maintained, with fairly serviceable, though strictly utilitarian, rooms. Its rates are inexpensive, considering its desirable location, only a five-minute walk from the Piazza San Marco and three short blocks from the Riva degli Schiavoni vaporetto stop. Singles (bathless only) go for 7,000 lire ($8.12); bathless doubles for 12,000 lire ($13.92); doubles with bath are 14,000 lire ($16.24), inclusive. All prices include a continental breakfast. The hotel's easy to spot, on the campo next to a news kiosk, where ice cream and chilled coconut are served. The Rio is open from March to mid-November.

Near La Fenice: San Fantin, 1930A Campiello La Fenice (tel. 31-401), is a modest and modernized little hotel with a classic facade in one of the choicest cultural and historical spots of Venice. Its entrance is forbidding with cannon balls forming part of its decor. Inside you're given a friendlier greeting. The rooms are simply furnished and reasonably comfortable. The most expensive singles rent for 8,000 lire ($9.28), and bathless doubles peak at 14,500 lire ($16.82). A double with bath costs 18,000 lire ($20.88). The hotel shuts down every year around mid-November, reopening its doors in the spring.

5. The Pick of the Pensions

Near the Salute: La Calcina, 780 Zattere al Gesuati (tel. 27-045), opens onto the bright Guidecca Canal in what used to be the English enclave of Venice before the area developed a broader base of tourism. In a less trampled, secluded, and dignified district of Venice, it's reached by taking the vaporetto to the Accademia station. John Ruskin, who wrote *The Stone of Venice,* stayed here in 1877, and he charted the ground for his latter-day countrymen. The pension is absolutely clean, but the furnishings are almost deliberately simple and unpretentious. The rooms are comfortable, and most of them come equipped with baths or showers. In peak season, the demi-pension rate ranges from 12,950 lire ($15.02) to 15,250 lire ($17.69) per person. The I.V.A. tax is extra. If there's no room at the inn, try the **Seguso** pension next door, which is comparable not only in price, but in general style and amenities.

Pensione alla Salute "Da Cici," 222 Dorsoduro (tel. 22-271), is a centuries-old palazzo in a secluded and charming part of Venice (vaporetto stop 14). It avoids the usual mass tourism features, linking itself with the inner image of the city. Poetically oriented, it's been an offbeat haven for numerous writers and artists, including Ezra Pound at one time. Right on a small waterway that empties into the Grand Canal, "Da Cici" is furnished in a standard way, though most serviceable. The friendliness of the reception and the level of cleanliness compensate. Full pension ranges from 12,800 lire ($14.85) to 16,500 lire ($19.14) in a single; from 18,950 lire ($21.98) for two persons in one room. It's preferred that you take at least demi-pension in high season. Rates are reduced substantially from October 31 to March 15. In summer, guests can dine in the garden, sampling good food.

Near the Rialto: Caneva, 5515 Ramo della Fava (tel. 28-118), sits on its own canal, midway between the Rialto Bridge and the Piazza San Marco. Most of its functional bedrooms overlook either the canal or courtyard, with its potted trees and balconies. The owner, Mr. Gino, keeps his rooms tidy and employs a friendly staff (the maids sing as they scrub). Most of his rooms are bathless, for which he charges singles a rate of 5,500 lire ($6.38); couples, 9,000 lire ($10.44), inclusive. A few rooms have private bath or shower, for which you pay more, of course. Breakfast is required.

On the Riva degli Schiavoni: Casa Paganelli, 4687 Riva degli Schiavoni (tel. 24-324), is not only in a breathtaking position, right on the lagoon, with the sea life floating by, but it's one of the more attractive low-cost places at which to stay in Venice. The art-conscious owner, Signor Paganelli, sees his little pension more as a miniature museum of modern art. He's installed picture windows in the front, placed a few excellent paintings in the lounge, and furnished it in the contemporary fashion, with large semi-tropical plants. Artists love to stay here (look for a painting left behind by Ben Nicholson). The rooms for sleeping are compatible with those who like simplicity, good beds, and plenty of space to put one's possessions out of sight. Breakfast is included in the room rates. Bathless singles go for 8,000 lire ($9.28); bathless doubles for 15,000 lire ($17.40), inclusive. Some rooms have a private bath or shower. For these the charge is an additional 2,500 lire ($2.90) for singles; 4,000 lire ($4.64) for doubles. The half-pension rate is 14,000 lire ($16.24) in a bathless single; 27,000 lire ($31.32) for two persons in a bathless double. Vaporetto stop 16.

Pensione Wildner, 4161 Riva degli Schiavoni (tel. 27-463), is an inn in a choice position, overlooking the lagoon, only a short walk from the Piazza San Marco. Wtih boats and gondolas bobbing outside your bedroom window, the setting seems ideal. But the interior is incongruous and unromantic, relying on uninspired modern. Nevertheless, the rooms are clean and comfortable, and you can take your meals (well-prepared, ample portions) outside at the sidewalk tables. In all, there are 20 rooms, and breakfast is included in the rates. The rates are most reasonable—8,000 lire ($9.28) in a bathless single; 15,000 lire ($17.40) in a bathless double, rising to 18,000 lire ($20.88) in a double with shower. The rate for full pension is 18,000 lire ($20.88) per person, inclusive. The Wildner is like an Italian version of a French country bistro—only with that view. Vaporetto stop 16.

Near Piazza San Marco: Doni Pensione, 4656 San Zaccaria (tel. 24-267), sits in a private position, off the lagoon, about a three-minute walk from St. Mark's. Most of its 11 bathless rooms either overlook a little canal, where four or five gondolas usually are tied up, or a garden with a tall fig tree. Utter simplicity prevails, especially in the pristine and down-to-earth bedrooms, but the level of cleanliness is high. The rates are compensatingly low. In season half board is required at 9,000 lire ($10.44), including service and taxes. Off season an inclusive 5,000 lire ($5.80) to 6,000 lire ($6.96) is charged for room and breakfast. The pension is at Vaporetto and motorboat stop 16.

Locanda Silva, 4423 Fondamenta del Rimedio (tel. 27-643), is officially classified beneath the fourth-class category of Italian hotels. But labels mean little when you see the good, clean rooms offered here at low prices. The tariff, including a continental breakfast, is 5,200 lire ($6.03) in a single, 8,750 lire ($10.15) in a double, and 11,850 lire ($13.75) in a triple. For a shower or bath, you are charged 600 lire (70¢) extra. A friendly reception awaits you from the owners, Signor and Signora Ettore. The location is most central, less than 200 yards from the Piazza San Marco.

READER'S PENSION SELECTION: "Right by the Guglie Bridge (walk down Lista di Spagna until you hit the canal, turn left, and you're right there) is **Casa Dalla Chiara,** 339 Cannaregio-Ponte delle Guglie (tel. 29-902). It's the private home of two charming women who rent out rooms. The home was originally a mansion with stone floors and steps, and the rooms are large and comfortably furnished. There is a small restaurant on the corner, and in the evenings the gondoliers tie up their gondolas and sit at the sidewalk tables. This is not a tourist area, but across the bridge are small shops and a market, where one can buy inexpensive fruits, pasta, or rolls for breakfast. The Dalla Chiara is quite busy in summer, so it's best to write ahead. Rates for these spotless rooms are 6,000 lire ($6.96) double; 8,000 lire ($9.28) triple; 11,000 lire ($12.76) for a four-bedded room; and 13,000 lire ($15.08) for five beds in a room" (Juliet Rothman, Annapolis, Md.).

6. On the Lido

A DELUXE HOTEL: Excelsior Palace Hotel, 40 Lungomare Marconi (tel. 60-201), is one of the most luxurious hotels in Italy, largely responsible for making the word Lido synonymous with a beach resort. At first glance, it appears to be a castle; no, a government building—no, a hotel of sweeping magnitude, with rooms that range in style and amenities from cozy singles to suites. All the doubles—spacious enough for tennis games—have private bathrooms or showers. The monument to La Dolce Vita is open only from May to September, and the charge for a single room ranges from 32,000 lire ($37.12); in a double, from 48,000 lire ($55.68).

The food is every bit as good as the viands dispensed at that other CIGA ringleader, the Gritti Palace. The Excelsior maintains its own beachfront, with individual cabanas for the jet-set habitués, and there is a heated swimming pool facing the sea. Throughout the hotel are many extras, such as a rustic bamboo drinking veranda; tavernas; an outside dinner theater with tables set around a raised stage where flamenco dancers perform; 10 tennis courts; and gardens. It's even got its own entertainment world—built in—a theatrical nightclub, "Chez-vous," with a rising floor. A memorable experience for those who can afford it. A private ferry will shuttle you back and forth between the Lido and the mainland.

A FIRST-CLASS HOTEL: Des Bains Grand Hotel, 17 Lungomare Marconi (tel. 765-921), is an enormous establishment, built in the grand era of European resort hotels, with its own wooded park and private beach with individual cabanas. So traditional is its ambience that it was used as the central stage for the film "Death in Venice." For delicious comfort, set apart from the intense drama of Venice itself, the Grand is a good choice, another member of the CIGA chain that dominates the deluxe and first-class field in Venice and on the Lido. Overlooking the sea, the May-to-September hotel has 250 well-furnished, fairly large bedrooms—all with private bathrooms or showers. The single rate ranges from 16,000 lire ($18.56) to 24,000 lire ($27.84), depending on the plumbing and the size of the room. The double rate ranges from 22,000 lire ($25.52) to 38,000 lire ($44.08), plus taxes.

Full pension will run from 30,000 lire ($34.80) to 43,000 lire ($49.88) per person, plus the service charge. Guests dine in a large veranda dining room, cooled by Adriatic breezes. The food is top rate, the service superior. Special features include many resort-type amenities: tennis courts; a large salt-water swimming pool; a private pier with water slide, diving board, and paddle wheel boats, and a park with shade trees and flowering shrubbery. The lounges are dignified, tastefully furnished. And finally, an orchestra plays for evening dancing. A motorboat shuttles you back and forth between Venice (or the mainland) and the Lido.

A MEDIUM-PRICED HOTEL: Quattro Fontane, 16 Via Quattro Fontane (tel. 760-227), is the most charming hotel on the Lido. The trouble is, a lot of people know that, so it's likely to be booked (and it's open April to September only). Like a chalet from the Dolomites, it's most popular with the discriminating English, who like a homey atmosphere, a garden, friendly management, rooms with superior amenities, and good food served at tables set under shade trees. What a contrast to the sterile modernity of the Casino, a short distance away. The directors are Mr. and Mrs. Bevilacqua (she's Scandinavian). Their hotel was recently enlarged, and it now offers 72 rooms, more than two thirds with private shower baths. The rate for a bathless single is 9,000 lire ($10.44); 14,000 lire ($16.24) with bath. Bathless doubles go for 20,000 lire ($23.30); with bath, 24,000 lire ($27.84). And full pension ranges from 20,000 lire ($23.30) to 27,000 lire ($31.32) per person, inclusive. The hotel lies about 50 yards from the beach.

A PENSION: The Villa Parco, 1 Via Rodi (tel. 760-015), nestles on the so-called unfashionable part of the Lido—hence its low price. A third-class pension with only 22 rooms, this villa is one of several built in the district. A turn-of-the-century atmosphere hangs over the area; the smell of honeysuckle is in the air—all compensating for the fact that you must walk to the beach. The unquestioned star choice of the low-budget field, the Villa Parco is well maintained and comfortable for a pension with such a low rating. The house is surrounded by its own garden with outside tables—ideal for quiet, relaxing interludes. And, appropriate for Venice, it's also near a canal. The rates for singles (bathless only) are 4,500 lire ($5.22). The bathless doubles cost 7,000 lire ($8.12); with bath 8,500 lire ($9.86), inclusive. The food is good and served in generous portions, with a full-pension rate ranging from 12,000 lire ($13.92) to 13,000 lire ($15.08) per person. The villa is open from April to September.

THE ENVIRONS: Villa Condulmer, outside Mogliano (tel. 450-001), is a 17th-century villa 10 miles from Venice. Surrounded by its own huge grounds, it accepts discerning visitors year round. Built on the ruins of a monastery, the villa still maintains its classic architectural richness, with ornately paneled walls, parquet floors, frescoed ceilings, antiques, and Venetian crystal chandeliers. Food from the hotel's own gardens is served in the intimate gold and white dining room. The drinking lounge is also cozy—containing a baronial fireplace. The bedrooms are graciously large, furnished in a classic deluxe style. The highest tariffs are charged from May to September. It's best to take half pension at that time, costing 20,000 lire ($23.20) per person. The hotel is really a resort, complete with an 18-hole golf course, two excellent tennis courts, and a large, free-form swimming pool.

Villa Cipriani, Asolo (tel. 521-66), is for the romanticist who'd enjoy staying in the house where the legendary actress, Eleonora Duse, and the poet, Robert Browning, once lived. The town itself is in peaceful hills, and is famous for its mild climate. It's about an hour's drive from Venice, a total of 40 miles, reached by the main road to Verona. The hotel is run by Signor Cipriani of Harry's Bar fame. Still maintaining its original architectural beauty, it has been handsomely converted to receive guests who like the quiet, the views, and the cypress and olive trees. The villa requires half board, and meals are served on the terraces. Open all year round. A single under those terms ranges from 28,000 lire ($32.48); a double, 40,000 lire ($46.40) for two. Rooms are attractively furnished, all 26 containing private baths.

7. The Restaurants of Venice

Although Venice doesn't grow much foodstuff, and is hardly a victory garden, it is bounded by a rich agricultural district and plentiful vineyards in the hinterlands. It is from the Adriatic that the city gets the choicest items on its menu, although the fish dishes, such as scampi, tend to be expensive. The many rich and varied specialties prepared in the Venetian kitchen will be surveyed in the restaurant recommendations to follow. For Italy, the eating establishments of the city are high priced, though there are many trattorie catering to the low-budget tourists. We'll first take up our fork at the most expensive, then descend in price level.

THE TOP RESTAURANTS: Antico Martini, 1980 San Marco Campo San Fantin (tel. 37-027), is elegantly situated, facing the celebrated Teatro della Fenice. The leading restaurant of Venice, it elevates the Venetian cuisine to its highest level, even—or especially—if you stick to the local fare. Because it serves such good food, it has enjoyed a long list of distinguished patrons, including Lord Olivier, Sir John Gielgud, Leonard Bernstein, Igor Stravinsky, and Balanchine. An excellent beginning is the risotto serenissima, made with a base of fennel hearts, fresh garden peas, and bits of sauteed bacon, stirred into a mound of rice, costing 2,400 lire ($2.78). For a main dish try the fegato alla veneziana (best when covered with a liberal sprinkling of freshly ground pepper), which is tender calf's liver fried with onions and served with a helping of polenta, a yellow cornmeal mush praised by Goldoni. The cost? 3,650 lire ($4.24). Other specialties: sogliola alla mugnaia (the finest sole meunière we've sampled in Italy) for 5,100 lire ($5.92). Also good is the roast baby lamb for 4,400 lire ($5.10). A complete meal will probably cost from $14 to $22. An interesting local wine, especially with fish dishes, is the yellow Tocai. Decor? Inside, the walls are paneled; elaborate chandeliers glitter overhead; gilt-framed oil paintings adorn the walls. Outside, the courtyard is favored in summer. The restaurant's in the tradition of a Venetian palazzo.

Actually, it was founded in 1720 as a coffee house, serving the popular Turkish brew in the heyday of trade with the Ottoman Empire. A wine grower from Tuscany acquired the coffee house as a bad debt in 1921. That long-ago proprietor was the grandfather of the present owner, Emilio Baldi, who runs the present Antico Martini with just the right amount of dash and flair. Open only for dinner and closed Tuesdays.

Quadri, 120 Piazza San Marco (tel. 22-105), is one of the most fashionable restaurants in all of Italy. If we awarded stars, we'd need a galaxy for this citadel of gourmet food. Of course, Quadri should be great: it's had almost two centuries to perfect itself. The richly embellished upstairs—resplendent in Venetian baroque—is reserved for a culinary extravaganza. For a memorable beginning, order fettuccine à la Cooper, 5,000 lire ($5.80) for two persons. Then you can get down to some serious dining, perhaps selecting scampi à la Quadri at 5,000 lire ($5.80) or grillade de poisson (fish), also 5,000 lire. Another heaven-sent chef's specialty is côte de veau serenissima, also 5,000 lire. Finally, a superb ending to a perfect meal is the glacé au four à la Quadri, 2,500 lire ($2.90). The setting on two levels is from the 17th and 18th centuries—brocaded walls, Venetian chandeliers, bombé chests, intricate mirrors. It's plush intimate, atmospheric. The restaurant closes November 1 and reopens April 1. However, in winter a coffee shop—right on the square—remains open, serving tea, sandwiches, and pastries from 9 a.m. to 10 p.m. Closed Mondays.

Harry's Bar, 1323 Calle Vallaresso (tel. 36-797), serves some of the best food in Venice. Its fame was spread by Ernest Hemingway. A. E. Hotchner, in his *Papa Hemingway,* quoted the writer as saying, "We can't eat straight hamburger in a Renaissance palazzo on the Grand Canal." So he ordered a five-pound "tin of Beluga caviar" to, as he said, "take the curse off it." Harry, by the way, is an Italian named Cipriani, an entrepreneur extraordinaire known for the standard of his cuisine and the level of his accommodations. His bar is a watering spot for martini-thirsty Americans—a wide mixture that includes both Madison Avenue types and the sunflower girls of Kansas. The vodka martini is dry and well chilled, and costs 1,300 lire ($1.51). Hemingway and Hotchner had Bloody Marys, now 1,700 lire ($1.97). Some superb libations are made with the juice of fresh peaches grown in the lagoon (one, called a Bellini, consists of champagne and fresh peach juice, truly delectable). The food is good, and you can have your choice of dining in the bar downstairs, or the room with a view upstairs. To begin with, we'd recommend the Venetian fish soup at 1,750 lire ($2.03), followed by the scampi thermidor with rice pilaf at 7,400 lire ($8.58), topped off by a chocolate mousse at 1,200 lire ($1.39). The proverbial club sandwich is yours at 3,100 lire ($3.60). It's open all year any day except Mondays.

Taverna La Fenice, 1938 San Marco (tel. 23-856), is one of the most romantic dining spots in Venice. In summer guests dine outside under a canopy, overlooking the Teatro della Fenice where Stravinsky introduced "The Rake's Progress." The service is smooth and efficient, and English is spoken. The most appetizing beginning is a selection of seafood antipasto at 2,800 lire ($3.25) per serving. The fish in this selection is caught fresh from the Adriatic. Two main-dish specialties include châteaubriand at 13,000 lire ($15.08) for two persons, and scaloppine alla crema e funghi (mushrooms) at 4,000 lire ($4.64). The restaurant also specializes in cannelloni alla Fenice at 1,500 lire ($1.74). Desserts average 1,500 lire ($1.74). The decor in the interior is elegant. Closed Wednesdays and from the end of November till Christmas.

La Caravella, 2398 Calle Larga XXII Marzo (tel. 708-901), is probably the most expensive restaurant in Venice—but worth it for that special occasion. Next door to the Hotel Saturnia-Internazionale, it attracts with its gracious ambience, an elegant pub atmosphere with time-mellowed paneling. Many of the specialties are featured nowhere else in town. For a different beginning, try a smooth gazpacho—the cold "liquid salad" of Andalusia—2,000 lire ($2.32). Standard dishes include châteaubriand for two persons at 12,900 lire ($14.96) and the spring chicken cooked in a paper bag at 4,200 lire ($4.87). However, the best item to order is one of the poached fish dishes, such as bass—all priced according to weight and served with a tempting sauce. The bouillabaisse in the style of Marseilles is also excellent at 4,900 lire ($5.68). After all that, the ice cream in champagne is welcome at 2,000 lire ($2.32). Closed Wednesdays and from September 15 to June 15.

Other Top Restaurants

Trattoria "Alla Colomba," 1665 San Marco-Piscina-Frezzeria (tel. 041-23-817), close to San Marco Square, is the queen of the trattorie of Venice. Owned by "propriétaire-conducteur" Giovanni Deana, who runs the excellent and previously recommended Bonvecchiati Hotel, the ristorante, like the hotel, is decorated with a small gallery of modern paintings, including works by well-known Italian and internationally known artists such as De Chirico, Campigli, Sironi, Picasso, Kokoschka, and Chagall. The popularity of the trattoria is mainly due to the excellence of its cuisine, which includes such specialties as minestre di fagioli (bean soup), risotto di frutti di mare alla Pescatora (risotto with seafood), risotto di funghi del Montello (risotto with mushrooms of the local hills of Montello), baccalà alla vicentina (milk-simmered dried cod, seasoned with onions, anchovies, and cinnamon and served with polenta), and granzeola (shellfish of the Adriatic). Fruits and vegetables are produced locally on the islands near Venice. The cost of an excellent meal is likely to run between 6,000 lire ($6.96) and 10,000 lire ($11.60).

A La Vecia Cavana, 4624-A Rio Terra SS. Apostoli (tel. 87-106), is off the tourist circuit, but is increasingly popular, even attracting an occasional movie star. "Cavana" is a place where gondolas are parked, a sort of liquid garage. The site of the restaurant used to be such a place. Decorated in the tavern style, it does some mouth-watering specialties such as tagliatelle alla carbonara at 1,000 lire ($1.16); fondue bourguignonne at 4,000 lire ($4.64); even a filetto al whiskey at 4,000 lire also. Desserts range in price from 600 lire (70¢) to 800 lire (93¢). Closed Mondays.

"al graspo de ua," 5093 Calle dei Bombaseri, is one bunch of grapes you'll want to pluck. For that special meal, it's a winner. Decorated in the old taverna style, it offers several dining rooms, whose chief feature is their antipasto and dessert tables—enough to make a Scandinavian smörgasbord chef turn green with envy. The dining room has a beamed ceiling, hung with garlic and copper bric-a-brac. Considered the best fish restaurant in Venice, "al graspo de ua" has been patronized by such celebs as Elizabeth Taylor, Jeanne Moreau, Rossano Brazzi, Giorgio di Chirico, even Melvin Laird. You can help yourself to all the hors d'oeuvres you want—known on the menu as "self-service mammouth"—for 3,500 lire ($4.06). A saner beginning might be the risotto di frutti di mare at 2,500 lire ($2.90). Among the pasta dishes, one especially recommendable is the vermicelli alle vongole (with baby clams), at 2,000 lire ($2.32). For 4,000 lire ($4.64), you çan order the gran fritto dell'Adriatico, a mixed treat of deep-fried fish from the Adriatic. Desserts are good, especially the peach melba at 1,500 lire ($1.74). The air-conditioned restaurant is connected with a low-cost albergo, near the Rialto Bridge (vaporetto stop 7). Closed Mondays.

MEDIUM-PRICED RESTAURANTS: Near La Fenice: Al Teatro, Campo Teatro "La Fenice," is a ristorante-pizzeria in a romantic setting on a piazzetta adjoining the opera house. You can let your mood dictate your dining spot for the evening, as there are several rooms from which to choose. In fair weather, tables are placed out on the charming little square. Downstairs, one can order scrumptious pizza (the best in town), a plate-sized one costing from 1,000 lire ($1.16) to 1,500 lire ($1.74). Besides pizzas, several regional dishes are offered, including risi e bisi (a soup made with rich broth, rice, and fresh spring peas) for 1,500 lire ($1.74). A noodle dish worthy of an award is spaghetti carbonara (made with butter, cheese, and bits of pork), 1,500 lire also. This is one of the many specialties the maître d' prepares right at your table. For dessert, try a mixed fruit salad (macedonia) with ice cream for 1,200 lire ($1.39). The upper-floor dining rooms are decorated in the rustic manner, seating everybody from young men with their dates to dowagers. Closed Tuesdays.

Ristorante da "Raffaele," 2347 San Marco, at the Ponte delle Ostreghe, has long been one of our favorite little canal-side restaurants in Venice, a place where one can absorb the charm and special atmosphere of the city. We've made so many visits here that the head waiter once ordered the chef to prepare us some special Venetian dishes, little knowing we were planning to include his establishment in a guide. It's a five-minute walk from the Piazza San Marco and a minute from the Grand Canal, near an arched bridge where the gondolas glide by. When featured, the bean soup is a delight, as are the seafood specialties, such as scampi, squid, or deep-fried fish from the Adriatic, for around 3,500 lire ($4.06).

All'Angelo, 408 San Marco Calle Larga, is the restaurant portion of a small hotel that draws a large clientele of artists. Paintings cover the bare brick walls. Here you can have some of the more popular Venetian specialties. From the à la carte listings, four are especially recommended: the mixed fish fry from the Adriatic at 2,800 lire ($3.25); tender calf's liver fried with onions, 2,900 lire ($3.36); scaloppine Marsala, 2,700 lire ($3.13); and calf's sweetbreads, also cooked in Marsala, also costing 2,700 lire. Seafaring tastes may be attracted to the Venetian bouillabaisse at 2,400 lire ($2.78) or the grilled sturgeon, 2,700 lire ($3.13). For those who flunked Italian, the menu's in English. The service is efficient without appearing to be so. No pretentious drama, but superb victuals. If the weather's right, aim for a sidewalk table.

Near the Accademia: Locanda Montin, 1147 Fondamenta Eremite, near San Trovaso (tel. 271-51), has for years been the traditional gathering place for the literati. Ezra Pound used to frequent the establishment. On its own quiet little canal, the inn is difficult to locate, as it's not at all in the business of trying to attract tourists. However, it's about a five-minute walk from the Accademia. If the weather is fair, try to get a seat in the outdoor garden out back. The cooking is traditional Venetian, featuring such dishes as fegato alla veneziana (liver and onions), risi e bisi (rice and peas), and a mixed fish fry. Expect to pay about 6,000 lire ($6.96) for a complete meal, including a carafe of the local wine.

Near the Rialto: Trattoria da Bruno, 5721 Castello Calle del Paradiso, is like a country taverna in the center of Venice, about halfway between the Rialto Bridge and the Piazza San Marco. On a narrow street, the restaurant attracts its crowds by grilling meats on an open hearth fire. Get your antipasto at the colorful counter and watch your prosciutto order being prepared—paper-thin slices of spicy flavored ham wrapped around breadsticks (grissini). In the right season, da Bruno does some of the finest game specialty dishes in Venice. If featured, try in particular its capriolo (roebuck) at 2,500 lire ($2.90) and its gagiano (pheasant), 2,200 lire ($2.55). A typical Venetian specialty—prepared well here—is the zuppa di pesce (fish soup) at 1,500 lire ($1.74). After that rich fare, you may settle for a macedonia of mixed fruit at 500 lire (58¢) for dessert. Closed Tuesdays.

Trattoria Madonna, 594 Calle de la Madonna, near the Rialto Bridge, is one of the most characteristic trattorie of Venice. Unfortunately, it's usually so crowded you can't get in. On a narrow street, it lures with its fish specialties. To get you started, we'd suggest the antipasto frutti di mare (fruits of the sea) at 2,000 lire ($2.32). At the fish counter, on ice, you can inspect the sea creatures you'd like to devour. The mixed fish fry is 3,000 lire ($3.48); the grilled eel, 4,000 lire ($4.64). Only aficionados like this latter entree. Desserts average around 500 lire (58¢).

La Vida, Campo San Giacomo dell Orio (near vaporetto stop No. 5), is for those who yearn nostalgically for the Venice of yesterday. At the turn of the century, it enjoyed patronage from a list of painters, many of whom were still imitating Giovanni Bellini and Giorgione. The setting has remained from another day, with even a library filled with volumes on Venetian lore. At a bar stool covered with velvet you can order one of the traditional syrup-flavored water beverages instead of the more jaded martini. Likewise, the cuisine is traditional, featuring most of the well-known Venetian dishes with an emphasis on rice more than pasta. The menu changes daily, and specialties are scrawled in bad hand-writing on a blackboard. Expect to pay 7,000 lire ($8.12) for a meal, including the regional wine. La Vida is lifeless on Mondays.

BUDGET RESTAURANTS: Near Piazza San Marco: **Al Gambero,** 4685 Calle dei Fabbri, is a canal-side restaurant with a sidewalk terrace, one of the best of the low-budget dining spots of Venice. The food is good and well prepared, with all sorts of taste treats. The least expensive way to dine here is to order a 3,300-lire ($3.83) set meal, which might include pastina in brodo (noodle soup), followed by either Hungarian goulash or calf's liver fried with onions in the Venetian style and accompanied by roast potatoes, with the fruit of the season or a selection of that delicious Italian cheese for dessert. However, we generally order from the à la carte list, which offers worthy specialties, including spaghetti Gambero style at 900 lire ($1.04). The fish dishes include mussels in the Venetian style for 1,300 lire ($1.51). Anyone with a sweet tooth and a discriminating palate will like the zabaglione with Marsala wine for dessert, 700 lire (81¢). There's a 13% service charge, plus 300 lire (35¢) cover.

Trattoria Nuova Grotta, 4538 Calle della Rasse, is an intimate place at which to dine, within walking distance of the Piazza San Marco. It offers a meal for 5,000 lire ($5.80), including spaghetti with clams, followed by fillet of sole, with vegetables and a salad, plus dessert, and a quarter of a liter of wine. An even cheaper meal, for 3,700 lire ($4.29), featured minestrone, boiled sturgeon, vegetables, salad, dessert and wine. The fish to be cooked is kept in a refrigerated showcase at the entry window, so you can take a look before deciding. The house specialty is the savory zuppa di pesce, a combination fish soup at 2,000 lire ($2.32). It's a freshly decorated little restaurant, with murals of old sailing ships. On nippy nights the tables near the open fire are favored. The trattoria is easy to find (take the vaporetto to stop 16). Closed Tuesdays.

Ristorante Gorizia "a la Valigia," 4697 Calle dei Fabbri (tel. 87-396), a short walk from the Piazza San Marco, next door to the Hotel Gorizia, is the best of the trattorie along this restaurant-studded street. It serves a 3,500-lire ($4.06) tourist menu that might begin with pasta or soup and follow with a house specialty, goulash, and end with a basket of fresh fruit. On the à la carte menu, served dishes are worthy, especially those that are most typical of the Venetian kitchen—small cuttlefish with polenta (the yellow cornmeal mush) for 2,000 lire ($2.32), the fried liver with onions in the Venetian style, also with polenta, for 2,000 lire also.

THE ATTRACTIONS OF VENICE

VENICE IS THE COURTESAN of Europe, appearing at times to have been created specifically to entertain her legions of callers. Ever since the body of St. Mark was smuggled out of Alexandria and entombed in the basilica, Venice has been hostess to a never-ending stream of visitors—famous and otherwise—from all over the world.

In the pages ahead, we'll explore her great art and architecture. But unlike Florence, Venice would reward her guests with treasures, even if they never ducked inside a museum or church. In the city on the islands, the frame eternally competes with the picture inside.

"For all its vanity and villainy," wrote Lewis Mumford, "life touched some of its highest moments in Venice."

To begin our search for its special and unique beauty, we'll head for—

1. St. Mark's Square

The **Piazza San Marco** was the heartbeat of the Serenissima in the heyday of Venice's glory as a seafaring republic, the crystallization of her dreams and aspirations. If you have only one day for Venice, you need not leave the square, as the city's major attractions, such as the Basilica of St. Mark and the Doge's Palace, are centered there or nearby.

The traffic-free square, inhabited by tourists and pigeons, and sometimes by the Venetians themselves, is a constant source of bewilderment and interest—its moods changing as quickly as the characters in a Goldoni play. If you rise at dawn, you can almost have the piazza to yourself, watching the sun come up—the sheen of gold mosaics glistening into a mystic effect of incomparable beauty. At mid-morning (9 a.m.) the overstuffed pigeons are fed by the city (if you're caught under the whir, you'll think you're witnessing a remake of Hitchcock's "The Birds"). At mid-afternoon the tourists reign supreme, and it's not surprising in July to witness fisticuffing over a camera angle. At sunset, when the two "Moors" in the Clock Tower strike the end of another day, lonely sailors begin a usually frustrated search for those hot spots that characterized Venice of yore, but not of today. Deep in the evening, the strollers parade by or stop for espresso at the fashionable Florian Caffé—and sip while listening to a band concert.

Thanks to the efforts of the conqueror of Venice, Napoleon, the square was unified architecturally, the emperor adding the Fabbrica Nuova, bridging the Old and New Procuratie. Flanked with medieval-looking palaces, Sansovino's Library, elegant shops and colonnades, the square is now finished—unlike the Piazza della Signoria at Florence. On the Piazza San Marco promenaded the wealthy of the old-world Europe of the 18th and 19th centuries. For specific sights to inspect individually, we'll first explore the:

BASILICA OF ST. MARK'S: The so-called "Church of Gold" dominates the square. One of the world's greatest and most richly embellished churches, it looks as if it had been moved intact from Istanbul. A conglomeration of styles, it owes a heavy debt to Byzantium, but incorporates other designs, such as Romanesque and Gothic, with free-wheeling abandon. Like Venice itself, it is adorned with booty from every corner of the city's once far-flung mercantile empire—capitals from Sicily, columns from Alexandria, porphyry from Syria, sculpture from old Constantinople.

The basilica is capped by a dome which—like a spider plant—sends off shoots, in this case a quartet of smaller-scaled cupolas. Spanning the facade is a loggia, surmounted by four famous St. Mark's horses—the "triumphal quadriga"—of uncertain origin, variously attributed to the 3rd or 4th centuries B.C. (though some claim later). The horses were once gilded, but are now tarnished. After the fall of Venice, Napoleon carted them off to Paris, but they were subsequently returned.

On the facade itself are rich marble slabs and mosaics that depict scenes from the lives of Christ and St. Mark. One of the mosaics re-creates the entry of the evangelist's body into Venice—transported on a boat, of course, St. Mark's body, hidden in a pork barrel, was smuggled out of Alexandria in 828 and shipped to Venice. The evangelist dethroned Theodore, the Greek saint who up to then had been the patron of the city that had "outgrown" him.

In the atrium are six cupolas filled with mosaics illustrating scenes from the Old Testament, including the legend of the Tower of Babel. Once the private chapel and pantheon of the doges, the basilica stuns with its interior—a wonderland of marbles, alabaster, porphyry, and pillars. Visitors walk in awe across the undulating multi-colored ocean floor, itself patterned with mosaics.

To the right is the admission-free Baptistery, dominated by the Sansovino-inspired baptismal font, on which a bronzed John the Baptist is ready to pour water. Look back at the aperture over the entryway to see a mosaic, the dance of Salome in front of Herod and his court. Wearing a star-studded russet-red dress and three white fox tails, Salome dances under a platter holding John's head. Far from being sexy, she is posturing, reminiscent of Ruth St. Denis. Her glassy face is that of a Madonna, not an enchantress.

After touring the Baptistery, proceed up the right nave to the doorway to the Treasury (Tesoro), open from 10 to 5:30 p.m., and charging 200 lire (23¢) for admission. The oft-looted Treasury contains the inevitable skulls and bones under glass, plus goblets, chalices, Gothic candelabra.

The entrance to the Presbytery is nearby (use the same ticket). In it, on the high altar, is the alleged sarcophagus of St. Mark, resting under a green marble "blanket," held up by four sculptured, Corinthian-styled alabaster columns. The Byzantine-styled "Pala d'Oro," from Constantinople, is the rarest treasure at St. Mark's—made of gold and studded with precious stones.

On leaving the basilica, head up the stairs in the atrium for the Marciano Museum and the Loggia dei Cavalli; open from 9 a.m. to 6 p.m., charging 200 lire (23¢) admission. The museum itself, with its mosaics and tapestries, is especially interesting, but walk out onto the loggia for a view of the Piazza San Marco and a close-up glimpse of that incomparable team of horses.

THE PALACE OF THE DOGES: Off St. Mark's Square, entered through the magnificent 15th-century Porta della Carta at the Piazzetta, the Doge's Palace is part of the legend and lore of Venice. Like a frosty birthday cake in pinkish-red marble and white Istrian stone, the Venetian-Gothic palazzo—with all the architectural intricacies of a paper doily—gleams in the tremulous Venetian light. Considered by many to be the grandest civic structure in Italy, it dates back to 1309, though a fire in 1577 destroyed much of the building.

If you enter from the Piazzetta, past the four porphyry Moors, you'll stand in the middle of the splendid Renaissance courtyard, one of the latest styles in a palace that has experienced the work of many architects of widely varying tastes. You can take the "giants' stairway" to the upper loggia—so called because of the two Sansovino mythological statues.

The fire made ashes of many of the palace's greatest masterpieces, and almost spelled doom for the building itself, as a new architectural fervor of the post-Renaissance was in the air. But sanity prevailed. Many of the greatest Venetian painters of the 16th century adorned the restored palace, replacing the canvases or frescoes of the old masters.

After climbing the Sansovino "stairway of gold," you'll enter some get-acquainted rooms. Proceed to the Anti-Collegio salon housing the palace's greatest art work—notably Veronese's "Rape of Europa," far left on the right-hand wall. One critic called the work "delicious." Tintoretto prevails with his "Three Graces" (to the left on the entrance wall) and his "Bacchus and Ariadne" (to the left on the wall opposite the entrance). Some critics consider the latter his supreme achievement. In the adjoining "Sala del Collegio," you'll find allegorical paintings on the ceiling by Veronese. Proceeding to the right, you enter the "Sala del Senato o Pregadi," with its allegorical painting by Tintoretto in the center of the ceiling.

In the "Sala del Consiglio dei Dieci," with its gloomy paintings, the dreaded Council of Ten (often called "The Terrible Ten" for good reason) used to assemble to decide whose head was in need of decapitation. In the antechamber, bills of accusation were dropped in the lion's mouth.

Now trek downstairs through the once-private apartments of the doges to the grand "Maggior Consiglio," with its allegorical "Triumph of Venice" on the ceiling, painted by Veronese. What makes the room outstanding is Tintoretto's "Paradise," over the Grand Council chamber—said to be "the largest oil painting in the world." Paradise seems to have an overpopulation problem, perhaps a too-optimistic point of view on Tintoretto's part. Tintoretto was in his 70s when he began this monumental work. He died only six years later. The second grandiose hall, entered from the grand chamber, is the "Sala dello Scrutinio," with paintings telling of past glories of Venice.

Re-entering the "Maggior Consiglio," follow the arrows on their trail across the Bridge of Sighs, linking the Doge's Palace with the Palazzo delle Prigioni, where the cellblocks are found, the ones that lodged the prisoners who felt the quick justice of the "Terrible Ten." The "sighs" in the bridge's name stemmed from the sad laments of the numerous victims led across it to certain torture and possible death. The cells themselves are just dank remnants of the horror of medieval justice. It was here that the state sentenced the adventurer Casanova in 1775, but he made a celebrated escape only a year later.

The palace is open daily from 10 a.m. to 3:30 p.m., and it charges 700 lire (81¢) per person.

PIAZZETTA SAN MARCO: If St. Mark's Square is the drawing room of Europe, then the satellite Piazzetta is the antechamber. Hedged in by the Doge's Palace, Sansovino's Library, and a side of St. Mark's, the tiny square faces the Grand Canal. Two tall granite columns are mounted by a winged lion, representing St. Mark, and a statue, supposedly that of the dethroned patron, St. Theodore, taming a "dragon." Both columns came from the East in the 12th century.

During the heyday of the Serene Republic, dozens of victims either lost their heads or were strung up here, many of them being first subjected to torture that would have made the Marquis de Sade flinch. One, for example, had his teeth hammered in, his eyes gouged out, and his hands cut off before being strung up. Venetian justice became notorious throughout Europe.

If you stand with your back to the canal, looking toward the south facade of St. Mark's Basilica, you'll see the so-called "Virgin and Bambino" of the poor baker, a mosaic which honors Pietro Fasiol (also Faziol), a young man unjustly sentenced to death on a charge of murder.

To the left of the entrance to the Doge's Palace are four porphyry figures, which, for want of a better description, the Venetians called "Moors." These puce-colored fellows are huddled close together, as if afraid. Considering the decapitations and torture that have occurred on the Piazzetta, we shouldn't wonder.

THE CAMPANILE: One summer night back in 1902, the bell tower of the Basilica of St. Mark's—suffering from years of rheumatism in the damp Venetian climate—gave out a warning sound that sent the elegant and fashionable coffee drinkers scurrying from the Florian Caffé in a dash for their lives. But the campanile gracefully waited till the next morning—July 14—before it tumbled into the piazza. The Venetians rebuilt their belfry, and it's now safe to ascend. In campanile-crazed Italy, where visitors must often ascend circuitous stairs, it's good to report that the Venetian counterpart has a modern elevator. For 500 lire (58¢), you can ride it for a pigeon's view of the city—any time in summer from 9 a.m. to 11:30 p.m. (it closes in the afternoon in winter). It's a particularly good vantage point for viewing the cupolas of St. Mark's Basilica.

THE CLOCK TOWER: At St. Mark's Square is one of the most typical and characteristic of Venetian scenes—that of the two Moors striking the bell atop the Clock Tower. The *torre* itself soars over the Old Procuratie. The clock under the winged lion not only tells the time, but is a boon to the astrologer in that it matches the signs of the Zodiac with the position of the sun. If the movement of the Moors striking the hour seems slow in today's fast mechanized world, remember how many centuries the poor wretches have been at their task without time off. The tower may be scaled from 9 to noon and from 3 to 6 (till 5 in winter), for a 200-lire (23¢) admission. After climbing the spiral staircase, you emerge through what looks like a submarine hatch. Puzzling sign: "Please do not strike the Moors." Shouldn't it be the other way around?

2. The Grand Canal

Peoria may have its Main Street, Paris its Champs Elysées—but Venice, for uniqueness, tops all of them with its Grand Canal. Lined with palazzi— many in the elegant Venetian-Gothic style—this great road of water is today filled with vaporetti, motorboats, and gondolas. Along the canal the boat moorings are like peppermint sticks. It begins dramatically at the Piazzetta San Marco on one side and Longhena's Salute Church on the opposite bank. At midpoint it is spanned by the Rialto Bridge, lined with budget shops. Eventually, the canal winds its serpentine course to the railway station. We can guarantee that there's not a dull sight en route.

Of course, the gloriously coiffured ladies Longhi painted have faded with high tide. Many of the lavish furnishings and tapestries that adorned the interiors of the palaces have been hauled off to museums or have ended up in the homes of the heirs of the rising mercantile class of two centuries ago. Venetian nobility, at one point in the sad decline of the city, didn't get less noble; they only went broke.

Some of the major and most impressive buildings along the Grand Canal may be visited, as they have been converted into galleries and museums (see below). Others have been turned into cooperative apartments. Venetian housewives aren't the incurable romantics that the foreign visitors are. A practical lot, these women can be seen stringing up their laundry in front of thousands upon thousands of tourists who subject their wash to the Mr. Clean test.

Along this canal one foggy day came Madame Amandine Lucile Aurore Dudevant, née Dupin (otherwise known as George Sand), with her effete, poetic young lover (Alfred de Musset), rescued from his mother's skirttails. John Ruskin came this way to debunk and expose in his *The Stones of Venice.* Robert Browning, burnt out from the loss of his beloved Elizabeth and (of a later day) his rejection at the hands of Lady Ashburton, came here to settle down in a palazzo, where he eventually died of a cold. Of more recent vintage, Eleanora Duse came this way with the young poet to whom she had given her heart, Gabriele d'Annunzio. Even Shakespeare came here in his fantasies (and intrepid guides will point out the "Palazzo de Desdemona").

3. Museums and Galleries

Venice is a city of art. Decorating her palazzi and adorning her canvases were artists such as Giovanni Bellini, Carpaccio, Giorgione, Titian, Lotto, Tintoretto, Veronese, Tiepolo, Guardi, Canaletto, and Longhi, to name the more important ones. In the museums and galleries to follow, important works by all these artists, are exhibited, as well as a number of modern surprises, such as the Guggenheim Collection. But if you have time for only one gallery, make it:

THE ACADEMY: At the Campo della Carità (vaporetto stop No. 12), the pomp and circumstance, the glory that was Venice, lives on in a remarkable collection of paintings spanning from the 14th to the 18th centuries. The hallmark of the Venetian school? Color and more color. From Giorgione to Veronese, from Titian to Tintoretto, with a Carpaccio cycle thrown in, the Academy has samples—often their best—of its most famous sons. We'll highlight only some of the most renowned masterpieces for the first timer in a rush.

Room I is the beginning both literally and figuratively, devoted mainly to works by 14th-century artists, such as Paolo and Lorenzo Veneziano, who crossed the Byzantine bridge into a Gothic garden (see his "Annunciation").

Room II livens considerably with Giovanni Bellini's "Madonna and Saint" (poor Sebastian, not another arrow), and Carpaccio's fascinating, though gruesome, work of mass crucifixion. In Room III head for the painting on the easel by the window, attributed to the great Venetian artist, Giorgione. On this canvas, he depicted the Madonna and Bambino, along with the mystic St. Catherine of Siena and John the Baptist (a neat trick for Catherine, who seems to have perfected transmigration to join the cast of characters).

Room IV contains two most important works with secular themes—Montagna's armored "St. George," with the dragon slain at his feet, and Hans Memling's 15th-century portrait of a young man. A most unusual "Madonna and Bambino" is by Cosmè Tura, the master of Ferrara who could always be counted on to give a new twist to an old subject. The Tuscan master, Piero della Francesca, is represented with "St. Jerome."

Room V is devoted primarily to the Madonnas and Bambini of Giovanni Bellini, expert in his harmonious blending of colors. None but major artists could stand the test of a salon filled with the same subjects, but under Bellini's brush each Virgin achieves her individual spirituality. Giorgione's "Tempest," displayed here, is the single most famous painting at the Academy. It depicts a baby suckling from the breast of its mother, while a man with a staff looks on. What might have emerged as a simple pastoral scene on the easel of a lesser artist comes forth under Giorgione as a picture of rare and exceptional beauty. Summer lightning pierces the sky, but the tempest seems in the background—far away from the figures in the foreground, who are menaced without knowing it.

In Room VII rests the masterpiece of Lorenzo Lotto, a melancholy portrait of a young man. Room X is dominated by Paolo Veronese's "The Banquet in the House of Levi"—in reality, a "Last Supper" that was considered a sacrilege in its day, forcing Veronese to change its name to indicate a secular work. Impish Veronese caught the hot fire of the Inquisition by including in the mammoth canvas dogs, a cat, midgets, blackamoors, Huns, and drunken revelers. Four large paintings by Tintoretto—noted for their swirling action and powerful drama—depict scenes from the life of St. Mark. Also by Tintoretto are the "Presentation of Jesus at the Temple" and his tragic, ghostly "Deposition." Finally, painted in his declining years (some have suggested in his 99th year before he died from the plague) is Titian's majestic "Pietà."

Room XI is filled with many other works by Veronese (an epic "Crucifixion," an "Annunciation," and the "Battle of Lepanto," in which the Venetians triumphed over the Turks) and Tintoretto (a golden "Cain and Abel," a "St. Jerome," and a "St. Andrew"). Tiepolo, the great decorative painter, has figures writhing across one wall, plus two curious 3-D works in the corners.

After a long and unimpressive walk, search out Canaletto's "Pirticato," in Room XVII. Room XX is heightened by Gentile Bellini's stunning portrait of St. Mark's Square, back in the days (1496) when the horses glistened with gold in the sunlight. All the works in this salon are intriguing, especially the re-creation of the "Palazzo di Rialto," then a covered wood bridge, by Carpaccio.

In Room XXI hangs the cycle of narrative paintings that Vittore Carpaccio did of St. Ursula for the Scuola (School) of S. Orsola. No. 578 is the most famous, showing Ursula asleep on her elongated bed, a dog nestled on the floor, as the angels come for a visitation. But all the works are excellent. A virtuoso performance by an artist. Finally, on the way out (Room XXIV), look for Titian's "Presentation of the Virgin," a fit farewell to this galaxy of great Venetian art.

The Academy is open from 9 a.m. to 1:30 p.m., daily, except Mondays, charging no admission. (Holidays, 9 to 12:30.)

CORRER MUSEUM: At the opposite end of St. Mark's Basilica—housed in the Procuratie Nuove—this museum traces the development of Venetian painting from the 14th to the 16th centuries. But on the second floor are the red and maroon robes once worn by the doges, plus some fabulous street lanterns, as well as an illustrated copy of *Marco Polo in Tartaria.* In Room 7 is Cosmè Tura's "La Pietà," a miniature of renown from the genius of the Ferrara school. This is one of his more gruesome works, a bony, gnarled Christ sprawled on the lap of the Madonna. In Room 8 search out a Schiavone "Madonna and Bambino" (No. 545), our candidate for the ugliest bambino ever depicted on canvas (no wonder the mother looks askance!).

Room 11 is one of the most important at the Correr, filled with three masterpieces: "La Pietà" by Antonello da Messina; a "Crucifixion" by Hugo van der Goes, the Flemish painter; and a "Madonna and Bambino" by Dieric Bouts, who depicted a baby suckling from his mother in a sensual manner. Room 13 is the star attraction of the Correr—the Bellini salon, including works by founding padre Jacopo and his son, Gentile. But the real master of the household was the other son, Giovanni, the major painter of the 15th-century Venetian school (see his "Crucifixion" and compare it with his father's treatment of the same subject).

In Room 14 is a small, though celebrated, portrait of St. Anthony of Padua by Alvise Vivarini, plus works by Bartolomeo Montagna. In Room 15 is the single most important work in the gallery—Vittore Carpaccio's "Two Venetian Ladies," popularly known as the "Courtesans." A lesser work, "St. Peter," with the daggers in him, hangs in the same room—perhaps a hara-kiri victim for his having to share quarters with "women like that!" The Correr, charging 500 lire (58¢) for admission, is open from 10 a.m. to 4 p.m. (Sundays—morning only—it's free).

CA' D'ORO: (vaporetto stop No. 6). This is one of the grandest and most handsomely embellished palaces along the Grand Canal. Though it contains the important **Franchetti Gallery,** the House of Gold (so named because its facade was once gilded) competes with its own paintings. Built in the first part of the 15th century, in the ogival style, it has a lacy Gothic look. Baron Franchetti, who restored and filled it with his own collection of paintings, sculpture, and furniture, presented it to Italy in World War I.

You enter into a stunning courtyard with a multi-colored patterned marble floor, filled with statuary (a lovely garden out back). Then proceed upstairs to the lavishly appointed palazzo itself. Directly opposite the entrance door is an art-filled room, in which the major painting is Titian's voluptuous Venus. She coyly covers one breast, but what about the other?

Also on this floor, in a special niche reserved for the masterpiece of the Franchetti collection, is Andrea Mantegna's icy cold "St. Sebastian," riddled with what must be a record number of arrows. The saint, like the goodly Christian martyr that he was, seems to be enjoying his pain.

On the same floor, again in a niche reserved for it, is Anthony Van Dyck's restored "Portrait of a Gentleman." You'll also find works by Carpaccio and Longhi. The rooms aren't numbered, nor are the paintings labeled—so you'll have to search them out. Don't fail to walk out onto the loggia for a view of the Grand Canal. The palace, which charges 150 lire for admission, is generally open daily, except Mondays, from 10 to 4 p.m. On admission-free Sundays, it's open till 1 p.m. Before heading to the palazzo, check at the Tourist Office to see if it's open, because it has recently been closed for repairs.

CA' REZZONICO: (vaporetto stop No. 11). This is a 17th- and 18th-century palace along the Grand Canal, where Robert Browning set up his bachelor headquarters. Pope Clement XIII also stayed here. It's a virtual treasure house, known for both its baroque paintings and furniture. First, you enter the Grand Ballroom, with its allegorical ceilings, then proceed through lavishly embellished rooms with Venetian chandeliers, brocaded walls, portraits of patricians, tapestries, gilded furnishings, and touches of chinoiserie. At the end of the first walk is the Throne Room, with its allegorical ceiling by Giovanni Battista Tiepolo.

On the first floor you can walk out onto a balcony for a view of the Grand Canal as the aristocratic tenants of the 18th century saw it. After this, another group of rooms follow, including the library. In these salons look for a bizarre collection of paintings. One, for example, depicts half-clothed women beating up a defenseless naked man (one amazon is about to stick a pitchfork into his neck, another to crown him with a violin!). In the adjoining room another woman seems ready to chop off a man's head, and in still another painting a woman is hammering a spike through a man's skull. Enough torture by the ladies to please Leopold von Sacher-Masoch!

Upstairs you'll find a survey of 18th-century Venetian art. As you enter the main room from downstairs, head for the first salon on your right (facing the Canal), which contains the best works of all, paintings from the brush of Pietro Longhi. His most famous work, "The Lady and the Hairdresser," is the first canvas to the right on the entrance wall. Others depict the life of the idle Venetian rich. On the rest of the floor are bedchambers, a chapel, and salons—some with badly damaged frescoes, including a romp of satyrs. Finally, on the top floor are more exhibits, principally majolica and Venetian costumes—and, the most interesting of all, a puppet theater. The palace is open from 10 a.m. to 4 p.m., and charges 500 lire (58¢) for admission. On admission-free Sundays, it's open from 9:30 a.m. till 12:30 p.m.

CA' PESARO: This museum is a gallery along the Grand Canal (take the vaporetto to station No. 5). The palace was designed—but not completed—by Longhena, the master of Venetian baroque in the 17th century. Most visitors may want to skip the relatively dull art of 19th-century Venice, and concentrate instead on modern works by foreign masters. In Room XVI, for example, are paintings by Kandinsky and Mark Tobey, as well as sculpture by Henry Moore, plus Max Ernst's "The Weatherman" and a miniature by Paul Klee. In Room XVII, the Sala De Lisi, are three works by Giorgio de Chirico—one of them is only a conventional portrait, but in the other two the Italian artist is at his metaphysical peak.

Also on the floor, but across the grand hall (room opening onto the Grand Canal), is Marc Chagall's expressive "Rabbi." And don't fail to see the salon devoted exclusively to the sculptures and sketches of Arturo Martini (1889-1947). In particular, his head of a young woman is filled with waiting and wonder. But, in contrast, he could also find inspiration in the past, providing a new interpretation of a classic theme: a bust of Medusa with her reptilian coiffure. The gallery, charging 250 lire (29¢) for admission, is open from 10 a.m. to 4 p.m. in summer.

GUGGENHEIM COLLECTION: At Ca' Venier dei Leoni, an unfinished palazzo, (vaporetto stop 14 or on foot from the Academy Gallery), is one of the most comprehensive and brilliant private art collections in the Western world, revealing both the foresight and critical judgment of its owner. The collection is housed in the Venetian home of Peggy Guggenheim (address: 701 San Gregorio). Her house, open free to the public, may be visited on Monday, Wednesday, and Friday from 3 to 5 p.m. No descriptions of the paintings or sculptures appear underneath them, and only a few are identifiable by legible signatures, but catalogs are for sale. Ms. Guggenheim, in the tradition of her family, has been a life-long patron of contemporary painters and sculptors. Founder of the Peggy Guggenheim Museum in New York in the 40s, she created one of the most avant-garde galleries for the works of contemporary artists. Critics were impressed not only by the high quality of the artists sponsored, but by her methods of displaying them.

As her private collection increased, she decided to find a larger showcase and selected Venice, steeped in long tradition as a haven for artists. While the Guggenheim Museum was going up in New York to Frank Lloyd Wright's specifications, she was creating her own gallery in Venice. Guests wander through her private home, enjoying art in an informal and relaxed way. Max Ernst was one of her early favorites, as was Jackson Pollock (she provided a farmhouse where he could develop his painting technique). Displayed here are works not only by Pollock and Ernst, but by Mark Tobey (see his satiric "Advance of History"), Picasso, Chagall, Delvaux, Hirshfield (his exploration of derrière), and a garden of modern sculpture.

Count yourself fortunate if you get to meet Peggy Guggenheim herself. A legend in her own time, she is a controversial, always colorful personality.

THE NAVAL MUSEUM AND ARSENAL: The Naval Museum at Campo S. Biasio (on the Riva degli Schiavoni) is filled with cannons (bronze lions, no less), ships' models, and fragments of old vessels dating back to the days when Venice was master of the Adriatic. The prize exhibit is in Room 9—a gilded model of the "Bucintoro," the great ship of the doge that surely would have made Cleopatra's barge look like an oil tanker. In addition, you'll find models of historic and modern fighting ships, of local fishing and rowing craft, and a collection of 24 Chinese junks, as well as a number of maritime *ex voto* from churches of Naples. The museum, charging 50 lire (6¢) for admission, is open from 8:30 a.m. to 2 p.m. Closed Tuesdays.

If you walk along the canal branching off from the museum, you'll soon reach the **Arsenal** at the Campo de l'Arsenal guarded by stone lions, Neptune with a trident, and other assorted ferocities. You'll spot it readily enough because of its two towers, flanking each side of the canal. The Arsenal in its day turned out galley after galley at speeds usually associated with wartime production.

ARCHAEOLOGICAL MUSEUM: On the Piazzetta San Marco, facing the Palace of the Doges, the museum is sheltered in the Procuratie Nuove. This museum, it appears, is little visited, in spite of the stream of tourists who idle by outside and in spite of its outstanding collection of Greek and Roman sculpture. Inside, you'll find the noblest heads of Rome, with a goodly assortment of gods and goddesses. Room VIII is graced with the best work—a Dying Gaul from a Greek original of the third century B.C., as well as Leda and the Swan, a Roman copy of a third-century-B.C. Greek original. The museum is open daily, except Monday, from 9:30 to 12:30 and from 3 to 6 p.m. (winter, 10 to 3), and charges 100 lire (12¢) admission. On admission-free Sundays, it closes at 1 p.m.

4. Scuole and Churches

SCHOOL OF SAN ROCCO: (vaporetto stop No. 10): Of the scuole of Venice, none is as richly embellished as this one, filled with epic canvases by Tintoretto. By a clever trick, he won the competition to decorate the darkly illuminated early 16th-century building. He began painting in 1564, and the work stretched on till his powers as an artist waned. The paintings sweep across the Upper and Lower Halls, mesmerizing the viewer with a kind of passion play. In the grand hallway, they depict New Testament scenes, devoted largely to episodes in the life of Mary (the "Flight into Egypt" among the best). In the top gallery are works illustrating scenes from both the Old and New Testaments, the most renowned being those devoted to the life of Christ. In a separate room is what is considered Tintoretto's masterpiece—his mammoth "Crucifixion," one of the world's most celebrated paintings. In it he showed his dramatic scope and sense of grandeur as an artist, creating a deeply felt scene that virtually comes alive—filling the viewer with the horror of systematic execution, thus transcending its original subject matter. The school, charging 500 lire (58¢) for admission, is open daily from 10 a.m. to 1 p.m.

SANTA MARIA DEI FRARI: Known simply as the Frari, this Venetian-Gothic church is at Campo dei Frari, only a short walk from the Scuola di San Rocco (vaporetto stop No. 10, S. Toma). The church is filled with some great art. First, the best—Titian's "Assumption" over the main altar, a masterpiece of soaring beauty, depicting the ascension of the Madonna on a cloud "puffed up" by floating cherubs. In her robe, but especially in the robe of one of the gaping saints below, "Titian red" dazzles as never before.

On the first altar to the left as you enter is Titian's second major work here—a "Madonna Enthroned," painted for the Pesaro family in 1526. Though lacking the power and drama of the Assumption, it, nevertheless, is a brilliant painting—in the use of both color and light effects. But Titian surely would turn redder than his Madonna's robes if he could see the latter-day, neoclassical tomb built for him on the opposite wall. The kindest word for it: large!

Facing it is a memorial to Canova, the Italian sculptor who led the revival of classicism. To return to more enduring art, head for the sacristy for a Giovanni Bellini triptych on wood, painted in 1488. The Madonna is cool and serene, one of Bellini's finest Virgins. The Franciscan friary is open from 10 a.m. to noon and from 2:30 to 5:30 p.m., and charges a well-spent 100 lire (12¢) for admission.

SCUOLA DI S. GIORGIO DEGLI SCHIAVONI: At St. Antonio Bridge (Fondamenta dei Furlani) off the Riva degli Schiavoni is the second important school to visit in Venice. Between 1502 and 1509, Vittore Carpaccio painted a pictorial cycle here of exceptional merit and interest. Of enduring fame are his works of St. George and the dragon, our favorite art in all of Venice—certainly the most delightful. For example, in one frame St. George charges the dragon on a field littered with half-eaten bodies and skulls. Gruesome? Not at all. Any moment you expect the director to call cut. The pictures relating to

St. Jerome, though appealing, don't compete with St. George and his ferocious dragon. The school is open from 9:30 a.m. to 12:30 p.m. and from 3:30 to 6 p.m. (10 to 12:30 on Sundays), for a 200-lire (23¢) admission charge, from October to April. The rest of the year the hours are from 10 a.m. till noon and from 3 to 5:30 p.m. It is closed Mondays.

CHIESA MADONNA DELL'ORTO: At Campo dell'Orto this church provides a good reason to walk to this fairly remote northern district of Venice (vaporetto stop No. 6). At the church on the lagoon, you'll be paying your final respects to Tintoretto. The brick structure with a Gothic front, is famed not only because of its paintings by that artist, but because the great master is buried in the chapel to the right of the main altar. At the high altar are Tintoretto's "Last Judgment" (on the right) and his "Sacrifice of the Golden Calf" (left)—two monumental paintings that curve at the top like a Gothic arch. Over the doorway to the right of the altar is Tintoretto's superb portrayal of the presentation of Mary as a little girl at the temple. The composition is unusual in that Mary is not the focal point—rather, a pointing woman bystander dominates the scene. The first chapel to the left (facing) of the main altar contains a masterly work by Cima de Conegliano, showing the presentation of a sacrificial lamb to the saints (the plasticity of John's body evokes Michelangelo). Finally, the first chapel on the left (as you enter) is graced with an exquisite Giovanni Bellini "Madonna and Bambino" (note the eyes and mouth of both mother and child, a work of consummate skill). There are two other pictures on the apse representing "The Presentation of the Cross to St. Peter" and "The Decapitation of St. Paul" (1551-1555). Besides the five paintings of the apse are works by Tintoretto and his school. Two paintings are by Palma the Younger: "The Annunciation" and "The Crucifixion" (where the influence of his master, Tintoretto, is seen).

THE CHURCH OF SAN SEBASTIANO: This is at Campo S. Bastian, and can be reached by waterbus line No. 5, stopping at San Basegio. It's also possible to tie in a visit here with one to Ca' Rezzonico. If so, take line No. 1, getting off at stop 11. Continue down Calle Larga S. Barnaba to San Sebastiano. In a city as rich in art as Venice, this small Renaissance church might easily have been overlooked. However, it's well worth a visit, as it contains the only frescoes of Paolo Veronese in Venice (also his first), plus canvases of exceptional beauty, the cycle illustrating the story of San Sebastian and of Esther. The master, who died in 1588, is buried near the side altar on the left. The church also contains paintings by Titian, Tintoretto, and an architectural monument by Sasovino. It is open, free, from 9 to noon and from 4 to 7 in summer (in winter its afternoon hours are from 3 to 5:30).

CHURCH OF SAN ZACCARIA: Behind St. Mark's Basilica on the square named after San Zaccaria is a Gothic church with a Renaissance facade. The church is filled with works of art, notably Giovanni Bellini's "Madonna Enthroned," painted with saints (second altar to the left). Many have found this one of Bellini's finest Madonnas, and it does have beautifully subdued coloring, though it appears rather static. Apply to the sacristan (offering) to see the Sister's Choir, with works (no major ones) by Tintoretto, Titian, Il Vecchio, Anthony Van Dyck, and Bassano. The paintings aren't labeled, but the sacristan will point out the names of the artists. In a separate room are five armchairs in which the Venetian doges of yore sat. And—the best for last—see the faded frescoes of Andrea del Castagno in the shrine honoring San Tarasio. The church is open from 10 a.m. till noon and from 4 to 6 p.m.

THE CHURCH OF S. GIORGIO: It sits on the little island of S. Giorgio Maggiore, across the water from the Piazzetta San Marco. To visit it, take the Giudecce-bound vaporetto (No. 5) on the Riva degli Schiavoni, getting off at the first stop, right in the courtyard of the church. The building was designed by Palladio, the great Renaissance architect of the 16th century—perhaps as a consolation prize for his not being chosen to rebuild the doge's burnt-out palace. The logical rhythm of the Vicenza architect is played here on a grand scale. But inside it's almost too stark (Palladio was not much on gilded adornment). The chief art hangs in the main altar—two epic paintings by Tintoretto—one to the left, the "Fall of Manna," and then the far more successful "Last Supper" to the right. It's interesting to compare Tintoretto's "Cena" with that of Veronese at the Academy. Afterward, you may want to take the elevator for 300 lire (35¢), to the top of the belfry for a view of the greenery of the island itself (look for the Greek-style Teatro Verde), the lagoon, and the Doge's Palace across the way. In a word, unforgettable! The church is open from 9 a.m. to noon and from 2 to 7:30 p.m.

SANTA MARIA DELLA SALUTE: Like the proud landmark that it is, this church—the pinnacle of the baroque movement in Venice—stands at the mouth of the Grand Canal, overlooking the Piazzetta San Marco (vaporetto stop No. 14). One of the most historic churches in Venice, it was built by Longhena in the 17th century as an offering to the Virgin for delivering the city from the grip of the plague. It was erected on enough pilings to support the Empire State Building (well, almost). Surmounted by a great cupola, the octagonal basilica makes for an interesting visit, as it houses a small art gallery in its sacristy (tip the custodian)—a marriage feast of Cana by Tintoretto, allegorical paintings on the ceiling by Titian, and a mounted St. Mark and poor St. Sebastian with his inevitable arrow. The latter works, however, did not earn for Titian the title of "Il Divino." The admission-free basilica is open from 7 to noon and from 3 to 7.

CHURCH OF SS. GIOVANNI E PAOLO: Also known as "Zanipolo". On the Campo of the same name, this church is often known as the pantheon of Venice, as it houses the tombs of many doges. One of the great Gothic churches of Venice, the building was erected between the 13th and 14th centuries. Inside, it contains art work by many of the most noted Venetian painters. As you enter, you'll find a retable (right aisle) by Giovanni Bellini (including a S. Sebastian plugged with arrows). In the Rosary Chapel are ceilings by Veronese, depicting New Testament scenes, including "The Assumption of the Madonna." To the right of the church is one of the world's best known equestrian statues—that of Bartolomeo Colleoni (paid for by the condottiere himself), sculptured in the 15th century by Andrea del Verrochio. The bronze has long been acclaimed as his masterpiece, though it was completed by another artist. The horse is far more beautiful than the armored military hero, who looks as if he had just stumbled upon a three-headed crocodile. To the left of the pantheon is the **Scuola di San Marco,** with its stunning Renaissance facade (it's now run as a civic hospital).

5. The Lido and Lagoon

Along the white sands of the Lido strolled a hand-holding Eleanora Duse and d'Annunzio (the *Flame of Life*); Goethe in Faustian gloom; a club-footed Byron trying to decide with whom he was in love that day; De Musset pondering the fickle ways of George Sand; Thomas Mann's Gustave von Aschenbach with his eye on Tadzio in *Death in Venice*. But gone is the relative isolation of yore. The De Mussets of today aren't mooning over lost loves: they're out chasing bikini-clad new ones.

Near the turn of the century, the Lido began to blossom into the fashionable beachfront resort it is today, complete with deluxe hotels and its Municipal Casino (see "Venice After Dark"). Currently frequenting the strip of sand are mustachioed Milano industrialists, movie stars, and wealthy Venetians hoping to take the curse off the August heat. But Lido prices aren't always stratospheric, now that a number of less expensive hotels and pensioni have opened to accommodate the increasing number of budget-minded tourists.

Even if you aren't lodging at the Lido, you may still want to come over for a swim in the Adriatic. And if you don't want to cross the thresholds of the rarefied citadels of hotel beachfront property—with huts lining the beach like a tribe of Swahili—you can try the Lungomare G. D'Annunzio Public Bathing Beach at the end of the Gran Viale (Piazzale Ettore Sorger), a long stroll from the vaporetto stop. You can book cabins—called *camerini*—and enjoy sand as good as that at the Excelsior. Rates change seasonally.

To reach the Lido, take vaporetto 6, which charges 150 lire (17¢) round trip (the ride takes about 15 minutes). The boat departs from a landing stage near the Doge's Palace.

But don't confine your look at the Venetian lagoon just to the Lido. Venice is surrounded by islands, at least three of which make for a memorable day's outing by inexpensive vaporetto transportation.

MURANO: In the lagoon is the island where glassblowers have for centuries performed oral gymnastics turning out those fantastic chandeliers (some with porpoise arms) that Victorian ladies used to prize so highly, along with heavily ornamented glasses so ruby red or so indigo blue you can't tell if you're drinking blackberry juice or pure wood-grain. Happily, the glassblowers are still plying their trade, though increasing competition—notably from Sweden —has forced a creeping sophistication into some of the designs. Still, the tasteful ware must be sought out in a glass menagerie where some of the animals (reptilian chalices) should never have been released, much less allowed inside your home.

Murano remains the chief expedition from Venice, but it doesn't take even second place in the beauty contests (Burano and Torcello are far shapelier). How to visit: you can combine a tour of Murano with a trip around the lagoon. For 150 lire, you take vaporetto 5 at Riva degli Schiavoni, a short walk from the Piazzetta San Marco. The boat docks at the landing platform at Murano where—lo and behold—the first furnace awaits conveniently. Perhaps too conveniently. One reader, Dennis Spencer Kahane, of Washington, D.C., writes that this showroom "has prices averaging between twice and thrice those found in the shops of Venice for comparable merchandise."

As you stroll through Murano, you'll find that the factory owners are only too glad to let you come in and see their age-old crafts (try to arrive in mid-morning when the furnaces are going full blast). These managements aren't altogether altruistic, of course. While browsing through the showrooms, you need stiff resistance to keep the salesmen at bay. And it's possible to bargain down the initial quoted offer by salesmen. Don't—repeat, don't—pay the marked price on any item. That's merely the figure at which to open negotiations.

An exception to that is made-on-the-spot souvenirs, which are turned out at Murano. For example, you might want to purchase a horse streaked with blue. The artisan takes a piece of incandescent glass, huffs, puffs, rolls it, shapes it, snips it. No sooner than it took Houdini to free himself, he has shaped a horse. The showrooms of Murano also contain a fine assortment of Venetian crystal beads, in every hue of the rainbow. You may find some of the best work to be the experiments of apprentices. On one recent occasion a clerk was trying to steer us toward a tawdry vase when we spied some delicately hued glass based on Etruscan designs. The clerk was apologetic—"just the work of students." But we purchased an exquisite Etruscan vase and a she-wolf whose distant ancestor suckled Romulus and Remus.

You can take the same ferry back, but why not get off at Fondamente Nuove, then slowly stroll through an unheralded section of the city which will bring you closer to the quiet charm and serene beauty of Venice?

BURANO: An island riddled with canals, Burano became world famous as a center of lace making, a craft that reached its pinnacle in the 18th century (recall Venetian point?). The visitor who can spare a morning to visit this island will be rewarded with a charming little fishing village far removed in spirit from the grandeur of Venice, but lying only half an hour away by ferry. The one-way fare is 120 lire, and boats leave from Fondamente Nuova, which overlooks the Venetian graveyard, well worth the trip all on its own.

The **Cemetery of St. Michele** is filled with greenery and birds, not to mention remarkable birthday-cake tombs. Such famous men as Igor Stravinsky, Ezra Pound, and Sergei Diaghilev, the founder of the Ballet Russe, are buried here. The guard at the entrance will supply a map. The crematorium is open from 5 to 6 p.m. on Tuesdays, Thursdays, and Saturdays.

Once at Burano, you'll discover that the houses of the islanders come in varied colors—sienna, robin's egg blue, barn red, butterscotch, mauve. If you need a focal point for your excursion, it should be the **Scuola Merletti** in the center of the fishing village at Piazza Baldassare Galuppi. The Burano School of Lace was founded in 1872 as part of a resurgence movement aimed at restoring the age-old craft that had earlier declined, giving way to such other lace-making centers as Chantilly and Bruges. By going up to the second floor, you can see the lacemakers, mostly young girls, at painstaking work, and can purchase hand-embroidered or handmade lace items.

After visiting the lace school, you can walk across the square to the **Duomo** and its leaning campanile (inside, look for the "Crucifixion" by Tiepolo).

If you're on the island at lunchtime, you may want to join a long line of celebrated people who have patronized the rather simple-looking *caratteristico* **Trattoria da Romano**, 223 Via Baldassare Galuppi (around the corner from the lace school). For about 4,500 lire ($5.22) per person, we recently enjoyed a superb dinner there, which consisted of risotto di pesce (the Italian version of the Valencian paella), followed by fritto misto di pesce, a mixed fish fry from the Adriatic, with especially savory bits of mullet, squid, and shrimp. The tab also included refreshing wine, fresh fruit, and service. Closed Tuesdays and November 12 to 30.

A 50-lire (6¢) boat ride takes you from Burano to:

TORCELLO: Of all the islands of the lagoon, Torcello—the so-called mother of Venice—offers the most charm. If Burano is behind the times, then Torcello is positively antediluvian. In the footsteps of Hemingway, you can stroll across a grassy meadow, traverse an ancient stone bridge, and step back into that time when the Venetians first fled from invading barbarians to create a virtual city to Neptune in the lagoon. Torcello has two major attractions: a church with Byzantine mosaics good enough to make the Empress Theodora at Ravenna turn as purple with envy as her robe, and a *locanda* (inn) that converts trippers into inebriated angels of praise. But, first, the spiritual nourishment before the alcoholic sustenance—

The **Church of S. Maria Assunta:** Founded in 639 A.D. and subsequently rebuilt, the church—whipped by the winds of the Adriatic—stands in a lonely grassy meadow. Beside it is a handsome campanile dating from the 11th century. It is visited chiefly (150-lire admission) because of its Byzantine mosaics. Clutching her child, the weeping Madonna in the apse is a magnificent sight. On the opposite wall is a powerful "Last Judgment." Byzantine artisans, it seems, were at their best in portraying hell and damnation. At S. Maria Assunta, they do not disappoint. In their Inferno they have re-created a virtual human stew, the fires stirred by wicked demons. Reptiles slide in and out of the skulls of cannibalized sinners.

After a whiff of this Dantesque nightmare, you'll need one of "Harry's" martinis.

The **Locanda Cipriani** (tel. 730-150), just across from the church, is an inn extraordinaire. The term locanda usually denotes an unusually inexpensive lodging, rated under the lowliest pension. But not so at this resting place. The country inn, well appointed with an open-air dining loggia, is owned by Giuseppe Cipriani, of Harry's Bar fame in Venice. His chef features a number of high-priced dishes, with suggested dinners on the menu ranging from 9,000 lire ($10.44) to 12,000 lire ($13.92) for a big spread, including service. Specialties: cannelloni, fish soup (most savory), a rice pilaf (delicious—a big, saffron-colored portion). American-styled drinks, including excellent martinis cost 900 lire ($1.04). For starters, try the gnocchi, a Roman-inspired dish, made with a semolina base. Closed from November 4 to mid-March. Incidentally, six rooms are available, and you can stay here in what must be the most remote inn in Venice, paying 36,000 lire ($41.76) per person for full board. The locanda is ideal for honeymooners.

Final warning: If you go on your own, don't listen to the friendly, but savvy, gondoliers who hover at the ferry quay. They'll tell you that both the church and the locanda are "miles away." Actually, they're both reached after a leisurely 12- to 15-minute stroll along the canal.

6. Venice After Dark

In olden days, wealthy Venetians were rowed down the Grand Canal, serenaded by gondoliers. To date, no one has improved on that age-old custom. But it can be expensive.

CAFES: Strolling through St. Mark's Square, having a cup of espresso at one of the cafes, and listening to a band concert may be even better. The two most famous cafe sites are the **Florian** and **Quadri**, both of which date back to the early 18th century. The Florian is romantically and elegantly decorated—pure Venetian salons with red plush banquettes, intricate and elaborate murals under glass, and art nouveau lighting and lamps. Considered the most fashionable and aristocratic rendezvous in Venice, the Florian roster of customers has included such figures as Casanova, Lord Byron, Goethe, Canova, De Musset, and Madame de Stäel.

The Quadri, on the other side of the square, also retains an old-world elegance. Wagner used to drop in for a drink when he was working on "Tristan and Isolde."

Both cafes have orchestras playing from 10:30 a.m. until midnight, but from April to November only. Three times a week there's a special musical treat when an 80-piece municipal band plays (Mondays, Thursdays, and Sundays from 9 to 11 p.m.). When music isn't playing, a cup of espresso costs 600 lire (70¢), a "white coffee," 700 lire (81¢). During concert periods, 400 lire (46¢) are added to all coffees served on the plaza. When the municipal band is playing, however, no such fee is assessed.

Want more in the way of nightlife? All right, but be warned: the Venetian nightclub owners may sock it to you when they present the bill. The Lido is the star bet in your search for twinkling colored lights, the featured attraction being the:

MUNICIPAL CASINO: If you want to risk your luck and your lire, you can take a 300-lire (35¢) boat ride on Line 28, leaving from the Piazzetta San Marco and delivering you to the landing dock of the Casino Municipale. The Italian government wisely forbids that its nationals cross the threshold, unless they're working on the staff. You're hit with a 5,500-lire ($6.38) entrance fee for the dubious privilege of entering the gambling salon, where you can then proceed to toss away your money on blackjack, roulette, baccarat, or whatever. In winter, the casino moves to the 17th-century **Vendramin-Calergi Palace** on the Grand Canal (incidentally, Wagner died here in 1883).

The **Night Club del Casino** features the best and most expensive entertainment on the Lido. In the same building as the Casino, it offers a floor show around midnight (striptease, dance numbers, solo singers). The price of the first drink is 5,500 lire ($6.38). Evening wear is mandatory during the film festival.

LIDO SPOTS FOR THE YOUNGER SET: The **Parco della Rose,** on the Gran Viale, a short walk from the vaporetto stop, draws a lively crowd of locals and visiting collegians in summer. The open-air pavilion is set in a garden, next to its own restaurant and pizzeria. In the pavilion itself, the usual peak-season charge is 2,000 lire ($2.32) for the entrance fee and your first drink. Pizzas go from 800 lire (93¢) to 1,200 lire ($1.39). There's dancing to a combo that's usually lively. Open from June to mid-September.

The newest club and in many ways more recommendable than the above is **Club 22,** 22 Lungomare Marconi. Like the others, it is mainly a fair weather operation which often stays open till 4 a.m. during the peak season. For your entrance fee and your first drink, expect to pay 1,500 lire ($1.74). The clients dance on a raised platform overlooking the Lido beach. To reach the night spot, take the vaporetto to the Lido, and get off and walk up Gran Viale. At the beach, turn to the right and go along the coast. If it's a good night, the sounds alone will tell you you're at the right place.

The **Piper Jockey Club,** 124 Lista di Spagna (tel. 71-66-43), is the leading discotheque of Venice. A young crowd is attracted to its beach location and avant-garde music, the latter usually presided over by a disc jockey. The latest in stereophonic sounds is played, and 500 people can find lots of space on two air-conditioned dance floors. In between rounds, you can enjoy drinks in an American bar. The entrance fee is 2,500 lire ($2.90) per person.

In Venice itself, you'll find:

FLOOR SHOWS & DANCING: The **Antico Martini,** Campo San Fantin, near La Fenice Theatre (tel. 24-121), is the best choice in the city for a more conventional nightclub visit, in an establishment catering to the post-30 set. But the strippers aren't one-tenth as appetizing as the dishes served in the superb restaurant on the same premises. The club itself is dressy, featuring both a floor show and an orchestra. You'll pay 5,000 lire ($5.80) for the first drink; 4,000 ($4.64) thereafter. . . . In summer, the **Settimo Cielo** (roof garden of the deluxe hotel, the Bauer Grünwald), 1440 San Moisè, is ideal for tripping the light fantastic under a Venetian moon—that is, if you don't mind shelling out 3,500 lire ($4.06) for your first drink, 2,300 lire ($2.67) thereafter. There's no floor show, but a good orchestra. Off season, the joint jumps in the taverna downstairs.

FOLK MUSIC: At the **Alla Grotta,** 407 Calle dell'Angelo, performers alternate between operatic arias and old Venetian love ballads, the audience occasionally joining in. And you can drown your own blues in purple wine. A bottle of vino, enough for five, costs 4,200 lire ($4.87); a beer or any other Italian drink is 2,300 lire ($2.67). In a cellar, the Grotta is somewhat touristy, but that's a characteristic it shares with nearly every other establishment in Venice. The action starts after dinner (and usually continues till 1 a.m.). . . . Another wine cellar, but this time for drinking only, is **Enoteca "al Vòlto,"** 4081 S. Luca, Calle del Vòlto, which offers excellent French, Hungarian, Italian, even African, wines at 100 lire (12¢) to 200 lire (23¢) per glass. The average bottle begins at 850 lire (99¢). Open till 10 p.m.

THE FILM FESTIVAL: Since 1932, Venice has played host to an annual festival of the cinema, usually beginning in the last days of August and running into the first two weeks of September. Steadily mushrooming in popularity, the festival today attracts top stars and directors, all accompanied by a glittering assortment of the so-called international set. Motion pictures are most often presented in their original languages, with Italian subtitles. Films are shown at the **Cinema Palace** on the Lido, near the Municipal Casino.

The very fortunate time their visit to Venice to coincide not only with the film festival, but with the spectacular **Regatta,** usually held on the first Sunday in September. The Grand Canal fills with richly ornamented craft, and spectators from the balconies of the palazzi watch the race of the gondolas. The regatta is an ancient Venetian custom—worth the trip to Venice just to see the period costumes.

THEATER-GOING: **La Fenice** is one of the most famous theaters in Europe, dating now from the 19th century (an earlier structure was gutted by fire). In the 18th-century heyday of La Fenice, Carlo Goldoni, a Venetian playwright and master of comedy, presented his buffoons night after night—and play after play—to the delight of high society. Italy has yet to produce another master of comedy to topple Goldoni from his pedestal near the Rialto Bridge. To cap the perfect visit, try to attend either a concert or an opera at this theater. While nearly all opera houses of Europe shut down in the summer, La Fenice remains operating in July—and offers everything from "Traviata" to the Leningrad Philharmonic Orchestra.

———————————

As the old travelogue used to say, "As the sun sinks over the Grand Canal, we bid a fond farewell to Venice." Coming up: three satellites that once were forced to declare their allegiance to the city built on the water.

Chapter XI

VERONA, PADUA, VICENZA

1. Verona
2. Padua
3. Vicenza

TEARING YOURSELF AWAY from the Piazza San Marco is a task for those of iron will. But Venice doesn't possess a regional monopoly on art or treasures. Of the cities of interest easily reached from Venice, three tower above the rest. They are **Verona,** the home of the eternal lovers, Romeo and Juliet; **Padua,** the city of Mantegna, with its frescoes by Giotto, and **Vicenza,** city of Palladio, with its streets of Renaissance palazzi and its villa-studded hills. The miracle of all of these cities is that Venice did not siphon off their creative drive completely, though the Serene Republic dominated them for centuries.

The first and most important sightseeing center is the longest distance from Venice—

1. Verona

The home of the pair of star-cross'd lovers, Verona was the setting for the most famous love story in the English language, Shakespeare's *Romeo and Juliet.* A long-forgotten editor of an old volume of the Bard's plays once wrote: "Verona, so rich in the associations of real history, has even a greater charm for those who would live in the poetry of the past." It's not known if a Romeo or a Juliet ever existed, but the remains of Verona's recorded past are much in evidence today. Its Roman antiquities, as only one example, are unequaled north of Rome itself.

In the city's medieval age of flowering under the despotic, cruel Scaligeri princes, Verona reached the pinnacle of its influence and prestige, developing into a town that even today is considered among the great art cities of Italy. The best-known member of the ruling Della Scala family, Can Grande I, was a patron of Dante. His sway over Verona has often been compared to that of Lorenzo the Magnificent over Florence.

THE SIGHTS: Verona is found alongside the snaking Adige River, about 71 miles from Venice. It's most often visited on a quickie half-day excursion from that city (easily reached on the autostrada), but Verona deserves more time.

It's meant for wandering and for contemplation. If you're rushed, head first to the old city to begin your exploring at the:

Piazza Dei Signori

Opening onto this square, the handsomest in Verona, is the Palazzo del Governo, where Can grande extended the shelter of his hearth and home to that fleeing Ghibelline, Dante Alighieri. The marble statue in the center of the square, the expression as cold as a Dolomite icicle, is of the "divine poet." But unintimidated pigeons perch on his pious head. Facing Dante's back is the late 15th-century Loggia del Consiglio, surmounted by five statues. The most attractive building on the square, the loggia is frescoed. Five different arches lead into the Piazza dei Signori, the innermost chamber of the heart of Verona. From the piazza, the arch to the right of building #1 will take you to the:

Arche Scaligere

These tombs, surrounded by highly decorative wrought iron, form a kind of open-air pantheon of the Scaligeri princes. One tomb—that of Cangrande della Scala—rests directly over the door of the Santa Maria Antica church, itself dating from the 12th century, with many Romanesque features. It is crowned by a copy of an equestrian statue (original one now at the Castelvecchio). The tomb nearest the door is that of Mastino II; the one behind it—and the most lavish of all—that of Cansignorio. Visiting hours in summer are from 9 a.m. to noon and from 3 to 6:30 p.m. (in winter, from 2:30 to 5:30 p.m.). The tombs are closed on holidays. Adjoining the Piazza dei Signori is the:

Piazza Delle Erbe

The old Roman forum, this lively, palace-flanked square is today the setting of the fruit and vegetable market . . . and milling Veronese, both shoppers and vendors. In the center of the square is a fountain dating from the 14th century and a Roman statue dubbed "The Virgin of Verona." The pillar at one end of the square—crowned by a chimera—symbolizes the many years that Verona was dominated by the Serenissima. Important buildings and towers include the House of Merchants, dating from the early years of the 14th century; the Gardello Tower built by one of the Della Scala princes; the restored former City Hall and the Lamberti Tower, soaring about 260 feet high; the Maffei Palace in the baroque style; and, finally, the Casa de Mazzanti.

From the vegetable market, you can walk down the **Via Mazzini,** the most fashionable street in Verona, to the **Piazza Bra,** where you'll find the neoclassical town hall and the Renaissance palazzo, the Gran Guardia. But the reason for a visit is to view:

The Arena

Evoking the Colosseum in Rome, the elliptically shaped amphitheater dates from the 1st century A.D. Standing today are four arches of the "outer circle" and a complete "inner ring." For nearly half a century, it's been the setting of a summer opera house, usually from mid-July to mid-August. More than 20,000 persons are treated to—say, Verdi, Mascagni, or a performance of Aïda, the latter considered by some to be the greatest operatic spectacle in the world. The Arena is open from 8 a.m. to 7 p.m. in summer (from 9 to noon and 2:30 to 4:30 in winter), and charges 100 lire (16¢) for admission.

Castelvecchio

Ordered built by Can Grande II in the 14th century, the Old Castle is alongside the Adige River (and reached by heading out the Via Roma). It stands near the Ponte Scaligera, the bridge bombed by the Nazis in World War II and subsequently reconstructed. The former seat of the Della Scala family, the restored castle has been turned into an **Art Museum,** with important paintings from the Veronese school, and works by other masters of Northern Italy. The most significant displays are on the upper floor.

In the Sala Monga is Jacopo Bellini's St. Jerome, in the desert with his lion and crucifix. Two sisterlike portraits of Saints Catherina and Veranda by Vittore Carpaccio grace the Sala Rizzardi Allegri. The Bellini family are also represented here—two lyrical Madonnas and Bambini by Giovanni (the master of that subject) and a blood-curdling "Crucifix" by his brother, Gentile.

Between the buildings is the most charming equestrian statue we've ever seen, that of Can Grande I, grinning like a buffoon, with a dragon sticking out of his back like a projectile. In the Sala Murari Dalla Corte Bra' is one of the most beguiling portraits in the castle—Giovanni Francesco Caroto's grinning red-haired boy with a caricature. The Sala di Canossa is a Tintoretto showcase —his "Madonna Nursing the Bambino," the "Presentation at the Temple," and his "Nativity."

In the Sala Bolognese Trevenzuoli is a rare self-portrait of Bernardo Strozzi. And finally, in the Sala Giuseppe Gazzola hangs an almost satirical portrait of an 18th-century Venetian patrician family by Longhi. The Castelvecchio owns what is perhaps the most delightful art in all of Verona—Pisanello's fresco of St. George freeing the Princess of Trebizond from the dragon. The castle is open from 9 a.m. to noon and from 3 to 6 p.m. in summer (from 2:30 to 4:30 in winter), and charges 200 lire (23¢).

Church of San Zeno

This near-perfect Romanesque church and campanile, at the Piazza San Zeno, a long walk along the river from the Castelvecchio, is graced with a stunning entrance—two pillars supported by puce-colored marble lions and surmounted with a rose window. On either side of the portal are bas reliefs depicting scenes from the Old and New Testaments, as well as a mythological story portraying Theodoric as a huntsman lured to hell (the king of the Goths defeated Odoacer in Verona). The panels—nearly 50 in all—on the bronze doors are a remarkable achievement of primitive art, sculptured perhaps in the 12th century. They reflect, of course, a naïve handling of their subject matter— see John the Baptist's head resting on a platter. The artists express themselves with such candor they achieve the power of a child's wonderbook. Inside, the church is divided into a central nave and two aisles. Somber, severe, it contains a major Renaissance work at the main altar, a triptych by Andrea Mantegna, showing the Madonna and Bambino enthroned with saints. Though not remarkable in its characterization, it reveals the artist's genius for perspective. The church is closed for a long time during lunch, not opening again till 3 in the afternoon.

Church of Sant' Anastasia

Piazza Sant'Anastasia. In the same square as the deluxe hotel, Due Torri, the church dates from the 13th century. Though its facade isn't complete, it nevertheless is considered the finest representation of the Gothic design in Verona. Many artists in the 15th and 16th centuries decorated the interior, though few of the works seem worthy of being singled out for special mention. The exception, however, is the Pellegrini Chapel, with the reliefs in terra-cotta by the Tuscan artist, Michele. The interior consists of one nave, flanked by two aisles, and the overall effect is impressive, especially the patterned floor. As you enter, look for two hunchbacks.

Il Duomo

At the Piazza del Duomo, the cathedral of Verona is outdistanced in interest by the Basilica of San Zeno, but it still merits a visit. A blend of the Romanesque and Gothic styles, its facade contains (lower level) sculptured reliefs by Nicolaus, made in the 12th century, depicting scenes of Roland and Oliver, who were two of the legendary dozen knightly paladins attending Charlemagne. In the left aisle (first chapel) is an "Assumption" by Titian. The other major work of art is the rood screen in front of the Presbytery, with Ionic pillars, designed by Samicheli.

Basilica of San Fermo

At the Piazza San Fermo, a Romanesque church dating from the 11th century forms the foundation of the 14th-century Gothic basilica that surmounts it. Through time, it's been used by both the Benedictines and the Franciscans. The interior is unusual, with a single nave and a splendid roof constructed of wood and exquisitely paneled. The most important work in the basilica is Pisanello's frescoed "Annunciation," to the left of the main entrance (at the Brenzoni tomb). Delicate and graceful, the work reveals the artist's keen eye for architectural detail and his bizarre animals.

Roman Theater

Originally built in the 1st century A.D., the Teatro Romano—now in ruins—climbs the foot of St. Peter's Hill. For nearly a quarter of a century, a Shakespearian festival has been staged here on certain dates in July and August, and, of course, it makes for a unique theater-going experience to see *Romeo and Juliet,* or *Two Gentlemen of Verona,* in this setting. The theater is across from the Adige River (take the Ponte di Pietra). The theater keeps the same hours as the Castelvecchio, but charges 200 lire (23¢) for admission. After seeing the remains of the theater, you can take an elevator to the 10th-century Santa Libera Church towering over it. In the cloister of St. Jerome is the **Roman Archaeological Museum,** with its interesting mosaics and Etruscan bronzes.

Giardino Giusti

These well-manicured, Italian-styled gardens, studded with cypress trees, form one of the most relaxing and coolest spots in all of Verona for pleasant strolls. You can climb all the way to the monster balcony for an incomparable view of the city. The romantic Arcadians of the 18th century met here in a setting appropriate to their idealized beliefs. To visit the gardens (open till sunset), you must pay a 100-lire admission charge. The gardens may be reached by crossing the Ponte Nuovo and heading down the Via Santa Maria in Organo, which becomes the Via Giardino Giusti.

Juliet's Tomb

Outside the city, the so-called "Tomba di Giulietta" is sheltered in a Franciscan monastery entered on the Via Luigi da Porto, off the Via del Pontiere. "A grave? O, no, a Lantern. . . . For here lies Juliet, and her beauty makes this vault a feasting presence full of light." Don't you believe it! Still, the cloisters, in the vicinity of the Adige River, are graceful. The "tomb" may be visited in summer from 9 a.m. to noon and 3 to 6:30 p.m. (in winter from 9 a.m. to noon and from 2:30 to 5:30 p.m.). An admission of 100 lire (12¢) is charged.

Sightseeing Tip

"Casa di Giulietta," (Juliet's House), 23 Via Capello, right off the Piazza delle Erbe, is the Information Tourist Office, Galleria Liston, 10 Piazza Bra (tel. 30-086), and you'll be able to pick up a good map before striking out on a tour of Verona. The house has a balcony and courtyard. With a little bit of imagination, it's not too difficult to imagine Romeo saying: "But, soft! what light through yonder window breaks? It is the east, and Juliet is the sun!"

Note: The Verona **Alitalia** office is at 61 Corso Porta Nuova (tel. 27-424).

HOTELS IN VERONA: Verona boasts a deluxe hotel, the Due Torri. After that, the level of accommodations drops considerably, making most of the lodgings more suitable for overnighting than lingering. Hotel rooms tend to be scarce during the Country Fair in March and the opera and theater season in July and August.

First-Class Hotels

Grand Hotel, 105 Corso Porta Nuova (tel. 22-570), was created out of the former Reichenbach Palace and equipped with thoroughly modern installations, all of which resulted in 60 well-furnished bedrooms, 40 of which have private baths or showers. With its ornate architecture and balcony "box seats," it sits grandly on a wide, tree-lined boulevard running between the railway station and the Roman Arena. Inside, the decor tends more toward functional modern, except for the traditional pieces in the lounge. The preferred bedrooms face the quieter rear garden, its flagstone walks cutting through clipped hedges. The generously large rooms have good amenities. Singles with bath in peak season go for 15,000 lire ($17.40). Bathless doubles rent for 18,000 lire ($20.88); with bath, 26,000 lire ($30.16), inclusive. In summer, there's an open-air dining terrace.

Colomba D'Oro, 10 Via C. Cattaneo (tel. 21-725), masquerades as an old villa in the center of town, with moss-green shutters and balconies. But inside it is efficiently organized to accommodate voyagers in an atmosphere that hovers between semi traditional and contemporary. The 55 bedrooms—all with private baths or showers—are nicely furnished, with matching fabrics and comfortable pieces. The single rate is 16,000 lire ($18.56). The high season charge for doubles is 26,500 lire ($30.74). The rates quoted are inclusive, though you'll be assessed 1,000 lire ($1.16) per person extra for air conditioning. The hotel's service is good, the management hospitable.

The Medium-Priced Range

Milano Hotel, 11 Vicolo Tre Marchetti (tel. 24-985), is a modern 110-bed hotel, one minute from the Roman Arena. Its public rooms are furnished in a functional style, using plastic, wrought iron, and "crouch modern" armchairs in the lobby. The bedrooms are neatly laid out with utilitarian simplicity but remain comfortable and restful. All the rooms have hot and cold running water, and many of them have either a private bath or shower. The bathless singles go for 5,500 lire ($6.38); with bath, 8,500 lire ($9.86). The bathless doubles rent for 10,000 lire ($11.60); with bath, 12,000 lire ($13.92), inclusive. Other facilities include a garage and an elevator.

Giulietta E Romeo, 3 Vicolo Tre Marchetti (tel. 23-554), has two balconies on the street facade, most appropriate for the Romeo and Juliet of today. By leaning out either balcony, you can easily see the Roman Arena. The hotel has a slight formality to it, with a fumed oak lobby in aging modern, though generally the atmosphere is more traditional. The recently remodeled hotel has 36 rooms, all with private bath or shower. The rate in a single room is 8,000 lire ($9.28). Doubles go for 14,000 lire ($16.24), inclusive.

The Budget Range

Aurora, Piazza delle Erbe (tel. 27-624), is a tower-sized building—three rooms on a landing—that stacks up six flights. But it can be fun if you're in a stair-climbing mood. This little non-elevator hotel opens off the Piazza delle Erbe, the center of the city. It's modest, immaculate, and comfortable. Many of the rooms overlook the colorful market square. Each floor has its own toilet and bath, and each room is equipped with an individual water basin. Bathless singles rent for 4,500 lire ($5.22); doubles without bath go for 7,000 lire ($8.12); and a handful of doubles with private bath run to 9,000 lire ($10.44), inclusive. Breakfast is an additional 1,200 lire ($1.39). The pension rate is 9,000 lire ($10.44), plus 15%.

Hotel Verona, 47 Corso Porta Nuova (tel. 27-241), is a lire-watcher's special. Perched on a wide, parkway avenue, halfway between the edge of the city and the Roman Arena, it's housed in a rather modern building. Though its lobby is cramped, the bedrooms themselves provide average comfort, with the usual amenities. Most importantly, the premises are kept clean. The hotel offers 25 bedrooms, with only a handful of the doubles having a private bath or shower. The rate for a bathless single is 4,500 lire ($5.22); with shower, 5,500 lire ($6.38). The bathless doubles—by far the majority—go for 7,000 lire ($8.12); with bath, 8,500 lire ($9.86), inclusive. No meals, other than a continental breakfast, are offered.

THE TOP RESTAURANTS: Ristorante 12 Apostoli, 3 Vicolo Corticella San Marco (near the Piazza delle Erbe, up the Via Pelliciai; tel. 24-680), is the oldest restaurant in Verona, in business for two centuries. It's a festive place at which to dine, steeped in tradition, with frescoed walls and two dining rooms separated by brick arches. It's operated by the two Gioco brothers. Giorgio is the artist of the kitchen, changing his menu daily in the best tradition of great chefs, while Franco directs the dining room. Just consider some of these delicacies: salmon baked in a pastry shell (the fish is marinated the day before, seasoned with garlic, stuffed with scallops); or chicken stuffed with shredded vegetables and cooked in four layers of paper! To begin with, we recommend the tempting antipasti alla Scaligera at 2,000 lire ($2.32). Another specialty is cotoletta 12 Apostoli at 4,000 lire ($4.64). Even the pasta e fagioli at 1,000 lire

($1.16) is superb. For your dessert, you can order the homemade cake, a big piece for 1,200 lire ($1.39). Count on spending at least 9,000 lire ($10.44) for a really top-notch repast with wine. The restaurant is closed on Mondays, but open otherwise from noon to 3 p.m. and from 7:30 to 10 p.m.

Ristorante Re Teodorico, Piazzale di Castel San Pietro (tel. 49-990), is perched in a choice scenic position, high on a hill at the edge of town, with a panoramic view of Verona and the Adige River. From its entrance, you descend a cypress-lined road to a ledge-hanging restaurant, suggestive of a lavish villa. Tables are set out on a wide flagstone terrace edged with a row of classical columns and an arbor of red and yellow rose vines. Specialties on the à la carte menu include fondue bourguignonne, 3,500 lire ($4.06) or fillet of sole cooked in white wine for 3,200 lire ($3.71), even the rognone di vitello (calf's kidneys) for 2,800 lire ($3.25). The desserts are as heavenly as the view, zabaglione in Marsala wine or a banana flambé with Cointreau, ranging from 800 lire (93¢) to 1,200 lire ($1.39).

Low-Cost Meals

Arche, 6 Via Scaligere (tel. 21-415), is a small bistro that's one of the finest of the budget dining taverns of Verona. Its position in the heart of the city is unbeatable, across the street from the tombs of the Gothic Scaligeri princes and on the same street as the so-called "House of Romeo," dating from the 13th century. The food is above average, well prepared, and served in generous portions. From the à la carte listings, you can begin with zuppa di pesce alla Chiggiotta (fish soup) at 1,000 lire ($1.16) or, perhaps, a risotto with frutti de mare (fruits of the sea) at 1,000 lire also. The chef specializes in grilled fish from the Adriatic, including branzini (bass), sogliole (sole), and rombi (turbot), at an average cost of 3,000 lire ($3.48) per dish. A good dessert is a piece of Florentine cake, zuccotto, 800 lire (93¢). Closed Tuesdays.

2. Padua (Padova)

Padua no longer looks as it did when Burton tamed shrew Taylor in the Zeffirelli adaptation of Shakespeare's *The Taming of the Shrew,* which was set in old Padua. But it remains a major art center of Venetia, some 25 miles west of Venice itself. A university that grew to fame throughout Europe was founded here as early as 1222 (in time, Galileo and the Poet Tasso were to attend).

Padua itself is sometimes known as "La Città del Santo" (the city of the saint), the reference being to St. Anthony of Padua, who is buried at a basilica the city dedicated to him. "Il Santo" was an itinerant Franciscan monk (who is not to be confused with St. Anthony of Egypt, the monastic hermit who could resist all temptations of the Devil). Padua lies about a 45-minute train ride from Venice, easily reached on a one-day return.

THE SIGHTS: If you're checking out 12 other cities on the same day you visit Padua, then we recommend that you confine your sightseeing to the (1) Cappella degli Scrovegni (Giotto frescoes) and (2) the Basilica di San Antonio.

Cappella Degli Scrovegni (Also Arena Chapel)

In the public gardens off the Corso Garibaldi, the modest (on the outside) chapel is the best reason for visiting Padua. Sometime around 1305 and 1306, Giotto did a cycle of more than 35 (remarkably well-preserved) frescoes inside, which (along with those at Assisi) form the basis of his claim to fame. Like an illustrated storybook, the frescoes unfold Biblical scenes. The third bottom panel (lower level on the right) depicts Judas kissing a most skeptical Christ, perhaps the most reproduced and widely known panel in the cycle. On the entrance wall is Giotto's "Last Judgment," with Hell winning out in sheer fascination. The master's representation of the "Vices and Virtues" is bizarre, revealing the depth of his imagination in personifying the nebulous evil or the elusive good. One of the most dramatic of the panels is the raising of Lazarus from the dead, a masterly balanced scene, rhythmically ingenious for its day. The swathed and cadaverous Lazarus, however, looks indecisive as to whether he'll join the living again. The chapel is open from 9 a.m. to 12:30 p.m. and from 2 to 6 p.m. (closed on Sundays), and charges 200 lire (23¢) for admission. Winter hours are from 1:30 to 4:30 p.m. An easy walk from the chapel leads to the:

Chiesa Degli Eremitani

One of the tragedies of Padua was that this church was bombed in World War II. Before that time, it housed one of the greatest art treasures in Italy, the Ovetari Chapel frescoed by Andrea Mantegna. The cycle of frescoes was the first significant work by Mantegna (1431-1506). The church was rebuilt, but you don't resurrect 15th-century frescoes, of course. Inside, in the chapel to the right of the main altar, are fragments left after the bombing, a preview of what we missed in Mantegna's work. The most interesting fresco saved is a panel depicting the dragging of St. Christopher's body through the streets. Note also the "Assumption of the Virgin." Mantegna is recommended even to those who don't like "religious painting." Like Da Vinci, the artist had a keen eye for architectural detail.

Basilica Di San Antonio

Piazza del Santo. Dating from the 13th century and dedicated to St. Anthony of Padua interred inside, the basilica is a hodgepodge of styles, with mainly Romanesque and Gothic features. It has as many cupolas as Salome had veils. Campanili and minarets combine to give it an Eastern appearance. Inside, it is richly frescoed and decorated—and usually swarming with pilgrims devoutly ritualistic to the point of paganism, touching "holy" marble supposed to have divine power. The strangest relic is in the Treasury, and that is said to be St. Anthony's seven-centuries-old tongue. The same tongue allegedly "converted" the sturgeon and the carp (from the legend of the saint preaching to the fishes).

The greatest art treasures are the Donatello bronzes at the main altar, with a realistic "Crucifix" (fluid, lyrical line) towering over the rest. Seek out, too, the Donatello relief depicting the removal of Christ from the cross, a unified composition expressing in simple lines the tragedy of Christ, the sadness of the mourners—an unromantic approach.

In front of the basilica is one of Italy's best known statues—this one by Donatello. Donatello broke with the regimentation and rigidity of medievalism in the 15th century by sculpturing an undraped David. Likewise, in the work in front of the basilica, he restored the lost art of the equestrian statue. Though the man it honors—called "Gattamelata"—is of little interest to art lovers, the statue is of prime importance. The large horse is realistic, as Donatello was a master of detail. He cleverly directs the eye to the forceful, commanding face of the Venetian military hero. Gattamelata was a dead ringer for Lord Laurence Olivier.

Civic Museum

Piazza del Santo (near the basilica). Of the museums sheltered in this building, the picture gallery is the most important—filled with minor works by major Venetian artists, dating back to the 14th century. Regrettably, the *pinacoteca* is badly lit, and it's difficult to view some of the works properly, even on sunny days. Except for a wooden "Crucifix" by Giotto in Salon 1, many of the best paintings are hung in Salon 2—two miniatures by Giorgione (Leda and her amorous swan, and a mother and child in a bucolic setting); Giovanni Bellini's "Portrait of a Young Man" (with a haircut that today would be considered chic); Jacopo Bellini's miniature "Descent into Limbo," with its childlike devils. Finally, the 15th-century Arras tapestry is displayed here. Other works in the rooms to follow include Veronese's martyrdom of St. Primo and St. Feliciano, plus Tintoretto's "Supper in Simone's House" and his "Crucifixion" (the latter probably the finest single painting in the gallery). The museum is open from 9 a.m. to 12:30 p.m. and from 3:30 to 6 p.m. (in winter, from 3 to 5), and charges 200 lire (31¢) for admission. On Sundays and holidays, the hours are from 9:30 to 1. Closed Mondays and Saturdays.

Palazzo Della Ragione

At the Piazza delle Erbe. Dating from the early 13th century, this "Palace of Law" is listed among the remarkable buildings of Northern Italy. Ringed with loggias and with a roof shaped like that of the hull of a sailing vessel, it sits in the market place of Padua. Climb the steps and enter the grandiose Salone, an assembly hall that's about 270 feet long. In the hall is a gigantic wooden horse dating from the 15th century. The walls are richly frescoed, the symbolic paintings replacing frescoes by Giotto and his assistants destroyed in a fire in 1420. The hall is open from 9 to 12:30 and from 2 to 6:30 from mid-March to mid-October, and the charge is 150 lire for admission. Morning hours remain the same off season, though in the afternoon it's open only from 1:30 to 4:30. On Sundays and holidays it closes at noon.

Note: The Padua **Alitalia** office is at 4 Galleria Brancaleon (tel. 662-222).

HOTELS IN PADUA: In the past few years, Padua has seen a spurt of hotel building, as many visitors are spending the night instead of limiting their visits to a half-day trek from Venice. Our recommendations embrace three price ranges, beginning with:

A First-Class Choice

Grande Albergo Storione, 2 Riviera Tito Livio (tel. 651-033), is one of the finest hotels in Padua, with 100 freshly groomed rooms—all with private baths. The hotel, with its severe facade, lies only a short walk from the heart of the city, the Piazza delle Erbe. The interior is modern, and the rear courtyard is built with arched pillars and a balustrade balcony. The large and airy public rooms have style and taste. The main living room contains a Venetian sedan chair and a bar in an alcove. The bedrooms reinforce the contemporary theme, with wide French doors, compact wood-grained furnishings—all built in, including bedside tables and desks. Everything is spotless. The rate in a single room is 17,000 lire ($19.72); 24,000 lire ($27.84) in a double, inclusive.

The Medium-Priced Range

Europa-Zaramella, 3 Largo Europa (tel. 661-200), is another modern winner, also built in the 60s, but in a price range lower than that of the Storione. Near the Padua post office, it contains 60 handsome bedrooms, all with private baths and air conditioning. The single rate ranges from 12,000 lire ($13.92) to 14,000 lire ($16.24); the double rate, from 18,500 lire ($21.46) to 20,000 lire ($23.20) inclusive. Considering the value, this is a bargain. The bedrooms are tasteful, with bare pastel walls and built-in furnishings, most compact and serviceable. The rooms open onto small balconies. The public rooms are enhanced by cubist murals, free-form ceramic plaques, and furniture placed in conversational groupings. The American bar is popular, as is the dining room. The Zaramella Restaurant features a good Paduan cuisine, with an emphasis on seafood dishes from the Adriatic.

The Budget Class

Albergo Al Giardinetto, 27 Prato della Valle (tel. 65-69-72), is in a quiet lane, near the sports palace. It's surrounded by gardens and trees, and the entrance gives the impression of a private mansion more than a hotel. An elevator takes you to your room, but we prefer the marvelous marble stairs. The bedrooms are large and well furnished, often with simple antiques. Floors, however, are covered with plastic tiles. Some of the matrimonial beds we recently saw appeared suitable for three persons. A single with bath goes for 5,600 lire ($6.50), and a double with bath costs 8,000 lire ($9.28). A few rooms with an extra bed for a third person go up to 10,000 lire ($11.60). The private baths are often attractive, with lavender tiles, and are kept immaculate and shining.

DINING IN PADUA: Isola di Caprera, 5 Via Marsilio da Padova (tel. 39-385), off the Piazza Frutta, is a two-in-one restaurant. The front section looks like a contemporary country tavern with a sophisticated decor. The rear dining room, slightly more formal, is on a lower level. The theme is set when you spot the mugs of beer or the pitchers of wine brought to your table. The well-prepared food—hale and hearty fare—is typical of the Venetian cuisine. From an à la carte menu, you might begin with spaghetti alla Bolognese at 900 lire ($1.04), then follow with the house specialty, spalta de macale glasseta, 3,500 lire ($4.06). Homemade cakes are priced from 700 lire (81¢), and wines begin at 2,500 lire ($2.90). Add 12% for service, plus a 500-lire (58¢) cover charge. Closed Tuesdays and from August 1 to 20.

Ristorante Al Santo, 63 via del Santo (tel. 27-953), is near the Piazza del Santo, opening widely under the arches of the via del Santo. There's a large grill where you're invited to admire the cooking. Inside, the atmosphere is typically Italian, with small tables covered by immaculate white napkins. While seated on comfortable wooden provincial chairs, you are surrounded by the many wine bottles offered for your taste. Although the à la carte selections are wide, we'd suggest you order from the tourist menu at a cost of 3,700 lire ($4.29). We recently enjoyed a brimming bowl of zuppa di verdura (a soup of greens), followed by an excellent broiled veal cutlet with tasty potatoes, then a basket of fresh fruit, plus a quart of red wine. The service is friendly and efficient.

A Famous Coffee House

Caffe Pedrocchi, 6 Piazzetta Pedrocchi, off the Piazza Cavour, is a neoclassical landmark—the spot the student visits to plot various sorts of mayhem, the philosopher to ponder (quite loudly) the merits of Hegel or Kant, the visitor to have a piece of pastry at 500 lire (58¢), and a cup of espresso at another 500 lire at one of the largest, most famous, and most romantic coffee houses in all of Italy. You haven't heard the heartbeat of Padua until you've been tanked up on Pedrocchi mocha.

3. Vicenza

In the 16th century, Vicenza was transformed into a virtual laboratory for the architectural experiments of Andrea Palladio, a Paduan who arrived there in 1523. One of the greatest architects of the Renaissance, Palladio peppered the city with palazzi and basilicas, and the surrounding hills with villas for patrician families.

The architect was particularly important to England and America. In the 18th century, Robert Adam was especially inspired by him, as reflected by many country homes in England today. Then, through the influence of Adam and others even earlier, the spirit of Palladio was imported across the waves to America (take, for example, Jefferson's Monticello or plantation homes in the antebellum South). Palladio even lent his name to this style of architecture —"Palladianism"—identified by regularity of form, massive, often imposing size, and an adherence to lines established in Ancient Greece and Rome.

THE SIGHTS: To introduce yourself to the "world of Palladio," head for the heart of Vicenza—

Piazza Dei Signori

In this classical square stands the **Basilica Palladiana** partially designed by Palladio. The loggias consist of two levels, the lower tier with Doric pillars, the upper with Ionic. In its heyday, this building was much frequented by the aristocrats among the Vicentinos, who were lavishly spending their gold for villas in the neighboring hills. They met here in a kind of social fraternity, probably to talk about the excessive sums being spent on Palladio-designed or inspired projects. Originally, the basilica was in the Gothic style, and served as the Palazzo della Ragione (justice). The roof collapsed following a 1945 bombing, but has been subsequently rebuilt. To the side is the Tower of the Piazza, dating from the 13th century and soaring approximately 270 feet high. Across from the basilica is the **"Loggia del Capitanio"** (guard), designed by Palladio in his waning years. On the square itself are two pillars, one supporting a chimera, another a saint.

Olympic Theater

The masterpiece of Palladio—ideal for performances of classical plays—is one of the world's greatest theaters (and still in use). It was completed in 1585, five years after Palladio's death, by his pupil, Vincenzo Scamozzi. The curtain went up on the Vicenza première of Sophocles' *Oedipus Rex.* The arena seats, in the shape of a half-moon, are encircled by Corinthian columns and balustrades. The simple proscenium is abutted by the arena. What ordinarily is the curtain in a conventional theater is a permanent facade, U-shaped, with a large central arch and a pair of smaller ones flanking it. These three openings have forced perspective on the raked stage. The reproductions represent the ancient streets of Thebes, combining architectural detail with trompe l'oeil. Above the arches (to the left and right) are rows of additional classic statuary on pedestals or in niches. Over the area is a dome, with trompe l'oeil clouds and sky, giving the illusion of an outdoor Roman amphitheater. At the Piazza Matteotti, the attraction may be visited from 9 a.m. to 12:30 p.m. and from 3 to 5:30 p.m. (till 4 p.m. in winter). It is closed Mondays. The cost: 150 lire (17¢).

City Museum

Across the street from the entrance to the Olympic Theater, the museum is housed in the Palace of Chiericati, one of the most outstanding buildings by Palladio. Begun in the mid-16th century, it was not finished until the latter 17th century, during the baroque period. Today, the palazzo is visited chiefly for its excellent collection of Venetian paintings on the second floor. Works by lesser-known artists, Paolo Veneziano, Bartolomeo Montagna and Jacopo Bassano, are displayed alongside paintings by such giants as Tintoretto, Veronese, Tiepolo. Notable items include Tintoretto's "Miracle of St. Augustine" in Room VII, as well as Veronese's "The Cherub of the Balustrade" and his "Madonna and Bambino" in the same salon. Also intriguing are Tiepolo's "Time and Truth" and Giovanni Battista Piazzetta's "Ecstasy of San Francesco" in Room XIV. The museum, at the Piazza Matteotti, keeps the same hours as the theater, except that it is closed on Mondays. It charges 100 lire (12¢) for admission.

Santa Corona Church

Off the Corso Palladio, a short walk from the Olympic Theater, the church was founded in the mid-13th century, and designed in the Gothic style. Much altered over the centuries, it should be visited if for no other reason than to see Giovanni Bellini's "Baptism of Christ" (fifth altar on the left—leave a small offering for turning on the light switch). In the left transept, a short distance away, is another of Vicenza's well-known works of art—this one by Veronese depicting the Three Wise Men playing tribute to the Christ child. The high altar with its intricate marble work is also of interest. A visit to Santa Corona is more rewarding than a trek to the Duomo (Cathedral), only of passing interest.

Basilica of Monte Berico

High on a hill overlooking the town and the surrounding villas, the Basilica is the Sacré Coeur of Vicenza. Lit at night, the church is reached by car or a hiker's walk up a colonnaded street. Inside, the basilica unveils the magnificence of the absolute. At night, red lanterns burn. But the real reason for climbing the hill is to walk out onto the belvedere near the church. You'll see the town spread beneath your feet—a sight of splendor day or night.

"La Rotonda"

Outside the town, past the "Arco delle Scalette" (the landmark "arch of the tiny steps" from the late 16th century), is another of the most famous creations of that maestro, Palladio. Like the Olympic Theatre, the Rotunda was started by Palladio but left for completion by his pupil, Scamozzi. Many great estates in Europe and America found their inspiration in this elegant, domed villa. The home is a private residence and therefore can't be visited. However, the grounds are open on Tuesdays, Thursdays, and Saturdays from 3 to 5 p.m., costing an admission of 500 lire (58¢).

Villa Valmarana

In the same area, this villa, often called the "Dwarf's Villa," rounds out the sights of Vicenza. This building is not a Palladio creation, having been designed as a private estate in the 17th century. It is visited today by those wishing to see frescoes by Giambattista Tiepolo. In splendid colors, Tiepolo depicted scenes from the *Iliad* and the *Aeneid*, Ariosto's *Roland the Mad*, and Tasso's *Jerusalem Delivered*. The still-inhabited villa may be visited on Thursdays, Saturdays, and Sundays from 10 a.m. to noon and every working day afternoon from 3:30 to 6:30 p.m.

HOTELS IN VICENZA: **Jolly Hotel Campo Marzio**, 21 Viale Roma (tel. 24-560), is the finest hotel in town when judged for amenities. A link in the Jolly chain that stretches from Trieste to Siracusa, Sicily, the first-class hotel is built just outside the heart of the city, with a view across park grounds to the hilltop Basilica of Monte Berico. There is a wide front veranda across the building where you can have drinks while enjoying the view. The hotel is built in the "no nonsense" school, designed for comfort, not frilly adornment. The bedrooms have contemporary furnishings, and many of them also enjoy private baths and showers. The rate for a bathless single is 11,100 lire ($12.88); 16,200 lire ($18.79) for a single with bath; 17,700 lire ($20.53) for a bathless double; 24,500 lire ($28.42) for a double with bath. There's plenty of free parking space for your car, as well as a restaurant on the premises where an average meal costs 5,800 lire ($6.73).

READERS' HOTEL SELECTIONS: "**Milano**, 5 Stradella dei Servi (tel. 23-438), is a very good hotel for the price. A single room is 3,000 lire ($3.48). It is three minutes from the station, served by bus No. 1. It's in the center of the historical district" (Madeleine Dutour-Gauzé, St. Germain-en-Laye, France). . . . "A very cozy hotel is the **Hotel Cristina**, 32 Corso S. Felice (tel. 34-280). A double room with bathroom may vary from 10,000 lire ($11.60) to 12,500 lire ($14.50). The breakfast is not included but can be had at the hotel whose owners make a point of giving up-to-date information about the many attractions of the lovely town. Since parking is sometimes difficult, the availability of an inside courtyard is a special blessing for the visitor" (Dr. Giovanni Patara, Rome, Italy).

WHERE TO DINE: The **Ristorante Padavena**, 93 Via Verona (tel. 24-340), is the finest dining spot in town, charging from 4,000 lire ($4.64) to 6,000 lire ($6.96) for a meal. A typical dinner may consist of pasta e fagioli, a pasta-bean dish that's a favorite in the Veneto region, baccalà alla vicentina (dried cod cooked in milk and spiced with everything from anchovies to cinnamon) served with slices of polenta (yellow corn meal), and, to top off the meal, fresh fruit and the local cheese. Closed Wednesday.

THE DOLOMITES AND TRIESTE

THE LIMESTONE DOLOMITES are a peculiar mountain formation of the northeastern Italian Alps. At times their peaks soar to a height of 10,500 feet. One of Europe's greatest natural attractions, the Dolomites are a year-round pleasure destination, with two high seasons: in midsummer, and then in winter when the skiers slide in.

At times the Dolomites form fantastic shapes, combining to create a landscape that looks primordial, with chains of mountains peaking like giant dragon's teeth in contrast to lofty masses of detritus. Clefts descend precipitously along jagged rocky walls, while at other points a vast flat tableland—spared by nature's fury—emerges.

Before we proceed to details, readers with an extra day or so to spare may first want to postpone their Dolomite adventure for a detour to:

1. Trieste

On the half-moon Gulf of Trieste, opening into the Adriatic, Trieste is 72 miles northeast of Venice. A shimmering, bright city, with many neo-classical buildings, it perches at a remote point in Italy. As a tourist center, it's got a long way to go, though Austrians on low budgets have heavily patronized the Trieste Riviera for years. The skimpy swimwear of the vacationing beauties from Vienna adds a delectable cosmopolitan air. Now that Yugoslavia is gaining in popularity, Trieste is drawing a broader base of visitors—including thousands from across the Atlantic who use the Adriatic port as a gateway to Tito's country.

As a seaport, Trieste has had a long and colorful history, with many changes of ownership. The Hapsburg emperor, Charles VI, declared it a free port in 1719. But by the time the 20th century rolled around, it was an ocean outlet for the Austro-Hungarian empire. Came the war and a secret deal among the Allies, and Trieste was ceded to Italy in 1918, marking its decline. In the late summer of 1943, Trieste again fell to foreign troops—this time the Nazis.

The arrival of Tito's army from Yugoslavia in the spring of 1945 changed its destiny once more. A post-war attempt to turn it into a Free Territory failed. In 1954, after many a hassle, the American and British troops withdrew as the Italians marched in, with the stipulation that the much-disputed Trieste would be maintained as a free port.

The heart of Trieste is the neo-classic **Piazza dell'Unita d'Italia,** said to be the largest in Italy fronting on the sea. Opening onto the square is the Town Hall with a clock tower, the Palace of the Government, and the main office of the Lloyd Triestino ship line. Flanking the square are numerous cafes and restaurants, popular at night with the denizens of Trieste who sip an apéritif, then later promenade along the seafront esplanade. After visiting the main square, you may want to view Trieste from an even better vantage point. If so, head up the hill for another cluster of attractions:

CATHEDRAL OF S. GIUSTO: Dedicated to the patron saint (Just) of Trieste, who was martyred in 303 A. D. The basilica was consecrated in 1330, incorporating a pair of churches that had been separate until then. The front is in the Romanesque style, enhanced by a medallion-like rose window. Inside, the nave is flanked by two pairs of aisles. To the left of the main altar are found the best of the Byzantine mosaics in Trieste (note especially the blue-robed Madonna and her child). The main altar and the chapel to the right contain less interesting mosaics. To the left of the basilica entrance is a small campanile from the 14th century, which you can scale on foot for a view of Trieste and its bay. At its base are preserved the remains of a Roman temple from the first century A.D. From the basilica you can walk to the nearby:

Castle

Constructed in the 15th century by the Venetians, this fortress maintained a sharp eye on the bay, watching for unfriendly visitors arriving from the Adriatic. Along its bastions, you have panoramic views of Trieste. The museum inside is of minor interest. In July and August, open-air performances—Hungarian dancers, whatever—are staged in the **Cortile delle Milizie.** The **Bottega del Vino,** an elegant taverna restored in 1967, caps your exploration within the city proper.

MIRAMARE: Overlooking the Bay of Grignano, the Castle was erected by Archduke Maximilian, the brother of Franz Joseph, the Hapsburg emperor of Austria. Maximilian, who married the Princess Charlotte of Belgium, was the commander of the Austrian navy in 1857. (In an ill-conceived move, he and "Carlotta" sailed to Mexico in 1864, where he became the emperor in an unfortunate reign. He was shot in 1867 in Querétaro, Mexico. His wife lived until 1927 in a château outside Brussels, having been driven insane by the Mexican episode.) On the ground floor of the castle, you can visit the bedroom of Maximilian (built like a ship's cabin) and that of Charlotte, as well as an impressive receiving room and more parlors, including a chinoiserie salon. Miramare, which is reached by line G from the Piazza Oberdan, may be visited on weekdays (except Mondays) from 9 to 1:30 for a 100-lire admission charge. On holidays, the hours are from 9 to 1, and the admission is only 50 lire. On admission-free Sundays, it's open from 9 to 1. Enveloping the Castle are magnificently designed park grounds (Parco di Miramare), ideal for pleasant strolls (no admission fee, open till sunset).

THE GIANT GROTTO: About nine miles from Trieste, you can visit the Giant Grotto, an enormous cavern, one of the most interesting phenomena of speleology. At a depth of 446 feet, it is the largest hypogean cave of the world. It's necessary to have a guide to take you along the paths and stairs. Admission is 500 lire (58¢), and guided visits are from 10 a.m. There are five tours a day in summer, four in winter. Near the entrance, is the Museum of Speleology, opened in 1963 and unique in Italy. The grotto can be reached either through Villa Opicina or by taking the Strada del Friuli beyond the Victory Lighthouse as far as Prosecco.

Note: In Trieste, the **Alitalia** office is at 15 Via Milano (tel. 61-506).

WHERE TO STAY: The **Citta di Parenzo,** 8 Via degli Artisti (tel. 61-259), is the economy special of Trieste. In the business district, it is, nevertheless, tucked away on a relatively secluded street. In charge of the pleasant little lobby is a friendly, English-speaking receptionist. Reached by an elevator, all the good-sized bedrooms have hot and cold running water, are moderately well decorated, and make for a good night's sleep (no sound of roaring Vespas and Fiats). The rate for the bathless singles is 6,000 lire ($6.96); 10,000 lire ($11.60) for the bathless doubles. The limited number of singles with bath or shower go for 8,000 lire ($9.28); doubles with bath for 14,000 lire ($16.24), inclusive. No meals other than a continental breakfast are served.

THE TOP RESTAURANTS: **Piccolo,** 8 Via S. Caterina (tel. 61-300) serves the best food in Trieste. Just off the main street (Corso Italia), it features fish—all the catches from the blue Adriatic. If you order fresh fish, a cart is wheeled to your table, and you make your own selection. To begin with, we'd recommend the assorted antipasto of the sea at 1,500 lire ($1.74). Another good beginning is the risotto alla Miramare, 1,200 lire ($1.39). Most main dishes average around 2,500 lire ($2.90). Closed Wednesdays and from July 1 to July 25.

Nuovo Dante, 12 Via Giosuè Carducci (tel. 24-038), is good, actually one of the most well-appointed dining rooms and snack bars in town. You're given a choice of dining salons, many preferring the dramatic tavern setting, with its beamed ceilings. One section is devoted to a smart pub. For starters, we'd recommend the savory antipasto misto pesce, an assortment of seafood hors d'oeuvres at 1,800 lire ($2.09). Recommended among the main dishes are the mixed seafood grill at 2,500 lire ($2.90) and the braciola alla Dante, also costing 2,500 lire. A grand dessert, if your appetite will permit, is the Gran Coppa gelato (ice cream) at 1,600 lire ($1.86). Closed Wednesdays.

Some 100 miles north of Venice is . . .

2. Cortina D'Ampezzo

This fashionable resort is your best center for exploring the snow-powdered Dolomites. Its reputation as a tourist mecca dates back before World War I, but its growth in recent years has been phenomenal. All it needs now to give St. Moritz the coup de grâce is for Princess Radziwill to take up residence in a chalet. Until that great day, Cortina d'Ampezzo draws throngs of nature lovers in summer, and both Olympic-caliber and neophyte skiers in winter. The Dolomite haven is a hotel owner's Shangri-la, charging maximum prices in July and August as well as in the three months of winter.

The town "signora" of propaganda once insisted: "Just say Cortina has *everything.*" Statements of propaganda chiefs, even when they come from charming Italian ladies, are suspect—but in this case she's nearly right. "Everything," in the Cortina context, means—first and foremost—people of every shape and hue: New York socialites in their old Balenciaga gowns rub elbows in late night spots with frumpy Bremen hausfraus. Young Austrian men, clad in Loden jackets and stout leather shorts, walk down the streets with feathers in their caps and gleams in their eyes. French girls in lime-yellow pants sample Campari at cafe tables, while the tweedy English sit at rival establishments drinking "tea like mother made."

Then, too, "everything" means location. Cortina is in the middle of a valley ringed by enough Dolomite peaks to cause Hannibal's elephants to throw up their trunks and flee in horror. Regardless of which road you choose for a motor trip, you'll find the scenery rewarding. Third, "everything" means good food. Cortina sets an excellent table, inspired by the cuisine of both Venice and Tyrol. Fourth, "everything" means sporting facilities in both summer and winter—chiefly golf, horseback riding, curling, tennis, fishing, mountain climbing, skiing, skating, and swimming. The resort not only has an Olympic Ice Stadium, but an Olympic bog track and ski jump (the 1956 Olympics were held at Cortina, publicizing the resort all over the world). In addition, it has a skiing school with 130 instructors. Recently inaugurated are an Olympic-sized ice-skating rink, a large indoor swimming pool, and Olympic downhill track, a cross-country track, plus an Olympic bobsleigh track and an Olympic ski-jumping hill (Italia).

Fifth, "everything" means top-notch hotels, pensions, private homes, even mountain huts for the rugged. Though the locations, facilities, types of service, price structures, and decor in these establishments vary considerably, we've never inspected an accommodation here that wasn't clean. Most of the architecture of Cortina, incidentally, seems more appropriate to Zell am See, Austria, than an Italian town.

In brief, Cortina is for the leisurely life—no fuss and bother about those dutiful visits to museums, basilicas, and historical monuments. The emphasis is on fun—fun from the early morning when the heartiest visitors gather at the funicular for an early lift to the peaks, fun till the last patron—his head reeling with Italian wine—exits from the lowliest taverna.

HOTELS IN CORTINA D'AMPEZZO: The pickings are ample—and in all price ranges.

The Medium-Priced Range

Park Hotel Victoria, 1 Corso Italia (tel. 32-46), is the best of the second-class hotels in the center of town, a modern structure created in the Tyrolean style, with many good-sized balconies opening onto views of the mountaintops. It's a successful place, combining the old chalet decor with contemporary, roomy areas and plenty of amenities (most rooms with private baths and plenty of steamheat in the winter months). The various living rooms and dining rooms are furnished with reproductions of old country furniture (bare-pine tables, peg-legged chairs). The regional fireplace with a raised hearth is the focal point for after-dinner gatherings. Open from June 29 to September and from December 20 to March, the hotel in high season charges 11,500 lire ($13.34) for a bathless single, 14,000 lire ($16.24) for a single with bath. The rate for a bathless double is 16,000 lire ($18.56); 20,000 lire ($23.20) for a double with bath, inclusive. And full pension is 25,000 lire ($29) per person, dropping to 20,000 lire ($23.20) per person off season.

Ancora, 62 Corso Italia (tel. 32-61), is a revamped hotel enclosed on two sides by terraces with outdoor tables and umbrellas—the town center for sipping and gossiping. Garlanded wooden balconies encircle the five floors, with most bedrooms opening directly onto these sunny porches. About half the well-furnished and comfortable bedrooms have private baths. The full-pension charge in peak season is 22,000 lire ($25.52) per person in a bathless room, 27,000 lire ($31.32) in an accommodation with bath, inclusive. Off season, these prices, respectively, drop to 16,000 lire ($18.56) per person and 20,000 lire ($23.20) per person. The bedrooms are especially pleasant—many with sitting areas—and you sleep under brightly colored woolen blankets. All is kept shiny clean; the service is polite and efficient, and the food is good.

The Budget Range

Menardi, 112 Via Majon (tel. 24-00), is an eye-catcher in the upper part of Cortina, looking like a great country inn, with its wooden balconies and white and green shutters. Its rear windows open onto a meadow of flowers and a view of the rough Dolomite crags. The inn dates back 800 years. It is now run by the Menardi family, who still know how to speak the old Dolomite tongue, Ladino. Decorated in the Tyrolean fashion, each bedroom has its distinct personality. Of the 40 bedrooms, 38 have private baths. The maximum rate charged in high season for a bathless double is 14,000 lire ($16.24); 16,000 lire ($18.56) in a double with bath, inclusive. The bathless singles go for 6,000 lire ($6.96); 9,000 lire ($10.44) in a single with bath. The full-pension rate ranges from 10,000 lire ($11.60) to 20,000 lire ($23.20) per person, inclusive. Considering what you get—the quality of the facilities, the reception, and the food—we'd rate this one as the best for the money in Cortina. The living rooms and dining room have homelike furnishings—lots of knickknacks, pewter, antlers, spinning wheels. The Menardi is open from June 15 to September 29 and from December 20 to March 20.

Nord, 1 Via Verra (tel. 47-07), on the edge of Cortina, is an Alpine-styled chalet. The walls in the bedrooms are white stucco; natural wood balconies on all sides give each one a spectacular view of the mountains and the nearby river. Owned and managed by the Ghedina brothers and their wives, it has a homelike, friendly atmosphere. The bedrooms are as clean and tidy as spring edelweiss. Of the hotel's 26 streamlined and smoothly functioning bedrooms, about half have private baths. Open from June 10 to October 10 and from December 20 to April 5, the hotel in high season charges, for full pension, from 16,500 lire ($19.14) to 18,000 lire ($20.88) per person, depending on the plumbing. Off season, the prices are only 13,500 lire ($15.66) to 15,000 lire ($17.40) per person. Tables and chairs are set out for viewing and drinking.

Rooms in Private Homes

The Tourist Office, 8 Piazzetta S. Francesco, has a list of all the private homes in and around Cortina that take in paying guests, lodging them family style for little cost. It's a good opportunity to live with a Dolomite family in comfort and informality. For information, you can get in touch with the Tourist Office. Even though there are nearly 3,500 rooms available, it's best to reserve in advance, especially from August 1 to 20 and from December 20 to January 7, when bookings reach their peak.

THE TOP RESTAURANTS: Al Foghèr, 12 Vai Paolo Grohmann (tel. 27-02), highly recommended by the Swiss Gourmet Society, is a combination restaurant and third-class hotel. The kitchen is first class, however, offering one of the most acclaimed cuisines in the Dolomites. The dining room's dominated by a big stove in the middle of the room, and several specialties are prepared on charcoal in full view of the diners. For 5,000 lire ($5.80), you can order this typical repast: tagliolini in brodo (a pasta in rich chicken broth), braciole di vitello (veal), followed by a flaky apple strudel. Al Foghèr's popular, and you may have to wait for space in one of the tiny salons furnished with ladder-back chairs and love seats. If you order a complete meal, choosing one of the specialties such as pigeon, quail, or lark, your tab is likely to run around 6,700 lire ($7.77), with wine and service added.

Restaurant Gambrinus, 28 Via Cesare Battisti (tel. 47-55), won't electrify you with the breathtaking view, but it will serve you some of the best food in this resort. The cuisine is redeeming, with its wholesome, hearty fare. Praiseworthy are the Hungarian goulash, chicken cacciatora with polenta, and zuppa degli Ussari. Innsbruck is 100 meters—not 100 miles—away when you order grilled beefsteak, Tyrolean style, for 2,500 lire ($2.90), or apple strudel for 500 lire (58¢). The pièce de résistance is the river trout, averaging around 2,500 lire ($2.90) per plate.

"Da Beppe Sello," 67 Via Ronco, is, in reality, a third-class hotel, but habitués of Cortina know it as a village-edge chalet providing regional meals that are generous and tasty. In summertime, the al fresco dining on the terrace is preferred; all other times, guests retreat inside the snug and pleasing Tyrolean-styled dining room. The restaurant's open from December to March and from June 1 to September 25. Look for some of these specialties: gnocchi di patate (potato dumplings) for 1,200 lire ($1.39), or roast chicken with savory bay leaves for 2,300 lire ($2.67)—delightful. The fried trout is superb, costing 2,500 lire ($2.90) per plate.

THE MAIN SIGHT: Though they may frighten the britches off you, Cortina's little cable cars climb halfway to the stars. Take at least one of them to the summit for a preview of what it's like to be a yodel away from the pearly gates. Most recently dedicated is the **"Arrow in the Sky,"** the name given the new cableway from Col Druscié (elevation 3,937 feet) to Tofana di Mezzo (elevation 10,643 feet). The travel time on the 2-billion-lire cableway is 15 minutes, and the round-trip cost is 3,500 lire ($4.06). At Tofana, skiing is possible through the end of June. On a clear day, you can see as far as Venice and Milan. Trips leave from 12 via dello Stadio every half hour in summer and every 20 minutes in winter, bringing you to the Tofana di Mezzo through the Col Druscié and Ra Valleys. However, you may be content with the **Tondy Di Faloria** funicular

that zips you to the first landing stage at Mandres, then sprouts wings and flies across the Dolomite peaks for an intimate glimpse. The round-trip ticket (and a return booking up there is highly recommended!) is 3,000 lire ($3.48). At the top of the second stage is a sun deck with chairs and a bar. In high season, both winter and summer, the funicular operates every hour from 9 a.m. to 8 p.m. For the frightened visitor, the Belvedere di Pocol at an altitude of 5,000 feet is accessible by taking the cable car from the Piazza Roma every hour, a round-trip fare costing 1,200 lire ($1.39). From that vantage point, you have a good view of Cortina and the valley.

NIGHTLIFE: The **King's Club,** 7 Via Majon (tel. 24-97), is a discotheque with a decor more suitable to a convention of Swiss yodelers. If your flight across the Dolomite peaks has not completely taken your breath away, you can do your number to all the now sounds at this discotheque. Abby Rand wrote, "The après-ski pageantry is like Vogue come to life. If the King's Club didn't exist, Michelangelo Antonioni would have had to invent it for a movie." But whatever you do, keep dancing, since the drinks here are about 4,500 lire ($5.22) apiece. . . . You've been disinherited? Stroll through the streets, find a taverna that's jumping, go in, have a beer from Bavaria, and enjoy the gemütlich atmosphere.

THE GREAT DOLOMITE ROAD: From Cortina d'Ampezzo in the east to Bolzano in the west is a circuitous route of 68 1/3 miles. It ranks among the grandest scenic drives in all of Europe. The first pass you'll cross (Falzarego) is about 11 miles from Cortina. At 6,900 feet above sea level, it offers a panoramic view. The next great pass is called Pordoi, at about 7,350 feet above sea level, loftiest point along the highway (you can take a cable car to the top). You'll find restaurants, hotels, and cafes. In the spring, edelweiss grows in the surrounding fields. After crossing the pass, you'll descend to the little resort of Canazei, then much later pass by the sea-blue Carezza Lake.

3. Bolzano

The terminus of the Great Dolomite Road (or the gateway, depending upon your approach), Bolzano is a town of mixed blood, reflecting the long rule that Austria enjoyed until 1919. Many names, including that of the town itself (Bozen), appear in German. As the recipient of considerable Brenner Pass traffic (55 miles north), the city is a melting pot of Italians and both visitors and residents from the Germanic lands. The capital of a province of the same name, Bolzano lies in the center of the Alto Adige region. It is traversed by two rivers, the Isarco and Talvera, one of which splits the town into two sections.

Bolzano makes a good headquarters for exploring the Dolomites and the scenic surroundings, such as Renon (Ritten in German) on the Alpine plateau, with its cogged rail cable; the village of San Genesio, reached by cable north of Bolzano; and Salten, 4,355 feet up, an Alpine tableland. Bolzano is a modern industrial town, yet a worthwhile sightseeing attraction in its own right. It has many esplanades for promenading along the river. The most interesting street is the colonnaded Via dei Portici. You can begin your stroll down this most colorful street of old buildings at either the Piazza Municipio or the Piazza delle Erbe, the latter a fruit market for the orchards of the province.

HOTELS IN BOLZANO: Park Hotel Laurin, 4 Via Laurino (tel. 47-500), recaptures the glamor of the past, the nostalgia of yesteryear. The 120 well-furnished and ample-sized bedrooms have private bathrooms. The only hotel in Bolzano in its first-class classification, the Park Laurin charges 19,500 lire ($22.62) in a single. The rate in a double is 34,000 lire ($39.44) inclusive. Its private garden is dominated by old shade trees and a flagstone-enclosed swimming pool. Guests are drawn to the high-beamed and spacious lounge, with its graceful brass chandeliers and its groupings of antiques and good reproductions, as well as its baronial fireplace and deeply set windows. The garden terrace is a sunpocket, ideal for lunches or breakfast. The evening meals are served in the interior dining room to the accompaniment of a softly playing orchestra or in the Parc-Restaurant in the garden with its comfortable open-air American bar. Full pension is 16,000 lire ($18.56) per person added to the cost of the room.

Grifone-Greif, 6 Piazza Walther (tel. 27-057), is under the same management as the already recommended Park Laurin. But its charges are cheaper, as it's rated second-class. Strategically on the Piazza Walther with its Salzburg spirit of ornate buildings and open-air cafes, the year-round Grifone-Greif has a traditional look out front, where there's a sidewalk cafe under a canopy. In the rear, however, is a garden swimming pool and a revamped modern facade with upper-floor balconies. The rooms vary in size and amenities, though all are comfortable and well maintained (140 in all, 110 of which have private baths). The rate in a bathless single is 12,000 lire ($13.92); 17,000 lire ($19.72) in a single with bath; 21,000 lire ($24.36) for a bathless double; 31,000 lire ($35.96) for a double with bath, inclusive. In fair weather, you can dine in the open-air restaurant, sheltered by a canopy. Excellent Tyrolean-styled and Italian meals are served in a garden atmosphere. Full pension is 13,100 lire ($15.20) per person added to the room cost.

Two Budget Hotels

Hotel Garni-Metropol, 14 Via Rosmini (tel. 21-767), is a 40-room sparklingly modern hotel, tastefully conceived, with low rates. Opened in 1967, it is embellished with some of the freshest amenities in Bolzano. A short block from the Talvera River, it offers a combined street-floor lounge, breakfast room, and wood-paneled bar, all with well-designed furnishings. An elevator takes one up to compact bedrooms, nicely coordinated with built-in pieces. Even the bathless rooms have slick basins set against marble, including a bidet. A twin-bedded room with bath goes for 11,000 lire ($12.76); 8,000 lire ($9.28) for a bathless double. The rate for a bathless single is 5,000 lire ($5.80); 6,500 lire ($7.54) with bath. Adjacent to the hotel is a private garage.

Herzog, 2 Piazza del Grano (tel. 26-267), is a small, old-world inn, in the heart of Bolzano. It is owned and managed by a genial couple, Maria and Walter Herzog, who have brought a personal style and charm to their venerated establishment. The Herzog attracts painters, poets and writers, who respond to the old atmosphere. Each room is decorated individually with hand-loomed rugs from Austria, hand-painted furniture, even some antiques from England. Many of the rooms have either private baths or showers. Open year-round, the hotel charges 5,000 lire ($5.80) in a bathless single. The bathless doubles go for 8,000 lire ($9.28); with bath, 11,000 lire ($12.76). Throughout the hotel are an attractive color scheme and furnishings—all fresh and airy. The little breakfast room overlooks the old piazza.

DINING IN BOLZANO: Chez Frederic, 12 Via Diaz (tel. 41-411), is altogether exceptional for the area, serving some of the finest food outside the major hotel dining rooms. Across the river, it is decorated in a pleasant, inviting style. In summer, tables are set outside in the courtyard. Everything is cooked to order and served in a polite and efficient manner. To begin your meal, we'd recommend an order of speck, a Tyrolean dish of meat sliced razor thin, the color of dried beef, costing 1,800 lire ($2.09). As a main dish, the pepper steak is also recommended at 3,500 lire ($4.06), though you may prefer the châteaubriand for two persons at 12,000 lire ($13.92). The chef's recommendation, and we concur, is fegato col uvetta (liver with grapes) at 2,500 lire ($2.90). Desserts range from 350 lire (41¢) to 1,000 lire ($1.16). Closed Sundays.

Gay, 1 Piazza della Mostra (tel. 27-870), is the best pizza parlor in Bolzano, the pies being served at outdoor tables in the evening in summer. You can order almost any kind of pizza you want, the prices averaging from 800 lire (93¢) to 1,500 lire ($1.74). The Gay is also a suitable restaurant, offering a delicious meal for about 3,300 lire ($3.83), including, on one recent occasion, tortellini in brodo, followed by gnocchi in the old style of the Piedmont district, then baccalà (codfish) with polenta, plus a salad and dessert—really a top-notch bargain. Popular with families, the restaurant is totally informal. In season, beer-drinking diners often stage their own concerts.

4. Merano

Once the capital of Tyrol (before Innsbruck), Merano (Meran) was ceded to Italy at the end of World War I, but it retains much of its Austrian heritage. In days gone by, it was one of the most famous resorts in Europe, drawing kings and queens and a vast entourage from many countries, who were attracted to the Alpine retreat by the grape cure. (The eating of luscious Merano grapes is supposed to have medicinal value.) After a slump, Merano is enjoying an upsurge in popularity, especially in autumn when the grapes are harvested. Before the last war, Merano also became known for its radioactive waters, in which ailing bathers supposedly secured relief for everything from gout to rheumatism.

The Passirio River cuts through the town (and along it are many promenades, evoking the heyday of the resorts of the 19th century). In the Valley of the Adige at the foot of Küchelberg, Merano makes a good base for excursions in several directions—particularly to Avelengo. A bus from Sandplatz will deliver you to a funicular connection, in which you can ascend about 3,500 feet above sea level to Avelengo, with its splendid vista and mountain hotels and pensions.

Merano itself is richly endowed with vacation-type facilities and attractions, such as open-air swimming pools at its Lido, tennis courts, and a race track (Grand Prix in September).

READER'S SIGHTSEEING TIP: "While wandering along the famous Tappeinerweg promenade in Merano, I happened upon a castle which houses a museum of Tyrolean folkways, the only one of its kind in the region. There is a blacksmith's workshop and a grain mill. At the same time it is a museum of comparative ethnology which exhibits artifacts belonging to a North African nomadic tribe, the Bedja. There is a room dedicated to Ezra Pound, who lived in Merano between 1958 and 1964, and completed his 'Centor' here. Exhibitions of painters and sculptors are held each summer, and classical concerts are presented in the courtyard. The **Museo Agricola** can be reached via Dorf Tirol (bus every hour on the hour from Merano) or on foot by climbing the Tappeinerweg. It is open every day except Tuesday, from 3 to 5 p.m., admission $1. The castle-museum is owned by the daughter and grandson of Ezra Pound, who are lovely people" (Nancy Stillman, Austin, Texas).

HOTELS IN MERANO: The resort is also well stocked with hotel beds, and offers many superior accommodations at inexpensive prices.

First-Class Choices

The **Bristol** (Grand Hotel), 14 Via Ottone Huber (tel. 23-361), is a semi-luxury hotel with 149 large, handsomely furnished bedrooms—each with its own private bath or shower. Some are equipped with ornate pieces, and private balconies envelop the building. Open from March to October, the Bristol is under the same ownership as the Bauer Grünwald in Venice. The hotel charges 21,000 lire ($24.36) in peak season for its single rooms; 38,000 lire ($44.08) for its doubles. The food (open-air restaurant) has been highly praised, and you'll be quoted rates from 23,000 lire ($26.68) to 29,500 lire ($34.22) per person for full pension. The I.V.A. tax is included. While the rooms are as comfortable and modern as one could wish, and the baths are handsomely tiled (with bidets), it is the roof garden with the heated swimming pool that holds the magnetic attraction.

Eurotel Astoria, 21 Via Winkel (tel. 25-442), is ahead of its time architecturally in the tradition of Le Corbusier—cellular modern raised on huge round pillars, the ground floor opening onto the surrounding garden. Each room has a private balcony for mountain viewing. Closed from November 15 to March 15, the hotel charges a peak season rate of 14,000 lire ($16.24) in a single; 25,000 lire ($29) in a double, inclusive of service, taxes, and breakfast. No pension terms are available, though there's a dining room on the premises—wood-paneled walls and picture windows opening onto the garden. The bedrooms have fine Scandinavian-oriented furnishings, with lots of built-in features, such as beds, desks, dressing and end tables. There is a sitting room area, making it ideal for longer stays, plus tiled baths in all the 114 rooms. Special features: medicinal radioactive baths and a heated open-air swimming pool.

The Medium-Priced Range

Eurotel Merano, 5 Via Garibaldi (tel. 24-316), has the same newness and contemporary atmosphere as its more prestigious sister hotel, the Eurotel Astoria. Near the center of Merano, close to the river, it is in a built-up business district. For freshness and functional design, it is the finest second-class establishment in Merano, offering 100 rooms, all with either private bathrooms or showers. Open year-round, the hotel charges 8,000 lire ($9.28) for a single, 14,000 lire ($16.24) double, inclusive. An attractively styled dining room is on the premises. Pension off season is 15,000 lire ($17.40) per person, rising to 18,000 lire ($20.88) per person in peak season. Special features: a garden with a bar, a garage, and a solarium.

The Budget Range

Sittnerhof, 58 Via Verdi (tel. 23-331), is a family-run chalet, as Tyrolean as a yodel. Just outside the center of town, it is set in the midst of vineyards and orchards (in the autumn it has its own homemade wine), and is, in reality, a small working farm—the barn, complete with horses and hay, is nearby. Beyond the barn, set aside in a little grassy meadow, is a flagstone-edged swimming pool, and despite the farm atmosphere, many of the handsomely rustic bedrooms have private tiled baths or showers (an annex across the way handles the overflow). The rate in a bathless single is 8,000 lire ($9.28); 9,500 lire ($11.02) for a single with bath; 8,000 lire ($9.28) per person for a bathless double; 9,000 lire ($10.44) per person for a double with bath. Meals (good

Austrian cooking) are served either in the cozy dining room, decorated in warm
tones, or else on the terrace, near a garden of flowers and bushes. Full-pension
terms range from 13,000 lire ($15.08) to 16,000 lire ($18.56). Off season, you'll
be quoted an even lower rate. Operated by the Brunner family, the Sittnerhof
invites with its relaxed, informal, and friendly atmosphere. English spoken.

DINING IN MERANO: The pension requirement is an old and established
tradition at Merano. But if you're lodging at a hotel that doesn't require meals,
or are just passing through for the day, then a fine choice for dining out is the
Forst-Forsterbräu, 90 Corso Libertà (tel. 23-336), a Tyrolean beer hall incon-
gruously encamped in a modern building. Actually, the restaurant features al
fresco dining out back, far more inviting in summer, and is usually stuffed
tighter than knockwurst with German tourists. The food is first rate, with an
average meal offered for between 4,000 lire ($4.64) and 6,000 lire ($6.96).
Service is included in the price, but the I.V.A. tax will be added. The Forster-
bräu is open from 9 a.m. to midnight, with meals served from 11:30 to 2:30 and
from 6:30 to 9:30. Closed Tuesdays.

A 35-mile drive south of Bolzano delivers us to:

5. Trento (Trent)

Another Northern Italian city that basks in its former glory, this medieval
town on the left bank of the Adige is known throughout the world as the host
of the Council of Trent (1545-1563). Beset with difficulties, such as the rising
tide of "infidels," the Ecumenical Council convened at Trent, a step that led
to the Counter-Reformation.

On the main rail line from the Brenner Pass, Trent today is visited mainly
as a stopover en route to other points. The city itself has much old charm, offset
somewhat by unbridled industrialization. For a quick glimpse of the old town,
head for the **Piazza del Duomo**, dominated by the **Cathedral of Trent.** Built
in the Romanesque style and much restored over the centuries, it dates from
the 12th century. In the center of the square is a mid-18th-century Fountain
of Neptune, armed with a triton.

The ruling Prince Bishops of Trent, who held sway till they were toppled
by the French in the early 19th century, resided at the medieval **Castello del
Buon Consiglio,** reached from the Via B. Clesio. Now the old Castle has been
turned into a National Museum, with only a fair collection of paintings and fine
art, some quite ancient, such as a mosaic from Roman times; and a Risorgimento Museum, containing mementos related to the period of national unification
between 1750-1870. The museum is open from 9 a.m. to noon and from 2 to
6 p.m. (it closes at 4:30 p.m. in winter). Entrance is free. Closed Mondays.

Though lean on attractions itself, Trent makes a good base for exploring
the sports resort of **Monte Bondone,** with its panoramic view (chair-lifts),
about 8½ miles from the city center; **Paganella,** slightly more than six miles
from Trent (the summit—nearly 7,000 feet high—is reached by cable); and the
Brenta Dolomites. The latter excursion, which will require at least a day for
a good look, will reward you with some of the finest mountain scenery in Italy.
From Trent, you'll first pass by **Lake Toblino,** then travel a winding, circuitous
road for much of the way, past jagged boulders. A 10-minute detour from the
main road is suggested at the turnoff to the Genova valley, with its untamed
scenery—at least to the thunderous **Nardis waterfall.** A good stopover point
is the fast-rising little resort of **Madonna di Campiglio.**

For those stopping over in Trent, we now consider:

HOTELS IN TRENT: Direly in need of a Counter-Reformation, the hotels of Trent are better for overnighters than fortnighters. In two different price ranges, our recommendations follow, beginning with the most expensive—

Grand Hotel Trento, 3 Via Alfieri (tel. 26-297), is a modern well-kept first-class hotel, considered the finest in Trent. It is clean, comfortable, and the bedrooms are well furnished, all with private baths. In peak season, the rate for a single is 10,000 lire ($11.60), and the charge for a double is 20,000 lire ($23.20), inclusive. The dining room and lounges are cavernous, and there's an American Bar, plus a garden.

Motel Agip, 168 Via Brennero (tel. 81-117), is a modern establishment in an industrial district of Trent. Opposite the railway tracks at the edge of town, it is true to the Agip chain tradition: pleasantly furnished bedrooms, trim, clean, and efficient. All its rooms contain private showers. Doubles go for 14,000 lire ($16.24); singles for 8,000 lire ($9.28). The lobby is in the contemporary rustico style.

DINING IN TRENT: **Birreria Forst,** 38 Via Oss-Mazzurana (tel. 26-399), is in the heart of Trent, decorated in the style of a Tyrolean tavern. Dining is on two levels, and the Germanic tone is set by the pretzels on a spike placed at each table. In a remodeled small palazzo, the Forst not only serves the best viands in Trent, it is also the most attractive place at which to dine. The chef prepares many flambé dishes well, including rognone (kidneys) al cognac. To begin your repast, however, we'd suggest the risotto cooked in champagne. Another good dish is fegato di vitello alla Veneziana (tender slices of veal liver prepared with onions). A choice of four set meals is offered at 3,500 lire ($4.06) each. Closed Mondays.

READER'S SIGHTSEEING TIPS: "In the Province of Trento, there is the very attractive and well-equipped resort of **Cavalese.** It can easily be reached by bus once you have used the main railway line from Rome to Bolzano. It is a very attractive summer and winter resort at a height of some 3,000 feet. I recommend **Pensione Dolomiti,** where a double room with bath will cost about 10,000 lire ($11.60) for full board, taxes included. The owners take care personally of the management of the hotel, and the cuisine is first class. No effort is spared by Signora Giuseppina to make the 30 guests feel at home in an area abundant in attractions.

"In the same valley where Cavalese lies, there is also 'le Alpi di **Pampeago.'** It is a major winter resort at a height of some 5,500 feet, equipped with chairlifts, ski lifts, cable cars, and proudly lists more than 40 miles of beautiful ski runs. There are hotels and boarding houses of all classes, and the best and most attractive is **Hotel Pampeago** (tel. 0462-83004), where a double room with bath can be had with full board for an average price of 18,000 lire ($20.88) per person, inclusive. The hotel assures first-class treatment of all its guests. The multilingual staff makes any stay enjoyable in a pleasant atmosphere" (Dr. Giovanni Patara, Rome, Italy).

From an Alpine landscape, we descend into the Lake District of Italy.

Chapter XIII

THE LAKE DISTRICT

1. Lake Garda
2. Lake Como
3. Lake Maggiore

FLOWER-BEDECKED promenades . . . lemon trees and villas . . . parks and gardens . . . tunnel-like roads . . . crystal-clear blue waters . . . great natural beauty. A Lake District holiday may sound a bit dated, like a penny-farthing bicycle or an aspidistra in the bay window. But the lakes themselves—notably Garda, Como, and Maggiore—combine to form one of the most enchanting splashes of scenery in Northern Italy.

Like the Lake District in Northwestern England, the Italian lakes have attracted poets and writers, everybody from Goethe to Gabriele D'Annunzio. But after World War II (Mussolini was strung up in Como), the Italian lakes seemed to be largely the domain of English and German women, the matronly types who prefer to do a lot of walking in groups. In our more recent swings through the district, we've noticed an increasing joie de vivre and a rising influx of the under-25 set, particularly at such resorts as Limone on Lake Garda.

Even if your time is limited, you'll want to have at least a look at:

1. Lake Garda
The most easterly of the Northern Italian lakes, Garda is also the largest, stretching 32 miles in length (and 11½ miles in width at its fattest point). Sheltered by mountains, its scenery, especially the part on the western shore that reaches from Limone to Salò, has often been compared to that of the Mediterranean: olive, orange, and lemon trees, even palms. The almost transparent lake is ringed with four art cities: Trent to the northeast, Brescia to the west, Manova (Mantua) to the south, and Verona to the east.

The eastern side of the lake is more rugged, less trampled, but the western resort-studded strip is far more glamorous to the first-timer. On the western side, a circuitous road skirts the lake through one molelike tunnel after another. You can park your car at several secluded belvederes for a panoramic lakeside view. In spring the scenery is splashed with color, everything from wild poppy beds to oleander. Garda is well served by buses, or else you can traverse the lake on steamers or motorboats, leaving from a number of harbors.

From our last stopover in Trent, it's only a 27-mile drive southwest to:

RIVA DEL GARDA: Astride the narrowing northern point of Garda, in the province of Trento, 195 feet above sea level, Riva is the oldest and most traditional resort along the lake. It consists of both an expanding new district and an old town, the latter centered at the Piazza III Novembre. On the harbor is the **Tower of Apponale,** dating from the 13th century, and the **Rocca,** built in 1124 and once owned by the ruling Scaligeri princes of Verona. The latter has been turned into a museum.

On the northern banks of the lake, between the Benacense plains and towering mountains, Riva offers the advantages of riviera and Dolomites. Its climate is classically Mediterranean, mild in winter and moderate in summer. Vast areas of rich green vegetation combine with the deep blue of the lake. Many come for health cures; others for business conferences, meetings, and fairs. Riva is popular with tour groups from the Germanic lands and from England. It is linked to the Brenner/Modena motorway (Rovereto Sud/Garda Nord exit), the railway (Rovereto station), and is near Verona Airport Villafranca.

Information is available from Azienda Autonoma di Siggiorno, Palazzo dei Congressi, 38066 Riva del Garda (tel. 0464-5444).

Hotels in Riva del Garda

A first-class choice, the **Lido Palace,** 10 Viale Carducci (tel. 52-664), is a grand lakeside retreat, surrounded by gardens and only a five-minute walk to the town center. The formal tree-lined drive reinforces the feeling of entering a private estate. The furnishings don't live up to the high architectural level, but the palazzo is spacious, with well-kept bedrooms decked out in standard modern. The 80-bedroom hotel, from July 1 till September 13, charges 15,000 lire ($17.40) for a double room with bath; 9,000 lire ($10.44) for a single. The cost of full board ranges from 13,000 lire ($15.08) to 16,000 lire ($18.56) per person in season, but only 9,000 lire ($10.44) to 14,000 lire ($16.24) per person at other times. Open from April 8 till October 15.

In the medium-priced bracket, the **Sole,** 35 Piazza III Novembre (tel. 52-686), apparently had far-sighted founders, snaring the best position on the waterfront. Although rated second-class by the government, and charging second-class prices, the hotel has all the amenities worthy of a first-class rating. It's an overgrown villa and has a large stack of rooms with arched windows and surrounding colonnades. Its interior has time-clinging traditional rooms. The beamed-ceilinged lounge centers around a cone-sloped hooded fireplace, with clusters of antique chairs set on islands of Oriental carpets. The character and quality of the bedrooms vary considerably according to their position (most of them have views of the lake). Some are almost suites, with living room areas; the smaller ones are less fortunate. Nevertheless, all the rooms are comfortable and are maintained spotlessly. The rate in a single room without bath is 6,000 lire ($6.96); 9,500 lire ($11.02) for a single with bath. The charge for a bathless double is 10,000 lire ($11.60); 14,000 lire ($16.24) for a double with bath, inclusive. The rates quoted are for high season only. Full pension is 12,000 lire ($13.92) per person, inclusive. You can dine in the formal interior room or on the flagstone lakeside terrace. It's a pleasant retreat.

Riva (Grand Hotel), 10 Piazza Garibaldi (tel. 52-340), open from April 10 to October 10, is a formal lakeside villa, with a row of palms in front, and a garden at the rear. In the center of everything, with good views of Garda, the hotel is quite big—130 rooms in all, about half with private baths. The furnishings are functional. Depending on the time of year, doubles without bath range from 9,800 lire ($11.37) to 16,800 lire ($19.49). With bath, the double rate goes from 11,900 lire ($13.80) to 18,700 lire ($21.69). The supplement for a single room is 2,000 lire ($2.32). A favorite gathering place for guests is the lounge, decorated in warm shades of copper brown. The Riva also maintains a 20-room annex, offering bathless rooms only (but with hot and cold running water).

In the budget category, the **Luise,** 9 Viale Rovereto (tel. 52-796), is a simple and compact modern hotel that offers you a lot for your lire. A block from the lake, near the town center, the Luise has 59 bedrooms—mostly with private baths or showers. The rooms are tastefully restrained, with the built-in essentials. Open year-round, the hotel charges 10,000 lire ($11.60) for its bathless doubles, 12,500 lire ($14.50) for its doubles with bath. The single rate is 8,000 lire ($9.28) in a bathless room, 10,000 lire ($11.60) with bath. Among its features are a walnut-paneled reception lounge, a modest but neat dining room, and a sidewalk terrace cafe. The full-pension rate ranges from 12,000 lire ($13.92) to 14,000 lire ($16.24) per person, inclusive.

Leaving Riva, the first resort you'll approach while heading south on the western shore (about six miles away) is:

LIMONE SUL GARDA: Characteristic of Garda's western shore is the *limonaie,* hillside terraces of lemon and orange groves. Taking its name from the fruit of the lemon trees, Limone is one of the liveliest resorts along the lake, drawing crowds of young people, probably because of its abundance of fourth-class hotels charging low prices.

Snuggling close to the lake, Limone is reached by descending a narrow, precipitous road. The village itself nestles on a narrow hunk of land space. Shopkeepers, faced with no building room, dug right into the rock (in one such resulting grotto, you can get a cavewoman coiffure). If you're bypassing Limone, you may still want to make a detour south of the village to the turnoff to **Tignale** in the hills. You climb a modern highway to the town for a sweeping overall vista of Garda, one of the most scenic spots on the entire lake.

Hotels in Limone Sul Garda

In the medium-priced range, **Le Palme** (tel. 94-006) is the best and most gracious hotel in Limone. It's a 16th-century, Venetian-styled palazzo, compactly set right at the water's edge, with its own private garden and lakeside terrace. Although extensively remodeled for the installation of more private baths, it retains many of its original architectural features. Three of its lounging salons open onto the side garden terrace, where there's a pair of 100-year-old palm trees. Throughout the hotel is a goodly mixture of Italian and French provincial furnishings, Victorian bric-a-brac, lots of brocade, silk, and gilt—but all homelike, no museum feeling here. Most of the bedrooms have a private bath or shower and intimate sun balconies. The furnishings combine the old and the new (the rooms decked out with the ornately painted Venetian furniture cost no more than those in more functional modern). Open April to October, the hotel charges 9,500 lire ($11.02) for a bathless single; 14,500 lire ($16.82) for a bathless double; and 15,700 lire ($18.21) for a double with bath or shower, inclusive. Full-pension terms range from 13,000 lire ($15.08) to 15,000 lire ($17.40). Le Palme is often more like a house party than a hotel. In fair weather, you can take meals on the dining terrace beside the water. The more formal dining room, with its Louis XV-styled chairs and decorative sculpture, opens onto the lake. Because of its popularity, it is best to make reservations.

GARDONE RIVIERA: In the province of Brescia, the western shore of Gardone Riviera is well equipped with a number of good hotels and sporting facilities. Its lakeside promenade attracts a wide range of predominantly European tourists for most of the year. When it used to be chic for patrician Italian families to spend their holidays by the lake, many of the more prosperous built elaborate villas not only in Gardone Riviera, but in neighboring Fasano (some of these have been converted to receive guests). The town also has the biggest manmade sight along the lake, which you may want to visit even if you're not lodging for the night.

The Main Sight

Vittoriale was once the private home of Gabriele D'Annunzio (1863-1938), the famous poet and military adventurer, another Italian who believed in "La Dolce Vita," even when he couldn't afford it! Most of the celebrated events in D'Annunzio's life—such as his love affair with Eleanora Duse, his bravura takeover as a self-styled commander of a territory being ceded to Yugoslavia—occurred before 1925. In the remaining years of his life and up until he died in the winter before World War II, the national hero lived the grand life at his private estate on Garda.

North of the town, Vittoriale is open from 8 a.m. to 6:30 p.m. (off season, from 8 a.m. to noon and from 2 to 6 p.m.), and charges 500 lire (58¢) for admission. The furnishings and decor passed for avant-garde in their day, but evoke the Radio City Music Hall of the 30s when viewed now. D'Annunzio's death mask is of morbid interest, and his bed with a "Big Brother" eye adds a curious touch of 1984 (over the poet's bed is a faun casting a nasty sneer!). The marble bust of Duse seems sadly out of place, but the manuscripts and old uniforms perpetuate the legend. In July and August, D'Annunzio plays are presented at the amphitheater on the premises. To sum up, a bizarre museum to a dated hero of yesteryear.

Hotels in Gardone Riviera

A first-class hotel, the **Eurotel Gardone Riviera** (tel. 21-161), is one of the most modern and streamlined to grace the Gardone Riviera skyline. For well-appointed comfort and amenities, we'd rate it higher than the traditional reigning queen in the first-class category, the Grand (the Eurotel is also cheaper). Closed from November 5 to December 20, it is one of the showcases of the fast-rising Eurotel chain, a "resident tourist cooperative." Built on the rise of a hill near the lake, it is a vast, sprawling, and contemporary structure, privately placed in its own gardens with landscaped terraces. Architecturally advanced, the hotel offers 80 rooms, compact with coordinated colors, all with private baths or showers. The peak-season rate for a single is 9,500 lire ($11.02); 21,000 lire ($24.36) in a double. The bed-and-breakfast rate is a maximum 12,000 lire ($13.92) per person in season. All the lounges are gracious, some opening Japanese fashion onto inner gardens. Special features: a free-form swimming pool, flower and lawn terraces, banks of rock gardens, tennis, and golf.

In the budget range, **Bellevue Hotel** (tel. 20-235), an old villa perched up from the main road, has many terraces surrounded by trees and flowers—and an unforgettable view. You can stay here, enjoying the advantages of lakeside villa life. Franco Pizzi, who owns and manages the hotel, opens his large rooms to guests from April to October. The furnishings in the bedrooms are ordinary modern, and everything is kept shipshape. The rate is 8,000 lire ($9.28) for a bathless double; 9,000 lire ($10.44) for a double with bath, inclusive. The lounges have more comfort than style, and the dining room is simple though the view through the arched windows and the quality of the meals themselves are excellent (no skimpy helpings here). The full-pension rate in high season ranges from 8,500 lire ($9.86) to 9,800 lire ($11.37) per person, inclusive.

At the southern side of Lake Garda stands our final stopover.

SIRMIONE: Perched at the tip of a narrowing strip of land, Sirmione juts out for 2½ miles into Lake Garda. Noted for its thermal baths (used in the treatment of deafness), the town is a major resort that blooms in spring and wilts in autumn. It's reached by heading north after veering from the autostrada connecting Milan and Verona.

The resort was a favorite of Giosuè Carducci, the Italian poet who won the Nobel Prize for literature in 1906. In Roman days, it was frequented by still another poet, Catullus. Today the **Grotte di Catullo** is the chief sight, an unbeatable combination of Roman ruins and a panoramic view of the water. You can wander at leisure through the remains of this once-great villa. At the far end of town, the grottoes are open from 9 a.m. to an hour before sunset; it closes Mondays. The admission is 100 lire (12¢) on weekdays.

At the entrance to the town stands the moated 13th-century **Castle** that once belonged to the powerful Scaligeri princes of Verona. Architecturally, the medieval castle is distinguished by its crenellated battlements. You can climb to the top and walk the ramparts. It is open (admission free) from 9:30 a.m. to 12:30 p.m. and from 3 to 6 p.m. (closes earlier off season; hours are from 10 to 12:30 and from 2 to 5). Closed Mondays.

Hotels in Sirmione

During the peak season, motorists sometimes have to have a hotel reservation to take their vehicle into the crowded confines of the town. In hotels, Sirmione is adequately endowed. The following are our recommendations:

A first-class choice is the **Villa Cortine Palace** (tel. 916-021), luxuriously set apart from the town center, surrounded by imposing and sumptuous gardens. The century-old grounds have a formal entrance through the fluted columns of a colonnade. There are winding lanes lined with cypress trees, wide-spreading magnolias, and flower-bordered marble fountains with classic sculpture. Through the trees emerges a partial view of the lake and the nearby private waterside beach area. A newer structure with well-furnished rooms and private baths has been built adjoining the mellowed and pillared main building. In comfort and convenience, the bedrooms are unequaled in Sirmione. Open from March to October, the hotel charges a peak-season rate of 12,000 lire ($13.92) in a bathless single; 13,000 lire ($15.08) in a single with bath; 25,000 lire ($29) in a double. The full-pension rate ranges from 26,000 lire ($30.16) to 27,500 lire ($31.90) per person, inclusive. The interior has one formal drawing room, with much gilt and marble, very palace-like.

In the medium-priced range is the **Olivi** (tel. 961-110), a creation of its sun-loving owner, Signor Bertini. Also an architect, he managed to erect a hotel where each room is light and view-oriented. Furthermore, its location is excellent, on the rise of a hill in a grove of olive trees, at the edge of town. The all-glass walls of the major rooms never let you forget you're in a garden spot of Italy. Even the compact and streamlined bedrooms—59 in all—have walls of glass leading out onto open balconies. Most of the rooms have private baths, for which couples pay 16,000 lire ($18.56) in high season; singles, 9,500 lire

($11.02). Open year round, the hotel charges from 18,000 lire ($20.88) to 20,000 lire ($23.20) per person for full pension in high season.

Flaminia Hotel, 8 Piazza Flaminia (tel. 916-078), is the best third-class hotel in Sirmione, with such facilities and amenities that the government allows it to charge prices slightly higher than some second-class hotels. One of the newer accommodations, it lies near the town center right on the lakefront, with a terrace extending out into the water. The bedrooms, all with private baths and telephones, come off fairly well, dominated as they are by French doors opening onto private balconies. Couples are charged a peak-season rate of 15,000 lire ($17.40), inclusive. A few singles are rented at 10,000 lire ($11.60). Open year round, the Flaminia charges 18,000 lire ($20.88) per person in summer for full pension, inclusive. The rooftop dining terrace, with its moss-green tiled floor, Chinese red garden chairs, all-glass windows, provides an excellent view of Garda—a fit background for well-prepared meals. The lounges are furnished with functional modern, such as bullfrog armchairs.

The budget-priced **Pensione Anna** (tel. 916-139) may not be right on the lake, but it's an island of good taste in a sea of uninspired modern hotels. Half a block from the Moat of the Castle, it has its own garden and rooftop sun terrace. It is the best and most personally run pension in town—not unlike an English inn, with some beamed ceilings and stone walls. The sitting room is exactly like a private home, where one has preserved the finest of the family antiques. The 18 bedrooms are also homelike mixing the old with the modern; each has hot and cold running water, a few have private baths, and most offer a pleasant view. Open from April to September, the pension charges 10,000 lire ($11.60) in a bathless single; 13,000 lire ($15.08) for a double with bath, inclusive. The dining room, with its low, arched ceiling and old-styled chairs, serves hearty, bountiful food.

Grifone ("The Griffin"), corner of via Dante, facing the side of the castle (tel. 9174), is an old mansion, completely renewed, with a lot of marble. The reception is tiny, but the rooms are comfortable, with matrimonial (king-sized) beds. Overlooking either the castle or the lake and gardens, most of the rooms contain private baths or showers. The cost of a single is 5,500 lire ($6.38), rising to 10,000 lire ($11.60) in a double. There is no pension situation, but you can eat at the Grifone Restaurant, with its quite modern atmosphere. The dining room provides a mixture of neo-rustic furniture with good service. There's a terrace right over the lake, with the castle on the side. The cooking is first class and only à la carte. Selections include minestrone at 800 lire (93¢); followed by osso bucco, 2,500 lire ($2.90), with vegetables of your choice. To finish, we'd suggest a delicious baked apple at 500 lire (58¢). The house wine is a real bargain at 800 lire (93¢) for half a bottle. Service is an extra 15%.

READER'S HOTEL SELECTION AT GARDA: "I am happy to point out a most picturesque and delightfully situated little town with quaint buildings of the 13th century, **Garda.** It is a little jewel, where peace, pleasant landscape, and well-organized beaches are the main attractions. I was particularly happy with **Hotel Vittoria,** Via Lungo Lago (tel. 624-065). It is perfect for those who seek quiet surroundings, spotless rooms, and excellent cuisine. The owners, Famiglia Maffezzoli, do their utmost to make guests happy. The hotel is some 15 yards from Garda Lake shore and the spacious garden in front of the building is normally used for breakfast or lunch. Prices vary from 8,000 lire ($9.28) to 12,000 lire ($13.92) for full board, taxes included, depending on the season or room. The cuisine is a major success of Signora Maffezzoli, ably helped by her daughter, Antonella. Look for the tagliatelle alla Antonella, brasato or polenta" (Dr. Giovanni Patara).

2. Lake Como

Everything noble, everything evoking love—that was how Stendhal characterized fork-tongued Lake Como. Others have called it "the looking glass of Venus." More than 30 miles north of Milan, it is, next to Garda, the most heavily visited of Italian lakes. A shimmering deep blue, the lake spans 2½ miles at its widest point. With its flower-studded gardens, its villas built for the wealthy of the 17th and 18th centuries, its mild climate, Larius (as it was known to the Romans) is among the most scenic spots in all of Italy.

For a short, but still fairly comprehensive, one-day motor tour, we suggest going first to Como at the southern tip of the lake. Como, the provincial capital, is an industrial town noted for its silk. From there, you can travel up the eastern shore of the west branch to Bellàgio, the best-known resort. From Bellàgio, you can either stop over or else traverse the lake by car ferry to Villa Carlotta and Tremezzo on the western shore, then head south down the strip to Milan again. We've found this to be a more scenic routing than along the eastern branch of Como, called the Laga di Lecco.

CERNOBBIO: Less than three miles northwest of Como, Cernobbio is a small, fashionable resort frequented by the wealthy of Europe because of its deluxe hotel, the 16th-century Villa d'Este. But its idyllic anchor on the lake has also attracted a less affluent tourist, who'll find a number of third- and even fourth-class accommodations as well.

The Budget Range

Hotel Asnigo (tel. 510-062). Commanding a view of Como from its hillside perch at Piazza Santo Stefano, this is a good little (23 bedrooms) albergo set in its own garden. Its special and subtle charms have long been known to a lake-loving set of British visitors. An Englishwoman writes: "Last summer I did something not recommendable to your readers: I went on a trip to Italy with my nephew and his wife from America, who quite frankly patronize a higher type of establishment than I do. Naturally, they were lured to the Villa d'Este on Como. I, fortunately, was able to find a splendid little third-class hotel in the hills, the Asnigo. The proprietor was most helpful; the meals flawless and beautifully served; the rooms (no w.c., but hot and cold running water) spotlessly clean and comfortable. After being a dinner guest one night at the Villa d'Este, I returned the hospitality the following evening by inviting my relatives for a most enjoyable meal at my pensione. At least, they learned that good food and comfort are not the sole domain of the deluxe hotel." We echo her sentiments. Incidentally, the hotel is open only from April to October 10, and charges from 9,500 lire ($11.02) for half pension, in a bathless room; 10,500 lire ($12.18) with bath. Off-season reductions are granted by the courteous management.

A 45-minute drive north from Como will take you to:

BELLAGIO: Sitting on a promontory at the point where Lake Como forks, Bellàgio is with much justification given the label of "The Pearl of Larius." A quiet, sleepy veil hangs over the town's arcaded streets and its little shops. Bellàgio is rich in memories, having attracted the fashionable, even royal visitors, such as King Leopold I of Belgium, who used to own the 18th-century Villa Giulia. To reach many of the spots in the town, you must climb streets that are really stairways. Its lakeside promenade blossoms with flowering shrubbery. From the town, visitors can take tours of Lake Como and enjoy several resort-type sports, such as rowing and tennis, or else they can lounge at Bellàgio Lido.

If time allows, try to explore the gardens of the **Villa Serbelloni,** the Bellàgio Study and Conference Center of the Rockefeller Foundation (not to be confused with the Grand Hotel Villa Serbelloni by the waterside in the village). The villa is not open to the public, but the park can be visited on guided tours starting at 10 a.m. and 4 p.m., and lasting for two hours. Tours are conducted daily except Sundays and holidays, from Good Friday to mid-October at a cost of 500 lire per person, the proceeds going to local charities.

You can also visit the **Grand Hotel Villa Serbelloni,** a deluxe hotel on the shore of the lake, also with a beautiful garden and park. The hotel is open from April 10 to October 10.

Hotels in Bellàgio

Good choices are available in a number of categories, in hotels that have appealed to everyone from Napoleon to Mark Twain. For the visitor who wants to find a retreat on the lake, Bellàgio emerges as the most suitable resort. Our recommendation follows.

In the medium-priced range there is **Du Lac** (tel. 950-320), a long-established hotel right in the center of town, with a street-front portico restaurant open to non-residents. It's a well-built place, recently redecorated, but its most recommendable feature is the rooftop garden with its lakeside view and the usually reliable sun shining down warmly. The hospitable proprietors keep their hotel open from April to October. The bedrooms—50 in all, most with private baths—are pleasant (some with lake views), decked out with chintz fabrics. The peak-season rate for a bathless double is 9,800 lire ($11.37); 14,000 lire ($16.24) for a double with bath. The single rate ranges from 5,000 lire ($5.80) in a bathless room to 9,000 lire ($10.44) with bath. Full pension averages from 10,000 lire ($11.60) to 14,000 lire ($16.24) per person.

READERS' HOTEL SELECTION: "**Haus Bethusy,** 28 Via Eugenio Vitali (tel. 950-135), offers an elegant and comfortable atmosphere. The terraces provide for relaxation in beautiful surroundings. A rowboat is also available for the use of guests. The charming hostess is Countess Elsa Bethusy. Bellagio can be reached by bus, which departs from the Como train station, or by a boat from Como. Call the countess for time schedules. A single room without bath costs 4,000 lire ($4.64); a double without bath, 6,500 lire ($7.54)" (The Martins and the Armaninos).

From Como, car ferries ply back and forth across the lake to **Cadenabbia** on the western shore. Cadenabbia itself is another lakeside resort, with hotels and villas, the most important of which you'll surely want to visit—

THE VILLA CARLOTTA: Directly south of Cadenabbia on the run to Tremezzo, the Villa Carlotta is the most-visited attraction on Lake Como—and with good reason. In a serene setting, the villa is graced with gardens of exotic flowers and blossoming shrubbery, especially rhododendrons and azaleas. Its beauty is tame, cultivated, much like a fairy-tale that recaptures the halcyon life available only to the very rich of the 18th century. Dating from 1747, the estate was named after a Prussian princess, Carlotta, who married the Duke of Saxony-Meiningen. Inside the villa are a number of art treasures, including Canova's "Cupid and Psyche," and a number of neo-classical statues by Bertel

Thorvaldsen, the famous Danish sculptor who died in 1844. Also displayed are neo-classical paintings, furniture, and a stone and bronze table ornament which belonged to viceroy Eugene Beauharnais. The villa is open March 1 to September 30 from 8:30 a.m. to 6:30 p.m. From October 1 to November 15, hours are from 9 a.m. to noon and from 2 to 2:30 p.m. The Carlotta closes from November 15 until March 1. Admission is 1,000 lire ($1.16). From the villa, it's only a minute's drive to:

TREMEZZO: Another popular west shore resort, Tremezzo opens ónto a panoramic view of Lake Como. Around the town is a district known as Tremezzina, with luxuriant vegetation that includes citrus trees, palms, cypresses, and magnolias. Tremezzo is the starting point for many excursions. Its accommodations are much more limited than those in Bellàgio, though it does boast—

A First-Class Hotel

Grand Hotel Tremezzo (tel. 40-446), is exactly that: a grand old hotel resting on a lakeside ledge, surrounded by spacious terraced gardens and keeping good company with the neighboring Villa Carlotta. Excellent architecturally, it has, alas, become a virtual showroom for manufacturers of plastic-type furniture. Still, the situation is ideal, especially under palm trees by the open-air swimming pool or on the lakeside Lido. The bedrooms are enormous, built when spaciousness was a prerequisite. More than half the rooms, furnished in a contemporary style, contain private baths and their own balconies. Low season here is from April to June 30 and from September 11 through October. From June 1 to September 10, the hotel charges its highest rates: 8,000 lire ($9.28) in a bathless single; 13,000 lire ($15.08) in a single with bath; 12,000 lire ($13.92) in a bathless double; 19,000 lire ($22.04) for a double with bath, inclusive. The full-pension rate ranges from 14,000 lire ($16.24) to 20,000 lire ($23.20) per person, inclusive. Most of the very pleasing meals, costing 6,000 lire ($6.96) are served on the lakeside terrace. In the rustic-styled discotheque, Escale, guests dance to records in an intimate candlelit atmosphere under beamed ceilings.

READERS' HOTEL SELECTION AT COMO: "Hotel Tre Re in Como is at 20 Via Beldoni (tel. 26-5374). After seven years of budget travel all around the world, we count this as one of our best finds. The rooms are clean, well lighted, and well heated. Beds are firm and full size, and above all, the hotel is open all year. A garage is available free, a plus, since overnight parking in central Como can be a problem. Its location in the center of old Como is ideal. The Standa Department Store is the only thing that mars a view of the cathedral one block away. It is only minutes from the narrow alleyways of the old city where antique stores and cheese shops are nestled cheek by jowl. A walk in the opposite direction brings you to the lake" (Barb and Larry Strong, Tunis, Tunisia).

3. Lake Maggiore

The shores of this lake wash up on the banks of Piedmont and Lombardy in Italy, but its more austere northern basin (Locarno, for example) lies in the mountainous region of Switzerland. At its longest point, it stretches a distance of more than 40 miles (and is 6½ miles at its widest stretch).

A wealth of natural beauty awaits the visitor: mellowed lakeside villas, dozens of gardens with lush vegetation, sparkling waters, magnificent panoramic views. A veil of mist seems to hover at times, especially in the early spring and late autumn.

Maggiore is a most rewarding lake to visit from Milan, especially because of the Borromean Islands in its center (most easily reached from Stresa). The fortunate visitor will be able to motor around the entire basin. But those on a more limited schedule may find the western, resort-studded shore the most scenic. From Milan, a drive northwest for about 51 miles will take you to Stresa, the major resort on Lake Maggiore.

The launching of a 320-by-18-foot floating fountain, with 110-foot, multicolored waterjets, on Lake Maggiore was part of an attempt to update the region's "belle epoque" image and to increase the popularity of the region.

STRESA: On the western shore, Stresa has skyrocketed from a simple village of fisherfolk to a first-class international resort. Its vantage on the lake is almost unparalleled, and its level of hotel accommodations is superior to that of the other Maggiore resorts of Italy. Scene of sporting activities and an international festival of Musical Weeks (beginning in late August), it swings into action in April, then dwindles in popularity at the end of October. Stresa is reached in one hour from Milan on the Simplon Railway.

Hotels in Stresa

We'll survey the best of accommodations in Stresa—in price categories ranging from deluxe to fourth class:

A deluxe hotel, the **Grand Hotel Et Des Iles Borromées** (tel. 30-431), comes on like a turn-of-the-century palace—the only luxury hotel in Stresa. Those baroque Victorians who created the establishment made it worthy of a diamond tiara. Run by the CIGA chain, it stands in the midst of its own park and gardens on the edge of town, opening onto the lake and the Borromean Islands. Along the lakefront are the hotel's private swimming terraces and cabanas. The public salons are furnished in a subdued manner, and the bedrooms—145 in all, 123 with shower baths—extend the theme, liberally using old pieces and fine reproductions. Most of the rooms have private balconies.

The hotel is open from April to October, and charges its highest prices from July to September. For a single room without bath, you'll pay 15,880 lire ($18.33); 23,720 lire ($27.51) in a single with bath. The charge for a bathless double is 27,280 lire ($31.65); 38,480 lire ($44.64) for a double with bath. The full-pension charge in high season ranges from 35,000 lire ($40.60) to 60,000 lire ($69.60). At night, there's dancing. Sports, such as tennis and water-skiing, reign supreme during the day.

The medium-priced range offers the **Hotel Astoria** (tel. 30-259), expressly for sun-seekers who want a modern hotel with its own heated swimming pool. Standing right on the lake, it features triangular balconies—one to each bedroom—jutting out for the view. Most of its streamlined, starkly furnished, but rather spacious bedrooms have private baths as well. Open from April to October, the hotel in high season charges 15,000 lire ($17.40) for a single with bath; 22,000 lire ($25.52) for a double with bath, inclusive. The full-pension rate reaches a peak of 25,000 lire ($29) per person. The public lounges have walls of glass opening toward the lake view and the garden. The portion of the dining room favored by most guests is the wide-paved, open-air, front terrace, where under shelter you dine on a good cuisine while enjoying Maggiore as the chef-d'oeuvre.

In the budget range, the **Hotel Moderno** (tel. 30-468), true to its name, is a contemporary, 49-bedroom establishment in the midst of the shopping section, about two blocks from the lake. Most of its front rooms have street balconies. The little reception lounge is meager, but the open-air dining room in the rear—shaded by vines—is especially pleasant and the food is good. Each bedroom, reached by elevator, has private bath or shower. Open March to September, the Moderno in peak season charges 6,000 lire ($6.96) for a single and 13,000 lire ($15.08) for a double, inclusive. Half pension, and we recommend it here, ranges from 9,000 lire ($10.44) to 13,000 lire ($15.08) per person, inclusive. A short walk will take you to the Moderno's private swimming pool and garden.

Meuble Primavera, 39 Via Cavour (tel. 31-286), is a recently built unit. The welcome from the owner, Signor Maurizio Ferraris, is friendly. He has the happy and relaxed temperament you expect from a host. His family-run hotel is kept immaculately clean. Fully tiled floors and Norwegian-styled wood furniture are used throughout. Some of the front bedrooms have windows over the Via Cavour, facing an old church. They also have balconies of red geraniums. A double with private bath runs between 7,800 lire ($9.05) and 8,500 lire ($9.86). A single begins as low as 4,000 lire ($4.64) without bath. Doubles without bath cost only 6,000 lire ($6.96). Breakfast is served in the first-floor lounge, where you may chat with Signor Maurizio at night over a glass of Grappa.

READER'S HOTEL SELECTION: "I found the owners of the **Hotel Ariston,** on the main boulevard, 60 Corso Italia (tel. 31195) quite friendly. For some reason, the hotel is listed as third class, which means the price per person for a single room, no bath, but a bidet and a toilet in the room, was 4,500 lire ($5.22)" (Janet H. Sutton, Los Angeles, Calif.).

Dining in Stresa

Taverna del Pappagallo, 38-45 Principessa Margherita, is an informal little garden restaurant and tavern operated by three brothers who turn out some of the best and least expensive meals in Stresa. Specialties of the house include gnocchi (semolina dumplings) for 700 lire (81¢); scallopine alla Milanese for 2,500 lire ($2.90); salamino allo spiedoe fagioli (grilled sausage with beans) for 1,500 lire ($1.74); and saltimbocca alla Romana (a veal and ham dish), 2,800 lire ($3.25)—unusually delicious. At night pizza is king (try the Pizza Regina) with prices going from 900 lire ($1.04) to 1,800 lire ($2.09). The taverna service is most friendly, with a personal family touch.

Bettolino della Carafa, 6 Via Mazzini, is a nice little trattoria with square wooden tables and chairs. The service is great. A set menu is offered for 3,500 lire ($4.06), which might include vegetable soup, fillets of trout, delicious green beans, and a tasty caramel custard. A la carte meals are also served, with main dishes costing from 1,500 lire ($1.74) to 3,000 lire ($3.48). A large choice of pizzas is also offered in the 800-lire (93¢) to 1200-lire ($1.39) range.

THE BORROMEAN ISLANDS: The heart of Lake Maggiore is occupied by this chain of tiny islands, which were turned into sites of lavish villas and gardens by the Borromeo clan. From the harbor at Stresa, you can buy an excursion ticket on a boat that will take you to the three major islands. In summer, a boat leaves about every 30 minutes, and the three-hour trip costs 4,000 lire ($4.64), including admission fees to the villas—which tend to be expensive.

The major stopover is on the **Isola Bella** (Beautiful Island), which should be visited if you have time for only one sight. Dominating the island is the 17th-century Borromeo Palazzo. When approached from the front, the figurines in the garden evoke the appearance of a wedding cake. On conducted tours, you are shown through the light and airy palace, from which the views are remarkable. Napoleon slept here. A special feature are the six grotto rooms, built piece by piece like a mosaic. In addition, there is a collection of quite good tapestries, with gory cannibalistic animal scenes that should appeal even to those who don't like tapestries. Outside, the white peacocks in the garden enchant year after year. If you don't purchase the overall ticket, you must pay 750 lire (87¢) to enter the palace and its grounds, which are open in season from 9 to noon and from 1:30 to 5:30.

The **Isola Madre** (Mother Island) is the largest of the chain visited chiefly because of its botanical gardens. On a guided tour, you are shown through a lush setting ripe with pomegranates, camellias, wisteria, rhododendrons, bougainvillea, hibiscus, hydrangea, magnolias, even a cypress tree from the Himalayas. In season, you can go on the garden tour from 8:30 a.m. to 12:30 p.m. and from 1:30 to 5:30 for a 650 lire-(75¢) entrance fee.

The **Isola dei Pescatori** (Fishermen's Island) is without major sights or lavish villas, but in many ways it is the most colorful. Less a stage setting than its other two sisters, it is inhabited by fishermen who live in colorful cottages. Good walks are possible in many directions.

Unless you have grown villa and garden weary, you may want to visit this final sight—

The Villa Taranto

Back on the mainland near the resort of Pallanza, north of Stresa, the botanical gardens spread over more than 50 acres of the Castagnola Promontory which juts out into Lake Maggiore. In this dramatic setting between the mountains and the lake, more than 20,000 species of plants from all over the world thrive in a well-tended and cultivated institution, begun in 1931 by a Scotsman, Captain Neil McEacharn. Plants range from rhododendrons and azaleas to specimens from such faraway places as Louisiana and Canada. Seasonal exhibits include fields of Dutch tulips (80,000 of them), Japanese magnolias, giant water lilies, cotton plants, and rare varieties of hydrangeas. The formal gardens of the villas are carefully laid out with ornamental fountains, statues, and reflection pools. Among the more ambitious creations of the gardens are the elaborate irrigation system which pumps water from the lake to all parts of the gardens, and the Terrace Gardens, complete with waterfalls and swimming pool. The villa gardens are open every day from 8:30 a.m. till sunset, from April 1 through October 31. Professional guides will take you on tours which last more than an hour. You may also take a round-trip boat ride from Stresa, which docks at the Villa Taranto pier adjoining the entrance to the gardens. The boat fare is 2,000 lire ($2.32), including the entrance fee. Otherwise, you pay an admission of 1,200 lire ($1.39).

Chapter XIV

MILAN AND FIVE LOMBARD CENTERS

**1. Milan
2. Bergamo
3. Brescia
4. Cremona
5. Mantua
6. Pavia**

THE VICISSITUDES OF the history of Italy are reflected in Lombardy as perhaps in no other region. All conquerors from barbarians to Napoleon have marched across its plain. Even Mussolini came to his end here. He and his mistress—both already dead—were strung up in a square in Milan as war-weary residents vented their rage upon the two bodies.

Among the most progressive of all the Italians, the Lombards have charted an industrial empire unequaled in Italy. Often the dream of the underfed and jobless worker in the south is to go to "Milano" for the high wages and the good life.

But Lombardy isn't all manufacturing. Milan, as we'll soon see, is filled to the brim with important attractions, and nearby are four old art cities— Bergamo, Brescia, Cremona, and Mantua (Mantova), as well as the Carthusian Monastery of Pavia.

1. Milan

Up to now we've been paying homage to the past. In the capital of Lombardy we meet the Italy of today and of tomorrow. The progressive Milanese are creating a powerful manufacturing and commercial metropolis, advanced in design and fashion. The past lingers on in its many art treasures spared from the heavy World War II bombing, including the Gothic Cathedral and Leonardo da Vinci's memorable "Last Supper." Nevertheless, the banking center of Italy—home to around two million people—is firmly entrenched in the 20th century.

As a railway terminus in the Po Valley, it is without peer in Italy: the Simplon, Bernina, and Gotthard lines link Northern Italy with the heartland of Europe. The city tends to be fiercely hot in summer (rooms with air conditioning are advised for those who can afford them) and fiercely cold in winter.

A word of warning: Milan really closes up in August, except for hotels, of course. Reader Pam King, of New Haven, Connecticut, writes: "It didn't really bother us, but some people might care, as it's a little eerie. We found only one out of every seven or eight stores open."

Note: The addresses of the **Alitalia** offices in Milan are 5 Via Albricci and 37 Via L. Sturzo. The Alitalia Representative Office is at the Air Terminal, 37 Via L. Sturzo (tel. 6281; booking 2836).

HOTELS IN MILAN: In the city is a superabundance of deluxe as well as first- and second-class hotels, most of which are big on comfort, but short on romance. In the third and fourth-class bracket and on the pension level, there are dozens of choices—many of which rank at the bottom of the totem pole of comparably classed establishments in all of Italy's major cities, with the exception of Naples.

The Deluxe Choices

Principe e Savoia, 17 Piazzale della Repubblica (tel. 62-30), near the railway station, is a blockbuster CIGA chain establishment. The interior of the old "wing" completely revamped and a modern building added, it is well on its way to becoming a small-scale Waldorf Astoria. Very substantial, very luxurious, it offers good solid comfort in an overscaled atmosphere. A great many lire were lavished on the furnishings and accoutrements, with well-styled period reproductions in ascendancy. The bedrooms themselves—many with private balconies and all with private baths or showers—are tastefully restrained and handsomely maintained. A single rents for 35,000 lire ($40.60); a double from 45,000 lire ($52.20), plus taxes. In the quiet and verdant rear garden, tables with umbrellas are set out for drinks and refreshments. Finally, you'll find the usual deluxe hotel facilities, such as an underground garage and banqueting halls, along with "My Grill," the choice of many a Milanese businessman seeking to impress his out-of-town client.

Hotel Palace, 20 Piazza della Repubblica (tel. 63-36), blithely ignores the pell-mell commercial world enveloping it, standing aloof on the slight rise of a hill, with a formal car entrance and a facade of 11 floors with tiers of balconies. It is near the railway station and its sister CIGA luxury hotel, the Principe e Savoia. An American bar and Grill Room are also on the premises. The food is top-notch, often attracting the well-heeled Milanese out for a night on the town. The decorating theme running through the public lounges and bedrooms blends modern and traditional furnishings. All of the rooms have private baths, and are air-conditioned or heated. The rate for a single with bath is 32,000 lire ($37.12); from 42,000 lire ($48.72) in a double. In the lounge bar you'll invariably meet someone from back home—that is, if you live in Easthampton or Palm Beach.

The First-Class Range

Aerhotel Executive, 45 Viale Sturzo (tel. 6294), inaugurated in 1973, is the largest hotel in Italy, with 420 double-bedded rooms. Managed by the hotel chain, Aerhotel, it was jointly created by Alitalia, CIGA (the biggest Italian hotel concern), and S.M.E. (one of the major Italian financial holdings, partly owned by the Italian government). It is adjacent to the Alitalia Air Terminal, most central. All rooms have private baths, air conditioning, radio, TV, and long-distance telephone (direct dialing to the U.S.A.). The modern furnishings and the service are most efficient. Well known is its Normanno Restaurant, with some of the best meat dishes in Milan. The decor is inspired by the French Norman style. You can have an excellent meal for 7,000 lire ($8.12). The Caravelle Restaurant, on the other hand, is ideal for a quick breakfast, business lunch, even a late snack. For a single room the rate is 27,000 lire ($31.32); 36,000 lire ($42.92) for a double. Public facilities include two bars (one with piano) and a garage for 500 cars.

Aerhotel Fieramilano, 20 Viale Boezio (tel. 3105), is managed by the same chain which operates Aerhotel Executive described above. Aerhotel is jointly owned by Alitalia, CIGA, and S.M.E. Near the Fiera Campionara, it is a first-class establishment offering 238 well-furnished and comfortable bedrooms, all with private bath and air conditioning. All the amenities are here—a restaurant, a bar, a snack bar, a coffee shop, a garage, and a garden—to ease you into life in the big city. A single with bath rents for 27,000 lire ($31.32), a double with bath for 37,500 lire ($43.50), including I.V.A. tax. A complete lunch or dinner costs 7,000 lire ($8.12) in the hotel's restaurant.

Hotel Cavour, 21 via Fatebenefratelli (tel. 65-09-83), is a leading first-class hotel, containing 110 rooms with private tub or shower baths. The cost is 30,000 lire ($34.80) in a double, 23,000 lire ($26.68) in a single, plus 9% I.V.A. tax. A continental breakfast is included. The modern decor is far better than average—in fact, rather elegant. The hotel is spotlessly clean, offering good service and an excellent location, a short walk from the Duomo and La Scala.

Windsor, 2 Via Galileo Galilei (tel. 637-151), which was erected and furnished in 1968, is an accomplishment. In spite of its "moderno," it maintains a warm ambience. A generous use of splashy and vibrant colors, plus a wise selection of traditional furnishings, with an accent on comfort, have made the Windsor a satisfactory hotel in its price range. A corner building of sienna-colored marble, it was built midway between the railway station and the Duomo on a tree-lined boulevard. Each of its 114 bedrooms comes equipped with a bath and shower, plus a direct-dial telephone, a radio, television, and your own drink-stocked refrigerator. You get free air conditioning as well, and there is also a garage. Singles rent for 21,500 lire ($24.94); doubles for 29,000 lire ($33.64). The accommodations contain wall-to-wall draperies, with built-in headboards and chests. Public facilities include a cozy, rather luxurious bar, as well as a dramatic dining room, with tall panels of wood and walls of curtained glass.

Marino alla Scala, 5 Piazza della Scala (tel. 867-803), seems to have been created for discriminating guests who enjoy the opera. Handy for some of the most famous singers who appear at La Scala, it has that operatic touch itself, with its highly stylized interior. There's a profusion of antiques, as well as velvet swags at the windows, an Empire bar, and a town-housey drawing room with crystal sconces and a chandelier. Even the bedrooms have been given a person-alized touch—some have brass beds, most have excellent furnishings, desks, and living areas, as well as well-maintained private bathrooms. The rate for a single is 21,700 lire ($25.17); 27,800 lire ($32.25) for couples. Breakfast is an extra 2,200 lire ($2.55).

De La Ville, 6 Via Hoepli (tel. 867-651), lies halfway between the Duomo and La Scala. Every one of its individual bedrooms has its own bath or shower and is air-conditioned. The restrained elegance of the bedrooms alone makes it worthwhile. With coordinated colors and fabrics, the furniture is well styled. For a single room, the rate is 25,000 lire ($29); 35,000 lire ($40.60) for a double. The lounges have comfortably traditional pieces, glossy marble floors, tapestry rugs, old clocks, and a china collection. Dining is most agreeable in the Vivero Restaurant. The De La Ville is under the same management as the Hotel Vesuvio in Naples and the Excelsior Vittoria in Sorrento.

The Medium-Priced Range

Hotel Augustus, 29 Via Napo Torriani (tel. 655-741), is just far enough away from the railway station to miss the commotion, yet close enough for convenience. It's a medium-sized hotel with 55 bedrooms, most compact and ultra modern. Throughout is a generous blending of marble, wood paneling, and contemporary furnishings. The rooms, though small, are well furnished, containing air conditioning and an occasional painted brass bed. Nearly all the bedrooms have either private baths or showers with freshly scrubbed appli-ances, including bidets. The recently built elevator hotel charges 15,000 lire ($17.40) in a single with bath; 22,000 lire ($25.52) for a double with bath. Every room has a "frigo-bar."

Casa Svizzera, 3 Via S. Raffaele (tel. 80-77-38), right off the Piazza Duomo, this is one of the newest, most modern hotels in the city center, now that it's been rebuilt. Two elevators service five floors of rooms. Soundproofing keeps out the noise. Air conditioning can be independently regulated in each accommodation. Each of the 75 bedrooms contains a private bath, renting from 21,500 lire ($24.94) in a single, from 28,500 lire ($33.06) in a double or twin-bedded room. These tariffs include a Swiss breakfast, but not the 12% tax. The bedrooms are furnished in a homey fashion. Features include paneled double windows, "frigo-bars," and TV sets.

The Budget Range

Hotel Adler, 10 Via Ricordi (tel. 221-441), is a small family-owned and operated place. The father or daughter will check you in; the mother will give you a good breakfast in the attractive garden in the rear. The family has been rewarded for their thoughtfulness and courtesies by a fast-increasing business. The older wing is absolutely immaculate, with good-sized rooms, but a more recent building has been thoroughly remodeled and contains a series of excellent, small, and compact rooms plus private baths or showers. The inclusive rate in a single is 4,500 lire ($5.22) without bath, 6,700 lire ($7.77) with bath. A double without bath is 8,100 lire ($9.40), increasing to 11,500 lire ($13.34) with bath. There is even an elevator. The hotel is just two blocks from the Piazza Loreto, which is on a subway line.

Albergo Bolzano, 21 Via Boscovich (tel. 665-037), offers an inexpensive way to live in Milan without compromising comfort. This little hotel, its rooms reached by elevator, is the domain of a family who speak only a little English, but welcome foreign visitors. Rooms with or without private shower baths are offered. The inclusive rate in a bathless single is 6,000 lire ($6.96); 8,000 lire ($9.28) in a single with bath; 10,500 lire ($12.18) for a bathless double; and 14,000 lire ($16.24) for a double with bath. The lounge is comfortable with leather armchairs, and tables open onto a covered grape arbor (a cool patio retreat on hot days). Breakfast served on the patio is the only meal offered.

Milano Pensione, 17 Via Napo Torriani (tel. 665-428), makes for an inexpensive stop near the railway station. Housed in an oldish building with an elevator, the second-class pension has an utterly plain foyer, reached by passing through a courtyard. No English is spoken; it's not really imperative anyway—Italians always seem to make themselves understood. The rooms are simple, quite bare in fact, but serviceable for those who must keep cost low. The bathless singles rent for 6,150 lire ($7.14); the bathless doubles go for 9,000 lire ($10.44); the charge is 13,000 lire ($15.08) in the doubles with complete bath. Other than a continental breakfast, no meals are offered.

READERS' HOTEL AND PENSION SELECTIONS: "Our last stop was Milan after an unseasonably cold and rainy April holiday. We discovered **Pensione Arno,** 17 Via Lazzaretto (tel. 652-782), a short walk from the railroad station. There we found warmth and hospitality in one of the most attractive and accommodating pensions of our trip. A double with shower was 9,650 lire ($11.20), dropping to 6,650 lire ($7.72) in a bathless double. Singles rent for 4,150 lire ($4.82)" (Mr. and Mrs. Richard E. Foley, Rochester, N.Y.). . . . "1 give the highest recommendation to **Pension Lima,** 47 Corso Buenos Aires (tel. 271-65-27). Gest. Guidotti Cerniglia and her daughter rent nine rooms of their elegantly furnished home on the second floor of a large apartment building. Although the pension is on a major thoroughfare, and less than a block from an underground station stop, the rooms are quiet because the pension faces a courtyard. Since her daughter was vacationing, I met only Gest. Guidotti, the mother. She brings rolls and espresso to your room in the morning at whatever time you specify. She answers questions about places to see and how to get there. She allows you to use her ironing facilities and to wash small amounts of clothes in the bathroom. A cultured, educated woman, she is delightful company. Although she speaks French (only her daughter speaks English), she is so charming and helpful, sign language would be sufficient. All this for only 3,800 lire ($4.41) for a single room, bathroom down the hall, and, of course, a continental breakfast included. Double rooms are available. Full pension (all meals) is offered when her daughter is there, but it isn't necessary to accept the meals to rent a room" (Janet H. Sutton, Los Angeles, Calif.). . . . "We highly recommend the **Hotel Leonardo,** around the corner from the Casa delle Studente at 10 Piazza Leonardo da Vinci. We had large, quiet rooms. There is a very nice, non-English-speaking owner. Cost: 6,800 lire ($7.89) for a double room without breakfast, but including taxes and services. It's a bit hard to find, since there is no number on the door outside" (Tom and Gale Lederer, Richmond, Calif.). . . . "**Hotel Due Giardini,** 46 Via Settala (tel. 220-093), is a small hotel consisting of two houses with a small garden between, very peaceful, and not far from the station. I paid 7,500 lire ($8.70) for a double with two beds. No breakfast. There was a shower (free) on each floor with hot water all day" (Mrs. Ingeborg Söderland, Stockholm, Sweden). . . . "**Hotel Pensione Londra,** 4 Piazza Argentina (tel. 228-400), charged 9,600 lire ($11.14) for a bathless double, including breakfast, service, and taxes. I can testify to its cleanliness and the comfort of its furnishings" (Dr. Heinz G. Vogelsang, Germany). . . . "The **Pensione Eva,** 17 Via Lazzaretto, a 10-minute walk from the train station, offers a clean double room for 6,500 lire ($7.54). A continental breakfast is 1,200 lire ($1.39) each, and a shower is 1,000 lire ($1.16). The service was very friendly" (M. and A. Axen, Prince George, B. C. Canada).

DINING IN MILAN: A happy experience. The cooking of Lombardy is distinctive, relying heavily on the country butter, and reaching its finest levels of accomplishment in Milan. Even the minestrone tastes different. The specialty: "risotto," rice cooked in consomme and flavored with saffron. The vines of Lombardy yield tender grapes, and the grapes are transformed into such delicious and aromatic wines as Barbagallo, Buttafucco, and something called "Inferno." The wide-ranging economic levels of the population—from textile manufacturer to working man—are reflected in the prices of the restaurants, ranging from the haute cuisine type to the simple pizza parlor. First, the most expensive—

First-Class Restaurants

Taverna Gran Sasso, 10 Piazza Principessa Clotilde (tel. 637-578), not only provides regional meals, but is a joyride as well. It is an old taverna, filled with lots of sentimental baubles. Its walls are crowded ceiling to floor with copper molds, ears of corn, strings of pepper and garlic, and cart wheels. A high open hearth burns with a charcoal fire, and a Sicilian cart is laden with baskets of bread, dried figs, nuts and kegs of wine. In addition, there are antique musical instruments, old Victrolas, crude chairs, even a cranking automatic piano and an antiquated telephone with an oversized brass mouthpiece. As you enter, you'll find a mellowed wooden keg of wine with a brass faucet (you're to help yourself, using glass mugs). The policy is country festive—that is, you can eat all you want for 8,000 lire ($9.28), including wine. The cuisine features a number of specialties from the Abruzzi district in the south of Italy—regional dishes such as maccheroni alla chitarra, a distinctively shaped macaroni with a savory meat sauce. The first course offers at least 10 choices; the second, two; the third, four; the fourth, five; and there are six or seven desserts to choose from for the final selection. The waiters and waitresses wear folk apparel, and they join in the spirit of the place—often singing folk songs. Not open on Sundays (closed in July).

Biffi Scala, 2 Via Filodrammatici (tel. 876-332), is near the Theatre Museum and the Teatro alla Scala on the Piazza della Scala. One of the top four restaurants of Milan, it draws a chic crowd, especially before and after opera performances. Either at the sidewalk tables or in the pleasantly decorated dining room, elegantly dressed women remind us that Milan is a city of fashion. The service is considerate and smooth, the menu exceptionally fine. Among the more appetizing dishes recommended is that reliable pre-main dish standard, "risotto," at 1,000 lire ($1.16). Valencian rice is also available at 3,500 lire ($4.06). The chef, we've found, does rognone trifolato (calf's kidneys sliced razor thin) extremely well, at a charge of 4,500 lire ($5.22). Other good main dishes include tournedos Scala at 5,000 lire ($5.80). The gâteaux Biffi Scala will be yours for 1,000 lire ($1.16). A bar and tearoom combination offers delicious pastries and stays open all day. Closed Sundays and for two weeks in August.

The Medium-Priced Bracket

Alfio-Cavour, 31 Via Senato (tel. 700-633), is noted for seafood, and particularly for its house specialty, a grand mixed fish grill for 5,000 lire ($5.80). The dining room oozes with atmosphere: modern sculpture, strings of onions, pineapples, squash, coconuts, hanging hams, corn, wine bottles, and sausages—enough trappings to adorn half the trattorie to the Swiss border. The winter garden is a delight. You don't merely eat well here, you feast. The chef has a number of specialties that he's perfected to an art—including the vermicelli with fresh tomatoes, 1,200 lire ($1.39). Also recommended is Adriatic sole sauteed in butter, 4,500 lire ($5.22). Desserts begin at 800 lire (93¢). Closed Mondays and from August 5 to August 31.

Trattoria Bagutta, 14 Via Bagutta (tel. 702-767), patronized heavily by artists, is the most celebrated of the trattorie in Milan. A venerable-looking establishment, it is slightly hard to find in its side street location. The Bagutta is famous for its caricatures—framed and frescoed—which cover its walls. Of the many large and bustling dining rooms, the rear with its picture windows is more enticing. The food is lushly tempting, drawing upon the kitchens of Lombardy, Tuscany, and Bologna for inspiration. Assorted antipasti are offered, ranging in price from 2,500 lire ($2.90) to 3,500 lire ($4.06). Main dish specialties include fried squid and scampi at 5,000 lire ($5.80); lingua e pure (tongue with mashed potatoes), 2,500 lire ($2.90); and scaloppine alla Bagutta, 3,500 lire ($4.06). The Bagutta enjoys a vogue among out-of-towners who consider it chic to patronize the sophisticated little trattoria, as opposed to the more deluxe restaurants. Closed Sundays and for part of August.

A Santa Lucia, 3 Via San Pietro all'Orto (tel. 793-155), pulls out hook, line, and sinker to lure with some of the best fish dinners in Milan. A festive place at which to dine, the restaurant is decked out with photographs of pleased celebs, who attest to the skill of its kitchen. At any time of the day you can order such specialties as a savory fish soup for 3,700 lire ($4.29), a meal in itself; fried baby squid, also 3,700 lire; or good-tasting sole for 4,000 lire ($4.64). Spaghetti alle vongole at 1,400 lire ($1.62) evokes the tang of the sea with its succulent clam sauce. At night, pizza reigns supreme. Try either the calzone of Naples, 1,300 lire ($1.51), or the pizza alla Napoletana at 1,200 lire ($1.39), the classic dish of the city on the bay. Both are made with mozzarella, on menus often translated in English as "buffalo cheese" for some peculiar reason. Closed Mondays and in August.

Low-Cost Restaurants

Biffi, in the Galleria Vittorio Emanuele (across from the Duomo), is the leading candidate for Stateside-type foodstuff. It's dramatically located in the most popular arcade of Milan. In fact, it's the Milan equivalent of Paris' Café de la Paix. You can select snacks or full meals served at sidewalk tables where you can people-watch. A typical beginning might include risotto alla Milanese at 800 lire (93¢), followed by chicken salad at 1,600 lire ($1.86), or beefsteak and potatoes, 2,500 lire ($2.90). Pizzas are also featured, averaging 900 lire ($1.04), though you'd pay 1,300 lire ($1.51) for calzone.

READER'S RESTAURANT SUGGESTION: "Our best restaurant find in Milan was the **Stella d'Oro da Giovanni,** 3 Via Donizetti (tel. 705-580). In the evening, one can order a number

of four-course meals for under $3, and get attentive service and linen napkins and tablecloths"
(Esther Kirschner, Huntington Woods, Mich.).

THE TOP ATTRACTIONS: Despite its modern architecture and industry,
Milan is a city of great art. The serious sightseer will give the metropolis at least
two days for exploration. If your schedule is frantic, see (1) Il Duomo; (2) da
Vinci's "Last Supper" at the Santa Maria della Grazie; and the important (3)
Brera Picture Gallery.

The Cathedral

In the very center of Milan, opening onto the heart of the city's life, the
Piazza del Duomo, the impressive lacy Gothic Cathedral ranks with St. Peter's
in Rome and the Cathedral at Seville, Spain, as the largest in the world. It is
479 feet long and 284 feet wide at the transepts. Dating from 1386, the church
has seen numerous architects and builders. The conqueror of Milan, Napoleon,
even added his own decorating ideas to the facade in the early years of the 19th
century. The imposing structure of marble is the grandest and most flamboyant
example of the Gothic style in Italy.

Built in the shape of a Latin cross, the cathedral is divided by soaring
pillars into five naves. The overall effect is like a marble-floored Grand Central
Station—that is, in space—with far greater dramatic intensity. In the crypt
rests the tomb of San Carlo Borromeo, the cardinal of Milan. In the crypt you
may visit for 100 lire (12¢) the treasure of the Cathedral, an exhibition of the
most precious liturgical furnishings of the sacristy. To experience the Duomo
at its most majestic, you must ascend to the roof, either by elevator for 300 lire
(35¢) or by steps for 150 lire (17¢), from which you can walk through a "forest"
of pinnacles, turrets, and marble statuary—like a promenade in an early Coc-
teau film. The gilded Madonna towers over the tallest spire, but there's a W.C.
on the roof, too, to remind one of life's practical side.

Santa Maria delle Grazie

Off the Corso Magenta, on the Piazza Santa Maria delle Grazie, this
Gothic church was erected by the Dominicans in the mid-15th century. A
number of its more outstanding features, such as the cupola, were designed by
the great Bramante. But "trippers" from all over the world flock here to gaze
upon a fresco in the convent next door. In what was once a refectory, the
incomparable Leonardo da Vinci adorned one wall with his "Last Supper."
Commissioned by Ludovico the Moor, the painting was finished about 1497.
The gradual erosion of the fresco makes for one of the more intriguing stories
in art. Narrowly escaping bombing in 1943, it was restored painstakingly in the
post-war years. What remains today, however, is Leonardo's "outline"—and
even it is suffering badly. As one Italian newspaper writer put it: "If you want
to see 'Il Cenacolo,' don't walk—run!" A painting of grandeur, the fresco
portrays Christ at the moment he announces to his shocked apostles that one
of them will betray him. Vasari called the portrait of Judas "a study in perfidy
and wickedness." The old refectory may be visited from 10 a.m. to 3 p.m. daily
and from 9 a.m. to 1 p.m. on Sundays and holidays. Entrance fee is 200 lire
(23¢).

Brera Picture Gallery

At 28 Via Brera, one of Italy's finest art galleries contains an exceptionally
good collection of both Lombard and Venetian masters. Like a Roman emper-

or, Canova's nude Napoleon—a toga draped over his shoulder—stands in the courtyard (fittingly, a similar statue ended up in the Duke of Wellington's town house in London). Among the notable works are a "Pietà" by Lotto in Room III; Giovanni and Gentile Bellini's "St. Mark Preaching in Alexandria" in Room V; and Andrea Mantegna's "Virgin and the Cherubs" in Room VII. In Room VIII are two of the most important prizes at the Brera—Mantegna's "Dead Christ" and Giovanni Bellini's "La Pietà," as well as Carpaccio's "St. Stephen Debating." Other paintings include Titian's "St. Jerome" in Room X; as well as Lombard art in Room XIII, including Bernardino Luini's "Virgin of the Rose Bush" and Andrea Solario's "Portrait of a Gentleman." Two of the greatest canvases hang in Room XXV—Piero della Francesca's "Virgin and Bambino Enthroned with Saints and Angels and the Kneeling Duke of Urbino in Armor," as well as a "Christ" by Bramante. In Room XXVI is Raphael's "Wedding of the Madonna," with a dancelike quality. The gallery, charging 150 lire for admission, is open daily except Monday from 9 a.m. to 2 p.m. On Sundays, the hours are from 9 a.m. to 1 p.m., and then it's free. On our last visit, only 10 pavilions were open. Check at the Tourist Office before visiting.

OTHER SIGHTS: **Poldi Pezzon Museum:** At 12 Via Manzoni, this is really a fabulous museum, done in great taste and rich with antique furnishings, tapestries, frescoes, and Lombard wood carvings. It also displays a remarkable collection of paintings by many of the old masters of Northern Italy, including Andrea Mategna's "Madonna and Child," Giovanni Bellini's "Cristo Morto," and Filippo Lippi's "Madonna, Angels, and Saint" (superb composition). One gallery is devoted entirely to Flemish artists, and on the top floor is a collection of ceramics and a large collection of clocks and watches. The museum grew out of a private collection donated to the city in 1871. It is open from 9:30 a.m. to 12:30 p.m. and from 2:30 to 5:30 p.m., and charges 500 lire (58¢) for admission. Closed Mondays; it is also open Thursday evenings, even in August.

Castle Sforzesco: At the Piazza Castello sits the Castle of Milan. The ancient seat of the ruling Visconti, it was rebuilt by Francesco Sforza, who launched another governing dynasty. It is believed that both Bramante and Leonardo da Vinci may have contributed architectural ideas to the fortress. Following extensive World War II bombings, it was painstakingly restored and turned into a Museum of Ancient Art. Displayed on the ground floor are sculpture from the fourth century A.D., medieval art from Lombardy, and armor. The most outstanding exhibit, however, is Michelangelo's "Rondanini Pietà," on which he was working the week he died. In the rooms upstairs, besides a good collection of ceramics, antiques, and bronzes, there is the important section of the picture gallery, rich in paintings from the 14th to the 18th centuries, including works by Lorenzo Veneziano, Mantegna, Lippi, Bellini, Crivelli, Foppa, Bergognone, Cesare da Sesto, Lotto, Tintoretto, Cerano, Procaccini, Morazzone, Guardi, and Tiepolo. The Castle is open from 9:30 a.m. to noon and from 2:30 to 5:30 p.m., and charges no admission. Closed Mondays.

Ambrosiana Picture Gallery: At 2 Piazza Pio XI, near the Duomo, the picture gallery and library were founded in the early 17th century by Cardinal Borromeo. On the second floor, the *pinacoteca* contains a remarkable collection of art, mostly from the 15th through the 17th centuries. Among the notable works are (Room I) a "Madonna and Angels" by Botticelli; works by Brueghel in Room VI (impressive detail, among the best art in the gallery); paintings by Lombard artists, including Bramatino's "Presepe," in earthy primitive colors, plus a curious miniature "Crucifix" by Andrea Solario, along with works by Bernardino Luini. In Room X is a large sketch by Raphael on which he labored before painting the "School of Athens" for the Vatican. The most celebrated treasures are the productions of Leonardo da Vinci's "Codice Atlantico." (In Milan, the master had as a patron the powerful Ludovico Sforza, known as "The Moor.") After seeing the sketches, you can only agree with Leonardo's evaluation of himself as a genius without peer. Attributed to him is a portrait of a musician, believed to have been that of Franchino Gaffurio. The library contains manuscripts of Virgil, shown for scientific examination only. The visiting hours are from 9:30 a.m. to 5 p.m., and the charge is 200 lire (23¢) for admission.

San Eustorgio: At 1 Piazza Sant'Eustorgio, this basilica and bell tower date from the 13th century, having been built in the Gothic style in the 13th century by patrician Milanese families. Originally, it was the tomb of Saint Eustorgio (fourth century A.D.). Inside, its greatest treasure is the "Cappella (chapel) Portinari" designed in 1462 by the Florentine, Michelozzo, in the style of the Renaissance (the sacristan will let you inside for 100 lire). The chapel is frescoed and contains a bas relief of angels at the base of the cupola. In the center is the intricately carved tomb, supported by marble statuary, of the 16th-century Florentine, Pietro Martire Vermigli, known as "Peter Martyr."

Sant'Ambrogio: At the Piazza Sant'Ambrogio, this church was originally erected by St. Ambrose in the later years of the fourth century A.D. The present structure was built in the 12th century in the Romanesque style. According to legend, St. Ambrose was said to have baptized St. Augustine at the basilica. The remains of St. Ambrose, encased in silver, rest in the crypt. The church itself, entered after passing through a quadrangle, is rather stark and severe, in the style of its day. The atrium is its most distinguishing architectural feature. In the apse are interesting mosaics from the 12th century. The Lombard tower at the side dates from 1128, and the facade with its two tiers of arches is impressive.

The **Cimitero Monumentale** (Monumental Cemetery), near the air terminal and beyond Stazione Garibaldi, has catered for more than 100 years to the whims of the elite of Milan's society. Actually, the only requirements for burial in the cemetery are first, that you are dead, and second, that there is a great deal of money available to buy your way into a plot. Some families have paid up to 200 million lire (more than $310,000) just for the privileges of burying their dead here. The graves are marked, not with brass plates or granite markers, but with Greek temples, elaborate obelisks, or such original works as an abbreviated version of Trajan's column.

This outdoor museum has become such an attraction that the superintendent has compiled an illustrated guidebook—a sort of "Who *was* who"—which is now in its second edition. Among the cemetery's outstanding sights are a sculpted "Last Supper" with bronze life-sized figures created for the Campari family. Several fine examples of art nouveau sculpture dot the hillside, and there's a tasteful example of "liberty" style architecture (Italy's version of art nouveau) in a tiny chapel designed to hold the remains of Arturo Toscanini's son who died in 1906. Among the notables buried here are Toscanini himself, Giuseppe Verdi, novelist Alessandro Manzoni, and members of the Olivetti (business machinery) and Motta (coffee and pastry) families.

MILAN NIGHTLIFE: As in Rome, many of the top nightclubs in Milan shut down for the summer, when the cabaret talent and bar girls pack their trunks and head for the hills or the seashore. Some clubs that remain open are more suited for Milano factory owners spending a night on the town with salesmen from Central Europe. Tabs tend to be stratospheric, entertainment second rate, and the atmosphere in many of them depressing.

If you have only a night for Milan and are here between mid-December and May, try to attend a performance at the world-famed **Teatro alla Scala.** Built to the designs of Piermarini, the neo-classic opera house was restored after World War II bomb damage. The most celebrated opera stars appear here, and the Milanese first-night audience is considered among the hardest to please in the world. Tickets may also be extremely hard to come by. First gallery seats range from 2,400 lire ($2.78) to 3,700 lire ($4.29). Second gallery seats average 2,200 lire ($2.55), though you may pick up less desirable ones for 1,600 lire ($1.86). Standing room is 500 lire (58¢).

We know of no better way of spending an evening in Milan than at **Bottega del Vino Scoffone,** 4 Via Victor Hugo, in the center of the city. Dating from 1700, this is one of the oldest and best known wine houses in Italy. At a stand-up bar, you can order wine by the glass, ranging in price from 100 lire (12¢) to 500 lire (58¢). However, you can also select a full bottle at one of the tables where there is waiter service. The selection is wide, including wines of Sicily, Sardinia, and Tuscany. The tavern also serves food, offering such dishes as ravioli at 650 lire (75¢), or roast veal at 1,800 lire ($2.09).

Using Milan as a base, you can drive 31 miles on the motorway northeast of the city to:

2. Bergamo

A two-in-one city, Bergamo is crowned by the hilltop Città Alta, the old walled town fortified by the Venetians during their long centuries of dominance. With the Bergamesque Alps in the background, it makes for a Lombard setting of dramatic intensity, earning the praise of Stendhal. At its base is the more modern Lower Town, with its wide streets and shops.

SIGHTSEEING IN BERGAMO: For the sightseer, the higher the climb the more rewarding the view. By funicular, you can go from the Higher Town to the hill of San Vigilo crowning it at its loftiest point. The Città Alta is replete with narrow circuitous streets, old squares, splendid monuments, and imposing and austere medieval architecture that prompted D'Annunzio to call it a city of muteness.

The heart of the Upper Town is the **Piazza Vecchia,** which has witnessed most of the town's upheavals and a parade of conquerors ranging from Attila to the Nazis. On the square is the Palazzo della Ragione, the town hall; an 18th-century fountain designed by Contarini; and the Palazzo Nuova of Scamozzi, the Library of Bergamo.

A vaulted arcade (in which students occasionally gather for song-fests) connects the Piazza Vecchia with the Piazza del Duomo. Opening onto the latter is the Cathedral of Bergamo, with little bite in its baroque teeth. The church on this square that is interesting is the **Santa Maria Maggiore.** D'Annunzio, in rough translation, said it seemed "to blossom in a rose-filtered light." Built in the Romanesque style, the church was founded in the 12th century. At a much later date it was baroqued on its interior, with its disturbingly busy ceiling. The Flemish and Tuscan tapestries displayed are exquisite, incorporating such themes as the "Annunciation" and the "Crucifixion." The choir dates from the 16th century, having been designed by Lotto. Fronting the main altar are a series of inlaid panels by Capodiferro di Lovere, depicting such themes as Noah and the Ark and David and Goliath.

Also opening onto the cathedral square is the **Colleoni Chapel,** honoring the already inflated ego of the Venetian military hero. The Renaissance chapel —its inlaid marble facade reminiscent of Florence—was designed by Giovanni Antonio Amadeo, who is chiefly known for his creation of the Certosa in Pavia, south of Milan. For the "condottiere," Amadeo built an elaborate tomb, surmounted by a gilded equestrian statue (Colleoni, of course, was the subject of one of the most famous equestrian statues in the world, now standing on a square in Venice.) The tomb sculptured for the soldier's daughter, Medea, is much less elaborate. Giovanni Battista Tiepolo painted most of the frescoes on the ceiling.

Facing the cathedral is the Baptistry, dating from the mid-14th century and rebuilt at the end of the 19th century. The original architect of the octagonal building was Giovanni da Campione.

In the Lower Town is Bergamo's chief attraction, the—

Carrara Academy

Filled with a wide-ranging collection of the works of home-grown artists, as well as Venetian and Tuscan masters, the Academy draws art lovers from all over the world. The gallery charges 200 lire (23¢). Summer hours are 9 a.m. to noon and 3 to 6 p.m.; winter hours, from 9 a.m. to noon and 2 to 5 p.m. On the top floor are the most important works—so head there first if your time is limited:

The Botticelli portrait of "Giuliano di Medici" is well known (Room II). Room III contains three different versions of Giovanni Bellini's standard subject, the "Madonna and Bambino"—all beauty, no power. It's interesting to compare his work with that of his brother-in-law, Andrea Mantegna, whose "Madonna and Bambino" is also displayed, as is Vittore Carpaccio's "Nativity of Maria," seemingly inspired by Flemish painters.

In Room IV you encounter a most original treatment of the tired theme of the "Madonna and Bambino"—this one the work of Cosmé Tura of Ferrara. In Room VI are a triptych by Lotto; a portrait of the "Holy Family with St. Catherine" (wonderful oval composition) by Lotto; and Raphael's "St. Sebastian." The entire wall space in Room IX is taken up with paintings by Moroni (1523-78), a local artist who seemingly did everybody's portrait who could affort it. In the salons to follow, foreign masters, such as Rubens, Van der Meer, and Jan Brueghel, are represented, along with Guardi's architectural renderings of Venice and Longhi's continuing parade of Venetian high society.

DINING AND SLEEPING AT AN INN: **Agnello d'Oro,** 22 Via Gombito (tel. 249-883), is a little spellbinder, an intimate, old-styled country inn right in the heart of the Città Alta, facing a handkerchief square with a splashing fountain. It's a beguiling background for good food or a good bed. When you enter the cozy reception lounge, with its scarlet and gold wooden chairs, you should ring an old bell to bring the owner away from the kitchen. You dine at pleasant, wooden tables, sitting on carved ladderback chairs.

Among the à la carte offerings are three worthy regional specialties. For starters, try casoncelli alla bergamasca, a succulent ravioli dish for 1,000 lire ($1.16); quaglie farcte (quail stuffed and accompanied by slices of the yellow cornmeal dish) for 2,000 lire ($2.32); and a homemade dessert, gelato alla zabajone caldo, for 700 lire (81¢). Wine is served in unusual pitchers. The dining room becomes the tavern lounge between meals, with many chess sets kept busy.

The rooms are quite good (some beds set in recesses) and nicely furnished. Hopefully, you'll get one of the front rooms, with French doors, heavy shutters, and miniature balconies with potted vines. Every accommodation has a private bath. The rate in a single is 6,000 lire ($6.96), 9,000 lire ($10.44) for a double.

WHERE TO DINE IN BERGAMO: In the heart of the Città Alta, the **Taverna dei Colleoni**, 7 Piazza Vecchia (tel. 232-596), is known to many a gourmet who journeys here to try regional dishes of exceptional merit. Architecturally it continues the design concept of the square. The sidewalk tables are popular in summer, and the view is part of the reward for dining there. Inside, the decor suggests medievalism, but with a fresh approach. The ceiling is vaulted; the chairs are leather, and there's a low-floor dining room with a wood-burning fireplace. The specialties include gnocchi verde alla Parma, 1,200 lire ($1.39), followed by entrecôte Bergamese, 3,300 lire ($3.83). A three-course meal with wine is offered for 5,000 lire ($5.80). Desserts range from 900 lire ($1.04) to 1,300 lire ($1.51). Closed Mondays.

3. Brescia

Near the lakes of Garda and Iseo, Brescia is an ancient town, the capital of a province of the same name. It is on the main route between Verona and Milan and makes for a good stopover. In the medieval period, it was a duchy, but it has known many rulers, including the Romans, the Scaligeri of Verona, the Visconti of Milan, and the Venetians. One of the most disastrous moments in its history was the looting and burning of the town by French troops under Gaston de Foix in 1512. The ferocity of its fight for independence from the Austrians in 1849 earned for it the title of Lioness of Italy. Its last battle was in the spring of 1945, when Allied forces seized the town.

The historic heart of town is the **Piazza della Loggia,** on which the Brescian Renaissance reached its fullest bloom architecturally. The Palazzo della Loggia itself dates from 1492, but was actually built in stages. The architecture on the square certainly owes a debt to other cities. The top part of the loggia evokes a Palladio design in Vicenza, and the clock tower *(orologio),* with its two "moors," is reminiscent of a similar tower on the Piazza San Marco in Venice. Also opening onto the square is the Monte Vecchio di Pietà, dating from 1484.

A short walk away will take you to the **Piazza del Duomo,** where you'll find both an old and a "new" cathedral, as well as the Broletto, the latter built in medieval times as the first town hall. It is joined by a tower, called the "Torre del Popolo." The "Duomo Vecchio" from the 11th century is often referred to as the Rotunda because of its shape. It was erected over a church dating from the sixth century A.D., and modernization has destroyed much of what must have been its original drama (be sure to explore the crypt). Adjoining is the rather juiceless New Cathedral designed by Giovanni Battista Lantana in the 17th century.

Actually, the most interesting attraction in Brescia is the:

Tosio-Martinengo Civic Picture Gallery: Right off the Piazza Moretto in the Martinengo da Barco Palace is a "pinacoteca," filled with the most important works of the artists of the Brescian school, as well as with a scattered sampling from the old masters of Northern Italy. The admission-free gallery is open from 9 a.m. to noon and from 2:30 to 5:30 p.m. (closed Sundays and holidays). Among the more notable works are Raphael's "The Redeemer" and Lotto's "The Adoration of the Shepherds." One salon is devoted to the leading painter of Brescia, Moretto (see his "Annunciation" and his "Christ and an Angel" from the 16th century) and to Romanino. Works by other leading Lombard artists, such as Moroni, Foppa (the chief force in the early Renaissance in Brescia), and Savoldo, are also displayed.

If time remains, try to visit the Capitolium, housing the **Civic Museum of the Roman Period,** at the Piazza del Foro. This Corinthian temple, built by Vespasian in 73 A.D., contains a prize exhibit: the "Statue of Victory," a Roman bronze (discovered in 1826) that was inspired by Praxiteles and his pupils. Additional exhibits include such bronzes as the "Bacchic Ass," as well as a collection of bas reliefs, ceramics, and mosaics. The civic museum keeps the same hours as the picture gallery.

Note: In Brescia, **Alitalia** has an office at 38 Corso Zanardelli (tel. 56-448).

WHERE TO DINE IN BRESCIA: La Sosta, 20 Via San Martino della Battaglia, off the Vittorio Emanuele II (tel. 295-603), is one of the main reasons to go to Brescia. The cuisine is excellent; the setting beguiling, making "The Stop" a well-named establishment. It's a preserved 17th-century stable, converted into a glamorous dining hall. At first glance, it seems more like a vaulted chapel of a royal palace, indicating that its former equine occupants were given the regal treatment. Tables are set along the aisles, the naves, and around tall marble pillars. Around the walls are equestrian paintings and prints. Look carefully at the pillars, and you'll see large rings where horses were once tied up. In the center aisle is a 20-foot food display table which guests preview before taking their seats. A temptation of antipasti or hors d'oeuvres costs 3,000 lire ($3.48). Recommendable main courses include sole meunière, again costing 3,000 lire, and filetto di bue (beef fillet) at 3,000 lire, also. If you use the side entrance, be sure to catch the vast open hearth where meats and fish are grilled. A few tables are set around the fire for more informal dining, a choice spot on nippy evenings. Closed Mondays and in August.

4. Cremona

This city of the violin is found on the Po River plain, 53 miles east of Milan. Music lovers from all over the world flock here, as it was the birthplace of Monteverdi (the father of modern opera), and of Stradivari, who made violin-making an art. Born in Cremona in 1644, Antonio Stradivari became the most famous name in the world of violin-making, far exceeding the skill of his teacher, Amati. The third great family name associated with the craft, Guarneri, was also of Cremona.

Most of the attractions of the city are centered on the harmonious **Piazza del Comune.** The Romanesque Cathedral dates from 1107, though its actual consecration was in 1190. Over the centuries, Gothic, Renaissance, even baroque elements were incorporated. In the typical Lombard style, the pillars of the main portal rest on lions, an architectural detail matched in the nearby octagonal Baptistery from the 13th century. Surmounting the portal are some marble statues in the vestibule, with a Madonna and Bambino in the center. The rose window over it, from the 13th century, is inserted in the facade like a medallion.

Inside, the cathedral consists of one nave flanked by two aisles. The pillars are draped with Flemish tapestries. Five arches on each side of the nave are admirably frescoed by such artists as Boccaccio Boccaccino (see his "Annunciation" and other scenes from the life of the Madonna, painted in the early 16th century). Other artists who worked on the frescoes were Gian Francesco Bembo ("Adoration of the Wise Men" and "Presentation at the Temple"); Gerolamo Romanino (scenes from the life of Christ); and Altobello Melone (a "Last Supper").

Beside the Cathedral is the **Torrazzo,** dating from the latter 13th century and enjoying a reputation as the tallest campanile (bell tower) in Italy. From the same period—and also opening onto the piazza—are the Loggia dei Militi and the Palazzo Comunale in the Gothic style as uniquely practiced in Lombardy.

5. Mantua

Once a duchy, Mantua knew a flowering of art and architecture under the ruling Gonzaga dynasty which held sway over the town for nearly four centuries. Originally an Etruscan settlement, later a Roman colony, it has known many conquerors, including the French and Austrians in the 19th century. Virgil, the great Latin poet, has remained its most famous son (he was born outside the city in a place called Andes).

Mantua is an imposing city, at times even austere, despite its situation near three lakes, Superior, di Mezzo, and Inferiore. It is easily reached from a number of cities in Northern Italy, lying about 25 miles from Verona, 95 miles from Milan, and 42 miles from Parma. It is very much a city of the past.

THE SIGHTS: If you're just passing through, at least try to save time for its chief attraction—

The Gonzaga Palace

At the Piazza Sordello, the ducal apartments of the Gonzagas may be visited. With more than 500 rooms and 15 courtyards, the group of palaces is considered by many to be the most remarkable in Italy—certainly when judged from the standpoint of size. Like Rome, the compound wasn't built in a day, or even in a century. The earlier buildings, erected to the specifications of the Bonacolsi family, date from the 13th century. The latter 14th century and early 15th saw the rise of the Castle of St. George, designed by Bartolino da Novara. The Gonzagas also added the Palatine Basilica of St. Barbara by Bertani.

Over the years, the historic monument of Renaissance splendor has suffered tremendous looting of its art treasures (Napoleon was responsible for carting off some of the greatest objets d'art from the collection of Isabella d'Este, who did much to turn Mantua into "La Città dell'Arte"). The Ducal Palace is open, as of this writing, from 9 a.m. to 2 p.m.; to 1 p.m. on Sundays (closed Mondays), and charges 150 lire (17¢) for admission. You are not admitted after 1 p.m.

A guide takes visitors on a tour, pointing out the many highlights. At times, as you wander from salon to salon, down ornately decorated corridor after corridor, you get an eerie feeling of unreality, as in the old film, "Last Year at Marienbad." The painting collection is rich, including works by Tintoretto, El Greco, Sustermans, Strozzi, and a "cut up" Rubens. A number of tapestries were woven in Brussels, based on designs by Raphael.

The display of classical statuary is impressive, gathered mostly from the various Gonzaga villas at the time of Maria Teresa of Austria. Among the more inspired sights are the "Zodiac Room," the "Hall of Mirrors," with a vaulted ceiling evoking Versailles, the "River Chamber," the "Apartment of Paradise," and the petite headquarters of a dwarf nearby. The most interesting and best-known room is the "Sala degli Sposi" (bridal chamber), frescoed by Andrea Mantegna in the castle. Winged cherubs appear over a balcony at the top of the ceiling. Look for a curious dwarf and a mauve-hatted figure that was Mantegna's self-portrait. A cavalry scene (al fresco) by Pisanello has been recently discovered. Two other sightseeing attractions include:

The Basilica of St. Andrew

Built to the specifications of Leon Battista Alberti, this church opens into the Piazza Mantegna, just off the Piazza Erbe, with its fruit vendors. The actual work on the basilica, started in the 15th century, was carried out by a pupil of Alberti, Luca Fancelli. The church was finally completed in 1782 when Juvara crowned it with a dome. As you enter, the first chapel to your left contains the tomb of the great Mantegna (the paintings are by the artist's son, except for the "Holy Family" by the old master himself). The sacristan will light it for you. In the crypt you'll encounter one of the more fanciful legends in the history of church relics: St. Andrew's claim to possess the blood of Christ, "the gift" of St. Longinus, the Roman soldier who is said to have pierced his side. Beside the basilica is a campanile (bell tower), dating from 1414.

The "Te" Palazzo

This Renaissance palace, built in the 16th century, is known for its frescoes by Giulio Romano and his pupils. At the edge of the city, it is reached on the Viale Te Federigo II. One of the Gonzagas ordered the villa built. The frescoes in the various rooms, dedicated to everything from horses to Psyche, rely heavily on mythology for subject matter. The Room of the Giants, the best known, has a scene depicting heaven venting its rage on the giants who have moved threateningly against it. To visit the palace, you must go on a guided tour. Summer hours are from 9 a.m. to 12:30 p.m. and from 3 to 6:30 p.m. In winter, hours are from 9:30 to 12:30 and from 2 to 4. Admission is 100 lire (12¢). Closed Mondays.

WHERE TO DINE IN MANTUA: Ai Garibaldini, 7 Via San Longino (tel. 29-237), does interesting and imaginative dishes, and has thereby become a favorite of those seeking such regional specialties as quadrucci alla provinciale (a flat pasta of the province) for 850 lire (99¢) or glassata (a gelatinized veal loaf) for 2,700 lire ($3.13). Most desserts—delicious and homemade—average around 600 lire (70¢). Closed July 26 to August 14.

READER'S HOTEL SELECTION: "About 10 minutes from the station is the **Albergo Virgilio**, 101 Corso Vittorio Emanuele (tel. 23-598). It's clean and comfortable, and the price includes use of the bathroom. A single room is 3,000 lire ($3.48); a double, 5,000 lire ($5.80)" (John Hayward, Aberdeen, South Africa).

6. Pavia

About 16 miles south of Milan, the **Certosa** (Charter-house) of Pavia marks the pinnacle of the Renaissance statement in Lombardy. The Carthusian monastery is five miles north of the town of Pavia itself. Gian Galeazzo Visconti founded the Certosa in 1396, but it was years before it was completed. The result: one of the most harmonious structures in Italy.

The facade, studded with medallions and adorned with strips of colored marble and sculptural work, was designed in part by Amadeo, who worked on the building in the latter 15th century. Inside, much of its rich decoration is achieved by frescoes reminiscent of an illustrated storybook. You'll find works by Perugino ("The ever-lasting father") and Bernardino Luini (a Madonna and Child). Ludovico the Moor, one of the patrons of Leonardo da Vinci, is buried in the north transept.

Through an elegantly decorated portal you enter the small cloisters, noted for their exceptional terra-cotta decorations. In the second and larger cloisters is a continuous chain of elaborate "cells," attached villas with their own private gardens and loggia. The monastery is open in summer from 9:30 to 12:30 and from 2 to 6 p.m., and charges 300 lire for admission. In winter the afternoon hours are from 1:30 to 4:30. Closed on Mondays.

PIEDMONT AND THE VALLE D'AOSTA

TOWERING, SNOW-CAPPED Alpine peaks . . . oleanders, poplars, and birch trees . . . sky-blue lakes . . . river valleys and flower-studded meadows . . . the chamois and the wild boar . . . medieval castles . . . Roman ruins and folklore . . . the taste of Vermouth on home ground . . . Fiats and fashion. Northwest Italy—a fascinating area to explore.

Piedmont is largely agricultural, though its capital, Turin, is one of Italy's front-ranking industrial cities (with more mechanics per square foot than in any other location in Europe). The influence of France is strongly felt, in both the dialect and the kitchen.

Valle D'Aosta (really a series of valleys) has traditionally been associated with Piedmont, but in 1948 it was given wide-ranging autonomy. Most of its residents (in this least populated district in Italy) speak French. Closing in the Valle D'Aosta to the north on the French and Swiss frontiers are the tallest mountains in Europe, including Mont Blanc (15,780 feet), the Matterhorn (14,690 feet), and Mount Rosa (15,200 feet). The road tunnels of Great St. Bernard and Mont Blanc (opened in 1965) connect France and Italy.

1. Turin

The capital of Piedmont, Turin gave birth to the Italian Risorgimento (unification). During the years when America was fighting its Civil War, Turin became the first capital of a unified Italy, a position it later lost to Florence. Much of the history of the city was associated with the House of Savoy, a dynasty that reigned for nine centuries, even presiding over the Kingdom of Italy. Victor Emmanuel II, the king of Sardinia (incidentally, Turin was the capital of Sardinia), was proclaimed king of Italy in 1861. The family ruled—at times in name only—until the monarchy was abolished in 1946.

Following extensive World War II bombings, Turin is prospering again, largely because of the Fiat manufacturers who base there. The city has been called the Detroit of Italy. Many buildings were destroyed, but much of its 17th- and 18th-century look remains. Turin is well laid out, with wide streets, historic squares, churches, and parks. For years it has had a reputation as the least visited and least known of Italy's major cities. Easily reached, Turin (Torino in Italian) is on the Po River, 140 miles west of Milan, 108 miles northeast of Genoa.

Note: In Turin, **Alitalia** has an office at 35 Via Lagrange (tel. 552-424).

HOTELS IN TURIN: Generally the hotels lack distinction, except in the expensive range. Like Milan, Turin is an industrial city first, a tourist center second. Most of its hotels were built after the war, with an eye toward modern comfort but not necessarily style. Our recommendations follow, beginning with:

The First-Class Range

Villa Sassi, 47 Via Traforo del Pino (tel. 890-556), is a classic, 17th-century-styled estate at the edge of the city, surrounded by its own park grounds and approached by a winding driveway. Now converted into a top-grade hotel and restaurant (see "Dining" below), it offers a dozen rooms to wayfarers. The original, impressive architectural details are still intact, including the wooden staircase in the entrance hall. The drawing room invites with its over-scaled mural and life-sized sculptured baroque figures holding bronze torchiers. The intimate drinking salon continues the same theme, with its draped red velvet walls, bronze chandelier, black dado, and low-seat cushions. Each bedroom has been decorated in individual style (the fabrics and colors are harmonious, and the furniture is a combination of antiques and reproductions). The manager, Giuliano Zonta, sees that all is run in a personal way, with "custom-made" service. The rooms have either private baths or showers, for which the single rate is 16,500 lire ($19.14); the double, 31,000 lire ($35.96). You may want to take full pension for 37,000 lire ($42.92) per person, inclusive, but a minimum stay of three days is required. Closed August 15 to September 1.

The Medium-Priced Range

Hotel Victoria, 4 Via Nino Costa (tel. 553-710), is a small but substantial hotel opening onto a tree-filled garden on a quiet street. Though simply designed, the bedrooms have a niceness to them—that is, they seem personal with shades of one color to a room. Soft apple-green walls, graceful dark green draperies, white wrought-iron beds, and velour armchairs add a certain charm. All 75 of the bedrooms have either a private shower or bath. The rate in a single room is 9,000 lire ($10.44); 13,500 lire ($15.66) in a double, inclusive. A continental breakfast is the only meal served.

The Budget Range

Hotel Bologna, 60 Corso Vittorio Emanuele (tel. 538-159), is a 58-bedroom hotel in an old-fashioned building, kitty corner from the railway station, and offering good, clean, and inexpensive rooms. Many guests carry their own luggage from the station to the hotel (the entrance is found under an arcade). Its lobby is neat and compact with good leather chairs. Although no English is spoken, you don't need a linguist to get yourself settled in a good room. Most of the bedrooms are bathless, though a few have private baths or showers. The single rate ranges from 5,500 lire ($6.38) to 7,500 lire ($8.70); the doubles from

9,000 lire ($10.44) to 11,900 lire ($13.69), inclusive. A continental breakfast at 800 lire (93¢) is the only meal served. If you're fortunate you may be assigned a room overlooking the Piazza Carlo Felice.

READER'S HOTEL SELECTION: "We found the third-class **Hotel Campo di Marte,** 7 Via XX Septembre (tel. 545-361), only a few minutes' walk from the station. The charge was 7,000 lire ($8.12) for a large, bathless double. No breakfast is served" (Warren H. Curry, Albuquerque, N. M.).

DINING IN TURIN: Turin gave the world Vermouth, for which martini drinkers have been in the eternal debt of the Carpano family. The Piedmont kitchen is another fragrant delight, differing in many respects from the Milanese, especially in its liberal use of garlic. What it lacks in subtlety is often made up in large portions of hearty fare.

The Top Restaurants

Villa Sassi, 47 Via Traforo del Pino, (tel. 890-556), is a spacious, 17th-century styled villa on the rise of a hill at the edge of the city. Against the background of a stylish, antique-decorated villa, a modern dining room has been built, with walls of glass extending toward the gardens (most of the tables have an excellent view). Most of the basic foodstuff is brought in from the villa's own farm—not only the vegetables, fruit, and butter but the beef as well. In the entranceway to the dining room is a showcase display of fresh fruits.

At the villa, it's recommended that you order à la carte unless you're a guest of the hotel. For starters, try either the risotto con rane (frog legs cooked with broth-simmered rice) for 1,600 lire ($1.86), or fonduta for 3,000 lire ($3.48), a Piedmont fondue, made with Fontina cheese, richly flavored with eggs, milk, and butter, to which the delicious white truffles of the region are added. Another local dish of Piedmont is agnolotti, a form of meat-stuffed pasta like ravioli, costing 1,600 lire ($1.86). If featured, you may want to try the prized specialty of the house: camoscio in salmi—that is, chamois (a goatlike antelope) prepared in a sauce of olive oil, anchovies, and garlic, laced with wine and served with polenta. Count on spending at least 10,500 lire ($12.18) to 18,000 lire ($20.88) for a complete dinner, plus 18% for service. You'll have a sumptuous meal. Closed Sunday evenings and Mondays from August 15 to September 1.

Del Cambio, 2 Piazza Carignano (tel. 546-690), is a classic and traditional restaurant of Old Turin. Here, you can dine in comparative grandeur, in a setting of white and gilt walls, crystal chandeliers, and gilt mirrors. It's utterly old world. The chef has received many culinary honors, and unfortunately, we have room to mention only a few of his specialties. To begin with, the assorted antipasti are excellent, costing 2,500 lire ($2.90) for a generous and savory helping. The best pasta dish is the regional angnolotti piemontesi at 1,200 lire ($1.39). Among the main dishes singled out for special praise are the costolette alla fagiolini with truffles at 3,500 lire ($4.06) and the fillet of sole at 3,500 lire also. Fresh vegetables of the day average around 600 lire (70¢) per serving. Rounding out the repast is a delicious tart, costing 1,000 lire ($1.16). Closed Sundays and from August 1 to 25.

BUDGET CHOICES: Ristorante Mauro, 21 Via Maria Vittoria (tel. 51-98-13), is the best of the low-cost trattorie. Generally packed (everybody loves a bargain!), it is within walking distance of the Piazza San Carlo. The food is conventional, but manages to have character, as the chef borrows freely from most of the gastronomic centers of Italy. An excellent pasta specialty is tortelloni di nagro alla cardinale at 650 lire (75¢). Most main dishes are in the 1,500-lire ($1.74) to 2,000-lire ($2.32) range. Desserts begin at 350 lire (41¢). Tuscan wine is offered in carafes at prices beginning at 1,800 lire ($2.09). Closed Mondays.

Ristorante San Secondo, 7-B Via San Secondo (tel. 54-21-82), is an attractive and very hospitable Sicilian restaurant, run by Sige Calabrò. The interior is decorated with rough unfinished offwhite walls, wood beams and panels, antique guns and iron objects on the walls. A choice of three separate dining rooms awaits guests. Specialties include spaghetti alla Siciliana (with tomato sauce and eggplant) at 900 lire ($1.04); bistecca alla Palermetana (with a mushroom sauce) at 2,500 lire ($2.90); tonno al ferri (fresh tuna fish, grilled) at 3,000 lire ($3.48); and Cassata Siciliana (fruit cake) at 1,000 lire ($1.16). Closed Mondays and for 10 days at Christmas.

SIGHTSEEING IN TURIN: To begin your exploration, head first for the **Piazza San Carlo,** the loveliest and most unified square in the city, covering about 3½ acres. Heavily bombed in the last war, it dates from the 17th century, and was built to the design of Carlo di Castellamonte. In the heart of the piazza is an equestrian statue of Emanuele Filiberto. The two churches are those of Santa Cristina and San Carlo. On the square, some of the most prestigious names in Italy have sat sipping coffee and plotting the unification of Italy. The most popular coffee house (and a good place to gather your energy for sightseeing) is the **Caffè Torino,** 204 Piazza San Carlo, where under the arcade you'll often see elegant Turinese who turn up for pastries, Campari . . . and much talk.

However, if your tastes are different, you may prefer **'l Caval 'd Brôns,** also on the Piazza San Carlo, before setting out to see the sights. It's a turn-of-the-century British-styled pub, with red flocked silk walls, red hanging lamps, and red plush tufted banquettes—altogether an ingratiating and regal setting for a rendezvous. You can order coffee, as well as regular drinks, beer, and snacks. It's a popular spot with the fashionable youth of Turin. Bottles of good Italian wine begin at 1,800 lire ($2.09).

Ready to go now?

You'll find the most interesting museums housed in the Guarini-designed, 17th-century **Science Academy Building,** 6 Via Accademia della Scienze. The collection of the **Egyptian Museum** is so vast that it's rated second only to the one at Cairo. Of the statuary, that of Rameses II is the best known, though there is one of Amenhotep II as well. A room nearby contains a rock-temple consecrated by Thutmosis III in Nubia. In the crowded wings upstairs, the world of the pharaohs lives on (one of the prize exhibits is the "Royal Papyrus," with its valuable chronicling of the Egyptian monarchs from the first through the 17th dynasties). The funerary art is exceptionally rare and valuable, especially the chapel built for Meie and his young wife, and an entirely reassembled tomb (that of Kha and Mirit, 18th dynasty), discovered in a well-preserved condition at the turn of the century. The museum is open from May 2 to September 30 from 10 a.m. to 1 p.m. and 3 to 6 p.m. and charges 150 lire (17¢) for admission (winter from 9 to 2). On Sundays and holidays it is open from 9 a.m. to 1 p.m. Closed Mondays.

In the same building, you can visit the **Sabauda (Savoy) Gallery,** one of the richest in Italy, whose collection was acquired over a period of centuries by the House of Savoy. It is open daily from 9 a.m. to 2 p.m. and Sundays from 9 a.m. to 1 p.m. Closed Mondays. The charge for admission is 150 lire (17¢).

The Academy has the largest exhibition of the Piedmontese masters, but is well endowed in Flemish art as well. Of the latter, the best known painting is Sir Anthony Van Dyck's "Three Children of Charles I." Other important works include Botticelli's "Venus," Memling's "Passion of Christ," Rembrandt's "Sleeping Old Man," Titian's "Leda," Mantegna's "Holy Conversation," Jan van Eyck's "The Stigmata of Francis of Assisi," Veronese's "Dinner in the House of the Pharisee," and intriguing paintings by the Brueghels.

The Cathedral: This Renaissance structure dedicated to John the Baptist is of major interest to visitors as it contains Guarini's Chapel of the **Holy Shroud.** Acquired by Emanuele Filiberto (whose equestrian statue you saw in the Piazza San Carlo), the shroud is purported to be the one that Joseph of Arimathea wrapped around the body of Christ when he was removed from the cross. Detailed charts in front of the holy relic claim to show evidence of a hemorrhage produced by the crown of thorns. The chapel, crowned by a baroque dome, is at the Piazza IV Marzo, a short walk from the entrance to the Royal Palace.

The Royal Palace: At the Piazza Castello, the palace that the Savoys called home was begun in 1645. Its halls, columned ballroom by Palagi, tea salon, and "Queen's Chapel" are richly baroqued. The original architect was Amedeo di Castellamonte, but numerous builders were to supply ideas and skill before the palazzo was finally completed. As in nearly all ducal residences of that period, the most bizarre room is the one bedecked with flowering chinoiserie. The throne room is of interest, as is the tapestry-draped Banqueting Hall. Le Nôtre, a Frenchman, mapped out the gardens, which may be visited from spring till autumn. The palace itself is open from 9 a.m. to 7 p.m. and the charge is 100 lire (12¢) for admission.

In the **Palazzo Madama,** also opening onto the Piazza Castello, is the **Civic Museum of Ancient Art.** It has something to please everybody, having evolved from a showcase of regional art to several major galleries displaying works from other areas and countries as well. Its prize is the painting, "Portrait of an Unknown Man," by Antonello da Messina. Works dating from the Romanesque period to the Renaissance are displayed in the initial rooms. Of interest are a "Madonna" by Barnaba da Modena; a codex, "The Very Rich Hours of Duc de Berry," with illustrations by Jan van Eyck and others; and a "Madonna and Bambino," a sculptural work by Tino da Camaino, dating from the 14th century. The baroque rooms on the second floor—the former state apartments —were occupied at separate times by the two "madames" for whom the palace is named (Madame Cristina of France lived here in the 17th century and Maria Giovanne Battista di Savoia-Nemours in the 17th and 18th centuries). On the third floor is a large collection of ceramics and porcelain, including some glass from the days of the Roman Empire. The museum is open from 9 a.m. to 7 p.m., and charges 100 lire (12¢) for admission. Closed Mondays.

Carlo Biscaretti di Ruffia Automobile Museum: At 40 Corso Unità d'Italia, outside the heart of the city, in a colossus of a modern exhibition hall, historic "buggies" are handsomely displayed. The exhibits span the years— ranging from a model of Valturio's "wind machine" (made 20 years before Columbus sailed for America!), to the first Fiat car (turn of the century), to a pre-World War II Mercedes-Benz. The museum is open daily, except Mondays, from 9:30 a.m. to 12:30 p.m. and from 3 to 7 p.m., and charges 500 lire (58¢) for admission. Off season hours are from 10 a.m. to 1:30 p.m. and from 3 to 5:30 p.m.

2. Aosta

In the capital of the Valle D'Aosta stands the Arch of Augustus, built in 24 B.C., the date of the Roman founding of the town. Aosta was important in Roman times, and the further remains of a theater, the Praetorian Gate, and the Forum provide other evidence of its occupation and growth under domination from the south.

The town is also enriched by its medieval relics. The Gothic church of Sant'Orso, founded in the 12th-century, is characterized by its landmark steeple designed in the Romanesque style. You can explore the crypt, but more interesting are the cloisters, with capitals of some three dozen pillars depicting Biblical scenes.

Lying on a major artery, Aosta makes for an important stopover point, either for overnighting or as a base for exploring the Valle D'Aosta or taking the cablecar to the Conca di Pila, the mountain that towers over the town. Our hotel recommendations follow.

HOTELS IN AOSTA: **Valle D'Aosta,** 174 Corso Ivrea (tel. 41-845), is in good modern design, the leading hotel in Aosta. Open year round, the first-class hotel is a prominent stopover for motorists using the Great Saint Bernard and Mont Blanc road tunnels into Italy. Owned by Rank Hotels Ltd., it is managed efficiently and well. An elevator takes you from the spacious lounges to the bedrooms. Each of the rooms contains wall-sized picture windows turned toward the view. The furnishings are restrained and tasteful, and each room has a bathroom. In high season (July 1 to October 1), the hotel charges from 16,500 lire ($19.14) to 27,000 lire ($31.32) in a twin-bedded room. If you wish, you can take all of your meals at the Valle D'Aosta, as the establishment maintains a first-class restaurant on the premises.

Corona e Posta, 28 Piazza E. Chanoux (tel. 22-23), placed prominently on the town square, looks as if it were a palace—and, true enough, it has a long history of royal habitation and visits. Built nearly 500 years ago, it was once the hunting lodge of the Earl of Bosses (the Duke of Aosta lived here). It remains one of the special old inns of the valley, a medium-priced establishment where the service and atmosphere are select and refined. The building retains much of its original character: ornate beamed ceilings, paneled walls, stained glass, marble fireplaces, and French-Victorian furnishings. Time has been kind to most of the bedrooms: the furnishings were accumulated over a number of years, and everything is personal. Many of the rooms contain private baths. In high season, the hotel charges 9,000 lire ($10.44) in a bathless single; 10,500 lire ($12.18) in a single with bath. For a bathless double, the tariff is 15,500 lire ($17.98), 17,000 lire ($19.72) with bath. Between the wings is a terrace where tables are set out for refreshments.

A Motel on the Outskirts

Motor Village Residence, Villair de Quart (tel. 62-258), is a cluster of alpine log chalets set on a hillside near the autostrada, a short drive south from Aosta. Frenchmen drive through the tunnel to spend the weekend here and enjoy the regional cooking. Built on terraces, near the main lodge, the chalets are compelling. You ascend wooden steps and enter into a bed-sitting room, furnished in the alpine fashion, except for the all-plastic bathroom units which seem more suitable for a trip to the moon. A double room with bath rents for 15,000 lire ($17.40), and the demi-pension rate is 11,000 lire ($12.76) per person.

In the main building, which also has some basic rooms rented when the chalets are filled, is the restaurant, Le Bourricot Fleuri. In addition to the intimate rustic bar with an open fireplace, there are two dining rooms, sharing the warmth of a fire on a raised hearth. Here steaks and chops, as well as mountain stream fish, are grilled to order. The decor consists of ladderback rushseated chairs, pine-paneled walls, and a generous use of vivid colors. Recommended is the menu gastronomique at 7,000 lire ($8.12). First, you're given a selection of about 20 kinds of hors d'oeuvres, both hot and cold, each regional. The typical main dish is a grilled steak, though you may prefer one of the roasts with vegetables. Next the cheese wagon is brought to your table, and you can sample the alpine varieties. A pastry wagon is also wheeled by, each selection richer, lighter, and more fattening than the one before. Finally, a fresh basket of fruit is placed at your table. Wine is served in ceramic pitchers.

A 22-mile drive from Aosta takes us to:

3. Courmayeur and Entrèves

Courmayeur is an international resort, with a "high season" attracting the alpine excursionist in summer, the ski enthusiast in winter. Its popularity was given a conside ble boost with the opening of the Mont Blanc road tunnel, feeding traffic from France into Italy (estimated run of the trip, 20 minutes). The cost for automobiles of up to 1,000 cm., 3,500 lire ($4.06) one way and 4,000 lire ($4.64) round trip. For cars up to 1,700 cm., 5,000 lire ($5.80) and 6,000 lire ($6.96) respectively; for cars up to 2,400 cm., 6,500 lire ($7.54) and 8,500 lire ($9.86) respectively.

With Europe's highest mountain in the background, Courmayeur sits snugly in a valley. To the north of the resort is the village of Entrèves, sprinkled with a number of chalets (some of which receive paying guests).

In the vicinity, you can take a cable car lift—one of the most unusual in Europe—across Mont Blanc all the way to Chamonix, France! A ride across glaciers that is altogether frightening, altogether thrilling, but for steel-nerved adventure seekers only. It's possible to break your trip into halves or quarters by booking a ride to one of the landing stages, then returning on the cable car going back. It's also possible to take a funicular to Cresta Arp, at 9,038 feet the closest balcony to Mont Blanc. Charging 6,000 lire ($6.96) round trip, the cable car runs every hour in season from 8:30 a.m. to 6 p.m.

HOTELS IN COURMAYEUR: Courmayeur has a number of good and attractive hotels, many of which are open only seasonally. We'll begin our survey with:

The Medium-Priced Range

Hotel Courmayeur, 156 Via Roma (tel. 82-323), is built in the alpine style. Right in the center of the village, it was constructed so that most of its rooms would have unobstructed views of the nearby mountains. A number of the bedrooms, furnished in the mountain chalet style, also have wooden balconies and private baths or showers. The hotel is open all year. In high season it charges from 16,200 lire ($18.79) to 18,200 lire ($21.11) in its doubles with shower or private baths. The full-pension tariff is 17,000 lire ($19.72) to 19,080 lire ($22.14) per person daily. I.V.A. is included.

The Budget Range

Hotel Del Viale, Viale Monte Bianco (tel. 82-227), resounds with the alpine theme. An old-style mountain chalet, it perches at the edge of town. Clients enjoy the indoor-outdoor life: the front terrace with tables set out under trees in fair weather, the cozy and pleasant rooms inside in chillier months. In the winter, guests gather in the taproom to enjoy après-ski life, drinking at the pine tables, warming their feet before the open fire. The house is enriched with such pieces as a large wooden pillar rescued from a wine press, exposed beams, hanging copper kettles, a grandmother's clock, pewter, and pots of flowers in the window. The bedrooms have a rustic air about them—natural wood, somewhat crude, but pleasant, comfortable, and very clean. The rooms have running water. In high season, the rate in a bathless single room is 7,000 lire ($8.12); 12,000 lire ($13.92) in a bathless double. The cost of full pension ranges from 16,000 lire ($18.56) to 18,000 lire ($20.88) per person. Meal time is a big occasion, and the food comes in generous portions, in the tradition of the Valdostan kitchen. The friendliness that prevails here turns wallflowers into edelweiss bouquets. Open year round.

Ange & Grand Hotel, 88 Via Roma (tel. 82-221), is like an overgrown inn that could have served as a convent. In the heart of town, it is L-shaped so as to provide for a large triangular entry courtyard. The long, low adjoining buildings have wooden balconies, shuttered windows, and tables with parasols set out along the front colonnade. The interior public rooms have vaulted ceilings and deep arches, but most of the furnishings are impersonal and simple. It is in the dining room that the Ange & Grand comes mostly to life (the Italian-alpine cooking is superb). The bedrooms—59 in all, some with private baths—are good sized, with semi-modern baths, and (in some cases) private balconies. Open from June 20 to September 30, the hotel in peak season charges from 6,500 lire ($7.54) to 8,000 lire ($9.28) in a single; from 9,000 lire ($10.44) to 12,000 lire ($13.92) in a double, depending on the plumbing. Full pension ranges in price from 12,000 lire ($13.92) to 16,000 lire ($18.56) per person. The private garden is pleasant, as is the tearoom where everyone gathers after strolls or mountain treks.

Hotel Ermitage, Località Ermitage, M. 1470 (tel. 82-283), is for those who are part goat: a rustic chalet high above the town center, reached by a narrow, winding road. It is set in an unspoiled mountain forest, with a small surrounding meadow and a view of Mont Blanc that is spellbinding. The back rooms open onto the woods, the front ones onto the mountain peaks and forests. Owned by Berta Chenoz, the Ermitage is open from June 28 to September 20. In all, there are 17 bedrooms, small and suitably furnished (hot and cold running water, but no private baths). The peak-season (July 10 to August 31) rate in a single is 3,500 lire ($4.06); 4,700 lire ($5.45) double. You can stay here in peak season and have all your meals for from 8,500 lire ($9.86) to 10,500 lire ($12.18) per person, inclusive. Signora Chenoz, who is graciousness herself, speaks English, and is shyly proud of the home cooking she provides (no synthetic ingredients—all fresh eggs, butter, milk).

DINING IN COURMAYEUR: **Al Vecchio Torchio,** 3 Via Roma (tel. 82-222), is a specialty restaurant of the Valdostan kitchen. It is an old taverna at the rear of the Moderno Hotel. In a setting of thick plaster walls, beamed ceilings, crude ladderback and reed chairs, and a large wooden wine press, the foodstuffs are served. All is presided over by a chef who often brings his dishes to you for inspection before cooking. Watch him build a jackstraw structure of twigs on the wide hearth to grill the steaks. The favorite dish of the house is fonduta (the Valdostan fondue of mountain cheese, milk, and eggs, prepared in a ceramic bowl with a wooden ladle) for 2,800 lire ($3.25). For the same price, you can also have a Swiss-styled fondue. Ever tried bagna cauda? This is one of the most savory dishes of both the Piedmont and Aostan cuisines. It's a sauce composed of garlic, olive oil, and anchovies (raw vegetables, usually celery sticks, are dipped into the heated sauce), and it's a memorable treat for 2,800 lire ($3.25). In season venison is offered at 3,500 lire ($4.06). The taverna is open in season from noon to 4 p.m. for lunch and from 8 till 1 a.m. Closed Tuesdays off season. At night, the pizza oven's going, with pies costing 900 lire ($1.04). To finish, you can have a plate of local cheese (Fontina) for 600 lire (70¢).

THE "CHALET OF GLUTTONY" AT ENTREVES: La Maison de Filippo (tel. 89-968), offers the complete gastronomic experience of the Valdostan kitchen in a *tipico* atmosphere. A colorful tavern, it is the creation of Leo Garin, who was once featured in both *Playboy* magazine and *Town & Country*. His establishment is for those who enjoy a rustic atmosphere, bountiful regional food, and a festive mood. The fare is served either in the mellowed rooms inside, or in the beer garden in summer, with a full view of Mont Blanc. Mr. Garin features local specialties on an all you can eat basis, charging around 5,500 lire ($6.38) for "the works." Some call his la maison the "Chalet of Gluttony."

A typical meal? The first course might begin with a selection of delicious hors d'oeuvres, followed by a two-foot-long platter of about 60 varieties of sausage, with a cutting board and knife. Then there will be a parade of pasta dishes. For a main course, you can pick everything from fondue to camoscio (chamois meat) to trout with an almond and butter sauce, to roast duck with an orange glaze. You may even prefer the Valdostan boiled dinner, with pungent ham hock, cabbage, and potatoes. Accompanying are huge hunks of coarse country bread from a wicker basket (the size of a laundry bin). For dessert, crêpes suzette are an ever-popular favorite, along with a selection of the regional cheese.

At the end of the banquet, an aptly titled grail of friendship makes for an exciting event. Meals are served until midnight, and the tavern is open year-round.

Many Frenchmen ride through Mont Blanc tunnel just to dine here. Inside, the three-story open hallway seems like a rustic barn, with an open worn wooden staircase leading to the various dining nooks. You pass casks of nuts, baskets of fresh fruit, window ledges with bowls of salad, fruit tarts, wooden boxes spilling over with spices, onions, gourds, and loaves of freshly baked bread. It's one of the most charming inns in all the valley.

A 31-mile drive northeast of Aosta takes us to:

4. Breuil-Cervinia

Fast rising as a ski resort, Breuil-Cervinia has enough alpine terrain to satisfy all but the most insatiable of scene-gulpers. With the Matterhorn (Cervino) towering majestically in the background, the resort occupies a superb setting, including a man-made one that has burst into full bloom in recent years. All its hotels and chalets have that new look to them, much like a Klondike town. The air is crystal fresh, and there are walks in all directions.

For the most exciting look at mountain scenery, take the run to the Plateau Rosa at 11,415 feet above sea level. A round-trip ticket on the funicular costs

6,000 lire ($6.96). In winter, you'll find about 75 ski instructors and more than a dozen ski lifts.

HOTELS IN BREUIL-CERVINIA: In hotels, Breuil-Cervinia is amply stocked, with new ones sprouting up along the hillside all the time. Our recommendations follow.

The Medium-Priced Range

Hotel President (tel. 94-476), is built on a curve, affording an unobstructed view of the Matterhorn. Its facade is done in the checkerboard fashion, with panels of wood alternating with windows—distinctive modern. There are ample, comfortable, and attractive facilities in the public rooms providing a good center for winter-time après-ski socializing. The living room has groups of leather wing chairs, arranged for post-hike conversations. Wood paneling lends warmth to the reception lounge and the dining room, the latter a fit background for the good Valdostan meals served. The bedrooms—48 in all, every one with private bath—are oversized, with well-chosen color schemes, compact built-in headboards, telephones, and bedlights. Breakfast tables are set before your picture window—and that is the best part of the day: coffee, a croissant, and the Matterhorn. The hotel charges 7,500 lire ($8.70) in a single, 15,000 lire ($17.40) in a double. Full pension is 18,000 lire ($20.88) per person, inclusive. The President is open from November 1 to May 2 and from July 1 to September 10.

The Budget Range

Chalet Valdôtain (tel. 94-428), is a family affair, offering a homey touch that makes it unique. The Morello family operates this roadside chalet at the edge of the village, near Lago Bleu (Lake Blue). An alpine structure, it makes a sophisticated use of wood and picture windows; and the bedrooms are tastefully restrained (a typical one has pine floors, and walls partly in white and partly in pine). The rate for a single is 6,000 lire ($6.96), 7,500 lire ($8.70) in a double. The peak-season charge for full pension is 10,500 lire ($12.18) per person, inclusive. Meals in the blue and white dining room are best in winter, when the logs are lit in the fieldstone fireplace. The get-together point is the espresso bar in natural wood paneling. Open from October 28 to May 10 and June 28 to September 28.

Leonardo Carrel (tel. 94-077), is an excellent refuge for skiers and mountain climbers, standing as it does at the foot of the Alps, with a stream at its edge, along with woods and pastures. Owned by Ada and Leonardo Carrel (a professional guide and ski instructor), it offers a chance to enjoy the simple alpine chalet life. The stone and wood house, with its overhanging roof (three tiers of sun balconies), is just outside the village. In it, the Carrels have provided a private bath or shower for every one of the 10 bedrooms, surprising for a hotel rated fourth class. The interior walls in most rooms are in knotty pine; accommodations are simply furnished. The price of a single in high season is 3,500 lire ($4.06), 5,500 lire ($6.38) in a double. The dining room, in knotty pine, with freshly starched white curtains and tablecloths, is an appropriate place for the meals prepared by Mrs. Carrel, who knows the specialties of the Valle D'Aosta. The hotel is open year-round.

READER'S SELECTION FOR THE BERNARD PASS: "About 45 minutes after leaving the Bernard Pass tunnel, we found a charming, new, and inexpensive hotel in a very small town. It was the **Hotel Baita,** Gran S. Bernardo, Etroubles (Aosta) (tel. 78-214). For four of us, the hotel charge was 10,000 lire ($11.60). An excellent dinner for four was about $14. The hotel is on a hill overlooking the town and is easy to find and drive to as you come down the mountains" (Fred Knirk, Hacienda Heights, Calif.).

From the alpine peaks of the Matterhorn, we descend to the beaches of the Italian Riviera.

GENOA, THE TWO RIVIERAS, ELBA

FOR YEARS THE RETREAT of the wintering wealthy, the twin Italian Rivieras now enjoy the broadest base of tourism. Even in winter (the average temperature in January hovers around the 50-degree Fahrenheit mark) the Rivieras are popular, though not for swimming. Most of the hotels charge high season prices then, unique for European beach resorts. The pleasant, balmy weather is made possible by the protection provided by the Ligurian Apennines that loom in the background.

The winding coastline of the Rivieras, especially the one that stretches from the French frontier to San Remo, is especially familiar to movie-goers, as it's been used as a background for countless flicks about sports car racing, jewel thieves, spy thrillers, even off-the-record romancers. Over the years, the northwestern coast of Italy has known the famous and the infamous, especially literary figures: Shelley (who drowned off the shore), D'Annunzio, Byron, Katherine Mansfield, George Sand, D. H. Lawrence.

The Mediterranean vegetation is luxuriant, characterized by pines, olives, citrus trees, cypresses. The Western Riviera—the Riviera di Ponente—from the border to Genoa is sometimes known as the Riviera of Flowers, because of its perfumey profusion of blossoms. Starting at the French border, Ventimiglia becomes the gateway city to Italy. Along the way you'll encounter the first big resort, Bardighera, followed by San Remo, the reigning queen, though her crown has been tarnished since her more lustrous days at the turn of the century.

Genoa, dividing the two Rivieras, is the capital of the Ligurian region—a big, bustling port city that has charm for those willing to spend time seeking out its subtleties.

On the Riviera di Levante (eastern), a triumvirate of small, dramatically situated resorts—Rapallo, Santa Margherita, and Portofino (the yachtsman's favorite)—take the edge. Proceeding down the coast, you'll come to Viareggio, a mammoth summer watering spa for low and middle-income Italians, though parts of it evoke a tawdry Coney Island atmosphere. La Spezia, a naval port perched on a gulf, is included not so much for its own attractions, but as a base for exploring the Cinque Terre. Finally, south of Pisa you can take a ferry at Piombino for the most isolated beach strips of them all, on the Isle of Elba in the Tuscan archipelago.

Starting at the French frontier, we'll base first in:

1. San Remo

Ever since the Emperor Frederick wintered here in a villa, the reputation of San Remo has grown, attracting first the turn-of-the-century wealthy, including many Frenchmen, Englishmen, and later the Americans. Positioned about 10 miles from the French frontier, 85 from Genoa, the flower-filled resort seems dated by today's standards, though attempts have been made to upgrade it. But its casino, race track, 18-hole golf course, its deluxe Royal Hotel, still attract the fashionable. Its climate is considered the mildest on the entire Western Riviera coast.

Even if you're just passing through, you might want to stop off and visit La Città Vecchia (also known as La Pigna), the old city on the top of the hill. Far removed in spirit from the burgeoning sterility near the water, old San Remo blithely ignores the present, capturing and holding the past behind the facades of its tiny houses on narrow, steep lanes. In the new town, the palm-flanked Passeggiata dell'Imperatrice attracts the promenader. For a scenic view, you can take the funicular to Monte Bignone at 4,265 feet.

HOTELS IN SAN REMO: There are plenty of accommodations in San Remo, in all price categories.

The Medium-Priced Range

Hotel Paradiso, 10 Via Roccastarone (tel. 85-112), is lodged on a hillside in a former residential sector now turned into a resort district. Few North Americans have visited here, though those who have have appreciated the family ownership, the quiet position, and the comfortable amenities. You enter onto a paved parking area. The rooms overlook the lower terrace, banked with semi-tropical vines and flowers. A recently built dining room has its own airy look, with three walls of glass. The old-fashioned drawing room, on the other hand, is decorated with a marble fireplace, gilt mirrors, and crystal chandeliers. A bar has been installed. The bedrooms are well furnished, and all contain a private bath or shower. Each balcony seemingly has a different color of potted geraniums, all the handiwork of the owner, Signora Gaiani. For full board, the tariffs range between 14,000 lire ($16.24) and 18,000 lire ($20.88) per person depending on the accommodation as well as the season. A double costs 15,000 lire ($17.40). Single rooms range between 8,000 lire ($9.28) and 8,700 lire ($10.09).

The Budget Range

Villa Ortea, 121 Via Alessandro Volta (tel. 83-054), is a renovated villa, only a few minutes' walk from the beach. At the rear of the original house, a much more modern bedroom addition has been incorporated. Half of the raised front terrace has an ultra-modern lounge; the other half is graveled and dominated by a high magnolia tree sheltering garden furniture. Open year-round, the hotel offers good accommodations, and the bedrooms are furnished with studio beds set against wall panels. Some of the doubles have private baths, and each room has hot and cold running water. The hotel charges 4,500 lire ($5.22) in a single without bath; 7,500 lire ($8.70) in a double without bath. The most expensive rooms, doubles with bath, go for 10,000 lire ($11.60). The full-pension tariff ranges in price from 9,500 lire ($11.02) to 10,500 lire ($12.18) per person. The dining room is simple, as are the good-tasting meals. The lounge, in contrast, is attractively decorated.

Hotel Juana, 70 Corso Matuzia (tel. 62-273), seems to have all the necessities for a pleasant stopover. Housed in a newish building, about a block or so from the beach (next to the tennis club), it is right on the main street of San Remo. It offers a cozy, rather simple and homelike accommodation, with blond maple bedroom furnishings in the contemporary idiom. The rooms are average sized, and nearly half of them have private baths. Open year-round, the Juana charges 4,000 lire ($4.64) in a bathless single; 5,500 lire ($6.38) in a single with bath. Doubles range in price from 7,000 lire ($8.12) to 8,500 lire ($9.86), inclusive. Full board ranges from 10,000 lire ($11.60) to 11,000 lire ($12.76) per person. The meals are excellent, served in a pleasant dining room with marble columns and bentwood chairs.

READERS' PENSIONE SELECTION: "Readers should not be put off by the fact that they will need to pay a 10-lire lift fee to get to the third floor **Pensione Matuzia,** 121 Via Matteotti int 4 (tel. 70-647). It's a five-minute walk from the railway station. The warm welcome and homey atmosphere at this spotless pensione are joys. The pensione is run by a charming young English couple, Joan and Tom Thompson, who provided us with a cup of tea or coffee, 'at the drop of a hat' and good wholesome English or Italian food on a full- or demi-pension basis. Our room cost us 6,000 lire ($6.96) for a double and single bed in a large room and an extra bed was thrown in for our youngest daughter free. The rooms are all equipped with hot and cold water, and hot showers and baths are available" (John and Barbara Turner, Veaumaris, Victoria, Australia).

DINING IN SAN REMO: In San Remo, you'll be introduced to the Ligurian cuisine, a table characterized by the Genovese style of cooking, with a heavy reliance on seafood dishes. If featured on the menu, try the buridda, which is the Ligurian version of the standard Mediterranean bouillabaisse. The white wines from the five villages—the Cinque Terre—are highly valued.

The Best Restaurants

Pesce d'Oro, 270 Corso Cavalloti (tel. 86-641), serves the finest food on the Italian Riviera! The location is so unprepossessing—right in the midst of dreary mechanics' alley—you'll think you're at the wrong address. However, once inside you should place yourself in the hands of Signor Visconti, who is both the chef and the owner. Perhaps he'll suggest a pasta to begin with, the lasagne al pesto (a sauce made with olive oil, garlic, pine seeds, cheese, and fresh basil), or the highly recommendable farfalline al'pizzico—a happy blending of potatoes, spinach-flavored pasta butterflies, and fresh string beans. Among the seafood dishes, the zuppa di frutti di mare is outstanding, as is the spiedino di scampi. Fresh fish is featured daily, except on Mondays when the "Golden Fish" is closed. Expect to pay anywhere from 8,000 lire ($9.28) to 10,000 lire ($11.60). Closed in June.

Rendezvous, 126 Via Matteotti (tel. 85-609), is a fine restaurant. Its fish specialties rate a rave; they change with the seasons and the catch. A brightly lit establishment in a commercial district of San Remo, it has an army of white-jacketed waiters in attendance. Many of the à la carte offerings have been found faultless—the cannelloni at 1,500 lire ($1.74); osso bucco at 4,000 lire ($4.64); sole—truly superb—at 3,300 lire ($3.83); chicken in gelatin, the hot weather favorite, at 3,000 lire ($3.48). A cover charge of 600 lire (70¢) is assessed, plus 15% for service. Closed Wednesdays and from July 1 to 22.

The Medium-Priced Range

La Lanterna, 8 Via Molo di Ponente al Porto, is a harborside restaurant where the smart set goes for top-notch fish dinners and a big whiff of local atmosphere. You'll find a good table under parasols, so you can keep an eye trained on the yachting set ("no darling, we're definitely not going to Hydra this year!"). Most dishes are beautifully cooked and served by a friendly, willing staff. The less expensive way to dine here is to order from the 3,500-lire ($4.06) fixed-price menu—including, for example, an excellent fish soup, called brodetto di pesce con crostini (a choice of about five other dishes), followed by a mixed Ligurian fish fry or a meat course, such as scaloppine in a Marsala wine sauce. Desserts are included in the price, but drinks are extra. There is another menu at 5,000 lire ($5.80), with more elaborate and unusual offerings.

Castel Doria, 53 Corso Nino Bixio (tel. 85-583), is a cafe-restaurant-tearoom overlooking the harbor. It does just honors to the Ligurian cuisine, especially in its fish dishes. Most recently, we tried a plate of succulent mussels, then followed with delicious fried fish and fresh fruit for dessert. If you don't like sea treats, the Castel Doria does the standard Italian dishes well, including gnocchi (semolina dumplings) or the veal cutlet Bolognese, always a favorite of the discriminating palate. Tempting trays of antipasti or hors d'oeuvres are prepared by the chef for 1,500 lire ($1.74). Two especially recommended dishes on the à la carte menu include riso alla marinara (seafood rice) at 1,800 lire ($2.09) and spiedino di gamberi (grilled shrimps with a special sauce added) at 4,000 lire ($4.64). The owner also owns some vineyards, which produce his specialty wines, "Castel Doria Rossese" and "Castel Doria Vermentino." Closed Wednesdays.

U Nostromû, 2 Piazza Sardi (tel. 80-767), is good for seafood and a nautical atmosphere. It has two entrances (one facing the port side), and it contains all the expected ship's trappings, including lanterns and netting. The square on which it sits is colorful—in a low-income district of San Remo, where laundry flaps in the wind from the overhead balconies. Inside, there is a cozy ambience, with colored tablecloths and friendly service. The dish to order here is risotto del pescatore (seafood rice) at 1,000 lire ($1.16). An excellent main course is gamberoni alla Nostromû (lobster) at 4,000 lire ($4.64). The zuppa di pesce (fish soup) is invariably superb, costing 2,200 lire ($2.55). A soothing finish is the zabaglione at 700 lire (81¢).

Low-Cost Dining

Il Bagatto, 145 Via Matteotti, provides inexpensive meals in a country tavern setting, complete with dark beams, provincial chairs, even overscaled pepper grinders brought to the tables. The location is in the shopping district of the town, about two blocks from the sea. The 3,500-lire ($4.06) and 4,500-lire ($5.22) fixed-price (drink extra) menus are limited in choice, but extremely well prepared. Our most recent dinner offered a choice of creamy lasagne or savory hors d'oeuvres. The scaloppina with marsala sauce was especially pleasing, as was (on another occasion) tender calf's liver with bacon. All orders were accompanied by potatoes and a choice of vegetables, then followed by crème caramel for dessert. We've found the à la carte dishes equally rewarding, including minestrone at 1,000 lire ($1.16) or the mixed fish fry at 3,500 lire ($4.06). And the pièce de résistance is the Valencian paella—a whopping order with delicious bite-sized pieces of fish floating in a sea of rice, costing 9,000 lire ($10.44) for two persons.

SAN REMO AFTER DARK: The high life holds forth at the **Casino.** For decades, fashionable visitors have frequented this temple, dining in the highest style in the elegant restaurant, reserving tables at the nightclub for dancing and drinks, or testing their luck with the chips. Like a white plaster palace— perhaps lacking the ornate lushness of its nearby sister, Monte Carlo—it stands pristine and restrained, catering to a rather conservative audience. The entrance fee to the Casino—a daily "tourist card"—costs 2,000 lire ($2.32). This charge gains you access to the Sala Comune, the general gaming room. The restaurant itself serves superb viands, a complete meal costing between 8,000 lire ($9.28) and 12,000 lire ($13.92), including service and tax. The night spot is like a small New York supper club. You pay 2,500 lire ($2.90) as a cover charge. The dance music—sometimes a modified rock—is occasionally augmented with change-of-pace vocalists. From July through September, there's a one-hour cabaret show, and in winter two orchestras play nightly. In high season, drinks average around 5,000 lire ($5.80), dropping to 3,500 lire ($4.06) in low season. The bartender can make at least 25 concoctions (he's used to odd requests.). From July to mid-September, the roof garden with a delightful view is open. Diners, American Express accepted.

The **Club 64,** 2 Via Verdi, near the Casino, is the swingingest place in town—the action overlapping in about half a dozen rooms. A background of modern art—sculpture and paintings—sets the contemporary scene, the rock music blending well. In private nooks, you squat on red Chinese stools behind iron grill cages. There's a tiny bar for drinks. The doors open wide every night at 10 p.m., lasting until 4 a.m. In July and August, admission (including one drink) is 2,500 lire ($2.90). A combo plays then. When records spin in the true discotheque fashion, the price of admission drops to only 2,000 lire ($2.32). Club 64 is favored by many Teutonic and English-speaking young people.

2. Genoa (Genova)

It was altogether fitting that "Genoa the Proud" (Superba) gave birth to Christopher Columbus. Its link with the sea and maritime greatness dates back to ancient times. However, Columbus did his hometown a disservice. By blazing the trail to the New World, he caused a devastating blow to Mediterranean ports in general, as the balance of trade shifted to newly developing centers on the Atlantic.

Even so, Genoa today is Italy's première port, ranking with Marseilles in importance. In its heyday (the 13th century), its empire rivaled that of Venice, extending from colonies on the Barbary Coast to citadels on the Euphrates. Apart from Columbus, its most famous son was Andrea Doria (the ill-fated ocean liner was named after him), who wrested his city from the yoke of French domination in the early 16th century.

Like a half moon, the port encircles the Gulf of Genoa. Its hills slope right down to the water, so walking is likely to be an uphill affair. Because of the terrain, it was quite late in Genoa's development that it saw the opening of the Christopher Columbus Airport.

The center of the city's maritime life, the **Harbor of Genoa** makes for an interesting stroll, particularly in the part of the old town bordering the water.

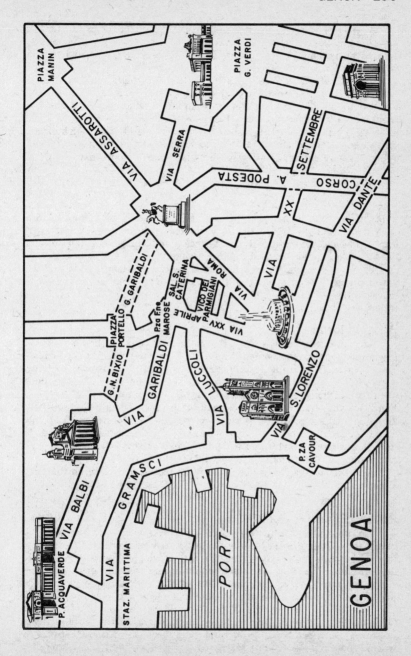

Sailors from many lands search for adventure and girls to entertain them in the little bars and cabarets occupying the back alleyways. Often the streets are merely medieval lanes, with foreboding buildings closing in like sheets blowing in the wind.

A word of warning: the harbor, particularly after dark, is not for the squeamish. It can be dangerous. If you go wandering, try not to be alone and leave as many valuables in safekeeping as possible. Genoa is rougher than Barcelona, more comparable to Marseilles.

The present harbor was the result of extensive rebuilding, following massive World War II bombardments that crippled its seaside installations. The best way to view the overall skyline is from a boat which you take from the Maritime Station at the Ponte dei Mille. The trip, lasting one hour, costs 1,500 lire ($1.74) per person. Along the way, you'll pass naval yards, shipbuilders, steelworks, and warehouses (yachtsmen anchor at Duca degli Abruzzi)—not a pretty picture entirely, but a fascinating landscape of industrial might.

Note: In Genoa, the **Alitalia** office is at 188 Via XII Ottobre (tel. 595-741).

THE SIGHTS: Back in the heart of the city, you'll surely want to stroll down the **Via Garibaldi**, the street of the patricians, on which noble Genovese families erected splendid palazzi in late Renaissance times. The guiding hand behind the general appearance and most of the architecture was Alessi, who grew to fame in the 16th century (he once studied under Michelangelo). Among the structures you'll want to visit, as they contain important galleries and museums, is the—

Palazzo Rosso

At 18 Via Garibaldi is this 17th-century palace, once the home of the Brignoles. Restored after bombings in World War II, it contains a good collection of paintings, with such exceptional works as an "Ecce Homo" by Caravaggio, a "St. Catherine" by Tintoretto, drawings by the bold Alessandro Magnasco of the 18th century. Perhaps its best known exhibit is Sir Anthony Van Dyck's portrait of Pauline Brignole from the original collection. Also displayed is a rare collection of old coins, ceramics, sculpture, and a horrific display of gilded baroque statuary. The admission-free gallery is open daily from 10 a.m. to noon and from 2 to 6 p.m. (closed Tuesdays all day and Sunday afternoons, but open Thursday nights till 10:30 p.m.).

Across from the red palace is the white palace, at No. 11 on the same street.

Palazzo Bianco Gallery

Donated to the city by the Duchess of Galliera, along with her collection of art, the palace was designed by Domenico Grimaldi in the 17th century, though its appearance today reflects the work of later architects. Also gravely damaged during the war, the palace was rebuilt afterward, its designers using the opportunity to reflect the most recent advances in museum planning. The most significant paintings—from the Dutch and Flemish schools—include Van Der Goes' "Jesus Blessing the Faithful," as well as works by Sir Anthony Van Dyck and Peter Paul Rubens. A wide-ranging survey of European artists is presented—with paintings by Zurbaran, and works by Bernardo Strozzi (a whole room) and Alessandro Magnasco (excellent painting of a scene in a Genovese garden). David's "Virgin of the Pappa" is impressive. On the main floor is an exhibition of Flemish tapestries reflecting superb skill. The admission-free gallery is open from 10 until noon and from 2 to 6 p.m. daily, excepting Sunday afternoons and Mondays. On Saturdays, it remains open till 10:30 p.m.

From the Via Garibaldi, you can head down the Via della Maddalena to the next attraction—

National Gallery

Housed in the Palazzo Spinola, 1 Piazza della Pellicceria, is another painting collection. (This palace was originally designed for the Grimaldi family in the 16th century as a private residence, though the Spinolas took it over eventually.) Its notable works include Sir Anthony Van Dyck's "Child and His Dog" and Joos Van Cleve's "Madonna in Prayer." The gallery, charging no admission, is open from 10 a.m. to 1:30 p.m. only, every day except Sundays and Mondays.

The Via Garibaldi eventually becomes the Via Balbi, another palazzi-flanked street. The chief attraction here is:

Royal Palace

At 10 Via Balbi, the Palazzo Reale dates from the early years of the 17th century, having been erected for the Balbi family, for whom the street itself is named. Like all Genovese palazzi, it has seen subsequent alterations, some of which marred the original designs. Filled with paintings and sculpture (works by Van Dyck, Guido Reni's "Magdalen"), it shines best in its Hall of Mirrors and Throne Room. The admission-free palace is open on Tuesdays, Thursdays, and Sundays from 9 a.m. to 1 p.m.

Although Genoa is noted for its medieval churches, towering over all of them is:

Cathedral of San Lorenzo

At the Piazza San Lorenzo (Lawrence), the cathedral is distinguished by its bands of black and white marble adorning the facade in the Pisan style. In its present form, it dates from the 13th century, though it was erected upon the foundation of a much earlier structure. Alessi, referred to earlier, designed the dome, and the campanile (bell tower) dates from the 16th century. The Chapel of John the Baptist, with interesting Renaissance sculpture, is said to contain the remains of the saint for whom it is named. The Treasury is worth a visit, especially for its Sacred Bowl, thought to be the Holy Grail when Crusaders brought it back from Caesarea in the early 12th century (eastern traders probably made goodly sums off naïve Christians pursuing relics of Christ for the church back home).

Cimitero di Staglieno

This has to be the most spectacular cemetery in the world. It is a collection of architectural wonders on a reduced scale—everything from a Gothic cathedral to an Egyptian pyramid, to a Romanesque basilica to a Moorish mosque. The schmaltzy Victorian statuary is larger than life. The tombs of the great families of Genoa are found here. Giusepe Mazzini, the Italian patriot, was buried here in 1872. The cemetery lies about 3 miles from the center of Genoa. Take road No. 45.

A last sight that tour buses are fond of visiting is the so-called **House of Columbus**, a modest, vine-covered building at the Piazza Dante, off the Vico

Dritto Ponticello (not to be visited inside). What it is, is an 18th-century reconstruction at the site of what may have been the house of the explorer.

HOTELS IN GENOA: Generally hotels are second rate but some good finds await those who search diligently. Warning: some of the cheap hotels and pensions in and around the waterfront are to be avoided! Our recommendations, however, are suitable for married couples or women traveling alone.

A Deluxe Choice

Colombia-Excelsior, 40 Via Balbi (tel. 261-841), is another CIGA chain prizewinner. Facing the tree-lined piazza opposite the front of the railway station, it is for the lover of the sumptuous life, with its art nouveau 19th-century poshness. Most sultans would (and do) feel at home in its main lounges, with their ornate vaulted ceilings, arched colonnades, stained glass, Turkish carpets, and crystal chandeliers. The only luxury hotel in Genoa, it has been revamped without losing its original character. The many salons, the ballroom, drawing room, grand staircase, and gilt "throne" chairs are impressive, but so are most of the elegant bedrooms, everything from roomy suites favored by the King of Belgium to the more stripped-down facilities in the single chambers. All the rooms have private baths and air conditioning. Year-round, singles with bath rent for 30,000 lire ($34.80), doubles with bath for 44,000 lire ($51.04)—to which you must add taxes. Little niceties and big comforts make it a special place at which to stay.

The First-Class Range

Bristol-Palace, 35 Via XX Settembre (tel. 592-541), has a number of features that make one's stay in Genoa special. Its obscure entrance behind colonnades on a commercial street is misleading. The salons and drawing rooms are furnished nicely with traditional pieces—many antiques are utilized, some of which appear to be of museum caliber. The dining room, in the Louis XVI style, is the most inspired—an ornately carved ceiling highlighting a mural of cloud-riding cherubs in the center. The larger of the bedrooms have an old-fashioned elegance, are spacious and comfortable, and most tastefully furnished. Most of the rooms have private baths, and all have the proper amenities, such as bedside lamps and telephones. The bathless rooms are less stylish, but still quite nice. Depending on the plumbing, singles range in price from 15,000 lire ($17.40) to 19,000 lire ($22.04), doubles from 25,000 lire ($29) to 32,000 lire ($37.12), including continental breakfast and service. Taxes will be added, plus air conditioning.

Plaza, 11 Via Martin Piaggio (tel. 893-642), is newer than its modified classic facade suggests. Its location is one of its finest assets, just off the well-laid-out Piazza Corvetto with its equestrian statue, flower-bordered walks, and trees. The interior of the well-run hotel has been completely renewed, providing comfort and convenience. The bedrooms—100 in all, with either private baths or showers—are above average. Many have tiny sitting areas and modern, functional furnishings, plus refrigerator bars. The inclusive rate in a single is 21,000 lire ($24.36); 37,000 lire ($42.92) in a double, with breakfast. Air conditioning is included. On the premises are an American bar and a grill room.

The Medium-Priced Range

Hotel Eliseo, 5 Via M. Piaggio (tel. 893-529), is a pleasant 41-room villa converted into a hotel and opening off the attractive old, tree-filled Piazza Corvetto. The owner, Signor Petrucci, has left his imprint of individuality. He has furnished the main living room with some Victorian and Empire pieces. In the dining room are the original frescoed ceiling, swag draperies, and French windows. The bedrooms are also stamped with personality, though the smaller singles have dated modern pieces. Most of the doubles, however, come equipped with furniture seemingly brought in from a palace—Venetian gilt, hand-painted beds, soft fabrics, fruitwood inlaid desks, and bombé chests. More than half the rooms have private baths or showers. Depending on plumbing, the single rate ranges from 10,300 lire ($11.95) to 12,000 lire ($13.92); the double rate from 19,600 lire ($22.74) to 21,700 lire ($25.17). The full-pension tariff goes from 18,000 lire ($20.88) to 22,000 lire ($25.52) per person, depending on the availability of private bath.

Park Hotel, 10 Corso Italia (tel. 311-040), overlooks the waterfront outside the city. A castle-styled villa, it is surrounded by its own gardens and entered through a covered gateway. It's more of a Victorian-styled establishment, with a tall square tower featuring a covered observation terrace. The interior is quite good, with a two-story entrance hallway, almost baronial, then an encircling staircase, glass ceiling, and antiques. The dining room is formal and dominated by a painted ceiling, and the Doric-columned lounge with its group of stylized bronze chairs is ideal for coffee or drinks. The bedrooms—19 in all, some with private baths or showers—vary widely in both size and decor (a few have balconies). Most of them are furnished with a blending of semi-modern and traditional. You can usually count on comfort and space. The bathless single rate is 7,300 lire ($8.47). Doubles with bath cost 14,000 lire ($16.24). The Park, which lies on the road to Portofino and Santa Margherita, has a good restaurant open to non-residents.

The Budget Range

Hotel Assarotti, 42 Via Assarotti (tel. 885-822), a substantial, well-run, 26-room establishment—no fuss, no frills—has been entirely renovated. Off a busy boulevard, it occupies a floor of a large building. The undersized lounges are furnished in a lackluster fashion, with deep leather armchairs. The bedrooms—all with modern private baths or showers—are nondescript in style but functional from the point of view of comfort (the larger, more handsome doubles are parceled out first). The single rate ranges from 4,200 lire ($4.87) to 5,600 lire ($6.50); doubles go for 9,200 lire ($10.67) to 10,500 lire ($12.18), inclusive. The service is personalized, and private parking is available.

Hotel Basilea, 1 Scalinata dell'Osservatorio (tel. 219-043), is a Genovese version of a stage set for "The Night of the Iguana." An old-styled villa on a steep hillside ledge, just five minutes up from the central railway station, it's an adventure for those in the mood. Its front terrace is surrounded by semi-tropical trees, plants, a fish pool, a caged hawk, an arbor, and tables set out for meals, drinks, or socializing. The bedrooms—16 in all, a handful of doubles with private baths—are consistent with the building: interesting but definitely of another era. The rate in a single room is only 3,500 lire ($4.06); 5,700 lire ($6.61) in a bathless double; 7,000 lire ($8.12) in a double with bath. The family-style meals are good (our last dinner, filet of sole grilled in butter, was delicious). For half board, expect to pay anywhere from 6,800 lire ($7.89) to 7,800 lire ($9.05), plus tax.

DINING IN GENOA: You'll find lots of colorful restaurants and trattorie, many of which are strung along the harbor. The Genovese cuisine has been praised for its imaginative kitchen. The following recommendations will give you several chances to judge it for yourself. By ordering anything with *pesto* at the end, you'll be sampling the best known regional concoction, a sauce made with olive oil, garlic, pine seeds, cheese, and fresh basil.

The Best Restaurants

Ristorante Vittorio al Mare, 11 Belvedere Firpo (tel. 310-085), right on the waterfront, lies at the edge of the city in the Boccadasse district. It's a modern establishment, with unmarred views of the sea, but its decor is so unprepossessing that you'd hardly know it serves the most delicious dishes in Genoa. The cuisine is not subtle, in the typical fashion of the seaport, but even such routine dishes as scalloppine al marsala or veal cutlet milanese, roast veal or grilled entrecôtes, seem distinguished here. The fish courses are most highly recommended, especially the mixed fish fry and the burrida (the local bouillabaisse with savory spices). The average meal ranges in price from 6,000 lire ($6.96) to 10,000 lire ($11.60). Only the finest ingredients are used, and the service generally pleases.

Ristorante Pichin, 6r Vico dei Parmigiani, at the Piazza Fontane Marose, (tel. 540-553), evokes a country inn, replete with hams hanging from the rafters, racks of wine bottles, baskets, and a raised fireplace and hearth for broiling. On its walls are framed awards for consistently maintaining a top-level Genovese kitchen. It is skillfully run (every waiter is expertly trained), and a heavenly number of à la carte specialties are offered. Generally, it's advisable to stick to the regional dishes. For example, the Pichin makes its own version of pasta—called trenette al pesto (paper-thin noodles seasoned with a sauce made of olive oil, basil, cheese, garlic, and pine seeds) at 1,200 lire ($1.39); or ravioli alla pichin at 1,400 lire ($1.62). The fish and meat courses are seemingly endless. However, you can't miss with the mixed grill at 4,500 lire ($5.22), or the sogliola alla mugnaia (sole in butter) at 4,300 lire ($4.99). For 1,000 lire ($1.16), you can have a delicious crème caramel, or a Florentine cake, zuccotto, also 1,000 lire. With many of your fish orders, you can sniff the wafting bouquet of a bottle of Coronata, a delicious yellowish wine. Closed Mondays and from August 1 to September 1.

The Medium-Priced Range

Piccolo, 33r Via Casaregis (tel. 312-419), is one of the most popular, modern, and attractive trattorie on the outskirts of Genoa near the sea. As in most of the Genovese eating establishments, seafood takes star billing. The servings are generally large, but quality isn't neglected for quantity. Practically every ravioli and risotto dish is impressive here, but the gastronomic treat is the local specialty, lasagne al pesto, at 1,000 lire ($1.16). In Genoa, this wide-noodle dish is served with the local sauce of olive oil, garlic, pine seeds, basil, and cheese. The variation on this is trenette al pesto at 900 lire ($1.04). The zuppa di pesce, a Ligurian bouillabaisse, is exceptionally tasty at 2,500 lire ($2.90). And for your main course, try the mixed fish fry at 2,500 also. Closed Thursdays.

Trattoria del Mario, 33r Via Conservatori del Mare, Piazza Banchi (tel. 298-467), is one of the best dining spots in the old town, offering a minimum of atmosphere but a maximum of taste. Its location may be somewhat hard to find, but the Genovese have been marking a trail to the door of Signor Camera. He's decidedly famous in the port city. His fine cooking seemingly grows more elaborate each year we sample it. He features such distinguished specialties as trenette al pesto, described earlier; pesce (fish) ai feri, and stoccafisso (dried cod) genovese. Expect to pay from 6,000 lire ($6.96) to 12,000 lire ($13.92) for a fine repast. Closed Saturdays.

The Budget Range

Gran Gotto, 11 Via Fiume (tel. 564-344), facing a park, is a topnotch trattoria with a good atmosphere and a fine kitchen. The concentration is on seafood, but the meat and pasta dishes aren't neglected either. In fact, the most typical offering—trenette al pesto—is quite famous, a pasta of paper-thin noodles (depending on the artistry of the chef) that is served with the characteristic sauce of Liguria, pesto, made with garlic, cheese, olive oil, basil, and pine seeds, for 1,000 lire ($1.16). The delicately simmered risotto is tempting at 1,000 lire also. The main dishes are most reasonably priced and of high standard, including the mixed fish fry at 3,300 lire ($3.83) or the French baby squid for the same price. The zuppa di pesce, like a Mediterranean bouillabaisse, has made many a luncheon for many a gourmet, and costs 3,500 ($4.06). The rognone al cognac, at 3,000 lire ($3.48) is another superb choice—tender calf's kidneys that have been cooked and delicately flavored in cognac. A favored spot with the Genovese themselves.

READER'S SIGHTSEEING TIP: "**Valenza Po,** between Genoa and Alessandria, is small. It has one hotel, one pension with restaurant, and one restaurant. Yet it's one of the three principal jewelry-making centers in Italy, with several thousand artisans (we were told 7,000 plus) working in gold and silver crafts. The **Orafa Valenzana,** at 1 Piazza Don Minzoni, has one of the most outstanding permanent exhibits of jewelry in Europe and attracts buyers and sellers from many foreign countries to the town.

There was not much choice in lodging or food, but our double room with breakfast, no bath, cost 7,000 lire ($8.12) at the **Hotel Croce di Malta,** 28 Via Lega Lombarda (tel. 913-49). The only restaurant in town (and I mean the only public eating place except the pension's restaurant) is the **Ristorante Il Caminetto,** 13-E Via Alfiere, about three blocks from the hotel. It serves very good food, and has a friendly, colorful atmosphere. Dinner never starts before 9 p.m., and the cost is about 4,500 lire ($5.22) per person" (Kenneth M. Castro, Murphys, Calif.).

3. Rapallo

A front-ranking seaside resort—known for years to a chic and wealthy crowd who live in villas studding the hillside—Rapallo occupies a remarkable site overlooking the Gulf of Tigullio. In deluxe accommodations, such as the Excelsior Palace, it is superior to either Santa Margherita or Portofino. But in the medium-priced to budget range, the average wayfarer will do better at the other two resorts.

In summer, the heart of Rapallo takes on a crowded, somewhat carnival air, as hordes of bathers occupy the rocky sands along the beach. In the area is an 18-hole golf course plus an indoor swimming pool, a riding club, and a very modern tourist harbor. You can also take a cable car to the Sanctuary di Montallegro, then walk to Monte Rosa for what is considered one of the finest views on the Ligurian coast.

HOTELS IN RAPALLO: We'll survey a select few before moving on to Santa Margherita.

The First-Class Range

Grand Hotel Bristol, 309 Via Aurelia Orientale (tel. 50-216), is nestled in its own miniature forest of palm trees at the edge of town, with a fine panorama of the Gulf of Tigullio. The best in its classification, it is fine for what it is—even edging up to the deluxe level in the scope of its facilities and its position. Like a great old villa, with a private bath and all the amenities (the doubles have small sitting areas and are furnished with traditional pieces). But, again, the view from your bedroom window is the most memorable feature. The hotel charges in high season a rate of 19,000 lire ($22.04) to 25,000 lire ($29) in a single; 26,500 lire ($30.74) to 30,000 lire ($34.80) in a double. The full-pension rate ranges from 29,000 lire ($33.64) to 37,000 lire ($42.92) per person. A beach with private cabañas is reserved for hotel guests, though the majority seem to prefer the outdoor salt-water swimming pool (heated in winter).

The Medium-Priced Range

Hotel Moderno & Royal, 6 Viale Gramsci (tel. 50-601), is a gracious, old 50-room villa, on the sea, with tables and umbrellas set out on its front terrace. Most of its public rooms have high-arched windows to drink in the view of the promenade, with its row of palm trees. Directly across the promenade is Rapallo's swimming beach—with its rows of flamboyantly colored cabañas and bikini-clad inhabitants. Almost all of the bedrooms have private baths or showers, and the furnishings are modern and comfortable. A single with bath costs 10,000 lire ($11.60), dropping to 8,000 lire ($9.28) without bath. Bathless doubles are tabbed at 13,000 lire ($15.08), rising to 17,000 lire ($19.72) with bath. Quite good meals are served in the pleasant dining room, with its crystal chandeliers and fruitwood provincial, cane-backed chairs. The full-pension rate, in a room with private bath, is 18,000 lire ($20.88) per person, inclusive. A minimum stay of three days is required. Before dinner drinks are offered on the arched loggia, where there's a constant parade of fellow sun seekers.

The Budget Range

Hotel Giulio Cesare, 62 Corso Colombo (tel. 50-685), is a surprise bargain for the Italian Riviera. A modernized four-story villa, painted in shades of salmon, it stands on the "right" side of Rapallo. The genial owner, Signor Orgiana, has been skillful in renovating the establishment, keeping expenses down in order to keep room rates lower. Lying on the coast road, about 90 feet from the sea, his hotel offers 33 bedrooms, mainly with private baths. The bedrooms, featuring a good view of the Gulf of Tigullio, are furnished with tasteful reproductions, resulting in a homelike ambience (most of them have sun balconies). The singles range in price from 4,500 lire ($5.22) to 5,900 lire ($6.84); the doubles from 7,000 lire ($8.12) to 8,900 lire ($10.32), inclusive. Ask for the rooms on the top floor if you want a better view and a quieter situation. The meals are prepared with flair, and fine ingredients are used (the fish dishes are superb). The full-pension rate ranges from 8,900 lire ($10.32) to 10,500 lire ($12.18) per person, inclusive. Closed for part of November.

The next stop along the drive is:

4. Santa Margherita

A fast-growing resort, Santa Margherita Ligure also occupies a beautiful position on the bay. With a most attractive harbor, usually thronged with fun-seeking life, the spa offers the widest range of accommodations in all price levels on the Eastern Riviera. Its promenade, palm trees swaying in the wind, and beds of flowers give it a festive appearance. But typical of the Riviera, its beach combines rock and sand.

HOTELS IN SANTA MARGHERITA: You'll find some exceptionally good values.

The First-Class Range

Park Hotel Suisse, 31 Via Favale (tel. 89-571), is set in its own garden nest above the town center, with a panoramic view of the sea and harbor. It has seven floors, all of extreme modern design, with deep private balconies which are al fresco living rooms for some of the bedrooms. On the lower terrace is a large, free-form, salt-water swimming pool surrounded by a terrace and an edge of semitropical vegetation. A modernistic water chute, diving boards, a cafe with parasol tables for refreshments, all give one the experience of seaside life without the disadvantages. The bedrooms opening onto the rear gardens, sans sea view, cost slightly less; the rooms are decked out with contemporary furnishings in strong, bold colors. Open March to November, the hotel in high season charges 20,000 lire ($23.20) for a single with bath, 35,000 lire ($40.60) for a double with bath. The full-pension rate is around 30,000 lire ($34.80) per person, but a minimum stay of three days is required. A few bathless singles and doubles are available for less, of course. Demi pension at 27,000 lire ($31.32) is required in high season.

The Medium-Priced Range

Hotel Laurin, 3 Corso Marconi (tel. 89-971), sits pueblo-like right on the town waterfront. Each level is stepped back so as to provide a long sun terrace in front of the bedrooms. Its canary-yellow facade and low white roof seem to reflect and intensify the Mediterranean sun. The living room, with its wall of wide windows, is furnished harmoniously. The dining room, in a restrained contemporary fashion, has wide windows letting in the warm sun through filmy curtains. Its second dining spot, an à la carte restaurant, La Broche, serves till midnight. All the bedrooms have built-in features—not too extreme, almost traditional. They have two large glass windows and a door opening onto the terrace and sea view. There is air conditioning for hot nights. Open all year, the hotel in high season charges from 10,000 lire ($11.60) to 16,500 lire ($19.14) in a single room, from 17,000 lire ($19.72) to 26,500 lire ($30.74) for a double, inclusive except for 1,000 lire ($1.16) assessed for air conditioning. The full-pension rate is 18,000 lire ($20.88) per person.

Hotel Tigullio et de Milan, 3 Via Rainusso (tel. 87-455), a two-minute walk from the central square and the beach, is one of the finest hotels in its classification—in fact, it rivals many a first-class establishment. Set back from the street and surrounded by a garden, it is graced by a sun loggia on the roof. The interior is different in a nice way: it has a distinct flair, as every room gives off an aura of restrained good taste and imagination. The reception lounge has marble floors, wood-paneled pillars, crude—yet sophisticated—provincial furniture. The rate for a single is 8,000 lire ($9.28), increasing to 12,000 lire ($13.92) in a double. The color themes are well chosen; the built-in furniture makes the rooms more spacious; an elevator takes guests to all bedrooms. Full pension is 17,000 lire ($19.72) per person. The hotel is open all year, and the management will grant as much as 10% discount between October 1 and May 1. The owners, incidentally, are Stefano and Lucia Trevella. Both speak English and are delighted to have North American guests.

The Budget Range

The **Hotel Conteverde,** 1 Via Zara (tel. 87-139), offers one of the freshest and warmest welcomes for the low-budget traveler in Santa Margherita. Only two blocks from the sea, the third-class hotel has been handsomely revamped, its rooms simple but more than adequate (a few private baths are available in the doubles). Directed by Dino Pizzi, the hotel is open year-round, charging in high season 5,000 lire ($5.80) in a bathless single; 8,000 lire ($9.28) for a bathless double; and 12,000 lire ($13.92) for a double with bath. The full-pension rate ranges from 9,500 lire ($10.44) to 12,000 lire ($13.92) per person, inclusive. The terrace in front of the hotel has swing gliders; the lounge, period furnishings—even rockers. All is consistent with the villa exterior of shuttered windows, flower boxes, and a small front garden and lawn where tables are set out for refreshments.

Hotel Jolanda, 8 Via Luisito Costa (tel. 87-513), is, in reality, two buildings joined together by a patio which serves as an open-air dining room. It is about two blocks from the sea and the Piazza Caprera. One of the Siamese halves is an old-styled villa, in the semi-baroque style, the other is in straightforward modern, with rows of balconies. There is no sea view, but the pension is on a peaceful little street, away from the noise of heavy traffic. Open year-round, the Jolanda in high season charges 5,000 lire ($5.80) in a bathless single, 9,500 lire ($11.02) in a bathless double. The most expensive room, a double with bath, is 10,500 lire ($12.18). The full-pension rate ranges from 10,000 lire ($11.60) to 11,000 lire ($12.76) per person. The decor is rather jazzy, but the welcome's nice.

DINING IN SANTA MARGHERITA: Hotels and pensions have the upper hand. However, a few select establishments offer quality meals.

La Posada, 47 Piazza Martiri della Libertà (tel. 87-444), provides a charming change of pace. Perched on the harbor, where the fishing boats tie up, it is a rustic little Spanish bodega that can be inexpensive or dear—depending entirely on what you order and your appetite. To begin your meal, we'd recommend a gazpacho at 800 lire (93¢), the "liquid salad" of Andalusia that's just right on a summer day. The chef does an appetizing zarzuela de mariscos at 3,000 lire ($3.48), shellfish flavored with garlic and interestingly spiced. With access to honest-to-goodness fish, the kitchen also turns out a Valencian paella at 2,000 lire ($2.32) for two. Paella, of course, is the classic saffron-flavored rice dish of Valencia, studded with tasty morsels of whatever the chef desires—everything from chicken to bits of shrimp. The bodega also serves a refreshing sangría, the national drink of Spain—red wine, soda water, slices of oranges and lemons, all swilled around in a pitcher of ice for 2,000 lire ($2.32). Closed Mondays.

Da Alfonso, 8 Piazza Martiri della Libertà (tel. 87-436), is an all-purpose restaurant, which has as its co-star a pizza oven, turning out 17 varieties to please the palate. Inside, there are vaulted ceilings, with hanging lanterns, rope chairs, and amusing drawings on the walls which are covered with a kind of monk's cloth. In summer, the favorite seats are at the sidewalk tables, where guests enjoy a view of the public gardens and the sea. On the à la carte menu, a shellfish pizza costs 1,500 lire ($1.74), an artichoke pizza the same. Special fish dishes include zuppa di pesce (a seafood soup) at 4,500 lire ($5.22), a gamberoni (lobster) alla Parigina, 5,000 lire ($5.80)—these latter dishes for big splurgers only. Da Alfonso is open every day around the clock.

NIGHTLIFE: Covo di Nord-est, 1 Lungomare Rossetti (tel. 86-558), is in an elegant position, right on the coast road, halfway between Santa Margherita and Portofino. Here you can dance to an orchestra or—on "off nights"—to records; the orchestra performs in the international Italian style. There is an entrance fee of 4,000 lire ($4.64), which includes the first drink. An additional libation costs 3,000 lire ($3.48). When a star is appearing, the entrance fee depends on the performer's box office. This club is slightly dressy. Again, the situation is dramatic—and can be romantic if you're in the mood.

Saltincielo, 2 Via Aurelia Occidentale (tel. 86-741), is suited for an adventure: a special place to drink and dance, up in the clouds away from it all. The skytop nightclub, on a mountain ledge, hangs over Santa Margherita, offering a panoramic look at Portofino as well. It has an outside terrace for drinks, an ideal way to enjoy the breathtaking view. Attracting a younger crowd, who flock around the stereophonic system. No meals are offered, but the drink minimum is 3,000 lire ($3.48) per person. The translation of the name of this bird's nest club: jump in the sky.

About a four-mile drive from Santa Margherita and we're at:

5. Portofino

Elizabeth Taylor makes her way from boutique to boutique, a "page boy" supplying fresh ice drinks, and village mothers thrusting bambini in her face (they've read in the tabs that she likes children). Later, a speedboat whisks Taylor Inc. to a palatial yacht moored off the peninsula. You're likely to see anybody and anything in Portofino—and usually do.

Favored by yachtsmen, the resort occupies an idyllic position on a quiet harbor that mirrors the pastel-washed little houses fronting it. In the 30s, it enjoyed a reputation with artists; later, a terribly chic crowd moved in—and they're still there, occupying villas in the hills and refusing to surrender completely to popsicle-eating "trippers" who mill in during the day. Then the expatriate, well-heeled habitués flee, only to re-emerge at the martini hour when the last tour bus has pulled out.

The thing to do in Portofino: during the day—but preferably before sunset —start on a walk that leads toward the tip of the peninsula. You'll pass by the entrance to an old castle (where a German baron once lived), old private villas, towering trees, and dark green vegetation, until you reach the lighthouse.

When you return to the main piazza, proceed to one of the two little drinking bars on the left side of the harbor that rise and fall in popularity.

A SIGHT TO SEE: The **Monte Museum,** at Portofino Vetta, high in the hills above the resort, contains a unique assemblage of 300 frescoes dating from the 10th to the 16th century. In a natural setting almost as beautiful as the contents themselves, the museum is the creation of industrialist Orlando Crotti. An avid lover of fresco art, Crotti spent 30 years seeking out and buying the works from churches, parishes, and prayer chapels. A sign at the entrance makes an unusual promise to its visitors. It states simply that the expense of operating the museum requires an admission contribution. "But if after you have visited the museum you consider that it was not worth the price of the ticket you paid for, tell us and we will reimburse you." Is the Monte Museum worth the price of admission? We can only state that, as yet, no one has asked for a refund.

HOTELS IN PORTOFINO: In hotels, Portofino is severely limited, and in high season you may have to book a room in nearby Santa Margherita or Rapallo. **The Splendido** is suitable as a luxury base if you've a yacht moored in the harbor below or have closed down your Palm Beach house for the summer. Otherwise, you may prefer one of the following recommendations.

The Medium-Priced Range

Albergo Nazionale (tel. 69-138), is at stage center—right on the harbor, with a wide canopy covering its restaurant tables. An old villa with many roof levels, it is modest, yet well laid out. Its interior rooms are tastefully decorated, and its little lounge has a brick fireplace, coved ceiling, antique furnishings, and good reproductions. Most of the bedrooms, furnished in a mixture of styles (hand-painted Venetian in some of the rooms), have a view of the harbor. Owner Bruno Briola should be congratulated for his work in improving and upgrading the physical plant. The food at the Nazionale is extremely good, the restaurant attracting a lively business among non-residents as well. Nearly all of its rooms have a private bath or shower, with singles renting for from 8,500 lire ($9.86) to 12,600 lire ($14.62); doubles for from 15,500 lire ($17.98) to 23,000 lire ($26.68), inclusive. The full-pension rate ranges from 18,000 lire ($20.88) to 23,000 lire ($26.68) per person, inclusive. In high season, you don't stand much of a chance to secure a room unless you plan to stay for a few days on the pension plan. Reductions are granted to off-season visitors.

Hotel Piccolo (tel. 69-015) lies just outside the village proper, above the narrow and twisting coastal roads. It possesses a dining terrace overlooking the sea. Down below the road, a steep path leads to a little public beach. The old villa—26 rooms to rent, most of them with private baths or showers—has been pleasantly decorated, all on an individual basis. The management and courteous staff do much to make one's stay enjoyable. Open from April to October 15, the hotel charges 9,000 lire ($10.44) for its single rooms, 16,000 lire ($18.56) for its doubles, inclusive. The full-pension rate ranges from 12,500 lire ($14.50) to 18,500 lire ($21.46) per person, inclusive. As you sit on the terrace, having your evening meal of homecooked dishes—the trees overhead, the sea down below—you, too, will want to return time and again to the Piccolo. Ask the house gardener to get you started on the almost hidden narrow path, providing a shortcut to the village through hedges, past stone walls and a little church.

The Budget Range

Hotel Eden (tel. 69-091), just 150 feet away from the harbor in the heart of the village, is a little 12-room albergo, a lone budget holdout in an otherwise high fashion resort. Set in its own garden (hence, its name), it is a good and friendly place at which to stay. While there is no view of the harbor, there is a winning vista from the front veranda, where breakfast is served. The hotel is run by a family, and life here is decidedly casual. Open year-round, the albergo charges 9,000 lire ($10.44) in a single, this rate increasing to 15,000 lire ($17.40) in a double with bath. The food is good, so the full-pension rate is recommended, costing a minimum of 15,000 lire ($17.40) per person.

RESTAURANTS IN PORTOFINO: Il **Pitosforo** (tel. 69-020), draws a raft of raves, and mostly likely cries of protest when the tab is presented. While not blessed with an especially distinguished decor, its position right on the harbor gives it all the native chic it needs (it's reached by climbing steps). The food is especially worthy. Zuppa di pesce, a delectable Ligurian fish soup, costs 6,500 lire ($7.54) per serving, though the bouillabaisse goes up to 8,500 lire ($9.86). Lasagne al pesto, wide noodles prepared in the Genovese sauce, is 1,500 lire ($1.74). Other fish dishes include the mussels alla marinara at 2,500 lire ($2.90). A number of Spanish dishes are offered as well, including gazpacho at 1,000 lire ($1.16) and Valencian paella at 6,500 lire ($7.54) for two, saffron-flavored rice studded with sea fruit and chicken. Expect to pay at least 15,000 lire ($17.40) per person for a meal. Closed Tuesdays and from January 6 to February 7.

Delfino (tel. 69-081), right on the harbor-fronting village square, is the other most fashionable dining spot in Portofino. Less expensive than Il Pitosforo, it offers virtually the same type of food, such as lasagne al pesto at 1,200 lire ($1.39). Again, the fish dishes provide the best reason for lifting your fork: mussels in a marinade at 2,200 lire ($2.55); zuppa di pesce at 6,000 lire ($6.96) —really a soup made of freshly caught fish with a secret spice blend; risotto with shrimp at 2,500 lire ($2.90); and a mixed fish fry, also 2,500 lire. The latter is exceptional, a whole platter loaded with shrimp, sole, squid, etc. If you can't stand fish—but are trapped into dining with those who do—then know that the chef at Delfino prides himself on his sage-seasoned vitello all'uccelletto, a roast veal with a gamey taste. The price: 3,000 lire ($3.48). Try and get a table near the front, so as to enjoy the parade of visitors and villagers. Closed Thursdays and from November 6 to December 20.

6. La Spezia

An important naval port in Italy, La Spezia lies at the center of the gulf of the writers, its waterfront promenade lined with palm trees. Heavily bombed in World War II because of its strategic military value, it is an essentially modern town today, about 70 miles south of Genoa.

La Spezia makes a good base for exploring sights—often remote—along the coast. For example, south of town, opening onto the gulf, is the little village of **San Terenzo,** which converts into a popular resort for young people in summer. Totally lacking the élan of the more highly polished beach meccas, it is unspoiled and unsophisticated—just as Shelley found it in 1822, the year he drowned off the coast. His Magni house is at 15 Via P. Mantegazza on the waterfront ("I still inhabit this divine bay, reading dramas, sailing, and listening to the most enchanting music").

The most exciting trip hereabouts is to the **Cinque Terre** (Five Lands)— five cliffside-hugging villages that rank among the least trampled on the Ligurian coast. Long cut off from the outside world, but accessible by rail, three of the villages have recently built roads. Eventually all of them are supposed to be accessible to motorists. Known for their delicious wines, they are called Riomaggiore, Manarola, Corniglia, Vernazza, and Monterosso al Mare (the latter the most popular among sandy beach devotees). A train stops in each village. Visitors can get off at one point and walk from one village to another along a path cut into the cliff. A strong guard rail affords some protection.

From April to September, motor boats service the area. These boats leave from and return to Portovenere, charging 5,000 lire ($5.80) for a round-trip ticket. Boats leave from Portovenere at 11 a.m., from Vernazza at 3 p.m. Boats

from La Spezia to Portovenere depart every half hour at a cost of 600 lire (70¢).
Service daily, including Sundays and holidays.

WHERE TO DINE: Piemontese, 63 Via Persio (tel. 38-215), ranks among our
favorites. A short walk from the harbor at the corner of a park, it is a simply
decorated establishment. The food and service are good, and inexpensive. The
chef's specialties include deviled chicken at 2,000 lire ($2.32) and a fish fry at
2,000 lire also, with tasty bits of shrimp and squid. Any number of good soup
and pasta dishes are featured at prices ranging from 400 lire (46¢) to 900 lire
($1.04). Other specialties include ossi buchi e funghi (mushrooms) at 2,300 lire
($2.67); taglietelline alla creola (noodles with tomato sauce, prosciutto, and
mushrooms) at 800 lire (93¢); and gamberoni all'Americana (large shrimp with
a very spicy cognac sauce), 3,500 lire ($4.06).

7. Isle of Elba

Lying slightly more than six miles from the mainland of Italy, Elba is the
largest island in an archipelago linked to Tuscany (Florence). (The string of
Tuscan islands, incidentally, includes the legendary Montecristo, 25 miles
south of Elba, made famous by the older Dumas in his *The Count of Monte
Cristo*—and now containing the remains of a Camaldulensian convent last
occupied in the mid-16th century. The tiny isle, lying between Leghorn and
Corsica, has become a natural preserve and bird sanctuary, administered by the
Forestry Service.)

Napoleon knew Elba well, but today it's being fast discovered by ever-
increasing numbers of foreign visitors, especially Germans, who value its low
prices and good accommodations. Italy has far more glamorous islands (Capri
and Ischia), but Elba makes for an excellent, less trampled base for a holiday
by the sea, with a minimum of sights. In many places—*still*—a rustic life holds
forth, the people suspicious of strangers, standoffish. But the growing number
of visitors coming over are necessarily changing the landscape—and even the
Elbani themselves, many of whom have known extremely hard times, are now
learning the wily ways of competing for tourist lire.

With 91 miles of coastline—and with lots of hidden coves and occasional
beaches away from the madding crowd—Elba presents the typical Mediterranean landscape of silvery olive trees and hill-climbing vineyards. Its climate
is mild, with a tendency toward dryness.

How to get there: a number of means are offered, principally from the port
of Piombino on the Italian mainland. The hydrofoil, taking less than 30
minutes, is the quickest, most efficient method. But motorists will want to
board one of the ferry boats that run between Piombino and Portoferraio
(capital of Elba) several times daily (there's more limited service in winter).
There is also a ferry service between Piombino and Porto Azzurro on the
southern coast of Elba. The fare is usually 2,000 lire ($2.32) per person one way,
with a small car being transported for about 11,000 lire ($12.76) one way. Space
is likely to be tight in summer—so reserve at one of the offices of the Società
di Navigazione Toscana at Piombino (also book your return from Elba).

Once on the island, you'll want to visit the chief manmade attraction:
Napoleon's Villa at San Martino, about three miles outside Portoferraio.
With everything—quite symbolically—in trompe l'oeil, the villa was the summer home of Napoleon, who ruled over the small principality of Elba following
his abdication on April 11, 1814. Only 45, the Corsican was impatient, launching many projects to keep his mind occupied. But it wasn't enough. In March

1815, he left Elba to begin the famous "Hundred Days" that culminated in Waterloo. He was never to return to Elba, of course, as he was exiled the next time to Saint Helena.

The villa itself is unimpressive, but rich in the memories of its former tenant. The apartments were occupied by Napoleon and Marshal Bertrand. On the grounds today is a 19th-century neo-classic museum (see the statue of Galatea by Canova). The residence is open from 9 to 1 and from 3 to 6 in season (9 to 2 in winter; 9 to 1 on Sundays), and charges 200 lire (23¢) admission, except on Sundays, when admission is free. Closed Mondays.

We'll dock first at:

PORTOFERRAIO: Elba's capital is a busy harbor, filled with traffic caused by the coming and going of visitors. However, it's not the loveliest spot at which to base for a holiday by the sea, as the resorts in the hinterlands offer far more idyllic settings. (In off season it provides a more suitable center, as many outlying hotels shut down then.) In the old town is the **Mulini Palazzina,** a Medici fortress containing Napoleon memorabilia. It charges the same admission and is open the same hours as Napoleon's Villa at San Martino, described above. Closed Thursdays.

Hotels in Portoferraio

The medium-priced range, the **Hotel Garden,** Località Schiopparello, just outside Portoferraio (tel. 966-043), is a pleasant oasis, set back from the water. A modern hotel, it stands in the midst of a garden of palm trees, pine groves, and terraces with views of the sea. The structure is a warm combination of natural stone walls and glass, especially the living and dining rooms. The bedrooms—56 in all, mostly with tiled baths or showers—are spacious, with shutter doors opening onto communal sun terraces. The furnishings are in the Nordic modern style. Open from April 22 to October 5, the hotel charges from 11,000 lire ($12.76) to 17,700 lire ($20.53) per person, including full pension (which is required, incidentally), plus tax and use of the beach. The food is excellent.

Even for a budget hotel, the **Ape Elbana** (tel. 92-245) is a super bargain. Opening onto a colorful square in the heart of town, it is an old villa, somewhat casual in its housekeeping, with a wide veranda which quickly converts every day into a social center. Staying here is like going Elban in an interesting way. The rooms have adequate comfort and come equipped with old furnishings, such as wooden beds with high head and foot boards, and rather antiquated plumbing. Bathless singles go for 3,200 lire ($3.71), bathless doubles for 5,000 lire ($5.80). Doubles with private bath rent for 7,300 lire ($8.47). Pension terms (not applicable for stays of only one day) range in price from 8,000 lire ($9.28) to 9,300 lire ($10.79) per person, inclusive. The meals served on the ground floor are most palatable, especially the fish dishes, such as sole sautéed in butter; the excellent, but basic, pastas; and fresh salads.

A drive along the north shore for about seven miles will take you to:

PROCCHIO: An attractive beach on a crystal blue bay, Procchio is one of the best-equipped resorts on Elba, particularly in hotels in the top brackets.

First-Class Hotels in Procchio

Hotel Del Golfo (tel. 523-565) is a self-sustaining private world, overlooking the Gulf of Procchio. A modern, three-story hotel, it stands on its own grounds at the inner bend of the bay, with a sandy beach. The parklike surroundings have many recreational facilities, including a free-form swimming pool with a flagstone terrace, cabañas, an open-air restaurant, and tennis courts. The hotel is built of stone and partially covered with bougainvillea. Most of the bedrooms have private balconies, where it's the custom to have your breakfast. The bedrooms are large, comfortable, and immaculate, some with air conditioning. High-season prices are charged from July 11 to August 20, and the hotel remains open from mid-May to mid-October. All the rooms have private baths or showers. In summer, singles range in price from 13,000 lire ($15.08) to 14,000 lire ($16.24); doubles from 16,000 lire ($18.56) to 20,000 lire ($23.20). The full-pension rate climbs from 25,000 lire ($29) to 30,000 lire ($34.80) per person, plus tax. Public rooms are spacious and modern. The dining room has a panoramic view of the sea, and the American bar is cozy.

Medium-Priced Hotels in Procchio

Hotel Désirée (tel. 907-502) sits in a topnotch position, off the coast road, with its own gardens and beach. Spacious and modern, it offers sun-pocket terraces. The furnishings in the public rooms may suggest air terminal modern, but the architecture is for those who like a sense of openness, light and happy colors, and tiled terraces with garden furniture set out for refreshments. There is a long dining room with two all-glass walls and another of native stone. The bedrooms are contemporary, with strong colors and streamlined furnishings—immaculately maintained. Désirée receives guests from April 25 to October 15. All rooms contain either private baths or showers. The highest tariffs are charged from June 28 till August 31, at which time full pension ranges in price from 17,000 lire ($19.72) to 19,000 lire ($22.04) per person. In June and September, the rate for full pension ranges from 13,500 lire ($15.66) to 15,500 lire ($17.98) per person, plus tax.

Continuing along the northern shore for another 4½ miles, we arrive at our terminus, the resort of:

MARCIANA MARINA: An unspoiled fishing village (at least for the moment!), Marciana Marina occupies a lovely setting. You can still see the fishermen sitting around weaving lobster baskets. We're not impressed with the town's first-class hotel, but one of its less expensive accommodations provides good value.

A Budget Hotel

Hotel Imperia, 12 Viale Amedeo (tel. 99-082), is a little gem: a remodeled hotel, just a few minutes from the sea. Built by a fisherman and his sons, it offers low prices. There is a modern lobby, and many of the bedrooms have balconies overlooking fig trees. No skimping was allowed in the furnishings: they are well-chosen contemporary pieces with an occasional provincial selection adding flair. Most of the bedrooms have brightly colored and compact tiled bathrooms. Open year-round, the hotel in high season asks 3,645 lire ($4.23) for a bathless single; 4,410 lire ($5.11) for a single with bath. The doubles range in price from 6,640 lire ($7.71) to 7,730 lire ($8.97). No pension terms are quoted.

Albergo Marinella, Marciana Marina (tel. 99-018), is a newly renovated seafront hotel and restaurant combination, right on the promenade. It's not only economical, but the food is especially good, and you're in the center of the promenade where the cafes provide the town's social activity. Behind the albergo's white and gold facade is a spacious lobby, with comfortable lounging chairs and an open fireplace. Away from the sea is a quiet and small informal garden, with brightly canopied chairs, swings, and tables. The bedrooms are stark white, each with one wall of wood paneling, plus minimum furnishings, though most of them have a view of the sea. All rooms are doubles, and each has a private bath as well. For half pension, the rate is 10,500 lire ($12.18) per person, increasing to 12,300 lire ($14.27) for full pension, plus I.V.A. High season is in July and August when reservations are required. The owner, Francesco Torino, is proud of his chef, Ciccio, who carefully selects fresh fish for his dinners every morning and serves his platters with the white Elban house wine from his own cellar. On the open but covered dining terrace, every table seems to be ringside.

The largest and most important resort on the southern shore is:

MARINA DI CAMPO: A base for trips to the celebrated Montecristo, Marina di Campo, studded with pine trees, is our favorite among the Elban resorts, offering the most superior accommodations (especially the Iselba). The sandy beach separating it from the sea—slightly more than a mile long—is most inviting, the quintessence of an Elban holiday. The pace is slow; the living's easy—so give it a try.

First-Class Hotels in Marina di Campo

Hotel Iselba (tel. 97-097) is, hands down, *the* place to stay in Elba. Its sophistication reaches across its borders to challenge similar establishments at more fashionable resorts. Like a world created for *Harpers Bazaar,* it lies on the south shore, a private compound of low natural fieldstone and glass buildings arranged part Japanese-style, part hacienda, along the sand dunes. Importantly, there is a private beach. The hotel stands in a grove of silvery beach firs, and some of the rooms open onto a flagstone-edged reflection pool, afloat with water lilies. The dining room of natural stone, with a rattan ceiling and garden chairs, has a waterside wall of glass. The cuisine is excellent, with Italian and international dishes mixing freely. Through clever architectural devices, the living rooms seem to reach out to take in the outdoors. Most of the guest rooms are in detached stone cottages, and many have private sitting rooms. Your bedroom might have a long refectory desk set in front of a wall of glass, opening onto a private terrace and pine trees. Excellent antiques are used unsparingly, and fine wood chests are often set against natural stone walls, brightened by a bowl of wild sand dune flowers. Full pension can go from 26,000 lire ($30.16) to 29,000 lire ($33.64) per person, inclusive. Open May 15 to October 15.

Where to Stay in Marina di Campo

Villa Nettuno (tel. 97-028) stands quietly in a small forest of baby pines, with an adjoining private beach. Its central building encompasses two dining rooms, lounges, and bedrooms—with additional motel-like accommodations tacked on. Full pension ranges from 14,500 lire ($16.82) to 18,000 lire ($20.88) per person, inclusive, from the day of opening, April 15, to closing, September 30. It is obligatory to take at least demi-pension. I.V.A. is added to all tariffs. All of the bedrooms have private showers, French doors, and balconies. The rooms themselves are chaste and severe, almost monastic; the living room is furnished in bold colors, but the design is impersonal.

In the southeast sector of the island is:

CAPOLIVERI: One of the choicest spots on the island—particularly noted for views of the sea—the colorful village of Capoliveri occupies one of the more recently emerging resort areas of Elba. It's in the vicinity of Porto Azzurro.

PORTO AZZURRO: The southeastern terminus of the ferry, Porto Azzurro is a colorful harbor, suitable for photographing and dining, but less so for overnighting (most accommodations in the town itself tend to the antique).

A Medium-Priced Hotel

Cala di Mola, Porto Azzurro (tel. 95-225), is a Mediterranean resort on the shore of the Gulf of Mola, only 2,400 yards from Porto Azzurro. It provides near luxurious accommodations at a fair price. The bedrooms are set back in hillside terraces, opening onto flower gardens and a double swimming pool area. Staircases set in rugged stone lead to each room, and purple bougainvillea is rampant. Greek-styled ceramic pots filled with red geraniums edge the wide sun terrace. Each accommodation has style and dignity, and is exceptionally cool, graced with chic traditional furniture reporductions, as well as bedcovers in bold, colorful stripes. A private sun terrace and breakfast balcony is provided. Full pension ranges from 12,000 lire ($13.92) to 16,900 lire ($19.60) per person, plus I.V.A. and pool charges. Dining is in a rustic-styled tavern, with reed-seated ladder-backed chairs, beams, wrought-iron wall lanterns, and deep arches. Antiques are used throughout the public rooms. The owner, Mr. Feliceiti, is a kind, hospitable Neapolitan.

Where to Dine

La Lanterna (tel. 95-026), offers invariably fresh-tasting fish dishes. The situation is also desirable, with terrace dining overlooking the water. Among specialties worth sampling are panzerotti all'Elbana (a local pasta) at 1,200 lire ($1.39); fried scampi and squid at 2,300 lire ($2.67); zuppa di cozze (a mussel soup in a savory marinade) at 2,000 lire ($2.32); sogliole in burro (sole sautéed in butter) at 2,600 lire ($3.02).

After Elba, we strike out along the western coastal route south till the Bay of Naples comes into view.

Chapter XVII

NAPLES, ISCHIA, POMPEII

1. Naples
2. The Environs
Ischia
4. Pompeii

IN PERHAPS THE MOST memorable novel to come out of World War II, *The Gallery* by John Horne Burns, there is this passage: "But I remember best of all the children of Naples. The scugnizz'. Naples is the greatest baby plant in the world. Once they come off the assembly line, they lose no time getting onto the streets. They learn to walk and talk in the gutters. Many of them seem to live there."

The milling Mediterranean city—known to the American G.I. of 1944— has changed drastically since its early post-war days. Yet its character seems unalterable. To the foreigner unfamiliar with the complexities of the multifarious "Italies" and their regional types, the Neapolitan is the quintessence of the country—easy to caricature (O Sole Mio?, Mamma Mia, Bel Canto). If a native who moved to Rome (Sophia Loren) evokes the Italian woman to you, you'll find more of her look alikes here than in any other city.

1. Naples

Naples is a city to be savored in bits and pieces, like the zuppa di pesce (fish soup). It is almost too much to take at once. But that is how the city comes upon you, like a runaway car, with tour ticket sellers, shoeshine boys, hotel hawkers, and pickpockets.

July and August can be extremely unpleasant in Naples, despite the air conditioning units in many of the hotels (some of which seem to blow out lukewarm heat). The average working male on the street solves the problem by pulling off his shirt. And no Neapolitan housewife gets overheated running up and down the steps to convey a message to someone on the street—a situation she handles by screaming out the window. Surely, the Neapolitans are the most spontaneous people on earth, wearing their emotions on the surface of their skin.

What Naples is, is a fantastic adventure. The best approach, from its bay, is idyllic—a port set against the backdrop of a crystal blue sky and volcanic mountains. "See Naples and Die" is apt. The rich attractions inside the city and

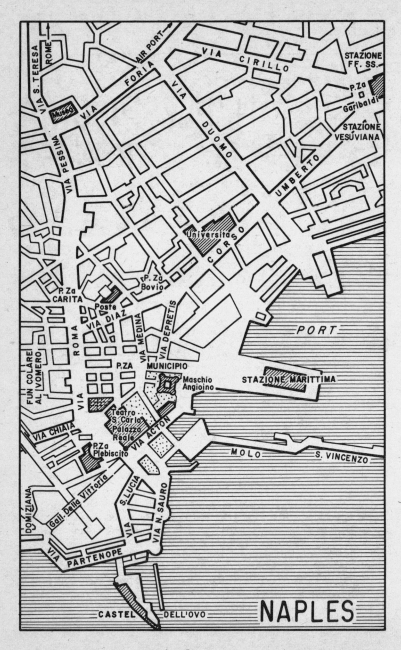

in the environs (Pompeii, Ischia, Vesuvius, the Phlaegrean Fields, Herculaneum) make Naples one of the five top tourist meccas of Italy. The inexperienced may have difficulty coping with it. The seasoned explorer will find it worthy ground, even venturing down side streets, some of which teem with prostitutes and a major source of their upkeep: the ubiquitous sailor.

The history of Naples (Palaeopolis of old) is ancient, the city having been founded by the Greeks (so it is believed) in the 6th century B.C. Early in the story, the Romans conquered the city, and it was later visited by such fun-and-sun-seeking emperors as Nero, as well as by poets (Virgil wrote *Georgics* here). Over the years it has known many conquerors—everyone from Roger II of Sicily to Charles of Anjou in the 13th century to the Americans in the 20th. The city was made the capital of the Kingdom of the Two Sicilies by Charles III of Spain in 1734. It is the second largest port in Italy, topped only by Genoa, and is also currently experiencing rapid industrial growth (it is the home of the ever-growing aircraft corporation, Aeritalia).

Note: In Naples, **Alitalia** has its office at 78 Via Miguel Cervantes (tel. 312-200).

Hotels in Naples: The hotels are vastly improved. The old "name" places are being restored, and new ones cropping up. Most of the large hotels lie in that colorful and popular district of Santa Lucia. Many of the first-class and deluxe establishments line the Via Partenope along the water. In and around the central railway station are other clusters, many built since the late 50s. Regardless of the price range in which you travel, there's a bed waiting for you in Naples.

The Deluxe Range

Hotel Excelsior, 48 Via Partenope (tel. 417-111), has a strong foothold on a most dramatic position in Naples—right on the waterfront, with views of Santa Lucia and Vesuvius. Owned by the prestigious hotel chain of CIGA, it recently underwent a total restoration and refurbishing. Resisting extreme contemporary furnishings, the management made every effort to create a gracious country homelike ambience. While there are many elegant and impressive details, such as Venetian chandeliers, Doric columns, wall-filling murals, and bronze torchiers, there is also an abundance of informality—pieces covered in muted chintz, Regency groups for drinking, provincial chairs in pale blue velvet in the drinking salon, a marble fireplace, and Biedermeier furniture. This same sophistication prevails in the bedrooms, where Oriental rugs blend harmoniously with traditional elements. Most of them are, in reality, bed-sitting rooms, suitable for entertaining. Under the excellent management of Massimo Rosati, there is no rubberstamp decor or welcome—individuality counts. All of the rooms are air-conditioned, and most of them contain a well-maintained private bathroom. Singles with bath go for 22,600 lire ($26.20) to 28,200 lire ($32.71); doubles for 38,480 lire ($44.64) to 47,440 lire ($55.03).

Hotel Vesuvio, 45 Via Partenope (tel. 417-044), is a handsome pink and white waterfront hotel. A good choice with genuine comfort, it features a dramatic view. The bedrooms are decorated in a traditional manner, with French doors leading to balconies in some. Every room is air-conditioned at no extra cost, and all bedrooms have private bathrooms or showers. A single ranges in price from 13,000 lire ($15.08) to 19,000 lire ($22.04); doubles go from 17,000 lire ($19.72) to 28,000 lire ($32.48). Service and air conditioning are included in these tariffs. There is a dining room right on the roof garden. The restaurant is a real magnet in summer. It was designed for both indoor and al fresco terrace dining, with views of the harbor—ideal at sunset. On the premises are an American-styled bar, a hairdresser, and a private garage.

The First-Class Range

Ambassadors Palace, 70 Via Medina (tel. 312-031), is—surprisingly enough—a skyscraper, Italian style. Neapolitans call it Il Grattacielo. Billing itself as the highest hotel in Italy, it stands as a landmark, a few blocks up from the central harbor. The interior designer, leery of cold modern, tried valiantly to infuse it with lushness. A long, ornately tiled dining gallery—on the top floor—has all-glass walls, sparked by a row of crystal chandeliers and made more intriguing by carved chairs. The marble-pillared lobby has touches of ornate gilt and a curlicue decor. The bedrooms, mostly large scaled, are more successful, with fine wood-grained desks, chairs, armoires, ornate wrought-iron beds, and Oriental rugs. Most of the rooms have a private bath or shower, as well as steam heat or air conditioning for which you must pay 700 lire (81¢) extra. The Ambassadors Palace charges 13,500 lire ($15.66) in a single with bath; 21,700 lire ($25.17) in a double with bath.

Parker's Hotel, 135 Corso Vittorio Emanuele (tel. 685-866), sits up and away from all the harbor commotion, and offers a gracious old-fashioned accommodation on one of the better hillside avenues of Naples. Built in the last century, it has palace-like features, created when architects cared about the beauty of their work. The dining room has drama—neo-classic walls, fluted pilasters, and ornate ceilings. Connected by deep molded arches, the various lounges and reception halls open off one another. The furnishings are also of another era—some fine antiques mixed with neutral chairs. The bedrooms—87 in all, mainly with private baths or showers—are furnished either with traditional pieces or in semi-modern. Some of the rooms are formal, in white and gold, with built-in wardrobes, hand-carved chairs, and coordinated fabrics. High-season rates are quoted from March 16 to October 31—from 5,800 lire ($6.73) to 8,800 lire ($10.21) in a single; from 12,500 lire ($14.50) to 20,000 lire ($23.20) in a double. Add the I.V.A. tax. During the low season, a 20% discount may be granted. Most of the rooms have panoramic views over tree tops of the bay.

The Medium-Priced Range

Hotel Britannique, 133 Corso Vittorio Emanuele (tel. 660-933), with its old-world atmosphere, its ingratiating Swiss family ownership, its hillside view of the Bay of Naples, is unquestionably our favorite in its classification. Wherever you look, you'll feel the imprint of the hospitality and the sustained good taste of the Löliger family (the son is now taking over full management), all of whom have the gentle, but firm, hand needed to manage a hotel. The Britannique is on the curve of a wide hillside boulevard, away from the harbor, providing a panoramic view of it from a distance. The drawing room has a fine, tall inlaid desk and some Victorian chairs arranged for after-dinner conversations. The dining room—entered through a greenhouse—is simple, serving delicious home-cooked meals. There's an ornate mahogany elevator to take you to your period bedroom, many of which have private baths. Some of the larger rooms have double sinks, old brass beds, and inlaid chests. Singles peak at 10,000 lire ($11.60); doubles at 17,500 lire ($20.30).

Hotel Miramare, 24 Via Nazario Sauro (tel. 611-550), has a superb position, seemingly thrust out toward the harbor on a dockside boulevard. It is central, sunny, and priced rather low for its classification. Its lobby evokes a little Caribbean hotel, with a semi-tropical look—airy with so-so furnishings. The lower bedrooms are much too noisy (the curse of most Neapolitan hotels), so request a quieter one upstairs. Open year round, the Miramare quotes a reduced off-season rate, but in summer you'll pay 13,000 lire ($15.08) in a bathless double, that tariff increasing to 16,500 lire ($19.14) in a double with bath, service and tax included. On the premises are an American bar, a restaurant-taverna, and a roof garden.

The Budget Range

Hotel Rex, 12 Via Paleopoli (tel. 416-102), is an inexpensive and pleasant hotel in the Santa Lucia district, almost backing up to the deluxe hotels half a block away on the bay. One of our most favored low-cost establishments, it spans half a block, though it has no elevator. A goodly percentage of the refurbished bedrooms are comfortable and large—each is scrubbed and polished daily and is nicely furnished. Many of the rooms have private bathrooms. The single rate ranges from 2,600 lire ($3.02) to 3,400 lire ($3.94); the double rate from 3,900 lire ($4.52) to 6,100 lire ($7.08), inclusive. No meals are served, other than a continental breakfast brought to your room.

Hotel Toledo e Regina, 352 Via Roma (tel. 412-825), is an old hotel that has been gutted and completely redone, becoming contemporary, utilitarian, and fresh. The restyling has been successful, and the hotel has a spacious lounge, featuring three French doors and an arched ceiling. Even the bedrooms —68 in all, a goodly percentage with private baths or showers—have been refurbished. They are extra large, with French doors and (in some cases) colorfully tiled baths, built-in beds, and wardrobes. Those without private bath have wash basins and modesty screens. The rate in a single room peaks at 4,900 lire ($5.68), the doubles going for a top 8,493 lire ($9.85), inclusive. No meals, other than a continental breakfast, are served.

READERS' HOTEL SELECTION: "We would like to recommend the **Hotel Manzoni,** 6 Vico Ferrovia (tel. 222-960). A pleasant man approached us as we were leaving the railway station. He had a mini-bus waiting and whisked us off, much to our surprise, only a short distance from the station. A friendly welcome awaited us, and we were impressed by the general appearance of the hotel. A clean, comfortable double room cost us 8,000 lire ($9.28) for bed and breakfast and use of an adjacent shower. By arrangement, dinner is available in the evening at a moderate cost. The situation was very convenient, within a short walk of trams from the nearby Piazza Garibaldi to the wharf for trips to Capri" (Mr. and Mrs. Robert T. Martin, Auckland, New Zealand).

THE NEAPOLITAN CUISINE: A mixed reaction. Naples is the home of pizza and spaghetti. If you're mad for either of those items, then you'll delight in sampling the authentic versions. However, if you like subtle cooking and have an aversion to olive oil or garlic, you'll not "fare" as well. At any rate, the waiters are likely to be a production themselves—even if your meal isn't. Our most expensive dining recommendations will come first.

Le Arcate, 249 Via Aniello Falcone (tel. 683-380), sits high up on a hillside, away from the harbor, but with a splendid view of the bay. Topping the list of most visitors, it is quite famous—and rightly so, as Signor Izzo has passed on all his recipes and techniques to his sons. The restaurant—on several levels—has wide picture windows to embrace the scenery, and everywhere there are tall palms, ferns, and flowers. The preferred tables are on the outer terrace, where you dine under a canopy of umorellas, surrounded by large pots of roses and geraniums.

From the à la carte menu, you'll want to try: prosciutto e fichi (spicy ham with figs) for 2,000 lire ($2.32) or antipasti assorti (an impressive array of hors d'oeuvres), also 2,000 lire. The fish selections are supreme: sautéed clams (vongole) at 2,500 lire ($2.90); assorted gulf fish at 2,000 lire ($2.32); and zuppa di pesce, the pièce de résistance of the house, a superb Neapolitan fish stew—with bits of octopus—in a savory marinade at 5,000 lire ($5.80). The non-fish dishes, prepared especially well, are the fillet of steak for 3,000 lire ($3.48), and the veal scaloppine with lemon, also 3,000 lire. To begin your meal, why not order maccheroni (macaroni) with four different kinds of cheese, a house specialty at 1,000 lire ($1.16)? Spaghetti alla carbonara (bits of pork, whipped egg, and Parmesan cheese) is flambéed at 1,500 lire ($1.74). And of course, you can always finish with crêpes suzette at 3,000 lire ($3.48). Finally, if you want to sample Neapolitan ice cream, then order la torre delle Arcate, 1,000 lire ($1.16) which is just that: a tower of delicious ice cream. Open April to October, it can be reached by bus No. 128, although a taxi is recommended.

Fish Dinners on the Harbor in Santa Lucia

The waterside restaurants of Naples are well known, provoking heated arguments among diners—both local and foreign—as to their relative merits. We've sampled most of them a number of times, finding wide differences. Our selections follow.

La Bersagliera, Banchina Santa Lucia (tel. 415-692), is one of the most popular restaurants in all of Naples, a delight on a hot night when half the city turns out to stroll through the district. Most of the tables are perched outside, right by the sea, where boats in rainbow colors bob up and down in the water and Neapolitan kids strip down and jump in for a dip—even though the swimming area can sometimes rival the polluted waters of New York's Hudson River.

Regardless of where you've had spaghetti before (even if it was in a tin can, the pasta soaking in its own sauce), you should try it here. Certain Neapolitans maintain they are the only ones who know how to prepare the dish right, claiming that the rest of the world serves "bastardized" versions of the thin ribbons. The most characteristic way of ordering it at La Bersagliera is with clams (vongole), for 1,200 lire ($1.39). And you may want to follow with the mixed fish fry at 2,200 lire ($2.55). If it's all too fishy, you can order chicken cacciatora, also 2,200 lire. A generous slice of cake finishes off the meal at 700 lire (81¢).

Don Pasquale, Via Mergellina, a short haul by taxi from the center, provided us with our finest repast during our latest rounds in Naples. As at Le Arcate, the chef is noted for his maccheroni (macaroni) with a quartet of different cheeses, costing 750 lire (87¢). It's so good you may be tempted to order another plate, but we'd suggest you go on to one of the tempting seafood platters or the tender entrecôte, paying on an average of 2,500 lire ($2.90) for a main course. A complete meal will likely run to 6,500 lire ($7.54), but it's well worth it. Closed Sundays.

An Inexpensive Trattoria

Da Marino, 118-120 Via Santa Lucia, is an excellent pizzeria-ristorante in the tourist-trodden Santa Lucia district, near many of the major hotels. It bills itself as a "meeting place of gourmets," but this is a rather fanciful and characteristic example of Neapolitan overstatement. What it is, is one of the best of the low-cost pizzerias, serving such superb pies as pizza marinara at 500 lire (58¢); pizza Margherita at 600 lire (70¢); or pizza made with salami and mozzarella at 900 lire ($1.04). No restaurant in Campania ignores the sea, so try, alternatively, either the fish soup at 2,500 lire ($2.90) or the mixed fish fry at 1,800 lire ($2.09). Closed Tuesdays.

Stateside Specialties

The **California,** 101 Via Santa Lucia, thinks of itself as "the original American luncheonette in Naples," with that old back home atmosphere. It provides a suitable oasis for those homesick and hankering for banana splits, ice-cream sundaes, ham & eggs, and pancakes. It's both a counter and a table affair, with a glassed-in sidewalk area where the English-speaking waiters are used to the ways of the families of the American Armed Forces. Offered are such typical items as a banana split, 1,200 lire ($1.39); a hamburger steak, 1,300 lire ($1.51); or a hot roast beef sandwich, 1,000 lire ($1.16). For the Texan, there's chili con carne at 1,300 lire ($1.51). The breakfast specials draw a lively U.S. clientele who order a plate of bacon and eggs for 1,000 lire ($1.16) as well as "authentic" Kellogg's corn flakes. The California is open from 7 a.m. to 3 a.m.

THE SIGHTS OF NAPLES: Before striking out for Pompeii or Capri, you should try to see some of the sights inside Naples. If you're hard pressed for time, then settle for the first two museums of renown.

The Best of the Museums

The **National Museum,** at the Piazza Museo, with its Roman and Greek sculpture, contains one of the most valuable archaeological collections in Europe—in particular the select Farnese acquisitions, plus mosaics and sculpture excavated at Pompeii and Herculaneum. Though the building dates from the 16th century, it was turned into a museum some two centuries later by Charles Bourbon.

In Room I (on the ground floor) is one of the treasures of the Farnese collections—the nude statues of Armodio and Aristogitone, the most outstanding in the room. A famous bas relief in Room II depicts Orpheus and his wife, Eurydice, with Mercury—from an original of the fifth century B.C.

Room III is enlivened by the nude statue of the spear-bearing Doryphorus, copied from a work by Polyclitus the elder and excavated at Pompeii. A gigantic, but weary Hercules—a statue of remarkable boldness—guards Room XII. A copy of an original by Lysippus, the fourth-century B.C. Greek sculptor for Alexander the Great, it was discovered in the Baths of Caracalla in Rome. On a more delicate pedestal is a decapitated, but exquisitely beautiful Venus (Aphrodite). In Room XIV is the Psyche of Capua (it's easy to see why Aphrodite was jealous!). Room XV displays the "Group of the Farnese Bull," presenting its pageantry of violence from the days of antiquity. A copy of either a second-or third-century B.C. Hellenistic statue—one of the most frequently reproduced of all sculptures—it was discovered at the Baths of Caracalla. The marble group depicts a scene in the legend of Amphion and Zethus who tied Dirce, wife of Lycus of Thebes, to the horns of a rampaging bull. After this, you will have seen the best of the works on this floor, except for a bust of Homer, a Greek original.

The galleries on the mezzanine are devoted to mosaics excavated from Pompeii and Herculaneum. Shown are scenes of cock fights, dragon-tailed satyrs, an aquarium, and—the finest item of all—Alexander Fighting the Persians in Room LXI.

On the top floor are housed some of the celebrated bronzes dug out of the Pompeii and Herculaneum lava and volcanic mud. Of particular interest is a tripod of satyrs with erections, a Hellenistic portrait of Berenice, a comically drunken satyr, a statue of a "Sleeping Satyr," and "Mercury on a Rock."

The museum is open from 9 a.m. to 3 p.m. (Sundays from 9 a.m. to 1 p.m.), and charges 100 lire (12¢) for admission. Closed Wednesdays.

The **Capodimonte National Gallery and Museum** in the 18th-century Palace of Capodimonte (built in the time of Charles III) stands in a park, haughtily removed from the squalor of Naples. It's got something to be smug about, as it houses one of Italy's finest picture galleries (an elevator takes visitors to the top floor).

In Room 2 are seven Flemish tapestries—made to the designs of Bernart Van Orley—showing grand-scaled scenes from the Battle of Pavia (1525), in which the forces of Francis I of France—more than 25,000 strong—lost to those of Charles V. Van Orley, who lived in a pre-Guernica day, obviously didn't consider war a horror, but a romantic ballet (Rudolf Nureyev would pirouette with envy at the "positions" of some of the soldiers).

In Room 4 hangs one of the *pinacoteca's* greatest possessions: Simone Martini's "Coronation" scene, depicting the brother of Robert of Anjou being crowned King of Naples by the Bishop of Toulouse. In Room 6 linger over the great Masaccio's "Crucifixion," bold in its expression of grief, in spite of a no-neck Christ. Room 7 is the most important—literally filled with the works of Renaissance masters, notably an "Adoration of the Bambino" by Luca Signorelli; a "Madonna and Bambino" by Perugino; a panel by Raphael; a "Madonna and Bambino with Angels" by Botticelli; and—the most beautiful of all—Filippino Lippi's "Annunciation and Saints."

In Room 10 is Raphael's "Holy Family and St. John" and a copy of his celebrated portrait of Pope Leo X. After several salons, look in Room 17 for Andrea Mantegna's "St. Eufemia" and his portrait of Francesco Gonzaga; brother-in-law Giovanni Bellini's "Circumcision" and "Transfiguration"; and Lotto's "Portrait of Bernardo de Rossi" and his "Madonna and Bambino with St. Peter." Room 19 is hung with Titians, with Danaë taking the spotlight from Pope Paul III.

Room 20 is devoted to Flemish art. Pieter Brueghel's "Blind Men" is an outstanding work, and his "Misanthrope" is devilishly powerful. Other foreign works include Hugo van de Goes' "Pietà" and Joos van Cleve's "Adoration of the Magi." In Room 21 climb the stairs for a panoramic view of Naples and the bay, a finer landscape than any you'll see inside. Two choice sketches in Room 23 include Raphael's "Moses" and Michelangelo's "Three Soldiers." In Room 31 you're treated to Velázquez' "Drinkers" and in Room 45 Goya's portraits of Charles IV and his errant queen.

The state apartments downstairs deserve a hurried inspection. Room after room is devoted to gilded mermaids, Venetian sedan chairs, ivory carvings, a porcelain chinoiserie salon (the best of all), tapestries, the Farnese armory (Room 90), and a large glass and china collection.

The museum is open from 9:30 a.m. to 3 p.m. (Sundays till 1 p.m.), and charges 150 lire (17¢) for admission. Closed Mondays.

Minor Attractions

National Museum of San Martino, in the Vomero residential district (bus No. 49 or 42), is magnificently situated on the grounds of the Castel Sant'Elmo. It was founded in the 14th century as a Carthusian monastery, but decayed badly until architects reconstructed it in the 17th century in the Neapolitan baroque style. Now a museum for the City of Naples, it displays stately carriages, historical documents, ship replicas, china and porcelain, silver, Campania paintings of the 19th century, military costumes and armor, and the lavishly adorned crib by Cuciniello. In Room 25 is a balcony that opens onto a fabulous view of Naples and the bay, as well as Vesuvius and Capri. Many come here just to stand on this belvedere in space and drink in the view. The colonnaded cloisters have curious skull sculpture on the inner balustrade. The "Certosa" (Charterhouse) may be visited from 9:30 a.m. to 1 p.m. for a 150-lire (17¢) admission. Closed Mondays.

The **Royal Palace**, at the Piazza Plebiscito, was designed by Domenico Fontana in the 17th century. The eight statues on the facade are of Neapolitan kings. In the heart of the city, the square itself is one of the most architecturally interesting in Naples, with a long colonnade and a church, San Francesco di Paolo, that evokes the style of the Pantheon in Rome. Inside the Palazzo Reale you can visit the royal apartments, lavishly and ornately adorned in the baroque style with colored marble floors, paintings, tapestries, frescoes, antiques and porcelain. Charles de Bourbon, son of Philip IV of Spain, became king of Naples in 1734. A great patron of the arts, he installed a Library in the Royal Palace, one of the greatest of the south, with more than 1,250,000 volumes. The palace may be visited from 9 a.m. to 2 p.m. (Sundays from 9 a.m. to 1 p.m.) for 100-lire (12¢) admission. Closed Mondays.

The **New Castle** (Castelnuovo) at the Piazza del Municipo, was ordered built in the late 13th century by Charles I, king of Naples, as a royal residence for the House of Anjou. Badly ruined, it was later virtually rebuilt in the mid-15th century by the House of Aragon. The castle is distinguished by a trio of three round imposing battle towers at its front. Between two of the towers—guarding the entrance—an Arch of Triumph was designed by Francesco Laurana to honor the expulsion of the Angevins by the forces of Alphonso I in 1442. It has been described by art historians as a masterpiece of the Renaissance. The Palatine Chapel in the center dates from the 14th century, and the City Commission of Naples meets in the Baron's Hall, designed by Segreta of Catalonia. The New Castle may be visited during the day; it charges no admission.

The **Church of Santa Chiara** (Clare), on the palazzi-flanked Via Mariano Semmola, was ordered built by Robert the Wise, king of Naples, in the early 14th century. It became the church for the House of Anjou. Though World War II bombers heavily blasted it, it has been returned somewhat to its original look, in the Gothic style as practiced by Provençal architects. The altar piece by Simone Martini is displayed at the Capodimonte Galleries (see above), leaving the Angevin royal sarcophagi as the principal art treasures, especially the tomb of King Robert himself in back of the main altar. The Cloister of the Order of the Clares was restored by Vaccaro in the 18th century—and is marked by ornate adornment, particularly in the tiles.

Finally, the **Castel dell'Ovo** ("The Castle of the Egg") is a 2,000-year-old fortress overlooking the Gulf of Naples. The site of the castle was important centuries before the birth of Christ, and was fortified by early settlers. In time a major stronghold guarding the bay was erected, and was duly celebrated by Virgil. In one epoch of its long history, it served as a state prison. The view from here is magnificent.

NAPLES AFTER DARK: A sunset walk through **Santa Lucia** and along the waterfront never seems to dim in pleasure, even if you've lived in Naples for 40 years straight. Visitors are also fond of riding around town in one of the *carrozzelle,* horse-drawn wagons. As the sun is setting, you may want to drop in at **Il Gabbiano,** 27 Via Partenope (tel. 411-666), a sophisticated and charming little bar with a glass-fronted facade overlooking the bay. A pre-dinner apéritif, such as a Dubonnet, costs 1,200 lire ($1.39). Beer is 1,000 lire ($1.16). The management promises, in a poem distributed to guests, that you will be left to dream "and perhaps to forget if you have in your heart a pain." If you reserve, you can join one of 30 diners in armchair comfort on the second floor, enjoying hamburger steak at 2,500 lire ($2.90) or entrecôte alla pizzaiola at 2,600 lire ($3.02).

From August 1 till September 30, Tourcar, I Piazza Matteotti (tel. 323-310), will book you on a **"Naples by Night"** tour, leaving at 9 p.m. and costing 6,000 lire ($6.96) per person. You're taken through the streets of the old city, stopping off at excavations which are illuminated at night. Finally, you visit a bar where you're given one drink and can listen to Neapolitan songs—old and new.

Or you can stroll by the glass-enclosed **Galeria Umberto,** off the Via Roma, in the vicinity of the Theater of San Carlo. The 19th-century gallery, which evokes many a memory for a G.I., is still standing today, though a little the worse for wear. It is a kind of social center for Naples. John Horne Burns used it for the title of his novel, *The Gallery,* in which he wrote: "In August 1944, everyone in Naples sooner or later found his way into this place and became like a picture on the wall of the museum." Through it walked Momma, Giulia, even the melancholy Desert Rat. Perhaps you will be a part of the frame as you're viewed sipping your apéritif.

Attending a performance at the **Theater of San Carlo** is to be savored like nectar from the gods. Summer productions are likely to include Puccini's "Madame Butterfly" or Verdi's "Aïda." And if you want to see just the theater, you can visit it during the day (9 a.m. to noon) for a 100-lire admission. The theater was originally built in the baroque style for the Bourbon king, Charles III, using such trappings as marble from Siena and crystal from Bohemia. It had to be rebuilt following an 1816 fire and was largely restored and renewed again after extensive bombings in World War II.

On its nightclub and cabaret circuit, Naples probably offers more sucker joints than any other port along the Mediterranean (American sailors are the major objects of prey). If you're starved for action, you'll find plenty of it—and you're likely to end up paying for it dearly and regretting it (maybe even worse.)

With Naples under our belt, we're ready to tackle the most interesting of the day excursions, beginning with:

2. The Environs

THE PHLAEGREAN FIELDS: One of the bizarre attractions of Southern Italy, the Campi Flegrei, as they are known, form a backdrop for a day's adventure of exploring west of Naples and along its bay. An explosive land of myth and legend, the fiery fields contain a semi-extinct volcano (Solfatara), the cave of the Cumaean Sibyl, Virgil's gateway to the "Infernal Regions," the ruins of thermal baths and amphitheaters built by the Romans, deserted colonies left by the Greeks—and lots more. Strike out along the Via Domiziana, stopping first at:

Solfatara

About 7½ miles west from Naples, in the vicinity of Pozzuoli, the ancient crater of Solfatara hasn't erupted since the final year of the 12th century—but it's been threatening to ever since. Like a fire-spouting dragon, it gives off sulfurous gases and releases scalding vapors through cracks in the earth's surface. In fact, the activity—or inactivity—of Solfatara has been observed for such a long time that the crater's name is used by Webster's dictionary to define any "dormant volcano" emitting vapors. The crater may be visited from 8:30 a.m. to 7 p.m. for a 500-lire (59¢) admission. On summer nights Solfatara is illuminated from 8 to 10:30, but only visitors on the organized night tours may visit it then.

A mile and a half away is:

Pozzuoli

A seaport, Pozzuoli opens onto a gulf of the same name, screened from the Bay of Naples by a promontory. Once the port of Rome, it has been treated unkindly by history, oft the victim of many conquerors who ransacked her. The ruins of an amphitheater, built in the last part of the first century A.D., testify to past greatness. Considered one of the finest surviving examples of the arenas of antiquity, it is particularly distinguished by its "wings"—which, considering their age, are in good condition. The remains can be seen where exotic beasts from Africa were caged before being turned loose in the ring to test their jungle skill against a gladiator. The amphitheater, which may be visited daily (except Monday) from 9 a.m. to two hours before sunset, is said to have entertained 40,000 spectators at the height of its glory. In another part of town, the Temple of Serapis was really the "Macellum," or market square, with some of its ruined pillars projecting up today. It was erected during the reign of the Flavian emperors.

Lago d'Averno

Ten miles west of Naples, near Baia, is a lake occupying an extinct volcanic crater. Known to the ancients as the Gateway to Hades, it was for centuries shrouded in superstition. Its vapors were said to produce illness and even death, and Averno could well have been the source of the expression—"still waters run deep." Fronting the lake are the ruins of what has been known as the Temple of Apollo from the first century A.D. and what was once commonly identified as the Cave of the Cumaean Sibyl. According to legend, the Sibyl is said to have ferried Aeneas, son of Aphrodite, across the lake, where he traced a mysterious spring to its source, the River Styx. In the first century B.C., Agrippa turned it into a harbor for Roman ships by digging out a canal.

Baia

In the days of Imperial Rome, the emperors—everybody from Julius Caesar to Hadrian—came here to frolic in the sun, while enjoying the comforts of their luxurious villas. Nero is said to have murdered his mother, Agrippina, at nearby Bacoli, with its Pool of Mirabilis. (The ancient "Baiae" was named for Baios, helmsman for Ulysses.) Parts of its illustrious past have been dug out. Ruins of scope and dimension were revealed, including both the Temple of Baiae and the Thermal Baths, said to have been among the greatest erected in Italy. You can explore this archaeological district from 9 to 3 daily, except Thursdays, for a 100-lire admission.

Cuma

Ancient Cumae was one of the first outposts of Greek colonization in what is now Italy. Twelve miles west of Naples, it is an abandoned town today, of interest chiefly because it is said to have contained the cave of the legendary Cumaean Sibyl. The cave of the oracle—really a gallery—was dug by the Greeks in the fifth century B.C. and was a sacred spot to them. Beloved by Apollo, the Sibyl is said to have written the *Sibylline Oracles,* a group of books of prophecy purchased—according to tradition—by Tarquin the Proud. You may visit not only the caves, but also the ruins of temples dedicated to Jupiter and Apollo (later converted into Christian churches), from 9 a.m. to one hour before sunset, for a 100-lire admission. On the Via Domitiana, to the east of Cuma, you'll pass the Arco Felice, an arch about 64 feet high, built by the Emperor Domitian in the first century A.D.

HERCULANEUM: The builders of Herculaneum (Ercolano in Italian) were still working to repair the damage caused by a 62 A.D. earthquake when Vesuvius erupted on that fateful August day in 79 A.D. Herculaneum, a much smaller town (about one-fourth the size of Pompeii), didn't start to come to light again until 1709 when Prince Elbeuf launched the unfortunate method of tunneling through it for treasures. The Prince was more intent on profiting from the sale of objets d'art than in uncovering a dead Roman town.

Subsequent excavations have been slow and sporadic. In fact, Herculaneum is not completely dug out today. One of the obstacles has been that the town was buried under a much heavier layer of volcanic mud than was Pompeii under its lava mass. Of course, this formed a greater protection for the buildings buried underneath—many of which were more elaborately constructed than those at Pompeii, as Herculaneum was a seaside resort for patrician families. The complication of having the slum of Resina resting over the yet-to-be excavated district has further impeded progress and caused urban renewal.

Although all the streets and buildings of Herculaneum hold interest, some ruins merit more attention than others. The baths (terme) are divided between those at the forum and those on the outskirts (Terme Suburbane in the vicinity of the more elegant villas). The municipal baths, which segregated the sexes, are larger, but the ones at the edge of town are more lavishly adorned. The Palestra was a kind of sports arena, where games were staged to satisfy the appetites of the spectacle-hungry denizens.

The typical plan for the average town house was to erect it around an uncovered atrium. In some areas, Herculaneum possessed the harbinger of the modern apartment house. Important private homes to seek out include the "House of the Bicentenary," the "House of the Wooden Cabinet," the "House of the Wooden Partition," and the "House of Poseidon (Neptune) and Amphitrite," the latter containing what is perhaps the best known mosaic discovered in the ruins.

The finest example of how the aristocracy lived is provided by a visit to the "Casa dei Cervi," named the House of the Stags because of sculpture found inside. Guides are fond of showing their male clients a statue of a drunken Hercules urinating. The best of the houses are locked and can only be seen by permission of the gatekeepers, who will expect small tips for their services.

The ruins may be visited daily from 9 a.m. to one hour before sunset, for a 150-lire admission. To reach the archaeological zone, take the regular train service from Naples on the Circumvesuviana Railway, a 20-minute ride leaving about every half hour from 387 Corso Garibaldi (or take bus No. 255 from the

Piazza Municipio). Otherwise, it's a 4½ mile drive on the autostrada to Salerno (turn off at Resina).

VESUVIUS: A volcano that has struck terror in Campania, Vesuvius looms menacingly over the Bay of Naples. The date—August 24, 79 A.D.—is well known, for it was then that Vesuvius burst forth and buried Pompeii, Herculaneum, and Stabiae under its mass of lava and volcanic mud. Many fail to realize that Vesuvius has erupted periodically ever since (thousands were killed in 1631), with the last major spouting of lava occurring in this century (it blew off the ring of its crater in 1906).

The approach to Vesuvius is dramatic, with the terrain growing forlorn and foreboding as you near the top. Along the way you'll see villas rising on its slopes and vineyards (the grapes produce an amber-colored wine known as Lacrimae Christi; the citizens of Pompeii enjoyed vino from this mountainside, as excavations revealed). Closer to the summit, the soil becomes the color of puce and an occasional wildflower appears.

Although it may sound like a dubious invitation to some (Vesuvius, after all, is an active volcano!), it is possible to visit the rim—or lips, so to speak—of the crater's mouth. As you look down into its smoldering core, you may recall that Spartacus—in a century before the eruption that buried Pompeii—hid in the hollow of the crater, which was then covered with vines. At the foot of Vesuvius, you can board a chair lift that will take you to the summit. The round-trip ticket is 1,000 lire ($1.16), and you must pay a guide 500 lire (58¢) per person once you reach the top. The chair lift operates year round: from 9 a.m. to 8 p.m., July through mid-September; from 9 to 7 in spring; from 9 to 6 in the autumn; and from 9 to 4, November through March. Though this isn't reported to alarm you, it was in 1944 that the chair lift—immortalized in the Italian song, "Funiculi Funiculà"—was destroyed in an eruption!

To reach Vesuvius from Naples, you can take the Circumvesuviana Railway, or (in summer only) a motor coach service from the Piazza Vittoria, which hooks up with bus connections at Pugliano, transporting visitors to the lower station of the chair lift.

OPLONTI: Excavations begun in 1967 under the modern town of Torre Annunziata, just ten miles north of Pompeii, have revealed an archaeological wonder that may well rival the discoveries of that ancient city. **Oplonti,** buried in the 79 A.D. eruption of Vesuvius which also destroyed Pompeii and Herculaneum, differs from the other cities in that it was strictly a residential community, having no market places or forums. Perhaps the businessmen of Pompeii commuted from Oplonti, or it may even have been a vacation resort center for wealthy Roman patricians.

The most important discovery to date in Oplonti is a magnificent Roman villa, 180 feet square, discovered in almost perfect condition in 1973. Its architecture and wall paintings reflect two distinct periods of Pompeiian styles, indicating that the villa was begun in the first century B.C. One of the most dramatic frescoes is a representation of Hercules in the Garden of the Hesperides. The villa also contains many of the original furnishings, including vases, mirrors, sculpture, and even personal objects such as combs. Although excavations are being hampered because the ancient city lies under a modern town, other villas are even now being uncovered under a government grant which should insure more rapid progress in this archaeological treasure ground.

CASERTA: Fifteen miles north of Naples, in the town of Caserta, is one of the largest and greatest palaces of Italy. The rectangular "Reggia," as it is known, was built in the 18th century for the Bourbon king of Naples, Charles III. The architect was Luigi Vanvitelli, who had dreams of Versailles. The other Bourbon king, Ferdinand IV, son of Charles III, lived here when the palace was completed in 1774. In World War II, the Allies commandeered it for use as a military headquarters, and the Nazi army in Italy surrendered here in the spring of 1945.

You can today visit the baroque State Apartments, with their rich furnishings of the 18th and 19th centuries (some of the present residents, in the grand tradition of the old days at the Louvre, still hang out their laundry). The apartments are open from 9 a.m. to 2 p.m. (admission-free Sundays till 1 p.m.), for a 150-lire (17¢) admission charge. Closed Mondays. The Parco Reale (royal park) is quite spectacular, costing 100 lire (12¢) to visit, but it's best to drive your car through at 150 lire (17¢) as it would take at least half a month to walk through it. Vanvitelli adorned the park with statuary, fountains, and cascading waterfalls. If you're not driving to Caserta, you can take a motor coach leaving about every half hour from the Piazza Umberto in Naples.

A First-Class Hotel

Reggia Palace Hotel, Viale Carlo III (tel. 58500), is a semi-luxurious stopover accommodation off the motorway between Rome and Southern Italy. Only seven miles from Naples, this completely air-conditioned hotel overlooks the famous Reggia di Caserta. It has built-in conveniences and is decorated in a modern Italian idiom, with a flourish of strong primary colors and sleek, yet comfortable, contemporary furnishings. The rooms are compact and tasteful, almost Mondrian in style, with white walls and off-white carpets, plus colorful bed covers and chairs. Each room has its own bath or shower and telephone, as well as a desk and dressing table. A single with a continental breakfast is 8,500 lire ($9.86), increasing to 15,000 lire ($17.40) in a double. On the half-pension plan, one person can stay here for 12,000 lire ($13.92) nightly. Meals are served in a spacious blue and white dining room, or else in the grill room. Drinks usually precede a repast, and they are provided in a womblike American bar, decorated in tones of blue and royal purple. On the grounds are a swimming pool, tennis courts, beauty parlor, record library, sauna, children's garden, and a gymnasium.

READER'S TOURING SUGGESTION (MONTELLA): "Montella is just outside of Naples. One can take a bus, taxi, or train to get there. Montella rests high and clean in lovely green mountains. You'll actually get the feel of what it's like to live as an Italian, in their gentle life style. The **Verteglia Hotel** Via M. Cianciulli (tel. 61-002), is the highest building in the town and affords a view. It's modern and immaculate. There are flowers everywhere. Signor Alfonso Gambone runs the hotel, bar, and restaurant, and his wife, Generosa, supervises the kitchen and does most of the cooking, which is comparable to some of the finest French and Chinese cuisine I have ever eaten. Ask for her veal cutlets or her pizza verdura. Try some of the local cheeses and butters; they are famous all the way to Venice. (That's what brought me here in the first place.) The butter is celebrated and has been for a couple of centuries. In pre-refrigeration days, it was necessary to transport protein for many months at sea without it spoiling. Exporters discovered a natural (no preservatives or chemicals) method—sealing the butter in cheese skins to cut off spoilage. The results, fantastic—a mild nutty tasting butter and you won't believe the cheeses. They are tied and hung, as are the butters, and aged in cellars. They make one of the last good buys in all of Europe, and can be thrown into suitcases and hauled about, or one can just mail home a few head of each. The hotel is just off the Piazza S. Bartoli. Each room has a telephone in it, each has a bath or a shower, and most have a terrace. The roof is for the use of the guests and is terraced. The hotel is frequented mostly by Italians as its low charges suggest.

"The most famous and experienced cheese maker of Montello, in fact, of the whole Neapolitan area, is Mario Carbone. Though he speaks little English, when it comes to the language of the palate, he understands and expresses all. I highly recommend visiting him and his factory" (Ralph DeStefano, Columbus, Ohio).

For our next trip, we head across the Bay of Naples to its largest island.

3. Ischia

Dramatically situated in the bay, Ischia is of volcanic origin. Some of its beaches are radioactive, and its thermal spas claim cures for most anything that ails you—be it "gout, retarded sexual development, or chronic rheumatism."

Called the Green Island or Emerald Island, Ischia is bathed in brilliant light and surrounded by sparkling waters that wash up on many sandy beaches (a popular one: Sant'Angelo). The island is studded with pine groves, and its vineyards produce well-known wines, such as Biancolella. Both a red and a white wine are named after Monte Epomeo, a dead (last eruption: 14th century) volcano that towers over the island (2,590 feet high). From its summit, a spectacular view unfolds before you. Other popular wines include the red and white Ischia, the latter a favorite accompaniment for most fish platters served on the island.

Ischia is fast rising in popularity, as the number of first-class hotels that went up in the 50s and 60s reveal. Many wealthy Italians prefer it to Capri, which they consider overrun by foreigners. Before the 50s, Ischia was secluded and relatively unknown, except for those who wanted a quiet oasis. Henrik Ibsen, for example, finished *Peer Gynt* at a villa near Casamicciola. The remoter points on the island, such as Forio with its fledgling art colony, remain relatively untouched by the invasion. The largest development and concentration of hotels is in the Port of Ischia.

From Naples, the island is reached by ferry boat, hydrofoil, or helicopter. The quickest and easiest way to reach Ischia is to book an aliscafi (hydrofoil) the one-way fare costing 1,800 lire ($2.09) per person. The hydrofoil leaves several times daily.

We'll dock first at:

PORTO D'ISCHIA: This dramatic harbor actually emerged from the crater of a long-dead volcano. Most of the population and the largest number of hotels, as mentioned, are centered here. Connected by a bridge, the Aragonese Castle once guarded the harbor from raids. At the castle lived Vittoria Colonna, the poetess and confidante of Michelangelo, to whom he wrote the celebrated letters. In accommodations, you are offered a good choice.

A First-Class Hotel

Hotel Moresco (tel. 991-122) is like a private hacienda in Old Mexico. You keep expecting Dolores Del Rio at any minute! Opposite the Excelsior, it is set a pace or two outside the center of Punta Molino. It is a private compound behind stone walls, with its gardens reaching to its own beach. Seemingly everything is designed for a whirling social life, with a strong accent on sun-seeking activities. There are tennis courts, a solarium, game rooms, and a Figure 8 swimming pool, with a Japanese bridge across its waist. Everywhere you look in the garden—filled with shady fir trees and semi-tropical plants—are lounge chairs. The hacienda, partially covered by magenta bougainvillea, has deeply set arches and balconies. The rooms are decked out for plush living.

Against a backdrop of Spanish arches, plaster walls, and beamed or vaulted ceilings, is a lavish arrangement of furniture in the Spanish theme, with brightly colored tiled floors, satins, tufted silk sofas, and ladderback chairs. The bedrooms—a total of 63, all with private baths or showers—have highly carved ornamental beds with strongly striped covers, heavy Spanish dressers and chests, and (in most cases) private balconies. Everywhere are large surfaces of vivid color contrasted with pristine white. Open from April 25 to October 12, the hotel in high season charges a peak 20,000 lire ($23.20) in a single, 36,000 lire ($41.76) in a double. The full-pension peaks at 32,000 lire ($37.12) per person.

Medium-Priced Accommodations

La Villarosa (tel. 991-316) is the finest pension in Ischia. Set in a garden of gardenias, banana, eucalyptus, and fig trees, it is like a private villa, charmingly furnished with antiques. The replicas of the past will either amuse or fascinate: a fruitwood spinet piano, a Regency console with a bronze candelabrum, a Victorian tiptop table, a high-backed wing chair, a Gothic love seat in tangerine, a Biedermeier card table. The dining room is in the informal country style, with terra-cotta tiles, lots of French windows, and antique chairs. The meals are a delight, served with a variety of offerings, including the local specialties. And what looks like a carriage house in the garden has been converted into an informal taverna, with more antiques—relaxing, attractive, and ingratiating. Open from April to October, the pension in high season charges 10,000 lire ($11.60) in a single room. Doubles rent for 14,000 lire ($16.24), inclusive. Full pension in summer is 18,000 lire ($20.88), inclusive, per person. The staff is exceptional, selected to maintain the personal atmosphere. The bedrooms are well kept, conveying a homelike flavor.

Floridiana (tel. 991-014) is a stately, low-built villa in the center of town, only a few minutes' walk from the beach. You arrive at its formal entrance with a large open doorway set back in a garden flanked by date palms. From the top peek colorful sun umbrellas used in the secluded rooftop solarium. The terrace in the rear has a good view of the surrounding gardens and the nearby sea and functions as the outdoor living room. The lower level, with tree-shaded walks, is for those nursing sunburns or for just relaxing under lemon trees. Others may prefer the American bar, or the swimming pool. Inside, one little salon is furnished tastefully with Victoriana—quite authentic and charming—though the public lounges rely heavily on plastic and bleached maple. The bedrooms have much in their favor: spaciousness, Nordic modern desks and beds, French doors opening toward private sun decks. The Floridiana is open from April to October, and charges high-season prices from July 1 to September 30. At that time, you'll pay 10,000 lire ($11.60) in a single with bath; 15,000 lire ($17.40) for a double with bath. The full-pension rate is from 14,000 lire ($16.24) to 20,000 lire ($23.20) per person.

Budget Accommodations

Villa Paradiso (tel: 991-501) is the fulfilled dream of Giuseppe Iacono. After a long 20-year pilgrimage to Minneapolis, he purchased this old family villa, and is now accepting paying guests from April to October. The white and green villa has its own garden, with date palms, orange and lemon trees, plus a front veranda and a flagstone terrace surrounded by well-kept flowers. But it is the forthright geniality of the owner that makes a stay here enjoyable—certainly not the decor. His staff prepares abundant meals and serves them in the Moorish dining room, with its three large windows covered with intricate wrought-iron screens. The bedrooms vary in size—some are overly spacious, with comfortable and efficient furnishings. A few have private baths. In high season, Signor Iacono charges 5,500 lire ($6.38) in a bathless single; from 10,000 lire ($11.60) to 12,000 lire ($13.92) in a double room, depending on the plumbing. The full-pension rate ranges from 10,500 lire ($12.18) to 14,000 lire ($16.24) per person. It's a two-minute walk from the beach, where you can rent your own changing cabin, European style, by the day or week.

READER'S HOTEL SELECTION: "Hotel Aragonese, Via G.V. Vico (tel. 99-24-31), was our most delightful find. We reserved a room sight unseen, and it turned out to be a gem. It is run by a big Italian family (the hotel is new), and the cooking is quite good. Our room with complete bath, balcony overlooking the thermal swimming pool (with water warm enough to enjoy a daily swim in early October), and three delicious meals a day was only $28 a day" (Mrs. Frank Haupt, Burkburnett, Texas).

Along the northern coast (frequent bus service) a short ride takes you to:

LACCO AMENO: Jutting up from the water, a rock named Il Fungo (the mushroom) is the landmark natural sight of Lacco Ameno. The spa is the center of the good life (and contains the best hotel accommodations on the entire island). People come from all over the world—either to relax on the beach and be served top-level food, or to take the cure. The radioactive waters at Lacco Ameno have led to the development of a modern spa with extensive facilities for thermal cures—everything from underwater jet massages to mud baths.

First-Class Accommodations

La Reginella (tel. 994-304), sits opposite its more glamorous sister, the Regina Isabella. It shares the same ownership and some of the facilities, but charges lower prices. Built as a large villa with many patios and tropical planting, the hotel is open year-round. The bedrooms—50 in all, each with a private bath or shower—are attractive, with coordinated colors and fabrics and French doors opening onto balconies. Rooms are air-conditioned, for which you must pay 1,200 lire ($1.39) extra. The singles in high season go for 14,600 lire ($16.94), the doubles for 26,100 lire ($30.28), taxes included. And full pension is a maximum 30,000 lire ($34.80) in a single room, 29,500 lire ($34.22) per person in a double room, taxes included. The dining room for al fresco meals has a coved ceiling and vines growing profusely around pillars. The inner dining area is quite pleasant and colorful; the reception lounge is brightened with floral chintz chairs. In the evenings guests seek out the Regina Isabella bar for music and dance. La Reginella guests may use two large thermal water swimming pools—one indoor, one open air—next door.

When Vesuvius erupted in 79 A.D., Pliny the Younger, who later recorded the event, thought the end of the world had come. For our next adventure, we head south from Naples to the scene of the long-ago excitement.

4. Pompeii

The ruined Roman city of Pompeii (Pompei in Italian)—dug out from the inundation of volcanic ashes rained on it by Vesuvius in the year 79 A.D.—has sparked the imagination of the world. At the excavations, the life of 20 centuries ago is vividly experienced.

Numerous myths have surrounded Pompeii—one of which is that a completely intact city was rediscovered. Actually the Pompeians—that is, those who escaped—returned to their city when the ashes had cooled and removed some of the most precious treasures from the thriving resort. They were the forerunners of the later archaeologists. But they left plenty behind to be uncovered at a later date and carted off to museums throughout Europe and America.

After a long medieval sleep, Pompeii was again brought to life in the late 16th century—quite by accident by the architect Domenico Fontana. However, it was in the mid-18th century that large-scale excavations were launched. Somebody once remarked that Pompeii's second tragedy was its rediscovery— that it really should have been left to its slumber for another century or two when it might have been taken care of better. The comment was prompted by the sad state of some of the present ruins and the poor maintenance in general. A UPI story reported: "Weeds have claimed the famous amphitheater, where signs warn that a wall is in danger of collapsing. The elements are destroying valuable frescoes in the patrician houses along Via dell' Abbondanza and in the gladiators' residence." The second major problem is theft. Although some of the finest mosaics, statuary, and frescoes have been removed to museums, much remains. On one of our most recent visits, a statue had been stolen the night before.

In December, 1975, the Italian Senate appropriated about $4.6 million for the protection and preservation of Pompeii.

Despite the hazards, Pompeii is one of the top attractions of Europe. Although the dedicated sightseer can spend hours roaming about Pompeii and spotting such details as propaganda posters for candidates for public office, the more hurried visitor may want to confine his or her look to some of the following most important ruins.

THE SIGHTS: The **House of Vetti,** for example, is the most elegant of the patrician villas, with an Etruscan courtyard, statuary (such as a two-faced Janus), paintings, and a black and red Pompeian dining room frescoed with Cupids. (At the entrance—behind the shutters—is an erotic fertility drawing, occasionally shown to men if no women are looking).

The second important villa, in the vicinity of the Porto Ercolano (Herculaneum Gate), lies outside the walls. Reached by going out the Viale alla Villa dei Misteri, it is the **House of Mysteries.** What makes the villa exceptional— aside from its architectural features—are its remarkable frescoes, depicting scenes associated with the sect of Dionysus (Bacchus), one of the cults that was flourishing in Roman times. These murals are relatively all that remain to reveal these initiation rites. Note in some of the backgrounds the Pompeian red.

In the center of town is the **Forum**—rather small, the heart of Pompeian life, known to bakers, merchants, and the wealthy aristocrats who lived luxuriously in the villas. Parts of the Forum were severely damaged in an earthquake 16 years before the eruption of Vesuvius and had never been repaired when the final destruction came. Three buildings that surround the Forum are the **Basilica** (the largest single structure in the city) and the **Temples of Apollo and Jupiter.** The **Stabian Thermae** (Baths)—where both men and women lounged and relaxed in between games of knucklebones—are in good condition, among the finest to come down to us from antiquity. Here you'll see some skeletons in plaster casts. The **Lupanare** titillates visitors with its so-called pornographic paintings. These frescoes are the source of the fattest tips to guides.

In the **Antiquarium** is a number of objects used in the day-to-day life of the Pompeians, including kitchen utensils, pottery, as well as mosaics and sculpture. Note the cast of a dog caught in the agony of death.

The excavations may be visited daily, except Mondays, from 9 a.m. till one hour before sunset for an admission fee of 150 lire (17¢). At the entrance you can hire a guide at a prescribed rate, which is currently fixed at 5,500 lire ($6.38) for one to two persons, 7,000 lire ($8.12) for three to five persons.

To reach Pompeii from Naples, take the 13½ mile drive on the autostrada to Salerno. If you need public transportation, you can board the Circumvesuviana Railway in Naples, departing every half hour. At the railway station in Pompeii, bus connections take you to the entrance of the excavations. There is an entrance about 50 yards from the railway station at Villa Misteri.

HOTELS IN POMPEII: Accommodations appear to be for earnest archaeologists only. The best of the lot follow, beginning with:

The Medium-Priced Range

Hotel Bristol (tel: 863-1625) is a small, three-story establishment, right in the center of modern Pompeii, opposite the railway station. It's been completely renovated and improved, with a telephone in every room. Bedrooms have balconies opening onto a street with much traffic, and the lobby is a "showroom" of plastic furnishings. But the bedrooms are pleasant; the baths are immaculate and serviceable. Open year-round, the hotel in high season charges 5,600 lire ($6.50) in a single with bath; 9,150 lire ($10.61) in a double, all of which have baths. The dining here is neutral, not bad.

The Budget Range

Motel Villa dei Misteri, Pompei Scavi (tel. 861-3593), is most suitable for motorists. About a mile and a half from the center of town, it offers 33 double rooms with private showers and toilets, renting for 6,000 lire ($6.96) a night. It's really a top-notch bargain. Along with its own little garden, it features both a swimming pool and a place to park your car.

Annunciazione, 83 viale Mazzini (tel. 863-13-24), barely qualifies in this hotel desert, but its rooms are comfortably furnished and kept clean. An older couple are in charge of the precincts, and they are most hospitable, but speak no English. Nevertheless, they seem to understand their foreign guests, anticipating their needs. Only 10 rooms are available, with singles renting for 4,000 lire ($4.64) and doubles for 6,000 lire ($6.96). A continental breakfast at 800 lire is the only meal served.

WHERE TO DINE: The **Ristorante Internazionale,** Via del Foro (tel. 861-0777), lies within the ruins of old Pompeii, near the Baths of the Forum. In fact, many of its dining tables are set out in the shade of a quadrangle of one of the Pompeian villas. An impressive two-part restaurant has been constructed —the main dining room under a skylight and a rustic snack bar where you can order self-service meals at a cost of 2,500 lire ($2.90) to 3,000 lire ($3.48) per meal, plus drink. The outside restaurant in an ancient Palestra has an à la carte menu and is a restful place at which to dine, serving until 7 p.m. (3 p.m. in winter). You might begin with spaghetti Internazionale, then follow with zuppa di pesce, another house specialty.

THE AMALFI COAST AND CAPRI

UNTAMED BEAUTY . . . hairpin curves on the serpentine road . . . jagged coasts with sandy beaches filled with bikini-clad bodies and peppermint-striped cabañas . . . olive groves and grape vines . . . rocky peaks floating in cerulean mists . . . secluded inlets once haunted by pirates . . . the wafting aroma of fragrant lemon blossoms . . . cliff-hanging villas of rich expatriates . . . grottoes sapphire blue and emerald green . . . brilliant, shimmering light adored by painters . . . sunsets beloved by romantics.

English-speaking people use the appellation, "See Naples and Die" for the bay and Vesuvius in the background. The Germans reserve the saying for the Amalfi Drive. A number of motorists do see the Amalfi Coast and die, as the road is dangerous—not designed for its current stream of traffic, such as summer tour buses that almost sideswipe each other to pass. It's hard to concentrate on the road for the sights. That eminent traveler, André Gide, called the drive "so beautiful that nothing more beautiful can be seen on this earth."

Capri and Sorrento have long been known to an international clientele. But the emergence into popularity of the resort-studded Amalfi Drive has been a recent phenomenon. Perhaps it was discovered by German officers, then later by the American and English servicemen (Positano was a British rest camp in the last months of the war). Later, the war over, many returned, often bringing their wives. The little fishing villages in time became front-ranking tourism centers, with hotels and restaurants in all categories, even nightclubs honky-tonking their attractions. Sorrento and Amalfi are in the vanguard, with the widest range of facilities; Positano is moving up in middle-class appeal, though it remains popular with artists; Ravello is still the choice of the discriminating few, such as Gore Vidal, desiring relative seclusion.

Giuseppe Prezzolini once wrote: "The bronzed youths who during the summer are seen wandering around the town and on the beaches deserve special mention for their part in adding a note of interest and appeal to the tourist trade. From many parts of the world, blonde and brunette girls and even some mature women, perhaps teachers who are seeking a romantic interlude from their bookish world, or the bored wealthy, or dissatisfied artists, have come here purposefully to find a Latin lover. Some have found one for a week or a month and some have even found husbands for the rest of their lives."

We'll add nothing to that, except to say that to cap off our Amalfi Coast adventure, we'll leave on a boat from Sorrento heading for Capri, which needs no advance billing. Three sightseeing attractions in this chapter—in addition to the towns and villages themselves—are worthy of a special pilgrimage: the Green Grotto between Amalfi and Positano, the Blue Grotto of Capri, and the Greek temples of the ancient Sybarite-founded city of Paestum, south of Salerno.

Heading down from Naples, we'll stop first at:

1. Sorrento

Borrowing from Greek mythology, the Romans placed the legendary abode of the Sirens—those wicked mermaids who lured seamen to their deaths by their sweet songs—at Surrentum (Sorrento). Ulysses resisted their call by stuffing the ears of his crew with wax and having himself bound to the mast of his ship.

Perched on high cliffs, overlooking the Bays of Naples and Salerno, Sorrento has been sending out its siren call for centuries—luring everybody from Homer to Lord and Lady Astor. It was the birthplace of Torquato Tasso, author of *Jerusalem Delivered*.

The streets in summer tend to be as noisy as a carnival. The hotels on the racing strip, the Corso Italia, need to pass out ear-plug kits when they tuck you in for the night. Hopefully, you'll have a hotel on a cliff-side in Sorrento with a view of the "sea of the sirens." If you want to swim in that sea, you'll find both paths and private elevators taking guests down.

HOTELS IN SORRENTO: In its first and second-class hostelries, Sorrento is superior to almost any resort in the south, offering accommodations in all price ranges.

The First-Class Range

Parco dei Principi, 1 Via Rota (tel. 878-2101), provides the best living in Sorrento, combining an integrated contemporary design with the past. The core of this cliffside establishment is the tastefully decorated 18th-century villa of Prince Leopold of Bourbon Sicily. Milan's distinguished architect, Gio Ponti, conceived the new building, and it is a well-coordinated hotel unit. Both houses are placed in the parkland—acres of semi-tropical trees and flowers, a jungle with avenues of towering palms, acacia, olive, scented lemon, magnolias.

Attention is divided between the view from the cliff of the Bay of Naples and Vesuvius and the swimming pool. The latter is irregularly shaped, designed so as not to disturb the century-old trees. In addition, a private elevator takes swimmers down the cliff to the private beach, festooned with gaily colored cabañas. There is a mooring pier for yachts, motorboats, and for water-skiing. Within the garden are tennis courts, mini-golf, and bowling. The Bourbon villa is the center for special events: concerts, a nightclub, and receptions. Most of the action, however, takes place in the new building, where the architect has used one dominant theme: the blue of the Mediterranean pervades throughout. The public rooms are generous and spacious, utilizing blue and white herring-bone tiled floors, cerulean blue furniture slickly designed. The bedrooms carry out the sky-blue theme, with striped floors, walls of glass leading to private balconies, built-in desks and headboards with accessories. The rooms are air-conditioned (individually controlled) and contain spick and span, well-func-tioning private bathrooms. Open from March 25 to October, the hotel charges 13,000 lire ($15.08) in a single with bath; 28,200 lire ($32.71) in a double with bath, plus service and taxes. The full-pension rate is 32,000 lire ($37.12) per person.

Grand Hotel Excelsior Vittoria, off the Piazza Tasso (tel. 878-1900), clings tenaciously to its faded 19th-century glamor. Surrounded by spacious semi-tropical gardens, with blossoming lemon and orange trees, it is built on the edge of a cliff. Three elevators take bathers down to its own private beach and cabañas, but, if you prefer, there's a large swimming pool. The grounds were designed and planted when grandeur was a prerequisite for a resort hotel. The terrace theme predominates, especially on the waterside where cold drinks are served at sunset while one gazes at Vesuvius across the bay. Inside, the atmosphere is old worldish, especially in the mellowed dining room, sitting festive and formal, with ornate, hand-painted ceilings that are a tangle of clouds, sprays of flowers, and clusters of cherubs. While seated at ivory and cane provincial chairs, you'll be served a top-notch Sorrento cuisine. But it is the panoramic view through the windows that makes dining here memorable.

The bedrooms—124 in all, most with private baths—have their own drama. Some of them come with balconies opening onto the perilous cliffside drop. The rooms have a wide mixture of furnishings, with many old pieces being retained while others are carted off to make way for more up-to-date accoutrements. From April 10 to September 30, the hotel quotes a price of 16,120 lire ($18.70) in a single with bath; 25,240 lire ($29.28) to 35,240 lire ($40.88) for a twin with private bath, inclusive. For full board, 14,500 lire ($16.82) is added to the room rate. The hotel is open year-round, granting a 20% reduction off the room rate in low season.

Hotel Cesare Augusto, Via degli Aranci (tel. 878-2700), is in a garden with orange and lemon trees, set back from the sea, off the Piazza Tasso. It's for those who want the latest in up-to-date amenities and are drawn to a highly polished, slick atmosphere. Its special feature is a rooftop swimming pool and terrace, and its contemporary design is reflected in the airy public lounges with marble tiled floors, the neat little wood-paneled bar, and—the most popular of all—the luncheon room with its wood-slat ceiling, booths and tables in islands of red. The bedrooms—120 in all, each with a private bath—are cool and crisp, almost Japanese-like in their simplicity. Tiled floors, low built-in pieces, win-dows and doors of glass leading to individual balconies, round out the picture. The hotel is open year-round, and charges high-season prices from mid-March till the end of October. At that time, expect to pay 22,000 lire ($25.52) for a double. The full-pension rate is 17,000 lire ($19.72) per person in a double, inclusive.

Hotel Imperial Tramontano, Via Vittorio Veneto (tel. 878-1940), when approached by boat from Naples, seems like an integral part of the high cliff from its imperious position right in the center of town. Built in the villa style, it not only offers rooms with view balconies, but some of its public lounges open onto garden patios. The drawing room, with English and Italian antiques, modifies its spaciousness by its informal treatment of its furnishings. The bar and drinking lounge are spiked with period pieces—many of them mahogany,

Victorian styled. The bedrooms, with their tiled floors, were designed for long stays. Some have arched French doors and balconies where you can have morning coffee. Most of the furnishings are well styled, using both antiques and reproductions. The rooms generally have their own private baths, with a bidet and shower. Rates in high season are 15,500 lire ($17.98) in a single with private bath; 20,000 lire ($23.20) for a double with bath, inclusive. Full pension is 20,000 lire ($23.20) per person, inclusive. In the garden, you can inhale the aroma of sweet-smelling trees and walk down paths of oleanders, hydrangea, acacia, coconut palms, and geraniums.

The Medium-Priced Range

Hotel Bellevue Syrena, Via Marina Grande (tel. 878-1024), is the best of the second-class hotels in Sorrento. Though only a short walk from the central square, it is perched right on the edge of a cliff. It is an 18th-century villa that has been handsomely converted and made ready to receive paying guests. The Fluss brothers prefer to cater to a select clientele instead of the routine tour groups. Most of their public rooms open onto gardens and plant-filled terraces; a private elevator takes guests down to the hotel's private beach. The bedrooms vary considerably in size, as this was originally built as a private home. Consequently, you may get the chamber of the former owner, or a single assigned to the tutor of his son. Open year-round, the hotel in high season charges from 4,500 lire ($5.22) to 6,000 lire ($6.96) in its singles; from 6,500 lire ($7.54) to 10,500 lire ($12.18) for its doubles, inclusive. Demi-pension ranges from 9,000 lire ($10.44) to 12,500 lire ($14.50) per person, inclusive, in high season. It's advisable to reserve in advance, as the hotel attracts a loyal following.

Hotel Minerva, Via del Capo (tel. 878-1011), is our personal favorite. Placed like a bird's nest up on a cliff, away from the town center (but walkable), it is an informal villa spread out along flower and tree-filled terraces. You enter by elevator on the coastal road, and are lifted up to one of the loveliest spots on the Sorrento coast. Over the years the villa has been continually improved, with private baths added to all bedrooms. The rooms have fine old furnishings, each one personally styled, with comfort and dignity. The Minerva is owned by Signora Cacace, an attractive Italian-Danish lady who speaks excellent English.

The well-prepared meals that come from the kitchen are served in the beamed-ceilinged dining room, where deeply set arched windows open onto the view. The inside living room has conversationally grouped, Nordic-styled armchairs, but the magnet is the veranda terrace (guests dine here in summer), with its pergola pillars supporting a bamboo roof. It has an old stone wall, with potted flowers, olive trees, and an outdoor bar where you can order drinks and watch the sun sink over Sorrento. There is also a swimming pool. Open from March 15 to December 31, the Minerva charges 8,500 lire ($9.86) in its single rooms; 15,000 lire ($17.40) for its doubles, inclusive. Half board is 11,000 lire ($12.76) per person. In low season, only breakfast is served.

Hotel Conca Park, Via del Capo (tel. 878-2962), is one of the most modern hotels in Sorrento. Set away from the sea, it creates its own interest with a front-yard swimming pool surrounded by a sun deck and cabañas. The dining room on the ground level seems geared to large travel groups. The lounge has nicely coordinated colors, sea blue and fudge brown, and furnishings tastefully set up for conversation groups. The bedrooms—145 in all, each with a private shower bath—are most complete, with French doors opening onto balconies with a view of the Bay of Naples. Furnishings are in a pristine style, with simple Nordic designs, and rooms are well maintained and comfortable. Open year-round, the hotel in high season charges 8,500 lire ($9.86) for a single; 15,000 lire ($17.40) for a double, including breakfast. Half board is 11,000 lire ($12.76) per person per day. The hotel is easy to find—up a narrow street at the edge of town (Conca), with a few orange trees at the rear of the pool.

Hotel Bristol, Via del Capo (tel. 878-1436), has been built pueblo style on a steep hillside at the edge of town. From every room it's possible to have a view of Vesuvius and the Bay of Naples. In a contemporary vein, the hotel lures with its good sense of decor and spaciousness, and with well-appointed public as well as private rooms. The dining room with its terrace and all-glass facade depends upon the bay and view for its bait. There's an outer sun-shaded terrace for afternoon drinks from the winter-garden bar. A discotheque, "Chez Nino," is near the large panoramic swimming pool. You can go for a game of mini-golf, or take a private descent to a reserved cabin at the beach. The bedrooms are warm and inviting, with bright covers and built-in niceties. Most of them have private baths and balconies. Open year-round, the hotel in high season charges 15,000 lire ($17.40) for full pension per person, reducing that to 8,000 lire ($9.28) per person for just a room and breakfast. Many double rooms are air-conditioned. An added draw is a Finnish sauna, plus a heated swimming pool.

Hotel La Terrazza, Via Luigi del Maio (tel. 878-1640), was someone's dream villa, set in a panoramic position on the edge of a cliff. Managed by Signor Apreda, it is now operated as a hotel and a restaurant (the latter open to non-residents), yet the private gateway and tree-shaded drive are still intact, as are the classic, tile-paved terraces with marble stairs, along with urns and statuary on its balustrade. Unusual tropical plants edge up to the homey red geraniums. The interior rooms are well adapted for use as a hotel—pleasant and colorful, though not especially chic, yet strong on good comfort. There is a lower level dining room, dug out of a cliff, with wide screen windows for the famous view. A winding stairway leads down to the swimming pier lined with parasols and striped cabañas. An intimate bar with rattan furnishings is popular, as are the solarium and the little terraces for drinks at sunset. Most of the bedrooms have either a private bath or shower. Open from March to October 15, the hotel in high season charges a peak 7,000 lire ($8.12) in a single; from 14,000 lire ($16.24) in a double. The full-pension rate is 12,000 lire ($13.92) per person.

The Budget Range

Villa di Sorrento, 6 Piazza Tasso (tel. 878-1068), is a pleasant villa right in the center of town. Romantic architecturally, it attracts with petite wrought-iron balconies, tall green shutters, and vines climbing the facade. The street is noisy, so the rooms in the rear are preferable. The interior has been renewed, and features furniture of the antique style. The rooms have small niceties such as bedside tables and lamps. All the accommodations have private bath or shower, some with terraces. There is an elevator as well. Open year-round, the hotel in high season charges 7,000 lire ($8.12) in its singles, 12,000 lire ($13.92) for its doubles, inclusive.

La Tonnarella, 31 Via del Capo (tel. 878-1153), is an old-fashioned villa at the outskirts of Sorrento, on a cliff-edge projection of garden terraces opening toward the sea. It's a popular place for dining, but welcomes guests who want sea-view rooms as well. The best feature here—apart from economy and the good meals—are the gardens with oleander, lemon, and eucalyptus trees. There is a bathing beach at the foot of the cliff, with elevator service provided. Eleven rooms are offered (doubles only), renting in high season at 7,500 lire ($8.70) with bath or shower, inclusive. Full pension (highly recommended) is 9,500 lire ($11.02) per person. The rooms are simple, but comfortable, and the view magnificent. All is operated by the Gargiulo family, who are proud of their kitchen. Space is provided for car parking.

READERS' HOTEL SELECTION: "**Hotel Garni Désirée,** 31 bis Via Capo (tel. 878-15-63), is a beautiful but cheap accommodation, offering every convenience at modest cost. The charge for a double with breakfast is 9,500 lire ($11.02). Our bedroom, with bath, shower, toilet, and bidet, had a balcony looking out onto a waterfall. Below that was a small beach. The building is in excellent condition. It was obviously a private home turned hotel (no restaurant), and a magnificent home at that. It is at the beginning of the Amalfi Drive, 1.5 kilometers from the center of town. There are good restaurants nearby, which is ideal as only breakfast is served. The tranquil hotel is run by Signor Silvio Gargiulo and his wife who speak English fluently. They are most friendly and helpful. We found March ideal here, with no tourist rush. The orchards were in full bloom, the weather fine" (Athol and Joan Sloman, Sydney, Australia).

DINING IN SORRENTO: Minervetta, Via Capodimonte (tel. 878-1098), is a cliff-hanging place, long considered one of the best restaurants in Sorrento, although many of the hotels offer, in our opinion, far better food. At the edge of town, most of the restaurant is hidden from the coastal road. Its position is winning, with wide and tall windows giving everyone a chance at the view: the Bay of Naples and old Vesuvius. You park your car on the roof and descend several flights to the simple dining room. Most diners begin with the cannelloni à la Minervetta at 750 lire (87¢), following with either grilled fish of the day at 2,000 lire ($2.32) or the fish soup at 3,000 lire ($3.48). The seafood salad at 1,500 lire ($1.74) is also recommendable. Try to have a sunset dinner here. Closed Tuesdays.

The **Villa Pompeiana,** attached to the Bellevue Syrena on the Via Marina Grande, is open to non-residents who enjoy its remarkable location. It's a little Pompeian-styled villa, built in part of Tivoli marble by Lord and Lady Astor, who wanted an ideal place—at the edge of a cliff—to enjoy the sunsets over Sorrento. At the tables set under the wisteria pergola, meals are served in an appetizing atmosphere of classical statues, semi-tropical trees and flowers. Dinners average around 5,000 lire ($5.80) including the cost of service and your beverage. Afternoon teas are also popular. Drinks, too, are served in the small patio of the villa, with its little center fountain and stone cherub. The owners, the Fluss brothers, occasionally offer classical concerts in summer which guests can attend for 600 lire (70¢).

"**O Parrucchiano,**" 73 Corso Italia (tel. 878-1321), offers a pleasant interlude on the busiest street in Sorrento. The pick of the trattorie, it is frequented by those who know they'll receive carefully prepared, handsomely served, economical meals in an attractive setting. The building is like an old taverna, the main dining room with an arched ceiling. On the terrace in the rear you can dine in a garden of trees, rubber plants, and statuary. The tourist menu here costs 3,500 lire ($4.06). Among the à la carte dishes, the classic items of Italian fare stand out, including the gnocchi (semolina dumplings) for 750 lire (87¢); the mixed fish fry from the Bay of Naples, only 1,800 lire ($2.09); and a tender veal cutlet Milanese for 1,400 lire ($1.62). Well recommended.

READER'S RESTAURANT SELECTION: "We wanted to eat an Italian meal in a restaurant under a grove of orange trees, and we found it in the **Ristorante degli Aranci,** 45-47 Via degli Aranci (tel. 878-2433). From the main street of Sorrento, turn left at the traffic lights into Via degli Aranci, walk up the hill and around the bend to the right (on the corner is a good supermarket), and soon you see a sign with an arrow, Ristorante degli Aranci. Walk up the narrow cobbled street and on your right is the restaurant, with white tablecloths under orange trees. We had cannelloni, 850 lire (99¢); mixed salad, 500 lire (58¢); vino rosso, 1,200 lire ($1.39) a full bottle. The menu

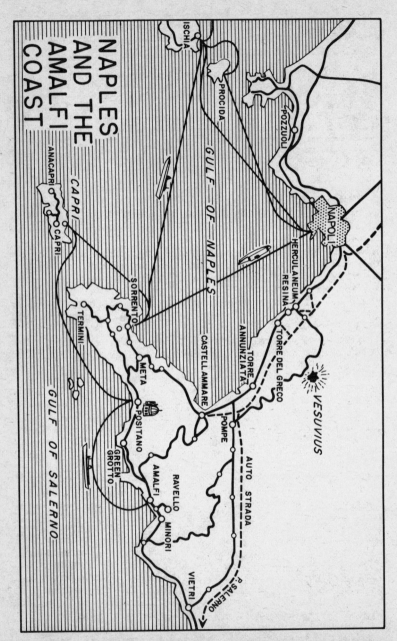

has all the usual veal, chicken, beef, and fish dishes at around 1,500 lire ($1.74). There are no extras, but taxes are included in the tariffs. If you want to save on sweets, buy a gelato from one of the street sellers on the way back. Choose from zabaglione, hazelnut, chocolate, coffee, and more" (Mrs. J. Hawley. St. Ives, New South Wales, Australia).

2. Positano

A hill-scaling, Moorish-styled village—traversed by only one road—on the southern strip of the Amalfi Drive, Positano opens onto the Tyrrhenian Sea with its legendary islands of the sirens. It has jack rabbited along the classic post-war route of many a European resort: a sleeping fishing village that was discovered by painters and writers (Paul Klee, Tennessee Williams), then was taken over by bohemia-sniffing main-drag visitors.

Today, smart boutiques adorn the village, and bikinis add vibrant colors to the mud-gray beach where you're likely to get pebbles in your sand castle. Attractive young people are in ascendancy in summer.

Prices have been rising sharply over the past few years. The 500-lire-a-night rooms—popular with sunset-painting artists—have gone the way of your baby teeth.

The topography of the village, you'll soon discover, is impossible. If you learn to climb the landscape with relative ease, you'll be qualified to hire out as a "scab" during the next donkey sitdown strike.

John Steinbeck once wrote: "Positano bites deep. It is a dream place that isn't quite real when you are there and becomes beckoningly real after you have gone."

Our hotel recommendations follow.

FIRST CLASS: San Pietro, (tel. 875-454), has only a miniature 15th-century chapel, projected out on a high cliff, for identification. A behind-the-scene elevator takes you down to the cliff ledges of what is the chicest resort along the entire Amalfi coast. By changing elevators at the reception lounge, you can descend even further to the swimming and boating cove, where you can sunbathe and enjoy the water in seclusion. The suite-like bedrooms are super glamorous, many containing picture windows beside one's bath tub (there's even a huge sunken Roman bath in one suite). Activities are both in and out of doors here. Bougainvillea is rooted on the terraces, reaching into the ceilings of many of the living rooms. The collection of antiques or reproductions is used lavishly in the living room. A dining room cut into the cliff with room-wide picture windows contains hundreds of arm-length strings of drying cherry tomatoes hanging overhead. San Pietro is the creation of the distinguished Carlo Cinque, who insists on no advertising, no signs, and zealously guards the privacy of each of his guests. Many are often distinguished, including Richard Burton or Laurence Olivier. One of the world's greatest dancers, Léonide Massine, owns an offshore island, and occasionally sails over to dine and spend the night. Naturally, staying here isn't cheap. Full pension costs from 32,000 lire ($37.12) to 40,000 lire ($46.40) per person.

La Sirenuse, 30 Via Colombo (tel. 875-066), offers an atmosphere in which taste reigns supreme. Everything exists for its sophisticated clientele, which includes numerous artists and writers. The owners, Mr. Aldo Sersale and Miss Anna Sersale, have taken this old villa—perched only a few minutes' walk up from the bay—and skillfully added new rooms and installed private baths. From many parts of the country, unusual furnishings were added: fine carved chests, 19th-century paintings and old prints, a spinet piano, upholstered pieces in bold colors, a Victorian settee. A typical touch: the drinking lounge has a polished wooden 16th-century cabinet, removed from an old jewelry shop.

The bedrooms—all with private baths—are infinitely varied, many with terraces overlooking the village. Your iron bed might be high and ornate, painted red, sharing the space with carved chests and refectory tables. Open year-round, the hotel charges high-season prices from April 1 to September 30:

20,000 lire ($23.20) in a single; 35,000 lire ($40.60) for a double, inclusive. Breakfast is included. Full pension is required in high season, for which guests who stay three days are charged 32,000 lire ($37.12) per person daily, inclusive. Meals on one of the three terraces are well served, the chef catering to the "international palate." You can also take a dip in the hotel's heated swimming pool.

MEDIUM-PRICED RANGE: Hotel L'Ancora, Via Colombo (tel. 875-318), is a standout choice in its classification. A hillside villa turned hotel, it basks in the atmosphere of a private club. It's fresh and sunny here, each room like a bird's nest on a cliff. Designed to accommodate the maximum of sun terraces and sheltered loggias for shade, the hotel is a five-minute climb from the beach (longer if you're past 30). Its main lounge has clusters of club chairs, tiled floors, and tear-drop chandeliers. But the bedrooms—catering to couples only—are the stars, with their individualized treatments. Well-chosen antiques, such as fine inlaid desks, are intermixed with more contemporary pieces. The bathrooms—one in each of the 18 rooms—are handsomely tiled and contain bidets, and each room opens onto a private terrace. Open from March to October, the hotel charges high-season prices from April 1 to September 30: 15,000 lire ($17.40) for a double, inclusive. Meals are served on the informal outdoor terrace, under a vine-covered sun shelter. The choice on the menu is excellent, with 14 items available for your first course, about 20 for your second. The full-pension rate in high season is 17,000 lire ($19.72) per person.

Casa Albertina, 4 Via Tavolozza (tel. 875-143), is a villa-styled guest house, reached by climbing a steep and winding road. Perched on the side of a hill, it offers a dramatic view of the coastline. The well-recommended hotel was built by the manager of La Sirenuse, who knows about good design and taste. Each bedroom is a gem: color coordinated in either mauve or blue. The rooms are furnished with well-selected pieces, such as gilt mirrors, fruitwood end tables, bronze bed lamps. Each accommodation has its own private bath, as well as wide French doors leading out to one's own balcony. You can have breakfast on the terra-cotta tiled terrace on your own garden furniture. Open year-round, the hotel charges its highest rates from April 1 to October 1: 8,000 lire ($9.28) in a single, 12,000 lire ($13.92) in a double. Full-pension terms are granted after a stay of three days: from 10,000 lire ($11.60) to 14,000 lire ($16.24) per person.

THE BUDGET RANGE: Hotel Vittoria, Via Fornillo (tel. 875-049), is a villa halfway up the hill, between the village and the waterfront. It has an old-styled gentility to it, with a family-type living room and a dining room and bar adjoining its wide-view terrace. Breakfast trays are set out at al fresco tables. The Vittoria provides good, though basic, living. Its immaculately kept doubles—private baths and comfortable furnishings—rent in high season for 8,500 lire ($9.86); a single room with bath or shower goes for 5,000 lire ($5.80). The food is good, and in season the full-pension rate is an inclusive 11,000 lire ($12.76) per person.

Casa Maresca, Viale Pasitea (tel. 875-140), looks like a gleaming white house in Northern Morocco. But it's a simple little hotel up from the water-front, and offering al fresco dining that lifts it above its second-class government classification. Known and frequented at times by artists and students, it is a good base for those who must keep costs low, yet don't want to compromise in comfort. The bedrooms—19 in all, mainly with private baths and windows opening onto views of the coast—rent in high season for 4,000 lire ($4.64) in a single with bath; 6,000 lire ($6.96) for a double with bath. The full-pension charge (typical Italian fare) ranges in price from 8,000 lire ($9.28). The hosts are Mario Maresca and his English wife, Pauline, who originally came here as a guest.

READER'S HOTEL SELECTION: "Hotel Pensione Italia, 85 Via Pasitea (tel. 875-024), is what a large number of us are looking for in Italy. Proprietor Luigi Montuori and his family run this villa with a fantastic view of the hills and sea. The dining terrace overlooks the sea and green hills. The food is fine Italian, and the joy and warmth you feel in this pension is outstanding. Mama Montuori does all the cooking, and daughter Rosaira is the English-speaking hostess. Rates range from 7,500 lire ($8.70) per person, including all meals, to 8,500 lire ($9.86) per person, depending on the month. It is near the entrance of Positano and has a terrace leading down to the beach" (Shirley Van Campen, Sacramento, Calif.).

DINING IN POSITANO: Buca di Bacco, Via Marina (tel. 875-004), right on the beach, is the top restaurant of Positano. Guests often stop off for a pre-dinner drink in the bar downstairs, then head for the second-floor dining room for their meals. The tone and theme of the "Buca" are set as you enter. On display are various special salads and fruits, including luscious black figs, and freshly peeled oranges in coconut or soaked in caramel. An abundant tray of tempting antipasti is brought to your table on request. An exciting opener is a salad made with fruits of the sea at 2,000 lire ($2.32), though you may prefer the zuppa di cozze (mussels) at 1,600 lire ($1.86), prepared with flair in a tangy sauce. Pasta dishes are priced from 1,000 lire ($1.16) to 2,000 lire ($2.32), and most meat courses run from 1,500 lire ($1.74) to 3,500 lire ($4.06).

3. Amalfi

From the 9th to the 11th centuries, the seafaring republic of Amalfi rivaled those great maritime powers, Genoa and Venice. Its maritime code, the Tavole Amalfitane, was used in the Mediterranean for centuries. But raids by Saracens and a flood in the 14th century devastated the city. Its power and influence weakened, until it rose again in modern times as the major resort on the Amalfi Drive.

From its position at the slope of the steep Lattari hills, it overlooks the Bay of Salerno. The approach to Amalfi is most dramatic, whether you come from Positano (our last stopover) or from Salerno, 15 miles to the east. Today, Amalfi depends almost exclusively on the tourist traffic, and the hotels and pensions in dead center are right in the milling throng of holiday makers. The finest and most highly rated accommodations lie on the outskirts.

THE SIGHTS: Evoking its rich past is **Il Duomo** in the center of town, named in honor of St. Andrew (Sant'Andrea), whose remains are said to be buried inside in the crypt. Reached by climbing steep steps, the cathedral is characterized by its black and white facade and its mosaics. Inside, there is one nave and two aisles, all richly baroqued. The cathedral dates back to the 11th century, though the present structure was rebuilt. Its bronze doors were made in Constantinople, and its campanile (bell tower) dates from the 13th century, erected partially in the Romanesque style. Adjoining the cathedral are the "Cloisters of Paradise," originally a necropolis for members of the Amalfitan "Establishment."

For your most scenic walk in Amalfi, start at the Piazza Duomo, heading up the Via Genova. The classic stroll will take you to the **"Valle dei Mulini,"** the Valley of the Mills, so called because of the paper mills along its rocky reaches. (The seafaring republic is said to have acquainted Italy with the use of paper.) You'll pass by fragrant gardens and scented citrus groves.

And for the biggest attraction of all, head west by car to the:

Emerald Grotto

This ancient cavern—known for its light effects—is a millenniums-old chamber of stalagmites and stalactites. Three miles west of Amalfi, the grotto is reached from the coastal road via a descent by elevator. Then you board a boat which traverses the eerie world of the grotto. The stalagmites—unique in that some are under water—form odd formations. Look for the underwater "crib." From June through September, the grotto is open from 8:30 a.m. to 6 p.m.; from 10 to 4 October to February; and from 9 to 5 from March to May. The charge is 1,000 lire ($1.16) for admission.

HOTELS IN AMALFI: In accommodations, we recommend the following, beginning with:

The First-Class Range

Cappuccini Convento (tel. 871-008) offers a chance to live in a former monastery. Throughout the centuries, various additions were made to the original chapter house, and in the year 1212 all was transformed, with the present still-functioning chapel being renovated and a cloister added. Its position is high above the edge of Amalfi, the sheer rock edges reached by cliff-scaling elevators—one to the garden terraces, the second to the old monastery itself. The monk's walk is a lengthy pergola running along the edge of a mountain, its round pillars supporting trellis work that holds aged purple bougainvillea. A vista of Amalfi and the coastline is spread before you.

Artists, painters, poets, statesmen, royalty—everybody from Theodore Roosevelt to Lady Hamilton to Longfellow to Gladstone—have signed the register. The main dining hall has its original cove ceiling, with dividing pillars. Light refreshments, even breakfast, are served on one of the terraces under a canopy. The bedrooms are converted monk cells—in some cases two have been joined together to provide more elbow room. Thirty-two rooms have private baths, 16 do not. High-season rates are charged from July 1 to September 30. Bathless singles rent for 5,000 lire ($5.80); 7,500 lire ($8.70) with bath. Doubles range from 9,500 lire ($11.02) to 13,000 lire ($15.08), depending on the plumbing. For demi-pension terms, a stay of three days is required: 11,500 lire ($13.34) to 13,500 lire ($15.66) per person. The private beach is reached by the elevators, and the garage charges 1,500 lire ($1.74) for your car, although free parking is available.

Excelsior Grand Hotel (tel. 871-344), outside Amalfi at Palavena, is a modern luxury hotel on the coast. Outdoing the positions of the nearby cliff-hanging monasteries, this extravaganza of avant-garde design is perched high up on a mountain. All of its rooms—about 90 with private baths—are angled toward the breathtaking view. You get the first glimmer of sunrise, the last rays of golden lights. The social center is the 100-foot terrazzo-edged swimming pool filled with filtered mountain spring water. For the lazier, a nearby garden shaded by umbrellas beckons. The hotel structure is unconventional. The core is a high octagonal glass tower rising above the central lobby, with exposed mezzanine lounges and an open staircase leading to the view. Wherever you go, the view is catered to, with softly chic furnishings arranged for sightseeing cultists.

The dining room, with mirrored pillars, ornate blue and white tiled floors, is a dignified place at which to sample the Italian cuisine with Gallic overtones. The bedrooms are individually designed, with plenty of room. The furnishings, chosen with a distinct flair, escape the curse of most hotel rooms. Many good reproductions, some antiques, king-sized beds, strongly colored tiled floors, all contrast with the stark white walls. The private balconies, complete with garden furniture, are the important feature. Open from April 15 to October 15, the hotel charges high-season rates from July 1 to mid-September: 10,000 lire ($11.60) in a single; 20,000 lire ($23.20) in a double. For full pension, you'll pay 20,000 lire ($23.20) to 22,900 lire ($26.56) per person.

For those who want a sea experience, the hotel has a private beach, to which it arranges transportation. Several spots were especially created for a festive stay: notably Bar Del Night, where an orchestra plays for dancing on weekends.

Hotel Luna e Torre Saracena (tel. 871-002) boasts a 13th-century cloister said to have been founded by St. Francis of Assisi. Now converted into a modern hotel, it is operated by the Barbaro brothers, who have aptly dubbed it a sun trap. A free-form swimming pool is nestled down on the rocks close to the sound of the surf and seagulls. The rather formal dining room has a coved ceiling, high-backed chairs, flowering draperies, arched windows opening toward the water, and good food (Italian and international) served in a friendly, efficient manner. The long corridors,—where monks of old used to tread—are now lined with colorful sitting areas and most unmonastic guests. The bedrooms have sea views, and most of them have private baths and terraces, compensating for their slightly dated modern furnishings. Open year-round, the hotel charges its highest prices from April 1 to September 30: from 12,000 lire ($13.92) in a single; 18,000 lire ($20.88) in a double. The full-pension rate is 24,000 lire ($27.84) per person. The hotel also has a nightclub, projecting out toward the sea. A romantic spot for whiling away a few hours in the evening. In summer, an orchestra plays for dancing.

The Medium-Priced Range

Caleidoscopio (tel. 871-220) is built in the villa style, above the town proper on the forward point of the mountainside, in the midst of lemon groves. A hotel minibus provides frequent trips to the town square, but life here is fairly self-contained. The lower terrace is graced with a swimming pool, and the next terrace has garden tables under umbrellas, ideal for breakfast or lunch. The next terrace up houses a spacious, curving dining room, with picture windows on two sides. There has been no skimping in the bedrooms, and all of them provide spaciousness and comfort, with French doors leading out to balconies. Open year-round, the hotel charges high-season prices from June 1 to September 30. At that time, the rate for a bathless single is 6,500 lire ($7.54); 8,000 lire ($9.28) in a single with shower. Doubles range from 11,000 lire ($12.76) to 14,000 lire ($16.24). Full pension costs from 12,000 lire ($13.92) to 13,500 lire ($15.66) per person daily. Aside from the view and the good food, the most enjoyable aspect of the hotel is its terraced gardens, with its old olive trees and scented lemon, the stone steps and paths leading past perfumed gardens. In addition, Caleidoscopio maintains a private beach.

Hotel Belvedere, Conca dei Marini (tel. 871-266), lodged below the coastal road outside Amalfi on the drive to Positano, possesses one of the best swimming pools in the entire area. Hidden from the view and noise of the heavily traveled road, it is in a prime position, thrust out toward the sea. Terraces of rooms and gardens descend to the water. Well-prepared Italian meals are served either inside (where walls of windows allow for views of the coast) or on the wide front terrace, with its white garden furniture. Signor Lucibello, who owns the hotel, sees to it that guests are made content, and provides, among other things, parking space for your car (a bus takes one into Amalfi). All 33 rooms have a freshly kept private bathroom to each well-furnished, but not stylish, bedroom. The facilities are serviceable and comfortable. Open from April to October, the aptly named Belvedere in high season charges 9,600 lire ($11.14) in a single; 17,600 lire ($20.42) for a double, inclusive. Full pension is a peak 20,200 lire ($23.20) per person, inclusive.

Hotel Miramalfi (tel. 871-247), on the western edge of Amalfi, lies below the coastal road and beneath a rocky ledge on its own beach. Family owned, and managed by Mario Mansi, it offers rooms that wrap around the curving contour of the coastline, giving each an unobstructed view of the sea. The stone swimming pier—used for sunbathing, diving, and the boarding of motor launches for water-skiing—is reached by a winding cliffside path, past terraces of grapevines. A space saver is the rooftop car park. The dining room is simple and unadorned, with glass windows and a few semi-tropical plants; the food is good and served in abundant portions. Breakfast is provided on one of the main terraces or on one's own balcony. Each bedroom—44 in all, mainly with private baths or showers—is well-equipped, with built-in headboards, fine beds, cool tiled floors, and efficient maintenance. Open year-round, the hotel in high season charges from 5,800 lire ($6.73) to 8,000 lire ($9.28) in its singles, from 11,130 lire ($12.92) to 15,000 lire ($17.40) for its doubles, the higher rate for rooms with bath. The inclusive charge for full pension ranges from 11,600 lire ($13.46) to 16,000 lire ($18.56) per person. There is a swimming pool and an elevator to the beach.

The Budget Range

Hotel Santa Rosa Ex-Monastero, at Conca dei Marini (tel. 871-214), could still please its monastic occupants of 1600, as nothing has been spoiled, and little has been changed to disturb the tranquility. This well-preserved retreat is perched in the clouds, high up on one of the winding roads out of Amalfi. Built on the edge of a projecting cliff, it offers a breathtaking view of the sea coast below. True, a few bathrooms have been slipped in here and there, but the long corridors—worn down by the sandals of the centuries—are uncarpeted. The cell-like rooms have comfortable beds, a few contemporary pieces of furniture, but on the whole they are severe and uncluttered.

Today, Mr. and Mrs. Enrico Caterina are the warm and gracious hosts. She and her husband inherited the hotel from her father, who once owned one of the greatest hotels in Europe, the San Domenico in Taormina. Open from April to September, the ex-monastery charges 7,500 lire ($8.70) for its singles, 11,500 lire ($13.34) for its doubles, inclusive. The full-pension charge is 14,000 lire ($16.24) per person, inclusive. Meals are prepared in the commodious former nuns' kitchen, equipped with long wooden work tables and a time-worn charcoal stove. On most occasions, dinners are served on the adjoining open terrace, with its stone walls and spectacular view. Natural ingredients are used, as you'll soon discover if you taste one of the moist and delicious homemade cakes. On nippy evenings, guests gather in the little salon, furnished with family-style antiques. The dynamic and friendly Signora Enrico is the catalyst. A very special place for very special people.

Hotel Bellevue (tel. 871-846), opening onto the sea, is ideal for couples (only) who want a modern hotel with all the up-to-date amenities. It is quite small—with only 23 doubles, all with private baths or showers—at the outer edge of Amalfi, offering good views, and right on the road. There is no garden, though other compensations make up for the lack. The bedrooms are cheerful, with fresh paint, tiled floors, and woodgrain contemporary furnishings. All the rooms have generous private terraces and are immaculately kept. Open year-round, the hotel in high season charges an inclusive 8,000 lire ($9.28) for a double room. And full pension is 8,000 lire per person, inclusive.

The Pick of the Pensions

Marina Riviera (tel. 71104), 50 yards from the beach, offers rooms and terraces overlooking the sea. Directly on the coastal road, it rises on terraces against the foot of the hills, with side verandas and balconies. There is a gracious dining room with high-backed provincial chairs, but meals in the open air are preferred. Two adjoining public lounges are traditionally furnished, and a small bar provides drinks whenever you want them. Rooms are simple, good sized (for the most part), and modestly furnished. The price for full pension is 6,500 lire ($7.54) per person daily, including service and I.V.A.

Hotel Zarino, (tel. 871-080) is a little hotel on the sea, run with characteristic Italian flair by Zarino Di Pino. The signor has created his own world. Autographed photos of old-time guests include Vittorio de Sica and Raymond Burr. Signor Di Pino, as head of the local Christian Democrat Party, is also pictured addressing the town populace from the top step of his former pension. For his completely adequate and serviceable rooms, he charges 2,500 lire ($2.90) in a bathless single, with doubles ranging from 3,500 lire ($4.06), inclusive. Full board is 6,400 lire ($7.42) per person in a bathless room, 7,500 lire ($8.70) per person with bath.

DINING IN AMALFI: La Caravella (tel. 871-029) is the best restaurant in Amalfi, and happily it's inexpensive. A grotto-like place, it's off the main street next to the road tunnel, only a minute from the beach. There's no pretense here: guests often dine in their bathing suits. The owner is Signor Di Pino, brother of the owner of Hotel Zarino. You get well-cooked, authentic Italian specialties, such as spaghetti Caravella, with a delicious fruit of the sea sauce, for 800 lire (93¢). Scaloppine alla Caravella is served with a tangy clam sauce for 1,600 lire ($1.86), and a big healthy portion of zuppa di pesce (fish soup) is yours for 2,000 lire ($2.32). You can also have a platter of the mixed fish fry, with crispy, tasty bits of shrimp and squid, for 1,600 lire ($1.86). An order of fresh fruit—served at your table in big bowls—costs 600 lire (70¢) per person. Closed in November.

4. Ravello

Known to personages ranging from Richard Wagner to Greta Garbo, Ravello is the choice spot along the Amalfi Drive. Its reigning celebrity at the moment is Gore Vidal who has purchased a villa in town as a writing retreat. The village seems to hang 1,100 feet between the Tyrrhenian Sea and some celestial orbit. From Amalfi, the sleepy (except for summer tour buses) village is approached by a wickedly curvaceous road cutting through the villa and vine-draped hills that hem in the Valley of the Dragone.

Celebrated in poetry, song, and literature are Ravello's two major attractions:

THE SIGHTS: The **Villa Cimbrone** is reached after a long walk past grape arbors and private villas. After ringing the bell for admission and paying a 300-lire (35¢) fee, you'll be shown into the vaulted cloisters (on the left as you enter). Note the grotesque bas relief. Later, you can stroll (everybody "strolls" in Ravello) through the gardens, past a bronze copy of Donatello's "David." Along the rose-arbored walkway is a tiny, but roofless, chapel. At the far end of the garden is a cliffside view of the Bay of Salerno, unfolding onto an unforgettable panorama that the devout might claim was the spot where Satan took Christ to tempt him with the world.

The **Villa Rufolo,** near the Duomo, was named for its founding patrician family in the 11th century. Once the residence of kings and popes, such as Hadrian IV, it is now remembered chiefly for its connection with Wagner. He composed an act of "Parsifal" here in a setting he dubbed the "Garden of Klingsor." Boccaccio was so moved by the spot he included it as background in one of his tales. Showing a Moorish influence, the architecture evokes the Alhambra at Granada. The large tower was built in what is known as the "Norman-Sicilian" influence. You can walk through the flower gardens leading to look-out points over the memorable coast line. The villa is open from March 1 to May 15, 9 a.m. to 1:30 p.m. and 2:30 to 6 p.m.; May 16 to May 30, 8:30 a.m. to 1:30 p.m. and 2:30 to 7 p.m.; June 1 to August 31, 9 a.m. to 8 p.m.; during September, 9:30 a.m. to 1:30 p.m. and 2:30 to 7 p.m.; during October, 9 a.m. to 1 p.m. and 2 to 6 p.m.; and November 1 to February 28, 9 a.m. to 1 p.m. and 2 to 5 p.m. Admission is 250 lire (29¢).

HOTELS IN RAVELLO: In accommodations, the choices at Ravello are somewhat limited in number, but big on charm.

The Medium-Priced Range

Hotel Palumbo (tel. 872-338) is our favorite elite retreat on the Amalfi coast. A 12th-century palace, it has been favored by the famous ever since Richard Wagner (who did a lot of composing here) persuaded the Swiss owners, the Vuilleumier family, to take in paying guests. To stay here is to understand why Max Reinhardt, Rossano Brazzi, Humphrey Bogart (filming "Beat the Devil"), Henry Wadsworth Longfellow, Edvard Grieg, Ingrid Bergman, Zsa Zsa Gabor, Gina Lollobrigida, and a young John Kennedy and his Jacqueline found its situation in the village ideal. Behind a high gateway wall—draped entirely in brilliant orange bougainvillea—is an entry courtyard, shaded by wide-spreading palm trees and an old well. Opening off the building are several terraces, with a spectacular view of the coast, 1,200 feet below.

The hotel offers gracious living in its series of drawing rooms, furnished informally, often with family antiques. Most of the pleasantly decorated bedrooms have nicely tiled baths and their own terraces. Open year-round, the hotel in high season charges from 9,400 lire ($10.90) to 11,800 lire ($13.69) in a single; from 13,900 lire ($16.12) to 18,000 lire ($20.88) in a double. Full pension goes from 19,800 lire ($22.97) to 21,800 lire ($25.29) per person, plus taxes. Meals show the influence of the Swiss-Italian ownership. Tables are set against windows so diners can enjoy the view. "Fill in" bookings are accepted. The Palumbo also offers its own production of "Episcopio" wine, served on the premises.

Hotel Caruso Belvedere (tel. 871-527) is a spacious, clifftop hotel, built into the 11th-century remains of what was once the d'Afflitto Palace and is now operated as a hotel by the Caruso brothers. It has semi-tropical gardens and a belvedere where the Bay of Salerno is spread before you. From here, you can look down the terraced mountain slopes and see the rows of grapes used to make the justly celebrated "Grand Caruso" wine on the premises. The entire atmosphere is gracious, and the indoor dining room has the original coved ceiling, plus elaborately tiled floors, caned-back chairs; it opens onto a wide terrace where meals are also served under a canopy. The cuisine is special here, especially the soufflés, vanilla or chocolate, light and cloudlike. Naturally, the locally produced wines are served: red, white, or rosé. The bedrooms—26 in all, mainly with private baths, but all with hot and cold running water—have character, some with paneled doors, some with antiques, and some with private terraces. Open year-round, the hotel in high season charges from 8,500 lire ($9.86) to 10,500 lire ($12.18) in a single; from 15,000 lire ($17.40) to 17,500 lire ($20.30) in a double, inclusive. Full pension is from 15,000 lire ($17.40) to 17,500 lire ($20.30) per person, inclusive. You'll never forget the arcaded walks, the Gothic arches, the pots of geraniums, the orange and purple bougainvillea, and the wine press with its large vats.

The Budget Range

Hotel Parsifal (tel. 871-524) is an exquisite little hotel, incorporating portions of the original convent founded in 1288 by Augustinian monks. These monks had an uncanny instinct for picking the best views, the most inspiring situations in which to build their retreats. The cloister, with stone arches and a tiled walk, has a multitude of potted flowers and vines, and the garden spots are the favorite of all, especially the one with a circular reflection pool. Chairs are placed for guests to watch the setting sun and firefly lights illuminating the twisting shore line. Dining is usually preferred on the trellis-covered terrace where bougainvillea and wisteria scents mix with that of lemon blossoms. The living rooms have bright and comfortable furnishings, set chastely against pure white walls. The bedrooms, while small, are tastefully arranged, and good strong colors are utilized (coordinated draperies and bedspreads blend with patterned tiled floors). A variety of accommodations are offered—with or without private bath—and a few rooms have terraces. In high season, the ex-convento charges from 3,500 lire ($4.06) to 6,000 lire ($6.96) for a single; from 6,000 lire ($6.96) to 9,500 lire ($11.02) for a double, inclusive. The full-pension rate ranges from 8,000 lire ($9.28) to 11,500 lire ($13.34) per person, inclusive.

Toro Hotel (tel. 871-520) and the Villa Amore (tel. 871-502) are real bargains—two small and charming villas converted to receive paying guests. The Toro—entered through a garden—lies just off the village square and the cathedral. It has semi-monastic architecture, with deeply set arches, long colonnades, and a tranquil character. The rooms may not have the finest decor—but at these prices, who complains? The owner is especially proud of the meals he serves (the dining room is also available to non-residents). Open year-round, the hotel in high season (April 1 to October 1) charges 3,500 lire ($4.06) for a bathless single, from 6,500 lire ($7.54) to 7,500 lire ($8.70) for a double, depending on the plumbing. The full-pension rate (minimum stay of three days for this price) ranges from 8,000 lire ($9.28) to 9,500 lire ($11.02) per person, inclusive. The Villa Amore charges the same prices. From some of its pleasantly furnished bedroom windows, there is a view of the coastline.

READER'S TOURING SUGGESTION: "Passing up Sorrento, Positano, and Amalfi because they were overrun with tourists, I discovered the little town of Minori, a short drive from Amalfi toward Salerno. It's a charming place, nestled in a cove surrounded by lemon groves, and Ravello on the mountain close by. It has a nice beach, and the hotels are modern, attractive, and reasonable. I stayed at **Hotel Caporal** (tel. 877-168). English is spoken, and they give thoughtful hospitality and excellent service. Mid-season, room with bath and half pension is 4,500 lire ($5.22); without bath, 3,500 lire ($4.06) per person. Tours from Minori go to Pompeii, Vesuvius, Naples, Capri, and other places" (Sarah D. Sands, Philadelphia, Pa.).

5. Salerno

Thirty miles south of Naples, the little seaport of Salerno, capital of its province, appears on the horizon. It became famous throughout the world on September 9, 1943, when Allied armies established a hard-fought-for beach-head and launched the invasion of the mainland of Europe, the beginning of the end of World War II. Most of its waterfront was destroyed in that daring attack by British commandos.

But there remain in the Old Town narrow streets from the Middle Ages and a Norman castle capping the hill in the background. The **Cathedral** is characterized by its 12th-century campanile (bell tower) in the Romanesque style. The bronze door (11th century) was shipped from Constantinople to grace Il Duomo, which was begun by Robert Guiscard. Inside is a remarkable medieval pulpit, held up by a dozen columns, with one decorative mosaic pillar standing aloof. In the crypt is the tomb of St. Matthew, the apostle.

Note: In Salerno, **Alitalia** has an office at 142 Corso Garibaldi (tel. 225-287).

HOTELS IN SALERNO: When stacked against the wonders and the variety of accommodations on the Amalfi Drive, Salerno is a poor sister. But it makes a suitable overnight stopover for motorists bound for Sicily.

Hotel Jolly Delle Palme, Lungomare Trieste (tel. 225-222), is the best in its first-class classification, set apart from the confusion of the heart of the city. It's at the northern tip of a waterside park, with a veranda overlooking the sea and the adjoining public bathing beach. This is a self-conscious modern establishment, totally functional—short on style, big on creature comforts. The bedrooms, however, are pleasantly furnished. Ask for the seaview bedrooms, as freight trains run right under the windows in back. Open year-round, the Jolly chain member charges 8,500 lire ($9.86) in a single with bath; a peak 21,000 lire ($24.36) in a double with bath.

Hotel Fiorenza, 145 Via Trento (tel. 351-160), is a surprising bedroom oasis in a hotel "desert," occupying the lower floors of a pint-sized "skyscraper" on the southern edge of the city. The medium-priced albergo is a cleancut modern establishment—neat and uncluttered, only a few hundred feet from the sea. It's in the contemporary style, with a gleaming glass lobby, especially well designed, with simple burlap draperies in primitive colors. The bedrooms are compact and Nordic designed, with built-in pieces. All the well-maintained rooms have private baths. The hotel charges 7,000 lire ($8.12) for its singles, 12,000 lire ($13.92) for its doubles, inclusive, with a continental breakfast costing an additional 1,200 lire ($1.39).

6. Paestum

Dating back to 600 B.C., the ancient Sybarite city of Paestum (Poseidonia) is about 25 miles south of Salerno. Abandoned for centuries, it fell to ruins. But the remnants of its past, excavated in the mid-18th century, are glorious—the finest heritage left from the Greek colonies that settled in Italy. The roses of Paestum—praised by the ancients—bloom two times yearly, splashing the landscape of the deserted city with a scarlet red, a fit foil for the salmon-colored temples that still stand in the archaeological garden.

The **Basilica** is a Doric temple, dating from the 6th century B.C., the oldest temple from the ruins of the Hellenistic world in Italy. The Basilica is characterized by nine columns fronting it and 18 flanking its sides. The Doric pillars are approximately five feet in diameter. Walls and ceiling, however, have long given way to decay. Animals were sacrificed to gods on the altar.

The **Temple of Neptune** is the most impressive of the Greek ruins at Paestum. It and the Temple of Hephaistos ("Theseum") in Athens remain the best-preserved Greek temples in the world, both dating from around 450 to 420 B.C. In front are six columns, surmounted by an entablature. Fourteen columns line the sides.

The **Temple of Caeres,** from the 6th century B.C., has 34 columns still standing and a large altar for sacrifices to the gods. The temple zone may be visited from 10 a.m. till sunset, for an admission fee of 150 lire. Using the same ticket, you can visit the **Archaeological Museum** across the road from the Caeres Temple. Open from 10 to 4, it displays the metopes removed from the treasury of the Temple of Hera (Juno). New discoveries have revealed hundreds of Greek tombs, which have yielded many Greek paintings. Archaeologists have called the find astonishing. In addition, other tombs excavated were found to contain clay figures, of a strongly impressionistic vein.

WHERE TO DINE: While at Paestum, you may want to take time out for lunch. If so, you'll find the **Nettuno Ristorante** (tel. 843-075) a special place at which to dine. Just at the edge of the ruins, it stands in a meadow, like a country inn or villa. The interior dining room has vines growing around in its arched windows, and from the tables there is a good view of the ruins. The ceilings are beamed, the room divided by three Roman stone arches. Outside, there is a terrace for dining, facing the temples—a marvelous stage for a Greek drama. Under pine trees, hedged in by pink oleander, you can order a complete meal for about 4,000 lire ($4.64), including such a typical selection as spaghetti with tomato sauce, beefsteak or roast chicken, a vegetable or salad, plus dessert. The à la carte suggestions include spaghetti with fillets in tomato sauce for 600 lire (70¢), veal cutlet for 2,000 lire ($2.32), and creme caramel for 500 lire (58¢).

7. Capri

The broiling dog-day July and August sun beating down on Capri illuminates a circus of human drama. The parade of visitors would give Ripley's "Believe It or Not" material for months. In the upper town, a vast snakelike chain of gaudily attired tourists promenades through the narrow quarters (many of the lanes evoking the Casbahs of North Africa).

The tired and retired roué, who often resembles the character ("the witch of Capri") that the late Noël Coward played in Tennessee Williams' screen adaptation, "Boom," casts a disdainful eye at the latest load of "competition": young girls disembarking at the harbor. Chicly dressed women, whose resemblance—however artificial—to Jacqueline Onassis is not coincidental, rush down the gangplank, only to vanish quickly to the sanctuary of their private villas in the hills.

Capri (pronounced Cápri, not Caprí as in the popular song) is an eternal re-enactment of the film, "Darling." That the Greeks called it "the island of the wild boars" provides a sardonic touch today. Before the big season rush is on, or after it's over, Capri is quite a different matter—an island of lush

Mediterranean vegetation (olives, vineyards, flowers), encircled by emerald waters, an oasis in the sun even before the days of that swinger, Tiberius, who moved the seat of the Empire here.

Writers, not only Coward himself, but D. H. Lawrence, have found Capri a haven. Some have written of it, including Axel Munthe *(The Story of San Michele)* and Norman Douglas *(Siren Land)*. The latter title is a reference to Capri's reputation as the "island of the sirens," a temptation to Ulysses.

REACHING THE ISLAND: You can go from Naples by hydrofoil in just 45 minutes. The hydrofoil *(aliscafi)* leaves several times daily (some stop at Sorrento). A one-way trip costs 1,800 lire ($2.09). The least expensive service is run by **Caremar**, Molo Beverello, in Naples. There is no need to have a car in tiny Capri, and they are virtually impossible to drive on the hairpin roads anyway. The island is serviced by funiculars, taxis, and buses.

"On the isle of Capri," your boat will dock at:

MARINA GRANDE: The least attractive of the island's communities, Marina Grande is the port, bustling with the coming and going of hundreds of visitors daily. It has a little sand-cum-pebble beach, on which you're likely to see American sailors—on shore leave from Naples—playing ball, occasionally upsetting a Coca-Cola over mamma and bambino.

If you're just spending the day on Capri, you should leave at once for the island's biggest attraction, the **Blue Grotto,** open from 9 a.m. till one hour before sunset. In summer, boats leave frequently from the harbor at Marina Grande, transporting passengers to the entrance of the grotto for 850 lire (99¢), round trip. Once at the grotto, you'll pay a 150-lire (17¢) entrance fee, plus the extra charge of 800 lire (93¢) for the boat that traverses the water.

You'll have to change boats to go under the low entrance to the cave. The toughened boatmen of Campania are unusually skilled at getting heavier passengers from the big boat into the skimpy craft with a minimum of volcanic spills.

The Blue Grotto is one of the most celebrated natural sights of Campania. Known to the ancients, it was later lost to the world until an artist stumbled upon it in 1826. Inside the caverna, light refraction (the sun's rays entering from an opening under the water) achieves the dramatic Mediterranean cerulean color. The effect is stunning, as thousands testify yearly.

If you wish, you can take a trip around the entire island, passing not only the Blue Grotto, but the Baths of Tiberius, the "Palazzo al Mare" built in the days of the Empire, the Green Grotto (less known), and the much-photographed rocks called the "Faraglioni." The motorboats circle the island in about 1½ hours, the fare costing 1,300 lire ($1.51) per person.

Connecting Marina Grande with Capri (the town) is a frequent-running funicular, charging 200 lire (23¢) for a round trip.

CAPRI: The main town is the center of most of the hotels, restaurants, and elegant shops—and the milling throngs. The heart of the resort is the Piazza Umberto I, like a grand living room. Most of the cafes opening onto the square charge stratospheric prices, so we recommend they be avoided on general principle.

Sightseeing in Capri

One of the most popular walks from the main square is down the Via Vittorio Emanuele, past the deluxe Quisisana, to the **Gardens of Augustus.** The park is the choice spot in Capri for views and relaxation. From this perch, you can see the legendary Faraglioni, the rocks, one inhabited by the "blue lizard." At the top of the park is a belvedere overlooking emerald waters and Marina Piccola. Nearby you can visit **The Certosa,** a Carthusian monastery honoring St. James when it was erected in the 14th century. The monastery is open daily from 9 to 1 and from 3 to sunset, and charges no admission.

Back at the Piazza Umberto I, head up the Via Longano, then the Via Tiberio, all the way to Mount Tiberio. Here you'll find the **Villa Jovis,** the splendid ruins of the celebrated estate from which Tiberius ruled the Empire from 27 to 37 A.D. Actually, the Jovis was one of a dozen villas that the depraved emperor erected on the island. Apparently, Tiberius couldn't sleep, so he wandered from bed to bed. From the ruins there is a view of both the Bay of Salerno and the Bay of Naples, as well as of the island itself. The ruins of the imperial palace may be visited from 9:30 a.m. to 4 p.m., for a 150-lire (17¢) admission fee.

Hotels in Capri

To find your own bed for the night shouldn't be too much of a problem. Capri is not just the exclusive enclave of the wealthy. Good accommodations, varying in style and taste, can be found in all price classifications.

To begin, our deluxe choice is the **Quisisana & Grand Hotel,** Via Came-relle (tel. 837-07-88), the favorite nesting place for a regular international clientele. More spacious than its central position would indicate, its private garden is shut off from the criss-cross tourism outside its front entrance. A large, rather sprawling, but imposing, structure, it offers a total of 130 bed-rooms—from cozy singles to ample suites—opening onto wide arcades with a view of the sea coast. The American bar (which seems appropriate to Berkeley Square, London) is the second most frequented spot on the premises, bowing to the swimming pool on the lower terrace. Under the trained eye of Mr. Roberto Ferraro, the main lounge has been entirely redone, with furnishings in antique gold.

There is a more formal dining room, with an entire wall of glass opening onto the park, but our preferred lunching spot is in the courtyard, where delicious meals are served under a suspended canopy. The head chef is preening proud of his fresh-tasting and attractively displayed fish dishes, as well as his lush fruit and vegetables. The bedrooms, as mentioned, vary greatly—furnished with both traditional and conservatively modern pieces. Open from mid-March to early November, the hotel charges a peak-season rate of 32,500 lire ($37.70) in a single, 48,800 lire ($55.68) in a double. Less expensive singles cost 22,400 lire ($25.98), and the cheapest doubles go for 33,600 lire ($38.98). Of course, you'll pay more for suites.

In the first-class range, the **Hotel Luna,** Giardini di Augusto (tel. 837-7035), is, in many ways, the best hotel on the entire island, worthy of a deluxe rating. On a cliff overlooking the sea and the rocks of Faraglioni, it is also between the Gardens of Augustus and the Carthusian monastery of St. James. The creature comforts of the 20th century have been combined nicely with the past. The furnishings have been chosen with a deep respect for excellent, tasteful reproductions of fine antiques—no jarring moderno here. Architectur-ally, the elaborately tiled designs for the floor set the pace. The atmosphere of the drinking lounge is clublike, and the dining room lures with blue draperies and ladderback chairs.

The bedrooms, a mixture of contemporary Italian pieces and a Victorian decor, are most successful—some incorporating wood and padded headboards and gilt mirrors over the desks, all consistently well styled. Some of the bedrooms have arched recessed private terraces overlooking the recently created garden of flowers and semi-tropical plants. The hotel is open from March 15 to November 10, and charges high-season rates from July through September. The tariff for a double ranges from 20,000 lire ($23.20) to 28,500 lire ($33.06); from 14,000 lire ($16.24) to 18,000 lire ($20.88) in a single. All rooms have handsome private bathrooms.

The medium-priced **Albergo Phoenicia,** 43 Corso Vittorio Emanuele III (tel. 837-0112), takes a deep bow to the past, even though of modern construction. Its lounges, dining room, and bedrooms are furnished with reproductions of provincial furniture. The main living room has brown leather furniture sitting on brown tiles, with overscaled green plants. Deep arches lead to smaller rooms, all with comfortable furniture for relaxing. The dining room has tall, reed-seated chairs set on avocado tiles overlooking a garden in the rear, where meals are served. The rooms, though small, are handsomely furnished and maintained. All the accommodations contain private baths. Singles rent for 8,000 lire ($9.28); doubles, 13,000 lire ($15.08). For full pension, one person pays 11,000 lire ($12.76) to 13,000 lire ($15.08) per day.

Hotel Al Gatto Bianco, 32 Via Vittorio Emanuele (tel. 837-0446), is a self-enclosed private world—a hothouse with no great view, but a friendly and warm atmosphere where good meals and good rooms take precedence. Its large restaurant, boasting "every Italian specialty," draws more clients than do the 44 well-furnished bedrooms, all with private baths. You can eat in the interior dining room, with its coved ceiling and arches, like Old Spain transported, or at one of the outdoor areas, where tables are set out under bamboo roofs. The interior of the "White Cat" is comfortable, in a manner to please the tea-drinking English (plenty of nooks with chintz-covered upholstered chairs and sofas). In fact, it's a flowery chintz paradise. Open from April to the first week of November, the hotel charges a peak 12,000 lire ($13.92) for a single with bath; 22,000 lire ($25.52) for a double with bath.

Hotel Flora, 26 Via Federico Serena (tel. 837-0629), in the more prestigious part of Capri, right on the street with chic boutiques, is a honey. It looks out onto the Monastery of St. James and the sea, and features terraces edged with oleander, bougainvillea, and geraniums. There are several tiled courtyards with garden furniture, pots of tropical flowers, and spots either to sunbathe or be cooled by the sea breezes. The public and the private rooms are a wise blend of the old and new. All of the 14 well-furnished double rooms have private baths. Open year-round, the hotel in high season charges a couple 21,500 lire ($24.94), including breakfast, service, taxes, and air conditioning.

La Vega, 10 Via Occhio Marino (tel. 837-04-81), is a sun-pocket little hotel nestled against the hillside, with a clear view of the sea. Each of the oversized rooms of this four-level building has private balconies overlooking the water. Below the rooms is a verdant garden of flowering bushes, and on the lower ledge is a splendid free-form swimming pool with a grassy border for sunbathing and a little bar for refreshments. Breakfast is served on a terrace surrounded by trees and large potted flowers. Double rooms with bath rent for 23,000 lire ($26.68), plus 9% for tax, though breakfast is included. The rooms have decoratively tiled floors and the beds have wrought-iron headboards.

The budget-priced **Villa Krupp,** Via Matteotti (tel. 837-0362), is a sun-pocket villa-turned-guest house, overlooking the Gardens of Augustus. Surrounded by shady trees, it offers a splendid view of the sea from its lofty terraces. A family-run place, it has the distinct advantage of intimacy—and is far removed from the hackneyed commercial tourist bustle that engulfs far too much of Capri. The front parlor is all glass, opening onto the seaside, with large semi-tropical plants set near Hong Kong chairs, all intermixed with painted Venetian-styled pieces. Your bedroom may be exceptionally large, with a fairly good bathroom. The villa has only 11 bedrooms, available from March 1 to November 15 for 6,000 lire ($6.96) in a single; 11,000 lire ($12.76) for a double. A continental breakfast is the only meal offered. To sum up, a top-notch choice for those desiring a personal, quiet holiday.

Manfredi Pagano, Villa Romana (tel. 771-021), is perhaps the oldest guest villa in Capri, near the town center, just minutes from the luxury boutiques. For many years, it stood vacant. But now it's been acquired by Signora Venere Federico, who runs several other hotels, including La Vega. Open from April 1 to September 30, the villa rises three stories, with tall arched green shutters and wide terraces for al fresco dining. Many of the bedrooms are quite large, with little wrought-iron balconies, though a few contain spacious terraces. The cost, including breakfast, is 13,000 lire ($15.08) in a double without bath, rising to 16,000 lire ($18.56) for two with bath.

READERS' PENSION SELECTION: "Our most outstanding experience was at **Pensione Villa Bianca,** 9 Via Belvedere Cesina (tel. 837-8016). Upon arriving, we were welcomed with open arms by the owner. Our immaculately clean, spacious double room, complete with terrace, bath, and a tiled floor, was 8,000 lire ($9.28) without breakfast. During our four-day stay, the owner could not do enough for us. He bargained with local shop owners and helped us choose the best pathways for delightful walks around Capri and Anacapri. A special treat for us included three indescribable, home-cooked, five-course meals. Try to time your visit with a full moon! It's a knockout" (Jim and Nancy Youngerman, Milwaukee, Wis.). . . . . "The **Pensione Belsito,** 11 Via Matermaria (tel. 837-0969), has a superb location overlooking the town, wide verandas, and crisply painted rooms. It has just been re-conditioned, and charges 8,000 lire ($9.28) for a-double with bathroom. The charming host speaks English. The view is really something" (John Hayward, Aberdeen, South Africa).

Restaurants in Capri

La Capannina, 14 Via Le Botteghe (tel. 770-732), is our favorite restaurant in all of Capri. It's not pretentious, although a host of famous people, ranging from film actresses to dress designers to royalty, patronize it. A trio of inside rooms is decorated in a sophisticated tavern manner, though the main draw in summer is the inner courtyard, with its ferns and hanging vines. At a table covered with a colored cloth, you can select the finest meals on the island. Wine is from vineyards owned by the restaurant. If featured, a fine opener is Sicilian macaroni at 1,000 lire ($1.16). Main-dish specialties include pollo (chicken) alla Capannina, 2,000 lire ($2.32), and scaloppine Capannina, also 2,000 lire. However, the most savory skillet of goodies is the zuppa di pesce (fish soup), garnered from the bay, at 3,000 lire ($3.48).

La Pigna, off the Via Lo Palazzo (tel. 837-0280), a short walk from the bus station, serves the finest meals for the money on the entire island, outside of the hotel dining rooms. A meal here is like attending a garden party in Capri, and this has been true since 1875. The owner, De Martino Giuseppina, loves flowers almost as much as good food. The ambience is one of a greenhouse, with purple petunias, red geraniums, and bougainvillea flourishing in abundance. The food is excellent, regardless of what you select, but try in particular the chicken supreme with mushrooms (the house specialty) for 2,200 lire ($2.55); the tortellini Bolognese for 1,200 lire ($1.39); and the ravioli alla Giuseppina, also 1,200 lire. A mixed salad costs 750 lire (87¢); assorted mouth-melting pastries are the same. A cover charge of 600 lire (70¢) is assessed, and 15% is added to the bill for service. The waiters are courteous and efficient; the atmosphere nostalgic, as guitarists stroll by singing sentimental love ballads. It is open till 2 a.m., serving from March 15 to the end of October.

Valentino, 7 Via Valentino, stands next door to the Gatto Bianco ("The White Cat"). In the boutique district, it is reached by going down a little alleyway. Once you reach the hotel, you climb steps to the right, leading to a little balconied terrace decorated with greenery. The food is well prepared, and the service is excellent. Recommendable is the risotto pescatore, a broth-simmered rice laced with fruits of the sea, 2,500 lire ($2.90). As in most restaurants of Capri, fish is the star. Main dishes at Valentino range from 1,800 lire ($2.09) to 3,000 lire ($3.48). Desserts are fairly routine, priced at 750 lire (87¢).

Faraglioni, 75 Via Camerelle, is a joy. Outside the main part of town, it sits on a little footpath. Strollers walk right through the sidewalk tables. Inside a rustic tavern atmosphere prevails. Our recent opener, riso alla pescatore, fisherman's rice, at 1,600 lire ($1.86), couldn't have been better. Our guest selected the mixed hors d'oeuvres at 1,800 lire ($2.09), and we ended up wishing we had ordered that, too. Fish, of course, is the main dish specialty, priced from 1,500 lire ($1.74) to 3,000 lire ($3.48). But for a change of pace, we recommend chicken Faraglioni, 2,500 lire ($2.90). It's delicious. Desserts average around 700 lire (81¢). Closed in winter.

Ristorante da Tonino Al Grottino, 27 Via Longano (tel. 837-0584), is our pick of the hard-to-find trattorie. Favored by personalities—everybody from Vittorio Gassman, Princess Soraya, Ted Kennedy to Ginger Rogers—it draws a constant stream of hungry diners. To reach it, walk down a narrow alleyway branching off from the Piazza Umberto I to an establishment not unlike a bistro in North Africa. The chef really knows how to rattle his pots and pans. Bowing to the influence of the nearby Neapolitan cuisine, he offers four different dishes of fried mozzarella cheese, any one highly recommended and costing only 800 lire (93¢) each. A big plate of the mixed fish fry from the seas of Campania goes for 1,800 lire ($2.09). The zuppa di cozze (clam soup) is a savory opener for 900 lire ($1.04), as is the ravioli alla Caprese for 800 lire (93¢). Truly succulent is a plate of crayfish in homemade mayonnaise for 1,900 lire ($2.20).

Da Gemma, 6 Via Madre Serafina, has long been a favorite with painters and writers. It's reached from the Piazza Umberto I by going up an arch-covered walkway, reminiscent of Tangier, Morocco. Some tables are arranged for the view. Everything's cozy and atmospheric. The cuisine is provincial, with a heavy reliance on fish dishes. The best beginning is the mussel soup at 1,500 lire ($1.74). Pizzas are also featured, ranging from 750 lire (87¢) to 1,000 lire ($1.16). The best main dish to order is the boiled fish of the day with creamy butter, priced according to weight. Desserts go from 500 lire (58¢) to 750 lire (87¢).

A particular lire watchers' favorite is **Raffaele Buonocore,** 28 Via Roma, a "tavola calda" and "rosticceria" for those on the leanest of budgets with the biggest of appetites. It dishes out precooked food in big pans fresh from the hot little kitchen. It's especially popular with young people who know they can get main meat dishes ranging from 1,700 lire ($1.97) to 2,300 lire ($2.67). Lasagne is 750 lire (87¢); cannelloni, also 750 lire; and fish dishes cost from 1,400 lire ($1.62) to 2,500 lire ($2.90). There is a service counter where you can point politely at the food that intrigues you.

ANACAPRI: Capri is really the upper town of Marina Grande. To see the upper town of Capri, you have to get lost in the clouds at Anacapri—more remote, secluded, and idyllic than the main resort, and reached by a daring 200-lire (23¢) round-trip bus ride, more thrilling than any roller coaster. One visitor once remarked that all autobus drivers to Anacapri "were either good or dead." At one point in its history, Anacapri was connected to its bigger sister only by the "Scala Fenicia," the Phoenician Stairs.

Disembarking at the Piazza della Victoria, you'll find a Caprian Shangri-la, a village of charming dimensions.

To continue your ascent to the top, you then hop aboard a chairlift to **Monte Solaro,** the loftiest citadel on the entire island at its lookout perch of 1,950 feet. The ride takes about 12 minutes and operates daily from 9:30 a.m. to sunset, charging 1,000 lire ($1.16) for a round-trip ticket. At the top, the spectacular panorama of the Bay of Naples is spread before you.

After your descent, you can head out to the **Villa San Michele** on the Via Capodimonte. This was the home of Axel Munthe, the Swedish author (*The Story of San Michele*), physician and friend of Gustav V, King of Sweden, who visited him several times on the island. The *casa* is left as Munthe (who died in 1949) furnished it, harmonious and tasteful. From the rubble and ruins of an imperial villa built underneath by Tiberius, Munthe purchased several bronzes, which are displayed inside. You can walk through the gardens for another in a series of endless panoramas of the island. Tiberius used to sleep out there al fresco and do various other things on hot nights! The villa may be visited from 9 a.m. to 6 p.m. for a 250-lire (29¢) admission fee.

Hotels in Anacapri

For a villa with a room for yourself, here are our recommendations, beginning with the first-class **Europa Palace** (tel. 837-0955). On the slopes of Monte Solaro, the Europa sparkles with moderno, turning its back on the past to embrace the semi luxury of today. Its designer, who had bold ideas, obviously loved wide open spaces, heroic proportions, vivid colors. For example, the lounge comes on strong with a Mediterranean blue ceiling and a gleaming tile floor, plus walls of glass opening onto extensive terraces. That's not all: it is built on three levels and "planted" with banana trees. There's an upper sun-bathing terrace where you can tan with a full view of the sea before you. The dining room, with its coved ceiling and arches, is adorned with tables of burnt orange. Arched windows open onto fir trees—a proper background for the top-level cuisine. The bedrooms are contemporary (some with sitting-room areas), using colors primitively bright. Naturally, every room has up-to-date amenities, such as private bathrooms, telephones, radios, and bedside lamps that look like white snakes jutting out of the wall! Open from April to October, the hotel in high season charges 14,000 lire ($16.24) for a single; from 25,000 lire ($29) double. Full pension is 24,000 lire ($27.84) to 27,000 lire ($31.32) per person inclusive. Most guests seem to make the swimming pool their outdoor living room.

In the medium-price range, there is the **Hotel San Michele di Anacapri** (tel. 837-1427), with its own spacious cliffside gardens and unmarred views. And, it has enough shady or sunny nooks to please everybody. Guests linger long and peacefully in its private and well-manicured gardens, the green trees softened by splashes of color from hydrangea and geraniums. The position of this contemporary, well-appointed hotel is just right: near Axel Munthe's Villa San Michele. The view for diners includes the Bay of Naples and Vesuvius. The lounges are pleasantly furnished in an older, more traditional vein, much like the appearance of a country house in France. The bedrooms carry out the same theme, with a deep curtsy to the past, but also with sufficient examples of today's amenities, such as tiled baths in most rooms, good beds, and plenty of space. Open year-round, the hotel in high season (July 1 to September 30) charges from 9,500 lire ($11.02) to 13,500 lire ($15.66) in a single; from 17,500 lire ($20.30) to 19,500 lire ($22.62) in a double, inclusive. The full-pension rate in high season ranges from 19,000 lire ($22.04) to 22,000 lire ($25.52) per person, inclusive. The same rates are quoted for Easter week. A small, 11-room annex, charging the same prices, handles the overflow. In the evenings, guests gravitate to the Green Lantern nightclub, like a taverna-styled grotto, where a guitarist strums the sentimental tunes of Naples.

The budget-priced **Hotel Bellavista** (tel. 771-463), only a two-minute walk from the main piazza, is an inexpensive modern retreat, saucily placed close to the first-class Caesar Augustus and offering the same panoramic view at much less cost. Ideal for young people, it uses electric, primary colors—a holiday place with authority. Lodged into a mountainside, it has large living and dining rooms as well as terraces opening toward a view of the sea. The breakfast and lunch terrace has garden furniture, a rattan-roofed sun shelter, and the cozy lounge has an elaborately tiled floor and a hooded fireplace on a raised hearth, ideal for nippy nights. The bedrooms are pleasingly contemporary (a few have a bed mezzanine, a sitting area on the lower level, and a private terrace). Bathless singles are 5,500 lire ($6.38), increasing to 7,200 lire ($8.35) with bath. Bathless doubles are 10,000 lire ($11.60), going up to 14,000 lire ($16.24) with bath. Full-pension terms are 14,000 lire per person.

Hotel Loreley (tel. 837-1440) has more to offer than economy: it's a cozy, immaculately kept accommodation, with a homey, genial atmosphere. Opened in 1963, it features an open-air veranda with a bamboo canopy, rattan chairs and, of course, a good view. The rooms overlook lemon-bearing trees that have (depending on the season) either scented blossoms or fruit. The bedrooms are quite large, with unified colors and enough furniture to make for a sitting room. A few of the rooms have private bath and balcony. Open year-round, the hotel charges high-season rates from March to October. For a single with breakfast, the tariff ranges from 5,500 lire ($6.38) to 6,500 lire ($7.54), increasing to 9,500 lire ($11.02) to 11,500 lire ($13.34) in a double, the higher rates for private baths. The hotel is approached through a white iron gate, past a stone wall. It lies off the road, toward the sea, and is surrounded by fig trees and geraniums.

After Anacapri, we descend to:

MARINA PICCOLA: A little fishing village and beach on the south shore, Marina Piccola is reached by walking down the Via Krupp (later you can take an autobus back up the steep hill to Capri). The village opens onto emerald and cerulean waters, with the Faraglioni rocks of the sirens jutting out at the far end of the bay.

Where to Dine

La Canzone del Mare (tel. 837-0589), is a memorable way to spend an afternoon in Marina Piccola. You dine here at a terrace restaurant, then later go for a swim in the luxurious free-form seaside pool. Built on several levels, the dining areas are shaded. This little compound of poshness was created by the legendary Gracie Fields, the English mill girl with the golden voice who became a star. After a full and dynamic career, starring in many films, countless vaudeville shows, and endless radio and television shows, Miss Fields (the wartime sweetheart of the British) fulfilled a goal at the end of her career by finding the loveliest spot she could in the Mediterranean. She opened this exclusive little restaurant and settled back to enjoy the leisurely life. Umberto Izzo manages everything and will welcome you to a meal, which is likely to run in the neighborhood of 6,000 lire ($6.96) to 10,000 lire ($11.60). Seafood dishes are specialties. Open April to October only.

Chapter XIX

SICILY, SARDINIA, AND SOUTHERN ITALY

SICILY, SARDINIA, and Southern Italy are ancient lands of myth and legend. The coastal waters washing up on their shores have carried with them a long parade of adventurers from the East.

The Greeks called Southern Italy and Sicily "Magna Graecia." The Mycenaeans plied their sailing craft into the early settlements of the south and made contact with its people a millennium and a half before the birth of Christ.

Too long neglected by foreign travelers wooed by the art cities of the north, the "boot of Italy," Sicily, and fast-rising Sardinia are today attracting greater and greater traffic.

HEADING SOUTH BY CAR: When you head south today, you won't have the transportation headache that plagued Goethe. The autostrada stretches all the way from Milan to Reggio Calabria, sticking out on the "big toe," the gateway to Sicily.

One day a bridge is supposed to connect Sicily with the mainland, a link that hasn't existed since the island broke away in unrecorded times. The project, it is estimated, would take at least eight years and cost at least a billion dollars. A major problem is that the span is to stretch across the Strait of Messina, a prime earthquake zone.

At present, one way to reach Sicily is to take a ferryboat from Reggio Calabria to Messina, costing only 200 lire (23¢) per passenger. Small cars are transported for 3,000 lire ($3.48) to 4,200 lire ($4.87). (Near Reggio Calabria, incidentally, is a much smaller community, **Scilla,** famous in Homeric legend. Mariners of old, such as Ulysses, crossed the Strait of Messina from here, and faced the double menace of the two monsters, Charybdis and Scylla.)

THE NAPLES TO PALERMO BOAT: One way to reach Palermo is by night ferry from Naples. The ferry leaves Naples at 9:30 p.m., arriving in Palermo the next morning at 6:45. The service is run by **Tirrenia S.A.,** whose offices in Palermo are at 385 Via Roma. A one-way fare is 33,000 lire ($38.28) in first class, 25,000 lire ($29) in second class. A small car is usually transported for 42,000 lire ($48.72). A special reduced price is offered on the return fare as long as you spend at least a week in Sicily.

Alitalia, by the way, flies directly to Palermo from Rome.

SICILY

Volcanic islands . . . skiing on the slopes of active Mount Etna . . . a sirocco from the Libyan deserts . . . horses with plumes and bells pulling gaily painted carts . . . old villas evoking scenes from "The Leopard" . . . the scent of almonds in the air . . . vineyards and citrus groves . . . Greek temples . . . coastal plains . . . classical dramas performed in theaters of antiquity . . . the aromatic fragrance of a glass of marsala after downing the Sicilian dessert, cassata.

Sicily, the largest of Mediterranean islands, is a land of dramatic intensity, like a drama by native son Luigi Pirandello. For centuries, its beauty and charm have attracted the greedy eye of foreigners: the Greeks, Romans, Vandals, Arabs, Normans, Swabians, and the Houses of Bourbon and Aragon.

Luigi Barzini wrote: "Sicily is the schoolroom model of Italy for beginners, with every Italian quality and defect magnified, exasperated and brightly coloured."

Of course, it is the people themselves—bound by tradition and local customs—that provide the greatest interest. But generalizations about the Sicilians may be increasingly difficult in the future, as the winds of change are blowing, especially among the young people. In fact, one young girl in Palermo may have taken a major step in the attainment of equal rights for women. She shocked the island when she refused to marry the cavalier young man who kidnaped and raped her. A thousand years of Sicilian tradition were swept aside! Her assailant got a 13-year prison sentence. (Being a practical people, the Italians usually drop all charges against any man who kidnaps and rapes a woman if the victim marries her assailant.)

The best centers for touring are Palermo, Agrigento, Syracuse, Catania, and Taormina. If you're considering anchoring into Sicily for a holiday, then Taormina occupies the best site, with the finest choice of hotels in all price ranges.

If you stick to the main road that skirts the coast, encircling the island, you'll get to see most of the major sights, veering inland for such gems as the Greek temple at Segesta and the active volcano of Mount Etna. In the Sicilian archipelago, the islands holding most interest for visitors are Lipari, Vulcano, and Stromboli, which can be visited on a day's excursion from Messina.

If you take a night boat from Naples, you'll arrive the next morning at:

1. Palermo

As the ferry boat docks in the Bay of Palermo, and you start spotting the blond, blue-eyed bambini all over the place, don't be surprised. If the fair-haired children don't fit your conception of what a Sicilian should look like, remember that the Normans landed here in 1060—six years before William the Conqueror put in at Hastings—and launched a campaign to wrest control of the island from the Arabs. Both elements were to cross cultures, a manifestation still seen today in Palermo's architecture—a unique style, Norman-Arabic.

The city is the largest port of Sicily, its capital, and the meeting place of a Regional Parliament granted numerous autonomous powers in post-war Italy. Against a backdrop of the citrus-studded Conca d'Oro plain and Monte Pellegrino, it is a city of wide boulevards, old quarters in the legendary Sicilian style (laundry lapping against the wind, smudged-face kids playing in the street), town houses, architecturally harmonious squares, baroque palaces, and modern buildings—many erected as a result of Allied bombings in 1943. Originally Palermo was founded by the Phoenicians, but it has known many conquerors, some of whom established courts of great splendor (Frederick II), others who brought decay (the Angevins).

If you want to combine sightseeing in Palermo with testing out the Sicilian beaches, then take a bus (Nos. 14 or 15) from the Piazza Giulio Cesare. One leaves every 15 minutes, heading for **Mondello,** where the Palermitans go for fun in the sun.

Note: In Palermo, the **Alitalia** offices are at 29 Via Libertá (tel. 584-533).

HOTELS IN PALERMO: Generally you'll find a poor lot, aided by a few fine choices that prove the exception to the rule. Hunt and pick carefully, as many hotels of Palermo are not suitable for the average international wayfarer. But that's not the case at any of the following recommendations.

A Deluxe Choice

Villa Igiea Grand Hotel, 1 Salita Belmonte (tel. 543-744), is a former stately seaside palace. A great old estate, now turned into one of the two top luxury hotels in Sicily, it's at the edge of the city, and is reached through a slumlike area. However, once inside its garden walls, all is happily transformed. Tall palms line the walks, and semi-tropical flowers cascade down the old stone walls. Opening onto the sea is a flagstone-edged, free-form swimming pool, near the ancient pillars of a ruined temple.

The palace itself is formal, with wide front verandas and balconies overlooking the sea. Inside, all is grand and glittering. You dine against a backdrop of paneled walls, ornate ceilings, sparkling chandeliers, and Venetian chairs. Top-quality meals are served by attentive waiters, used to the most fastidious of guests. And dinners are also served on the lushly furnished veranda, close to the flowers, plants, and birds. The lounges are furnished in le grand hotel manner, with antiques. Even the furnishings of the bedrooms appeal to antique collectors, with accommodations varying from sumptuous suites with private terraces and sea views to garden rooms of lesser size and glamor. All 91 rooms have private baths, some evoking Victoria's day. Open year-round, the hotel charges high-season rates from March 1 to November 1: 22,600 lire ($26.22) in a single, 37,950 lire ($44.02) in a double. Full pension ranges from 35,000 lire ($40.60) to 39,000 lire ($45.24) per person. In the evenings guests are drawn to a kind of grotto-like nightclub and bar, where there is a grill.

The First-Class Range

Grand Albergo & Delle Palme, 398 Via Roma (tel. 583-933), has let history and time pass it by, but it is a record of Palermo's former grandeur. Those who enjoy the atmosphere and appurtenances of another era will be happily ensconced here. Built in the heart of the city, in the manner of a grand palace, the hotel can look with pride to its architectural inheritance. There is a marble fountain in the lobby, where diamond-covered ladies must have enjoyed their sparkle! Palm trees, the glass-covered dining room, bronze torchiers, antiques sprinkled throughout, complete the atmosphere. In honor of Richard Wagner, who wrote portions of "Parsifal" here, the management has named the ballroom lobby after his composition. The furnishings of the bedrooms carry out the mellowed old traditional theme, and all of the "chambers" have old-fashioned private baths. Open year-round, the hotel charges from 10,000 lire ($11.60) to 14,000 lire ($16.24) in a single; 16,000 lire ($18.56) to 20,000 lire ($23.20) in a double. The full-pension rate is 23,500 lire ($27.26).

Jolly Hotel del Foro Italico, Foro Italico (tel. 235-842), is a glass and steel structure that provides accommodations in stark moderno. Off a busy boulevard (the Foro Italico facing the Gulf of Palermo), it invites with shafts of pale blue supporting triangular balconies. Try for the bedrooms on the upper floors or at the rear, which are quieter. One of the best of the new hotels (and popular for Sicilian wedding receptions), it offers a contemporary atmosphere, including a swimming pool. The public rooms are efficient, bright colors and serviceable furnishings combined with pieces upholstered in velvet. In the bedrooms, all is well organized, with lots of built-in pieces, private bathrooms, bedside lamps, telephones, and comfortable beds. Open year-round, the hotel boasts 304 bedrooms, making it the largest hostelry in the city. For a single, it charges 16,450 lire ($19.08), increasing to 24,400 lire ($28.30) in a double, breakfast included. On the premises are a restaurant and an American bar. The Jolly also has a garden, plus a wide parking area.

The Medium-Priced Range

Motel Agip, Via della Regione Siciliana (tel. 403-102), does for the second-class range of hotels what the Jolly does for the first: that is, it provides a fresh, modern accommodation for those who want up-to-date amenities. Typical of the Agip chain (owned by a gasoline company), this entry on the Palermo hotel scene offers relatively low prices for excellent comfort and value. It's on a wide boulevard at the edge of the city, which makes it more suitable for motorists. The rooms with private bath are choice—immaculate and compact, with well-planned features, furnished in the traditional motel style, and with good, comfortable beds. Open throughout the year, the 100-room motel charges 8,500 lire ($9.86) in a single with bath, 14,000 lire ($16.24) in a double with bath. There is air conditioning, though on low voltage. On the premises is a modern restaurant, dispensing the usual Italian dishes.

Hotel Ponte, 99 Via Francesco Crispi (tel. 243-621), is a modern building on the main dockside boulevard, one of the best of the second-class hotels near the city center. Its lobby invites with glistening marble floors, large mood-setting murals, deep "comfy" lounge chairs, and a good sense of style. All of the rooms have private baths and contemporary furnishings, and many offer balconies. You'll find numerous details usually associated with first-class hotels, including a bidet and shower in the bath, bedside lamps, and a little sitting room area. The rate in a single is 8,000 lire ($9.28), rising to 13,000 lire ($15.08) in a double. Air conditioning is provided for those nights when the sirocco from Africa blows in. In the dining room you'll be served good, rather abundant, meals.

Hotel Centrale, 327 Corso Vittorio Emanuele (tel. 586-201), in the heart of the city, tries valiantly to create that country estate look inside, with much chintz used in the lounges, plus crystal, even bowls of flowers. Rooms near the street, as in most Palermo hotels, tend to be noisy (and ear plugs are a good bet). In the vicinity of one of the landmarks of the city, the "Quattro Canti," the aptly named Centrale offers fairly good bedrooms, most of which have private baths or showers. The bedrooms, like the lobby, have numerous homey touches—some traditional furnishings, some contemporary. The rate ranges from 4,500 lire ($5.22) to 7,500 lire ($8.70) in a single, from 8,500 lire ($9.86) to 12,000 lire ($13.92) in a double.

Grande Albergo Sole, 291 Corso Vittorio Emanuele (tel. 24-88-89), is a pleasant second-class hotel near the center of town. All rooms—comfortable and fresh-looking—come with telephones, radios, and air conditioning. Singles range from 4,500 lire ($5.22) to 7,500 lire ($8.70); twin-bedded rooms from 8,500 lire ($9.86) to 12,000 lire ($13.92), depending on the plumbing. Pension is from 13,500 lire ($15.66) to 17,100 lire ($19.84) per person. Extras include a television room, day and night restaurants, and a roof garden and terrace for sunbathing.

The Budget Range

Hotel Sausele, 12 Via Vincenzo Errante (tel. 237-524), is a modern little hotel in the neighborhood of the railway station, the best in a rundown area. It's owned and managed by a Swiss-born gentleman, Monsieur Sausele, who has created a friendly and clean establishment in the tradition of his former homeland. Run efficiently, it is a modest, but quite pleasant, albergo. The lounges have been furnished in a homey manner, and the dining room, with natural brick walls, has a country inn look to it. Bedrooms are simple, with contemporary built-ins, most adequate for a good night's rest, and all rooms have hot and cold running water (a few with private baths). Air conditioning is available. The bathless singles go for 4,500 lire ($5.22), the bathless doubles for 7,000 lire ($8.12). The rate in a single with bath is 6,000 lire ($6.96); 9,000 lire ($10.44) for a double with bath, inclusive. Meals are quite good, there is top-notch service, and the pension rate ranges from 10,500 lire ($12.18) to 13,500 lire ($15.66) per person, inclusive.

Moderno Albergo, 276 Via Roma (tel. 588-683), is housed on the upper floor of an old-fashioned building right in the center of the city. There's an elevator to take you to the reception lounge, with its combined desk and bar. All is informal here, compact and cluttered, but warm and friendly. The bedrooms have the simple comforts, such as good beds, hot and cold running water, and telephones. The rate in a bathless single is 3,500 lire ($4.06), increasing to 5,000 lire ($5.80) with bath. A bathless double costs 6,000 lire ($6.96), peaking at 7,500 lire ($8.70) with bath.

RESTAURANTS IN PALERMO: Take your pick, they come in all shapes and sizes, and in all price ranges.

The Top Restaurant

Gourmand's, 37 Via della Libertà (tel. 206-431), is the best restaurant in Palermo for introducing yourself to the rich, aromatic cooking of Sicily. To begin with, try the Sicilian specialty of maccheroni con le sarde. The pièce de résistance of local pastas, it is spaghetti covered with a rich sauce of fresh sardines, bits of fennel tops, pine seeds, and olive oil. Foreigners sometimes have to cultivate a taste for it, but we are most sympathetic to it. Afterward you may want to follow with some of the chef's superb fish dishes, such as scampi. Fish forms one of the mainstays of the Sicilian diet and economy, and the chef at Gourmand's prepares platters with style and flourish. You may also want to sample some of the island's wines, such as one of the varieties of Corvo (the waiter will guide you). And to end your meal, it's traditional to order the wine of Sicily, marsala, a fit accompaniment to dessert. For a complete, well-rounded repast, expect to pay around 7,500 lire ($8.70), plus 18% for service. Closed Sundays and from July 15 to September 30.

The Medium-Priced Range

There are two regional restaurants in Palermo that, frankly, deserve more acclaim than they traditionally receive. Favored is **Al Ficodindia**, 64 Via Emerico Amari (tel. 203-214), translated as "The Inn of the Cactus Fruit." Its decor is typically Sicilian, a rustic tavern setting for the savory viands dispensed here. The table of antipasti is about the best we've encountered in Sicily, each succulent item going for anywhere from 1,000 lire ($1.16) to 1,550 lire ($1.80) for the more expensive produce. On our recent rounds, one diner kept going back for more and more until the waiter pleaded, "But, sir, you should order a main dish." The roast kid (caprettu o furnu) is the chef's specialty, as is a delicious tournedos accompanied by a sauce that contains, among other ingredients, prosciutto. About the cheapest you can get by for is 4,000 lire ($4.64), although your tab could easily run as high as 4,800 lire ($5.57), depending on how many trips you take to the antipasti table.

THE TOP SIGHTS: "The four corners" of the city, the **Quattro Canti di Città,** is in the heart of the old town. At the junction of the Corso Vittorio Emanuele and the Via Maqueda, the ruling Spanish of the 17th century influenced the design of this grandiose baroque square, replete with fountains and statues. From here you can walk to:

Piazza Bellini

This square is the most attractive of the plazas of the old city. In an atmosphere reminiscent of the setting for an operetta, you're likely to hear strolling singers with guitars entertaining pizza eaters. Opening onto it is the Church of Santa Maria dell'Ammiragli (also known as "La Martorana"), erected in 1143 with a Byzantine cupola by an admiral to Roger II. Its decaying, but magnificent, bell tower was built from 1146-1185. Also fronting the square are the Church of San Cataldo, erected in 1160 in the Arab-Byzantine style with a trio of faded pink cupolas, and the Church of Santa Caterina, from the 16th century.

Adjoining the square is the **Piazza Pretoria,** dominated by a fountain designed in Florence in 1554 for a villa, but acquired by Palermo about 20 years later.

A short walk will take you to the:

Cathedral of Palermo

On the Corso Vittorio Emanuele, the cathedral is a curious spectacle where East meets West. It was built in the 12th century on the foundation of an earlier basilica which had been converted by the Arabs into a mosque. The cathedral—much altered over the centuries—was founded by an English archbishop, known as Walter of the Mill. The "porch," built in the 15th century on the southern front in the Gothic style, is an impressive architectural feature. But the cupola, added in the late 18th century, detracts from the overall appearance, and the interior was revamped unsuccessfully at the same time, a glaring incongruity in styles. In the "pantheon" of royal tombs is that of the emperor, Frederick II, in red porphyry under a canopy of marble. The cathedral is open from 9 to noon and from 3 to one hour before sunset.

The other church worthy of note is:

San Giovanni Degli Eremiti

Saint John of the Hermits, on the Via dei Benedettini Bianchi. Perhaps in an atmosphere appropriate for the recluse it honors, this little church with its twin-columned cloisters is one of the most idyllic spots in all of Palermo. A medieval veil hangs heavy in the gardens, especially on a hot summer day as you wander around in its cloisters with their citrus blossoms and flowers. Ordered built by Roger II in 1132, the church happily adheres to its Arabic influence, surmounted by pinkish cupolas, while showing the Norman style as well. San Giovanni is open from 9 to 1 and from 3 p.m. to one hour before sunset in summer (otherwise, 9 to 4).

In the vicinity is the:

Palace of the Normanni

Palace of the Normans, at the Piazza del Parlamento, contains one of the greatest art treasures in Sicily, the **Cappella Palatina** (Palatine Chapel). Erected at the request of Roger II in the 1130s, it is considered the finest example of the Arabic-Norman style of design and building. The effect of the mosaics inside is awe inspiring. Almond-eyed biblical characters from the Byzantine art world—in lush colors—create a panorama of epic pageantry, illustrating such Gospel scenes as the Nativity. The overall picture is further enhanced by inlaid marble and mosaics and pillars made of granite shipped from the east. For a look at still further mosaics, this time in a more secular vein depicting scenes of the hunt, you can visit the Hall of Roger II upstairs, the seat of the Sicilian Parliament. The palace is open from 9 a.m. to 1 p.m. and from 3 to 6.

The two most important national museums follow.

National Gallery of Sicily

The **Palazzo Abbatellis,** on the Via Alloro, houses the National Gallery, with important collections of traditional as well as modern art, including works by local painters of the 15th century. On the ground floor is a particularly good collection of medieval sculpture. In Room 2 is the gallery's second most famous work, the 15th-century fresco, "Triumph of Death," in all its gory magnificence. A horsebackriding skeleton, representing death, tramples his victims under hoof. In Room 4 is Francesco Laurana's slanty-eyed Eleonora d'Aragona, and in Room 5 you'll find seven grotesque "Drôleries" painted on wood. Of the paintings on the second floor, "L'Annunziata" by Antonello da Messina, a portrait of the Madonna with depth and originality, is one of the most celebrated paintings in Italy. The palace, built in the Gothic-Renaissance style, is open from 9 a.m. to 1:30 p.m., except Mondays, and charges 150 lire (17¢) for admission.

National Museum

On the Piazza Olivella, is an ex-convento, one of the greatest archaeological collections in Southern Italy, where the competition's stiff. Many works displayed here were excavated from Selinunte, once one of the major towns in "Magna Graecia" (Greater Greece). See, in particular, the Sala di Selinunte, displaying the celebrated metopes that adorned the classical temples, as well as slabs of bas relief. The gallery also owns important sculpture from the Temple of Himera. The collection of bronzes is exceptional, including the athlete and the stag discovered in the ruins of Pompeii (a Roman copy of a Greek original) and a bronze ram that came from Syracuse, dating from the 4th century B.C. Among the Greek sculpture is "The Pouring Satyr," excavated at Torre del Greco (a Roman copy of a Greek original by Praxiteles). The museum is open daily, except Monday, from 9 a.m. to 2 p.m., and charges 250 lire (29¢) for admission.

The final attraction in the city is the most bizarre of all.

Catacombe Cappuccini

At the Piazza Cappuccini, on the outskirts of Palermo, the catacombs evoke the Horrors of Rue Morgue. The fresco—the Triumph of Death—dims by comparison to the real thing. The catacombs, it was discovered, contained a preservative that helped to mummify dead people. Sicilians, everyone from nobles to maids, were buried here in the 19th century, and it was the custom on Sunday to go and visit Uncle Luigi to see how he was holding together! If he should fall apart, he was wired together again or wrapped in burlap sacking. The last person buried in the catacombs was placed to rest in 1920—a little girl almost lifelike in death. But many Sicilians of the 19th century are in fine shape considering—with eyes, hair, clothing fairly intact (the convent could easily be turned into a museum of costume). Some of the expressions on the faces of the skeletons take the fun out of Halloween. A grotesque ballet! The catacombs may be visited from 9 a.m. to 12:30 p.m. and from 3 to sunset (contribution expected).

A 20-minute drive from Palermo takes visitors to the most important attraction in the environs:

Church of Monreale

The town of Monreale is five miles from Palermo, crawling up Mount Caputo and opening onto the Conca d'Oro plain. If you don't have a car, you can reach it by taking trolleybus No. 8 or 9 from the Piazza Indipendenza in Palermo. The Normans under William II founded a Benedictine monastery at Monreale some time in the 1170s. Near the ruins of that monastery a great cathedral was erected. Typical of the Alhambra at Granada, the relatively drab facade gives little indication of the riches inside.

The interior is virtually covered throughout with shimmering mosaics, illustrating scenes from the Bible, such as the story of Adam and Eve or Noah and the Ark. The art work provides a distinctly original interpretation to the old, rigid Byzantine form of decoration. The mosaics make for an Eastern look despite the Western-style robed Christ reigning over his kingdom. The ceiling is ornate, even gaudy. On the north and west facade of the church are two bronze doors in relief depicting biblical stories. The cloisters should also be visited. Built in 1166, they consist of twin mosaic columns, every other pair an original design (the lava inlay was hauled from the active volcano, Mount Etna). You can visit them from 9 to 1 and from 3 to 6 for a 100-lire admission.

(If you're looking for a room or a good meal at Monreale, you'll find both at **Park Hotel Carrubella,** 1 Corso Umberto (tel. 411-507). This modern cliff-side hotel, about four miles from Palermo, is furnished with some semi-luxurious touches, including main lounge gilt mirrors, sculpture, and marble. Bedrooms are pleasantly decorated, many with balconies affording a view of the Conca d'Oro. All accommodations are equipped with private baths, air conditioning, and telephones. Singles cost from 6,000 lire ($6.96) to 6,500 lire ($7.54); doubles, 10,800 lire ($12.53) to 11,500 lire ($13.34). A meal ordered à la carte averages around 3,000 lire ($3.48) to 4,000 lire ($4.64). Sun terraces with fountains, a TV room, a modest nightclub/ discotheque, a roof garden with view, and free coach service to Palermo and the Mondello Lido (a private beach) form a tempting combination of elements.)

READER'S SIGHTSEEING TIP: "From Palermo we took a side trip to Bagheria, to the east for 20 miles, where the **Villa Palagonia** stands. No one who visits Palermo should fail to see this villa. Built by an eccentric, deformed nobleman at the beginning of the 18th century, it has a garden full of grotesque statuary. Atop the garden wall are stone dwarfs and other freaks, some of them playing musical instruments. One of the rooms in the palace has a ceiling with mirrors, which creates a bizarre illusionistic effect. Anyone with a taste for the strange and grotesque will be intrigued by the Villa Palagonia. Goethe has an interesting passage on this villa in his travel diary" (Dr. Alfred Dorn, Long Island City, New York).

2. Segesta

Now deserted, Segesta (41 miles southwest of Palermo) was the ancient city of the Elymi, a people of mysterious origin, although they have been linked by some to the Trojans. As the major city in the west of Sicily, it was brought into a series of conflicts with the rival power nearby, Selinus (Selinunte). From the sixth through the fifth centuries B.C., there were near constant hostilities. The Athenians came from the east to aid the Segestans in 415 B.C., but the expedition ended in failure forcing the city to turn eventually for help to Hannibal of Carthage.

Twice in the fourth century B.C., it was besieged and conquered, once by Dionysius and again by Agathocles, the latter a particularly brutal victor who tortured, mutilated, or made slaves of most of the citizenry. Recovering eventually, Segesta in time turned on its old (but dubious) ally, Carthage. Like all Greek cities of Sicily, it ultimately fell to the Romans.

Today it is visited by those wishing to see its remarkable Doric temple, dating from the fifth century B.C. Though never completed, it is in an excellent state of preservation (the entablature still remains). The temple was far enough away from the ancient town to have escaped leveling during the "scorched earth" days of the Vandals and Arabs.

From its position on a lonely hill, the Doric temple commands a majestic setting. Although you can scale the hill on foot, you're likely to encounter Sicilian boys trying to hustle you for a donkey ride.

In another spot on Mount Barbaro a theater—built in the Greek style into the rise of the hill—has been excavated. It was erected in the third century B.C.

The Sicilian regional government has approved plans to develop a 350-acre park between the ancient town, the Greek theater, and the sanctuary. An archaeological laboratory will be constructed in the park.

In the car park leading to the temple is a cafe for refreshments.

3. Selinunte

One of the lost cities of ancient Sicily, Selinunte traces its history to the seventh century B.C. when immigrants from Megara Hyblaea (Syracuse) set out to build a new colony. They succeeded, erecting a city of power and prestige adorned with many temples. But that was like calling attention to a good thing. As earlier mentioned, much of Selinunte's fate was tied up with seemingly endless conflicts with the Elymi people of Segesta. Siding with Selinunte's rival, Hannibal virtually leveled the city in 409 B.C. Despite an attempt, the city was never to recover its former glory, and fell into ultimate decay.

Today, it is an archaeological garden, its temples in scattered ruins, the mellowed stone—the color of honey—littering the ground as if an earthquake had struck (as one did in ancient times). From 9 a.m. till one hour before sunset, you can walk through the monumental zone, exploring such relics as the remains of the Acropolis, the heart of old Selinunte. Parts of it have been partially excavated and reconstructed, as much as is possible with the bits and fragments remaining.

The temples, in varying states of preservation, are designated by alphabetical lettering. Temple E, in the Doric style, contains fragments of an inner temple. Standing on its ruins before the sun goes down, you can look out across the water that washes up again on the shores of Africa, from which the Carthaginian fleet emerged to destroy the city. The temples are dedicated to such mythological figures as Apollo and Hera (Juno). Most of them date from the sixth and fifth centuries B.C. Temple G, in scattered ruins, was one of the largest erected in Sicily, and was built in the Doric style.

On the southern coast of Sicily, Selinunte lies 76 miles below Palermo, or 70 miles west of Agrigento.

4. Agrigento

Greek colonists from Gela (Caltanissetta) named it Akragas when they established a beachhead here in the sixth century B.C. In time, their settlement grew to become one of the most prosperous cities in Magna Graecia (Greater Greece). A great deal of that growth is attributed to the despot, Phalaris, who ruled from 571 to 555 B.C. and is said to have roasted his victims inside a brazen bull, eventually meeting the same fate himself.

Empedocles, the Greek philosopher and politician (also credited by some as the founder of medicine in Italy) was the most famous son of Akragas, born around 490 B.C. He formulated the four elements theory (earth, fire, water, and air), modified by the agents, love and strife. In modern times, the town produced Luigi Pirandello, the playwright (*Six Characters in Search of an Author*), who won the Nobel Prize in 1934.

Like nearby Selinunte, the city was attacked by war-waging Carthaginians, the first assault in 406 B.C. In the third century B.C., the Carthaginians and Romans played Russian roulette with the city until it finally succumbed to Roman domination by 210 B.C. The city was then known as Agrigentum.

The modern part of the present town (in 1927 the name was changed from Girgenti to Agrigento) occupies a hill site. The narrow streets—Casbah-like—date back to the influence of the conquering Saracens. Heavy Allied bombing in World War II necessitated much rebuilding.

Note: The **Alitalia General Sales Agent** is at 10 Piazza Roma (tel. 29217 or 25949).

Below the town stretch the long reaches of "La Valle dei Templi," containing some of the greatest Greek ruins in the world.

THE VALLEY OF THE TEMPLES: Writers are fond of suggesting that Greek ruins be viewed either at dawn or sunset. Indeed, their mysterious aura is heightened then. But for details you can search them out under the bright cobalt blue Sicilian sky. The backdrop for the temples is idyllic, especially in spring when the striking almond trees blossom into pink. Riding out the Strada Panoramica, you'll first approach (on your left):

The **Temple of Juno** (Giunone): With many of its Doric columns restored, this temple was erected sometime in the mid-fifth century B.C., at the peak of a construction boom that skipped across the celestial globe honoring the deities. As you climb the blocks, note the remains of a cistern, as well as a sacrificial altar in front. There are good views of the entire valley from the perch here.

The **Temple of Concord,** next, ranks along with the Temple of Hephaistos (the "Theseum") in Athens as the best preserved Greek temple in the world. Flanked by 13 columns on its side, along with six in front and six in back, the temple was built in the peripteral hexastyle. You'll see the clearest example in Sicily of what an inner temple was like. In the late sixth century A.D., the pagan structure was transformed into a Christian church, which may have saved it for posterity, although today it has been stripped down to its classical purity.

The **Temple of Hercules** is the most ancient, dating from the sixth century B.C. Badly ruined (only eight pillars are standing) it once ranked in size with the Temple of Zeus. At one time the temple sheltered a celebrated statue of Hercules. The infamous Gaius Verres, the Roman magistrate who became an especially bad governor of Sicily, attempted to steal the image as part of his temple-looting tear on the island.

The **Temple of Jupiter** (Zeus) was the largest in the valley, similar in some respects to the Temple of Apollo at Selinunte. In front of the structure was a large altar. The giant on the ground was one of several telamones (atlases) used to support the edifice.

The so-called **Temple of Dioscuri,** with four Doric columns intact, is a "pasticcio"—that is, it is composed of fragments from different buildings. At various times it has been designated as a temple honoring Castor and Pollux, the twin sons of Leda and deities of seafarers; or Demeter (Ceres), the goddess of marriage and of the fertile earth, and Persephone, the daughter of Zeus who became the symbol of spring.

The temples can usually be visited from 9 a.m. till one hour before sunset.

The **National Archaeological Museum** stands near the Church of Saint Nicholas, on Contrada S. Nicola, and is open generally from 9 to 1, charging no admission. It is closed on Mondays. Its single most important exhibit is a head of the god, Telamon, from the Temple of Jupiter. The collection of Greek vases is also impressive. Many of the artifacts on display were dug up when Agrigento was excavated.

HOTELS IN AGRIGENTO: Only a fair lot is offered, but they are compensatingly inexpensive, the best choices falling in the medium-priced range:

Jolly Hotel dei Templi, Viallagio Mosè SS 115 (tel. 25725), is the best of the new establishments, rated "first class A." It's a completely modern structure, boasting a swimming pool, in the Valley of the Temples, with excellent views of the ruins. Accommodations are air conditioned and contain balconies. In a double with bath, the rate is from 13,800 lire ($16.01) to 17,200 lire ($19.95). A single with bath costs from 8,400 lire ($21.34) to 10,400 lire ($12.06). Some three-bedded rooms are available at 24,000 lire ($27.84). The well-furnished lodgings come complete with radio and television as well. On the premises are a bar and an international restaurant.

Hotel Jolly, 1 Piazzale Roma (tel. 29-190) is a completely modern structure in the center of town on a busy thoroughfare (again, those trusty ear plugs would be nice). It is neat, compact, and self-contained in this hotel wilderness where style, even comfort, is at a premium. The rooms—52 in all, mainly with private baths or showers—are furnished with "blond" contemporary pieces, acceptably serviceable. The charge for a bathless double is from 8,300 lire ($9.63) to 10,300 lire ($11.95); 12,000 lire ($13.92) to 15,100 lire ($17.52) with bath. The singles range from 4,200 lire ($4.87) to 9,500 lire ($11.02). On the premises is a restaurant.

Hotel Della Valle, Via dei Templi (tel. 26-966), is a bandbox, 88-bedroom hotel, between the town and the temples, most suitable for an overnight stopover. A good designer was employed to coordinate the layout, the structural lines, and the furnishings. The beige marble floor of the lounge, the gold velour furnishings, the blue ceiling and draperies give a sense of style. Even the drinking lounge, with its American bar, has neat wood paneling and comfortable sofas and armchairs. Sicilian meals are served against a pleasantly contemporary background. The mood is restful in the simple bedrooms—all with air conditioning, private baths or showers—which feature parquet floors, stark white walls, classic colored draperies, and modern headboards with zebra grain. The singles go for 7,950 lire ($9.22), the doubles for 13,300 lire ($15.43). The exterior, incidentally, is misleading, somewhat like a Y.M.C.A.

Villa Belvedere, 20 Via S. Vito (tel. 20051), has a bouquet of reasons to recommend it. First, its position is good, built on the Rock of Athena, with views of the temples and the African sea. In addition, on the premises is an international library with a collection of Greek coins and vases, plus minerals, wild flowers, and butterflies of Sicily. Adjoining the villa is a Roman garden with subtropical and Sicilian flora, as well as an astronomical instrument. The rooms are simply, though pleasantly, furnished. Bathless singles rent for 3,600 lire ($4.18), increasing to 8,000 lire ($9.28) in a double with bath.

Fifty-four miles south from Catania you'll find:

5. Syracuse (Siracusa)

Of all the Greek cities of antiquity that flourished on the coast of Sicily, Siracusa was the most important, a formidable competitor of Athens in the West. In the heyday of its power, it dared take on Carthage, even Rome. At one time, its wealth and size were so great as to be unmatched by any other city in Europe.

On a site on the Ionian Sea, colonizers from Corinth founded the city about 735 B.C. Much of its history was to be linked to the despots, beginning in 485 B.C. with Gelon, the "tyrant" of Gela who subdued the Carthaginians at Himera. Siracusa came under attack from Athens in 415 B.C., but the main Athenian fleet was destroyed and the soldiers on the mainland captured.

Dionysius I was one of the greatest despots, reigning over the city at the time of its particular glory in the fourth century B.C., when it extended its influence as a sea power. But in 212 B.C., the city fell to the Romans who, under Marcellus, sacked it of its riches and art. Incidentally, in this rape Siracusa lost its most famous son: the Greek physicist and mathematician, Archimedes, who was slain in his study.

Note: In Syracuse, **Alitalia** has offices at 88 Corso Matteotti (tel. 20-055).

THE SIGHTS: West of the modern town (take the Viale Rizzo) is the archaeological garden, peppered with the most important sightseeing attractions, beginning with the:

Greek Theater

On Temenite Hill, this was one of the great theaters of the classical period. Hewn from rocks during the reign of Hieron I in the fifth century B.C., the ancient seats have been largely eaten away by time. You can, however, still stand on the remnants of the stone stage where plays by Euripides were presented. In the time of Hieron II in the third century B.C.—a "term" that lasted through a golden jubilee—the theater was much restored. In spring the Italian Institute of Ancient Drama presents classical plays, works by Euripides, Aeschylus. and Sophocles. In other words, the show hasn't changed in 2.000 years.

Roman Amphitheater

This was erected at the time of Augustus. It ranks among the top five amphitheaters left by the Romans in Italy. Like the Greek theater, part of it was carved from rock. Unlike the Greek theater and its classical plays, the Roman amphitheater tended toward more "gutsy" fare. Gladiators—prisoners of war and exotic blacks from Africa—faced each other with tridents and daggers, or naked slaves would be whipped into the center of a to-the-death battle between wild beasts. Either way the victim lost. If his combatant—man or beast—didn't do him in, the crowd would often scream for the ringmaster to slice his throat. The amphitheater is near the entrance to the park, but it can also be viewed in its entirety from a belvedere on the panoramic road.

Latomia Del Paradiso

The most famous of the ancient quarries, this was one of four or five "latomies" from which stones were hauled to erect the great monuments of Siracusa in her day of glory. On seeing one of the caves, Michelangelo de Caravaggio is reputed to have dubbed it, "The Ear of Dionysius," because of its unusual shape like that of a human ear. But what an ear! Nearly 200 feet long. You can enter the inner chamber of the grotto where the tearing of paper sounds like a gun shot. It is said that the despot Dionysius used to force his prisoners into the "ear" at night, where he was able to hear every word they said. But this story—widely reported—is dismissed by some scholars as fanciful. Nearby is the "Grotta dei Cordari," where ropemakers plied their ancient craft. The profession is still demonstrated today, but only for the benefit of visitors.

The archaeological park, charging 100 lire for admission, is open from 9 a.m. to 1 p.m. and from 4 to 8 p.m. in summer (closes at sunset in winter). Not in the monumental park, but nearby, are the:

Catacombs of St. John (Giovanni)

These honeycombed tunnels upon tunnels of empty coffers evoke the catacombs along the Appian Way in Rome. The early Christian burial grounds may be visited from 9 a.m. to noon and from 2 p.m. till sunset for an admission of 100 lire. The world down below is approached from the Chiesa di S. Giovanni, from the third century A. D., though the present building is of a much later date. The crypt of St. Marcianus lies under what was reportedly the first cathedral erected in Sicily. The catacombs are at the end of the Viale S. Giovanni.

Latomia Di Cappuccini

At the Piazza Cappuccini, this is the second most important stone quarry from Ancient Siracusa. Recently converted into a "grotto" garden, it is believed that this may have been one of the quarries that quartered the poor wretches from Athens who lost the battle on sea and land against the troops of Siracusa and were taken as prisoners. The "jail," from which there was no escape, was particularly horrid, as the defeated soldiers weren't given food and were packed together like cattle and allowed to die slowly. But all is lovely and tranquil today, with peacocks prancing by. The Latomia keeps the same hours as the archaeological park, and charges 50 lire for admission.

THE ISLAND OF ORTYGIA:

Its beauties praised by Pindar, the island—reached by crossing the Ponte Nuova—was the heart of Siracusa, having been founded by the Greek colonists from Corinth. In Greek mythology, it is said to have been ruled by Calypso, the daughter of Atlas, the sea nymph who detained Ulysses (Odysseus) for seven years on the island.

Heading out the Foro Italico, you'll come to the **Fountain of Arethusa,** also famous in mythology. Alpheius, the river god, son of Oceanus, is said to have fallen in love with the sea nymph, Arethusa. The nymph turned into this spring or fountain, but Alpheius became a river and "mingled" with his love. According to legend, the spring ran red when bulls were sacrificed at Olympus.

Also on the island are two other worthy attractions:

The **National Archaeological Museum,** at 14 Piazza del Duomo, surveys the Greek, Roman and Early Christian epochs in sculpture and fragments of archaeological remains. Of the statues, the best known (special room on the ground floor) is the headless Venus Anadyomene, dating from the Hellenic period in the second century B.C. The museum is open from 9 to 1 and from 3:30 to 6, and charges 100 lire for admission; Sundays, open only from 9 to 1.

Also at the Piazza del Duomo, the **Cathedral of Syracuse,** with a baroque facade, was built over the ruins of the Temple of Minerva, and employs the same Doric columns. The temple was erected after Gelon the tyrant defeated the Carthaginians at Himera in the fifth century B.C. The Christians converted it into a basilica in the seventh century A.D.

HOTELS IN SYRACUSE: The supply is limited, but most adequate and generally inexpensive.

The First-Class Range

Hotel Park, 22/B Via Falisto (tel. 32-789), is the preferred choice in Syracuse for those wanting a completely modern hotel with up-to-date amenities. We prefer it to the Jolly, which is in the center of the city on a noisy street. It provides a most serviceable refueling stop between trips of exploration through the Greek ruins. The atmosphere is rather impersonal, but all is immaculately maintained (and those comfortable beds). The bedrooms themselves—104 in all, each one with private bath or shower—are spacious, kept shiny and clean (some have pleasant view balconies opening toward the sea). Singles go for 8,500 lire ($9.86); doubles for 13,500 lire ($15.66); full-pension terms are quoted at 13,000 lire ($15.08) per person. The meals are in the typically Italian style, quite good, far superior to some of the restaurants inside the town, which are often unfortunate experiences. And finally, the Park is in a quiet residential section of Syracuse.

The Medium-Priced Range

Hotel Bellavista, 4 Via Diodoro Siculo (tel. 36-912), is trying hard to become modern. It's hidden away on a lane in a quiet residential section, surrounded by flowering trees and vines. Family owned and run, the hotel has an annex in the garden for overflow guests. The main lounge has a sense of space, with black leather chairs and large, semi-tropical plants. The bedrooms are informal and most comfortable, often furnished with traditional pieces. Most of the rooms have their own sea-view balconies, and a number of them have either private baths or showers. The rate for a single room ranges from 6,500 lire ($7.54) to 7,500 lire ($8.70); for a double, 11,000 lire ($12.76) to 13,000 lire ($15.08). The full-pension rate ranges from 14,500 lire ($16.82) to 15,500 lire ($17.98) per person daily.

Panorama, 33 Via Necropoli Grotticelle (tel. 92-122), near the entrance to the city, on a rise of Temenite Hill, is a bandbox modern, 51-bedroom hotel, built on a busy street, about five minutes from the Greek Theater or Roman Amphitheater. It is not a motel, but does provide parking space. Inside, a most contemporary accommodation, with Nordic-styled furnishings, awaits you. The bedrooms are pleasant, and completely up-to-date with comfortable but utilitarian pieces. All of the rooms have either a private bath or shower, with singles going for 7,400 lire ($8.58), doubles for 10,500 lire ($12.18). On the premises is a hotel dining room, serving good meals with competent service. The full-pension charge is 12,500 lire ($14.50) per person.

The Budget Range

Riviera, 9 Via Eucleida (tel. 28-240), is a good choice for those who prefer a decidedly informal place at which to stay. The villa-turned-hotel stands on a blind street, opening toward the sea. Family run, it is "Operation Bootstrap," with the savings and earnings earmarked for renovations and decoration. At the heart of it all is the vitality of the rather exuberant Sicilians. A terrace pool with a diving board is being built for swimmers. The bedrooms are furnished with modern pieces—totally spotless and comfortable. Depending on the plumbing, singles range in price from 3,600 lire ($4.18) to 5,000 lire ($5.80); doubles from 6,000 lire ($6.96) to 7,200 lire ($8.35). There's an elevator, and the lounges face the sea.

Neapolis, 14 Via Carlo Forlanini (tel. 31-853), is a basic little modern hotel out near the temple ruins, in the vicinity of the Hotel Panorama. It provides a most adequate and inexpensive accommodation in any one of its 21 rooms, a great many of which have private baths. Furnished in Italian moderno, the hotel is in a fairly quiet residential area, and offers clean rooms and comfortable beds. Rates in a single range from 3,600 lire ($4.18) to 4,800 lire ($5.57); in a double with private bath or shower, the price is 7,200 lire ($8.35). Family-style meals are served—generous portions, good cooking—at the full pension charge of 7,500 lire ($8.70) to 8,500 lire ($9.86) per person daily.

READER'S HOTEL SELECTION: "I stayed one night at the **Hotel Centrale,** 141 Corso Umberto (tel. 25-528), which cost 2,500 lire ($2.90) in a single room and 400 lire (46¢) extra for use of the bath. A double is 5,000 lire ($5.80). I think it would be listed as a third-class hotel. It is only 200 yards from the railway station and on the main road, which crosses a bridge to the old town on Ortygia island" (G. Costin, Artarmon, Australia).

DINING IN SYRACUSE: Ristorante Bandiera, 2 Via Eritrea (tel. 28-546), is ideal for those who want to dine at an old taverna, found near the entrance to the bridge leading to the Città Vecchia (Old Town). Restored, it is a mellow building, close to the fishing boats. It has a certain charm, and the cuisine is dedicated to the best of Sicilian dishes. A reliable dish is the zuppa di pesce (fish soup) from the Ionian Sea at 3,200 lire ($3.71). An alternate choice is the zuppa di cozze at 1,800 lire ($2.09), a plate brimming with fresh mussels in a savory marinade. Among the asciutte, the Sicilian cannelloni at 750 lire (87¢) is good. The meat dishes feature a number of choices from the kitchens of Latium, Tuscany, and Emilia-Romagna, and average around 2,500 lire ($2.90). Desserts cost 600 lire (70¢).

North from Syracuse for 37 miles or south from Taormina for 32 miles will deliver you to:

6. Catania

Ranking in growth next to Palermo, the second city of Sicily is a suitable stopover base if you're planning a jaunt up Mount Etna. Largely industrial (sulfur factories), the important port opens onto the Ionian Sea. In 1692 an earthquake virtually leveled the city, and Etna has rained lava on it on many occasions—so its history is fraught with natural disasters.

Yet somehow Catania has learned to live with Etna, but her presence is everywhere. For example, in certain parts of the city you'll find hardened remains of lava flows, all a sickly purple color. Grottoes in weird shapes, almost fantasy like, line the shore and boulder-like islands rise from the water.

The present look of Catania—earning for it the title of "the baroque city"—stems from the last earthquake. Splitting the city is the **Via Etnea,** flanked with 18th-century "palazzi." The locals are fond of strolling through the **Bellini Garden,** named to honor Vicenzo Bellini, the young (dead at 32) composer of such operas as "Norma" and "La Sonnambula," who was born in Catania in 1801.

The **Piazza del Duomo** is also of interest, owing much of its look to Vaccarini, who designed the cathedral facade, the City Hall, and the "Elephant Fountain" in the center. The elephant, made of lava, supports an obelisk from the east. The **Cathedral of Catania,** in which the body of Bellini was interred after its 40-year "exile" in Paris, was created by Roger I in the late 11th century, but had to be reconstructed after the earthquake.

Catania also possesses the remains of a **Greek Theater** and a **Roman Amphitheater,** the latter dating from around the second century A.D. Both may be visited in summer from 9 a.m. to 1 p.m. and from 3:30 p.m. till sunset.

A ferry service, the *M/S Petrarca,* is on the Naples-Catania run. The ferry leaves Naples on Monday and Tuesday at 7 p.m. reaching Catania the following morning at 9. A one-way fare costs 33,000 lire ($38.28) in first class, 25,000 lire ($29) in second class. Small cars are usually transported for 42,000 lire ($48.72). A fare reduction is granted on the return voyage if your stay in Sicily is at least seven days.

Note: In Catania, **Alitalia** has an office at 111 Corso Sicilia (tel. 278729).

HOTELS IN CATANIA: Mediocre for the most part. A few good selections follow.

The First-Class Range

Hotel Excelsior, Piazza G. Verga (tel. 224-706), is actually a businessman's hotel. Opening onto a modern square, it is built with a facade of arcaded balconies branching off from the bedrooms, and each of these 151 rooms has either a private bath or shower. The furnishings themselves evoke "Born Yesterday"—with lots of shiny fabric, tufted headboards, electric colors. The hotel charges 15,000 lire ($17.40) in a single; 24,000 lire ($27.84) for a double, inclusive. All is air-conditioned, a lifesaver in Catania, one of the hottest cities of Europe. The roof garden with its covered pergola is pleasant, and the bar with its gleaming terrazzo serves the purpose.

Central Palace, 218 Via Etnea (tel. 224-706), is not quite as big as the Excelsior, but it provides the same de luxe style with more classic furniture. There's a definite touch of the modern about it. All its rooms have private baths and toilets, telephones, and air conditioning. Singles cost 13,000 lire ($15.08); doubles, 19,500 lire ($22.60).

Jolly Hotel Trinacria, 13 Piazza Trento (tel. 228-960), is a recently built hotel right in the heart of the city, a concoction of moderno splashed with pink, raspberry, and olive. Ideal for professional travelers, it is compact, comfortable, and offers fair service. Each room, public or private, is functional, but there the aesthetic story ends. Still, all 159 of the well-furnished rooms (lift-top mirror for dressing tables, showers with bidets) have handsomely maintained private bathrooms. Inclusive rate in a single is 19,100 lire ($22.16); 31,800 lire ($36.89) for a double. Full pension is quoted at 28,000 lire ($32.48) to 31,300 lire ($36.31) per person inclusive. In honor of Bellini's composition, the spaghetti is "alla Norma." All bedrooms have air conditioning.

The Budget Range

The **Hotel Moderno**, 9 Via Alessi (tel. 226-250), recently underwent a metamorphosis designed to upgrade its social standing. As a result, it is now one of the preferred choices in Catania for those wanting to cut corners. Only a short walk from the Piazza del Duomo, it stands at the end of a dead-end street, so the rooms tend to be quiet, a rare condition in noisy Catania. If your room has been renovated, chances are you'll find it pleasantly furnished and agreeable. All doubles, with shower bath, cost 11,000 lire ($12.76) to 12,000 lire ($13.92). Bathless singles go for 5,000 lire ($5.80), 7,500 lire ($8.70) with a private shower bath.

A Motel in Ognina—Budget Range

Motel Agip, Km. 92 on S.S. 114 Orientale Sicula (tel. 242-780) is a gap filler for those who don't want to press on to Taormina for the night. It's a tidy, compact, modern little motel, just outside the city. Owned by the gas company and bearing the familiar (throughout Italy) sign of a fire-breathing, six-legged beast, it offers a comfortable night's rest in a bedroom that is well-furnished and outfitted with a private bath and the routine amenities. The rate in a single room is 8,000 lire ($9.28), 13,500 lire ($15.66) for a double, inclusive. Try to avoid the front rooms because of the heavy traffic passing by. On the premises is a hustle-bustle restaurant dispensing plain victuals to passing motorists. Suitable for hunger, but only ordinary for the fastidious diner.

A de luxe resort at Cannizzaro

Hotel Baia Verde, Litoreanea Cannizzaro (tel. 245-650), lies only seven kilometers from Catania and compares with a Hollywood-style de luxe residence. It's angle shaped to provide a certain privacy for the balconies of each room. The well-furnished doubles or singles are reached from outside corridors. The furnishings are first class, the lobby being especially treated in modern, with a mixture of leather and wood. All accommodations contain private baths, and the charge for a single is 14,000 lire ($16.24); a double, 22,000 lire ($25.52). Full pension is 24,500 lire ($28.42) per person. The hotel stands right above the sea and has a swimming pool for those who don't want to chance their luck on the rocks. In the dreamy restaurant, prices for a complete luncheon or dinner are in the 6,000 lire ($6.96) to 8,000 lire ($9.28) range.

A Resort Hotel at Acitrezza

Albergo I Faraglioni, Lungomare dei Ciciopi (tel. 631-286), is a seafront cement-built "silo" tower hotel, some 11 miles north of Catania, a most comfortable stopover. The fortress-like architecture provides most bedrooms with a view of the sea. Surrounding the hotel are sun terraces, where you can get a tan. Most of the accommodations have rich, deep colors and are skillfully styled in a contemporary manner. The hotel is air conditioned. The high-season rate in a single is 9,500 lire ($11.02), rising to 17,500 lire ($20.30) in a double. Good food is served in the warmly decorated and wood-paneled Danish style dining room, with its overscaled planters for subtropical plants. In the evening, guests congregate in the spacious and circular nightclub for dancing and drinks.

DINING IN CATANIA: La Siciliana di la Rosa.

52a Viale Marco Polo (tel. 376-400). Several rooms, some in the garden, give this restaurant a hearty atmosphere or else an intimate one. It depends on your mood. The inner rooms are more folkloric than the outer ones. In the garden you can select from fresh fish displayed in a cold glass freezer. The menu is written in Sicilian, which is not quite Italian, but the attentive waiters will help you translate it into English. The choice of platters is not wide, but copious enough. The average meal with wine will cost from 4,500 lire ($5.22) to 5,000 lire ($5.80). The cooking is excellent. Most recently we enjoyed a typical Sicilian plate of antipasti called Riggatoni maritata, large noodles cooked in a vine-ripened tomato sauce, with mushrooms and little bits of meat, a meal in itself, at a cost of 1,200 lire ($1.39). Main dishes are in the 2,000-lire ($2.32) to 2,500-lire ($2.90) range. Fish plates are priced by weight. Try the local wine but be careful, as it's quite strong. It has a similar taste to certain California wines. Closed Wednesdays.

La Fazenda, 47 Viale 20 Settembre (tel. 221-026). A bar is in front, a sunken tavern dining room in the rear. Placed on a tiled floor are counter stools or banquettes. The outlook is contemporary, the culinary emphasis on grills on the open hearth and pizzas in the evening, the latter ranging from 400 lire (46¢) to 1,000 lire ($1.16). A good beginning is the seafood salad at 1,400 lire ($1.62), recommended only to those who like squid. Main dishes include rognone cognac (kidneys) at 2,000 lire ($2.32) and the cotoletta Milanese at 2,400 lire ($2.78). Most diners, however, prefer the grilled fish of the day, priced according to weight. Closed Mondays.

Caviezel, 70 Piazza Europa (tel. 370-445), stands at the end of the Corso Italia. The restaurant is in the delicatessen style, offering snacks as well as main meals. The choice of food is great and very appetizing. Among the snacks, fine meals are obtainable from 1,200 lire ($1.39) and up. In the restaurant section, the food is more expensive, a three-course lunch (no dinner) in the 4,000-lire ($4.64) to 6,000-lire ($6.96) range, depending on your choice.

READERS' ENTERTAINMENT SUGGESTION: "The marionette shows done with three-foot, 35-pound puppets telling stories of medieval warfare and chivalry are amazing. Cost: 800 lire (93¢) at one theater, 1,400 lire ($1.62) at the others. A list of theaters is available from the tourist office. Shows are held nightly, and no reservations are needed. There are four theaters in Palermo, but none of them comes anywhere close in drama or excitement to the theater in Acireale, near Catania" (Tom and Gale Lederer, Richmond, Calif.).

MOUNT ETNA: Looming menacingly over the coast of Eastern Sicily, Mount Etna is the highest and largest active volcano in Europe. The peak changes in size over the years, but is currently listed somewhere in the neighborhood of 10,800 feet. Etna has been active in modern times (in 1928 the little village of Mascali was buried under its lava), and eruptions in 1971 rekindled the fears of Sicilians.

Etna has figured in history and in Greek mythology. Empedocles, the fifth century B. C. Greek philosopher, is said to have jumped into its crater as a sign that he was being delivered directly to Mount Olympus to take his seat among the gods. It was under Etna that Zeus crushed the multi-headed, viper-riddled dragon, Typhoeus, thereby securing domination over Olympus. Hephaestus, the god of fire and blacksmiths, was believed to have made his headquarters in Etna, aided by the single-eyed Cyclopes.

The Greeks warned that whenever Typhoeus tried to break out of his "jail," lava erupted and earthquakes cracked the land. Granted that, the monster must have nearly escaped on March 11, 1669, date of one of the most violent eruptions recorded, destroying Catania about 17 miles away.

By road the approach from below is quite idyllic, past orange and lemon trees, as well as the vineyards from which both a red and white wine—known as Etna—is made. As you near the cable car lift at Rifugio Sapienza, the landscape becomes more rugged and bleak. Operating between 8:30 a.m. and sunset daily, the lift takes visitors to the intermediate stop and then to the rim of the crater. At that point you'll have to make arrangements to be transported in a jeep. Hearty types walk the distance, more than an hour's jaunt through lava ashes. The trip costs 6,000 lire ($6.96). The grounds around the station evoke the setting for a science fiction film of earth persons landing on Mars. However, as of this writing, tourists can go only as high as the intermediate stop on the cableway, at about 7,500 feet.

Because of Etna's more than 3½ miles of ski tracks and snow-covered slopes at 8,000 feet above sea level, it is popular with skiers in winter. But even in July and August, the weather will be cold, so dress accordingly.

7. Piazza Armerina & Enna

PIAZZA ARMERINA: This hill town is a base for exploring **Villa Imperiale,** four miles south of the town on the road to Mazzarino. In the contrada of Casale, the villa is renowned for its superb Roman mosaics. Dating from the third or fourth century B. C., it is attributed to Maximianus Herculeus, co-emperor with Diocletian, and is open from 9 a.m. to 1 p.m. and from 4 to 7:30 p.m., charging 100 lire for admission. In winter, the morning hours are the same, but in the afternoon it opens from 2 p.m. until sunset.

These polychrome mosaics feature such themes as 10 maidens in bikinis, the bathers, Roman circus sports, sea myths, a massage parlor, hunting, exotic beasts, and the "Labors of Hercules."

To reach the villa, you'll need either a car or a taxi. Four people can share a cab for around 4,500 lire ($5.22), round trip.

Accommodations

You can spend the night in Piazza Armerina at the medium-priced **Jolly,** Via C. Altacura (tel. 81-333). It is the best hotel here and is rated first class by the government. Only a few of the rooms are bathless, the rest have full comfort facilities. Furnishings are so-so, as is the food. Bathless singles go for 5,650 lire ($6.56), increasing to 7,800 lire ($9.05) with bath. The least expensive doubles, those without bath, go for only 9,700 lire ($11.25), but you must pay 13,150 lire ($15.25) for a complete shower bath. Meals are served in an air-conditioned restaurant, and drinks are available on the terrace. Expect to spend 6,000 lire ($6.96) to 7,000 lire ($8.12) for a complete luncheon or dinner, including local wine.

ENNA: This is an attractive town in the center of Sicily, 52 miles northeast from Agrigento. From here, one of the most exciting panoramas in all of Sicily unfolds from the Pisan Tower of the medieval castle on the top of the hill. In addition, the facade of the cathedral is a curiosity.

In Enna one can stay at the **Albergo Enna,** 43 Via Sant'Agate (tel. 21-882). Readers Tom and Gale Lederer, Richmond, Calif., write: "It has simple but adequate double rooms without private baths for 2,600 lire ($3.02) a night." Singles go for 1,800 lire ($2.09), all tariffs subject to 6% tax. Though this hotel is only rated fourth class, it's among the cheapest in town.

Halfway between Messina and Catania—about 32 miles in either direction —is:

8. Taormina

Runaway bougainvillea . . . silvery olive branches . . . a cerulean blue sky . . . cactuses adorning the hills like modern sculpture . . . pastel plastered walls . . . garden terraces of geraniums . . . trees laden with oranges and lemons . . . ancient ruins.

Dating from the fourth century B.C., Taormina hugs close to the edge of a cliff overlooking the Ionian Sea. Writers for English Sunday supplements rave of its unspoiled charms and enchantment. The sea, even the railroad track, lie down below, connected by bus routes. Looming in the background is Mount Etna, the active volcano. Noted for its mild climate, the town enjoys a year-round season.

The **Greek and Roman Theater** is the most celebrated monument, offering a view of rare beauty of Mount Etna and the sea coast. On the slope of Mount Tauro, the Greeks at an unrecorded time hewed the theater out of rock, but the Romans remodeled and modified it greatly for their amusement. The conquering Arabs, who seemed intent on devastating the town in the tenth century, slashed away at it. On the premises is an antiquarium, containing not only artifacts from the classical period, but early Christian ones as well. The theater is open from 9 a.m. to 1 p.m. and from 3:30 to one hour before sunset, and charges 150 lire for admission.

The other thing to do in Taormina is to walk through the **Giardino Pubblico,** a flower-filled garden overlooking the sea, a choice spot for views as well as a place to relax. At a bar in the park, you can order alcoholic drinks.

HOTELS IN TAORMINA: The best in Sicily—in fact, the finest in Southern Italy after you head south of Amalfi. All price levels and accommodations are offered, from sumptuous suites to army cots. Expect to be required to take either half or full pension.

A Deluxe Choice

San Domenico Palace, 5 Piazza San Domenico (tel. 23-701), is one of the great old hotels of Europe, converted from a 14th-century Dominican monastery, complete with cloisters. Overhauled, it almost begrudgingly boasts air conditioning and a flower-edged swimming pool. Its position is legend to discriminating travelers—high up from the sea coast, on several different levels surrounded by terraced gardens of almond, orange, and lemon trees. In the 19th century, it blossomed as a hotel, with no expense spared, and was a favorite of the elite: kings, artists, writers, statesmen. *Time* magazine once quoted the night porter as recalling when winter was the busy season ". . . and in those days as few as three titled families would fill the whole hotel with their retinues, and it took a mule train to fetch their belongings from the railroad station. Today (spring and summer are the peak seasons) they come with a flight bag containing a change of underwear."

The large medieval courtyard is planted with semi-tropical trees and flowers (bougainvillea never so purple). The encircling enclosed loggia—the old vaulted-ceilinged cloister—is decorated with potted palms and ecclesiastical furnishings (high-backed carved choir stalls, wooden angels and cherubs, religioso paintings in oil). Off the loggia are great refectory halls turned into sumptuously furnished lounges. While antiques are everywhere, the atmosphere is not museumlike, but gracious, with excellent traditional upholstered chairs and sofas. Ornate ceilings climb high, and arched windows look out onto the view. Dining in the main hall is a pleasant event. The cuisine is supervised by a masterful chef. The bedrooms, opening off the cloister, would surely impress a cardinal. One-of-a-kind furniture has been ingeniously utilized—elaborate carved beds, gilt, Chinese red, provincial pieces, Turkish rugs, Venetian chairs and dressers. Behind the scenes are many amenities, including private bathrooms in all rooms. But staying here is expensive: from 16,550 lire ($19.26) to 27,000 lire ($31.32) in a single; from 28,300 lire ($32.83) to 44,350 lire ($51.45) in a double. The pension rate peaks at 50,600 lire ($58.70) per person. To all tariffs, a 12% tax is added. The hotel is open year-round.

The First-Class Range

Jolly Hotel Diodoro, 75 Via Bagnoli Croce (tel. 23-312), is one of the most luxurious of the first-class hotels. Actually it was built and designed privately, and then taken over by the Jolly chain, which is as if one of the Jolly boys had suddenly married a lovely princess and brought her into the fold. The designing of everything—the public lounges, the bedrooms—is well-coordinated, on a high taste level. The dining room, with tall windows on three sides, is projected out toward the sea and Mount Etna. If there's sun in Taormina, you'll find it here. The outdoor swimming pool is also a suntrap; you can bathe, swim, and enjoy the view of mountains, trees, and flowers. The bedrooms are tasteful and comfortable, with well-designed furniture and the latest gadgets. Each room (all 103 are with private bath or shower) is angled toward the sea, with wide open windows. The bed-and-breakfast rate in a single room is 19,000 lire ($22.04), increasing to 36,600 lire ($42.46) in a double. The half-pension tariff is 26,000 lire ($30.16) per person.

Grande Albergo Capo Taormina, at Mazzaro, three miles from Taormina (tel. 24-000), is a world unto itself, nestled atop a rugged cape projecting into the Ionian Sea. Designed by one of Italy's most famous architects, Minoletti, it is newly built. There are five floors on five wide sun terraces, plus a salt-water swimming pool at the edge of the cape. Elevators take you through 150 feet of solid rock to the beach below. Bedrooms are handsomely furnished and well proportioned, with wide glass doors opening onto private sun terraces. The highest tariffs are charged from December 15 to January 15 and from April 1 to October 30. Full-board rates at those times go for 11,000 lire ($12.76) in a single, rising to 19,500 lire ($22.62) in a double. Pension is 28,000 lire ($32.48) per person, and a 6% tax is added. You can coddle yourself in the air-conditioned rooms, enjoying color television, a refrigerator bar, plus an adjoining tiled bath. There are two bars—one intimate, the other more expansive with an orchestra for dancing. The lobby blends the cultures of Rome, Carthage, and Greece, and an open atrium reaches skyward through the center. The food is lavishly presented, and is effectively enhanced by inexpensive Sicilian wines.

Bristol Park Hotel, 92 Via Bagnoli Croce (tel. 23-006), is one of the all-out comfort hotels built high on the cliffside at the edge of Taormina. Close to the public gardens of Duca di Cesarò, it offers a spectacular view of the coastline and Mount Etna from most of its private sun balconies. The interior decor is amusing: tufted satin, plush, and ornate. In contrast, the bedrooms are pleasingly traditional, excellent for a long stay, with private baths and air conditioning. The owners quote low-season prices from mid-January through February and from June 6 to July 20. The rate in a single room is from 8,000 lire ($9.28) to 10,600 lire ($12.30); from 17,000 lire ($13.92) to 19,700 lire ($22.85) in a double. Full pension goes from 18,000 lire ($20.88) to 25,000 lire ($29) per person, plus tax. The dining room, with its shield back chairs and arched windows framing the view, offers international meals, with an occasional Sicilian dish. There's a private beach with free deck chairs and parasols, plus bus service to the beach.

Excelsior Palace, 6 Via Toselli (tel. 23-101), seems like a Venetian palace, lost on the end ridge of the mountain fringe of Taormina. As foreboding as a fortress on two sides, the severity dissolves inside into style and comfort. The gardens at the back have terraces of scented semi-tropical flowers, date palms, yucca, and geraniums. The view of Etna and the sea coast below is of a rare enchantment. Renovated successfully, the hotel is managed so that superior facilities and service await all guests. The drawing room is somewhat formal (excellent for a cotillion), and the drinking lounge with provincial stools is intimate. On silk chairs, you can sit in the pleasant dining room and be served Sicilian and international meals. The air-conditioned bedrooms have plenty of space and are decorated in a traditional manner. A single with bath rents for 9,300 lire ($10.79), a double with bath for 17,050 lire ($19.78). And full pension goes for 19,000 lire ($22.04) per person. Tax is extra. You can swim at the hotel's seaside annex, and the kitchen staff will pack you a picnic lunch.

Villa Sant'Andrea, at Mazzaro' Taormina Mare (tel. 23-125), may not be high up in Taormina itself, but it's at the base of the mountain, directly on the sea, where you can swim off its own private beach. A villa was converted into a first-class hotel. It's English run (the English can always find those delightful little retreats), and it receives guests from April through October. You'll feel like part of a house party. Rooms have informality, a homelike prettiness, with a winning dining terrace where you can enjoy good food. Accommodations are air conditioned as well, with either a private bath or shower. For half board, including the price of your room, you pay 20,500 lire ($23.78) per person daily, plus I.V.A.

The Medium-Priced Range

Hotel Continental, 1 Via Dionisio (tel. 23-805), a recently built second-class establishment, has that special flair, as well as all the required contemporary facilities. It is in the upper part of town, from which there is a wide, unmarred view. Across its flat roof is a solarium exposed to the power of the Sicilian sun. On lower levels the bedrooms overlook a garden dominated by full-bearing orange trees and a free-form lily pond and fountain. Each room opens onto a wide veranda, large enough to make one's living area significantly more spacious. You will want to have your morning breakfast here, or to rest quietly in the evening. The rooms themselves (all doubles with private bath) have built-in pieces and petite sitting rooms near view windows. The rate in a single is 9,000 lire ($10.44); 14,000 lire ($16.24) in a double, inclusive. Full pension is 14,000 lire ($16.24) per person, inclusive. The main lounge is furnished in the contemporary idiom, with plenty of space for conversational groups and large semi-tropical plants, and the air-conditioned dining room is subdued in Danish modern.

Villa Belvedere, 79 Via Bagnoli Croce (tel. 23-791), is a gracious old villa bathed in Roman gold near the Giardino Pubblico. In its garden is a heated swimming pool. From the cliffside terrace in the rear—a social center for guests—is *that* view: the clear blue sky, the gentle Ionian Sea, the cypress-studded hillside, and menacing Mount Etna looking as if she's about to blow her top—the same view, incidentally, enjoyed by clients at the more expensive first-class hotels nearby. The formal entrance is enhanced by potted plants and wall-covering vines, and the interior living rooms of this generations-old, family-run establishment would captivate Elizabeth Barrett Browning. The bedrooms are simple, and the antique furnishings removed during World War II are gradually being restored. Many of the rooms have private baths, but all have hot and cold running water. Singles range from 6,700 lire ($7.77) to 9,000 lire ($10.44); doubles from 12,000 lire ($13.92) to 15,000 lire ($17.40), including breakfast. The villa is open from March till November 15 only.

Medium-Priced Pensions

Villa San Pancrazio, 22 Via Luigi Pirandello (tel. 23-252), is a special place for special people. Built on the site of a Roman villa and set in the second-largest garden in Taormina, it lures painters, philosophers, writers, even Queen Juliana of the Netherlands—those seeking the serene life. The overgrown gardens, quiet and heavily scented with flowers and orange blossoms, boast a tennis court. The former Dutch owner did her own archaeological probings, and thereby found the original cistern, which she opened and converted to a recreation room. But when government experts tried to remove from the garden a mosaic from Roman days, she sat down upon it, threatening, "Over my dead body!"

Inside, the main rooms surround a central glass-covered courtyard. There is a quadrangle of marble pillars with deep arches. The homey array of furnishings reveals the well-traveled background of the owners: Indonesian relics, carved chests, screens, batik hangings, bronzes, as well as large urns and pots of palms. The bedrooms—17 in all, many with private baths—are large and old-fashioned with a mélange of furnishings. Time worn, but time loved. The hotel charges from 6,000 lire ($6.96) to 8,000 lire ($9.28) in a single, from 10,500 lire ($12.18) to 15,000 lire ($17.40) for a double. Breakfast is included. It's close to a cableway for the beach.

Budget Accommodations

Villa Paradiso, 6 Via Roma (tel. 239-22), is at the top of our list for readers seeking some of the finest cooking in Taormina (see our dining recommendations). The immaculate and charming five-story hotel is at one end of the main street of town, in the vicinity of the Greek theater and overlooking the public gardens and tennis courts. The creation of the ingratiating Signor Salvatore Martorana, it is a moderately priced center for those who want to live well and dine expansively. He loves his establishment, and that attitude is reflected in the personal manner in which the living room is furnished, with good antiques and reproductions. Each of the 33 bedrooms is individually decorated, containing a balcony and private bath or shower. In high season full pension (highly recommended) is from 16,000 lire ($18.56) to 18,800 lire ($21.81) per person, inclusive. Guests spend many sunny hours on the rooftop solarium, or in the informal drinking bar and lounge where wallflowers are rare. It's air conditioned throughout. There's also a television room for guests, plus two elevators.

Villa Le Terrazze, 172 Corso Umberto (tel. 23-913), is entered from the main street, amid numerous shops, yet its rear rooms open onto a garden. A favorite with visitors seeking homelike comforts, it is small and compact (only 12 rooms, nine baths); yet several of the well-furnished bedrooms have private terraces. The high-season rate in a bathless single is 2,100 lire ($2.44), while similar doubles range in price from 4,250 lire ($4.93) to 6,750 lire ($7.83). The cooking is quite good; the portions generous; and full-pension arrangements are only 8,900 lire ($10.32) per person. There's an annex a two-minute walk away, where the cost is slightly less.

READERS' PENSION SELECTION: "We found by chance the **Pension Fortuna** run by a pleasant English lady, Mrs. E. Fuller, 33 Via Damianoroseo (tel. 24-586). We had a well-furnished double room with wash basin, hot and cold water, and a good continental breakfast for 7,000 lire ($8.12), minimum of three days. The cost is 8,800 lire ($10.21), minimum of three days, with bathroom. The rooms have a sea view and a view toward Mt. Etna" (Mrs. Agnes Johnson, Royal Oak, Auckland, New Zealand). . . . "We stayed at the **Casa Emmi**, 31 Via Zecca (tel. 23-332), where we had a double room without bath for 3,500 lire ($4.06), which included free use of a spotless bathroom. A double with private bath is 4,000 lire ($4.64), plus tax. There are no singles. The host and hostess are very hospitable, and give free maps of the area upon arrival. We lingered on several days here as it was so beautiful and the accommodation so congenial. There is even a furnace to dry those wet shoes and hastily laundered shirts. The pension is about two minutes from the place where the buses deposit visitors" (John Hayward, Aberdeen, South Africa).

DINING AT TAORMINA: The **Villa Paradiso**, 6 Via Roma (tel. 23922), enjoys a reputation among many Taormina habitués as the best place in town for Sicilian meals. Reached by an elevator, it's on the fifth floor of the aforementioned hotel; the altitudinal dining perch makes it unique in the town. With great flair, owner Salvatore Martorana provides dinners delicious and memorable, including a 6,500-lire ($7.54) tourist menu that offers a wide choice. He prepares many specialties, such as brandy-flavored lobster all'Antonio served with rice "al dente" 5,000 lire ($5.80) or risotto con gamberi. The fresh shrimp is first sautéed in garlic, and then a tomato sauce flavored with cognac or brandy is added. The rice, served separately, is cooked with spices, fried lightly, then baked. Spaghetti alla carrettiera is best for starters: the sauce is made of olive oil, tuna fish, and small vegetables which were soaked in a marinade.

9. The Aeolian Islands

The Greeks who came this way in the sixth century B.C. believed the Aeolian, or Lipari, Islands were the home of Aeolus, king of the winds. Volcanic activity on these islands has been reported since ancient times.

In Messina province, the islands have a "Y" shape, the northern tip formed by **Stromboli**, which was popularized in the Ingrid Bergman film. **Vulcano** forms the southern tip. Both these islands have volcanic activity, the crater at Stromboli being the most spectacular. The largest island in the archipelago is **Lipari,** which produces a malmsey-type wine. Lipari also contains a most important museum, devoted to archaeology. Many invaders have passed this way, including the Romans, the Saracens, the Carthaginians, the Normans. In Mussolini's day, the islands were used as places of banishment for political prisoners.

For the reader willing to make the journey, the islands form one of the most exciting itineraries in Southern Italy. Dr. John A. Fust, of Erie, Pennsylvania, wrote, "The Aeolian Islands are a world apart, at least after the high season, and are certainly recommended to anyone who is interested in a change. We stayed at the **Gattopardo Park Hotel** (tel. 911-035), in Lipari for 14,000 lire ($16.24) per person, in a large room with full bath and really first-class meals at the best restaurant on the island, Filippino.

Side-trips to Stromboli should be planned, staying overnight to climb up the volcano, if possible. **Villaggio Stromboli** (tel. 30-59) on Stromboli is run by Mr. Salvatore Tesoriero who speaks English and is very accommodating. His is a fourth-class hotel, and the rate is from 7,500 lire ($8.70) to 8,500 lire ($9.86) in a double room, the latter with a complete bath."

DO-IT-YOURSELF TOURS: Surface-skimming hydrofoils and other craft connect Sicily and its offshore Aeolian Islands. You purchase tickets to Vulcano from the S.A.S. company in Milazzo, about 20 miles west of Messina. The address is 14 Via Luigio Rizzo (tel. 921-8200). The cost is 2,000 lire ($2.32) for a one-way ticket. Usually there are four departures in summer, three in winter. Also at this office you can obtain information about other departures, including connections to Stromboli and Lipari. These hydrofoil schedules are subject to frequent change without notice, so have your hotel check in advance before striking out.

SARDINIA

"Unconquered Sardinia" was what D.H. Lawrence called it. But that is no longer the case. Once overrun with bandits and malaria, Sardinia, if predictions hold true, will one day be flooded with visitors. Aga Khan's Costa Smeralda, the so-called Emerald Coast in the northeast, has already experienced that phenomenon.

Of course, away from the deluxe hotels and chic discotheques of the Emerald Coast, the land of the banditti, the family clan, and the vendetta is still pretty much what it has always been in the hinterlands. Some of the Sards still follow a life style not far removed from the days of feudalistic Europe.

Its proud people reflect the heritage of an ancient civilization. They knew many invaders, including the Carthaginians, the Phoenicians, the Byzantine knights, the Saracens, the Pisans, the Genoese, and the Spaniards who ruled them for four centuries. The Sards are considered among the proudest and hardest working of all Italians.

Encircled by miles of silver-white sandy beaches, rocky coasts, bays, and gulfs, Sardinia is also an island of mountains and hills. Among Mediterranean islands, it is second in size, bowing only to Sicily. It's a rocky, gnarled land of primordial beauty, some of it little changed since biblical days. In the interior are sand-colored villages where many Sards live in poverty. Scattered throughout the island are the ruins of thousands of towerlike nuraghi—homes of Sardinia's former inhabitants. They have been called "ponderous labyrinths."

Our first stopover is in its largest city.

10. Cagliari

The capital of Sardinia, Cagliari is on the southern part of the island, and is completely surrounded by sea and hills. Alitalia will easily fly you there from either Milan or Rome. Though well known to the Greeks and the Romans, its appearance is modern, except for the old medieval quarter which occupies a long narrow hill running north and south.

For one of the best views, head for the large terrace at the south of the hill, the **Passeggiata Umberto I.** From here you can see the harbor, the lagoon, and the lower city.

THE SIGHTS: The **Cathedral** contains some of the city's most important works of art. Built in the 13th century, in Pisan style, it is a combination of the Romanesque and Gothic. Its most prized possession is its collection of pulpits by Maestro Guglielmo (these once stood in Il Duomo at Pisa). The 18th-century baroque tomb of Martin II of Aragon is impressive, as are the tombs of the Princes of the House of Savoy. Yet another important work of art is a triptych by Gerard David, the Flemish artist.

Another church which merits a visit is **San Saturnino,** built in the style of a Greek cross and tracing its history back to the fifth century.

Actually, the greatest treasures are in the **National Archaeological Museum,** near the Torre di San Pancrazio. It is open daily, except Monday, from

9 a.m. to 2 p.m., charging 150 lire (17¢) for admission. Winter hours are from 8:30 a.m. to 2:30 p.m. (Sundays, it closes at 1 p.m.).

Massive monuments left over from medieval days include the **Torre dell' Elefante** from 1307 and the **Torre di San Pancrazio** from 1305.

North of the town is a **Roman Amphitheater,** the largest such ruin in Sardinia, its impressive cellars carved out of a rock. In summer, opera is performed in front of an international crowd.

Its beach of **Poetto** stretches for some six miles, from the Margine Rosso (Red Bluff) to Sella del Diavolo (the Devil's Saddle). The beach is easily reached by public transportation from Cagliari.

WHERE TO STAY: **Hotel Mediterraneo,** Lungomare Cristoforo Colombo (tel. 301-271), is very central and enjoys a quiet position. It is the leading hotel in the city, having been inaugurated in 1965. The location is right on the sea, overlooking the well-known Golfo degli Angeli. All the well-furnished accommodations contain private baths or showers, balconies, radios, and the usual modern comforts. Singles cost 13,000 lire ($15.08); doubles, 22,000 lire ($25.52). In addition, the restaurant in the hotel offers a variety of national and international dishes, an average meal costing 6,000 lire ($6.96). The Mediterraneo receives guests all year round.

Jolly Hotel Regina Margherita, 44 Viale Regina Margherita (tel. 651-971), lies two blocks up the street from the Stazione Marittima at the harbor. Frankly, it's more of a businessman's hotel than a resort accommodation. Rising seven stories high, it is briskly modern—its lounges and bedrooms decorated in a straightforward and contemporary style, but serviceable and comfortable. Singles with bath cost 19,100 lire ($22.16); doubles, also with bath, 33,700 lire ($39.09). The food is fair, a complete luncheon or dinner going for 7,100 lire ($8.24).

Hotel Sardegna, 50 Via Lunigiana (tel. 286-245), has a capacity of 71 rooms, all with bath (mainly showers). The location is on the outskirts of the city, exactly at the entrance to the Strada Statale 131. That makes the Sardegna a better selection for motorists. The furniture in the rooms is new; the standard of cleanliness high, and the comfort reasonable. Singles rent for 9,500 lire ($11.02); doubles, 15,000 lire ($17.40). The average cost of a meal at the hotel is 5,000 lire ($5.80).

Less expensive is **Motel Agip,** Circonvallazione Pirri (tel. 860-612), which is on the outskirts of town and most beneficial to motorists. You can count on it being clean and reasonably comfortable—and not much else. The accommodations are basic, furnished in a no-nonsense contemporary idiom. All 57 of the rooms contain complete shower baths, with singles costing 8,500 lire ($9.86) and doubles peaking at 14,000 lire ($16.24). The beds are comfortable, and it's easy to check in. Suitable for an overnight stopover only.

WHERE TO DINE: **Del Corsaro,** 28 Viale Regina Margherita (tel. 64-318), offers the finest food in Cagliari. It's under the direction of the Deidda family, who see to it that the quality of the produce, and its preparation, are first rate. The cuisine stands side by side with the fine wines of Sardinia, helping to give the island a reputation as one of Italy's leading gastronomical regions. To begin your meal, we'd suggest an order of malloreddus—little dumplings of cornflour, flavored with saffron. They are served with a sprinkling of grated goat cheese, known as pecorino. If you want to continue sampling local dishes, ask for salsiccia brasata (a form of dry Sardinian sausage). Many other fine and more recognizable meat, poultry, and fish dishes are offered as well. Expect to pay from 6,000 lire ($6.96) to 10,000 lire ($11.60) for a complete meal, including wine. Closed Tuesdays.

La Pineta, 108 Via della Pineta (tel. 30-33-13), is a ristorante pizzeria, among the best in the capital. As an appetizer, prosciutto is featured, usually in three different ways, costing a high 2,000 lire ($2.32). The chef offers three specialties: spiedino (brochette) alla Pineta at 1,800 lire ($2.09); medaglioni di filetto allo spiedo (also on a brochette), 2,800 lire ($3.25); and saltimboca della casa, a variation of the popular Roman dish, 2,500 lire ($2.90). Also preferred, though ordered first, is an antipasto di mare, with an assortment of sea fruits, 1,800 lire ($2.09). The food is most acceptable, as is the service.

Italia, 30 Via Sardegna (tel. 657-987), is a modern, bustling ristorante rosticceria. We always go here for one dish—and is it ever good. It's called porchetto allo spiedo, and it costs 3,000 lire ($3.48) per serving. This most typical dish of Sardinia is suckling pig spit roasted and highly spiced. Also good is a brochette of mixed meat (carne mista) at 2,000 lire ($2.32). The fish dishes are also good, averaging 2,200 lire ($2.55) in price. For a minestre, we'd recommend gnocchetti sardi at 750 lire (87¢). This dish, described earlier, is made of corn flour and saffron, then covered with a sprinkling of grated goat cheese. Hanging from the ceiling of this bandbox contemporary restaurant is a two-story high cluster of spindle lights, illuminating the main dining rooms and the wooden mezzanine. It's a harmonious balance of stark white and wood tones, with Cardinal red and rush-bottomed chairs. Closed Sundays.

Sa Ziminera, 31 Via Trento (tel. 65-89-26), thrives in an atmosphere of rustic simplicity. Near the Roman Amphitheater, the restaurant keeps alive the traditions of the Sardinian countryside in its food and decor. You expect to see a plump woman come bursting from the kitchen at any moment, her arms loaded down with homemade breads or vegetables fresh-picked from the garden. The breads and pastries are indeed homemade, and help round out the hearty meals served here. For openers, you might try the spaghetti with regional sauce, 750 lire (87¢), or an antipasto for 1,800 ($2.09). For the main course, you could choose the spiedino alla contadina (literally, peasant on a spit); a tasty roast of pork cooked over an open fire, 1,800 lire also; or a simpler dish such as pork bracciole, again 1,800 lire, or grilled mullet, 1,500 lire ($1.74). Sa Ziminera is open every day except Monday. Closed from August 15 to September 15.

RESORTS IN THE ENVIRONS: If you're on vacation, it's far better to anchor in at **Santa Margherita,** 25 miles south of Cagliari on the southwest shore of the Gulf of Angels. You can then visit the capital for half-day shopping jaunts and sightseeing excursions. The pine woods skirt the coast, and fine sandy beaches and cliffs extend for five miles.

The **Hotel Castello,** Santa Margherita di Pula (tel. 92531), is the creation of the English-based Trust Houses Forte. It's a self-contained holiday world set in 55 acres of wooded coastal land, with nearly a half mile of sandy beach. Lofty, pine-covered mountains drop down to the seafront terrain. Architecturally, the hotel borrows heavily from Sardinian concepts and decor, avoiding the impersonal international style. Except for instruction costs, everything, within reason, is included in the price of a room: a sauna bath, a children's playground, six tennis courts, a cinema, plus a swimming pool and various water sports.

The core of the Castello has two arms of bedrooms reaching out toward the sea, embracing a lavishly designed garden, the pool, walks under pine trees, as well as the waterfront beach club, with its tee-pee styled, frond-built unbrellas, the Beachcomber Restaurant, and Lido Bar. In addition, you can sip an apéritif at the Bar Bandière before dining at the Ristorante Cavalieri. The latter is an operetta version of a Sardinian tavern, with high-sloped beamed ceilings, regional chairs, and large lantern chandeliers. The cuisine is Sardinian, accompanied by the fresh sparkling wines of the island. We especially recommend the pasta dishes. The King's Road discothèque alternates live music with recordings. Yet another relaxation center is the Beer Cellar, where you can informally chat with fellow guests, drinking steins of imported beer.

The accommodations are superb, with luxurious, though semi-rustic, furnishings. Most rooms are separated by wide sweeping arches and furnished with pastel-painted furniture and tiled floors. Another draw is the private terraces. Tariffs vary according to season and view, with the highest tabs charged from July 15 to September 15. A double room costs 28,000 lire ($32.48). For full pension, the range is from 31,000 lire ($35.96) to 34,000 lire ($39.44) per person.

The **Forte Hotel Village,** Santa Margherita di Pula (tel. 921-531), is less expensive than its adjoining sister hotel, the previously recommended Castello. However, it has the same high taste level, and the public and recreational facilities are shared. Its core is the piazza, with its boutiques, main buildings, even a church. The accommodation bungalows, secluded in a pine grove, encircle this piazza. Its architecture is an idealized African-Mediterranean, with tiled roofs and covered loggias with arches. The simply but pleasingly furnished bungalows are for two, three, and four guests, each having a private bath and terrace. Prices: a bungalow for two, for example, rents for anywhere from 28,000 lire ($32.48) to 35,000 lire ($40.60). However, the basic singles in the main building go from 14,500 lire ($16.82). Full-pension rates are 28,000 lire ($32.48) per person. Drinks at the bar and sports instruction are extra.

Hotel Capo Boi, Villasimius (tel. 79-225), lies about 28 miles from Cagliari on the east coast. Swiss owned, it offers everything that modern comfort stands for: a good international cuisine, including the best Italian regional dishes, personal attention from the staff, a large private sand beach and a wide private territory, but above all beauty, tranquility, and spaciousness. Under the full-pension plan, singles pay 20,900 lire ($24.24); doubles, 37,800 lire ($43.85) in low season. In high season, the full-pension plan is 40,900 lire ($47.44) in a single, 65,800 lire ($76.33) for two persons in a double. The hotel is closed from November to April.

11. Alghero

On the northwest coast, this former Aragonese fishing port is considered Sardinia's most beautiful town. Because of its heavy Catalan influence, it's been called a "Little Barcelona." Encircled by ancient ramparts, it is built on a rocky ledge above the sea. Flowers and palms grow in profusion, the entire setting crowned by the town's cathedral spire.

Alitalia connects Alghero to Rome and Milan by efficient air service.

THE SIGHTS: Best for exploring is the **Città Vecchia** or Old Town, somewhat Moorish in flavor. Two miles north of the town is an excellent bathing beach. Not too far away at Porto Conte is one of the most stunning undersea caves in the Mediterranean, the **Grotta di Nettuno.** Neptune's Grotto may be reached by sea or land. If you elect the latter method, you'll go along the Escala del Cabirol or Stairway of Goats. A wealth of stalactites lines the walls of the enclosures of the cave. Check with the tourist office in Alghero for boat departures to the caves, and allow at least three hours. Expect to pay at least 2,500 lire ($2.90), including admission to these spectacular caves.

UPPER BRACKET ACCOMMODATIONS: The **Villa Las Tronas,** Lungomare Dante (tel. 975-390), was, until recently, the residence of the remnants of the Italian royal family who used it for their holidays in Sardinia. Each room has a view of the sea and the bay, the latter considered by many the most beautiful in the Mediterranean. Surrounded by cultivated gardens, it stands near craggy rocks and tiny beaches. The architectural lushness of the villa has been retained, including the paneled silk walls, the parquet floors, the large gilt mirrors, the sconces, and the baroque furniture. The simplified, contemporary dining room has a baby-pink and skyblue color scheme. Best of all are the 19th-century chairs and the view of the sea. Bedrooms are simpler and harmoniously decorated. Each contains a private bath. It's customary to take full board in high season: 30,500 lire ($55.38) in a single, 28,000 lire ($32.48) per person in a double. These tariffs drop approximately 4,000 lire ($4.64) per person off season (September 16 to June 30). If there is no room at the main hotel, guests are housed in the annex, paying from 24,000 lire ($27.84) to 26,500 lire ($30.74) per person for full board. I.V.A. is extra. The hotel is open all year.

BUDGET ACCOMMODATIONS: **Eleonora,** Zona Calabona (tel. 97-92-36), gets A-minus for its modernity and comfort, and a C for style. Its bedrooms, set honeycomb style in a six-floor building, in one of the most attractive sections of Alghero, are 800 yards from the town center, but only 30 yards from the sea coast. Bedrooms are furnished, for the most part, in blond modern. Many have private view terraces. Rooms are equipped with private shower baths as well. In high season, the full-pension rate per person is 12,000 lire ($13.92), dropping to 10,000 lire ($11.60) off season. Rates include service, I.V.A. is extra. The lounge is powder-puff dressy, with crystal and pleated velvet upholstered furniture. There's also a dancing tavern, with draped fish nets, and strawberry pink and blue walls. Most guests prefer the terrace and swimming pool.

La Margherita, 70 Via Sassari (tel. 97-90-06), is a modest downtown hotel with an attractive stone-arched facade studded with balconies. Best of all is a rooftop terrace where you can order refreshments while scanning other rooftops and the bay. The lobby and lounge are serviceable and clean. The bedrooms are simplified in a homey modern, each with central heating and private bath. Full pension is 12,100 lire ($14.04) in high season, including I.V.A.

12. The Emerald Coast

The owners of motor yachts nod to each other at the harbor at Porto Cervo. The white sands attract some of the best-looking bodies in Europe. The Costa Smeralda in northeast Sardinia is a luxurious vacation haven "ruled" by his highness, the Aga Khan. The spiritual leader of some 15 million Ismaili Muslims arrived in 1961, and the coast hasn't been the same since.

Along with the Costa Smeralda Consortium, he transformed some 25,000 acres of savage coastal land into luxury villas, deluxe hotels, and marinas. Some of the excesses, such as high-rise buildings, that tended to mar the Italian Riviera have been outlawed. Buildings were commissioned to architects who were instructed to make them seem like part of the landscape.

Unless you arrive on a yacht in the tradition of the king of Greece, you may want to make the trek from the mainland at Civitavecchia aboard a car ferry. The **Tirrenia Line** runs from Civitavecchia to Olbia where you can make connections to your destination on the Emerald Coast. One-way cabin fares are 12,000 lire ($13.92) for first class, 9,000 lire ($10.44) for second class. If you don't want to rent a cabin, reclining "aircraft seats" go for 9,600 lire ($11.14) in first class, 6,500 lire ($7.54) in second class.

Motorists will be able to take some interesting excursions. For example, at **Olbia,** where the car ferries from Civitavecchia dock, there is San Semplicio, a Romanesque church, dating from the 11th century.

The **Arcipelago della Maddalena** lies right off the Emerald Coast. Car ferries link it with Palau. **La Maddalena** is the largest island and a favorite seaside resort. From there you can cross a causeway to the island of **Caprera,** where you'll find the former house and tomb of Garibaldi, the Italian patriot, soldier, revolutionary, and political leader.

Finally, you may want to go on a shopping expedition to **Nuoro,** in the central part of the island, where you can seek out Sardinian handicrafts, such as carpets, rush baskets, floral and damasked tapestries, lace from Bosa, ceramics and terracotta, wood carvings, decorated leather work, and earrings in filigree covered with pearls and garnets in the shape of mulberries.

A FIRST-CLASS QUARTET: Cala di Volpe, Cala di Volpe (tel. 96-083), is built irregularly and low in earth tones—a structure that looks like a Moorish-African village sprawling on a sand bar. You may be surprised to discover it's all new. It's purposefully deceiving. The tiled roofs, the patina of the white walls, and the flowers and plants on the patios and terraces look as if they've always been there. Irwin Shaw, the best-selling novelist, called it "for the spoiled darlings of our age." Its French architect, Monsieur Couelle, labeled the result an "operetta." He was perhaps referring to the deliberate campaign to give the resort immediate rustico. Each air-conditioned bedroom has a balcony with a view of the sea. Your bedroom walls may have rough plastered walls, perhaps in butter yellow, with reproductions of Italian antiques. The high season lasts from July 1 to September 15, and during this period full pension is 58,300 lire ($67.63) per person. At other times tariffs drop to 39,300 lire ($45.59) per person, plus 6% I.V.A. The hotel is open only from April 15 to September 30. The public facilities are vast, including an Olympic-sized swimming pool, a grill room, a nightclub, tennis courts, a private beach, and barbecue. Three hundred yards away is the 18-hole Robert Trent Jones championship golf course. Take along your chicest resort attire.

Pitrizza, Arzachena-Liscia di Vacca (tel. 92-000), is also under the aegis of the Aga Khan. It was built originally as a deluxe hotel, but now functions under a first-class rating. It's another remarkably skillful recreation of a group of six villas, inspired by Sardinian architecture. Native stone was used, and inside typical handicrafts were employed effectively. In fact, the interior bursts with contemporary taste and conveniences. The villas are clustered around a main clubhouse, which has a cozy and rustic drinking bar and lounge, plus an informal living and dining room. From the clubhouse an extensive terrace opens onto the sea. The swimming pool is sumptuous. Beachboys, lavish buffets, multi-lingual waiters, fleets of boats—hardly the comforts of home. Enjoying this luxury has been everybody from Elie Rothschild to Sam Spiegel. The hotel is open from May 15 to September 30, charging its highest rates from July 1 to September 15. At that time full pension is 63,300 lire ($73.43) per person. This full-board rate is lowered to 47,700 lire ($55.33) per person at other times.

Romazzino Beach Hotel, Arzachena-Rumazzino (tel. 96-020), is a first-class resort, directly on the bay, with its own sandy beach. The establishment is built to simulate a village, and has sprawling bedroom wings. Each bedroom contains a private sea-view balcony as well. The accommodations are handsomely furnished, often with ornate brass beds, reproductions of antiques, parquet floors, tasseled bed throws, and private lounge areas. In high season, the full-pension rate is a peak 70,000 lire ($81.20) per person daily. The hotel is open from May to October, lowering its full-pension rate off season to 50,000 lire ($58). The cuisine is a combination of Sardinian and international, emphasizing regional pasta dishes. In the evenings guests dance to discotheque music, often enjoying folk dances performed by the local villagers. Guests are offered beachside meals at a barbecue and pizza stand, as well as in the main dining room.

Cervo, 07020 Porto Cervo (tel. 92-003), is a yacht owner's paradise, yet its tariffs are cheaper than the recommendations above. Near the center of town, it was built right at the edge of the harbor. It, too, is an idealized version of a Sardinian village. Life here is lush, pampered, and chic. Rooms are built in a hacienda style opening onto flower gardens, vine-covered vista arbors, and sun-pocket rustic patios. You'll probably join other guests for apéritifs in the main patio, with its wicker chairs or in the informal, bamboo-sheltered luncheon area. Another social center is around the free-form swimming pool, with its adjoining refreshment and luncheon terrace. A cluster of tennis courts, even an indoor pool and barbecue, round out the facilities. The interior lounges and dining room are well designed and handsomely furnished. The hotel is open year-round, charging its highest tariffs from July 1 to September 15. At that time, the bed-and-breakfast rate is 42,400 lire ($49.18) per person. In the low season this drops to 34,000 lire ($39.44) per person. In winter, bed and breakfast is offered at a rate of 16,000 lire ($18.56) per person. In both high and low season. The cost of any additional meal is 8,000 lire ($9.28).

After touring Sicily and Sardinia, you can cross back over to the mainland for a totally different look at Italy.

SOUTHERN ITALY—APULIA

Known to the Italians as "La Puglia," the district of Apulia encompasses the most southeastern section of Italy, known as the heel of the geographic boot. It is the country's gateway to the Orient, but more specifically, for most North Americans, the gateway to Greece from the port of Brindisi. Through it marched the Crusader, and even earlier, the Roman on his way to the possessions in the East.

For most foreigners, it is a little-known, but fascinating, region of Italy, embracing some of its most poverty-stricken areas and some of its most interesting sections (see the Trulli District). Many signs of improved living conditions are in the air, however.

The land is rich in archaeological discoveries, and some of its cities were shining sapphires in the crown of Magna Graecia (Greater Greece). The Ionian and Adriatic Seas wash up upon its shores, which have seen the arrival of cross-currents of civilizations.

13. The Abruzzi

Although Abruzzo is the central region of peninsular Italy, it is considered a southern kingdom. It lies between the central Apennine chain and the Adriatic Sea, and can easily be reached from Rome on the Rome'L'Aquila-Adriatic

Sea motorway. This mountainous agricultural land is symbolized by the goat-skin-jacketed shepherd.

The best center for exploring is the capital at:

L'Aquila

In the Aterno Valley, L'Aquila is an artistic and cultural center, as well as a resort in both summer and winter.

Its **Basilica of San Bernardino** is from the 15th century. The harmonious facade—the most distinguishing feature of this magnificent building—was the work of Cola d'Amatrice. The interior is roofed by a polychrome ceiling carved from wood in the baroque style. In the right aisle is a chapel containing the mausoleum of St. Bernardino of Siena who died at L'Aquila.

The second major sight is the **Castle,** an imposing example of 16th-century military art erected by the Spanish governors. Its galleries now contain the National Museum of Abruzzo, with exhibitions of Roman archaeological findings, plus an outstanding collection of medieval art.

The **Basilica of S. Maria di Collemaggio** is a masterpiece of Abruzzi Romanesque-Gothic art, and it's considered one of the most beautiful of the late medieval churches of Italy. It is characterized by a facade of white and pink stone, as well as three rose windows and three portals.

Finally, the **Fountain of 99 Spouts** is connected to the legend of L'Aquila, which claims that the town was created by a miracle, with 99 quarters surrounding 99 castles, 99 churches, and 99 fountains. The fountain is said to date from the 13th century, though it was subsequently remodeled. At the time of its construction, it was one of the largest and most beautiful of the fountains of Italy.

Where To Stay

Hotel Duca degli Abruzzi, 10 Viale Duca degli Abruzzi (tel. 283-41), is one of the newest and most impressive hotels in L'Aquila, overlooking the city. A first-class choice, it offers bedrooms that are spacious and cheered by the use of bright colors. Many are individually decorated and often architecturally interesting. Singles range in price from 8,300 lire ($9.63) to 9,000 lire ($10.44); doubles, 14,200 lire ($16.47). There are many public lounges as well, with comfortable overscaled chairs. The best feature of the hotel is its panoramic restaurant, "Il Tetto," which is air conditioned, offering a typical Abruzzese cuisine as well as international dishes. A typical lunch, not including wine, but with the view thrown in free, goes for 5,000 lire ($5.80).

Where To Dine

Tre Marie, 3 Via Tre Marie (tel. 201-91), is the domain of the Scipioni family who have decorated the tavern in the *caratteristico* style of Abruzzo. It offers the finest food in the entire province, and many Roman gourmets drive out just for lunch or dinner. The owner, Guiseppe Scipioni, is a painter, and proudly displays a painting depicting the Tre Marie, three legendary ladies, Cleofe, Maddalena, and Vergine. The entire ceiling is decoratively studded with handmade and locally painted dishes. Even your service plates are handmade, each one different. The setting is persuasive and winning, and Tre Marie has been around long enough to gather a patina.

The food coming out of the kitchen is superb, featuring specialties of the region. The cuisine is rich and healthy, but doesn't betray the ingredients that have brought fame to this mountain gastronomy. For an appetizer, we'd suggest the local prosciutto e salame, 1,800 lire ($2.09). The ham is lean and tasty. Worthy of praise are the pasta dishes, none more notable than maccheroni alla chitarra, 1,200 lire ($1.39). This macaroni dish is so named because it is cut on a special utensil of beech-wood and steel strings made by artisans. The pasta is dressed in a ragoût. For a main meat dish, we'd suggest involtini Tre Marie at 2,200 lire ($2.55). This is a rolled meat choice in a piquant sauce. Two well-recommendable vegetable courses include fagioli al pomodoro (beans and tomatoes) at 800 lire (93¢) and lenticchie (lentils) alla paesana, also 800 lire. The dessert specialty is dolce Tre Marie all'ananas at 800 lire. For the wine, we'd suggest vino rosé paesano bottiglia, 1,500 lire ($1.74). Closed Mondays.

14. Taranto

A seaport 44 miles west of Brindisi, Taranto lent its name to both the tarantula (who haunts the hinterlands) and the tarantella, a dance that was supposed to free the victim from the spider's sting. Now a tarantella is the most popular folk dance of Southern Italy, characterized by hops and foot tapping.

THE SIGHTS: For the best view of the city, walk along the waterfront promenade, the **Lungomare Vittorio Emanuele.** The heart of the old town lies on an island, separating the Mare Piccolo from the Mare Grande. On the Ionian Sea, Taranto is one of Italy's most important naval bases. As such, it was the first to be hit by Allied bombs in 1940. The British occupied it in the autumn of 1943.

Earlier, in 927, the Saracens swept over the city, and leveled it. But before that time, it was the most prestigious city of Magna Graecia, having been established by colonists as early as the eighth century B.C. The evidence of that former glory rests today in the:

National Museum

At 41 Corso Umberto, this museum offers an extensive assemblage of figured terra-cottas, Grecian vases, goldware, classical sculpture, coins, and Roman mosaics. In Sala I and II you'll find Cupid, Aphrodite, and all the gang. Galleries IV through VI exhibit important finds from the excavated necropolis at Taranto, dating from the sixth to the second centuries B.C. Some of the pottery, originating at Corinth in the seventh and sixth century B.C., is among the most exceptional in the world. The designs of many of the Greek vases and terra-cottas would be considered sophisticated by today's standards (Picasso must have been inspired by some of the women). In Sala XII is enough jewelry to make Tiffany blush. The corridors contain figurines expertly arranged. The gallery, one of the great archaeological museums of Italy, is open from 9 a.m. to 2 p.m. daily, except Monday, and charges 150 lire (17¢) for admission every day except Sundays (when it's free).

Note: Alitalia doesn't have an office here, but a handling agent will help you at 51 Corso Umberto (tel. 22-051).

HOTELS IN TARANTO: Surprisingly good if you pick and choose carefully.

The First-Class Range

Hotel Delfino, 66 Viale Virgilio (tel. 39-981), stands on the waterfront, much like a beach club, with a swimming pool and garden overlooking the sea.

The magnet is the elaborately tiled sun deck, with its garden furniture and potted semi-tropical plants. There's a cozy country-style drinking lounge and bar, with ladderback chairs, wood paneling, and sheer white draperies. The dining room serves excellent fish dishes (try Taranto oysters!) in an attractive setting of paneled pillars and sea-view windows. A typical double room offers pale tiled floors, Scandinavian-styled wood-grained built-in furniture, vibrantly colored bed covers, and nut-brown armchairs in front of the view-window and balcony. Each bedroom has its own sparklingly clean bath, and the single rooms maintain the same taste level. Open year-round, the 222-room hotel charges 13,000 lire ($15.08) in a single; 21,400 lire ($24.82) in a double, including service, air conditioning, and I.V.A.

The Medium-Priced Range

Hotel Plaza, 46 Via D'Aquino (tel. 91-925), is our choice for those who want some style with their comforts. This ultra-modern 112-bedroom establishment opens onto a pleasant main square, with each chamber possessing its own balcony. Inside, it's a forest of shiny marble, with classic furnishings, a haven for those wanting a dignified background, contemporary amenities, and plenty of attentive service. The bedrooms are equally stylish and consistently well maintained, with coordinated furnishings and fabrics. Air conditioning, telephones, private baths with showers and bidets complete the picture. Singles cost 9,000 lire ($10.44). A double with shower or bath goes for 15,000 lire ($17.40).

The Budget Range

Hotel Miramare, 4 Via Roma (tel. 22-854), is quite a bargain for the area. It's a 57-bedroom, old-fashioned hotel, near the water. You check into the postage-stamp lobby, then are transported to the upstairs rooms by elevator. The bedrooms themselves are decidedly unchic, but contain the routine comforts and amenities. They are well maintained. Many of the rooms are quite large, with three or four beds, ideal for families. The front rooms overlook the water. Bathless singles go from 3,400 lire ($3.94) to 4,000 lire ($4.64). In a single with bath, the tariff peaks at 6,000 lire ($6.96). Bathless doubles cost 6,500 lire ($7.54), a top 9,500 lire ($11.02) with bath.

RESTAURANTS IN TARANTO: **Al Gambero,** 4 Vico Del Ponte (tel. 42-431), is one of the leading restaurants of Southeastern Italy, devoted, of course, to the world of fish dishes (Taranto is famous for its oysters and black mussels). It overlooks the bobbing boats in the harbor and the fish market of the old city. Diners have a choice of al fresco tables or the inside rooms of this big, two-story restaurant. The decor is interesting, enlivened by a collection of contemporary paintings. Two specialties make excellent beginnings. One is antipasti frutti di mare at 2,000 lire ($2.32); the other, spaghetti al Gambero, at 1,000 lire ($1.16) to 3,200 lire ($3.71). Expect to pay from 5,000 lire ($5.80) to 8,000 lire ($9.28) for a complete meal, including the local wine. Closed Tuesdays.

15. Brindisi

The Italian word *brindisi,* has entered the language of the world as a toast in 19th-century operas, such as Verdi's "La Traviata." It is, of course, a major seaport on the Adriatic, used in ancient times as well as now as a gateway to Greece and such other points east as Israel and Turkey.

Known to the Romans as Brundisium, it was the terminus of the Appian Way, a fact noted at the harbor by a commemorative column crowned with carvings of the deities. Many famous Romans passed through here: Augustus and Marc Antony to make peace, Cicero to write of it, and Virgil to die in 19 B.C. As an important seaport, it figured in many of the historical movements of Europe, such as the Crusades. In more recent times, it was a strategic Adriatic port in both World Wars, falling to the Allies in the wake of the late-summer invasion in 1943.

Incidentally, some Brindisi food specialties which we've chosen not to recommend include gnummarieddi (goat entrails in envelopes, spit cooked) and stacchiodde (ears covered with tomato sauce).

Note: In Brindisi, the **Alitalia** office is at 53 Corso Garibaldi (tel. 24-981).

HOTELS IN BRINDISI: Here are four recommendations, in three price ranges.

The First-Class Range

Internazionale, 26 Lungomare Regina Margherita (tel. 23-905), is like a palace, with a small courtyard, placed importantly on the harbor in full view of the departing and arriving vessels. Though it has been considerably updated, it still attracts those who favor an old-fashioned ambience. The entrance lobby has a vaulted ceiling and arches dividing it into various areas. In spite of the architecture, the furnishings are modern. The larger bedrooms have ornate paneled doors and marble fireplaces, though the furnishings are a mishmash. However, there is plenty of comfort. In rooms with private baths, the single rate is 9,000 lire ($10.44); it's 16,800 lire ($19.49) in a double. The restaurant, incidentally, provides good fish dishes. The Internazionale is only 400 yards from the main pier for car ferries to Greece, and is 300 yards from the Maritime Station Building where liners dock en route to Mediterranean ports, Africa, India, and the Far East.

Hotel Jolly, 149 Corso Umberto I (tel. 22-941), is the other first-class hotel in Brindisi, a total contrast to the antiquated Internazionale. It's so modern, in fact, that it tends to be a bit aesthetically sterile. The popular chain hotel is right on the station plaza. Between boats it provides real comfort, with all the modern amenities. There is a good-sized restaurant and grill on the premises, but the "plastico" lounge is best by passed quickly for the quite satisfactory bedrooms upstairs—most with private baths. In high season, singles rent for 15,300 lire ($17.75); doubles for 19,000 lire ($22.04) to 26,600 lire ($30.86).

The Medium-Priced Range

Hotel Corso, 88 Corso Roma (tel. 24-128), is Brindisi's 20th-century answer to New York's Flatiron Building. The six-floor, wedge-shaped hotel is built in the center of town, with wrap-around bedroom balconies, totally modern throughout, except for the provincial decor. Its lounge has ladderback, reed-seated armchairs, cedar paneling, an open cantilevered staircase, large fig plants, and a baroque cherub as mascot. The same informal charm permeates the dining room, with its wood paneling and country-style chairs. The bedrooms combine modern with traditional pieces, a most functional and uncluttered style of decorating. Rooms are with and without private baths. In a single, rates peak at 6,000 lire ($6.96); in a double, at 12,000 lire ($13.92).

The Budget Range

Hotel Europa 2, 31 Corso Roma (tel. 22-424), is on a main business drag, a few blocks from the ferry to Greece. It is a very simple and unassuming hotel that offers merely satisfactory accommodation for those who have to be economical. The owners, the Nobile brothers, are also the proprietors of La Lanterna restaurant (see below). A bathless double rents for 6,500 lire ($7.54), that rate going up to 8,500 lire ($9.86) in a double with bath.

DINING IN BRINDISI: La Lanterna, 6 Piazza Della Vittoria (just beside the Post Office, tel. 24-950), owned by the Nobile brothers, is a chalet-styled modern restaurant with food that rates a rave. Under an open-beamed ceiling, you sit on rustic chairs as the hors d'oeuvres are spread before you, a stunning array with many of the chef's favorites. From the à la carte menu, the specialties are: maccheronecini alla contadina (pieces of veal and sheep cheese in a thick tomato stew) for 700 lire (81¢); risotto alla pescatora (rice cooked in broth in a seafood sauce) for 700 lire also; grigliato alla Lanterna (mixed grill with pork, liver, sausage, and veal) for 2,000 lire ($2.32); scaloppine al Madeira (veal scaloppine in a Madeira wine sauce), 2,000 lire; and fritto di calamari e gamberi (fried squid and shrimp), also 2,000 lire. Closed Mondays.

Forty miles northwest of Brindisi is the heart of the:

16. Trulli District

The center of the area is the little village of **Alberobello,** a colony of bee-hive houses called *trulli.* What is a *trullo?* Unique in Europe, the houses are whitewashed and characterized by their conically shaped roofs of soil-colored stones. Often a house will have more than one of these small cupolas, even a second story, most often reached by a ladder and used for sleeping.

The narrow cobbled streets of what must be Italy's most fantastic village take you past *trullo* after *trullo.* The total effect is one of unreality, a feeling enhanced by the strange markings on the roofs, symbols whose meaning is lost to history. You can walk through the heart of the harmonious little settlement, perhaps even take a peek inside one or two if an invitation is forthcoming. The denizens of the town aren't averse to earning an extra lire, even if it means having a stranger poking around inside their casa.

WHERE TO STAY: Dei Trulli (tel. 721-130) offers unique living in one-of-a-kind bee-hive houses, almost a village unto itself. Modern plumbing and appropriate furnishings have been installed in each *trullo,* affording guests an opportunity to go native in a comfortable manner. You sleep in a bungalow that may have one, two, even three cones—circular buildings wedged together in the Siamese fashion. One will be your entryway with bath, another the bedroom, and a third the sitting and dining rooms with a brick fireplace. All double rooms contain private baths, and couples pay 16,500 lire ($19.14) to 20,500 lire ($22.62) nightly. For full pension, the tariff ranges from 16,000 lire ($18.56) to 21,000 lire ($24.36) per person.

Astoria, 11 Viale Bari (tel. 721-190), is a pleasant and intimate second-class hotel run in a personal way. In a village dedicated almost totally to the *trulli,* it is surprising to find a contemporary place at which to stay. Four floors high, the building contains an elevator; the tone here is oriented toward Nordic design and decor. The lobby is tasteful, with glistening marble floors, shiny black armchairs, wall panels, and a bar area of wood, brass, and wrought iron. The bedrooms, each with its own bath, are furnished in a utilitarian manner, with matching wood pieces and combination chests of drawers with lift-top mirrors that convert to dressing tables. The rate for a single room is 11,000 lire ($12.76), 16,000 lire ($18.56) in a double. There is a fresh and airy dining room, with soft, white draperies (and good home cooking, including the wines of Apulia).

17. The Spur of Italy

Called The Gargano, the mountainous woodsy promontory is the Spur of Italy. It's best seen in the autumn when you can enjoy the colors of the Umbrian Forest. Featuring such trees as maple, ash, cedar, and chestnut, it's quite a sight. The world here has a timeless quality. Unspoiled salt lake areas are found at Lesina and Varano. Bathing and aquatic sports are prevalent because of the mild climate and calm sea. The coast is a series of cliffs, rocks, caves, islets, and beaches. In addition to nature's wild and varied landscape, the promontory is rich in historic interest, showing off monuments that are Byzantine, Romanesque, Norman, and medieval.

You can reach Gargano by driving north from Bari, using **Manfredonia** as your gateway. If you're crossing Italy from Rome, Foggia is also a gateway. It lies 25 miles from Manfredonia. The port, dominated by its Angevin castle, was teeming with knights and pilgrims in medieval days. Venetian ships carried them across the sea on their Crusades. You'll find a decent hotel there if you plan to spend the night—**Gargano** 2 Viale Beccarini (tel. 220-39). All its adequately furnished accommodations contain private baths, with singles peaking at 6,000 lire ($6.96); doubles, 11,000 lire ($12.76).

Or you can drive only three kilometers away to **Siponto,** on the sea. The village is noted for its **Church of S. Maria,** dating from 1117 and built in the Pisan-Romanesque style. Standing in lonely pines, the church is all that remains of the old city of Siponte.

Siponto has two suitable hotels if you're planning to stay over. One is **Apulia** (tel. 221-65), charging 6,000 lire ($6.96) in a single with bath, that tariff rising to 10,000 lire ($11.60) in a double with bath. Less preferred is **Cicolella** (tel. 214-63), which offers simply furnished rooms with and without private baths. The top single rate is 4,000 lire ($4.64), increasing to 10,000 lire ($11.60) in a double with private bath.

From Manfredonia, you can take steamship services to the **Tremiti Islands,** running once daily during the summer and three times weekly in winter. Hydrofoil service is available between Termoli and Tremiti six times daily during the summer only. Service is provided by Aliscafo "Nibbio."

Motorists will find the principal town in the interior, **Monte Sant' Angelo,** in the great Umbrian Forest, to be a good starting point for a tour. From here you can venture into a landscape of limes, laurels, towering yews, along with such animal life as foxes and gazelles. Narrow passageways, streets that are virtual stairways, and little houses washed a gleaming white, characterize the town. The site of the town, standing on a spur, is most interesting, commanding great views. Before leaving the town, you may want to visit the **Sanctuary of San Michele,** in the Romanesque-Gothic style. The campanile is octagonal, dating from the last years of the 1200s.

If you continue east along the coast, you can stop off at **Mattinata,** rising above the plain and planted with olive trees.

From here, you can drive to the farthest point along the coast, **Vieste.** Here, rooted firmly in the sea, stands a legendary monolith. The rock is linked to the woeful tale of Vesta, a beautiful girl supposedly held prisoner on the stone by jealous sirens. Many grottoes along the coast can be explored by boat.

In and around here you will find some of the finest accommodations along the coast. The best place to stay at Viesta is **Pizzomunno Residence** (tel. 0884/78741), offering good food and handsomely furnished rooms, costing 15,000 lire ($17.40) in a single and 26,000 lire ($30.16) in a double. All the well-maintained rooms contain private baths. From your bedroom window, you'll have a view of the coast and the sea beyond.

An even more tranquil oasis is the **Albergo del Faro** (tel. 79011) at Baia di Pugnochiuso. This is really a tourist complex, built on a hill site right above the coast. The hotel project was built as the pilot scheme of a tourist center. Here you'll find shops, places to eat, swimming pools, tennis courts, clay pigeon shooting, sailing, and motorboats. Rooms are furnished in a streamlined Nordic modern style, with good color schemes. Obligatory pension costs from 22,000 lire ($25.52) to 28,000 lire ($32.48) per person daily.

18. Wind-Down Holidays

After a whirlwind tour of Italy, you can wind down and extend your visit by taking a week-long **Valtur Holiday.** No more museums, no more traffic-clogged cities—just peace and tranquility. Valtur has created a series of hotel villages in Southern Italy, often laid out in wooded areas and always built in advanced architectural design. The villages are constructed to look out onto the sea. Major ones include **Ostuni Marina,** a hotel-village on the Ostuni coast, 18 miles north of Brindisi; **Pollina,** in the province of Palermo, Sicily, nine miles east toward Cefalù on road No. 113; **Capo Rizzuto,** on the Ionian Sea in a setting of 6,000-year-old olive trees in the province of Catanzaro, 14 miles south of the city of Crotone in Southern Italy; **Brucoli,** on the southeast coast of Sicily, 18 miles from Catania airport; and **Alimini,** close to Otranto, six miles south of Lecce, 62 miles south of Brindisi.

In high season, from July 5 to August 22, an adult pays from 170,000 lire ($197.20) to 230,000 lire ($266.80) for a week at one of the hotel villages, everything included. Tariffs are reduced for children, of course. In the intermediate season, the adult charge is reduced to 150,000 lire ($174), and is lowered further to 125,000 lire ($145) in the off season. These rates, by the way, are only indicative and are subject to change without notice.

Activities are plentiful at these villages, and include nightclubs, barbecues, and sports. The accommodations are equipped with baths and toilets, and villages come with such facilities as restaurants, bars, swimming pools, and shopping centers. At lunch and dinner, wine is free, and you can drink as much as you want.

Valtur Holidays is made possible by a group of concerns, such as banks and key national and international organizations, including Alitalia and the Automobile Club d'Italia.

For information and reservations, apply to Valtur, 377 Via del Corso, Rome (tel. 678-4634 or 678-4588).

READERS' TIP: "Because of a shortage of 100-lire (12¢) bills in circulation, some provinces are printing their own 100 lire notes backed by local banks and *good only in that province.* We acquired several of these in Venice and found we could not spend them in Florence. A helpful clerk at the Banco Toscano in Florence exchanged them for us. We also encountered the same problem in Naples. Please advise travelers to spend this 'local currency' in the locality where it was issued to avoid problems" (Mark and Donna Rand, San Francisco, Calif.).

CURRENCY EXCHANGE

Here's how your U.S. dollar will translate into local currency. The basic unit of Italian currency is the lira. This chart is based on an exchange rate of 863 lire to the U.S. dollar. As we go to press, this rate appears to be stable, but, with world economic conditions being what they are, it's always best to confirm the up-to-date official rate of exchange before you go to Italy, by checking with your bank here at home.

LIRE	U.S.$	LIRE	U.S.$
50	$ .06	6,000	$ 6.96
75	.09	7,000	8.12
100	.12	8,000	9.28
250	.29	9,000	10.44
500	.58	10,000	11.60
750	.87	11,000	12.76
1,000	1.16	12,000	13.92
1,500	1.74	13,000	15.08
2,000	2.32	14,000	16.24
3,000	3.48	15,000	17.40
4,000	4.64	20,000	23.20
5,000	5.80	30,000	34.80

For her help in editing and preparing this guide, we are grateful to Margaret Foresman, longtime managing editor of *The Key West Citizen*. And for their research in the field, we acknowledge the efforts of Judy Baragli, Dr. Richard Adamany, and Pierre Français.

ARTHUR FROMMER, INC.
380 MADISON AVE., NEW YORK, N.Y. 10017   Date_____

Friends:
Please send me (postpaid) the books checked below:

$10-A-DAY GUIDES
(In-depth guides to low-cost tourist accommodations and facilities.)

☐ Europe on $10 a Day $4.95
☐ England on $15 a Day $4.50
☐ Greece on $10 a Day $3.95
☐ Hawaii on $15 & $20 a Day $4.50
☐ India (plus Sri Lanka and Nepal) on $5 & $10 a Day $3.95
☐ Ireland on $10 a Day $4.50
☐ Israel on $10 & $15 a Day $3.95
☐ Mexico and Guatemala on $10 a Day............................$4.95
☐ New Zealand on $10 a Day $3.95
☐ New York on $15 a Day $3.95
☐ Scandinavia on $15 & $20 a Day $4.50
☐ South America on $10 & $15 a Day $4.50
☐ Spain and Morocco (plus the Canary Is.) on $10 & $15 a Day ...$4.50
☐ Turkey on $5 & $10 a Day $3.95
☐ Washington, D.C. on $10 & $15 a Day $3.95

DOLLAR-WISE GUIDES

(Guides to tourist accommodations and facilities from budget to deluxe, with emphasis on the medium-priced.)

☐ England ....$4.50   ☐ Italy $4.50
☐ France ....$4.50   ☐ Portugal $3.95
☐ Germany ....$3.95   ☐ California $4.50

THE ARTHUR FROMMER GUIDES

(Pocket-size guides to tourist accommodations and facilities in all price ranges.)

☐ Athens ....$1.95   ☐ London $1.95
☐ Boston ....$1.95   ☐ Los Angeles $1.95
☐ Honolulu ....$1.95   ☐ New York $1.95
☐ Ireland/Dublin/Shannon ...$1.95 ☐ Paris $1.95
☐ Las Vegas ....$1.95   ☐ Rome $1.95
☐ Lisbon/Madrid/Costa del Sol $1.95 ☐ San Francisco $1.95
                                   ☐ Washington, D.C. $1.95

By the Council on International Educational Exchange

☐ Whole World Handbook ....$2.95   ☐ Where to Stay USA $2.95
(A student guide to work, study and travel   (A guide to accommodations in all 50
worldwide.)   states costing from 50¢ to $10 per night.)

Enclosed is my check or money order for $_____

NAME_____

ADDRESS_____

CITY_____STATE_____ZIP_____